[JOINT COMMITTEE PRINT]

GENERAL EXPLANATION OF TAX LEGISLATION ENACTED IN 2015

Prepared by the Staff

of the

JOINT COMMITTEE ON TAXATION

MARCH 2016

U.S. GOVERNMENT PUBLISHING OFFICE

WASHINGTON : 2016

JOINT COMMITTEE ON TAXATION

114TH CONGRESS, 2ND SESSION

SENATE
ORRIN G. HATCH, Utah,
  Chairman
CHUCK GRASSLEY, Iowa
MIKE CRAPO, Idaho
RON WYDEN, Oregon
DEBBIE STABENOW, Michigan

HOUSE
KEVIN BRADY, Texas,
  Vice Chairman
SAM JOHNSON, Texas
DEVIN NUNES, California
SANDER M. LEVIN, Michigan
CHARLES B. RANGEL, New York

THOMAS A. BARTHOLD, *Chief of Staff*
BERNARD A. SCHMITT, *Deputy Chief of Staff*

SUMMARY CONTENTS

	Page
Part One: Slain Officer Family Support Act of 2015 (Public Law 114–7)	3
Part Two: Medicare Access and Chip Reauthorization Act of 2015 (Public Law 114–10)	5
Part Three: Don't Tax Our Fallen Public Safety Heroes Act (Public Law 114–14)	7
Part Four: Highway and Transportation Funding Act of 2015 (Public Law 114–21)	9
Part Five: Defending Public Safety Employees' Retirement Act (Public Law 114–26)	10
Part Six: Trade Preferences Extension Act of 2015 (Public Law 114–27)	12
Part Seven: Surface Transportation and Veterans Health Care Choice Improvement Act of 2015 (Public Law 114–41)	24
Part Eight: Airport and Airway Extension Act of 2015 (Public Law 114–55)	42
Part Nine: Surface Transportation Extension Act of 2015 (Public Law 114–73)	44
Part Ten: Bipartisan Budget Act of 2015 (Public Law 114–74)	45
Part Eleven: Surface Transportation Extension Act of 2015, Part II (Public Law 114–87)	85
Part Twelve: Fixing America's Surface Transportation Act ("Fast Act") (Public Law 114–94)	86
Part Thirteen: Consolidated Appropriations Act, 2016 (Public Law 114–113)	99

CONTENTS

	Page
INTRODUCTION	1

Part One: Slain Officer Family Support Act of 2015 (Public Law 114–7) 3
    A. Acceleration of Income Tax Benefits for Charitable Cash Contributions for Relief of the Families of New York Police Department Detectives Wenjian Liu and Rafael Ramos (sec. 2 of the Act) 3

Part Two: Medicare Access and Chip Reauthorization Act of 2015 (Public Law 114–10) 5
    A. Increase Continuous Levy Authority on Payments to Medicare Providers and Suppliers (sec. 413 of the Act and sec. 6331(h) of the Code) 5

Part Three: Don't Tax Our Fallen Public Safety Heroes Act (Public Law 114–14) 7
    A. Exclusion of Certain Compensation Received by Public Safety Officers and Their Dependents (sec. 2 of the Act and sec. 104(a) of the Code) 7

Part Four: Highway and Transportation Funding Act of 2015 (Public Law 114–21) 9
    A. Extension of Highway Trust Fund Expenditure Authority (sec. 2001 of the Act and secs. 9503, 9504, and 9508 of the Code) 9

Part Five: Defending Public Safety Employees' Retirement Act (Public Law 114–26) 10
    A. Early Retirement Distributions to Federal Law Enforcement Officers, Firefighters, and Air Traffic Controllers in Governmental Plans (sec. 2 of the Act and sec. 72(t) of the Code) 10

Part Six: Trade Preferences Extension Act of 2015 (Public Law 114–27) 12

TITLE IV—EXTENSION OF TRADE ADJUSTMENT ASSISTANCE 12

		Page
A.	Extension and Modification of Health Coverage Tax Credit (sec. 407 of the Act and sec. 35 of the Code)	12

TITLE VIII—OFFSETS 17

A.	Time for Payment of Corporate Estimated Taxes (sec. 803 of the Act and sec. 6655 of the Code)	17
B.	Payee Statement Required to Claim Certain Education Tax Benefits (sec. 804 of the Act and secs. 25A and 222 of the Code)	18
C.	Special Rule for Educational Institutions Unable to Collect Taxpayer Identification Numbers of Individuals with Respect to Higher Education Tuition and Related Expenses (sec. 805 of the Act and sec. 6724 of the Code)	18
D.	Increase Penalty for Failure to File Information Returns and Payee Statements (sec. 806 of the Act and secs. 6721 and 6722 of the Code)	19
E.	Child Tax Credit Not Refundable For Taxpayers Electing To Exclude Foreign Earned Income From Tax (sec. 807 of the Act and sec. 24 of the Code)	21

Part Seven: Surface Transportation and Veterans Health Care Choice Improvement Act of 2015 (Public Law 114–41) 24

TITLE II—REVENUE PROVISIONS 24

A.	Extension of Highway Trust Fund Expenditure Authority (sec. 2001 of the Act and secs. 9503, 9504, and 9308 of the Code)	24
B.	Funding of Highway Trust Fund (sec. 2002 of the Act and sec. 9503(f) of the Code)	24
C.	Modification of Mortgage Reporting Requirements (sec. 2003 of the Act and sec. 6050H of the Code)	25
D.	Consistent Basis Reporting between Estate and Person Acquiring Property from Decedent (sec. 2004 of the Act and secs. 1014 and 6035 of the Code)	26
E.	Clarification of 6-Year Statute of Limitations in Case of Overstatement of Basis (sec. 2005 of Act and sec. 6501 of the Code)	28

		Page
F.	Tax Return Due Date Simplification (sec. 2006 of the Act and secs. 6071, 6072, and 6081 of the Code)	30
G.	Transfers of Excess Pension Assets to Retiree Health Accounts (sec. 2007 of the Act and sec. 420 of the Code)	34
H.	Equalization of Highway Trust Fund Excise Taxes on Liquefied Natural Gas, Liquefied Petroleum Gas, and Compressed Natural Gas (sec. 2008 of the Act and sec. 4041 of the Code)	35

TITLE IV—VETERANS PROVISIONS 37

    A. Exemption in Determination of Employer Health Insurance Mandate (sec. 4007(a) of the Act and sec. 4980H of the Code) 37

    B. Eligibility for Health Savings Account Not Affected by Receipt of Medical Care for a Service–Connected Disability (sec. 4007(b) of the Act and sec. 223 of the Code) 40

Part Eight: Airport and Airway Extension Act of 2015 (Public Law 114–55) 42

    A. Extension of Spending Authority and Taxes Funding Airport and Airway Trust Fund (secs. 201 and 202 of the Act and secs. 4083, 4801, 4261, 4271, and 9502 of the Code) 42

Part Nine: Surface Transportation Extension Act of 2015 (Public Law 114–73) 44

    A. Extension of Highway Trust Fund Expenditure Authority (sec. 2001 of the Act and secs. 9503, 9504, and 9508 of the Code) 44

Part Ten: Bipartisan Budget Act of 2015 (Public Law 114–74) 45

TITLE V—PENSIONS 45

    A. Mortality Tables and Extension of Current Funding Stabilization Percentages to 2018, 2019, and 2020 (secs. 503–504 of the Act, sec. 430 of the Code, and secs. 101(f) and 303 of ERISA) 45

TITLE XI—REVENUE PROVISIONS RELATED TO TAX COMPLIANCE 51

		Page
A.	Partnership Audits and Adjustments (sec. 1101 of the Act and secs. 6221–6241 of the Code)	51
B.	Partnership Interests Created by Gift (sec. 1102 of the Act and secs. 704(e) and 761(b) of the Code)	83

Part Eleven: Surface Transportation Extension Act of 2015, Part II (Public Law 114–87) 85

    A. Extension of Highway Trust Fund Expenditure Authority (sec. 2001 of the Act and secs. 9503, 9504, and 9508 of the Code) 85

Part Twelve: Fixing America's Surface Transportation act ("FAST ACT") (Public Law 114–94) 86

Division C—Finance 86

TITLE XXXI—HIGHWAY TRUST FUND AND RELATED TAXES 86

    A. Extension of Highway Trust Fund Expenditure Authority (secs. 31101 of the Act and secs. 9503, 9504, and 9508 of the Code) 86

    B. Extension of Highway-Related Taxes (sec. 31102 of the Act and secs. 4041, 4051, 4071, 4081, 4221, 4481, 4483, and 6412 of the Code) 87

    C. Additional Transfers to the Highway Trust Fund (sec. 31201 of the Act and sec. 9503 of the Code) 88

    D. Transfer to Highway Trust Fund of Certain Motor Vehicle Safety Penalties (sec. 31202 of the Act and sec. 9503 of the Code) 90

    E. Appropriation From Leaking Underground Storage Tank Trust Fund (sec. 31203 of the Act and secs. 9503 and 9508 of the Code) 90

TITLE XXXII—OFFSETS 91

    A. Revocation or Denial of Passport in Case of Certain Unpaid Taxes (sec. 32101 of the Act and secs. 6320, 6331, 7345 and 6103(k)(11) of the Code) 91

    B. Reform of Rules Related to Qualified Tax Collection Contracts, and Special Compliance Personnel Program (secs. 32102–32103 of the Act and sec. 6306 of the Code) 93

		Page
C.	Repeal of Modification of Automatic Extension of Return Due Date for Certain Employee Benefit Plans (sec. 32104 of the Act and secs. 6058 and 6059 of the Code)	96

Part Thirteen: Consolidated Appropriations Act, 2016 (Public Law 114–113) ... 99

Division P—Tax–Related Provisions ... 99

A.	High Cost Employer-Sponsored Health Coverage Excise Tax (secs. 101–103 of the Act and sec. 4980I of the Code)	99
B.	Annual Fee on Health Insurance Providers (sec. 201 of the Act and sec. 9010 of the Patient Protection and Affordable Care Act)	102
C.	Miscellaneous Provisions	103

	1.	Extension and phaseout of credits with respect to facilities producing electricity from wind (secs. 301–302 of the Act and secs. 45 and 48 of the Code)	103
	2.	Modification of energy investment credit (sec. 303 of the Act and sec. 48 of the Code)	104
	3.	Credit for residential energy efficient property (section 304 of the Act and 25D of the Code)	107
	4.	Treatment of transportation costs of independent refiners (sec. 305 of the Act and sec. 199 of the Code)	108

Division Q—Protecting Americans From Tax Hikes Act of 2015 ... 110

TITLE I—EXTENDERS ... 110

A.	Permanent Extensions	110

	1.	Reduced earnings threshold for additional child tax credit made permanent (sec. 101 of the Act and sec. 24 of the Code)	110
	2.	American opportunity tax credit made permanent (sec. 102 of the Act and sec. 25A of the Code)	112
	3.	Modification of the earned income tax credit made permanent (sec. 103 of the Act and sec. 32 of the Code)	114

Page

4. Extension and modification of deduction for certain expenses of elementary and secondary school teachers (sec. 104 of the Act and sec. 62(a)(2)(D) of the Code) 117

5. Extension of parity for exclusion from income for employer-provided mass transit and parking benefits (sec. 105 of the Act and 132(f) of the Code) 118

6. Deduction for State and local sales taxes (sec. 106 of the Act and sec. 164 of the Code) 119

7. Special rule for qualified conservation contributions made permanent (sec. 111 of the Act and sec. 170(b) of the Code) 121

8. Tax-free distributions from individual retirement plans for charitable purposes (sec. 112 of the Act and sec. 408(d)(8) of the Code) 124

9. Extension and expansion of charitable deduction for contributions of food inventory (sec. 113 of the Act and sec. 170 of the Code) 128

10. Extension of modification of tax treatment of certain payments to controlling exempt organizations (sec. 114 of the Act and sec. 512 of the Code) 131

11. Extension of basis adjustment to stock of S corporations making charitable contributions of property (sec. 115 of the Act and sec. 1367 of the Code) 132

12. Extension and modification of research credit (sec. 121 of the Act and secs. 38 and 41 and new sec. 3111(f) of the Code) . 133

13. Extension and modification of employer wage credit for employees who are active duty members of the uniformed services (sec. 122 of the Act and sec. 45P of the Code) 139

14. Extension of 15-year straight-line cost recovery for qualified leasehold improvements, qualified restaurant buildings and improvements, and qualified retail improvements (sec. 123 of the Act and sec. 168 of the Code) 140

15. Extension and modification of increased expensing limitations and treatment of certain real property as section 179 property (sec. 124 of the Act and sec. 179 of the Code) 143

16. Extension of treatment of certain dividends of regulated investment companies (sec. 125 of the Act and sec. 871(k) of the Code) 145

17. Extension of exclusion of 100 percent of gain on certain small business stock (sec. 126 of the Act and sec. 1202 of the Code) . 146

18. Extension of reduction in S corporation recognition period for built-in gains tax (sec. 127 of the Act and sec. 1374 of the Code) 147

19. Extension of subpart F exception for active financing income (sec. 128 of the Act and secs. 953 and 954 of the Code) 150

20. Extension of temporary minimum low-income housing tax credit rate for non-Federally subsidized buildings (sec. 131 of the Act and sec. 42 of the Code) 152

21. Extension of military housing allowance exclusion for determining whether a tenant in certain counties is low-income (sec. 132 of the Act and secs. 42 and 142 of the Code) 153

22. Extension of RIC qualified investment entity treatment under FIRPTA (sec. 133 of the Act and secs. 897 and 1445 of the Code) 155

B. Extensions Through 2019 156

1. Extension of new markets tax credit (sec. 141 of the Act and sec. 45D of the Code) .. 156

2. Extension and modification of work opportunity tax credit (sec. 142 of the Act and secs. 51 and 52 of the Code) 158

3. Extension and modification of bonus depreciation (sec. 143 of the Act and sec. 168(k) of the Code) 164

		Page
4. Extension of look-through treatment of payments between related controlled foreign corporations under foreign personal holding company rules (sec. 144 of the Act and sec. 954(c)(6) of the Code)		171

C. Extensions Through 2016 172

1. Extension and modification of exclusion from gross income of discharges of acquisition indebtedness on principal residences (sec. 151 of the Act and sec. 108 of the Code) 172

2. Extension of mortgage insurance premiums treated as qualified residence interest (sec. 152 of the Act and sec. 163 of the Code) 174

3. Extension of above-the-line deduction for qualified tuition and related expenses (sec. 153 of the Act and sec. 222 of the Code) 175

4. Extension of Indian employment tax credit (sec. 161 of the Act and sec. 45A of the Code) 177

5. Extension and modification of railroad track maintenance credit (sec. 162 of the Act and sec. 45G of the Code) 178

6. Extension of mine rescue team training credit (sec. 163 of the Act and sec. 45N of the Code) 179

7. Extension of qualified zone academy bonds (sec. 164 of the Act and sec. 54E of the Code) 180

8. Extension of classification of certain race horses as three-year property (sec. 165 of the Act and sec. 168 of the Code) 182

9. Extension of seven-year recovery period for motorsports entertainment complexes (sec. 166 of the Act and sec. 168 of the Code) 183

10. Extension and modification of accelerated depreciation for business property on an Indian reservation (sec. 167 of the Act and sec. 168(j) of the Code) 184

XIII

Page

11. Extension of election to expense mine safety equipment (sec. 168 of the Act and sec. 179E of the Code) 185

12. Extension of special expensing rules for certain film and television productions; special expensing for live theatrical productions (sec. 169 of the Act and sec. 181 of the Code) 186

13. Extension of deduction allowable with respect to income attributable to domestic production activities in Puerto Rico (sec. 170 of the Act and sec. 199 of the Code) ... 188

14. Extension and modification of empowerment zone tax incentives (sec. 171 of the Act and secs. 1391 and 1394 of the Code) 189

15. Extension of temporary increase in limit on cover over of rum excise taxes to Puerto Rico and the Virgin Islands (sec. 172 of the Act and sec. 7652(f) of the Code) 195

16. Extension of American Samoa economic development credit (sec. 173 of the Act and sec. 119 of Pub. L. No. 109–432) 196

17. Suspension of medical device excise tax (sec. 174 of the Act and sec. 4191 of the Code) 198

18. Extension and modification of credit for nonbusiness energy property (sec. 181 of the Act and sec. 25C of the Code) 200

19. Extension of credit for alternative fuel vehicle refueling property (sec. 182 of the Act and section 30C of the Code) 202

20. Extension of credit for electric motorcycles (sec. 183 of the Act and sec. 30D of the Code) 203

21. Extension of second generation biofuel producer credit (sec. 184 of the Act and sec. 40(b)(6) of the Code) 203

22. Extension of biodiesel and renewable diesel incentives (sec. 185 of the Act and sec. 40A of the Code) 204

23. Extension of credit for the production of Indian coal facilities (sec. 186 of the Act and sec. 45 of the Code) 207

24. Extension of credits with respect to facilities producing energy from certain renewable resources (sec. 187 of the Act and secs. 45 and 48 of the Code) 208

25. Extension of credit for energy-efficient new homes (sec. 188 of the Act and sec. 45L of the Code) 209

26. Extension of special allowance for second generation biofuel plant property (sec. 189 of the Act and sec. 168(l) of the Code) 210

27. Extension of energy efficient commercial buildings deduction (sec. 190 of the Act and sec. 179D of the Code) 211

28. Extension of special rule for sales or dispositions to implement FERC or State electric restructuring policy for qualified electric utilities (sec. 191 of the Act and sec. 451(i) of the Code) 213

29. Extension of excise tax credits and payment provisions relating to alternative fuel (sec. 192 of the Act and secs. 6426 and 6427 of the Code) 215

30. Extension of credit for fuel cell vehicles (sec. 193 of the Act and sec. 30B of the Code) 216

TITLE II—PROGRAM INTEGRITY 217

1. Modification of filing dates of returns and statements relating to employee wage information and nonemployee compensation to improve compliance (sec. 201 of the Act and secs. 6071 and 6402 of the Code) 217

2. Safe harbor for *de minimis* errors on information returns, payee statements, and withholding (sec. 202 of the Act and secs. 6721 and 6722 of the Code) 220

3. Requirements for the issuance of ITINs (sec. 203 of the Act and sec. 6109 of the Code) 222

4. Prevention of retroactive claims of earned income credit, child tax credit, and American Opportunity Tax Credit (secs. 204, 205, and 206 of the Act and secs. 24, 25A and 32 of the Code) 225

		Page
5.	Procedures to reduce improper claims (sec. 207 of the Act and secs. 24, 25A, 32, and 6695 of the Code)	227
6.	Restrictions on taxpayers who improperly claimed credits in prior year (sec. 208 of the Act and secs. 24, 25A and 6213 of the Code)	231
7.	Treatment of credits for purposes of certain penalties (sec. 209 of the Act and secs. 6664 and 6676 of the Code)	235
8.	Increase the penalty applicable to paid tax preparers who engage in willful or reckless conduct (sec. 210 of the Act and sec. 6694 of the Code)	237
9.	Employer identification number required for American opportunity tax credit (sec. 211 of the Act and secs. 25A and 6050S of the Code)	238
10.	Higher education information reporting only to include qualified tuition and related expenses actually paid (sec. 212 of the Act and sec. 6050S of the Code)	239

TITLE III—MISCELLANEOUS PROVISIONS 240

    A. Family Tax Relief 240

1. Exclusion for amounts received under the work colleges program (sec. 301 of the Act and sec. 117 of the Code) 240

2. Modification of rules relating to section 529 programs (sec. 302 of the Act and sec. 529 of the Code) 241

3. Modification to qualified ABLE programs (sec. 303 of the Act and sec. 529A of the Code) 244

4. Exclusion from gross income of certain amounts received by wrongly incarcerated individuals (sec. 304 of the Act and new sec. 139F of the Code) 248

5. Clarification of special rule for certain governmental plans (sec. 305 of the Act and sec. 105(j) of the Code) 249

	Page
6. Rollovers permitted from other retirement plans into SIMPLE retirement accounts (sec. 306 of the Act and sec. 408(p)(1)(B) of the Code)	250
7. Technical amendment relating to rollover of certain airline payment amounts (sec. 307 of the Act and sec. 1106 of the FAA Modernization and Reform Act of 2012)	252
8. Treatment of early retirement distributions for nuclear materials couriers, United States Capitol Police, Supreme Court Police, and diplomatic security special agents (sec. 308 of the Act and sec. 72(t) of the Code)	255
9. Prevention of extension of tax collection period for members of the Armed Forces who are hospitalized as a result of combat zone injuries (sec. 309 of the Act and secs. 6502 and 7508(e) of the Code)	256

B. Real Estate Investment Trusts 257

1. Restriction on tax-free spinoffs involving REITs (sec. 311 of the Act and secs. 355 and 856 of the Code) 262

2. Reduction in percentage limitation on assets of REIT which may be taxable REIT subsidiaries (sec. 312 of the Act and sec. 856 of the Code) 265

3. Prohibited transaction safe harbors (sec. 313 of the Act and sec. 857 of the Code) ... 265

4. Repeal of preferential dividend rule for publicly offered REITS; authority for alternative remedies to address certain REIT distribution failures (secs. 314 and 315 of the Act and sec. 562 of the Code) ... 267

5. Limitations on designation of dividends by REITs (sec. 316 of the Act and sec. 857 of the Code) 267

6. Debt instruments of publicly offered REITs and mortgages treated as real estate assets (sec. 317 of the Act and sec. 856 of the Code) 269

7. Asset and income test clarification regarding ancillary personal property (sec. 318 of the Act and sec. 856 of the Code) 270

	Page
8. Hedging provisions (sec. 319 of the Act and sec. 857 of the Code)	271
9. Modification of REIT earnings and profits calculation to avoid duplicate taxation (sec. 320 of the Act and secs. 562 and 857 of the Code)	273
10. Treatment of certain services provided by taxable REIT subsidiaries (sec. 321 of the Act and sec. 857 of the Code)	274
11. Exception from FIRPTA for certain stock of REITs; exception for interests held by foreign retirement and pension funds (secs. 322 and 323 of the Act and secs. 897 and 1445 of the Code)	277
12. Increase in rate of withholding of tax on dispositions of United States real property interests (sec. 324 of the Act and sec. 1445 of the Code)	284
13. Interests in RICs and REITs not excluded from definition of United States real property interests (sec. 325 of the Act and sec. 897 of the Code)	285
14. Dividends derived from RICs and REITs ineligible for deduction for United States source portion of dividends from certain foreign corporations (sec. 326 of the Act and sec. 245 of the Code)	286
C. Additional Provisions	287
1. Provide special rules concerning charitable contributions to, and public charity status of, agricultural research organizations (sec. 331 of the Act and secs. 170(b) and 501(h) of the Code)	287
2. Remove bonding requirements for certain taxpayers subject to Federal excise taxes on distilled spirits, wine, and beer (sec. 332 of the Act and secs. 5061(d), 5173(a), 5351, 5401 and 5551 of the Code)	290
3. Modification to alternative tax for certain small insurance companies (sec. 333 of the Act and sec. 831(b) of the Code)	291
4. Treatment of timber gains (sec. 334 of the Act and sec. 1201 of the Code)	294

	Page
5. Modification of definition of hard cider (sec. 335 of the Act and sec. 5041 of the Code)	295
6. Church plan clarification (sec. 336 of the Act and sec. 414 of the Code)	296

D. Revenue Provisions 305

1. Updated ASHRAE standards for energy efficient commercial buildings deduction (sec. 341 of the Act and sec. 179D of the Code) 305

2. Excise tax equivalency for liquefied petroleum gas and liquefied natural gas (sec. 342 of the Act and sec. 6426 of the Code) . 307

3. Exclusion from gross income of certain clean coal power grants (sec. 343 of the Act) 308

4. Clarification of valuation rule for early termination of certain charitable remainder unitrusts (sec. 344 of the Act and sec. 664(e) of the Code) 309

5. Prevention of transfer of certain losses from tax indifferent parties (sec. 345 of the Act and sec. 267 of the Code) 311

6. Treatment of certain persons as employers with respect to motion picture projects (sec. 346 of the Act and new sec. 3512 of the Code) 313

TITLE IV—TAX ADMINISTRATION 316

A. Internal Revenue Service Reforms 316

1. Duty to ensure that Internal Revenue Service employees are familiar with and act in accordance with certain taxpayer rights (sec. 401 of Act and sec. 7803 of the Code) 316

2. Prohibition of use of personal e-mail for official government business (sec. 402 of the Act) 317

3. Release of information regarding the status of certain investigations (sec. 403 of the Act and sec. 6103 of the Code) 318

4. Require the Secretary of the Treasury to describe administrative appeals procedures relating to adverse determinations of tax-exempt status of certain organizations (sec. 404 of the Act and sec. 7123 of the Code) 320

5. Require section 501(c)(4) organizations to provide notice of formation (sec. 405 of the Act, secs. 6033 and 6652 of the Code, and new sec. 506 of the Code) 325

6. Declaratory judgments for section 501(c)(4) and other exempt organizations (sec. 406 of the Act and sec. 7428 of the Code) 330

7. Termination of employment of Internal Revenue Service employees for taking official actions for political purposes (sec. 407 of the Act and sec. 1203(b) of the Internal Revenue Service Restructuring and Reform Act of 1998) 331

8. Gift tax not to apply to gifts made to certain exempt organizations (sec. 408 of the Act and sec. 2501(a) of the Code) 333

9. Extend the Internal Revenue Service authority to require a truncated Social Security Number ("SS") on Form W–2 (sec. 409 of the Act and sec. 6051 of the Code) . 335

10. Clarification of enrolled agent credentials (sec. 410 of the Act) 336

11. Partnership audit rules (sec. 411 of the Act and secs. 6225, 6226, 6234, 6235, and 6031 of the Code) 336

B. United States Tax Court 340

1. Filing period for interest abatement cases (sec. 421 of the Act and sec. 6404 of the Code) 340

2. Small tax case election for interest abatement cases (sec. 422 of the Act and secs. 6404 and 7463 of the Code) 341

3. Venue for appeal of spousal relief and collection cases (sec. 423 of the Act and sec. 7482 of the Code) 342

	Page
4. Suspension of running of period for filing petition of spousal relief and collection cases (sec. 424 of the Act and secs. 6015 and 6330 of the Code)	342
5. Application of Federal rules of evidence (sec. 425 of the Act and sec. 7453 of the Code)	343
6. Judicial conduct and disability procedures (sec. 431 of the Act and new sec. 7466 of the Code)	344
7. Administration, judicial conference, and fees (sec. 432 of the Act; Code sec. 7473 and new secs. 7470 and 7470A of the Code)	345
8. Clarification relating to the United States Tax Court (sec. 441 of the Act and sec. 7441 of the Code)	346
Appendix: Estimated Budget Effects of Tax Legislation Enacted in 2015	349

INTRODUCTION

This document,[1] prepared by the staff of the Joint Committee on Taxation in consultation with the staffs of the House Committee on Ways and Means and the Senate Committee on Finance, provides an explanation of tax legislation enacted in 2015. The explanation follows the chronological order of the tax legislation as signed into law.

For each provision, the document includes a description of present law, explanation of the provision, and effective date. Present law describes the law in effect immediately prior to enactment and does not reflect changes to the law made by the provision or by subsequent legislation. In a case where a Committee report accompanies a bill, this document is based on the language of the report. For a bill with no Committee report but with a contemporaneous technical explanation prepared and published by the staff of the Joint Committee on Taxation, this document is based on the language of the explanation.

Section references are to the Internal Revenue Code of 1986, as amended, unless otherwise indicated.

Part One is an explanation of the provisions of the Slain Officer Family Support Act of 2015 (Pub. L. No. 114–7).

Part Two is an explanation of the revenue provision of the Medicare Access and Chip Reauthorization Act of 2015 (Pub. L. No. 114–10).

Part Three is an explanation of the Don't Tax Our Fallen Public Safety Heroes Act (Pub. L. No. 114–14).

Part Four is an explanation of the revenue provisions of the Highway and Transportation Funding Act of 2015 (Pub. L. No. 114–21).

Part Five is an explanation of the Defending Public Safety Employees' Retirement Act (Pub. L. No. 114–26).

Part Six is an explanation of the revenue provisions of the Trade Preferences Extension Act of 2015 (Pub. L. No. 114–27).

Part Seven is an explanation of the revenue provisions of the Surface Transportation and Veterans Health Care Choice Improvement Act of 2015 (Pub. L. No. 114–41).

Part Eight is an explanation of the revenue provisions of the Airport and Airway Extension Act of 2015 (Pub. L. No. 114–55).

Part Nine is an explanation of the revenue provisions of the Surface Transportation Extension Act of 2015 (Pub. L. No. 114–73).

Part Ten is an explanation of the revenue provisions of the Bipartisan Budget Act of 2015 (Pub. L. No. 114–74).

---

[1] This document may be cited as follows: Joint Committee on Taxation, *General Explanation of Tax Legislation Enacted in 2015* (JCS–1–16), March 2016.

Part Eleven is an explanation of the revenue provisions of the Surface Transportation Extension Act of 2015, Part II (Pub. L. No. 114–87).

Part Twelve is an explanation of the revenue provisions of Fixing America's Surface Transportation Act ("FAST Act") (Pub. L. No. 114–94).

Part Thirteen is an explanation of the revenue provisions of the Consolidated Appropriations Act, 2016 (Pub. L. No. 114–113).

The Appendix provides the estimated budget effects of tax legislation enacted in 2015.

The first footnote in each Part gives the legislative history of the Act explained in that Part.

PART ONE: SLAIN OFFICER FAMILY SUPPORT ACT OF 2015

(PUBLIC LAW 114–7) [2]

A. Acceleration of Income Tax Benefits for Charitable Cash Contributions for Relief of the Families of New York Police Department Detectives Wenjian Liu and Rafael Ramos (sec. 2 of the Act)

Present Law

Tax exemption for charitable organizations

Organizations described in section 501(c)(3) (generally, charitable organizations) are exempt from Federal income taxation under section 501(a). A section 501(c)(3) organization must be organized and operated exclusively for exempt purposes, and no part of the net earnings of such an organization may inure to the benefit of any private shareholder or individual. An organization is not organized or operated exclusively for one or more exempt purposes unless the organization serves a public rather than a private interest. Thus, an organization described in section 501(c)(3) generally must serve a charitable class of persons that is indefinite or of sufficient size.

Deduction for charitable contributions

In general, under present law, taxpayers may claim an income tax deduction for charitable contributions. The charitable deduction generally is available for the taxable year in which the contribution is made. The tax benefit of a charitable contribution, however, often is not realized until the following calendar year when the tax return is filed.

A donor who claims a charitable deduction for a contribution of money, regardless of amount, must maintain as a record of the contribution a bank record or a written communication from the donee showing the name of the donee organization, the date of the contribution, and the amount of the contribution.[3] In addition to the foregoing recordkeeping requirements, substantiation requirements apply in the case of charitable contributions with a value of $250 or more.[4] No charitable deduction is allowed for any contribution of $250 or more unless the taxpayer substantiates the contribution by a contemporaneous written acknowledgment of the contribution by the donee organization.

---

[2] H.R. 1527. The House passed H.R. 1527 on March 25, 2015. The Senate passed the bill without amendment on March 27, 2015. The President signed the bill on April 1, 2015.
[3] Sec. 170(f)(17).
[4] Sec. 170(f)(8).

Explanation of Provision

Acceleration of donor's tax benefit for charitable contribution

The provision permits a taxpayer to treat a charitable contribution of cash made between January 1, 2015, and April 15, 2015, as a contribution made on December 31, 2014, if such contribution was for the relief of the families of slain New York Police Department detectives Wenjian Liu and Rafael Ramos. Thus, the effect of the provision is to give a calendar-year taxpayer who makes charitable contributions of cash for the relief of such detectives' families between January 1, 2015, and April 15, 2015, the opportunity to accelerate the tax benefit. Under the provision, such a taxpayer may realize the tax benefit of the contribution by taking a deduction on the taxpayer's 2014 income tax return.

The provision clarifies the recordkeeping requirement for monetary contributions eligible for the accelerated income tax benefits described above. With respect to such contributions, a telephone bill will satisfy the recordkeeping requirement if it shows the name of the donee organization, the date of the contribution, and the amount of the contribution. Thus, for example, in the case of a charitable contribution made by text message and chargeable to a telephone or wireless account, a bill from the telecommunications company containing the relevant information will satisfy the recordkeeping requirement.

The provision also clarifies that a contribution described in the provision that is made on or after December 20, 2014, will not fail to qualify for a charitable deduction, or for the acceleration of the deduction under the provision, merely because the contribution is for the exclusive benefit of the families of the slain detectives.

Payment by organization treated as related to organization's exempt purpose

Under the provision, certain payments are treated as: (1) related to the purpose or function constituting the basis for the organization's exempt status; and (2) are not treated as inuring to the benefit of any private individual, if the payments are made in good faith using a reasonable and objective formula that is consistently applied. Such payments include payments made: (1) on or after December 20, 2014, and on or before October 15, 2015; (2) to the spouse or any dependent (as defined in section 152 of the Code) of slain New York Police Department detectives Wenjian Liu or Rafael Ramos; and (3) by an organization that is exempt from tax under section 501(a) (determined without regard to such payments).

Effective Date

The provision is effective on the date of enactment (April 1, 2015).

PART TWO: MEDICARE ACCESS AND CHIP REAUTHORIZATION ACT OF 2015 (PUBLIC LAW 114–10) [5]

A. Increase Continuous Levy Authority on Payments to Medicare Providers and Suppliers (sec. 413 of the Act and sec. 6331(h) of the Code)

Present Law

In general

Levy is the administrative authority of the IRS to seize a taxpayer's property, or rights to property, to pay the taxpayer's tax liability.[6] Generally, the IRS is entitled to seize a taxpayer's property by levy if a Federal tax lien has attached to such property,[7] the property is not exempt from levy,[8] and the IRS has provided both notice of intention to levy[9] and notice of the right to an administrative hearing (the notice is referred to as a "collections due process notice" or "CDP notice" and the hearing is referred to as the "CDP hearing")[10] at least 30 days before the levy is made. A levy on salary or wages generally is continuously in effect until released.[11] A Federal tax lien arises automatically when: (1) a tax assessment has been made; (2) the taxpayer has been given notice of the assessment stating the amount and demanding payment; and (3) the taxpayer has failed to pay the amount assessed within 10 days after the notice and demand.[12]

The notice of intent to levy is not required if the Secretary finds that collection would be jeopardized by delay. The standard for determining whether jeopardy exists is similar to the standard applicable when determining whether assessment of tax without following the normal deficiency procedures is permitted.[13]

The CDP notice (and pre-levy CDP hearing) is not required if: (1) the Secretary finds that collection would be jeopardized by delay; (2) the Secretary has served a levy on a State to collect a Federal tax liability from a State tax refund; (3) the taxpayer subject to the levy requested a CDP hearing with respect to unpaid employment taxes arising in the two-year period before the beginning of the taxable period with respect to which the employment tax levy is served; or (4) the Secretary has served a Federal contractor levy.

---

[5] H.R. 2. The House passed H.R. 2 on March 26, 2015. The Senate passed the bill without amendment on April 14, 2015. The President signed the bill on April 16, 2015.
[6] Sec. 6331(a). Levy specifically refers to the legal process by which the IRS orders a third party to turn over property in its possession that belongs to the delinquent taxpayer named in a notice of levy.
[7] *Ibid.*
[8] Sec. 6334.
[9] Sec. 6331(d).
[10] Sec. 6330. The notice and the hearing are referred to collectively as the CDP requirements.
[11] Secs. 6331(e) and 6343.
[12] Sec. 6321.
[13] Secs. 6331(d)(3) and 6861.

In each of these four cases, however, the taxpayer is provided an opportunity for a hearing within a reasonable period of time after the levy.[14]

Federal payment levy program

To help the IRS collect taxes more effectively, the Taxpayer Relief Act of 1997[15] authorized the establishment of the Federal Payment Levy Program ("FPLP"), which allows the IRS to continuously levy up to 15 percent of certain "specified payments" by the Federal government if the payees are delinquent on their tax obligations. With respect to payments to vendors of goods, services, or property sold or leased to the Federal government, the continuous levy may be up to 100 percent of each payment.[16] For payments to Medicare providers and suppliers, the levy is up to 15 percent for payments made within 180 days after December 19, 2014. For payments made after that date, the levy is up to 30 percent.[17]

Under FPLP, the IRS matches its accounts receivable records with Federal payment records maintained by Treasury's Bureau of Fiscal Service ("BFS"), such as certain Social Security benefit and Federal wage records. When these records match, the delinquent taxpayer is provided both the notice of intention to levy and the CDP notice. If the taxpayer does not respond after 30 days, the IRS can instruct BFS to levy the taxpayer's Federal payments. Subsequent payments are continuously levied until such time that the tax debt is paid or the IRS releases the levy.

Explanation of Provision

The present limitation of 30 percent of certain specified payments is increased to 100 percent.

Effective Date

The provision is effective for payments made after 180 days after the date of enactment (April 16, 2015).

---

[14] Sec. 6330(f).
[15] Pub. L. No. 105–34.
[16] Sec. 6331(h)(3).
[17] Pub. L. No. 113–295, Division B.

PART THREE: DON'T TAX OUR FALLEN PUBLIC SAFETY HEROES ACT (PUBLIC LAW 114–14) [18]

A. Exclusion of Certain Compensation Received by Public Safety Officers and Their Dependents (sec. 2 of the Act and sec. 104(a) of the Code)

Present Law

Amounts received under a workmen's compensation act as compensation for personal injuries or sickness are excluded from gross income.[19] This exclusion applies to amounts received by an employee under a workmen's compensation act, or under a statute in the nature of a workmen's compensation act that provides compensation to employees for personal injuries or sickness incurred in the course of employment, as well as to compensation paid under a workmen's compensation act to the survivor or survivors of a deceased employee.[20]

Under the Omnibus Crime Control and Safe Streets Act of 1968, if the Bureau of Justice Assistance ("BJA"), an agency of the U.S. Department of Justice, determines that a public safety officer has died as the direct and proximate result of a personal injury sustained in the line of duty, the BJA will pay a monetary benefit to surviving family members or other beneficiary ("public safety officer survivor's benefit").[21] In addition, if the BJA determines that a public safety officer has become permanently and totally disabled as the direct and proximate result of a personal injury sustained in the line of duty, the BJA will pay a monetary benefit to the public safety officer ("public safety officer disability benefit").[22]

With respect to payments made by the Law Enforcement Assistance Administration (a previous agency of the U.S. Department of Justice) under the Public Safety Officers' Benefits Act of 1976 to a surviving dependent of a public safety officer who died as the direct and proximate result of a personal injury sustained in the line of duty, the Internal Revenue Service has ruled that the payments are made under a statute in the nature of a workmen's compensation act and are thus excluded from gross income.[23]

Explanation of Provision

The provision amends the Code to provide a specific exclusion from gross income for amounts paid (1) by the BJA as a public safety officer survivor's benefit or public safety officer disability

---

[18] H.R. 606. The House passed H.R. 606 on May 12, 2015. The Senate passed the bill without amendment on May 14, 2015. The President signed the bill on May 22, 2015.
[19] Sec. 104(a)(1).
[20] Treas. Reg. sec. 1.104–1(b).
[21] 42 U.S.C. sec. 3796(a).
[22] 42 U.S.C. sec. 3796(b).
[23] Rev. Rul. 77–235, 1977–2 C.B. 45.

benefit, or (2) under a State program that provides monetary compensation for surviving dependents of a public safety officer who has died as the direct and proximate result of a personal injury sustained in the line of duty, except that the exclusion does not apply to any amounts that would have been payable if the death of the public safety officer had occurred other than as the direct and proximate result of a personal injury sustained in the line of duty.

Effective Date

The provision is effective on the date of enactment (May 22, 2015).

PART FOUR: HIGHWAY AND TRANSPORTATION FUNDING ACT OF 2015 (PUBLIC LAW 114–21) [24]

A. Extension of Highway Trust Fund Expenditure Authority (sec. 2001 of the Act and secs. 9503, 9504, and 9508 of the Code)

Present Law

Under present law, the Internal Revenue Code (sec. 9503) authorizes expenditures (subject to appropriations) to be made from the Highway Trust Fund (and Sport Fish Restoration and Boating Trust Fund and Leaking Underground Storage Tank Trust Fund) through May 31, 2015, for purposes provided in specified authorizing legislation as in effect on the date of enactment.

Explanation of Provision

This provision extends the authority to make expenditures (subject to appropriations) from the Highway Trust Fund (and Sport Fish Restoration and Boating Trust Fund and Leaking Underground Storage Tank Trust Fund) through July 31, 2015.

Effective Date

The provision is effective on date of enactment (May 29, 2015).

---

[24] H. R. 2353. The House passed H. R. 2353 on May 19, 2015. The bill passed the Senate without amendment on May 23, 2015. The President signed the bill on May 29, 2015.

PART FIVE: DEFENDING PUBLIC SAFETY EMPLOYEES' RETIREMENT ACT (PUBLIC LAW 114-26) [25]

A. Early Retirement Distributions to Federal Law Enforcement Officers, Firefighters, and Air Traffic Controllers in Governmental Plans (sec. 2 of the Act and sec. 72(t) of the Code)

Present Law

An individual who receives a distribution from a qualified retirement plan before age 59½, death, or disability is subject to a 10-percent early withdrawal tax on the amount includible in income unless an exception to the tax applies.[26] Among other exceptions, the early distribution tax does not apply to distributions made to an employee who separates from service after age 55 (the "separation from service" exception), or to distributions that are part of a series of substantially equal periodic payments made for the life, or life expectancy, of the employee or the joint lives, or life expectancies, of the employee and his or her beneficiary (the "equal periodic payments" exception).[27]

Under a special rule for qualified public safety employees, the separation from service exception applies to distributions from a governmental defined benefit pension plan if the employee separates from service after age 50 (rather than age 55). A qualified public safety employee is an employee of a State or political subdivision of a State if the employee provides police protection, firefighting services, or emergency medical services for any area within the jurisdiction of such State or political subdivision.

Explanation of Provision [28]

The provision revises the special rule for applying the separation from service exception to qualified public safety employees.[29] First, the definition of qualified public safety employee is expanded to include Federal law enforcement officers, Federal customs and border protection officers, Federal firefighters, and air traffic controllers.[30]

---

[25] H.R. 2146. The House passed H.R. 2146 on May 12, 2015. The Senate passed the bill with an amendment on June 4, 2015. The House passed the bill with a further amendment on June 18, 2015. The Senate agreed to the House amendment on June 24, 2015. The President signed the bill on June 29, 2015.

[26] Sec. 72(t).

[27] Sec. 72(t)(2)(iv) and (v). Section 72(t)(4) provides a recapture rule under which, in general, if the series of payments eligible for the equal periodic payments exception is modified within five years of the first payment or before age 59½, an additional tax applies equal to the early withdrawal tax that would have applied in the absence of the exception.

[28] See Part Thirteen, Division Q, Title III, Item A.8 for an explanation of a related amendment.

[29] This provision also allows a qualified public safety employee to modify a series of payments to which the equal periodic payments exception has applied without being subject to the recapture rule described above.

[30] These positions are defined by reference to the provisions of the Civil Service Retirement System and the Federal Employees Retirement System.

In addition, the special rule is extended to distributions from governmental defined contribution plans (rather than just governmental defined benefit plans).[31]

Effective Date

The provision is effective for distributions after December 31, 2015.

---

[31] Under section 7701(j), the Federal Thrift Savings plan is treated as a qualified defined contribution plan.

PART SIX: TRADE PREFERENCES EXTENSION ACT OF 2015 (PUBLIC LAW 114–27) [32]

TITLE IV—EXTENSION OF TRADE ADJUSTMENT ASSISTANCE

A. Extension and Modification of Health Coverage Tax Credit (sec. 407 of the Act and sec. 35 of the Code)

Present Law

Health Coverage Tax Credit

Eligible coverage months

In the case of an eligible individual, a refundable tax credit is provided for 72.5 percent of the individual's premiums for qualified health insurance of the individual and qualifying family members for each eligible coverage month beginning in the taxable year.[33] The credit is commonly referred to as the health coverage tax credit ("HCTC"). The credit is available only with respect to amounts paid by the individual for the qualified health insurance.

Eligibility for the credit is determined on a monthly basis. In general, an eligible coverage month is any month if (1) the month begins before January 1, 2014, and (2) as of the first day of the month, the individual is an eligible individual, is covered by qualified health insurance, the premium for which is paid by the individual, does not have other specified coverage, and is not imprisoned under Federal, State, or local authority. In the case of a joint return, the eligibility requirements are met if at least one spouse satisfies the requirements.

Eligible individuals

An eligible individual is an individual who is (1) an eligible Trade Adjustment Assistance ("TAA") recipient, (2) an eligible alternative TAA recipient or an eligible reemployment TAA recipient, or (3) an eligible Pension Benefit Guaranty Corporation ("PBGC") pension recipient. In general, an individual is an eligible TAA recipient for a month if the individual (1) receives for any day of the

---

[32] H.R. 1295. The House Committee on Ways and Means reported H.R. 1295 on April 13, 2015 (H.R. Rep. No. 114–71). The House passed the bill on April 15, 2015. The Senate passed the bill with an amendment on May 14, 2015. The House agreed to an amendment to the Senate amendment on June 11, 2015. The Senate concurred in the House amendment with a further amendment on June 24, 2015. The House agreed to the Senate amendment on June 25, 2015. The President signed the bill on June 29, 2015. In addition, the House Committee on Ways and Means reported H.R. 1892 (Trade Adjustment Assistance Reauthorization Act of 2015) on May 8, 2015 (H.R. Rep. No. 114–108) and the Senate Committee on Finance reported S. 1268 (An Original Bill to Extend the Trade Adjustment Assistance Program, and for Other Purposes) on May 12, 2015 (S. Rep. No. 114–44).

[33] Qualifying family members are the individual's spouse and any dependent for whom the individual is entitled to claim a dependency exemption. Any individual who has certain specified coverage is not a qualifying family member.

month a trade readjustment allowance under the Trade Act of 1974 or would be eligible to receive such an allowance but for the requirement that the individual exhaust unemployment benefits before being eligible to receive an allowance and (2) with respect to such allowance, is covered under a required certification. An individual is an eligible alternative TAA recipient or an eligible reemployment TAA recipient for a month if the individual participates in a certain program under the Trade Act of 1974 and receives a related benefit for the month. Generally, an individual is an eligible PBGC pension recipient for any month if the individual (1) is age 55 or over as of the first day of the month and (2) receives a benefit for the month, any portion of which is paid by the PBGC. A person who may be claimed as a dependent on another person's tax return is not an eligible individual. In addition, an otherwise eligible individual is not eligible for the credit for a month if, as of the first day of the month, the individual has certain specified coverage, such as certain employer-provided coverage or coverage under certain governmental health programs.

Qualified health insurance

Qualified health insurance eligible for the credit is: (1) coverage under a COBRA continuation provision;[34] (2) State-based continuation coverage provided by the State under a State law that requires such coverage; (3) coverage offered through a qualified State high risk pool; (4) coverage under a health insurance program offered to State employees or a comparable program; (5) coverage through an arrangement entered into by a State and a group health plan, an issuer of health insurance coverage, an administrator, or an employer; (6) coverage offered through a State arrangement with a private sector health care coverage purchasing pool; (7) coverage under a State-operated health plan that does not receive any Federal financial participation; (8) coverage under a group health plan that is available through the employment of the eligible individual's spouse; (9) coverage under individual health insurance[35] if the eligible individual was covered under individual health insurance during the entire 30-day period that ends on the date the individual became separated from the employment which qualified the individual for the TAA allowance, the benefit for an eligible alternative TAA recipient or an eligible reemployment TAA recipient, or a pension benefit from the PBGC, whichever applies ("30-day requirement"); and (10) coverage under an employee benefit plan funded by a voluntary employee beneficiary association ("VEBA")[36] established pursuant to an order of a bankruptcy court (or by agreement with an authorized representative).[37]

Qualified health insurance does not include any State-based coverage (i.e., coverage described in (2)–(7) in the preceding paragraph) unless the State has elected to have such coverage treated as qualified health insurance and such coverage meets certain con-

---

[34] COBRA continuation provision is defined by section 9832(d)(1).
[35] For this purpose, "individual health insurance" means any insurance that constitutes medical care offered to individuals other than in connection with a group health plan. Such term does not include Federal- or State-based health insurance coverage.
[36] See section 501(c)(9) for the definition of a VEBA.
[37] See 11 U.S.C. sec. 1114.

sumer-protection requirements.[38] Such State coverage must provide that each qualifying individual is guaranteed enrollment if the individual pays the premium for enrollment or provides a qualified health insurance costs eligibility certificate and pays the remainder of the premium. In addition, the State-based coverage cannot impose any pre-existing condition limitation with respect to qualifying individuals. State-based coverage cannot require a qualifying individual to pay a premium or contribution that is greater than the premium or contribution for a similarly situated individual who is not a qualified individual. Finally, benefits under the State-based coverage must be the same as (or substantially similar to) benefits provided to similarly situated individuals who are not qualifying individuals.

A qualifying individual for this purpose is an eligible individual who seeks to enroll in the State-based coverage and who has aggregate periods of creditable coverage [39] of three months or longer, does not have other specified coverage, and is not imprisoned. However, State-based coverage that satisfies any or all of the consumer-protection requirements for State-based coverage with respect to all eligible individuals is also qualified health insurance for purposes of HCTC.[40]

Qualified health insurance does not include coverage under a flexible spending or similar arrangement or any insurance if substantially all of the coverage is for excepted benefits.

Advance payment of HCTC

The credit is available on an advance payment basis by means of payments by the Department of the Treasury ("Treasury") once a qualified health insurance costs credit eligibility certificate is in effect.[41] In some cases, Treasury may also make retroactive payments on behalf of a certified individual for qualified health insurance coverage for eligible coverage months occurring before the first month for which an advance payment is otherwise made on behalf of the individual. With respect to any taxable year, the amount which is allowed as HCTC for an eligible individual for a taxable year is reduced (but not below zero) by the aggregate amount of advance HCTC payments on behalf of the eligible individual for months beginning in the taxable year.

Premium assistance credit

For taxable years ending after December 31, 2013, a refundable tax credit (the "premium assistance credit") is provided for eligible individuals and families who purchase health insurance through an American Health Benefit Exchange.[42] The premium assistance credit, which is refundable and payable in advance directly to the insurer, subsidizes the purchase of certain health insurance plans through an American Health Benefit Exchange.

The premium assistance credit is available for individuals (single or joint filers) with household incomes between 100 and 400 per-

---

[38] For guidance on how a State elects a health program to be qualified health insurance for purposes of the credit, see Rev. Proc. 2004–12, 2004–1 C.B. 528.
[39] Creditable coverage is determined under section 9801(c).
[40] See Q&A–10 of Notice 2005–50, 2005–2 C.B. 14.
[41] Sec. 7527.
[42] Sec. 36B.

cent of the Federal poverty level ("FPL") for the family size involved who are not eligible for certain other health insurance. The premium assistance credit amount is generally the lower of (1) the premium for the qualified health plan in which the individual or family enrolls, and (2) the premium for the second lowest cost silver plan [43] in the rating area where the individual resides, reduced by the individual's or family's share of premiums.

If the premium assistance credit received through advance payment exceeds the amount of premium assistance credit to which the taxpayer is entitled for the taxable year, the liability for the overpayment must be reflected on the taxpayer's income tax return for the taxable year, subject to a limitation on the amount of such liability. For taxpayers with household income below 400 percent of FPL, the liability for the overpayment for a taxable year is limited to a specific dollar amount which varies depending on the taxpayer's household income as a percentage of FPL.

Explanation of Provision

Extension of HCTC

The provision amends the definition of eligible coverage month for HCTC purposes to include months beginning before January 1, 2020, if the requirements for an eligible coverage month are otherwise met.[44]

Election of HCTC

In order to coordinate eligibility for the premium assistance credit with eligibility for HCTC, under the provision, to be eligible for the HCTC for any eligible coverage month during a taxable year, the eligible individual must elect the HCTC. Further, except as the Secretary of Treasury may provide, the election applies for that coverage month and all subsequent eligible coverage months during the taxable year, must be made no later than the due date, with any extension, for filing his or her income tax return for the year, and is irrevocable. Further, the period for assessing any deficiency attributable to the election (or revocation of the election, if permitted) does not expire before one year after the date on which the Secretary of Treasury is notified of the election (or revocation). The taxpayer is not entitled to the premium assistance credit for any coverage month for which the individual elects the HCTC.

Qualified health insurance

The provision eliminates the 30-day requirement as a requirement for individual health insurance to be qualified health insurance for purposes of the HCTC, but the provision adds a requirement that the individual health insurance not be purchased through an American Health Benefit Exchange. The provision otherwise extends pre-2014 law for qualified health insurance, including the rules for State-based coverage, and the treatment of

---

[43] A qualified health plan is categorized by level (bronze, silver, gold or platinum), depending on its actuarial value, that is, the percentage of the plan's share of the total costs of benefits under the plan. A silver level plan must have an actuarial value of 70 percent.

[44] Title IV of the Act also provides for extension to June 30, 2021, of certain expired provisions of the Trade Act of 1974, Pub. L. No. 93–618, as amended, including provisions related to individuals eligible for trade adjustment assistance.

COBRA continuation coverage and coverage under certain VEBAs as qualified health insurance.

Advance payment

In the case of an eligible individual on whose behalf advance HCTC payment or advance premium assistance payment is made for months occurring during a taxable year and who subsequently elects HCTC for any eligible months,[45] the individual's income tax liability is increased by the amount of the advance payment, but then offset by the amount of the HCTC allowed to the individual.[46] If the individual on whose behalf the advance HCTC payment is made does not elect HCTC but instead claims the premium assistance credit for any coverage months, the increase in tax liability equal to the advance payment is offset by the amount of the allowable premium assistance credit, and any remaining tax liability attributable to the advance payment (and advance premium assistance payment, if any) is limited in the same way as if the advance HCTC payment had instead been advance premium assistance payment.

Under the provision, the Secretary of Treasury is directed to establish, no later than one year after date of enactment of the provision, a new program for making advance HCTC payments to providers of insurance on behalf of enrolled eligible individuals. The program shall only provide retroactive payments for coverage months occurring after the end of such one year period.

Agency outreach

The Secretaries of the Treasury, Health and Human Services, and Labor and the Director of the PBGC are directed to carry out programs of public outreach, including on the Internet, to inform potential HCTC-eligible individuals of the extension of HCTC availability and the availability of the election to claim such credit retroactively for coverage months beginning after December 31, 2013.

Effective Date

The provision is generally effective for coverage months in taxable years beginning after December 31, 2013. For any taxable year beginning after December 31, 2013, and before the date of enactment (June 29, 2015), the election to claim the HCTC may be made any time on or after the date of enactment and before the expiration of the 3-year period of limitation with respect to such taxable year[47] and may be made on an amended income tax return. The requirement that, in order to be qualified health insurance, individual health insurance not be purchased through an American Health Benefit Exchange is effective for coverage months in taxable years beginning after December 31, 2015.

---

[45] Receipt of advance HCTC payments during a year does not in itself constitute an election of the HCTC for the year.

[46] If a premium assistance credit is also allowed to the individual for months before the first month for which the HCTC is elected, the amount of the individual's allowed premium assistance credit is also taken into account in applying the offset.

[47] Sec. 6511(a).

TITLE VIII—OFFSETS

A. Time for Payment of Corporate Estimated Taxes (sec. 803 of the Act and sec. 6655 of the Code)

Present Law

In general, corporations are required to make quarterly estimated tax payments of their income tax liability.[48] For a corporation whose taxable year is a calendar year, these estimated tax payments must be made by April 15, June 15, September 15, and December 15. The amount of any required estimated payment is 25 percent of the required annual payment.[49] The required annual payment is 100 percent of the tax liability for the taxable year or the preceding taxable year. The option to use the preceding taxable year is not available if the preceding taxable year was not a 12-month taxable year or the corporation did not file a return in the preceding taxable year showing a liability for tax. Further, in the case of a corporation with taxable income of at least $1 million in any of the three immediately preceding taxable years, the option to use the preceding taxable year is only available for the first installment of such corporation's taxable year.[50] In addition, in the case of a corporation with assets of at least $1 billion (determined as of the end of the preceding taxable year), the installment due in July, August or September of 2017, is increased to 100.25 percent of the payment otherwise due.[51] For each of the periods affected, the next required installment is reduced accordingly (*i.e.*, the payment due in October, November, or December of 2017 is reduced by the amount that the prior payment was increased).

Explanation of Provision

In the case of a corporation with assets of at least $1 billion (determined as of the end of the preceding taxable year), the provision increases the amount of the required installment of estimated tax otherwise due in July, August, or September of 2020 by 8 percent of that amount (determined without regard to any increase in such amount not contained in the Internal Revenue Code) (*i.e.*, the installment due in July, August or September of 2020, is increased to 108 percent of the payment otherwise due). The next required installment is reduced accordingly (*i.e.*, the payment due in October, November, or December of 2020 is reduced by the amount that the prior payment was increased).

Effective Date

The provision is effective on the date of enactment (June 29, 2015).

---

[48] Sec. 6655.
[49] Sec. 6655(d)(1).
[50] Sec. 6655(d)(2) and (g)(2).
[51] African Growth and Opportunity Amendments, Pub. L. No. 112–163, sec. 4.

B. Payee Statement Required to Claim Certain Education Tax Benefits (sec. 804 of the Act and secs. 25A and 222 of the Code)

Present Law [52]

The Code contains provisions providing for either a credit against tax or an above-the-line deduction for certain amounts paid for qualified tuition and related expenses.[53]

Under section 6050S of the Code, eligible educational institutions that enroll individuals for any academic period are required to furnish, both to the IRS and to the student, an information return known as Form 1098–T. Among the information the educational institution is required to remit is (i) either the aggregate amount of payments received, or the aggregate amount billed, for qualified tuition with respect to the student to whom the Form 1098–T pertains; and (ii) the aggregate amount of grants received by such individual for payment of costs of attendance that are administered and processed by the institution during the calendar year.

Explanation of Provision

Under the provision, except as provided by the Secretary, no taxpayer may claim the credits for qualified tuition and related expenses, or the deduction for qualified tuition and fees, unless the taxpayer receives a statement required under section 6050S of the Code (the Form 1098–T), containing both the identifying information of the taxpayer (including the taxpayer's taxpayer identification number) as well information related to the calculation of the relevant credits and deduction.[54] In the case of a taxpayer who claims the credit or deduction with respect to an eligible student who is a dependent, the eligible student's receipt of the Form 1098–T will suffice for purposes of this requirement.

Effective Date

The provision is effective for taxable years beginning after the date of enactment (June 29, 2015).

C. Special Rule for Educational Institutions Unable to Collect Taxpayer Identification Numbers of Individuals with Respect to Higher Education Tuition and Related Expenses (sec. 805 of the Act and sec. 6724 of the Code)

Present Law

Eligible educational institutions that enroll individuals for any academic period are required to furnish, both to the IRS and to the

---

[52] This description of present law does not incorporate changes made to the tuition reporting requirements in the "Protecting Americans From Tax Hikes Act of 2015," Pub. L. No. 114–113. See Part Thirteen, Division Q, Title II, item 10.

[53] Secs. 25A and 222. For a detailed description of these provisions, see description of the "Protecting Americans From Tax Hikes Act of 2015," Pub. L. No. 114–113, secs. 102 and 153, *infra*.

[54] This information is required under section 6050S(b)(2)(B). The requirement to report tuition amounts either billed or paid under section 6050S(b)(2)(B)(i) was subsequently modified as a result of changes made to the tuition reporting requirements in the "Protecting Americans From Tax Hikes Act of 2015," Pub. L. No. 114–113, described *infra*. That modification required that institutions report only amounts paid, rather than amounts billed.

student, an information return known as Form 1098–T.[55] Among the information the educational institution is required to remit is the taxpayer identification number ("TIN") of the student to whom the form relates.[56]

A penalty under section 6721 or 6722 of the Code may apply to a payee that fails to include the information required on the Form 1098–T.[57] The Treasury regulations provide for a waiver of the section 6721 and 6722 penalties in the case of institutions that fail to include a correct TIN of the student. Such institutions will not be liable for these penalties if the failure to include the correct TIN was due to reasonable cause.[58] Reasonable cause may be established if the failure arose from events beyond the institution's control, such as failure of the student to furnish a TIN. However, the regulations require that the institution establish that it acted in a "responsible manner" both before and after the failure. The Treasury regulations set out detailed guidelines regarding the solicitation of TINs by the institution for purposes of making this determination.

Explanation of Provision

Under the provision, no penalty shall be imposed on an eligible educational institution under sections 6721 or 6722 solely by reason of failing to provide a correct TIN of an individual as required under section 6050S, if such institution makes, at the time of the filing of the Form 1098–T, a true and accurate certification under penalties of perjury that it has complied with standards promulgated by the Secretary for obtaining such individual's TIN.

Effective Date

The provision is effective for returns required to be made, and statements required to be furnished, after December 31, 2015.

D. Increase Penalty for Failure to File Information Returns and Payee Statements (sec. 806 of the Act and secs. 6721 and 6722 of the Code)

Present Law

Failure to comply with the information reporting requirements of the Code results in penalties, which may include a penalty for failure to file the information return,[59] to furnish payee statements,[60] or to comply with other various reporting requirements.[61] No penalty is imposed if the failure is due to reasonable cause.[62]

---

[55] Sec. 6050S.
[56] Sec. 6050S(b)(2)(A); Treas. Reg. sec. 1.6050S–1(b)(2)(ii)(A).
[57] Treas. Reg. sec. 1.6050S–3(f)(1), (2). The section 6721 penalty is applicable to information returns (*i.e.*, statements required to be remitted to the IRS under section 6050S), while the section 6722 penalty is applicable to payee statements (*i.e.*, statements required to be remitted to the taxpayer under section 6050S).
[58] Treas. Reg. sec. 1.6050S–3(f)(3).
[59] Sec. 6721.
[60] Sec. 6722.
[61] Sec. 6723. The penalty for failure to comply timely with a specified information reporting requirement is $50 per failure, not to exceed $100,000 per calendar year.
[62] Sec. 6724.

Any person who is required to file an information return, or furnish a payee statement, but who fails to do so on or before the prescribed due date, is subject to a penalty that varies based on when, if at all, the information return is filed. Both the failure to file and failure to furnish penalties are adjusted annually to account for inflation.

If a person files an information return after the prescribed filing date but on or before the date that is 30 days after the prescribed filing date, the amount of the penalty is $30 per return ("first-tier penalty"), with a maximum penalty of $250,000 per calendar year. If a person files an information return after the date that is 30 days after the prescribed filing date but on or before August 1, the amount of the penalty is $60 per return ("second-tier penalty"), with a maximum penalty of $500,000 per calendar year. If an information return is not filed on or before August 1 of any year, the amount of the penalty is $100 per return ("third-tier penalty"), with a maximum penalty of $1,500,000 per calendar year. If a failure to file is due to intentional disregard of a filing requirement, the minimum penalty for each failure is $250, with no calendar year limit.

Lower maximum levels for this failure to file correct information return penalty apply to small businesses. Small businesses are defined as firms having average annual gross receipts for the most recent three taxable years that do not exceed $5 million. The maximum penalties for small businesses are: $75,000 (instead of $250,000) if the failures are corrected on or before 30 days after the prescribed filing date; $200,000 (instead of $500,000) if the failures are corrected on or before August 1; and $500,000 (instead of $1,500,000) if the failures are not corrected on or before August 1.

Any person who is required to furnish a payee statement who fails to do so on or before the prescribed filing date is subject to a penalty that varies based on when, if at all, the payee statement is furnished, similar to the penalty for filing an information return discussed above. A first-tier penalty is $30, subject to a maximum of $250,000, a second-tier penalty is $60 per statement, up to $500,000, and a third-tier penalty is $100, up to a maximum of $1,500,000. Lower maximum levels for this failure to furnish correct payee statement penalty apply to small businesses. For purposes of the penalty, small businesses are firms having average annual gross receipts for the most recent three taxable years that do not exceed $5 million. The maximum penalties for small businesses are: $75,000 (instead of $250,000) if the failures are corrected on or before 30 days after the prescribed filing date; $200,000 (instead of $500,000) if the failures are corrected on or before August 1; and $500,000 (instead of $1,500,000) if the failures are not corrected on or before August 1.

In cases in which the failure to file an information return or to furnish the correct payee statement is due to intentional disregard, the minimum penalty for each failure is $250, with no calendar year limit. No distinction is made between small businesses and other persons required to report.

Explanation of Provision

The provision increases the penalties to the following amounts for information returns or payee statements due after December 31, 2015. The first-tier penalty is $50 per return, with a maximum penalty of $500,000 per calendar year. The second-tier penalty increases to $100 per return, with a maximum penalty of $1,500,000 per calendar year. The third-tier penalty increases to $250 per return, with a maximum penalty of $3,000,000 per calendar year.

The provision also increases the lower maximum levels applicable to small businesses, as follows. The maximum penalties for small businesses are: $175,000 if the failures are corrected on or before 30 days after the prescribed filing date; $500,000 if the failures are corrected on or before August 1; and $1,000,000 if the failures are not corrected on or before August 1.

For failures or misstatements due to intentional disregard, the penalty per return or statement increases to $500, with no calendar year limit. As with present law, there is no distinction between small businesses and other persons required to report in such cases.

Effective Date

The provision applies to information returns required to be filed and payee statements required to be furnished after December 31, 2015.

E. Child Tax Credit Not Refundable For Taxpayers Electing To Exclude Foreign Earned Income From Tax (sec. 807 of the Act and sec. 24 of the Code)

Present Law [63]

Child tax credit

An individual may claim a tax credit for each qualifying child under the age of 17. The amount of the credit per child is $1,000.[64] A child who is not a citizen, national, or resident of the United States cannot be a qualifying child.[65]

The aggregate amount of child credits that may be claimed is phased out for individuals with income over certain threshold amounts. Specifically, the otherwise allowable child tax credit is reduced by $50 for each $1,000 (or fraction thereof) of modified adjusted gross income over $75,000 for single individuals or heads of households, $110,000 for married individuals filing joint returns, and $55,000 for married individuals filing separate returns. For purposes of this limitation, modified adjusted gross income includes certain otherwise excludable income earned by U.S. citizens or residents living abroad or in certain U.S. territories, described below.[66]

The credit is allowable against both the regular tax and against the alternative minimum tax ("AMT"). In addition, a taxpayer is al-

---

[63] This description of present law does not incorporate changes made to the child tax credit in the "Protecting Americans From Tax Hikes Act of 2015," Pub. L. No. 114–113. See Part Thirteen, Division Q, Title I, item A.1.
[64] Sec. 24(a).
[65] Sec. 24(c).
[66] Sec. 24(b).

lowed an "additional child tax credit" which is refundable to the extent the credit exceeds the taxpayer's income tax (reduced by non-refundable credits).[67] The additional child tax credit is equal to 15 percent of earned income in excess of a threshold dollar amount (the "earned income" formula).[68] The threshold dollar amount is $3,000 for taxable years beginning before 2018 ($10,000 indexed for inflation since 2001 for taxable years beginning after 2017). For purposes of determining the additional child credit, earned income includes only earned income that is taken into account in determining taxable income. As a result, a citizen living abroad who earns more than the maximum section 911 exclusion (discussed below) will have residual earnings taken into account in determining taxable income, and thus will potentially be eligible for the additional child credit. For example, a married couple with earnings of $113,800 in 2015 would have earnings that exceeded the maximum section 911 exclusion by $13,000, or $10,000 in excess of the additional child credit refundability threshold of $3,000. If they had two qualifying children, the family would be potentially eligible for child credits of $1,800 ($200 of the otherwise allowed child credits is lost due to the income based phase-out of the child credit). The couple faces no U.S. regular income tax liability on the $13,000 against which to claim the credit. However, the couple is eligible for refundable child credits of $1,500 (15 percent of $10,000). In contrast to this couple, a couple earning less than the maximum section 911 exclusion and who claimed the exclusion would have no earnings taken into account in determining taxable income, and thus would not be eligible for the additional child credit. Thus certain higher income citizens working abroad face lower U.S. tax liabilities than lower income citizens working abroad.

Families with three or more children may determine the additional child tax credit using the "alternative formula," if this results in a larger credit than determined under the earned income formula. Under the alternative formula, the additional child tax credit equals the amount by which the taxpayer's social security taxes exceed the taxpayer's earned income tax credit ("EITC").

Earned income is defined as the sum of wages, salaries, tips, and other taxable employee compensation plus net self-employment earnings. Combat pay is treated as earned income taken into account in determining taxable income, regardless of whether it is excluded from gross income for other purposes.

Foreign earned income exclusion

A U.S. citizen or resident living abroad may be eligible to elect to exclude from U.S. taxable income certain foreign earned income and foreign housing costs.[69] This exclusion applies regardless of whether any foreign tax is paid on the foreign earned income or housing costs. To qualify for these exclusions, an individual (a "qualified individual") must have his or her tax home in a foreign country and must be either (1) a U.S. citizen[70] who is a bona fide

---

[67] Secs. 24(d) and 6401(b).
[68] Sec. 24(d)(1)(B)(i).
[69] Sec. 911.
[70] Generally, only U.S. citizens may qualify under the bona fide residence test. A U.S. resident alien who is a citizen of a country with which the United States has a tax treaty may, however,

resident of a foreign country or countries for an uninterrupted period that includes an entire taxable year, or (2) a U.S. citizen or resident present in a foreign country or countries for at least 330 full days in any 12-consecutive-month period.

The maximum amount of foreign earned income that an individual may exclude in 2015 is $100,800.[71] The maximum amount of foreign housing costs that an individual may exclude in 2015 is, in the absence of Treasury adjustment for geographic differences in housing costs, $16,128.[72] The combined foreign earned income exclusion and housing cost exclusion may not exceed the taxpayer's total foreign earned income for the taxable year. The taxpayer's foreign tax credit is reduced by the amount of the credit that is attributable to excluded income.

Explanation of Provision

Under the provision, a taxpayer who elects to exclude from gross income for a taxable year any amount of foreign earned income or foreign housing costs may not claim the refundable portion of the child tax credit for the taxable year.

Effective Date

The provision is effective for taxable years beginning after December 31, 2014.

---

qualify for the section 911 exclusions under the bona fide residence test by application of a non-discrimination provision of the treaty.

[71] Sec. 911(b)(2)(D)(i). This amount is adjusted annually for inflation. The exclusion amount is taken against the lowest marginal tax rates. See sec. 911(f).

[72] Sec. 911(c)(1) and (2). The Secretary of the Treasury has authority to issue guidance making geographic cost-based adjustments. See sec. 911(c)(2)(B). The Secretary has exercised this authority annually. The most recent guidance, Notice 2015–33 (April 14, 2015), includes adjustments for many locations. Under these adjustments, the maximum housing cost exclusion for any geographic area is $114,300 for expenses for housing in Hong Kong, China.

PART SEVEN: SURFACE TRANSPORTATION AND VETERANS HEALTH CARE CHOICE IMPROVEMENT ACT OF 2015 (PUBLIC LAW 114–41) [73]

TITLE II—REVENUE PROVISIONS

A. Extension of Highway Trust Fund Expenditure Authority (sec. 2001 of the Act and secs. 9503, 9504, and 9308 of the Code)

Present Law

Under present law, the Internal Revenue Code (sec. 9503) authorizes expenditures (subject to appropriations) to be made from the Highway Trust Fund (and Sport Fish Restoration and Boating Trust Fund and Leaking Underground Storage Tank Trust Fund) through July 31, 2015, for purposes provided in specified authorizing legislation as in effect on the date of enactment.

Explanation of Provision

This provision extends the authority to make expenditures (subject to appropriations) from the Highway Trust Fund (and Sport Fish Restoration and Boating Trust Fund and Leaking Underground Storage Tank Trust Fund) through October 29, 2015.

Effective Date

The provision is effective on the date of enactment (July 31, 2015).

B. Funding of Highway Trust Fund (sec. 2002 of the Act and sec. 9503(f) of the Code)

Public Law No. 110–318, "an Act to amend the Internal Revenue Code of 1986 to restore the Highway Trust Fund balance" transferred, out of money in the Treasury not otherwise appropriated, $8,017,000,000 to the Highway Trust Fund effective September 15, 2008. Public Law No. 111–46, "an Act to restore sums to the Highway Trust Fund and for other purposes," transferred, out of money in the Treasury not otherwise appropriated, $7 billion to the Highway Trust Fund effective August 7, 2009. The Hiring Incentives to Restore Employment Act transferred, out of money in the Treasury not otherwise appropriated, $14,700,000,000 to the Highway Trust Fund and $4,800,000,000 to the Mass Transit Account in the High-

---

[73] H.R. 3236. The House passed H.R. 3236 on July 29, 2015. The bill passed the Senate without amendment on July 30, 2015. The President signed the bill on July 31, 2015.

way Trust Fund.[74] The HIRE Act provisions generally were effective as of March 18, 2010.

Moving Ahead for Progress in the 21st Century ("MAP–21")[75] provided that, out of money in the Treasury not otherwise appropriated, the following transfers were to be made from the General Fund to the Highway Trust Fund:

	FY 2013	FY 2014
Highway Account	$6.2 billion	$10.4 billion
Mass Transit Account		$2.2 billion

MAP–21 also transferred $2.4 billion from the Leaking Underground Storage Tank Trust Fund to the Highway Account in the Highway Trust Fund.

The Highway and Transportation Funding Act of 2014 transferred $7.765 billion from the General Fund to the Highway Account of the Highway Trust Fund, $2 billion from the General Fund to the Mass Transit Account of the Highway Trust Fund, and $1 billion from the Leaking Underground Storage Tank Trust Fund to the Highway Account of the Highway Trust Fund.[76] The provisions were effective August 8, 2014.

Explanation of Provision

The provision provides that out of money in the Treasury not otherwise appropriated, the following transfers are to be made from the General Fund to the Highway Trust Fund: $6.068 billion to the Highway Account and $2 billion to the Mass Transit Account.

Effective Date

The provision is effective on the date of enactment (July 31, 2015).

C. Modification of Mortgage Reporting Requirements (sec. 2003 of the Act and sec. 6050H of the Code)

Present Law

Any person who, in the course of a trade or business during a calendar year, received from an individual $600 or more of interest during a calendar year on an obligation secured by real property (such as mortgage interest) must file an information return with the IRS and must provide a copy of that return to the payor.[77] The information return generally must include the name, address, and taxpayer identification number of the individual from whom the interest was received, and the amount of the interest and points received for the calendar year.

---

[74] The Hiring Incentives to Restore Employment Act (the "HIRE" Act), Pub. L. No. 111–147, sec. 442.

[75] Moving Ahead for Progress in the 21st Century Act ("MAP–21"), Pub. L. No. 112–141, sec. 40201(a)(2), and sec. 40251.

[76] Highway and Transportation Funding Act of 2014, Pub. L. No. 113–159, sec. 2002.

[77] Sec. 6050H.

Explanation of Provision

Under the provision, the following additional information is required to be included in information returns filed with the IRS and statements furnished to the payor with respect to a debt secured by real property: (i) the amount of outstanding principal on the mortgage as of the beginning of the calendar year, (ii) the loan origination date, and (iii) the address (or other description in the case of property without an address) of the property securing the debt.

Effective Date

The provision applies to returns required to be made, and statements required to be furnished, after December 31, 2016.

D. Consistent Basis Reporting Between Estate and Person Acquiring Property From Decedent (sec. 2004 of the Act and secs. 1014 and 6035 of the Code)

Present Law

The value of an asset for purposes of the estate tax generally is the fair market value at the time of death or at the alternate valuation date.[78] The basis of property acquired from a decedent is the fair market value of the property at the time of the decedent's death or as of an alternate valuation date, if elected by the executor.[79] Under regulations, the fair market value of the property at the date of the decedent's death (or alternate valuation date) is deemed to be its value as appraised for estate tax purposes.[80] However, the value of property as reported on the decedent's estate tax return provides only a rebuttable presumption of the property's basis in the hands of the heir.[81] Unless the heir is estopped by his or her previous actions or statements with regard to the estate tax valuation, the heir may rebut the use of the estate's valuation as his or her basis by clear and convincing evidence. The heir is free to rebut the presumption in two situations: (1) the heir has not used the estate tax value for tax purposes, the IRS has not relied on the heir's representations, and the statute of limitations on assessments has not barred adjustments; and (2) the heir does not have a special relationship to the estate which imposes a duty of consistency.[82]

Explanation of Provision

The provision amends section 1014 generally to require consistency between the estate tax value of property and basis of property acquired from a decedent. Under the provision, if the value of property to which the provision applies has been finally determined for estate tax purposes, the basis in the hands of the recipient can be no greater than the value of the property as finally determined. If

---

[78] Secs. 2031 and 2032.
[79] Sec. 1014. See section 1022 for special basis rules apply to property acquired from an electing estate of a decedent who died during 2010.
[80] Treas. Reg. sec. 1.1014–3(a).
[81] See Rev. Rul. 54–97, 1954–1 C.B. 113, 1954.
[82] See Technical Advice Memorandum 199933001, January 7, 1999.

the value of such property has not been finally determined for estate tax purposes, then the basis in the hands of the recipient can be no greater than the value reported in a required statement. The provision applies to property the inclusion of which in the decedent's estate increased the liability for estate tax on such estate, but does not include any property of an estate if the liability for such tax does not exceed the credits allowable against such tax. For purposes of the provision, the value of property has been finally determined for estate tax purposes if: (1) the value of the property is shown on an estate tax return, and the value is not contested by the Secretary before the expiration of the time for assessing estate tax; (2) in a case not described in (1), the value is specified by the Secretary and such value is not timely contested by the executor of the estate; or (3) the value is determined by a court or pursuant to a settlement agreement with the Secretary.

An executor of a decedent's estate that is required to file an estate tax return under section 6018(a) is required to report to both the recipient and the IRS the value of each interest in property included in the gross estate. A person that is required to file an estate tax return under section 6018(b) (returns by beneficiaries) is required to report to each other person holding a legal or beneficial interest in property to which the return relates and to the IRS the value of each interest in property included in the gross estate. The required reports must be furnished by the time prescribed by the Secretary, but in no case later than the earlier of 30 days after the return is due under section 6018 or 30 days after the return is filed. In any case where reported information is adjusted after a statement has been filed, a supplemental statement must be filed not later than 30 days after such adjustment is made.

The provision grants the Secretary authority to prescribe regulations necessary to carry out the provision, including the application of the provision when no estate tax return is required to be filed and when the surviving joint tenant or other recipient may have better information than the executor regarding the basis or fair market value of the property.

The provision applies the penalty for failure to file correct information returns under section 6721, and failure to furnish correct payee statements under section 6722, to failure to file the new information returns required under the proposal. Additionally, the provision applies the accuracy-related penalty under section 6662 to any inconsistent estate basis. For this purpose, there is an inconsistent estate basis if the basis of property claimed on a return exceeds the basis as determined under the above-described new rules that generally require consistency between the estate tax value of property and the basis of property acquired from a decedent under section 1014.

Effective Date

The provision is applicable to property with respect to which an estate tax return is filed after the date of enactment (July 31, 2015).

E. Clarification of 6-Year Statute of Limitations in Case of Overstatement of Basis (sec. 2005 of Act and sec. 6501 of the Code)

Present Law

Taxes are generally required to be assessed within three years after a taxpayer's return is filed, whether or not it was timely filed.[83] There are several circumstances under which the general three-year limitations period does not begin to run. If no return is filed,[84] if a false or fraudulent return with the intent to evade tax is filed, if private foundation status is terminated, or a gift tax for certain gifts is not properly disclosed, the tax may be assessed, or a proceeding in court for collection of such tax may commence without assessment, at any time.[85]

Other exceptions to the general rule result in an extension of the limitations period otherwise applicable. For example, the limitation period may be extended by taxpayer consent.[86] Failure to disclose or report certain information may also result in extensions of the statute of limitations. For example, failure to disclose a listed transaction as required under section 6011 on any return or statement for a taxable year will result in an extension that ensures that the limitations period remains open for at least one year from the date the requisite information is provided. The limitation period with respect to such transaction will not expire before the date which is one year after the earlier of (1) the date on which the Secretary is provided the information so required, or (2) the date that a "material advisor" (as defined in section 6111) makes its section 6112(a) list available for inspection pursuant to a request by the Secretary under section 6112(b)(1)(A).[87] In addition to the exceptions described above, there are also circumstances under which the three-year limitations period is suspended.[88]

A separate limitations period of six years from the date a return is filed is established for substantial omissions of items from gross income. For a trade or business, the term "gross income" means the total amount received or accrued from the sale of goods or services (if such amounts are required to be shown on the return) prior to diminution by the cost of such sales or services (generally, gross receipts). An omission from gross income is substantial if the omission exceeds 25 percent of the gross income reported on the return or the amount omitted is attributable to a foreign financial asset within the meaning of section 6038D (without regard to dollar thresholds and regulatory exceptions to reporting based on existence of duplicative disclosure requirements) and exceeds $5,000.[89]

---

[83] Sec. 6501(a). Returns that are filed before the date they are due are deemed filed on the due date. See sec. 6501(b)(1) and (2).
[84] Sec. 6501(c)(3).
[85] Sec. 6501(c)(1) and (2).
[86] Sec. 6501(c)(4).
[87] Sec. 6501(c)(10).
[88] For example, service of an administrative summons triggers the suspension either (1) beginning six months after service (in the case of John Doe summonses) or (2) when a proceeding to quash a summons is initiated by a taxpayer named in a summons to a third-party recordkeeper. Judicial proceedings initiated by the government to enforce a summons generally do not suspend the limitation period.
[89] Sec. 6501(e)(1). Similar six year limitations periods are established for estate and gift taxes as well as excise taxes, based on 25 percent omissions from items required to be reported on the relevant tax returns. See secs. 6501(e)(2) and 6501(e)(3).

Amounts that are adequately disclosed on a return, even if not reflected in the amount recorded as gross income, are generally not considered to have been omitted for purposes of determining whether the 25 percent threshold was exceeded. An amount is considered to have been adequately disclosed on a return if it is presented in a manner that is "adequate to apprise the Secretary of the nature and amount of such item."[90]

The six-year statute was enacted in 1954, patterned on an earlier five-year limitations period, with several differences.[91] The earlier statute was shortly thereafter the subject of an opinion of the U.S. Supreme Court, in which the Court held that the statute was clear on its face in requiring an omission of income to trigger the exception.[92] Neither the present statute nor its predecessor explicitly addresses the treatment of overstatements of basis.

A series of courts have considered the issue of whether a basis overstatement on a return may be considered an omission from a taxpayer's income for purposes of the limitations period. The cases dealt with adjustments to "listed" transactions[93] on partnership returns. The litigation results varied, with the result often depending upon the view of the deciding court regarding the vitality of the opinion in *The Colony, Inc.*[94] In cases in which the taxpayer prevailed, the courts generally followed the principle set forth in *The Colony, Inc.*, that "the extended period of limitations applies to situations where specific income receipts have been 'left out' in the computation of gross income and not when an understatement of gross income resulted from an overstatement of basis."

The Secretary promulgated regulations intended to resolve the issue going forward, making it explicit that the portion of income understated by reason of an overstated basis is to be included in determining whether an understatement constituted a 25 percent omission for purposes of the statute of limitations.[95]

In *Home Concrete & Supply, LLC. v. United States*, the U.S. Supreme Court held that an overstatement of basis that contributes to an understatement of income due is not itself considered to be an omission of income, without regard to whether the return re-

---

[90] Sec. 6501(e)(1)(B).

[91] Section 275(c) of the Internal Revenue Code of 1939 stated in its entirety "If the taxpayer omits from gross income an amount properly includible therein which is in excess of 25 per centum of the amount of gross income stated in the return, the tax may be assessed, or a proceeding in court for the collection of such tax may be begun without assessment, at any time within 5 years after the return was filed." 53 Stat. at Large 86 (1st Sess., 76th Cong. 1939). It did not include language comparable to subparagraph 6501(e)(1)(B)(ii), requiring adequacy of disclosure, nor did it distinguish between gross receipts of a trade or business and other income.

[92] *The Colony, Inc., v. Commissioner*, 357 U.S. 28 (1958).

[93] "Listed transactions" refers to transactions that are the same or substantially similar to transactions that the IRS has identified in a published notice as potentially abusive and therefore subject to the reporting requirements under section 6011, notwithstanding the fact that the transaction may not otherwise trigger the reporting requirements.

[94] The Federal, Ninth and Fourth Circuit Courts of Appeals and the U.S. Tax Court held for the taxpayers. See *Salman Ranch Ltd. v. United States*, 573 F.3d 1362 (Fed. Cir. 2009); *Bakersfield Energy Partners v. Commissioner*, 128 T.C. 207 (2007), aff'd, 568 F.3d 767 (9th Cir. 2009); and *Home Concrete & Supply, LLC. v. United States*, 634 F.3d 249 (4th Cir. 2011), aff'd 132 S. Ct. 1836 (2012), for proceedings consistent with the holding in *Home Concrete & Supply, LLC.*). The Tenth Circuit held for the government in *Salman Ranch Ltd. v. Commissioner*, (647 F.3d 929 (10th Cir. 2011), cert. granted, judgment vacated and remanded, (132 S. Ct. 2100 (2012) for proceedings consistent with the holding in *Home Concrete & Supply, LLC.*).

[95] Treas. Regs. secs. 301.6229(c)(2)–1 and 301.6501(e)–1. The Federal Circuit granted deference to the regulations issued subsequent to its *Salman Ranch* opinion and held for the government. *Grapevine Imports, Ltd. v. United States*, 636 F.3d 1368 (Fed. Cir. 2011) cert. granted, judgment vacated and remanded, 132 S. Ct. 2099 (2012).

veals the computation of basis.[96] In deciding in favor of the taxpayer, the Supreme Court followed its interpretation of the word "omits" in the predecessor to section 6501 in *The Colony, Inc.* Having previously interpreted an unambiguous term in the statute, the Court held that the contrary interpretation by the Secretary in Treasury regulations was invalid.

Explanation of Provision

The provision provides that in determining whether an amount greater than 25 percent of gross income was omitted from a return, an understatement of gross income by reason of an overstatement of unrecovered cost or other basis is an omission of gross income, without regard to whether or not the amount of unrecovered cost or basis claimed is disclosed on the return.

Effective Date

The provision is effective for returns filed after the date of enactment (July 31, 2015), as well as to any other return for which the assessment period specified in section 6501 had not yet expired as of that date.

F. Tax Return Due Date Simplification (sec. 2006 of the Act and secs. 6071, 6072, and 6081 of the Code)

Present Law

Persons required to file income tax returns[97] must file such returns in the manner prescribed by the Secretary, in compliance with due dates established in the Code, if any, or by regulations. The Code includes a general rule that requires income tax returns to be filed on or before the 15th day of the fourth month following the end of the taxable year, but certain exceptions are provided both in the Code and in regulations.

A partnership generally is required to file a Federal income tax return on or before the 15th day of the fourth month after the end of the partnership taxable year.[98] For a partnership with a taxable year that is a calendar year, for example, the partnership return due date (and the date by which Schedules K–1 must be furnished to partners) is April 15. However, a partnership is allowed an automatic five-month extension of time to file the partnership return and the Schedule K–1s (to September 15 in the foregoing example) by submitting an application on Form 7004 in accordance with the rules prescribed by the Treasury regulations.[99]

---

[96] 132 S. Ct. 1836; 182 L. Ed. 2d 746 (2012).

[97] Section 6012 provides general rules identifying who must file an income tax return, while other Code provisions referenced herein specifically address filing requirements of partnerships, corporations, and other entities.

[98] Secs. 6031, 6072.

[99] Sec. 6081. Treas. Reg. sec. 1.6081–2. See Department of the Treasury, Internal Revenue Service, *2011 Instructions for Form 1065, U.S. Return of Partnership Income*, p. 3. Unlike other partnerships, an electing large partnership is required to furnish a Schedule K–1 to each partner by the first March 15 following the close of the partnership's taxable year (sec. 6031(b)). However, an electing large partnership is allowed an automatic six-month extension of time to file the partnership return and the Schedule K–1s by submitting an application on form 7004 in accordance with the rules prescribed by the Treasury Regulations. Treas. Reg. sec. 1.6081–2(a)(2).

A C corporation or an S corporation generally is required to file a Federal income tax return on or before the 15th day of the third month following the close of the corporation's taxable year. For a corporation with a taxable year that is a calendar year, for example, the corporate return due date is March 15.[100] However, a corporation is allowed an automatic six-month extension of time to file the corporate return (to September 15 in the foregoing example) by submitting an application on Form 7004 in accordance with the rules prescribed by the Treasury regulations.[101]

To assist taxpayers in preparing their income tax returns and to help the Internal Revenue Service ("IRS") determine whether such income tax returns are correct and complete, present law imposes a variety of information reporting requirements on participants in certain transactions.[102] The primary provision governing information reporting by payors requires an information return by every person engaged in a trade or business who makes payments aggregating $600 or more in any taxable year to a single payee in the course of the payor's trade or business.[103] Payments subject to reporting include fixed or determinable income or compensation, but do not include payments for goods or certain enumerated types of payments that are subject to other specific reporting requirements.[104] Detailed rules are provided for the reporting of various types of investment income, including interest, dividends, and gross proceeds from brokered transactions (such as a sale of stock) paid to U.S. persons.[105]

The payor of amounts described above is required to provide the recipient of the payment with an annual statement showing the aggregate payments made and contact information for the payor.[106] The statement must be supplied to taxpayers by the payors by January 31 of the year following the calendar year for which the return must be filed. Payors generally must file the information return with the IRS on or before the last day of February of the year following the calendar year for which the return must be filed,[107]

---

[100] Secs. 6012, 6037, 6072. Section 6012(a)(2) provides that every corporation subject to taxation under subtitle A shall be required to file an income tax return. Section 6037, which governs the returns of S corporations, provides that any return filed pursuant to section 6037 shall, for purposes of chapter 66 (relating to limitations) be treated as a return filed by the corporation under section 6012. Section 6072, which sets forth the due dates for filing various income tax returns, provides that returns of corporations with a taxable year that is a calendar year under section 6012 (and section 6037 based on the language in that section) are due March 15.

[101] Section 6081(b) provides that a corporation is allowed an automatic extension of three months to file its income tax return if the corporation files the form prescribed by the Secretary and pays on or before the due date prescribed for payment, the amount properly estimated as its tax. However, section 6081(a) provides that the Secretary may grant an automatic extension of up to six months to file and the Treasury regulations do so provide. Treas. Reg. sec. 1.6081–3.

[102] Secs. 6031 through 6060.

[103] Sec. 6041(a). The information return generally is submitted electronically as a Form-1099 or Form-1096, although certain payments to beneficiaries or employees may require use of Forms W-3 or W-2, respectively. Treas. Reg. sec. 1.6041–1(a)(2).

[104] Sec. 6041(a) requires reporting as to fixed or determinable gains, profits, and income (other than payments to which section 6042(a)(1), 6044(a)(1), 6047(c), 6049(a), or 6050N(a) applies and other than payments with respect to which a statement is required under authority of section 6042(a), 6044(a)(2) or 6045). These payments excepted from section 6041(a) include most interest, royalties, and dividends.

[105] Secs. 6042 (dividends), 6045 (broker reporting) and 6049 (interest) and the Treasury regulations thereunder.

[106] Sec. 6041(d).

[107] Treas. Reg. sec. 31.6071(a)–1(a)(3)(i).

unless they file electronically, in which event the information returns are due March 31.[108]

Payors also must report wage amounts paid to employees on information returns. For wages paid to, and taxes withheld from, employees, the payors must file an information return with the Social Security Administration ("SSA") on or before the last day of February of the year following the calendar year for which the return must be filed.[109] However, the due date for information returns that are filed electronically is March 31.

Under the combined annual wage reporting ("CAWR") system, the SSA and the IRS have an agreement, in the form of a Memorandum of Understanding, to share wage data and to resolve, or reconcile, the differences in the wages reported to them. Employers submit Forms W-2, Wage and Tax Statement (listing Social Security wages earned by individual employees), and W-3, Transmittal of Wage and Tax Statements (providing an aggregate summary of wages paid and taxes withheld) directly to SSA.[110] After it records the Forms W-2 and W-3 wage information in its individual Social Security wage account records, SSA forwards the Forms W-2 and W-3 information to IRS.[111]

U.S. persons who transfer assets to, and hold interests in, foreign bank accounts or foreign entities may be subject to self-reporting requirements under both Title 26 (the Internal Revenue Code) and Title 31 (the Bank Secrecy Act) of the United States Code. With respect to account holders, a U.S. citizen, resident, or person doing business in the United States is required to keep records and file reports, as specified by the Secretary, when that person enters into a transaction or maintains an account with a foreign financial agency.[112] Regulations promulgated pursuant to broad regulatory authority granted to the Secretary in the Bank Secrecy Act[113] provide additional guidance regarding the disclosure obligation with respect to foreign accounts and require filing FinCEN Report 114, Report of Foreign Bank and Financial Accounts ("FBAR"), by June 30 of the year following the year in which the $10,000 filing threshold is met.[114] The FBAR is required to be filed electronically with the Treasury Department through the FinCEN BSA E-filing Sys-

---

[108] Secs. 6011(e) and 6071(b) apply to "returns made under subparts B and C of part III of this subchapter"; Treas. Reg. sec. 301.6011–2(b), mandates use of magnetic media by persons filing information returns identified in the regulation or subsequent or contemporaneous revenue procedures and permits use of magnetic media for all others.

[109] Treas. Reg. sec. 31.6051–2; IRS, "Filing Information Returns Electronically," Pub. 3609 (Rev. 12–2011); Treas. Reg. sec. 31.6071(a)–1(a)(3)(i).

[110] Pub. L. No. 94–202, sec. 232, 89 Stat. 1135 (1976) (effective with respect to statements reporting income received after 1977).

[111] Employers submit quarterly reports to IRS on Form 941 regarding aggregate quarterly totals of wages paid and taxes due. IRS then compares the W-3 wage totals to the Form 941 wage totals.

[112] 31 U.S.C. sec. 5314. The term "agency" in the Bank Secrecy Act includes financial institutions.

[113] 31 U.S.C. sec. 5314(a) provides: "Considering the need to avoid impeding or controlling the export or import of monetary instruments and the need to avoid burdening unreasonably a person making a transaction with a foreign financial agency, the Secretary of the Treasury shall require a resident or citizen of the United States or a person in, and doing business in, the United States, to keep records, file reports, or keep records and file reports, when the resident, citizen, or person makes a transaction or maintains a relation for any person with a foreign financial agency."

[114] 31 C.F.R. sec. 103.27(c). The $10,000 threshold is the aggregate value of all foreign financial accounts in which a U.S. person has a financial interest or over which the U.S. person has signature or other authority.

tem.¹¹⁵ Failure to file the FBAR is subject to both criminal¹¹⁶ and civil penalties.¹¹⁷ The regulations do not provide for extensions of time in which to file the FBAR.

Explanation of Provision

The provision includes the following changes: (i) filing deadline for partnerships and S corporations precede the due dates of their individual and corporate investors and (ii) the due date for filing returns by C corporations to be determined under general rule, with effect that it is a later return than under present law. It also includes statutory confirmation that six-month extension for time to file corporate income tax return is automatic, and requires regulatory updates to the rules regarding extension of time to file a return, including changes to conform the FBAR filing due date with income tax filing dates for individuals.

Filing deadlines for business income tax returns

The provision accelerates the due date for filing of Federal income tax returns of partnerships and S corporations by one month, to the 15th day of the third month following the close of the taxable year. It also removes C corporations from the scope of the exception to the general rule that requires income tax returns to be filed by the 15th day of the fourth month after the end of a taxable year, with the result that C corporation returns are generally due on or before the 15th day of the fourth month following the close of a taxable year, with the exception of certain C corporations electing a fiscal year ending on June 30. For those C corporations, the first return for which the due date as amended applies is the return with respect to a fiscal year beginning in 2026.

Extensions of time to file tax returns

The provision modifies the statute (consistent with current Treasury regulations) to grant an automatic six-month extension of time to file a Federal corporate income tax return, with two exceptions. First, C corporations with a taxable year ending on June 30 are granted a seven-month extension for returns with respect to taxable years beginning before January 1, 2026. For C corporations with a taxable year ending on December 31, the extension available for taxable years beginning before January 1, 2026 is five months. As with present law, the eligibility for the automatic extension is contingent on the corporation filing the form prescribed by the Secretary and paying all tax estimated to be due on or before the due date prescribed for payment.

The provision requires that the Treasury Department modify its regulations to conform the extension periods prescribed to the following terms. The maximum extension for the returns of partnerships using a calendar year is a six-month period ending on September 15. The maximum extension for the returns of trusts using

---

¹¹⁵ See http://bsaefiling.fincen.treas.gov/main.html. The predecessor form, Treasury Form TD F 90–22.1, was filed with the IRS Detroit Computing Center.

¹¹⁶ 31 U.S.C. sec. 5322 (failure to file is punishable by a fine up to $250,000 and imprisonment for five years, which may double if the violation occurs in conjunction with certain other violations).

¹¹⁷ 31 U.S.C. sec. 5321(a)(5).

a calendar year is a 5½ month period ending on September 30. The maximum extension for the returns of employee benefit plans using a calendar year is an automatic 3½ month period ending on November 15.[118] The maximum extension for the returns of tax-exempt organizations using a calendar year is an automatic six-month period ending on November 15. The due date for forms relating to the Annual Information Return of Foreign Trust with a United States Owner for calendar year filers is April 15 with a maximum extension for a six-month period ending on October 15.

FBAR due date conformity with income tax filing

In addition to requiring modification of the regulatory deadlines established for extensions of time to file income tax returns, the provision also requires that regulations establishing the due date for the form required under FBAR be amended. Under the provision, the FBAR due date is April 15 with regulatory authority to grant an extension of up to a six-month period ending on October 15. The provision permits the Secretary to waive any penalties for failure to file a timely request for an extension if the reporting period to which the penalty relates is the first period for which the taxpayer was subject to the FBAR requirements.

Effective Date

Changes to the filing due dates for partnerships, S corporations and C corporations are effective for returns for taxable years beginning after December 31, 2015, with one exception. For returns for C corporations with fiscal years ending on June 30, the amended due date does not apply until taxable years beginning after December 31, 2025.

The requirements that the Secretary revise certain filing due dates and extensions for taxable years beginning after December 31, 2016 are effective upon date of enactment (July 31, 2015).

Finally, the automatic six-month extension of time to file corporate income tax returns is effective for taxable years beginning after December 31, 2015 of all corporations, with the exceptions of C corporations with taxable years ending either June 30 or December 31. For years beginning before January 1, 2026, C corporations with a taxable year ending June 30 are permitted a seven month extension of time to file rather than six months. For C corporations with a taxable year ending December 31, the maximum extension of time to file for years beginning before January 1, 2026 is five months rather than six months.

G. Transfers of Excess Pension Assets to Retiree Health Accounts (sec. 2007 of the Act and sec. 420 of the Code)

Present Law

Subject to various conditions, a qualified transfer of excess assets of a defined benefit plan may be made to a retiree medical account or life insurance account within the plan to fund retiree health

---

[118] The provision relating to returns of employee benefit plans was repealed by section 32104 of the Fixing America's Surface Transportation ("FAST") Act, Pub. L. No. 114–94, as described in Part Twelve, Title XXXII, item C.

benefits and group term life insurance benefits ("applicable retiree benefits").[119] For this purpose, excess assets generally means the excess, if any, of the value of the plan's assets over 125 percent of the sum of the plan's funding target and target normal cost for the plan year (as defined under the funding rules for single-employer plans). A qualified transfer does not result in plan disqualification, is not a prohibited transaction, and is not treated as a reversion. No deduction is allowed to the employer for (1) a qualified transfer, or (2) the payment of applicable retiree benefits out of transferred funds (and any income thereon).

In order for the transfer to be qualified, accrued retirement benefits under the plan generally must be 100-percent vested as if the plan terminated immediately before the transfer (or in the case of a participant who separated in the one-year period ending on the date of the transfer, immediately before the separation). In addition, at least 60 days before the date of a qualified transfer, the employer must notify the Secretary of Labor, the Secretary of the Treasury, employee representatives, and the plan administrator of the transfer, and the plan administrator must notify each plan participant and beneficiary of the transfer.[120]

No more than one qualified transfer may be made in any taxable year. For this purpose, a transfer to a retiree medical account and a transfer to a retiree life insurance account in the same year are treated as one transfer. No qualified transfer may be made after December 31, 2021.

Explanation of Provision

Under the provision, no qualified transfers may be made after December 31, 2025. Thus, qualified transfers are permitted through that date.

Effective Date

The provision is effective on the date of enactment (July 31, 2015).

H. Equalization of Highway Trust Fund Excise Taxes on Liquefied Natural Gas, Liquefied Petroleum Gas, and Compressed Natural Gas (sec. 2008 of the Act and sec. 4041 of the Code)

Present Law

The Code imposes an excise tax on gasoline, diesel fuel, kerosene, and certain alternative fuels at the following rates:[121]

---

[119] Sec. 420. Qualified transfers of excess assets are generally made within single-employer defined benefit plans, but are permitted also within multiemployer plans.

[120] Sec. 101(e) of the Employee Retirement Income Security Act of 1974.

[121] These fuels are subject to an additional 0.1-cent-per-gallon excise tax to fund the Leaking Underground Storage Tank ("LUST") Trust Fund (secs. 4041(d) and 4081(a)(2)(B)). That tax is imposed as an "add-on" to other existing taxes.

[122] Diesel-water emulsions are taxed at 19.7 cents per gallon (sec. 4081(a)(2)(D)).

[123] The rate of tax is 24.3 cents per gallon in the case of liquefied natural gas, any liquid fuel (other than ethanol or methanol) derived from coal, and liquid hydrocarbons derived from biomass. Other alternative fuels sold or used as motor fuel are generally taxed at 18.3 cents per gallon. "Alternative fuel" also includes compressed natural gas. The rate for compressed natural gas is 18.3 cents per energy equivalent of a gallon of gasoline. See sec. 4041(a)(2) and (3).

Gasoline	18.3 cents per gallon
Diesel fuel and kerosene	24.3 cents per gallon [122]
Alternative fuels	24.3 and 18.3 cents per gallon [123]

The Code imposes tax on gasoline, diesel fuel, and kerosene upon removal from a refinery or on importation, unless the fuel is transferred in bulk by registered pipeline or barge to a registered terminal facility.[124] The imposition of tax on alternative fuels generally occurs at retail when the fuel is sold to an owner, lessee or other operator of a motor vehicle or motorboat for use as a fuel in such motor vehicle or motorboat.

Liquefied natural gas ("LNG") and liquefied petroleum gas (also known as propane) are classified as alternative fuels. LNG is taxed at the same per gallon rate as diesel, 24.3 cents per gallon. According to the Oak Ridge National Laboratory, diesel fuel has an energy content of 128,700 Btu per gallon (lower heating value) and LNG has an energy content of 74,700 Btu per gallon (lower heating value). Therefore, a gallon of LNG produces approximately 58 percent of the energy produced by a gallon of diesel fuel.

Liquefied petroleum gas is taxed at the same per gallon rate as gasoline, 18.3 cents per gallon. According to the Oak Ridge National Laboratory, gasoline has an energy content of 115,400 Btu per gallon (lower heating value), and liquefied petroleum gas has an energy content of 83,500 Btu per gallon (lower heating value). Therefore, a gallon of liquefied petroleum gas produces approximately 72 percent of the energy produced by a gallon of gasoline.

Compressed natural gas is taxed at 18.3 cents per energy equivalent of a gasoline gallon of gasoline. In Notice 2006–92, the IRS provided that this rate is 18.3 cents per 126.67 cubic feet of compressed natural gas.

Explanation of Provision

The provision changes the tax rate of LNG to a rate based on its energy equivalent of a gallon of diesel and changes the tax rate of liquefied petroleum gas to a rate based on its energy equivalent of a gallon of gasoline.

Specifically, the provision provides that liquefied petroleum gas is taxed at 18.3 cents per energy equivalent of a gallon of gasoline. For this purpose, "energy equivalent of a gallon of gasoline" means, with respect to liquefied petroleum gas, the amount of such fuel having a Btu content of 115,400 (lower heating value), which is 5.75 pounds of liquefied petroleum gas.

LNG is taxed at 24.3 cents per energy equivalent of a gallon of diesel fuel. For this purpose, "energy equivalent of a gallon of diesel" means, with respect to a liquefied natural gas fuel, the amount of such fuel having a Btu content of 128,700 (lower heating value), which is 6.06 pounds of liquefied natural gas.

Compressed natural gas is taxed at 18.3 cents per energy equivalent of a gallon of gasoline, which is 5.66 pounds of compressed natural gas.

---

[124] Sec. 4081(a)(1).

Effective Date

The provision is effective for fuel sold or used after December 31, 2015.

TITLE IV—VETERANS PROVISIONS

A. Exemption in Determination of Employer Health Insurance Mandate (sec. 4007(a) of the Act and sec. 4980H of the Code)

Present Law

Employer shared responsibility for health coverage

In general

Under the Patient Protection and Affordable Care Act ("PPACA"),[125] as amended by the Health Care and Education Reconciliation Act of 20101A[126] (referred to collectively as the "Affordable Care Act" or "ACA"), an applicable large employer may be subject to a tax, called an "assessable payment," for a month if one or more of its full–time employees is certified to the employer as receiving for the month a premium assistance credit for health insurance purchased on an American Health Benefit Exchange or reduced cost-sharing for the employee's share of expenses covered by such health insurance.[127] As discussed below, whether an applicable large employer owes an assessable payment and the amount of any assessable payment depend on whether the employer offers its full-time employees and their dependents the opportunity to enroll in minimum essential coverage under a group health plan sponsored by the employer and, if it does, whether the coverage offered is affordable and provides minimum value.[128]

Definitions of full-time employee and applicable large employer

For purposes of applying these rules, full-time employee means, with respect to any month, an employee who is employed on average at least 30 hours of service per week. Hours of service are to be determined under regulations, rules, and guidance prescribed by the Secretary of the Treasury ("Secretary"), in consultation with the Secretary of Labor, including rules for employees who are not compensated on an hourly basis.

---

[125] Pub. L. No. 111–148.

[126] Pub. L. No. 111–152.

[127] Sec. 4980H. This is sometimes referred to as the employer shared responsibility requirement or employer mandate. An applicable large employer is also subject to annual reporting requirements under section 6056. Premium assistance credits for health insurance purchased on an American Health Benefit Exchange are provided under section 36B. Reduced cost-sharing for an individual's share of expenses covered by such health insurance is provided under section 1402 of PPACA. For further information on these provisions, see Part II.B–D of Joint Committee on Taxation, *Present Law and Background Relating to the Tax-Related Provisions in the Affordable Care Act* (JCX–6–13), March 4, 2013, available at www.jct.gov.

[128] Under the ACA, these rules are effective for months beginning after December 31, 2013. However, in Notice 2013–45, 2013–31 I.R.B. 116, Part III, Q&A–2, the Internal Revenue Service ("IRS") announced that no assessable payments will be assessed for 2014. In addition, in 2014, the IRS announced that no assessable payments for 2015 will apply to applicable large employers that have fewer than 100 full-time employees and full-time equivalent employees and meet certain other requirements. Section XV.D.6 of the preamble to the final regulations, T.D. 9655, 79 Fed. Reg. 8544, 8574–8575, February 12, 2014.

Applicable large employer generally means, with respect to a calendar year, an employer who employed an average of at least 50 full-time employees on business days during the preceding calendar year.[129] Solely for purposes of determining whether an employer is an applicable large employer (that is, whether the employer has at least 50 full-time employees), besides the number of full-time employees, the employer must include the number of its full-time equivalent employees for a month, determined by dividing the aggregate number of hours of service for that month (up to a maximum of 120 for any employee) of employees who are not full-time employees for the month by 120. In addition, in determining whether an employer is an applicable large employer, members of the same controlled group, group under common control, and affiliated service group are treated as a single employer.[130]

Assessable payments

If an applicable large employer does not offer its full-time employees and their dependents minimum essential coverage under an employer-sponsored plan for a month and at least one full-time employee is certified as receiving for the month a premium assistance credit or reduced cost-sharing, the employer may be subject to an assessable payment of $2,0001A[131] (divided by 12 and applied on a monthly basis) multiplied by the number of its full-time employees minus 30, regardless of the number of full-time employees so certified. For example, in 2016, Employer A fails to offer minimum essential coverage and has 100 full-time employees, 10 of whom receive premium assistance credits for the entire year. The employer's assessable payment is $2,000 for each full-time employee over the 30-employee threshold, for a total of $140,000 ($2,000 multiplied by 70 (100 – 30)).

Generally, an employee who is offered minimum essential coverage under an employer-sponsored plan is not eligible for a premium assistance credit or reduced cost-sharing unless the coverage is unaffordable or fails to provide minimum value.[132] However, if an employer offers its full-time employees and their dependents minimum essential coverage under an employer-sponsored plan and at least one full-time employee is certified as receiving a premium assistance credit or reduced cost-sharing (because the coverage is unaffordable or fails to provide minimum value), the em-

---

[129] Additional rules apply, for example, in the case of an employer that was not in existence for the entire preceding calendar year.

[130] The rules for determining controlled group, group under common control, and affiliated service group under section 414(b), (c), (m) and (o) apply for this purpose. If the group is an applicable large employer under this test, each member of the group is an applicable large employer and subject to the employer shared responsibility requirement even if the member by itself would not be an applicable large employer. In addition, in determining assessable payments (as discussed herein), only one 30-employee reduction in full-time employees applies to the group and is allocated among the members ratably based on the number of full-time employees employed by each member.

[131] For calendar years after 2014, the $2,000 dollar amount, and the $3,000 dollar amount referenced herein, are increased by the percentage (if any) by which the average per capita premium for health insurance coverage in the United States for the preceding calendar year (as estimated by the Secretary of Health and Human Services ("HHS") no later than October 1 of the preceding calendar year) exceeds the average per capita premium for 2013 (as determined by the Secretary of HHS), rounded down to the nearest $10.

[132] Under section 36B(c)(2)(C), coverage under an employer-sponsored plan is unaffordable if the employee's share of the premium for self-only coverage exceeds 9.5 percent of household income, and the coverage fails to provide minimum value if the plan's share of total allowed cost of provided benefits is less than 60 percent of such costs.

ployer may be subject to an assessable payment of $3,000 (divided by 12 and applied on a monthly basis) multiplied by the number of such full-time employees. However, the assessable payment in this case is capped at the amount that would apply if the employer failed to offer its full-time employees and their dependents minimum essential coverage. For example, in 2016, Employer A offers minimum essential coverage and has 100 full-time employees, 20 of whom receive premium assistance credits for the entire year. The employer's assessable payment before consideration of the cap is $3,000 for each full-time employee receiving a credit, for a total of $60,000 ($3,000 multiplied by 20). The cap on the assessable payment is the amount that would have applied if the employer failed to offer coverage, or $140,000 ($2,000 multiplied by 70 (100 − 30)). In this example, the cap therefore does not affect the amount of the assessable payment, which remains at $60,000.

TRICARE and veterans health programs

The Military Health System provides active and retired members of the armed forces and their families (including certain survivors and former spouses) with medical coverage, primarily through the TRICARE program.[133] The TRICARE program offers various health plans, including a managed care option and fee-for-service options.

The Veterans Health Administration ("VHA"), within the Department of Veterans Affairs, provides certain veterans and family members (including certain survivors) with medical coverage through its health care programs.[134] Enrolled veterans are provided a medical benefits package that covers a range of medical care, including inpatient, outpatient, and preventive services. Medical coverage for eligible family members of veterans is provided through the Civilian Health and Medical Program of the Department of Veterans Affairs ("CHAMPVA").[135]

Explanation of Provision

Under the provision, solely for purposes of determining whether an employer is an applicable large employer (and possibly subject to an assessable payment), an individual is not taken into account as an employee for the month if the individual has medical coverage for the month under (1) a program for members of the armed forces, including coverage under the TRICARE program, or (2) under a VHA health care program, as determined by the Secretary of Veterans Affairs, in coordination with the Secretary of Health and Human Services and the Secretary. The provision affects only the determination of applicable large employer status, not whether an employer that is an applicable large employer, after application

---

[133] 110 U.S.C. chapter 55. Under section 5000A(f)(1)(A)(iv), this coverage satisfies the requirement under ACA that individuals have minimum essential coverage.

[134] 138 U.S.C. chapters 17 and 18.

[135] Under section 5000A(f)(1)(A)(v), minimum essential coverage includes coverage under a VHA health care program, as determined by the Secretary of Veterans Affairs, in coordination with the Secretary of Health and Human Services and the Secretary. Under Treas. Reg. sec. 1.5000A–2(b)(1)(v), the medical benefits package that enrolled veterans receive and CHAMPVA coverage are minimum essential coverage, as well as the comprehensive health care program for certain children of Vietnam Veterans and Veterans of covered service in Korea who are suffering from spina bifida.

of the provision, is subject to an assessable payment or the amount of any assessable payment.

Effective Date

The provision applies to months beginning after December 31, 2013.

B. Eligibility for Health Savings Account Not Affected by Receipt of Medical Care for a Service-Connected Disability (sec. 4007(b) of the Act and sec. 223 of the Code)

Present Law

An individual with a high deductible health plan and no other health plan (other than a plan that provides certain permitted insurance or permitted coverage) is generally eligible to make deductible contributions to a health savings account ("HSA"), subject to certain limits (an "eligible individual"). HSA contributions made on behalf of an eligible individual by an employer are excludible from income and wages for employment tax purposes. Eligibility for HSA contributions is generally determined monthly, based on the individual's status and health plan coverage as of the first day of the month. Contributions to an HSA cannot be made once an individual is enrolled in Medicare.

An individual with other coverage in addition to a high deductible health plan is still eligible to make HSA contributions if such other coverage is permitted insurance or permitted coverage. Permitted insurance is: (1) insurance if substantially all of the coverage provided under such insurance relates to (a) liabilities incurred under worker's compensation law, (b) tort liabilities, (c) liabilities relating to ownership or use of property (*e.g.,* auto insurance), or (d) such other similar liabilities as the Secretary of the Treasury may prescribe by regulations; (2) insurance for a specified disease or illness; and (3) insurance that provides a fixed payment per day (or other period) for hospitalization. Permitted coverage is coverage (whether provided through insurance or otherwise) for accidents, disability, dental care, vision care, or long-term care. Coverage under certain health flexible spending arrangements or health reimbursement arrangements is also permitted.

Under IRS guidance, an otherwise eligible individual who is eligible for medical benefits under a program of the Department of Veterans Affairs ("VA"), but who has not actually received such benefits during the preceding three months, is an eligible individual.[136] However, an individual is not eligible to make HSA contributions for any month if the individual has received VA medical benefits at any time during the previous three months unless the benefits are for permissible coverage or preventive care.[137]

Explanation of Provision

Under the provision, an individual does not fail to be treated as an eligible individual for any period merely because the individual

---

[136] Notice 2004–50, 2004–2 C.B. 196, Q&A–5.
[137] Notice 2004–50, Q&A–5; Notice 2008–59, 2008–2 C.B. 123, Q&A–9.

receives hospital care or medical services under any law administered by the VA for a service-connected disability.[138]

The provision does not otherwise change the application of the present-law rule for individuals eligible for VA medical benefits. Thus, an otherwise eligible individual who is eligible for VA medical benefits, but who has not actually received such benefits during the preceding three months, continues to be an eligible individual. However, an individual is not eligible to make HSA contributions for any month if the individual has received VA medical benefits at any time during the previous three months unless the benefits are for permissible coverage or preventive care or for a service-connected disability.

Effective Date

The provision applies to months beginning after December 31, 2015.

---

[138] For this purpose, the definition of service–connected disability under 38 U.S.C. sec. 101(16) applies.

PART EIGHT: AIRPORT AND AIRWAY EXTENSION ACT OF 2015 (PUBLIC LAW 114–55) [139]

A. Extension of Spending Authority and Taxes Funding Airport and Airway Trust Fund (secs. 201 and 202 of the Act and secs. 4083, 4801, 4261, 4271, and 9502 of the Code)

Present Law

Taxes dedicated to the Airport and Airway Trust Fund

Excise taxes are imposed on amounts paid for commercial air passenger and freight transportation and on fuels used in commercial and noncommercial (i.e., transportation that is not "for hire") aviation to fund the Airport and Airway Trust Fund.[140] The present aviation excise taxes and rates are as follows:

Tax (and Code section)	Tax Rates
Domestic air passengers (sec. 4261)	7.5 percent of fare, plus $4.00 (2015) per domestic flight segment generally [141]
International air passengers (sec. 4261)	$17.70 (2015) per arrival or departure [142]
Amounts paid for right to award free or reduced rate passenger air transportation (sec. 4261).	7.5 percent of amount paid
Air cargo (freight) transportation (sec. 4271)	6.25 percent of amount charged for domestic transportation; no tax on international cargo transportation

Tax (and Code section)	Tax Rates
Aviation fuels (sec. 4081): [143]	
Commercial aviation	4.3 cents per gallon
Non-commercial (general) aviation:	
Aviation gasoline	19.3 cents per gallon
Jet fuel	21.8 cents per gallon
Fractional aircraft fuel surtax (sec. 4043)	14.1 cents per gallon

The Airport and Airway Trust Fund excise taxes (except for 4.3 cents per gallon of the taxes on aviation fuels and the 14.1 cents

---

[139] H.R. 3614. The House passed H.R. 3614 on September 28, 2015. The Senate passed the bill without amendment on September 29, 2015. The President signed the bill on September 30, 2015.

[140] Air transportation through U.S. airspace that neither lands in nor takes off from a point in the United States (or the 225-mile zone, described below) is exempt from the aviation excise taxes, but the transportation provider is subject to certain "overflight fees" imposed by the Federal Aviation Administration pursuant to Congressional authorization.

[141] The domestic flight segment portion of the tax is adjusted annually (effective each January 1) for inflation (adjustments based on the changes in the consumer price index (the "CPI")). Special rules apply to air transportation between the continental United States and Alaska or Hawaii and between Alaska and Hawaii. The portion of such transportation that is not within the United States (e.g., the portion over the Pacific Ocean) is not subject to the 7.5-percent domestic air passenger excise tax. In addition to this pro-rated ad valorem tax, an $8.90 (2015) international tax rate for the excluded portion of the travel is imposed. The domestic flight segment component of tax applies under the same rules as for flights within the continental United States. Further, transportation within Alaska or Hawaii is taxed in the same manner as domestic transportation within the continental United States.

[142] The international arrival and departure tax rate is adjusted annually for inflation (measured by changes in the CPI).

per gallon fractional aircraft fuel surtax) are scheduled to expire after September 30, 2015. The 4.3-cents-per-gallon fuels tax rate is permanent.

With respect to fractional aircraft, the exemption from the excise tax on commercial transportation for fractional aircraft is scheduled to expire after September 30, 2015.[144] The fractional aircraft fuel surtax expires after September 30, 2021.

Airport and Airway Trust Fund expenditure provisions

The Airport and Airway Trust Fund was established in 1970 to finance a major portion of national aviation programs (previously funded entirely with General Fund revenues). Operation of the Trust Fund is governed by parallel provisions of the Code and authorizing statutes.[145] The Code provisions govern deposit of revenues into the Trust Fund and approve expenditure purposes in authorizing statutes as in effect on the date of enactment of the latest authorizing Act. The authorizing Acts provide for specific Trust Fund expenditure programs.

No expenditures are permitted to be made from the Airport and Airway Trust Fund after September 30, 2015. The purposes for which Airport and Airway Trust Fund monies are permitted to be expended are fixed as of the date of enactment of the FAA Modernization and Reform Act of 2012; therefore, the Code must be amended in order to authorize new Airport and Airway Trust Fund expenditure purposes.[146] The Code contains a specific enforcement provision to prevent expenditure of Trust Fund monies for purposes not authorized under Code section 9502.[147] This provision provides that, should such unapproved expenditures occur, no further aviation excise tax receipts will be transferred to the Trust Fund. Rather, the aviation taxes will continue to be imposed, but the receipts will be retained in the General Fund.

Explanation of Provision

The Act extends through March 31, 2016, the taxes, exemptions, and expenditure authority that were scheduled to expire on September 30, 2015.

Effective Date

The provision is effective on the date of enactment (September 30, 2015).

---

[143] Like most other taxable motor fuels, aviation fuels are subject to an additional 0.1-cent-per-gallon excise tax to fund the LUST Trust Fund.
[144] Sec. 4261(i).
[145] Sec. 9502 and 49 U.S.C. sec. 48101, *et. seq*.
[146] Sec. 9502(d).
[147] Sec. 9502(e)(1).

PART NINE: SURFACE TRANSPORTATION EXTENSION ACT OF 2015 (PUBLIC LAW 114-73) [148]

A. Extension of Highway Trust Fund Expenditure Authority (sec. 2001 of the Act and secs. 9503, 9504, and 9508 of the Code)

Present Law

Under present law, the Internal Revenue Code (sec. 9503) authorizes expenditures (subject to appropriations) to be made from the Highway Trust Fund (and Sport Fish Restoration and Boating Trust Fund and Leaking Underground Storage Tank Trust Fund) through October 29, 2015, for purposes provided in specified authorizing legislation as in effect on the date of enactment.

Explanation of Provision

This provision extends the authority to make expenditures (subject to appropriations) from the Highway Trust Fund (and Sport Fish Restoration and Boating Trust Fund and Leaking Underground Storage Tank Trust Fund) through November 20, 2015.

Effective Date

The provision is effective on date of enactment (October 29, 2015).

---

[148] H.R. 3819. The House passed H.R. 3819 on October 27, 2015. The bill passed the Senate without amendment on October 28, 2015. The President signed the bill on October 29, 2015.

PART TEN: BIPARTISAN BUDGET ACT OF 2015 (PUBLIC LAW 114–74) [149]

TITLE V—PENSIONS

A. Mortality Tables and Extension of Current Funding Stabilization Percentages to 2018, 2019, and 2020 (secs. 503–504 of the Act, sec. 430 of the Code, and secs. 101(f) and 303 of ERISA) [150]

Present Law

Minimum funding rules

A defined benefit plan maintained by a single employer is subject to minimum funding rules that generally require the sponsoring employer to make a certain level of contribution for each plan year to fund plan benefits.[151] The minimum funding rules for single-employer defined benefit plans were substantially revised by the Pension Protection Act of 2006 ("PPA").[152]

Minimum required contributions

In general

The minimum required contribution for a plan year for a single-employer defined benefit plan generally depends on a comparison of the value of the plan's assets, reduced by any prefunding balance or funding standard carryover balance ("net value of plan assets"),[153] with the plan's funding target and target normal cost.

---

[149] H.R. 1314. The House Ways and Means Committee reported H.R. 1314 on April 13, 2015 (H.R. Rep. No. 114–67). The House passed the bill on April 15, 2015. The Senate passed the bill with an amendment on May 22, 2015. The House agreed to an amendment to the Senate amendment on October 28, 2015. The Senate agreed to the House amendment on October 30, 2015. The President signed the bill on November 2, 2015.

[150] Sections 501–502 of the Act change the premiums required to be paid to the Pension Benefit Guaranty Corporation with respect to single-employer defined benefit plans under sections 4006–4007 of the Employee Retirement Income Security Act of 1974 ("ERISA").

[151] Secs. 412 and 430; ERISA secs. 302–303. For purposes of whether a plan is maintained by a single employer, certain related entities, such as the members of a controlled group, are treated as a single employer. Different funding rules apply to multiemployer and certain multiple-employer defined benefit plans, which are types of plans maintained by two or more unrelated employers. A number of exceptions to the minimum funding rules apply. For example, governmental plans (within the meaning of section 414(d)) and church plans (within the meaning of section 414(e)) are generally not subject to the minimum funding rules. Under section 4971, an excise tax generally applies if the minimum funding requirements are not satisfied.

[152] Pub. L. No. 109–280. The PPA minimum funding rules for single-employer plans are generally effective for plan years beginning after December 31, 2007. Subsequent changes were made by the Worker, Retiree, and Employer Recovery Act of 2008 ("WRERA"), Pub. L. No. 110–458; the Preservation of Access to Care for Medicare Beneficiaries and Pension Relief Act of 2010 ("PRA 2010"), Pub. L. No. 111–192; and the Moving Ahead for Progress in the 21st Century Act, Pub. L. No. 112–141, and the Highway and Transportation Funding Act of 2014, Pub. L. No. 113–159, discussed further herein.

[153] The value of plan assets is generally reduced by any prefunding balance or funding standard carryover balance in determining minimum required contributions. A prefunding balance results from plan contributions that exceed the minimum required contributions. A funding standard carryover balance results from a positive balance in the funding standard account that ap-

Continued

The plan's funding target for a plan year is the present value of all benefits accrued or earned as of the beginning of the plan year. A plan's target normal cost for a plan year is generally the present value of benefits expected to accrue or to be earned during the plan year.

If the net value of plan assets is less than the plan's funding target, so that the plan has a funding shortfall (discussed further below), the minimum required contribution is the sum of the plan's target normal cost and the shortfall amortization charge for the plan year (determined as described below).[154] If the net value of plan assets is equal to or exceeds the plan's funding target, the minimum required contribution is the plan's target normal cost, reduced by the amount, if any, by which the net value of plan assets exceeds the plan's funding target.

Shortfall amortization charge

The shortfall amortization charge for a plan year is the sum of the annual shortfall amortization installments attributable to the shortfall bases for that plan year and the six previous plan years. Generally, if a plan has a funding shortfall for the plan year, a shortfall amortization base must be established for the plan year.[155] A plan's funding shortfall is the amount by which the plan's funding target exceeds the net value of plan assets. The shortfall amortization base for a plan year is: (1) the plan's funding shortfall, minus (2) the present value, determined using the segment interest rates (discussed below), of the aggregate total of the shortfall amortization installments that have been determined for the plan year and any succeeding plan year with respect to any shortfall amortization bases for the six previous plan years. The shortfall amortization base is amortized in level annual installments ("shortfall amortization installments") over a seven-year period beginning with the current plan year and using the segment interest rates (discussed below).[156]

The shortfall amortization base for a plan year may be positive or negative, depending on whether the present value of remaining installments with respect to amortization bases for previous years is more or less than the plan's funding shortfall. If the shortfall amortization base is positive (that is, the funding shortfall exceeds the present value of the remaining installments), the related shortfall amortization installments are positive. If the shortfall amorti-

---

plied under the funding requirements in effect before PPA. Subject to certain conditions, a prefunding balance or funding standard carryover balance may be credited against the minimum required contribution for a year, reducing the amount that must be contributed.

[154] If the plan has obtained a waiver of the minimum required contribution (a funding waiver) within the past five years, the minimum required contribution also includes the related waiver amortization charge, that is, the annual installment needed to amortize the waived amount in level installments over the five years following the year of the waiver.

[155] If the value of plan assets, reduced only by any prefunding balance if the employer elects to apply the prefunding balance against the required contribution for the plan year, is at least equal to the plan's funding target, no shortfall amortization base is established for the year.

[156] Under PRA 2010, employers were permitted to elect to use one of two alternative extended amortization schedules for up to two "eligible" plan years during the period 2008–2011. The use of an extended amortization schedule has the effect of reducing the amount of the shortfall amortization installments attributable to the shortfall amortization base for the eligible plan year. However, the shortfall amortization installments attributable to an eligible plan year may be increased by an additional amount, an "installment acceleration amount," in the case of employee compensation exceeding $1 million, extraordinary dividends, or stock redemptions within a certain period of the eligible plan year.

zation base is negative, the related shortfall amortization installments are negative. The positive and negative shortfall amortization installments for a particular plan year are netted when adding them up in determining the shortfall amortization charge for the plan year, but the resulting shortfall amortization charge cannot be less than zero (that is, negative amortization installments may not offset normal cost).

If the net value of plan assets for a plan year is at least equal to the plan's funding target for the year, so the plan has no funding shortfall, any shortfall amortization bases and related shortfall amortization installments are eliminated.[157] As indicated above, if the net value of plan assets exceeds the plan's funding target, the excess is applied against target normal cost in determining the minimum required contribution.

Mortality tables

In general

In determining the present value of benefits for purposes of a plan's target normal cost and funding target, specific mortality tables prescribed by the IRS generally must be used.[158] These tables are to be based on the actual experience of pension plans and projected trends in such experience. In prescribing tables, the IRS is required to take into account results of available independent studies of mortality of individuals covered by pension plans. In addition, the IRS is required (at least every 10 years) to revise any table in effect to reflect the actual experience of pension plans and projected trends in such experience. The currently applicable mortality tables are specified in regulations, as updated in subsequent IRS guidance.[159]

Substitute mortality table

In some cases, a separate mortality table (a "substitute" mortality table) may be used upon request of the plan sponsor and approval by the IRS.[160] Two requirements must be met in order for a substitute mortality table to be used: (1) the table must reflect the actual experience of the pension plans maintained by the plan sponsor and projected trends in general mortality experience, and (2) there must be a sufficient number of plan participants, and the pension plans must have been maintained for a sufficient period of time, to have credible information necessary for purposes of requirement (1). In addition, a substitute mortality table generally may not be used for any plan unless (1) a separate mortality table is established and used for each other plan maintained by the plan

---

[157] Any amortization base relating to a funding waiver for a previous year is also eliminated.

[158] Sec. 430(h)(3) and ERISA sec. 303(h)(3). Separate mortality tables are required to be used with respect to disabled participants.

[159] Treas. Reg. sec. 1.430(h)(3)–2, as updated by Notice 2008–85, 2008–42 I.R.B. 905, for valuation dates occurring in 2009–2013, Notice 2013–49, 2013–32 I.R.B. 127, for valuation dates occurring in calendar years 2014 and 2015, and Notice 2015–53, 2015–33 I.R.B. 190, for valuation dates occurring in calendar year 2016. These tables are based on the tables contained in a report issued by the Society of Actuaries in July 2000, the RP–2000 Mortality Tables Report, after a study of mortality experience for retirement plan participants. Notices 2013–49 and 2015–53 discuss the Society of Actuaries' recent studies and reports on mortality experience for retirement plan participants and the expectation that the Treasury Department and IRS will issue proposed regulations providing updated mortality tables.

[160] Sec. 430(h)(3)(C) and ERISA sec. 303(h)(3)(C).

sponsor and, if the plan sponsor is a member of a controlled group, each member of the controlled group, and (2) the requirements for using a substitute mortality table are met with respect to the mortality table established for each plan, taking into account only the participants of that plan, the time that plan has been in existence, and the actual experience of that plan.

In general, a substitute mortality table may be used during the period of consecutive year plan years (not to exceed 10) specified in the plan sponsor's request. However, a substitute mortality table ceases to be in effect as of the earlier of (1) the date on which there is a significant change in the participants in the plan by reason of a plan spinoff or merger or otherwise, or (2) the date on which the plan actuary determines that the table does not meet the requirements for being used, as described above.

Treasury regulations and IRS guidance provide details as to the requirements for a substitute mortality table and the procedure for requesting approval to use a substitute mortality table.[161]

Interest rate used to determine target normal cost and funding target

The minimum funding rules for single-employer plans also specify the interest rates that must be used in determining the present value of benefits for purposes of a plan's target normal cost and funding target. Present value is generally determined using three interest rates ("segment" rates), each of which applies to benefit payments expected to be made from the plan during a certain period.[162]

The first segment rate applies to benefits reasonably determined to be payable during the five-year period beginning on the plan's annual valuation date;[163] the second segment rate applies to benefits reasonably determined to be payable during the 15-year period following the initial five-year period; and the third segment rate applies to benefits reasonably determined to be payable after the end of that 15-year period. Under the funding rules as enacted in PPA ("PPA" rules), each segment rate is a single interest rate determined monthly by the Secretary of the Treasury, on the basis of a corporate bond yield curve, taking into account only the portion of the yield curve based on corporate bonds maturing during the particular segment rate period. The corporate bond yield curve used for this purpose reflects the average, for the 24-month period ending with the preceding month, of yields on investment grade corporate bonds with varying maturities and that are in the top three quality levels available.[164] The Internal Revenue Service ("IRS") publishes the segment rates each month.

Under the Moving Ahead for Progress in the 21st Century Act ("MAP–21") and the Highway and Transportation Funding Act of

---

[161] Treas. Reg. sec. 1.430(h)(3)–2; Rev. Proc. 2008–62, 2008–2 C.B. 935, superseding Rev. Proc. 2007–37, 2007–1 C.B. 1433.

[162] Sec. 430(h)(2) and ERISA sec. 303(h)(2).

[163] Subject to an exception for small plans with no more than 100 participants, the annual valuation date for a plan must be the first day of the plan year.

[164] Solely for purposes of determining minimum required contributions, in lieu of the segment rates, an employer may elect to use interest rates on a yield curve based on the yields on investment grade corporate bonds for the month preceding the month in which the plan year begins (that is, without regard to the 24-month averaging described above) ("monthly yield curve"). If an election to use a monthly yield curve is made, it cannot be revoked without IRS approval.

2014 ("2014 Highway Act"), for plan years beginning after December 31, 2011, a segment rate determined under the PPA rules is adjusted if it falls outside a specified percentage range of the average segment rates for a preceding period. In particular, if a segment rate determined under the PPA rules is less than the applicable minimum percentage in the specified range, the segment rate is adjusted upward to match the minimum percentage. If a segment rate determined under the PPA rules is more than the applicable maximum percentage in the specified range, the segment rate is adjusted downward to match the maximum percentage. For this purpose, an average segment rate is the average of the segment rates determined under the PPA rules for the 25-year period ending September 30 of the calendar year preceding the calendar year in which the plan year begins. The Secretary is to determine average segment rates on an annual basis and may prescribe equivalent rates for any years in the 25-year period for which segment rates determined under the PPA rules are not available. The Secretary is directed to publish the average segment rates each month.

The specified percentage range (that is, the range from the applicable minimum percentage to the applicable maximum percentage) for a plan year is determined by reference to the calendar year in which the plan year begins as follows:
- 90 percent to 110 percent for 2012 through 2017,
- 85 percent to 115 percent for 2018,
- 80 percent to 120 percent for 2019,
- 75 percent to 125 percent for 2020, and
- 70 percent to 130 percent for 2021 or later.

Annual funding notice

The plan administrator of a single-employer defined benefit plan must provide an annual funding notice to each participant and beneficiary, each labor organization representing participants or beneficiaries, and the Pension Benefit Guaranty Corporation ("PBGC").[165] In addition to the information required to be provided in all funding notices, in the case of a single-employer defined benefit plan, the notice must include (1) the plan's funding target attainment percentage for the plan year to which the notice relates and the two preceding plan years, (2) the value of the plan's assets and benefit liabilities (that is, the present value of benefits owed under the plan) for the plan year and the two preceding years, determined in the same manner as under the funding rules, and (3) the value of the plan's assets and benefit liabilities as of the last day of the plan year to which the notice relates, determined using the fair market value of plan assets (rather than value determined under the funding rules) and, in computing benefit liabilities, the interest rates used in computing variable-rate PBGC premiums.[166]

---

[165] ERISA sec. 101(f). Annual funding notice requirements, with some differences, apply also to multiemployer and multiple–employer plans.

[166] In applying the funding rules, the value of plan assets may be determined on the basis of average fair market values over a period of up to 24 months. PBGC variable-rate premiums are based on a plan's unfunded vested benefit liabilities, computed using the first, second and third segment rates as determined under the PPA rules (without the adjustments applicable for funding purposes), but based on a monthly corporate bond yield curve, rather than a yield curve reflecting average yields for a 24-month period.

Additional information must be included in a single-employer plan's annual funding notice in the case of an applicable plan year. For this purpose, an applicable plan year is any plan year beginning after December 31, 2011, and before January 1, 2020, for which (1) the plan's funding target, determined using segment rates as adjusted to reflect average segment rates ("adjusted" segment rates), is less than 95 percent of the funding target determined without regard to adjusted segment rates, (2) the plan has a funding shortfall, determined without regard to adjusted segment rates, greater than $500,000, and (3) the plan had 50 or more participants on any day during the preceding plan year. Specifically, the notice must include (1) a statement that MAP–21 and the 2014 Highway Act modified the method for determining the interest rates used to determine the actuarial value of benefits earned under the plan, providing for a 25-year average of interest rates to be taken into account in addition to a two-year average, (2) a statement that, as a result of MAP–21 and the 2014 Highway Act, the plan sponsor may contribute less money to the plan when interest rates are at historical lows, and (3) a table showing, for the applicable plan year and each of the two preceding plan years, the plan's funding target attainment percentage, funding shortfall, and the employer's minimum required contribution, each determined both using adjusted segment rates and without regard to adjusted segment rates.

Explanation of Provision

Mortality tables

The provision relates to the requirement that there must be a sufficient number of plan participants, and the pension plans must have been maintained for a sufficient period of time, to have credible information, in order for a substitute mortality table to be used. Under the provision, the determination of whether plans have credible information is to be made in accordance with established actuarial credibility theory. The provision specifies that this standard permits the use of tables that reflect adjustments to the generally applicable mortality tables prescribed by the IRS if the adjustments are based on the actual experience of the pension plans maintained by the plan sponsor and projected trends in general mortality experience.[167]

Applicable minimum and maximum percentages and annual funding notice

The provision revises the specified percentage ranges (that is, the range from the applicable minimum percentage to the applicable maximum percentage of average segment rates) for determining whether a segment rate must be adjusted upward or downward. Under the provision, the specified percentage range for a plan year is determined by reference to the calendar year in which the plan year begins as follows:
- 90 percent to 110 percent for 2012 through 2020,

---

[167] The provision specifies also that this standard is materially different from rules relating to substitute mortality tables in effect on the date of enactment of the provision, including Rev. Proc. 2007–37.

- 85 percent to 115 percent for 2021,
- 80 percent to 120 percent for 2022,
- 75 percent to 125 percent for 2023, and
- 70 percent to 130 percent for 2024 or later.

In addition, for purposes of the additional information that must be provided in a funding notice for an applicable plan year, an applicable plan year includes any plan year that begins after December 31, 2011, and before January 1, 2023, and that otherwise meets the definition of applicable plan year.

Effective Date

The provision applies to plan years beginning after December 31, 2015.

TITLE XI—REVENUE PROVISIONS RELATED TO TAX COMPLIANCE

A. Partnership Audits and Adjustments (sec. 1101 of the Act and secs. 6221–6241 of the Code)

Present Law

Reporting requirements of partnerships generally

For Federal income tax purposes, a partnership is not a taxable entity. Instead, a partnership is a conduit and the items of partnership income, deduction, gain, loss, and credit are taken into account on the partners' income tax returns. A partnership is required to file an annual information return setting forth items of partnership information necessary to carry out the income tax (Form 1065).[168] A partnership is also required to furnish to each partner a statement of such partnership information as is relevant to the partner's income tax (Schedule K–1).[169] For taxable years beginning after December 31, 2015, partnership returns and partner statements are generally due by the 15th day of the third month after the end of the partnership taxable year.[170]

Rules relating to audit and adjustment procedures for partnerships

There are three sets of rules for tax audits and adjustments for partners and partnerships. First, for partnerships with more than 100 partners and that so elect, the electing large partnership rules enacted in 1997 apply.[171] Relatively few partnerships have made this election. Second, for partnerships with more than 10 partners or with passthroughs as partners (and that are not electing large partnerships), the TEFRA rules enacted in 1982 apply.[172] Under these two sets of rules, partnership items generally are determined at the partnership level under unified procedures. Third, for part-

---

[168] Sec. 6031(a).
[169] Sec. 6031(b).
[170] See sec. 6072(b) as amended by Pub. L. No. 114–41, sec. 2006 (114th Congress). For taxable years beginning after December 31, 2015, a partnership can request a six-month extension of time to file. See also Department of the Treasury, Internal Revenue Service, *2011 Instructions for Form 1065, U.S. Return of Partnership Income*, p. 4.
[171] Secs. 6240–6255.
[172] Secs. 6221–6234. TEFRA refers to the Tax Equity and Fiscal Responsibility Act of 1982 (Pub. L. No. 97–248), in which these rules were enacted.

nerships with 10 or fewer partners that have not elected the TEFRA audit rules, audit and adjustment rules applicable generally to taxpayers subject to the Federal income tax apply.[173]

For a partnership with few partners that does not elect to be governed by TEFRA rules, the tax treatment of an adjustment to a partnership's items of income, gain, loss, deduction, or credit is determined for each partner in separate proceedings, both administrative and judicial. These are known as deficiency proceedings. Adjustments to items of income, gains, losses, deductions, or credits of the partnership generally are made in separate actions for each partner. Particularly in the case of a partnership with partners in different locations, this may result in separate judicial determinations in different courts that are potentially subject to different appellate jurisdiction. Prior to the 1982 enactment of TEFRA, these had been the rules for all adjustments with respect to partners, regardless of the number of partners in the partnership.

TEFRA rules

Unified rules

TEFRA established unified rules. These rules require the tax treatment of all "partnership items" to be determined at the partnership, rather than the partner, level. Partnership items are those items that are more appropriately determined at the partnership level than at the partner level, as provided by regulations.[174] The IRS may challenge the reporting position of a partnership by conducting a single administrative proceeding to resolve issues with respect to all partners.

The rationale stated in 1982 for adding new rules for partnerships was that "[d]etermination of the tax liability of partners resulted in administrative problems under prior law due to the fragmented nature of such determinations. These problems became excessively burdensome as partnership syndications have developed and grown in recent years. Large partnerships with partners in many audit jurisdictions result in the statute of limitations expiring with respect to some partners while other partners are required to pay additional taxes. Where there are tiered partnerships, identifying the taxpayer is difficult." [175]

The TEFRA rules do not, however, change the process for collecting underpayments with respect to deficiencies at the partner (not the partnership) level, though a settlement agreement with respect to partnership items binds all parties to the settlement.[176]

---

[173] Secs. 6231 and 6201 *et seq.*

[174] Sec. 6231(a)(3). Any item that is affected by a partnership item (for example, on the partner's return) is an "affected item." Affected items of a partner are subject to determination at the partner level. Sec. 6231(a)(5).

[175] See Joint Committee on Taxation, *General Explanation of the Revenue Provisions of the Tax Equity and Fiscal Responsibility Act of 1982* (JCS–38–82), December 31, 1982, p. 268. Additional reasons for the 1982 change mentioned include the problems of duplication of administrative and judicial effort, inconsistent results, difficulty of reaching settlement, and inadequacy of prior-law filing and recordkeeping requirements for foreign partnerships with U.S. partners.

[176] Sec. 6224(c). The IRS has set forth procedures for entering into such partnership audit settlement agreements, which are summarized in Part F of Chief Counsel Notice 2009–27, "Frequently Asked Questions Regarding The Unified Partnership Audit And Litigation Procedures Set Forth In Sections 6221–6234," IRS CC Notice 2009–027, August 21, 2009.

Tax Matters Partner

The TEFRA rules establish the Tax Matters Partner as the primary representative of a partnership in dealings with the IRS. The Tax Matters Partner is a general partner designated by the partnership or, in the absence of designation, the general partner with the largest profits interest at the close of the taxable year. If no Tax Matters Partner is designated, and it is impractical to apply the largest profits interest rule, the IRS may select any partner as the Tax Matters Partner.

Notice requirements: notice required to partners separately

The IRS generally is required to give notice of the beginning of partnership-level administrative proceedings and any resulting administrative adjustment to all partners whose names and addresses are furnished to the IRS. For partnerships with more than 100 partners, however, the IRS generally is not required to give notice to any partner whose profits interest is less than one percent.

Partners must report items consistently with the partnership

Partners are required to report partnership items consistently with the partnership's reporting, unless the partner notifies the IRS of inconsistent treatment. If a partner fails to notify the IRS of inconsistent treatment, the IRS can assess that partner under its math error authority. That is, the IRS may make a computational adjustment and immediately assess any additional tax that results.[177] Additional tax attributable to an adjustment of a partnership item is assessed against each of the taxpayers who were partners in the year in which the understatement of tax liability arose.

Partners' limited ability to challenge partnership treatment

Partners have rights to participate in administrative proceedings at the partnership level, and can request an administrative adjustment or a refund for the partner's own separate tax liability. To the extent that a settlement is reached with respect to partnership items, all partners are entitled to consistent treatment.[178]

Statute of limitations

Absent an agreement to extend the statute of limitations, the IRS generally cannot adjust a partnership item for a partnership taxable year if more than three years have elapsed since the later of the filing of the partnership return, or the last day for the filing of the partnership return (without extensions). The statute of limitations is extended in specified circumstances such as in the case of a false return, a substantial omission of income, or no return.

One-year period

If the administrative adjustment is timely made within the limitations period described above, the tax resulting from that adjustment, as well as the tax attributable to affected items, including related penalties or additions to tax, must be timely assessed. The

---

[177] Secs. 6222 and 6230(b).
[178] Sec. 6224.

period in which the tax must be assessed against the partners does not expire before one year following the date on which the final partnership administrative adjustment may no longer be petitioned to the U.S. Tax Court or, if a petition was filed, a decision of the court with respect to such petition is final.[179]

Adjudication of disputes concerning partnership items

After the IRS makes an administrative adjustment, the Tax Matters Partner (and, in limited circumstances, certain other partners) may file a petition for readjustment of partnership items in the Tax Court, the district court in which the partnership's principal place of business is located, or the Court of Federal Claims.

Electing large partnership audit rules

Definition of electing large partnership

In 1997, an additional audit system was enacted for electing large partnerships.[180] The 1997 legislation also enacted specific simplified reporting rules for electing large partnerships.[181] The provisions define an electing large partnership as any partnership that elects to be subject to the specified reporting and audit rules, if the number of partners in the partnership's preceding taxable year is 100 or more.[182]

The rationale stated in 1997 for adding new audit rules for large partnerships was that "[a]udit procedures for large partnerships are inefficient and more complex than those for other large entities. The IRS must assess any deficiency arising from a partnership audit against a large number of partners, many of whom cannot easily be located and some of whom are no longer partners. In addition, audit procedures are cumbersome and can be complicated further by the intervention of partners acting individually."[183]

Unified rules

As under the TEFRA partnership rules, electing large partnerships and their partners are subject to unified audit rules. Thus, the tax treatment of partnership items is determined at the partnership, rather than the partner, level.

Partnership representative

Each electing large partnership is required to designate a partner or other person to act on its behalf. If an electing large partnership fails to designate such a person, the IRS is permitted to designate any one of the partners as the person authorized to act on the partnership's behalf.

Notice requirements: separate partner notices not required

Unlike the TEFRA partnership audit rules, the IRS is not required to give notice to individual partners of the commencement of an administrative proceeding or of a final adjustment. Instead,

---

[179] Sec. 6229(d) and (g).
[180] Secs. 6240–6255, enacted by the Taxpayer Relief Act of 1997, Pub. L. No. 105–34.
[181] Secs. 771–777.
[182] Sec. 775.
[183] See Joint Committee on Taxation, *General Explanation of Tax Legislation Enacted in 1997* (JCS–23–97), December 17, 1997, p. 363.

the IRS is authorized to send notice of a partnership adjustment to the partnership itself by certified or registered mail. The IRS may give proper notice by mailing the notice to the last known address of the partnership, even if the partnership had terminated its existence.

Partners must report items consistently with the partnership

Under the electing large partnership audit rules, a partner is not permitted to report any partnership items inconsistently with the partnership return, even if the partner notifies the IRS of the inconsistency. The IRS may adjust a partnership item that was reported inconsistently by a partner and immediately assess any additional tax without first auditing the partnership.[184]

Adjustments flow through to persons that are partners in the year in which the adjustment takes effect

Unlike the TEFRA partnership audit rules, however, partnership adjustments generally flow through to the partners for the year in which the adjustment takes effect.[185] Thus, the current-year partners' share of current-year partnership items of income, gains, losses, deductions, or credits are adjusted to reflect partnership adjustments that take effect in that year. The adjustments generally do not affect prior-year returns of any partners (except in the case of changes to any partner's distributive shares).

Partnership's payment of imputed underpayment is permitted

In lieu of passing through an adjustment to its partners, the partnership may elect to pay an imputed underpayment. The imputed underpayment generally is calculated by netting the adjustments to the income, gain, loss, or deductions of the partnership and multiplying that amount by the highest Federal income tax rate (whether individual or corporate). Adjustments to credits are taken into account as increases or decreases in the amount of tax. A partner may not file a claim for credit or refund of his allocable share of the payment. A partnership may make this election only if it meets requirements set forth in Treasury regulations designed to ensure payment (for example, in the case of a foreign partnership).

Regardless of whether a partnership adjustment passes through to the partners, an adjustment must be offset if it requires another adjustment in a year that is after the adjusted year and before the year the adjustment that was made takes effect.

For example, assume that an electing large partnership expenses a $1,000 item in year one. However, on audit in year four, it is determined that the item should have been capitalized and amortized ratably over 10 years rather than deducted in full in year one. The $900 adjustment for the improper deduction ($1,000 minus the year one amortization of $100) is offset by $100 of adjustments for amortization deductions in each of years two and three. The adjustment in year four is $700 (that is, $1,000 minus $300, the sum of the first three years' ratable amortization of $100 per year), apart

---

[184] Sec. 6241(b).
[185] Sec. 6242.

from any interest or penalty. The year four partners are required to include an additional $700 in income for that year. The partnership ratably amortizes the $700 in years four to 10.

Partnership, not partners separately, is liable for any penalties and interest

The partnership, rather than the partners individually, generally is liable for any interest and penalties that result from a partnership adjustment. Interest is computed for the period beginning on the return due date for the adjusted year and ending on the earlier of the return due date for the partnership taxable year in which the adjustment takes effect or the date the partnership pays the imputed underpayment. Thus, in the above example, the partnership is liable for four years' worth of interest (on a declining principal amount).

Penalties (such as the accuracy and fraud penalties) are determined on a year-by-year basis (without offsets) based on an imputed underpayment. All accuracy penalty criteria and waiver criteria (such as reasonable cause or substantial authority) are determined as if the partnership were a taxable individual. Accuracy and fraud penalties are assessed and accrue interest in the same manner as if asserted against a taxable individual.

Any payment (for Federal income taxes, interest, or penalties) that an electing large partnership is required to make is nondeductible.

If a partnership ceases to exist before a partnership adjustment takes effect, the former partners are required to take the adjustment into account, as provided by regulations. Regulations are also authorized to prevent abuse and to enforce efficiently the audit rules in circumstances that present special enforcement considerations (such as partnership bankruptcy).

Partners cannot request refunds separately

The IRS may challenge the reporting position of a partnership by conducting a single administrative proceeding to resolve the issue with respect to all partners. Unlike the TEFRA partnership audit rules, however, partners have no right individually to participate in settlement conferences or to request a refund.

Timing of Schedules K-1 to partners

An electing large partnership is required to furnish copies of information returns (Schedule K-1, Partner's Share of Income, Deductions, Credits, etc.) to partners by March 15 following the close of the partnership's taxable year (often a calendar year).[186]

Statute of limitations

Absent an agreement to extend the statute of limitations, the IRS generally cannot adjust a partnership item for a partnership taxable year if more than three years have elapsed since the later of the filing of the partnership return or the last day for the filing of the partnership return. The statute of limitations is extended in

---
[186] Sec. 6031(b).

specified circumstances such as in the case of a false return, a substantial omission of income, or no return.

Adjudication of disputes concerning partnership items

As under the TEFRA rules, a partnership adjustment can be challenged in the Tax Court, the district court in which the partnership's principal place of business is located, or the Court of Federal Claims. However, only the partnership, and not partners individually, can petition for a readjustment of partnership items.

If a petition for readjustment of partnership items is filed by the partnership, the court with which the petition is filed has jurisdiction to determine the tax treatment of all partnership items of the partnership for the partnership taxable year to which the notice of partnership adjustment relates, and the proper allocation of such items among the partners. Thus, the court's jurisdiction is not limited to the items adjusted in the notice.

Explanation of Provision

Repeal of TEFRA and electing large partnership rules

Generally for returns filed for partnership taxable years beginning after 2017, the provision repeals the tax reporting provisions and voluntary centralized audit procedures for electing large partnerships, as well as the TEFRA partnership audit and adjustment rules. In place of the repealed procedures, a centralized system for audit, adjustment, assessment, and collection of tax applies to all partnerships, except those eligible partnerships that have filed a valid election out. Electing out of the centralized system leaves applicable the present-law rules for deficiency proceedings. The centralized system is located in subchapter C of chapter 63 of the Code.

In General

Determination at partnership level

Under the centralized system, the audit of a partnership takes place at the partnership level. Any adjustment to items of income, gain, loss, deduction, or credit of a partnership for a partnership taxable year, and any partner's distributive share thereof, generally are determined at the partnership level.[187] Any tax attributable to these items generally is assessed and collected at the partnership level. The applicability of any penalty, addition to tax, or additional amount that relates to an adjustment of any item of income, gain, loss, deduction, or credit of a partnership for a partnership taxable year or to any partner's distributive share thereof is determined at the partnership level. Unlike prior law, distinctions between partnership items and affected items are no longer made. An underpayment of tax determined as a result of an examination of a taxable year is imputed to the year during which the adjustment is finally determined, and generally is assessed against and collected from the partnership with respect to that year rather than the reviewed year.

---

[187] Sec. 6221(a).

Under the centralized system, a partnership may seek modification of the imputed underpayment amount by providing the Secretary with specified information about the tax status of partners and about the nature and amount of items of income or gain, by means of reviewed-year partners filing amended returns with payment, or on the basis of other factors in regulations or guidance. A partnership may elect an alternative to partnership payment of the imputed underpayment in which each reviewed-year partner is furnished a statement of the partner's share of the adjustments (similar to Schedule K–1) and each such reviewed-year partner increases its tax for the year the statement is furnished. A partnership may file an administrative adjustment request.

Rules are provided relating to statutes of limitation and other applicable time periods, interest and penalties, judicial review, and other aspects of the centralized system under the provision.

Election out

The centralized system is applicable to any partnership unless it meets eligibility requirements and has made a valid election out for a taxable year.[188]

100 or fewer statements

A partnership may elect out of the centralized system (and it and its partners are governed by the present-law deficiency proceedings) for a partnership taxable year if it meets eligibility requirements. One of the eligibility requirements is that for the taxable year, the partnership is required to furnish 100 or fewer statements under section 6031(b) (Schedules K–1) with respect to its partners.

A further eligibility requirement for a partnership to make the election is that each of its partners is an individual, a deceased partner's estate, a C corporation, a foreign entity that would be required to be treated as a C corporation if it were a domestic entity, or an S corporation (provided special rules are met). A partnership with a foreign entity as a partner can meet this eligibility requirement if, under the rules of section 7701, the foreign entity would be taxable as a C corporation if it were domestic; that is, the foreign entity has elected to be, or is, treated as a per se corporation under the check-the-box regulatory rules under section 7701.[189] A C corporation partner that is a regulated investment company ("RIC") or a real estate investment trust ("REIT") does not prevent the partnership from being able to elect out, provided the applicable requirements are met.

Example

For example, a partnership is formed to conduct a joint venture between two corporations, X and Y. X's domestic C corporation subsidiary, W, owns a 50-percent interest in the partnership, and Y's domestic C corporation subsidiary, Z, owns a 50-percent interest in the partnership. The partnership is required to furnish two statements (Schedules K–1), one to W and one to Z. The partnership is

---

[188] Sec. 6221(b).
[189] See Treas. Reg. sec. 301.7701–2 and –3.

eligible to elect out of the centralized system for the taxable year, provided that the partnership meets the requirements (described below) as to the time and manner of electing out, including (among other requirements) disclosing to the Secretary the names and employer identification numbers of W and Z.

Time and manner of election out

The election is to be made with a timely-filed return of the partnership taxable year to which the election relates; the election is valid only for that year. The election must include the name and taxpayer identification number of each partner of the partnership in the manner prescribed by the Secretary. The partnership must notify each of its partners of the election in the manner prescribed by the Secretary.

S corporation partners

For a partnership with a partner that is an S corporation to elect out, the partnership is required to include with its election (in the manner prescribed by the Secretary) a disclosure of the name and taxpayer identification number of each person with respect to whom the S corporation must furnish a statement under section 6037(b) for the S corporation's taxable year ending with or within the partnership's taxable year for which the election is made. This requirement is met if the partnership discloses the name and taxpayer identification number of each S corporation shareholder with respect to which a statement (Schedule K–1) is required to be furnished under section 6037(b). These statements required to be furnished by the S corporation are treated as statements required to be furnished by the partnership for purposes of the 100-or-fewer-statements criterion for the partnership's eligibility to elect out.

Example

For example, if a partnership has 50 partners, 49 of which are individuals and one of which is an S corporation with 30 shareholders all of whom are individuals, the partnership is treated as being required to furnish 80 statements. This is the sum of 49 statements for individual partners, one statement for the S corporation partner, and 30 statements for individuals with respect to whom the S corporation must furnish statements. The partnership meets the 100-or-fewer-statements criterion for the partnership's eligibility to elect out.

Foreign partners

The Secretary may provide for an alternative form of identification of any foreign partners (for example, if the foreign partners do not have U.S. taxpayer identification numbers) for purposes of the requirement of disclosure of the name and taxpayer identification number of each partner by the partnership.

Other persons as partners

The Secretary may by regulation or other guidance identify other types of partners to whom rules similar to the special rules in the case of a partner that is an S corporation can apply. This guidance shall take into account, for purposes of applying the 100-or-fewer-statements criterion,[190] each direct and indirect interest in the partnership of any person to which a statement (comparable to the partner statement under section 6031(b)) is required to be furnished by any person. Such guidance may also take into account any person with respect to which a comparable statement is not required to be furnished but which has an interest (direct or indirect) in the partnership. Further, such guidance shall require the partnership to disclose to the Secretary the name and taxpayer identification number of each person with respect to which a statement (comparable to the partner statement under section 6031(b)) is required to be furnished and of other persons with an interest (direct or indirect) in the partnership.

Examples

For example, assume that a partner of a partnership is a disregarded entity such as a State-law limited liability company ("LLC") with only one member, a domestic corporation. Such guidance may provide that the partnership can make the election if the partnership includes (in the manner prescribed by the Secretary) a disclosure of the name and taxpayer identification number of each of the disregarded entity and the corporation that is its sole member, and each of them is taken into account as if each were a statement recipient in determining whether the 100-or-fewer-statements criterion is met.

As another example, such guidance may provide that a partnership with a trust as a partner can make the election if the partnership includes (in the manner prescribed by the Secretary) a disclosure of the name and taxpayer identification number of the trustee, each person who is or is deemed to be an owner of the trust, and any other person that the Secretary determines to be necessary and appropriate, and each one of such persons is taken into account as if each were a statement recipient in determining whether the 100-or-fewer-statements criterion is met. Similar guidance may be provided with respect to a partnership with a partner that is a grantor trust, a former grantor trust that continues in existence for the two-year period following the death of the deemed owner, or a trust receiving property from a decedent's estate for a two-year period.

As a further example, to the extent that such rules are consistent with prompt and efficient collection of tax attributable to the income of partnerships and partners, such guidance may provide rules permitting election out in the case of a partnership (the first partnership) with one or more direct or indirect partners which are themselves partnerships. Under any such guidance with respect to tiered partnerships, the sum of all direct and indirect partners (including each partnership and its partners) may not exceed 100 persons with respect to which a section 6031(b) statement must be furnished, and each partner must be identified. That is, eligibility of the first partnership to make the election requires the first partnership to include (in the manner prescribed by the Secretary) a disclosure of the name and taxpayer identification number of each direct partner of the first partnership and each indirect partner (in-

---

[190] Sec. 6221(b)(1)(B).

cluding each partnership and its partners) in every tier, and requires that each is taken into account in determining whether the 100-or-fewer-statements criterion is met.

Requirement of consistency with partnership return

The centralized system imposes a consistency requirement. A partner on its return must treat each item of income, gain, loss, deduction or credit attributable to a partnership in a manner that is consistent with the treatment of such income, gain, loss, deduction, or credit on the partnership return.[191] An underpayment that results from a failure of a partner to conform to the partnership reporting of an item is treated as a math error on the partner's return and cannot be abated under section 6213(b)(2).[192] The underpayment may be subject to additions to tax.

Notice of inconsistent position

If the partnership has filed a return but the partner's treatment on the partner's return is (or may be) inconsistent with the partnership's return, or if the partnership has not filed a return, the math error treatment and nonabatement treatment do not apply if the partner files a statement identifying the inconsistent position.[193] Further, a partner is treated as having complied with the obligation to file a statement identifying the inconsistent position in the circumstance in which the partner demonstrates to the satisfaction of the Secretary that the treatment of the item on the partner's return is consistent with the treatment of the item on the statement furnished to the partner by the partnership, and the partner elects the application of this rule.

A final decision in an administrative or judicial proceeding with respect to a partnership under the centralized system is binding on the partnership and all partners of the partnership.[194] In contrast, a final determination in an administrative or judicial proceeding with respect to a partner's identified inconsistent position is not binding on the partnership if the partnership is not a party to the proceeding.[195] No inference is intended that the partnership is bound by any other proceeding to which it is not a party, such as an administrative or judicial proceeding with respect to a partner's unidentified inconsistent position.

Partners bound by actions of partnership; designation of partnership representative

For purposes of the centralized system, the partnership acts through its partnership representative. The partnership representative has the sole authority to act on behalf of the partnership under the centralized system.[196] Under the centralized system, the partnership and all partners of the partnership are bound by actions taken by the partnership.[197] Thus, for example, partners may not participate in or contest results of an examination of a partner-

---

[191] Sec. 6222(a).
[192] Sec. 6222(b).
[193] Sec. 6222(c).
[194] Sec. 6223(b).
[195] Sec. 6222(d).
[196] Sec. 6223(a).
[197] Sec. 6223(b).

ship by the Secretary. A partnership and all partners of the partnership are also bound by any final decision in a proceeding with respect to the partnership brought under the centralized system of subchapter C. Thus, for example, a settlement agreement entered into by the partnership, a notice of final partnership adjustment with respect to the partnership that is not contested, or the final decision of the court with respect to the partnership if the notice of final partnership adjustment is contested, bind the partnership and all partners of the partnership.

Each partnership is required to designate a partner (or other person) with a substantial presence in the United States as the partnership representative. A substantial presence in the United States enables the partnership representative to meet with the Secretary in the United States as is necessary or appropriate, and facilitates communication during the audit process and during any other proceedings in which the partnership is involved. In any case in which such a designation by the partnership is not in effect, the Secretary may select any person as the partnership representative.

Partnership Adjustments

Partnership adjustments by the Secretary

The centralized system provides that any adjustment to items of income, gain, loss, deduction, or credit of a partnership for a partnership taxable year, and any partner's distributive share thereof, are determined at the partnership level. Any tax attributable to these items is assessed and generally is collected at the partnership level as an imputed underpayment paid by the partnership.

Reviewed year and adjustment year

For purposes of the centralized system, the reviewed year means the partnership taxable year to which the item being adjusted relates. For example, in an examination by the Secretary of a partnership's taxable year 2018, 2018 is the reviewed year.[198]

The adjustment year means (1) in the case of an adjustment pursuant to the decision of a court (under the centralized system's judicial review provisions), the partnership taxable year in which the decision becomes final; (2) in the case of an administrative adjustment request, the partnership taxable year in which the administrative adjustment request is made; or (3) in any other case, the partnership taxable year in which the notice of final partnership adjustment is mailed.[199] For example, in the case of adjustments with respect to partnership taxable year 2018 resulting in an imputed underpayment assessed in 2020 that the partnership then litigates in Tax Court, the decision of which is not appealed and becomes final in 2021, the adjustment year is 2021.

Payment of imputed underpayment by the partnership

Any adjustment to items of income, gain, loss, deduction, or credit of a partnership for a partnership taxable year, and any partner's distributive share thereof, are determined at the partnership level. In the event of any adjustment by the Secretary in the

---

[198] Sec. 6225(d)(1).
[199] Sec. 6225(d)(2).

amount of any item of income, gain, loss, deduction, or credit of a partnership, or any partner's distributive share, that results in an imputed underpayment, the partnership is required to pay the imputed underpayment in the adjustment year.[200]

Interest at partnership level

Interest due is determined at the partnership level and accrues at the rate applicable to underpayments.[201]

Adjustment that does not result in imputed underpayment

Any adjustment by the Secretary in the amount of any item of income, gain, loss, deduction, or credit of a partnership, or any partner's distributive share, that does not result in an imputed underpayment is taken into account by the partnership in the adjustment year. The amount of the adjustment is treated as a reduction in non-separately stated income or an increase in non-separately stated loss (whichever is appropriate). It may also be appropriate to treat the amount of an adjustment as a reduction (or increase) in a separately stated amount of income, gain, loss, or deduction. The amount of an adjustment in a credit is taken into account as a separately stated item.[202]

Determination of imputed underpayment amount

An imputed underpayment of tax with respect to a partnership adjustment for any reviewed year is determined by netting all adjustments of items of income, gain, loss, or deduction and multiplying the net amount by the highest rate of Federal income tax applicable either to individuals or to corporations that is in effect for the reviewed year.[203] Any adjustments to items of credit are taken into account as an increase or decrease, as the case may be, in the figure resulting from this multiplication. Any net increase or decrease in loss is treated as a decrease or increase, respectively, in income. Netting is done taking into account applicable limitations, restrictions, and special rules under present law.

Examples

Example.—Assume that a partnership reports the following items on its return for taxable year 2018 (dollar amounts in thousands):
- rental income of $100
- depreciation deduction of <$70>
- interest expense deduction of <$20>
- deduction for compensation paid of <$50>

In an examination of the partnership's taxable year 2018, the Secretary determines that depreciation was <$80>, not <$70>, for the year. (Assume that this change does not affect depreciation in other taxable years.) The Secretary also finds that $5 of rental in-

---

[200] Sec. 6225(a)(1).
[201] Sec. 6621(a)(2). Rules relating to interest, penalties, and additions to tax are further described below.
[202] Sec. 6225(a)(2).
[203] Sec. 6225(b)(1). The rule for determining the imputed underpayment applies except as provided in subsection 6225(c), which provides that the Secretary shall establish procedures under which the imputed underpayment amount may be modified consistent with requirements imposed thereunder.

come was omitted, for total rental income of $105, not $100, for the year. The adjustment reflecting an increase of $5 of rental income is netted with the adjustment reflecting the <$10> change in the depreciation (both ordinary in character and not subject to differing limitations or restrictions). The resulting adjustment is a net increase in loss of <$5>. There is no imputed underpayment. For the adjustment year (not 2018, the reviewed year), the partnership has an increase in non-separately stated loss of <$5> (or a reduction in non-separately income of <$5>).

Example.—As another example, assume a partnership reports the following items on its return for taxable year 2019 (dollar amounts in thousands):
- ordinary income of $300
- long-term capital gain (from asset sales) of $125, long-term capital loss (from asset sales) of <$75>, for a net long-term capital gain of $50
- depreciation deduction of <$100>
- tax credit of $5

In an examination of the partnership's taxable year 2019, the Secretary adjusts these items as follows and finds:
- ordinary income of $500 (a $200 adjustment)
- long-term capital gain of $200 (a $75 adjustment) and long-term capital loss of <$25> (a <$50> adjustment), for a net long-term capital gain of $175 (a $125 adjustment)
- depreciation deduction of <$70> (a <$30> adjustment)
- tax credit of $3 (a <$2> credit adjustment)

These are netted under the provision as follows. The adjustments to ordinary income and to the ordinary depreciation deduction are netted: $200 minus <$30> yields $230. The adjustments to long-term capital gain and loss are netted: $75 minus <$50> yields $125. The adjustments total $355. Assume that the highest rate of Federal income tax applicable to individuals or corporations in 2019 is 39.6 percent. The product of $355 and 39.6 percent is $140.58. The credit adjustment of <$2> increases that figure, yielding an imputed underpayment of $142.58 (not taking into account possible modifications further described below). The partnership pays the imputed underpayment in the adjustment year.

Determining imputed underpayment amount: adjustments to distributive shares

In determining an imputed underpayment, any adjustment that reallocates the distributive share of any item from one partner to another is taken into account by disregarding any decrease in any item of income or gain and disregarding any increase in any item of deduction, loss, or credit.[204]

Example

For example, assume that a partnership has two partners, L and M. Under the partnership agreement, $100 of rental income is allocated to L and $70 of depreciation and interest deductions are allocated to M for the taxable year. The Secretary notifies the partnership and the partnership representative of an administrative pro-

---
[204] Sec. 6225(b)(2).

ceeding initiated at the partnership level with respect to the partnership's return for 2024. Assume that the Secretary determines that the $70 distributive share of depreciation and interest deductions should be reallocated from M to L. The imputed underpayment of the partnership is determined without decreasing the $100 of rental income by the $70 of depreciation and interest deductions. The adjustment is a $70 increase in income. Assume that the highest rate of Federal income tax applicable to individuals or corporations in 2024 is 39.6 percent. The product of $70 and 39.6 percent is $27.72, the amount of the imputed underpayment. However, the partnership may implement procedures for modifying the imputed underpayment as so determined.

Modification of imputed underpayment amount

When an audit of a partnership is commenced, the Secretary notifies the partnership and the partnership representative of the administrative proceeding initiated at the partnership level. The Secretary also notifies the partnership and the partnership representative of any proposed partnership adjustment developed during the proceeding.[205] The Secretary must establish procedures for modification of the amount of an imputed underpayment.[206] One or more modification procedures may be implemented by the partnership after the initiation of the administrative proceeding, including before any notice of proposed adjustment. These procedures include the filing of amended returns by reviewed year partners, determination of the imputed underpayment without regard to the portion of it allocable to a tax-exempt partner, and modification of the applicable highest tax rates, including determining the portion of an imputed underpayment to which a lower rate applies.[207] In addition, the Secretary may by regulations or guidance provide for additional procedures to modify imputed underpayment amounts on the basis of factors that the Secretary determines are necessary or appropriate to carry out the function of the modification provisions, that is, to determine the amount of tax due as closely as possible to the tax due if the partnership and partners had correctly reported and paid while at the same time to implement the most

---

[205] Sec. 6231(a)(1) and (2).

[206] Sec. 6225(c).

[207] See section 411 of the Protecting Americans from Tax Hikes Act of 2015 (Division Q of Pub. L. No. 114–113). Under the provision, certain section 469(k) passive activity losses can reduce the imputed underpayment of a publicly traded partnership under the centralized system. The imputed underpayment can be determined without regard to the portion of the underpayment that the partnership demonstrates is attributable to (*i.e.*, would be offset by) specified passive activity losses attributable to a specified partner. The amount of the specified passive activity loss is concomitantly decreased, and the partnership takes the net decrease into account as an adjustment in the adjustment year with respect to the specified partners to which the net decrease relates. A specified passive activity loss for any specified partner of a publicly traded partnership means the lesser of the section 469(k) passive activity loss of that partner which is separately determined with respect to the partnership (1) for the partner's taxable year in which or with which the reviewed year of the partnership ends, or (2) for the partner's taxable year in which or with which the adjustment year of the partnership ends. A specified partner is a person who continuously meets each of three requirements for the period starting with the partner's taxable year in which or with which the partnership reviewed year ends through the partner's taxable year in which or with which the partnership adjustment year ends. These three requirements are that the person is a partner of the publicly traded partnership; the person is an individual, estate, trust, closely held C corporation, or personal service corporation; and the person has a specified passive activity loss with respect to the publicly traded partnership.

efficient and prompt assessment and collection of tax attributable to the income of the partnership and partners.

Anything required to be submitted pursuant to the modification of the amount of an imputed underpayment must be submitted to the Secretary not later than the close of the 270-day period beginning on the date the notice of a proposed partnership adjustment is mailed, unless the 270-day period is extended with the consent of the Secretary.

Any modification of the amount of an imputed underpayment is made only upon approval of the modification by the Secretary.

Modification procedures: amended returns of reviewed year partners

Payments made by reviewed year partners with amended returns can reduce the amount of an imputed underpayment.[208] Procedures for modification provide that the amount of an imputed underpayment is determined without regard to the portion of the underpayment taken into account by payment of tax included with amended returns of the reviewed year partners. The amended return relates to the taxable year of the partner that includes the end of the reviewed year of the partnership. The amended return is to take into account all adjustments in the amount of any item of income, gain, loss, deduction, or credit of the partnership (or any partner's distributive share) properly allocable to each partner, along with changes for any other taxable year with respect to which any tax attribute is affected by reason of the adjustments. Payment of any tax due is to be included with the amended return. In the case of an adjustment that reallocates the distributive share of any item from one partner to another, this modification procedure is only available if amended returns for the reviewed year are filed by all partners affected by the adjustment.

Modification procedures: tax-exempt partners

Procedures for modification provide for determining the amount of the imputed underpayment without regard to the portion of it that the partnership demonstrates is allocable to a partner that would not owe tax by reason of its status as a tax-exempt entity for the reviewed year.[209] For this purpose, a tax-exempt entity means (1) the United States, any State or political subdivision thereof, any possession of the United States, or any agency or instrumentality of any of these, (2) an organization (other than a cooperative) that is exempt from Federal income tax, (3) any foreign person or entity, and (4) any Indian tribal government determined by the Secretary in consultation with the Secretary of the Interior to exercise governmental functions. Under this procedure for modification, the partnership demonstrates the amounts of adjustments that are allocable to the tax-exempt partner and the resulting portion of the imputed underpayment allocable to that partner.[210]

---

[208] Sec. 6225(c)(2).
[209] Sec. 6225(c)(3).
[210] Secs. 6225(c)(3) and 168(h)(2)(A).

Modification procedures: modification of applicable highest tax rates

Procedures for modification provide for taking into account a rate of tax lower than the highest rate of Federal income tax applicable either to individuals or to corporations that is in effect for the reviewed year, for certain types of taxpayers or types of income.[211]

The partnership may demonstrate that a portion of an imputed underpayment is allocable to a partner that is a C corporation, and for that C corporation partner, the highest marginal rate of Federal income tax (35 percent in 2016, for example) for ordinary income and capital gain[212] for the reviewed year is lower than the highest marginal rate of Federal income tax for individuals (39.6 percent in 2016, for example). For a C corporation, the highest marginal rate of Federal income tax is the highest rate of tax specified in section 11(b).

Similarly, the partnership may demonstrate that a portion of an imputed underpayment relates to an item of long-term capital gain or qualified dividend income that is allocable to a partner who is an individual, and that the highest rate of tax with respect to that item of long-term capital gain or qualified dividend income for the reviewed year (20 percent for 2016, for example) is lower than the highest rate of Federal income tax applicable to individuals for the reviewed year (39.6 percent in 2016, for example). The highest rate for the type of income and type of taxpayer applies under the modification. An S corporation is treated as an individual for this purpose.

In general, the portion of the imputed underpayment to which the lower rate applies with respect to a partner is determined by reference to the partner's distributive share of items of income, gain, loss, deduction, and credit to which the imputed underpayment relates. However, if the partner's distributive share differs among items, then the portion of the imputed underpayment to which the lower rate applies is determined by reference to the amount of the partner's distributive share of net gain or loss if the partnership had sold all of its assets at their fair market value as of the close of the reviewed year. For example, adjustments are made to a partnership's rental income from property A and its depreciation deductions with respect to property B. A corporate partner has a 20 percent distributive share of rental income from property A, a 15 percent distributive share of depreciation deductions from property B, and a 20 percent distributive share of any gain in the reviewed year. However, if the partnership had sold its assets at fair market value as of the close of the reviewed year, the gain would have been $100, and based on its capital account, the corporate partner's distributive share would have been $20. Thus, the portion of the imputed underpayment to which the lower rate applies with respect to the corporate partner is 20 percent.

---

[211] Sec. 6225(c)(4).
[212] The Secretary has regulatory authority under the provision, including authority to acknowledge or identify the types of income, gain, deduction, and loss to which the lower rate applies. See also section 411 of the Protecting Americans from Tax Hikes Act of 2015 (Division Q of Pub. L. No. 114–113). A lower rate of tax may be taken into account in the case of either capital gain or ordinary income of a partner that is a C corporation.

Modification procedures: additional procedures

Additional procedures to modify the amount of an imputed underpayment may be provided by the Secretary on the basis of factors the Secretary determines are necessary or appropriate to carry out the purposes of the provision. These procedures allow partnerships to demonstrate tax attributes or information with respect to the reviewed year and with respect to reviewed year partners that could permit modification of the imputed underpayment to more closely approximate the amount of tax due with respect to the reviewed year if the partnership and partners had correctly reported and paid the tax due.

In the absence of regulations or guidance specifically addressing the manner in which these modifications or calculations are made, it is anticipated that partnerships will furnish to the Secretary the necessary documentation, data, and calculations to determine the amount of the reduction of the imputed underpayment with a reasonably high degree of accuracy.

Alternative to payment of imputed underpayment by partnership

As an alternative to partnership payment of the imputed underpayment in the adjustment year, the audited partnership may elect to furnish to the Secretary and to each partner of the partnership for the reviewed year a statement of the partner's share of any adjustments to income, gain, loss, deduction and credit as determined in the notice of final partnership adjustment.[213] In this case, each such partner takes these adjustments into account and pays the tax as provided under the provision.[214]

Payment by reviewed year partners in year that includes date of the statement

The reviewed year partner's tax is increased for the partner's taxable year that includes the date of the statement.

Amount of the reviewed year partner's adjustment

The reviewed year partner's tax is increased by an amount equal to the aggregate of the adjustment amounts as determined under the provision. This includes the amount by which the partner's tax would increase if the partner's distributive share of the adjustment amounts were included for the partner's taxable year that includes the end of the reviewed year, plus the amount by which the tax would increase by reason of adjustment to tax attributes in years after that year of the partner and before the year of the date of the statement. Tax attributes in any subsequent taxable year are required to be appropriately adjusted.

Penalties, additions to tax, additional amounts

Penalties, additions to tax, and additional amounts are determined at the partnership level;[215] each reviewed year partner is

---

[213] Sec. 6226(a).
[214] Sec. 6226(b).
[215] Secs. 6221 and 6226(c).

liable for its share of the penalty, addition to tax, and additional amount.[216]

Interest at partner level from reviewed year, with adjustments

In the case of an imputed underpayment for which the election under this provision is made, interest is determined at the partner level.[217] Interest is determined from the due date of the partner's return for the taxable year to which the increase is attributable. Interest is determined taking into account any increases attributable to a change in tax attributes for an intervening tax year. The rate of interest determined at the partner level is the underpayment rate as modified under the provision, that is, the rate is the sum of the Federal short-term rate (determined monthly) plus 5 percentage points.

Time and manner of making election

The partnership may make this election not later than 45 days after the notice of final partnership adjustment.[218] The election is revocable only with the consent of the Secretary. The election may be made whether or not the partnership files a petition for judicial review of the notice of final partnership adjustment.[219]

The partnership may make the election within 45 days from the notice of final partnership adjustment, and within 90 days from the notice of final partnership adjustment may file a petition for readjustment with the Tax Court, district court, or Court of Federal Claims.[220] Upon the final court decision, dismissal of the case, or settlement, the partnership is to implement the election by furnishing statements (at the time and manner prescribed by the Secretary) to the reviewed year partners showing each partner's share of the adjustments as finally determined. As part of any settlement, for example, it is contemplated that the Secretary may permit revocation of a previously made election, and the partnership may pay at the partnership level.

Time and manner of furnishing statement

The statement is to be furnished to the Secretary and to partners within such time and in such manner as is prescribed by the Secretary. In the absence of such guidance, the statements are to be furnished to the Secretary and to all partners within a reasonable period following the last day on which to make the election under this provision. The date the statement is furnished (as well as the date of the statement) is the date the statement is mailed, for this purpose.

Information furnished on statement to the Secretary and to partners

The statement furnished to the Secretary and to partners is to include the amounts of and tax attributes of the adjustments allocable to the recipient partner. Under regulatory authority, the Sec-

---

[216] Sec. 6226(c).
[217] Sec. 6226(c)(2).
[218] Sec. 6226(a)(1).
[219] Sec. 6226(d). See section 411 of the Protecting Americans from Tax Hikes Act of 2015 (Division Q of Pub. L. No. 114–113).
[220] Sec. 6234.

retary may require the statement to show the amount of the imputed underpayment allocable to the recipient partner. In addition, the statement is to include the name and taxpayer identification number of the recipient partner. The Secretary may require that the statement include such additional information as is necessary or appropriate to carry out the purposes of the provision, such as the address of the recipient partner and the date the statement is mailed.

Treatment of tiered partnerships and other tiered entities

Tiered partnerships.—In the case of tiered partnerships, a partnership that receives a statement from the audited partnership is treated similarly to an individual [221] who receives a statement from the audited partnership. That is, the recipient partnership takes into account the aggregate of the adjustment amounts determined for the partner's taxable year including the end of the reviewed year, plus the adjustments to tax attributes in the following taxable years of the recipient partnership. The recipient partnership pays the tax attributable to adjustments with respect to the reviewed year and the intervening years, calculated as if it were an individual (consistently with section 703), for the taxable year that includes the date of the statement. The recipient partnership, its partners in the taxable year that is the reviewed year of the audited partnership, and its partners in the year that includes the date of the statement, may have entered into indemnification agreements under the partnership agreement with respect to the risk of tax liability of reviewed year partners being borne economically by partners in the year that includes the date of the statement. Because the payment of tax by a partnership under the centralized system is nondeductible, payments under an indemnification or similar agreement with respect to the tax are nondeductible.

Deficiency dividends.—A recipient partner that is a RIC or REIT and that receives a statement from an audited partnership including adjustments for a prior (reviewed) year may wish to make a deficiency dividend [222] with respect to the reviewed year. Guidance coordinating the receipt of a statement from an audited partnership by a RIC or REIT with the deficiency dividend procedures is expected to be issued by the Secretary.

Administrative adjustment request by partnership

A partnership may file a request for an administrative adjustment in the amount of one or more items of income, gain, loss, deduction, or credit of the partnership for a partnership taxable year.[223] Following the filing of the administrative adjustment request, the partnership may apply most of the procedures for modification [224] in a manner similar to modification of an imputed underpayment under new section 6225(c). Like the partnership audit, tax resulting from the adjustment may be paid by the partners in

---

[221] See section 703, which states, "the taxable income of a partnership shall be computed in the same manner as in the case of an individual . . .".
[222] Sec. 860.
[223] Sec. 6227.
[224] Not including the modifications pursuant to filing of amended returns of reviewed year partners in new section 6225(c)(2).

the manner in which a partnership pays an imputed underpayment in the adjustment year under new section 6225. Alternatively, the adjustment may be taken into account by the partnership and partners, and the tax paid by reviewed year partners upon receipt of statements showing the adjustments, similar to new section 6226.[225] However, in the case of an adjustment (pursuant to a partnership's administrative adjustment request) that would not result in an imputed underpayment, any refund is not paid to the partnership; rather, procedures similar to the procedure for furnishing reviewed year partners with statements reflecting the requested adjustment apply, with appropriate adjustments.

Time for making administrative adjustment request

A partnership may not file an administrative adjustment request more than three years after the later of (1) the date on which the partnership return for the year in question is filed, or (2) the last day for filing the partnership return for that year (without extensions).

In no event may a partnership file an administrative adjustment request after a notice of an administrative proceeding with respect to the taxable year is mailed.

Tiered partnerships

In the case of tiered partnerships, a partnership's partners that are themselves partnerships may choose to file an administrative adjustment request with respect to their distributive shares of an adjustment. The partners and indirect partners that are themselves partnerships may choose to coordinate the filing of administrative adjustment requests as a group to the extent permitted by the Secretary.

Procedural Rules

In general[226]

The new centralized system provides rules governing notices, time limitations, restrictions on assessment and the imposition of interest and penalties in the context of a partnership adjustment.[227] The provisions include specific grants of regulatory authority to address the identification of foreign partners, the manner of notifying partners of an election out of centralized procedures, the manner in which a partnership representative is selected, and the extent to which the new centralized system may be applied before the generally applicable effective date.

Notice of proceedings and adjustments

The centralized system contemplates three types of principal notifications by the Secretary to the partnership and the partnership representative in the course of an administrative proceeding with respect to that partnership. The notifications also apply to any proceeding with respect to an administrative adjustment request filed

---

[225] Sec. 6227(b)(2); interest is computed at the underpayment rate (sec. 6621(a)(2)) without substituting "5 percentage points" for "3 percentage points" as under section 6226(c)(2)(C).
[226] Secs. 6231 through 6235.
[227] Secs. 6231–6235.

by a partnership.[228] These notices are (1) notice of any administrative proceeding initiated at the partnership level; (2) notice of a proposed partnership adjustment resulting from the proceeding; and (3) notice of any final partnership adjustment resulting from the proceeding. Such notices are sufficient if mailed to the last known address of the partnership representative or the partnership, even if the partnership has terminated its existence.

A notice of proposed adjustments informs the partnership of any adjustments tentatively determined by the Secretary and the amount of any imputed underpayment resulting from such adjustments. The issuance of a notice of proposed partnership adjustment begins the running of a period of 270 days in which to supply all information required by the Secretary in support of a request for modification. During that same period, the Secretary may not issue a notice of final partnership adjustment.[229] The Secretary is required to establish procedures and timeframes for the modification process in published guidance, which may include conditions under which extensions of time in which to submit final documentation of a modification request may be permitted by the Secretary.[230]

With the issuance of a notice of final partnership adjustment to the partnership, a 90-day period begins during which the partnership may seek judicial review of the partnership adjustment. The issuance of a notice of final partnership adjustment also marks the beginning of the 45-day period in which the partnership may elect the alternative payment procedures.[231] Further notices of adjustment or assessments of tax against the partnership with respect to the partnership taxable year that is the subject of the notice of final partnership adjustment are prohibited during the period in which judicial review may be sought or during which a judicial proceeding is pending (absent a showing of fraud, malfeasance, or misrepresentation of a material fact).[232]

Any notice of partnership adjustment may be rescinded by the Secretary, if the partnership consents. If the notice is rescinded, it is a nullity, and does not confer a right to seek judicial review, nor does it bar issuance of further notices.

Assessment, collection and payment

An imputed underpayment is assessed and collected in the same manner as if it were a tax imposed for the adjustment year under the Federal income tax.[233] The general provisions for assessment, collection and payment under subtitle F of the Code apply unless superseded by rules of the new centralized system. As a result, an imputed underpayment may be assessed against a partnership if the partnership agrees with the results of the examination, following the expiration of the 90th day after issuance of a notice of final partnership adjustment without initiation of judicial proceedings, or in the case of timely judicial proceedings, following the entry of final decision of such proceedings. If no court proceeding is initiated within the 90-day period, the amount that may be as-

---

[228] Secs. 6231(a) and 6227.
[229] Sec. 6231(a).
[230] Sec. 6225(c)(7).
[231] Sec. 6226.
[232] Sec. 6231(b).
[233] Sec. 6232.

sessed against the partnership is limited to the imputed underpayment shown in the notice.[234]

In the case of an administrative adjustment request for which the adjustment is determined and taken into account by the partnership in the partnership taxable year in which the request is made,[235] the imputed underpayment is required to be paid when the request is filed, and is assessed at that time. If the administrative adjustment request is subsequently audited and results in an imputed underpayment greater than that reported and paid with the originally filed request, the additional amount of the imputed underpayment may be assessed in the same manner and subject to same restrictions as any other imputed underpayment determined after examination.

Restrictions on assessment, levy, and collection

The centralized system provides a limitation on the time for assessment of a deficiency as well as levy and court proceedings for collection. Except as otherwise provided, no assessment of a deficiency may be made, and no levy or court proceeding for collection of any amount resulting from an adjustment may be made, begun, or prosecuted with respect to the partnership taxable year in issue before the close of the 90th day after the day that a notice of final partnership adjustment was mailed. If a petition for judicial review is filed,[236] no such assessment may be made and no such levy or court proceeding may be made, begun, or prosecuted before the decision of the court has become final.[237]

A premature action (i.e., one that violates the limitation on the time of assessment, levy, and court proceeding for collection) may be enjoined in the proper court, including the Tax Court.[238] This rule applies notwithstanding the general rule prohibiting suits for the purpose of restraining the assessment or collection of any tax.[239] The Tax Court has no jurisdiction to enjoin any such premature action unless a timely petition for judicial review has been filed,[240] and then only in respect of the adjustments that are the subject of the petition.

Several exceptions to the restrictions on assessment are provided.[241] First, rules similar to the math error authority under section 6213(b) are permitted as exceptions to the restrictions on assessment described above. The exceptions apply to instances in which a partnership is notified that adjustments to its return are necessary to correct errors arising from mathematical or clerical errors and in the case of a tiered partnership that fails to prepare its partnership return consistently with that of the partnership in which it is a partner. In the case of an inconsistent return position, the rules similar to those in section 6213(b) (providing for subsequent abatement of any resulting assessments if challenged within

---

[234] Sec. 6232(e).
[235] Secs. 6232(a) and 6227(b)(1).
[236] Sec. 6234.
[237] Sec. 6232(b).
[238] Sec. 6232(c).
[239] Sec. 7421(a).
[240] Sec. 6234.
[241] Sec. 6232(d).

60 days) are not applicable. Finally, a partnership may waive the restrictions on the making of any partnership adjustment.

Interest and penalties

Interest

In general, interest due is determined at the partnership level and accrues at the rate applicable to underpayments.[242] Two periods are relevant in computing the total interest due: the period in which the imputed underpayment of income tax exists, and the period attributable only to late payment of any imputed underpayment after notice and demand. For an imputed underpayment, interest accrues for the period from the due date of the return for the reviewed year until the due date of the adjustment year return, or, if earlier, payment of the imputed tax. If the imputed underpayment is not timely paid with the return for the adjustment year, interest is computed from the return due date for the adjustment year until payment.

If the partnership elects the alternative payment method under section 6226, under which the underpayment is determined at the partner level, the interest due is computed at the partner level. The underpayment interest begins to accrue from the due date of the return for the taxable year to which the increase is attributable, at a rate two percentage points higher than the rate otherwise applicable to underpayments.

Penalties

Generally, the partnership is liable for any penalty, addition to tax, or additional amount.[243] These amounts are determined at the partnership level as if the partnership were an individual who was subject to Federal income tax for the reviewed year, and the imputed underpayment were an actual underpayment or understatement for the reviewed year.

A penalty, addition to tax, or additional amount may apply with respect to an adjustment year return of a partnership in the event of late payment of an imputed underpayment, or, in the case of an election by the partnership under section 6226, with respect to the adjustment year return of a partner. In such cases, the penalty for failure to pay applies.[244] For purposes of accuracy-related and fraud penalties, the determination is made by treating the imputed underpayment as an underpayment of tax.[245]

Judicial review of partnership adjustment

A partnership may seek judicial review of a notice of final partnership adjustment within 90 days after the notice is mailed. Judicial review is available in the U.S. Tax Court, the Court of Federal Claims or a U.S. district court for the district in which the partnership has its principal place of business.

With respect to judicial review in either the Court of Federal Claims or a U.S. district court, jurisdiction is contingent on the

---

[242] Sec. 6621(a)(2).
[243] Sec. 6233(a)(1)(B).
[244] Secs. 6233(b)(3)(A) and 6651(a)(2).
[245] Secs. 6662, 6662A, 6663, and 6664.

partnership depositing with the Secretary, on or before the date of the petition, an amount equal to the full imputed underpayment. The deposit is not treated as a payment of tax other than for purposes of determining whether interest on any underpayment as ultimately determined would be due. The proceeding under this provision is a de novo proceeding, and determinations made pursuant to the proceeding are subject to review to the same extent as any other decision, decree or judgment of the court in question.

Once a proceeding is initiated, a decision to dismiss the proceeding (other than a dismissal because the notice of final partnership adjustment was rescinded under section 6231(c)), is a judgment on the merits upholding the final partnership adjustments.

Period of limitations on making adjustments

In general, the Secretary may adjust an item on a partnership return at any time within three years of the date a return is filed (or the return due date, if the return is not filed) or an administrative adjustment request is made. The time within which the adjustment is made by the Secretary may be later if a notice of proposed adjustment[246] is issued, because the issuance of a notice of proposed partnership adjustment begins the running of a period of 270 days in which the partnership may seek a modification of the imputed underpayment. Although the partnership generally is limited to 270 days from the issuance of that notice to seek a modification of the imputed underpayment, extensions may be permitted by the IRS. During the 270-day period, the Secretary may not issue a notice of final partnership adjustment.

After the timely issuance of a notice of proposed adjustment resulting in an imputed underpayment, the notice of final partnership adjustment may be issued no later than either the date which is 270 days after the partnership has completed its response seeking a revision of an imputed underpayment, or, if the partnership provides an incomplete or no response, no later than 330 days after the date of a notice of proposed adjustment.[247]

The partnership may consent to an extension of time within which a partnership adjustment may be made. In addition, the provision contemplates that the Secretary may agree to extend the period of time in which the request for modification is submitted, under procedures to be established for submitting and reviewing requests for modification. If an extension of the time within which to seek a modification is granted, a similar period is added to the time within which the Secretary may issue a notice of final partnership adjustment. The procedures for modifications of imputed underpayments are required to provide rules that exclude from any

---

[246] Sec. 6231.

[247] See section 411 of the Protecting Americans from Tax Hikes Act of 2015 (Division Q of Pub. L. No. 114–113), which rectifies the unintended conflict between section 6231 (barring the Secretary from issuing the notice of final partnership adjustment earlier than the expiration of the 270 days after the notice of a proposed adjustment) and section 6235 (requiring that a notice of final partnership adjustment be filed no later than 270 days after the notice of proposed adjustment in the case of a partnership that does not seek modification of the imputed underpayment). As amended, section 6235 provides that a notice of final partnership adjustment to a partnership that does not seek modification of an underpayment in response to a notice of proposed adjustment may be issued up to 330 days (plus any additional number of days that were agreed upon as an extension of time for taxpayer response) after the notice of proposed adjustment.

underpayment of tax the portion of adjustments that may have already been taken into consideration on amended returns filed by partners and for which the allocable underpayment of tax was paid.

Several exceptions similar to those generally applicable outside the context of partnerships are provided to the limitations period. In the case of a fraudulent return or failure to file a return, a partnership adjustment may be made at any time. If a partnership files a return on which it makes a substantial omission of income within the meaning of section 6501(e)(1)(A), the Secretary may make adjustments to the return within six years of the date the return was filed.

In addition, if a notice of final partnership adjustment described in section 6231 is mailed, the limitations period is suspended for the period during which judicial remedies under section 6234 may be pursued or are pursued and for one year thereafter. Where a partnership elects to apply section 6226, this provision operates to ensure that the period in which the Secretary may assess the resulting underpayment due from each partner is open for at least one year after proceedings at the partnership level have concluded. The partner who is responsible for paying an underpayment arising from the partnership reviewed year must compute such tax with respect to his taxable year in which or with which the partnership reviewed year ends, and pay the additional tax with the return for the year in which the partnership mails the statements to partners under section 6226. Because the additional tax arises from an adjustment at the partnership level that is binding on the partner, the partner may neither contest the merits of the partnership adjustment, nor may the partner claim the Secretary is time-barred with respect to such adjustment.

Examples

The interaction of the notice requirements of new section 6231 and the limitations period with regard to adjustments to partnership returns that result in imputed underpayments under new section 6235 is illustrated in this example regarding a partnership's taxable year 2018.

On March 15, 2019, it files a timely income tax return for the taxable year 2018. Absent any other activity by the Secretary or the partnership, the general three-year limitations period in which any item on the return may be adjusted expires in three years, on March 15, 2022.

On December 15, 2020, the Secretary notifies the partnership that it intends to initiate an administrative proceeding with respect to the 2018 partnership return. That notice neither shortens nor extends the period in which partnership adjustments may be made by the Secretary, but it ends the period in which the partnership may submit an administrative adjustment request with respect to that taxable year.

On September 15, 2021, the Secretary issues a notice of proposed adjustments that result in an imputed underpayment. Issuance of this notice triggers a period of 270 days during which the Secretary may not issue a notice of final partnership adjustment and within which the partnership must submit all required documentation in support of a request for modification of the imputed underpayment. This 270-day periods ends on June 15, 2022, which is later than the expiration of the otherwise applicable limitations period. The deadline for issuance of a notice of final partnership adjustment will depend upon whether and how the partnership responds to the proposed notice of adjustments.

If nothing further is received from the partnership, the Secretary may issue a notice of final partnership adjustment no later than 330 days after the notice of proposed adjustments (i.e., within 60 days after the expiration of the 270-day period in which partnership was permitted to respond). Because the 330th day after September 15, 2021, falls on Sunday, August 14, 2022, the final date on which the Secretary may issue a notice of final partnership adjustment is Monday, August 15, 2022.[248]

The partnership may instead respond to the notice with a timely request for modification of the imputed underpayment but ask for additional time to complete its submission in support of the request for modification. For example, the Secretary may grant a timely request for 45 additional days, allowing the partnership until Monday, August 1, 2022, to submit its complete response.

- If the partnership fails to provide the required information by August 1, 2022 and no further extension is granted, then the Secretary may issue a notice of final partnership adjustment no later than September 30, which is 60 days after August 1, 2022 (the end of the 270-day period plus the additional time that was granted to the taxpayer to provide its complete response).
- If the partnership instead provides its complete response on August 1, a notice of final partnership adjustment may be issued up to 270 days after the date on which the information required by the Secretary was submitted, or April 28, 2023. During this 270-day period ending with April 28, 2023, the Secretary is expected to review the information that was submitted and revise the adjustments that were proposed if appropriate.

In the alternative, consider a variation of the above facts in which the partnership submits an administrative adjustment request on June 1, 2020 that corrects several errors on its timely-filed 2018 return. The administrative adjustment request results in an imputed underpayment of tax, which the partnership pays in full, with interest from March 15, 2019 (the filing date of the return) when it submits the administrative adjustment request. On December 15, 2020, the Secretary notifies the partnership that he will initiate an administrative proceeding with regard to taxable year 2018. On September 15, 2021, the Secretary issues a notice of proposed adjustments to the partnership 2018 return.

As a result of submitting an administrative adjustment request, the period in which partnership adjustments to the taxable year 2018 may be made is extended to June 1, 2023, the date that is three years from the date the administrative adjustment request is submitted. Because that date is later than all of the extensions described in the preceding scenarios, the Secretary may issue a notice

---

[248] See section 7503.

of final partnership adjustments on or before June 1, 2023, provided that such notice is issued after expiration of the 270-day period within which the partnership must respond to the notice of proposed adjustments issued September 15, 2021. The issuance of a notice of proposed adjustments cannot shorten the limitations period for making an adjustment to the partnership return.

Issues raised by the partnership in its administrative adjustment request may be the subject of inquiry by the Secretary in several ways. If the original partnership return may be the subject of an examination, the administrative adjustment request is likely to be reviewed as part of that process. Alternatively, the administrative adjustment request may be subject to examination on its own. Interest on an imputed underpayment accrues from March 15, 2019, the unextended due date of the 2018 timely return until payment, whether the examination was prompted by the return or solely by the administrative adjustment request. However, full payment of the reported underpayment reported on the administrative adjustment request, plus interest calculated through the date of the administrative adjustment requests, ends accrual of additional interest with respect to that portion of the underpayment ultimately determined that was reported on the administrative adjustment request. If an increase in the imputed underpayment reported by the partnership results from the relevant examination, the additional tax that should have been reported and paid with the administrative adjustment request submitted during 2020 will incur interest from March 15, 2019, unextended due date of the 2018 return, to the date the amount is paid.

In addition, the issues presented in the administrative adjustment request may be relevant to determining the correct treatment of items reported by the partnership on returns for other periods. For example, the year in which the request is filed may be subject to examination for issues related to the items that were the subject of the administrative adjustment request. In that case, information from taxable year 2018 is relevant, regardless of whether an examination of 2018 is opened. However, no imputed underpayment for 2018 may be determined without initiating an administrative proceeding with respect to that year.

Definitions and Special Rules

Definitions and special rules [249]

Partnership

The term partnership means any partnership required to file a return under section 6031(a). This includes any partnership described in section 761 that is required to file a return.

Partnership adjustment

The term partnership adjustment means any adjustment in the amount of any item of income, gain, loss, deduction, or credit of a partnership, or any partner's distributed share thereof.

---

[249] Sec. 6241.

Return due date

The term return due date means, with respect to the taxable year, the date prescribed for filing the partnership return for such taxable year (determined without regard to extensions).

Payments nondeductible

No deduction is allowed under the Federal income tax for any payment required to be made by a partnership under the centralized system of partnership audit, assessment, and collection.

Under the centralized system, the flowthrough nature of the partnership under subchapter K of the Code is unchanged, but the partnership is treated as a point of collection of underpayments that would otherwise be the responsibility of partners. The return filed by the partnership, though it is an information return, is treated as if it were a tax return where necessary to implement examination, assessment, and collection of the tax due and any penalties, additions to tax, and interest.

A basis adjustment (reduction) to a partner's basis in its partnership interest is made to reflect the nondeductible payment by the partnership of the tax. Specifically, present-law section 705(a)(2)(B) applies, providing that the adjusted basis of a partner's interest in a partnership is the basis of the interest determined under applicable rules relating to contributions and transfers, and decreased (but not below zero) by expenditures of the partnership that are not deductible in computing its taxable income and not properly chargeable to capital account. Concomitantly, the partnership's total adjusted basis in its assets is reduced by the cash payment of the tax. Thus, parallel basis reductions are made to outside and inside basis to reflect the partnership's payment of the tax. Partners, former partners, and the partnership may have entered into indemnification agreements under the partnership agreement with respect to the risk of tax liability of former or new partners being borne economically by new or former partners, respectively. Because the payment of tax by a partnership under the centralized system is nondeductible, payments under an indemnification or similar agreement with respect to or arising from the tax are nondeductible.

Partnerships having principal place of business outside the United States

For purposes of judicial review following a notice of final partnership adjustment, a principal place of business located outside the United States is treated as located in the District of Columbia.

Suspension of period of limitations on making adjustment, assessment or collection

The provision includes a rule similar to the present-law rule [250] to conform the automatic stay of the Bankruptcy Code (Title 11) with the limitations period applicable under the centralized system for partnership adjustments. Any statute of limitations period provided under the centralized system on making a partnership adjustment, or on assessment or collection of an imputed under-

---

[250] Sec. 6213(f).

payment, is suspended during the period the Secretary is prohibited by reason of the Title 11 case from making the adjustment, assessment, or collection. For adjustment or assessment, the relevant statute of limitations is extended for 60 days thereafter. For collection, the relevant statute of limitations is extended for six months thereafter.

In a case under Title 11, the 90-day period to petition for judicial review after the mailing of the notice of final partnership adjustment [251] is suspended during the period the partnership is prohibited by reason of the Title 11 case from filing such a petition for judicial review, and for 60 days thereafter.

Treatment where partnership ceases to exist

If a partnership ceases to exist before a partnership adjustment under the centralized system is made, the adjustment is taken into account by the former partners of the partnership, under regulations provided by the Secretary. Whether a partnership ceases to exist for this purpose is determined without regard to whether there is a technical termination of the partnership within the meaning of section 708(b)(1)(B). The successor partnership in a technical termination succeeds to the adjustment or imputed underpayment, absent regulations to the contrary. A partnership that terminates within the meaning of section 708(b)(1)(A) is treated as ceasing to exist. In addition, a partnership also may be treated as ceasing to exist in other circumstances or based on other factors, under regulations provided by the Secretary. For example, for the purpose of whether a partnership ceases to exist under new section 6241(7), a partnership that has no significant income, revenue, assets, or activities at the time the partnership adjustment takes effect may be treated as having ceased to exist.

Extension to entities filing partnership return

If a partnership return (Form 1065) is filed by an entity for a taxable year but it is determined that the entity is not a partnership (or that there is no entity) for the year, then, to the extent provided in regulations, the provisions of this subchapter are extended in respect of that year to the entity and its items of income, gain, loss, deduction, and credit, and to persons holding an interest in the entity.

For example, assume two taxpayers purport to create a partnership for taxable year 2018, and a Form 1065 is filed for that year. The partnership is the subject of an audit under the centralized system for 2018, and pursuant to the provisions for judicial review, the partnership is determined by a court not to exist as partnership. Nevertheless, the rules of the centralized system apply to the items of income, gain, loss, deduction and credit, and to the two taxpayers, in respect of 2018. An imputed underpayment may be collected from the purported partnership in the adjustment year pursuant to new section 6225. Alternatively, the purported partnership representative may elect (at the time and in the manner prescribed by the Secretary) under new section 6226 to issue statements to the two taxpayers, which purported to hold partnership

---

[251] Sec. 6234.

interests for the reviewed year. To the extent of the adjustments, each of the two taxpayer's tax may be increased for the taxpayer's taxable year that includes the date of the statement. In this situation, the amount of the increase for each of them is amount by which the taxpayer's tax would increase if the taxpayer's share of the adjustment amounts were included for the taxpayer's taxable year that includes the end of the reviewed year, plus the amount by which the tax would increase by reason of adjustment to tax attributes in years after that year of the taxpayer and before the year of the date of the statement.

Related provisions

Binding nature of partnership adjustment proceedings

The provision clarifies that the merits of an issue that is the subject of a final determination in a proceeding brought under the centralized system [252] is among the issues that are precluded from being raised at a collection due process hearing (in connection with the right to, and opportunity for, such a hearing prior to a levy on any property or right to any property under present law).[253] The provision does not restrict the authority of the Secretary to permit an opportunity for administrative review, similar to the Collection Appeals Program,[254] nor does it limit a partner's right to seek review of the conduct of collection measures, such as whether notices of Federal tax lien or notice of intent to levy were timely issued.

For example, assume that a partnership is audited with respect to taxable year 2018. One of the adjustments reflects the partnership's omission of income of $1,000 in calculating partnership taxable income. Following receipt of the notice of final partnership adjustment, the partnership decides not to litigate. The partnership elects to issue statements to reviewed year partners, whose tax is increased for the partner's taxable year that includes the date of the statement, 2021. Reviewed year partner A's adjustment is $100, resulting in an increase in tax of $35, but partner A does not pay the increased amount of tax. The time for the partnership to litigate the adjustments has elapsed and the notice of final partnership adjustment is a final determination. Prior to any levy on any property or right to any property of partner A in connection with collection of the $35 tax, partner A has the right to and is afforded the opportunity for a hearing (the collection due process hearing). At the hearing, partner A may not raise the issue of whether the $1,000 (or A's $100 share of it) was properly includable in determining partnership taxable income, because a final determination

---

[252] That is, a proceeding brought under subchapter C of chapter 63 of the Code.

[253] Section 6330 establishes the requirement that the IRS provide notice of potential collection action and offer an opportunity for a hearing before an impartial officer, and identifies which issues may be raised at such hearing and which are precluded. Issues permitted to be raised include the underlying liability only if the taxpayer did not receive a notice of deficiency or otherwise have an opportunity to contest the liability. Prior to amendment, the issues that were precluded listed those that were the subject of any previous administrative or judicial proceeding. Treas. Reg. 301–6330. The Secretary's power to levy is set forth in present-law section 6331.

[254] For example, under TEFRA, the IRS permits partners to raise computational issues, interest abatement questions and other collection due process rights in administrative appeals in order to assure consistency in the handling of the cases, even though the partners are precluded from questioning the substance of the partnership adjustment. See Internal Revenue Manual, paragraph 8.22.8.19, TEFRA Partnerships.

with respect to the issue was made in a proceeding brought under the centralized system. The result is the same if the partnership had decided to seek judicial review and the final determination of the court is that the $1,000 is includable in determining partnership taxable income.

Restriction on authority to amend partner information statements

The provision provides that partner information returns (currently Schedules K–1) required to be furnished by the partnership [255] may not be amended after the due date of the partnership return to which the partner information returns relate. The due date takes into account the permitted extension period. For example, the Schedules K–1 furnished by a partnership with respect to its taxable year 2020 may not be amended after the due date for the partnership 2020 return. If the partnership has a calendar taxable year, the due date for its partnership 2020 return is September 15, 2021 (taking into account the permitted 6-month extension following the due date of March 15, 2021), after which date the Schedules K–1 for 2020 may no longer be amended.[256] The partnership may, however, file an administrative adjustment request pursuant to new section 6227, and the partnership may pay any resulting imputed underpayment at the partnership level.

Example

For example, assume that a partnership files its Form 1065 for taxable year 2020 on March 15, 2021. On November 3, 2021, the partnership discovers an omission from income for 2020. The partnership may not issue amended Schedules K–1 to its partners for 2020. However, the partnership may file an administrative adjustment request and pay the underpayment consistently with new section 6227(b)(1) for the partnership taxable year in which the administrative adjustment request is made. In this situation, the partnership does not furnish amended Schedules K–1 to the partners and the partners do not file amended Federal and State income tax returns with respect to the omitted income.[257]

Effective Date

The provision applies to returns filed for partnership taxable years beginning after December 31, 2017. The provision relating to administrative adjustment requests applies to requests with respect to returns filed for partnership taxable years beginning after December 31, 2017. The provision relating to the election of a partnership to furnish statements to partners (section 6226) applies to

---

[255] The requirement of furnishing partner information returns is imposed by section 6031(b). See section 411 of the Protecting Americans from Tax Hikes Act of 2015 (Division Q of Pub. L. No. 114–113), correcting a conforming amendment to strike the last sentence of section 6031(b) under prior law, which sentence related to repealed provisions on electing large partnerships.

[256] This rule does not, however, preclude the filing of amended returns of reviewed-year partners pursuant to the procedure for modification of an imputed underpayment in section 6225(c)(2).

[257] The partnership that files the administrative adjustment request is not precluded from furnishing under section 6227(b)(2) an adjusted statement (similar to a Schedule K–1) to each reviewed-year partner, who is then required to pay tax attributable to the partnership adjustment (as provided under guidance provided by the Secretary).

elections with respect to returns filed for partnership taxable years beginning after December 31, 2017.

A partnership may elect for the provisions of the centralized system (other than the election out under section 6221(b)) to apply to any return of the partnership filed for partnership taxable years beginning after the date of enactment and before January 1, 2018. This election is made at such time and in such form and manner as the Secretary of the Treasury may prescribe. A partnership may not elect out of the centralized system under section 6221(b) in combination with this election.

A partnership may choose to make this election, for example, to be eligible before 2018 to pay at the partnership level, to obviate the need to furnish amended Schedules K–1 to correct a partnership-level error, or to obviate the need for partners receiving amended Schedules K–1 to file amended Federal and State income tax returns. A partnership may not elect out of the centralized system under section 6221(b) in combination with this election.

B. Partnership Interests Created by Gift (sec. 1102 of the Act and secs. 704(e) and 761(b) of the Code)

Present Law

Under present law, a partnership includes an unincorporated organization that carries on any business, financial operation, or venture which is not otherwise treated as a trust, estate, or corporation under the Internal Revenue Code.[258] The Supreme Court has stated that the test of a partnership is "whether considering all the facts . . . the parties in good faith and acting with a business purpose intended to join together in the present conduct of the enterprise".[259] A partner means a member of a partnership.[260]

Present law also provides that the manner in which a person acquires a capital interest is not determinative of whether that person is recognized as a partner for income tax purposes. If he owns a capital interest in a partnership in which capital is a material income-producing factor, whether or not the interest was derived by purchase or gift from any person, the owner is treated as a partner.[261] The predecessor of this provision was enacted in 1951 to prevent the IRS from denying partner status to a taxpayer who shared actual ownership of the partnership's income-producing capital on the basis that the interest was acquired from a family member.[262] According to the legislative history, "Your committee's amendment makes it clear that, however the owner of a partnership interest may have acquired such interest, the income is taxed to the owner, if he is the real owner. If the ownership is real, it does not matter what motivated the transfer to him or whether the business benefitted from the entrance of the new partner."[263] The focus of the legislation was on which party (transferor or transferee) actually owns a partnership interest, not on whether a par-

---

[258] Sec. 761(a). See also sec. 7701(a)(2).
[259] *Commissioner v. Culbertson*, 337 U.S. 733, 742 (1949).
[260] Sec. 761(b).
[261] Sec. 704(e)(1).
[262] Pub. L. No. 82–183, sec. 340(a).
[263] S. Rep. No. 781, 82d Cong., 1st Sess., 38, 39 (1951): H.R. Rep. No. 586, 82d Cong., 1st Sess. 32 (1951).

ticular interest qualifies as a partnership interest. The provision states the general principle that income derived from capital is taxed to the owner of the capital.[264]

In a partnership known as Castle Harbour, LLC, two foreign banks held interests, the nature of which was the subject of dispute for income tax purposes. At the trial level, the District Court held that the tax-indifferent banks were partners even though the interest was not "bona fide partnership equity participation"[265] because the interest met the definition of a capital interest within the meaning of section 704(e)(1).[266] Thus, the tax-indifferent banks were partners to which income could be allocated. The trial court was reversed on appeal.[267]

Explanation of Provision

The provision clarifies that, in the case of a capital interest in a partnership in which capital is a material income-producing factor, the determination of whether a person is a partner with respect to the interest is made without regard to whether the interest was derived by gift from any other person. The provision strikes paragraph (1) of section 704(e) and modifies the definition of partner in section 761 to eliminate any argument that the provision provides an alternative test as to whether the holder of a capital interest is a partner with respect to that interest, or whether the interest constitutes a capital interest in a partnership.

The provision is intended to retain the present-law determination of which person (for example, the donor or the donee) is a partner. The provision is not intended to change the principle that the real owner of a capital interest is to be taxed on the income from the interest, regardless of the motivation behind or the means of the transfer of the interest. Thus, as under present law, the fact that an individual received such a partnership interest by gift from a family member does not determine whether that individual is (or is not) a partner.

The provision places the new provision in section 761, relating to definitions, rather than section 704, relating to a partner's distributive share.[268]

Effective Date

The provision applies to partnership taxable years beginning after December 31, 2015.

---

[264] See 4 Bittker and Lokken, *Federal Taxation of Income, Estates, and Gifts,* para. 86.3.1, at 86–29 (3rd ed. 2003). "The reference to 'ownership' of a capital interest is odd because it is a pervasive principle of tax law, seemingly needing no repetition for a limited class of assets, that income from property transferred by gift is thereafter taxed to the donee."

[265] *TIFD III-E, Inc. v. United States,* 459 F.3d 220 (2d Cir. 2006), reversing and remanding 342 F.Supp. 2d 94 (D. Conn. 2004). TIFD III-E, Inc. was tax matters partner for Castle Harbour, LLC.

[266] *TIFD III-E, Inc. v. United States,* 660 F. Supp. 2d 367 (D. Conn. 2009).

[267] *TIFD III-E, Inc. v. United States,* 666 F.3d 836 (2d Cir. 2012).

[268] The predecessor to section 704(e)(1) was located in the definitions at section 3797(a)(2) of the Internal Revenue Code of 1939. It was placed at section 704(e)(1) when the Code was recodified as the Internal Revenue Code of 1954.

PART ELEVEN: SURFACE TRANSPORTATION EXTENSION ACT OF 2015, PART II (PUBLIC LAW 114–87) [269]

A. Extension of Highway Trust Fund Expenditure Authority (sec. 2001 of the Act and secs. 9503, 9504, and 9508 of the Code)

Present Law

Under present law, the Internal Revenue Code (sec. 9503) authorizes expenditures (subject to appropriations) to be made from the Highway Trust Fund (and Sport Fish Restoration and Boating Trust Fund and Leaking Underground Storage Tank Trust Fund) through November 20, 2015, for purposes provided in specified authorizing legislation as in effect on the date of enactment.

Explanation of Provision

This provision extends the authority to make expenditures (subject to appropriations) from the Highway Trust Fund (and Sport Fish Restoration and Boating Trust Fund and Leaking Underground Storage Tank Trust Fund) through December 4, 2015.

Effective Date

The provision is effective on date of enactment (November 20, 2015).

---

[269] H.R. 3996. The House passed H.R. 3996 on November 16, 2015. The bill passed the Senate without amendment on November 19, 2015. The President signed the bill on November 20, 2015.

PART TWELVE: FIXING AMERICA'S SURFACE TRANSPORTATION ACT ("FAST ACT") (PUBLIC LAW 114–94) [270]

DIVISION C—FINANCE

TITLE XXXI—HIGHWAY TRUST FUND AND RELATED TAXES

A. Extension of Highway Trust Fund Expenditure Authority (secs. 31101 of the Act and secs. 9503, 9504, and 9508 of the Code)

Present Law

In general

Under present law, revenues from the highway excise taxes, as imposed through October 1, 2016, generally are dedicated to the Highway Trust Fund. Dedication of excise tax revenues to the Highway Trust Fund and expenditures from the Highway Trust Fund are governed by the Code.[271] The Code authorizes expenditures (subject to appropriations) from the Highway Trust Fund through December 4, 2015, for the purposes provided in authorizing legislation, as such legislation was in effect on the date of enactment of the Surface Transportation Extension Act of 2015, Part II.

Highway Trust Fund expenditure purposes

The Highway Trust Fund has a separate account for mass transit, the Mass Transit Account.[272] The Highway Trust Fund and the Mass Transit Account are funding sources for specific programs.

Highway Trust Fund expenditure purposes have been revised with each authorization Act enacted since establishment of the Highway Trust Fund in 1956. In general, expenditures authorized under those Acts (as the Acts were in effect on the date of enactment of the most recent such authorizing Act) are specified by the Code as Highway Trust Fund expenditure purposes. The Code provides that the authority to make expenditures from the Highway Trust Fund expires after December 4, 2015. Thus, no Highway Trust Fund expenditures may occur after December 4, 2015, without an amendment to the Code.

Section 9503 of the Code appropriates to the Highway Trust Fund amounts equivalent to the taxes received from the following:

---

[270] H.R. 22. The House passed H.R. 22 on January 6, 2015. The Senate Committee on Finance reported H.R. 22 on February 12, 2015 (S. Rep. No. 114–3). The Senate passed H.R. 22 with an amendment on July 30, 2015. The conference report was filed on December 1, 2015 (H. Rep. No. 114–357) and was passed by the House on December 3, 2015, and the Senate on December 3, 2015. The President signed the bill on December 4, 2015.

[271] Sec. 9503. The Highway Trust Fund statutory provisions were placed in the Internal Revenue Code in 1982.

[272] Sec. 9503(e)(1).

the taxes on diesel, gasoline, kerosene and special motor fuel, the tax on tires, the annual heavy vehicle use tax, and the tax on the retail sale of heavy trucks and trailers.[273] Section 9601 provides that amounts appropriated to a trust fund pursuant to sections 9501 through 9511, are to be transferred at least monthly from the General Fund of the Treasury to such trust fund on the basis of estimates made by the Secretary of the Treasury of the amounts referred to in the Code section appropriating the amounts to such trust fund. The Code requires that proper adjustments be made in amounts subsequently transferred to the extent prior estimates were in excess of, or less than, the amounts required to be transferred.

Explanation of Provision

The provision provides for expenditure authority through September 30, 2020.[274] The Code provisions governing the purposes for which monies in the Highway Trust Fund may be spent are updated to include the FAST Act.

Effective Date

The provision is effective on the date of enactment (December 4, 2015).

B. Extension of Highway-Related Taxes (sec. 31102 of the Act and secs. 4041, 4051, 4071, 4081, 4221, 4481, 4483, and 6412 of the Code)

Present Law Highway Trust Fund Excise Taxes

In general

Six separate excise taxes are imposed to finance the Federal Highway Trust Fund program. Three of these taxes are imposed on highway motor fuels. The remaining three are a retail sales tax on heavy highway vehicles, a manufacturers' excise tax on heavy vehicle tires, and an annual use tax on heavy vehicles. A substantial majority of the revenues produced by the Highway Trust Fund excise taxes are derived from the taxes on motor fuels. The annual use tax on heavy vehicles expires October 1, 2017. Except for 4.3 cents per gallon of the Highway Trust Fund fuels tax rates, the remaining taxes are scheduled to expire after October 1, 2016. The 4.3-cents-per-gallon portion of the fuels tax rates is permanent.[275] The six taxes are summarized below.

---

[273] Sec. 9503(b)(1).

[274] Cross-references to the reauthorization Act in the Code provisions governing the Sport Fish Restoration and Boating Trust Fund are also updated to include the FAST Act. In addition the date references in the Code provisions governing the Leaking Underground Storage Tank Trust Fund, and the Sport Fish Restoration and Boating Trust Fund are also updated.

[275] This portion of the tax rates was enacted as a deficit reduction measure in 1993. Receipts from it were retained in the General Fund until 1997 legislation provided for their transfer to the Highway Trust Fund.

Highway motor fuels taxes

The Highway Trust Fund motor fuels tax rates are as follows:[276]

Gasoline	18.3 cents per gallon
Diesel fuel and kerosene	24.3 cents per gallon
Alternative fuels	18.3 or 24.3 cents per gallon generally[277]

Non-fuel Highway Trust Fund excise taxes

In addition to the highway motor fuels excise tax revenues, the Highway Trust Fund receives revenues produced by three excise taxes imposed exclusively on heavy highway vehicles or tires. These taxes are:

1. A 12-percent excise tax imposed on the first retail sale of the following articles: truck chassis and bodies, truck trailer and semitrailer chassis and bodies, and tractors of the kind chiefly used for highway transportation in combination with a trailer or semitrailer (generally, the taxes apply to trucks having a gross vehicle weight in excess of 33,000 pounds and trailers having such a weight in excess of 26,000 pounds);[278]

2. An excise tax imposed on highway tires with a rated load capacity exceeding 3,500 pounds, generally at a rate of 0.945 cents per 10 pounds of excess;[279] and

3. An annual use tax imposed on highway vehicles having a taxable gross weight of 55,000 pounds or more.[280] (The maximum rate for this tax is $550 per year, imposed on vehicles having a taxable gross weight over 75,000 pounds.)

The taxable year for the annual use tax is from July 1st through June 30th of the following year. For the period July 1, 2016, through September 30, 2016, the amount of the annual use tax is reduced by 75 percent.[281]

Explanation of Provision

The provision generally extends present-law taxes through September 30, 2022. The heavy vehicle use tax is extended through September 30, 2023.

Effective Date

The provision is effective October 1, 2016.

C. Additional Transfers to the Highway Trust Fund (sec. 31201 of the Act and sec. 9503 of the Code)

Present Law

Public Law No. 110–318, "an Act to amend the Internal Revenue Code of 1986 to restore the Highway Trust Fund balance" trans-

---

[276] Secs. 4081(a)(2)(A)(i), 4081(a)(2)(A)(iii), 4041(a)(2), 4041(a)(3), and 4041(m). Some of these fuels also are subject to an additional 0.1-cent-per-gallon excise tax to fund the Leaking Underground Storage Tank Trust Fund (secs. 4041(d) and 4081(a)(2)(B)).

[277] See secs. 4041(a)(2), 4041(a)(3), and 4041(m).

[278] Sec. 4051.

[279] Sec. 4071.

[280] Sec. 4481.

[281] Sec. 4482(c)(4) and (d).

ferred, out of money in the Treasury not otherwise appropriated, $8,017,000,000 to the Highway Trust Fund effective September 15, 2008. Public Law No. 111–46, "an Act to restore sums to the Highway Trust Fund and for other purposes," transferred, out of money in the Treasury not otherwise appropriated, $7 billion to the Highway Trust Fund effective August 7, 2009. The Hiring Incentives to Restore Employment Act transferred, out of money in the Treasury not otherwise appropriated, $14,700,000,000 to the Highway Trust Fund and $4,800,000,000 to the Mass Transit Account in the Highway Trust Fund.[282] The HIRE Act provisions generally were effective as of March 18, 2010.

Moving Ahead for Progress in the 21st Century ("MAP–21")[283] provided that, out of money in the Treasury not otherwise appropriated, the following transfers were to be made from the General Fund to the Highway Trust Fund:

	FY 2013	FY 2014
Highway Account	$6.2 billion	$10.4 billion
Mass Transit Account		$2.2 billion

MAP–21 also transferred $2.4 billion from the Leaking Underground Storage Tank Trust Fund to the Highway Account in the Highway Trust Fund.

The Highway and Transportation Funding Act of 2014 transferred $7.765 billion from the General Fund to the Highway Account of the Highway Trust Fund, $2 billion from the General Fund to the Mass Transit Account of the Highway Trust Fund, and $1 billion from the Leaking Underground Storage Tank Trust Fund to the Highway Account of the Highway Trust Fund.[284] The provisions were effective on August 8, 2014.

The Surface Transportation and Veterans Health Care Choice Improvement Act of 2015, provided, out of money not otherwise appropriated, the following transfers from the General Fund to the Highway Trust Fund: $6.068 billion to the Highway Account, and $2 billion to the Mass Transit Account. The provision was effective July 31, 2015.

Explanation of Provision

The provision provides that out of money in the Treasury not otherwise appropriated, the following transfers are to be made from the General Fund to the Highway Trust Fund: $51,900,000,000 to the Highway Account and $18,100,000,000 to the Mass Transit account.

Effective Date

The provision is effective on the date of enactment (December 4, 2015).

---

[282] The Hiring Incentives to Restore Employment Act (the "HIRE" Act), Pub. L. No. 111–147, sec. 442.

[283] Moving Ahead for Progress in the 21st Century Act ("MAP–21"), Pub. L. No. 112–141, sec. 40201(a)(2), and sec. 40251.

[284] Highway and Transportation Funding Act of 2014, Pub. L. No. 113–159, sec. 2002.

D. Transfer to Highway Trust Fund of Certain Motor Vehicle Safety Penalties (sec. 31202 of the Act and sec. 9503 of the Code)

Present Law

Present law imposes certain civil penalties related to violations of motor vehicle safety.

Explanation of Provision

The provision deposits the civil penalties related to motor vehicle safety in the Highway Trust Fund instead of in the Treasury's General Fund.

Effective Date

The provision is effective for amounts collected after the date of enactment (December 4, 2015).

E. Appropriation From Leaking Underground Storage Tank Trust Fund (sec. 31203 of the Act and secs. 9503 and 9508 of the Code)

Present Law

Fuels of a type subject to other trust fund excise taxes generally are subject to an add-on excise tax of 0.1-cent-per-gallon to fund the Leaking Underground Storage Tank ("LUST") Trust Fund.[285] For example, the LUST excise tax applies to gasoline, diesel fuel, kerosene, and most alternative fuels subject to highway and aviation fuels excise taxes, and to fuels subject to the inland waterways fuel excise tax. This excise tax is imposed on both uses and parties subject to the other taxes, and to situations (other than export) in which the fuel otherwise is tax-exempt. For example, off-highway business use of gasoline and off-highway use of diesel fuel and kerosene generally are exempt from highway motor fuels excise tax. Similarly, States and local governments and certain other parties are exempt from such tax. Nonetheless, all such uses and parties are subject to the 0.1-cent-per-gallon LUST excise tax.

Liquefied natural gas, compressed natural gas, and liquefied petroleum gas are exempt from the LUST tax. Additionally, methanol and ethanol fuels produced from coal (including peat) are taxed at a reduced rate of 0.05 cents per gallon.

Explanation of Provision

The provision transfers $100 million on the date of enactment (December 4, 2015), $100 million on October 1, 2016, and an additional $100 million on October 1, 2017, from the LUST Trust Fund to the Highway Account of the Highway Trust Fund.

Effective Date

The provision is effective on the date of enactment (December 4, 2015).

---

[285] Secs. 4041, 4042, and 4081.

TITLE XXXII—OFFSETS

A. Revocation or Denial of Passport in Case of Certain Unpaid Taxes (sec. 32101 of the Act and secs. 6320, 6331, 7345 and 6103(k)(11) of the Code)

Present Law

The administration of passports is the responsibility of the Department of State.[286] The Secretary of State may refuse to issue or renew a passport if the applicant owes child support in excess of $2,500 or owes certain types of Federal debts, such as expenses incurred in providing assistance to an applicant to return to the United States. The scope of this authority does not extend to rejection or revocation of a passport on the basis of delinquent Federal taxes. Although issuance of a passport does not require a social security number or taxpayer identification number ("TIN"), the applicant is required under the Code to provide such number. Failure to provide a TIN is reported by the State Department to the IRS and may result in a $500 fine.[287]

Returns and return information are confidential and may not be disclosed by the IRS, other Federal employees, State employees, and certain others having access to such information except as provided in the Internal Revenue Code.[288] There are a number of exceptions to the general rule of nondisclosure that authorize disclosure in specifically identified circumstances, including disclosure of information about federal tax debts for purposes of reviewing an application for a Federal loan[289] and for purposes of enhancing the integrity of the Medicare program.[290]

Explanation of Provision

In general

Under the provision, the Secretary of State is required to deny a passport (or renewal of a passport) to a seriously delinquent taxpayer and is permitted to revoke any passport previously issued to such person. In addition to the revocation or denial of passports to delinquent taxpayers, the Secretary of State is authorized to deny an application for a passport if the applicant fails to provide a social security number or provides an incorrect or invalid social security number. With respect to an incorrect or invalid number, the inclusion of an erroneous number is a basis for rejection of the application only if the erroneous number was provided willfully, intentionally, recklessly or negligently. Exceptions to these rules are permitted for emergency or humanitarian circumstances, including the issuance of a passport for short-term use to return to the United States by the delinquent taxpayer.

The provision authorizes limited sharing of information between the Secretary of State and Secretary of the Treasury. If the Commissioner of Internal Revenue certifies to the Secretary of the

---

[286] "Passport Act of 1926," 22 U.S.C. sec. 211a et seq.
[287] Sec. 6039E.
[288] Sec. 6103.
[289] Sec. 6103(l)(3).
[290] Sec. 6103(l)(22).

Treasury the identity of persons who have seriously delinquent Federal taxes as defined in this provision, the Secretary of the Treasury or his delegate is authorized to transmit such certification to the Secretary of State for use in determining whether to issue, renew, or revoke a passport. Certification of a seriously delinquent tax debt under this provision is added to the list of actions for which the time in which the action must be performed may be postponed due to the taxpayer's service in a combat zone.[291] Applicants whose names are included on the certifications provided to the Secretary of State are ineligible for a passport. The Secretary of State and Secretary of the Treasury are held harmless with respect to any certification issued pursuant to this provision.

Applicable only to "seriously delinquent tax debt"

The provision applies only to "seriously delinquent tax debt," which includes any outstanding Federal tax liability (including interest and any penalties) in excess of $50,000 [292] for which a notice of lien or a notice of levy has been filed. With respect to debts for which a notice of lien has been filed, the debt is considered seriously delinquent only if the taxpayer's administrative review rights have been exhausted or lapsed. The amount is to be adjusted for inflation annually, using calendar year 2014, and a cost-of-living adjustment. Even if a tax debt otherwise meets the statutory threshold, it may not be considered seriously delinquent if (1) the debt is being paid in a timely manner pursuant to an installment agreement or offer-in-compromise, or (2) collection action with respect to the debt is suspended because a collection due process hearing or innocent spouse relief has been requested or is pending.

Taxpayer safeguards

Several measures ensure that the IRS corrects erroneous certifications and considers actions taken by a taxpayer after action has been initiated under this provision if such actions would have the effect of removing the debt from the category of seriously delinquent debt. These measures include limits on the authority of the Commissioner, notification requirements, standards under which the Commissioner may reverse the certification of serious delinquency, and limits on authority to delegate the certification process.

The Commissioner may not delegate the authority to provide certification of a seriously delinquent tax debt except to a Deputy Commissioner for Services and Enforcement, or to a Division Commissioner (the head of an IRS operating division). Neither official may redelegate such authority.

The Commissioner must inform taxpayers regarding the procedures in three ways. First, the possible loss of a passport is added to the list of matters required to be included in notices to taxpayer of potential collection activity under sections 6320 or 6331. Second, the Commissioner must provide contemporaneous notice to a taxpayer when the Commissioner sends a certification of serious delinquency to the Secretary. Finally, in instances in which the Com-

---

[291] Sec. 7508(a).
[292] The amount is indexed to inflation annually, based on calendar year 2015.

missioner decertifies the taxpayer's status as a delinquent taxpayer, he is required to provide notice to the taxpayer at the same time as the notice to the Secretary of the Treasury.

The decertification process provides a mechanism under which the Commissioner can correct an erroneous certification or end the certification because the debt is no longer seriously delinquent, due to certain events subsequent to the certification. If after certifying the delinquency to the Secretary, the IRS receives full payment of the seriously delinquent tax debt; the taxpayer enters into an installment agreement under section 6159; the IRS accepts an offer in compromise under section 7122; or a spouse files for relief from joint liability, the Commissioner must notify the Secretary that the taxpayer is not seriously delinquent. In each instance, the "decertification" is limited to the taxpayer who is the subject of one of the above actions. In the case of a claim for innocent spouse relief, the decertification is only with respect to the spouse claiming relief, not both spouses. The Commissioner must generally decertify within 30 days of the event that requires decertification.

The Commissioner must provide the notice of decertification to the Secretary of the Treasury, who must in turn promptly notify the Secretary of State of the decertification. The Secretary of State must delete the certification from the records regarding that taxpayer.

In addition, the provision allows limited judicial review of a wrongful certification (or failure to decertify) in a Federal district court or the U.S. Tax Court. If the court determines that the certification is erroneous, the court may order the Secretary of the Treasury to notify the Secretary of State of the error. No other relief is authorized.

Effective Date

The provision is effective on the date of enactment (December 4, 2015).

B. Reform of Rules Related to Qualified Tax Collection Contracts, and Special Compliance Personnel Program (secs. 32102–32103 of the Act and sec. 6306 of the Code)

Present Law

Code section 6306 permits the IRS to use private debt collection companies to locate and contact taxpayers owing outstanding tax liabilities of any type[293] and to arrange payment of those taxes by the taxpayers. There must be an assessment pursuant to section 6201 in order for there to be an outstanding tax liability. An assessment is the formal recording of the taxpayer's tax liability that fixes the amount payable. An assessment must be made before the IRS is permitted to commence enforcement actions to collect the amount payable. In general, an assessment is made at the conclusion of all examination and appeals processes within the IRS.[294]

---

[293] This provision generally applies to any type of tax imposed under the Internal Revenue Code.

[294] An amount of tax reported as due on the taxpayer's tax return is considered to be self-assessed. If the IRS determines that the assessment or collection of tax will be jeopardized by

Continued

Several steps are involved in the deployment of private debt collection companies. First, the private debt collection company contacts the taxpayer by letter.[295] If the taxpayer's last known address is incorrect, the private debt collection company searches for the correct address. Second, the private debt collection company telephones the taxpayer to request full payment.[296] If the taxpayer cannot pay in full immediately, the private debt collection company offers the taxpayer an installment agreement providing for full payment of the taxes over a period of as long as five years. If the taxpayer is unable to pay the outstanding tax liability in full over a five-year period, the private debt collection company obtains financial information from the taxpayer and will provide this information to the IRS for further processing and action by the IRS.

The Code specifies several procedural conditions under which the provision would operate. First, provisions of the Fair Debt Collection Practices Act apply to the private debt collection company. Second, the employees of private sector debt collection companies are prohibited from committing any act or omission which employees of the IRS are prohibited from committing in the performance of similar services. Third, subcontractors are prohibited from having contact with taxpayers, providing quality assurance services, and composing debt collection notices; any other service provided by a subcontractor must receive prior approval from the IRS.

The Code creates a revolving fund from the amounts collected by the private debt collection companies. The private debt collection companies are paid out of this fund. The Code prohibits the payment of fees for all services in excess of 25 percent of the amount collected under a tax collection contract.

The Code provides that up to 25 percent of the amount collected may be used for IRS collection enforcement activities. The law also requires Treasury to provide a biennial report to the Committee on Finance and the Committee on Ways and Means. The report is to include, among other items, a cost benefit analysis, the impact of the debt collection contracts on collection enforcement staff levels in the IRS, and an evaluation of contractor performance.

The Omnibus Appropriations Act of 2009 (the "Act"), which made appropriations for the fiscal year ending September 30, 2009, included a provision stating that none of the funds made available in the Act could be used to fund or administer section 6306.[297] Around the same time, the IRS announced that the IRS would not renew its contracts with private debt collection agencies.[298]

Explanation of Provision

Qualified tax collection contracts

The provision requires the Secretary to enter into qualified tax collection contracts for the collection of inactive tax receivables. In-

---

delay, it has the authority to assess the amount immediately (sec. 6861), subject to several procedural safeguards.

[295] The provision requires that the IRS disclose confidential taxpayer information to the private debt collection company. Section 6103(n) permits disclosure of returns and return information for "the providing of other services . . . for purposes of tax administration."

[296] The private debt collection company is not permitted to accept payment directly. Payments are required to be processed by IRS employees.

[297] Pub. L. No. 111–8, March 11, 2009.

[298] IR–2009–19, March 5, 2009.

active tax receivables are defined as any tax receivable (i) removed from the active inventory for lack of resources or inability to locate the taxpayer, (ii) for which more than 1/3 of the applicable limitations period has lapsed and no IRS employee has been assigned to collect the receivable; and (iii) for which, a receivable has been assigned for collection but more than 365 days have passed without interaction with the taxpayer or a third party for purposes of furthering the collection. Tax receivables are defined as any outstanding assessment which the IRS includes in potentially collectible inventory.

The provision designates certain tax receivables as not eligible for collection under qualified tax collection contracts, specifically a contract that: (i) is subject to a pending or active offer-in-compromise or installment agreement; (ii) is classified as an innocent spouse case; (iii) involves a taxpayer identified by the Secretary as being (a) deceased, (b) under the age of 18, (c) in a designated combat zone, or (d) a victim of identity theft; (iv) is currently under examination, litigation, criminal investigation, or levy; or (v) is currently subject to a proper exercise of a right of appeal. The provision grants authority to the Secretary to prescribe procedures for taxpayers in Presidentially declared disaster areas to request relief from immediate collection measures under the provision.

The provision requires the Secretary to give priority to private collection contractors and debt collection centers currently approved by the Treasury Department's Financial Management Service on the schedule required under section 3711(g) of title 31 of the United States Code, to the extent appropriate to carry out the purposes of the provision.

The provision adds an additional exception to section 6103 to allow contractors to identify themselves as such and disclose the nature, subject, and reason for the contact. Disclosures are permitted only in situations and under conditions approved by the Secretary.

The provision requires the Secretary to prepare two reports for the House Committee on Ways and Means and the Senate Committee on Finance. The first report is required annually and due not later than 90 days after each fiscal year and is required to include: (i) the total number and amount of tax receivables provided to each contractor for collection under this section, (ii) the total amounts collected by and installment agreements resulting from the collection efforts of each contactor and the collection costs incurred by the IRS; (iii) the impact of such contacts on the total number and amount of unpaid assessments, and on the number and amount of assessments collected by IRS personnel after initial contact by a contractor, (iv) the amount of fees retained by the Secretary under subsection (e) and a description of the use of such funds; and (v) a disclosure safeguard report in a form similar to that required under section 6103(p)(5).

The second report is required biannually and is required to include: (i) an independent evaluation of contactor performance; and (ii) a measurement plan that includes a comparison of the best practices used by private collectors to the collection techniques used by the IRS and mechanisms to identify and capture information on successful collection techniques used by the contractors that could be adopted by the IRS.

Special compliance personnel program

The provision requires that the amount that, under current law, is to be retained and used by the IRS for collection enforcement activities under section 6306 of the Code be instead used to fund a newly created special compliance personnel program. The provision also requires the Secretary to establish an account for the hiring, training, and employment of special compliance personnel. No other source of funding for the program is permitted, and funds deposited in the special account are restricted to use for the program, including reimbursement of the IRS and other agencies for the cost of administering the qualified debt collection program and all costs associated with employment of special compliance personnel and the retraining and reassignment of other personnel as special compliance personnel. Special compliance personnel are individuals employed by the IRS to serve either as revenue officers performing field collection functions, or as persons operating the automated collection system.

The provision requires the Secretary to prepare annually a report for the House Committee on Ways and Means and the Senate Committee on Finance, to be submitted no later than March of each year. In the report, the Secretary is to describe for the preceding fiscal year accounting of all funds received in the account, administrative and program costs, number of special compliance personnel hired and employed as well as actual revenue collected by such personnel. Similar information for the current and following fiscal year, using both actual and estimated amounts, is required.

Effective Date

The provision relating to qualified tax collection contracts applies to tax receivables identified by the Secretary after the date of enactment (December 4, 2015). The requirement to give priority to certain private collection contractors and debt collection centers applies to contracts and agreements entered into within three months after the date of enactment, and the new exception to section 6103 applies to disclosures made after the date of enactment. The requirement of the reports to Congress is effective on the date of enactment.

The provision relating to the special compliance personnel program applies to amounts collected and retained by the Secretary after the date of enactment.

C. Repeal of Modification of Automatic Extension of Return Due Date for Certain Employee Benefit Plans (sec. 32104 of the Act and secs. 6058 and 6059 of the Code)

Present Law

An employer that maintains a pension, annuity, stock bonus, profit-sharing or other funded deferred compensation plan (or the plan administrator of the plan) is required to file an annual return containing information required under regulations with respect to the qualification, financial condition, and operation of the plan.[299] The plan administrator of a defined benefit plan subject to the minimum funding requirements [300] is required to file an annual actuarial report.[301] These filing requirements are met by filing an Annual Return/Report of Employee Benefit Plan, Form 5500, and providing the information as required on the form and related instructions.[302]

Similarly, the Employee Retirement Income Security Act of 1974 ("ERISA") requires the administrator of certain pension and welfare benefit plans to file annual reports disclosing certain information to the Department of Labor ("DOL") and, with respect to some defined benefit plans, to the Pension Benefit Guaranty Corporation ("PBGC").[303] Plan administrators also comply with these ERISA filing requirements by filing Form 5500.

Forms 5500 are filed with DOL, and information from Forms 5500 is shared with the IRS and PBGC.[304] Form 5500 is due by the last day of the seventh month following the close of the plan year.[305] DOL and IRS rules allow the due date to be automatically extended by 2 months if a request for extension is filed.[306] Thus, in the case of a plan that uses the calendar year as the plan year, the extended due date for Form 5500 is October 15.

Under the Surface Transportation and Veterans Health Care Choice Improvement Act of 2015, in the case of returns for taxable years beginning after December 31, 2015, the Secretary of the Treasury is directed to modify appropriate regulations to provide that the maximum extension for the returns of employee benefit plans filing Form 5500 is an automatic 3 month period ending on November 15 for calendar-year plans.[307]

---

[299] Sec. 6058.

[300] Sec. 412. Most governmental plans (defined in section 414(d)) and church plans (defined in section 414(e)) are exempt from the minimum funding requirements.

[301] Sec. 6059.

[302] Treas. Reg. secs. 301.6058–1(a) and 301.6059–1. Form 5500 consists of a main form and various schedules, some of which require additional information to be included. The schedules that must be filed and the additional information that must be included with Form 5500 depend on the type and size of plan. A simplified annual reporting form, Annual Return/Report of Small Employee Benefit Plan, Form 5500–SF, is available to certain plans (covering fewer than 100 employees) that are subject to reporting requirements under ERISA and the Code. References herein to Form 5500 include Form 5500–SF.

[303] ERISA secs. 103, 104, and 4065. Most governmental plans and church plans are exempt from ERISA, including the ERISA reporting requirements. ERISA section 3004 requires that, when the IRS and DOL carry out provisions relating to the same subject matter, they must consult with each other and develop rules, regulations, practices and forms designed to reduce duplication of effort, duplication of reporting, and the burden of compliance by plan administrators and employers. Under ERISA section 4065, the PBGC is required to work with the IRS and DOL to combine the annual report to PBGC with reports required to be made to those agencies.

[304] Form 5500 filings are also publicly released in accordance with section 6104(b) and Treas. Reg. section 301.6104(b)–1 and ERISA sections 104(a)(1) and 106(a).

[305] Under ERISA section 104(a)(1), the annual report is due within 210 days after the close of the plan year or within such time as provided by regulations to reduce duplicative filings. DOL and IRS regulations provide for filing at the time required by the forms and instructions issued by the agencies. 29 C.F.R. sec. 2520.104a–5(a)(2) and Treas. Reg. secs. 301.6058–1(a)(4) and 301.6059–1(a).

[306] Treas. Reg. sec. 1.6081–11(a). Instructions for Form 5500 also provide for an automatic extension of time to file the Form 5500 until the due date of the Federal income tax return of the employer maintaining the plan if (1) the plan year and the employer's tax year are the same; (2) the employer has been granted an extension of time to file its federal income tax return to a date later than the normal due date for filing the Form 5500; and (3) a copy of the application for extension of time to file the Federal income tax return is maintained with the records of the Form 5500 filer. An extension granted by using this automatic extension procedure cannot be extended beyond a total of 9° months beyond the close of the plan year.

[307] Sec. 2006(b)(3) of Pub. L. No. 114–41 (July 31, 2015). See Part Seven, Title II, item F.

Explanation of Provision

The provision repeals the provision in the Surface Transportation and Veterans Health Care Choice Improvement Act of 2015 that provides for an automatic 3 month extension of the due date for filing Form 5500. Thus, the extended due date for Form 5500 is determined under DOL and IRS rules as in effect before enactment of the Surface Transportation and Veterans Health Care Choice Improvement Act of 2015.

Effective Date

The provision is effective for returns for taxable years beginning after December 31, 2015.

PART THIRTEEN: CONSOLIDATED APPROPRIATIONS ACT, 2016 (PUBLIC LAW 114–113)[308]

DIVISION P—TAX-RELATED PROVISIONS

A. High Cost Employer-Sponsored Health Coverage Excise Tax (secs. 101–103 of the Act and sec. 4980I of the Code)

Present Law

In general

Effective for years beginning after December 31, 2017, an excise tax is imposed on the provider of applicable employer-sponsored health coverage (the "coverage provider") if the aggregate cost of the coverage for an employee (including a former employee, surviving spouse, or any other primary insured individual) exceeds a threshold amount (referred to as "high cost health coverage").[309] The tax is 40 percent of the amount by which aggregate cost exceeds the threshold amount (the "excess benefit").

The annual threshold amount for 2018 is $10,200 for self-only coverage and $27,500 for other coverage (such as family coverage), multiplied by a one-time health cost adjustment percentage.[310] This threshold is then adjusted annually (including for 2018) by an age and gender adjusted excess premium amount.[311] The age and gender adjusted excess premium amount is the excess, if any, of (1) the premium cost of standard FEHBP coverage for the type of coverage provided to an individual if priced for the age and gender characteristics of all employees of the employer, over (2) the premium cost of standard FEHBP coverage if priced for the age and gender characteristics of the national workforce. For this purpose, standard FEHBP coverage means the per employee cost of Blue Cross/Blue Shield standard benefit coverage under the Federal Employees Health Benefit Program.

---

[308] H.R. 2029. The House passed H.R. 2029 on April 30, 2015. The Senate passed the bill with an amendment on November 10, 2015. The House agreed to amendments to the Senate amendment on December 17, and December 18, 2015, and the bill, as amended, passed the House on December 18, 2015. The Senate agreed to the House amendments on December 18, 2015. The President signed the bill on December 18, 2015.

[309] Sec. 4980I, which was added to the Code by section 9001 of PPACA and amended by section 10901 of PPACA and section 1401 of HCERA.

[310] The health cost adjustment percentage is 100 percent plus the excess, if any, of (1) the percentage by which the cost of standard FEHBP coverage for 2018 (determined according to specified criteria) exceeds the cost of standard FEHBP coverage for 2010, over (2) 55 percent.

[311] Under section 4980I, the 2018 threshold amounts are increased by $1,650 for self-only coverage or $3,450 for other coverage in the case of certain retirees and participants in a plan covering employees in a high-risk profession or repair or installation of electrical or telecommunications lines. For years after 2018, the threshold amounts (after application of the health cost adjustment percentage), and the increases for certain retirees and participants in a plan covering employees in a high-risk profession or repair or installation of electrical or telecommunications lines, are indexed to the Consumer Price Index for Urban Consumers ("CPI–U") (CPI–U increased by one percentage point for 2019 only), rounded to the nearest $50.

The excise tax is determined on a monthly basis, by reference to the aggregate cost of applicable employer-sponsored coverage for the month and 1/12 of the annual threshold amount. The excise tax is not deductible for income tax purposes.[312]

Applicable employer-sponsored coverage and determination of cost

Subject to certain exceptions, applicable employer-sponsored coverage is coverage under any group health plan offered to an employee by an employer that is excludible from the employee's gross income or that would be excludible if it were employer-sponsored coverage.[313] Thus, applicable employer-sponsored coverage includes coverage for which an employee pays on an after-tax basis. Applicable employer-sponsored coverage includes coverage under any group health plan established and maintained primarily for its civilian employees by the Federal government or any Federal agency or instrumentality, or the government of any State or political subdivision thereof or any agency or instrumentality of a State or political subdivision.

Applicable employer-sponsored coverage includes both insured and self-insured health coverage, including coverage in the form of reimbursements under a health flexible spending arrangement ("health FSA") or a health reimbursement arrangement and contributions to a health savings account ("HSA") or Archer medical savings account ("Archer MSA").[314] In the case of a self-employed individual, coverage is treated as applicable employer-sponsored coverage if the self-employed individual is allowed a deduction for all or any portion of the cost of coverage.[315]

For purposes of the excise tax, the cost of applicable employer-sponsored coverage is generally determined under rules similar to the rules for determining the applicable premium for purposes of COBRA continuation coverage,[316] except that any portion of the cost of coverage attributable to the excise tax is not taken into account. Cost is determined separately for self-only coverage and other coverage. Special valuation rules apply to certain retiree coverage, health FSAs, and contributions to HSAs and Archer MSAs.

Calculation of excess benefit and imposition of excise tax

In determining the excess benefit with respect to an employee (*i.e.,* the amount by which the cost of applicable employer-spon-

---

[312] Sec. 275(a)(6), referring to taxes imposed by chapter 43.

[313] Section 106 provides an exclusion for employer-provided coverage.

[314] Some types of coverage are not included in applicable employer-sponsored coverage, such as long-term care coverage, separate insurance coverage substantially all the benefits of which are for treatment of the mouth (including any organ or structure within the mouth) or of the eye, and certain excepted benefits. Excepted benefits for this purpose include (whether through insurance or otherwise) coverage only for accident, or disability income insurance, or any combination thereof; coverage issued as a supplement to liability insurance; liability insurance, including general liability insurance and automobile liability insurance; workers' compensation or similar insurance; automobile medical payment insurance; credit-only insurance; and other similar insurance coverage (as specified in regulations), under which benefits for medical care are secondary or incidental to other insurance benefits. Applicable employer-sponsored coverage does not include coverage only for a specified disease or illness or hospital indemnity or other fixed indemnity insurance if the cost of the coverage is not excludible from an employee's income or deductible by a self-employed individual.

[315] Section 162(l) allows a deduction to a self-employed individual for the cost of health insurance.

[316] Sec. 4980B(f)(4).

sored coverage for the employee exceeds the threshold amount), the aggregate cost of all applicable employer-sponsored coverage of the employee is taken into account. The threshold amount for self-only coverage generally applies to an employee. The threshold amount for other coverage applies to an employee only if the coverage provides minimum essential coverage to the employee and at least one other beneficiary and the benefits provided do not vary based on whether the covered individual is the employee or other beneficiary. For purposes of the threshold amount, any coverage provided under a multiemployer plan is treated as coverage other than self-only coverage.[317]

The excise tax is imposed on the coverage provider.[318] In the case of insured coverage (*i.e.*, coverage under a policy, certificate, or contract issued by an insurance company), the health insurance issuer is liable for the excise tax. In the case of self-insured coverage, the person that administers the plan benefits ("plan administrator") is generally liable for the excise tax. The person that administers the plan benefits includes the plan sponsor if the plan sponsor administers benefits under the plan. In the case of employer contributions to an HSA or an Archer MSA, the employer is liable for the excise tax.

The employer is generally responsible for calculating the amount of excess benefit allocable to each coverage provider and notifying each coverage provider (and the IRS) of the coverage provider's allocable share. In the case of applicable employer-sponsored coverage under a multiemployer plan, the plan sponsor is responsible for the calculation and notification.[319]

Explanation of Provision

Changes related to the excise tax

The Act includes two provisions that make changes with respect to this excise tax. One provision delays the effective date for the excise tax until years beginning after December 31, 2019, thereby delaying by two years (from 2018 to 2020) the year when the excise tax first becomes effective. However, the provision retains the 2018 threshold amount and provides the same adjustments to that amount for purposes of determining the threshold amounts for 2020 and subsequent years, and adjustments thereto. Thus, the threshold amounts that apply in 2020 and subsequent years include the same cost-of-living adjustments to the 2018 threshold amounts that apply under present law.

---

[317] As defined in section 414(f), a multiemployer plan is generally a plan to which more than one employer is required to contribute and that is maintained pursuant to one or more collective bargaining agreements between one or more employee organizations and more than one employer.

[318] The excise tax is allocated pro rata among the coverage providers, with each responsible for the excise tax on an amount equal to the total excess benefit multiplied by a fraction, the numerator of which is the cost of the applicable employer-sponsored coverage of that coverage provider and the denominator of which is the aggregate cost of all applicable employer-sponsored coverage of the employee.

[319] The employer or multiemployer plan sponsor may be liable for a penalty if the total excise tax due exceeds the tax on the excess benefit calculated and allocated among coverage providers by the employer or plan sponsor.

The other provision eliminates the denial of the deduction of the excise tax for income tax purposes.[320]

GAO study of suitable benchmarks for age and gender adjustment

The Act includes a provision that directs the Government Accountability Office to report to the Committee on Finance of the Senate and the Committee on Ways and Means of the House on (1) the suitability of the use of the premium cost of standard FEHBP coverage as a benchmark for the age and gender adjustment of the applicable dollar limit with respect to the excise tax and (2) recommendations regarding any more suitable benchmarks for the age and gender adjustment. The report is to be provided not later than 18 months after the date of enactment (December 18, 2015) and to be prepared in consultation with the National Association of Insurance Commissioners.

Effective Date

The provisions are effective on the date of enactment (December 18, 2015).

B. Annual Fee on Health Insurance Providers (sec. 201 of the Act and sec. 9010 of the Patient Protection and Affordable Care Act[321])

Present Law

An annual fee applies to any covered entity engaged in the business of providing health insurance with respect to United States ("U.S.") health risks.[322] The aggregate annual fee for all covered entities is the applicable amount. The applicable amount is $8 billion for calendar year 2014, $11.3 billion for calendar years 2015 and 2016, $13.9 billion for calendar year 2017, and $14.3 billion for calendar year 2018. For calendar years after 2018, the applicable amount is indexed to the rate of premium growth.

The aggregate annual fee is apportioned among the providers based on a ratio designed to reflect relative market share of U.S. health insurance business. For each covered entity, the fee for a calendar year is an amount that bears the same ratio to the applicable amount as (1) the covered entity's net premiums written during the preceding calendar year with respect to health insurance for any U.S. health risk, bears to (2) the aggregate net written premiums of all covered entities during such preceding calendar year with respect to such health insurance.

Explanation of Provision

The provision applies a one-year moratorium to the annual fee on health insurance providers for calendar year 2017.

---

[320] The Act provides that section 275(a)(6) that denies a deduction for taxes imposed by chapter 43 does not apply to this excise tax.
[321] "PPACA", Pub. L. No. 111–148, as amended.
[322] Sec. 9010 of PPACA.

Effective Date

The provision is effective upon date of enactment (December 18, 2015).

C. Miscellaneous Provisions

1. Extension and phaseout of credits with respect to facilities producing electricity from wind (secs. 301–302 of the Act and secs. 45 and 48 of the Code)[323]

Present Law

Renewable electricity production credit

An income tax credit is allowed for the production of electricity from qualified energy resources at qualified facilities (the "renewable electricity production credit").[324] Qualified energy resources comprise wind, closed-loop biomass, open-loop biomass, geothermal energy, municipal solid waste, qualified hydropower production, and marine and hydrokinetic renewable energy. Qualified facilities are, generally, facilities that generate electricity using qualified energy resources. To be eligible for the credit, electricity produced from qualified energy resources at qualified facilities must be sold by the taxpayer to an unrelated person.

SUMMARY OF CREDIT FOR ELECTRICITY PRODUCED FROM CERTAIN RENEWABLE RESOURCES

Eligible electricity production activity (sec. 45)	Credit amount for 2015[1] (cents per kilowatt-hour)	Expiration[2]
Wind	2.3	December 31, 2014
Closed-loop biomass	2.3	December 31, 2014
Open-loop biomass (including agricultural livestock waste nutrient facilities).	1.2	December 31, 2014
Geothermal	2.3	December 31, 2014
Municipal solid waste (including landfill gas facilities and trash combustion facilities).	1.2	December 31, 2014
Qualified hydropower	1.2	December 31, 2014
Marine and hydrokinetic	1.2	December 31, 2014

[1] In general, the credit is available for electricity produced during the first 10 years after a facility has been placed in service.
[2] Expires for property the construction of which begins after this date.

Election to claim energy credit in lieu of renewable electricity production credit

A taxpayer may make an irrevocable election to have certain property which is part of a qualified renewable electricity production facility be treated as energy property eligible for a 30 percent investment credit under section 48. For this purpose, qualified facilities are facilities otherwise eligible for the renewable electricity production credit with respect to which no credit under section 45 has been allowed. A taxpayer electing to treat a facility as energy property may not claim the renewable electricity production credit. The eligible basis for the investment credit for taxpayers making this election is the basis of the depreciable (or amortizable) prop-

---

[323] The Senate Committee on Finance reported S. 1946 ("Tax Relief Extension Act of 2015") on August 5, 2015 (S. Rep. No. 114–118). See sec. 157 of the bill as reported.
[324] Sec. 45. In addition to the renewable electricity production credit, section 45 also provides income tax credits for the production of Indian coal and refined coal at qualified facilities.

erty that is part of a facility capable of generating electricity eligible for the renewable electricity production credit.

Explanation of Provision

For qualified wind power facilities, the provision extends for two years the full renewable electricity production credit and the election to claim the energy credit in lieu of the electricity production credit, through December 31, 2016. For wind facilities the construction of which begins in 2017, the credits are extended at a rate equal to 80 percent of the otherwise available credit rate. For wind facilities the construction of which begins in 2018, the credits are extended at a rate equal to 60 percent of the otherwise available credit rate. For wind facilities the construction of which begins in 2019, the credits are extended at a rate equal to 40 percent of the otherwise available credit rate.

Effective Date

The provision takes effect January 1, 2015.

2. Modification of energy investment credit (sec. 303 of the Act and sec. 48 of the Code)

Present Law

In general

A nonrefundable, 10-percent business energy credit[325] is allowed for the cost of new property that is equipment that either (1) uses solar energy to generate electricity, to heat or cool a structure, or to provide solar process heat or (2) is used to produce, distribute, or use energy derived from a geothermal deposit, but only, in the case of electricity generated by geothermal power, up to the electric transmission stage. Property used to generate energy for the purposes of heating a swimming pool is not eligible solar energy property.

The energy credit is a component of the general business credit.[326] An unused general business credit generally may be carried back one year and carried forward 20 years.[327] The taxpayer's basis in the property is reduced by one-half of the amount of the credit claimed. For projects whose construction time is expected to equal or exceed two years, the credit may be claimed as progress expenditures are made on the project, rather than during the year the property is placed in service. The credit is allowed against the alternative minimum tax.

Special rules for solar energy property

For periods prior to January 1, 2017, the credit for otherwise eligible solar energy property is increased to 30 percent. In addition, equipment that uses fiber-optic distributed sunlight to illuminate the inside of a structure is solar energy property eligible for the 30-percent credit. For periods after December 31, 2016, the credit rate reverts to 10 percent and fiber optic property no longer qualifies.

---

[325] Sec. 48.
[326] Sec. 38(b)(1).
[327] Sec. 39.

Fuel cells and microturbines

The energy credit applies to qualified fuel cell power plants, but only for periods prior to January 1, 2017. The credit rate is 30 percent.

A qualified fuel cell power plant is an integrated system composed of a fuel cell stack assembly and associated balance of plant components that (1) converts a fuel into electricity using electrochemical means, and (2) has an electricity-only generation efficiency of greater than 30 percent and a capacity of at least one-half kilowatt. The credit may not exceed $1,500 for each 0.5 kilowatt of capacity.

The energy credit applies to qualifying stationary microturbine power plants for periods prior to January 1, 2017. The credit is limited to the lesser of 10 percent of the basis of the property or $200 for each kilowatt of capacity.

A qualified stationary microturbine power plant is an integrated system comprised of a gas turbine engine, a combustor, a recuperator or regenerator, a generator or alternator, and associated balance of plant components that converts a fuel into electricity and thermal energy. Such system also includes all secondary components located between the existing infrastructure for fuel delivery and the existing infrastructure for power distribution, including equipment and controls for meeting relevant power standards, such as voltage, frequency and power factors. Such system must have an electricity-only generation efficiency of not less than 26 percent at International Standard Organization conditions and a capacity of less than 2,000 kilowatts.

Geothermal heat pump property

The energy credit applies to qualified geothermal heat pump property placed in service prior to January 1, 2017. The credit rate is 10 percent. Qualified geothermal heat pump property is equipment that uses the ground or ground water as a thermal energy source to heat a structure or as a thermal energy sink to cool a structure.

Small wind property

The energy credit applies to qualified small wind energy property placed in service prior to January 1, 2017. The credit rate is 30 percent. Qualified small wind energy property is property that uses a qualified wind turbine to generate electricity. A qualifying wind turbine means a wind turbine of 100 kilowatts of rated capacity or less.

Combined heat and power property

The energy credit applies to combined heat and power ("CHP") property placed in service prior to January 1, 2017. The credit rate is 10 percent.

CHP property is property: (1) that uses the same energy source for the simultaneous or sequential generation of electrical power, mechanical shaft power, or both, in combination with the generation of steam or other forms of useful thermal energy (including heating and cooling applications); (2) that has an electrical capacity of not more than 50 megawatts or a mechanical energy capacity of not more than 67,000 horsepower or an equivalent combination of electrical and mechanical energy capacities; (3) that produces at least 20 percent of its total useful energy in the form of thermal energy that is not used to produce electrical or mechanical power, and produces at least 20 percent of its total useful energy in the form of electrical or mechanical power (or a combination thereof); and (4) the energy efficiency percentage of which exceeds 60 percent. CHP property does not include property used to transport the energy source to the generating facility or to distribute energy produced by the facility.

The otherwise allowable credit with respect to CHP property is reduced to the extent the property has an electrical capacity or mechanical capacity in excess of any applicable limits. Property in excess of the applicable limit (15 megawatts or a mechanical energy capacity of more than 20,000 horsepower or an equivalent combination of electrical and mechanical energy capacities) is permitted to claim a fraction of the otherwise allowable credit. The fraction is equal to the applicable limit divided by the capacity of the property. For example, a 45 megawatt property would be eligible to claim 15/45ths, or one third, of the otherwise allowable credit. Again, no credit is allowed if the property exceeds the 50 megawatt or 67,000 horsepower limitations described above.

Additionally, systems whose fuel source is at least 90 percent open-loop biomass and that would qualify for the credit but for the failure to meet the efficiency standard are eligible for a credit that is reduced in proportion to the degree to which the system fails to meet the efficiency standard. For example, a system that would otherwise be required to meet the 60-percent efficiency standard, but which only achieves 30-percent efficiency, would be permitted a credit equal to one-half of the otherwise allowable credit (i.e., a 5-percent credit).

Election of energy credit in lieu of section 45 production tax credit

A taxpayer may make an irrevocable election to have certain qualified facilities placed in service after 2008 and whose construction begins before January 1, 2015, be treated as energy property eligible for a 30-percent investment credit under section 48.[328] For this purpose, qualified facilities are facilities otherwise eligible for the renewable electricity production tax credit with respect to which no credit under section 45 has been allowed. A taxpayer electing to treat a facility as energy property may not claim the production credit under section 45.

Explanation of Provision

The provision extends and modifies the increased credit rate, but only with respect to property that uses solar energy to generate electricity, to heat or cool a structure, or to provide solar process heat. The credit rate is 30 percent for 2017, 2018 and 2019; 26 percent for 2020; and 22 percent for 2021. The credit rate is 10 percent for 2022 and thereafter, as provided for under present law. The

---

[328] See section 302 of the Act relating to an extension of the January 1, 2015, date in the case of wind facilities.

credit rate is determined by the year in which construction of the property commences, and applies at the time the property is placed in service. Property must be placed in service prior to December 31, 2023, to qualify for a credit rate in excess of 10 percent.

Effective Date

The provision is effective on the date of enactment (December 18, 2015).

3. Credit for residential energy efficient property (section 304 of the Act and 25D of the Code)

Present Law

In general

Present law (sec. 25D) provides a personal tax credit for the purchase of qualified solar electric property and qualified solar water heating property that is used exclusively for purposes other than heating swimming pools and hot tubs. The credit is equal to 30 percent of qualifying expenditures.

Section 25D also provides a 30 percent credit for the purchase of qualified geothermal heat pump property, qualified small wind energy property, and qualified fuel cell power plants. The credit for any fuel cell may not exceed $500 for each 0.5 kilowatt of capacity.

The credit is nonrefundable. The credit with respect to all qualifying property may be claimed against the alternative minimum tax.

The credit applies to property placed in service prior to January 1, 2017.

Qualified property

Qualified solar electric property is property that uses solar energy to generate electricity for use in a dwelling unit. Qualifying solar water heating property is property used to heat water for use in a dwelling unit located in the United States and used as a residence if at least half of the energy used by such property for such purpose is derived from the sun.

A qualified fuel cell power plant is an integrated system comprised of a fuel cell stack assembly and associated balance of plant components that (1) converts a fuel into electricity using electrochemical means, (2) has an electricity-only generation efficiency of greater than 30 percent, and (3) has a nameplate capacity of at least 0.5 kilowatt. The qualified fuel cell power plant must be installed on or in connection with a dwelling unit located in the United States and used by the taxpayer as a principal residence.

Qualified small wind energy property is property that uses a wind turbine to generate electricity for use in a dwelling unit located in the U.S. and used as a residence by the taxpayer.

Qualified geothermal heat pump property means any equipment which (1) uses the ground or ground water as a thermal energy source to heat the dwelling unit or as a thermal energy sink to cool such dwelling unit, (2) meets the requirements of the Energy Star program which are in effect at the time that the expenditure for such equipment is made, and (3) is installed on or in connection with a dwelling unit located in the United States and used as a residence by the taxpayer.

Additional rules

The depreciable basis of the property is reduced by the amount of the credit. Expenditures for labor costs allocable to onsite preparation, assembly, or original installation of property eligible for the credit are eligible expenditures.

Special proration rules apply in the case of jointly owned property, condominiums, and tenant-stockholders in cooperative housing corporations. If less than 80 percent of the property is used for nonbusiness purposes, only that portion of expenditures that is used for nonbusiness purposes is taken into account.

Explanation of Provision

The provision extends the credit for five years, through December 31, 2021, but only with respect to qualified solar electric property and qualified solar water heating property. The provision modifies the credit rate, reducing it to 26 percent for property placed in service in 2020 and 22 percent for property placed in service in 2021.

Effective Date

The provision is effective on January 1, 2017.

4. Treatment of transportation costs of independent refiners (sec. 305 of the Act and sec. 199 of the Code)

Present Law

In general

Present law provides a deduction from taxable income (or, in the case of an individual, adjusted gross income [329]) that is equal to nine percent of the lesser of the taxpayer's qualified production activities income or taxable income (determined without regard to the section 199 deduction) for the taxable year.[330] For taxpayers subject to the 35-percent corporate income tax rate, the nine-percent deduction effectively reduces the corporate income tax rate to just under 32 percent on qualified production activities income.[331]

In general, qualified production activities income is equal to domestic production gross receipts reduced by the sum of: (1) the costs of goods sold that are allocable to those receipts; and (2) other expenses, losses, or deductions which are properly allocable to those receipts.[332]

Domestic production gross receipts generally are gross receipts of a taxpayer that are derived from: (1) any sale, exchange, or other

---

[329] For this purpose, adjusted gross income is determined after application of sections 86, 135, 137, 219, 221, 222, and 469, without regard to the section 199 deduction. Sec. 199(d)(2).

[330] Sec. 199.

[331] This example assumes the deduction does not exceed the wage limitation discussed below.

[332] Sec. 199(c)(1). In computing qualified production activities income, the domestic production activities deduction itself is not an allocable deduction. Sec. 199(c)(1)(B)(ii). See Treas. Reg. secs. 1.199–1 through 1.199–9 where the Secretary has prescribed rules for the proper allocation of items of income, deduction, expense, and loss for purposes of determining qualified production activities income.

disposition, or any lease, rental, or license, of qualifying production property [333] that was manufactured, produced, grown or extracted by the taxpayer in whole or in significant part within the United States; [334] (2) any sale, exchange, or other disposition, or any lease, rental, or license, of qualified film [335] produced by the taxpayer; (3) any lease, rental, license, sale, exchange, or other disposition of electricity, natural gas, or potable water produced by the taxpayer in the United States; (4) construction of real property performed in the United States by a taxpayer in the ordinary course of a construction trade or business; or (5) engineering or architectural services performed in the United States for the construction of real property located in the United States.[336]

The amount of the deduction for a taxable year is limited to 50 percent of the W-2 wages paid by the taxpayer, and properly allocable to domestic production gross receipts, during the calendar year that ends in such taxable year.[337]

Limitation for oil related qualified production activities income

With respect to a taxpayer that has oil related qualified production activities income, the nine percent deduction is reduced by three percent of the least of the taxpayer's oil related qualified production activities income, qualified production activities income, or taxable income (determined without regard to the section 199 deduction).[338] The term "oil related qualified production activities income" means the qualified production activities income attributable to the production, refining, processing, transportation, or distribu-

---

[333] Qualifying production property generally includes any tangible personal property, computer software, and sound recordings. Sec. 199(c)(5).

[334] When used in the Code in a geographical sense, the term "United States" generally includes only the States and the District of Columbia. Sec. 7701(a)(9). A special rule for determining domestic production gross receipts, however, provides that for taxable years beginning after December 31, 2005, and before January 1, 2017, in the case of any taxpayer with gross receipts from sources within the Commonwealth of Puerto Rico, the term "United States" includes the Commonwealth of Puerto Rico, but only if all of the taxpayer's Puerto Rico-sourced gross receipts are taxable under the Federal income tax for individuals or corporations for such taxable year. Secs. 199(d)(8)(A) and (C), as extended by section 170 of the Act. In computing the 50-percent wage limitation, the taxpayer is permitted to take into account wages paid to bona fide residents of Puerto Rico for services performed in Puerto Rico. Sec. 199(d)(8)(B).

[335] Qualified film includes any motion picture film or videotape (including live or delayed television programming, but not including certain sexually explicit productions) if 50 percent or more of the total compensation relating to the production of the film (including compensation in the form of residuals and participations) constitutes compensation for services performed in the United States by actors, production personnel, directors, and producers. Sec. 199(c)(6).

[336] Sec. 199(c)(4).

[337] For purposes of the provision, "W-2 wages" include the sum of the amounts of wages as defined in section 3401(a) and elective deferrals that the taxpayer properly reports to the Social Security Administration with respect to the employment of employees of the taxpayer during the calendar year ending during the taxpayer's taxable year. Elective deferrals include elective deferrals as defined in section 402(g)(3), amounts deferred under section 457, and, for taxable years beginning after December 31, 2005, designated Roth contributions (as defined in section 402A). See sec. 199(b)(2). The wage limitation for qualified films includes any compensation for services performed in the United States by actors, production personnel, directors, and producers and is not restricted to W-2 wages. Sec. 199(b)(2)(D), effective for taxable years beginning after December 31, 2007.

[338] Sec. 199(d)(9). For example, assume a C corporation (the "taxpayer") has qualified production activities income of $750,000—of which $650,000 is oil related qualified production activities income—taxable income of $2,000,000, and has paid sufficient domestic production wages to not be subject to the wages paid limitation for the taxable year. The taxpayer's tentative section 199 deduction of $67,500 ($750,000 * 9 percent) is reduced by $19,500 ($650,000 * 3 percent), resulting in a section 199 deduction of $48,000 for the taxable year ($67,500 – $19,500).

tion of oil, gas, or any primary product thereof (as defined in section 927(a)(2)(C) prior to its repeal).[339]

Explanation of Provision

For taxpayers in the trade or business of refining crude oil and who are not major integrated oil companies (within the meaning of section 167(h)(5)(B), determined without regard to clause (iii) thereof), the provision provides that in computing oil related qualified production activities income, only 25 percent of the properly allocable costs related to the transportation of oil are allocated to domestic production gross receipts. This has the effect of increasing oil related qualified production activities income for independent refiners with transportation costs that are properly allocable to domestic production gross receipts.[340]

Effective Date

The provision applies to taxable years beginning after December 31, 2015, and before January 1, 2022.

DIVISION Q—PROTECTING AMERICANS FROM TAX HIKES ACT OF 2015

TITLE I—EXTENDERS [341]

A. Permanent Extensions

Part 1—Tax Relief for Families and Individuals

1. Reduced earnings threshold for additional child tax credit made permanent (sec. 101 of the Act and sec. 24 of the Code)

An individual may claim a tax credit of $1,000 for each qualifying child under the age of 17. A child who is not a citizen, national, or resident of the United States cannot be a qualifying child.

---

[339] See also Prop. Treas. Reg. sec. 1.199–1(f) (REG–136459–09) where the Secretary has proposed guidance on oil related qualified production activities income. Prop. Treas. Reg. sec. 1.199–1(f) will apply to taxable years beginning on or after the date the final regulations are published in the Federal Register.

[340] Continuing the above example, assume the taxpayer has properly allocable oil related transportation costs of $100,000 that were included in determining the qualified production activities income noted above. Under this provision, the taxpayer will only allocate $25,000 of such costs to domestic production gross receipts. Thus, the taxpayer's oil related qualified production activities income of $650,000 and qualified production activities income of $750,000 will each increase by $75,000 ($100,000 – $25,000), resulting in oil related qualified production activities income of $725,000 and qualified production activities income of $825,000. Hence, the taxpayer's tentative section 199 deduction of $74,250 ($825,000 * 9 percent) is reduced by $21,750 ($725,000 * 3 percent), resulting in a section 199 deduction of $52,500 for the taxable year ($74,250 – $21,750) (compared to $48,000 under present law).

[341] The Senate Committee on Finance reported S. 1946 ("Tax Relief Extension Act of 2015") on August 5, 2015 (S. Rep. No. 114–118). The bill generally extended expiring provisions through 2016 with some modifications. The House Committee on Ways and Means reported the following bills relating to the modification and making permanent or extending certain expiring provisions: H.R. 629 ("Permanent S Corporation Built-in Gain Recognition Period Act of 2015") on February 9, 2015 (H.R. Rep. No. 114–15), H.R. 630 ("Permanent S Corporation Charitable Contribution Act of 2015") on February 9, 2015 (H.R. Rep. No. 114–16), H.R. 641 ("Conservation Easement Incentive Act of 2015") on February 9, 2015 (H.R. Rep. No. 114–17), H.R. 644 ("America Gives More Act of 2015") on February 9, 2015 (H.R. Rep. No. 114–18), H.R. 637 ("Permanent IRA Charitable Contribution Act of 2015") on February 9, 2015 (H.R. Rep. No. 114–20), H.R. 636 ("America's Small Business Tax Relief Act of 2015") on February 9, 2015 (H.R. Rep. No.114–21), H.R. 622 ("State and Local Sales Tax Deduction Fairness Act of 2015") on April 6, 2015 (H.R. Rep. No. 114–51), H.R. 880 ("American Research and Competitiveness Act of 2015") on

The aggregate amount of child credits that may be claimed is phased out for individuals with income over certain threshold amounts. Specifically, the otherwise allowable aggregate child tax credit amount is reduced by $50 for each $1,000 (or fraction thereof) of modified adjusted gross income ("modified AGI") over $75,000 for single individuals or heads of households, $110,000 for married individuals filing joint returns, and $55,000 for married individuals filing separate returns. For purposes of this limitation, modified AGI includes certain otherwise excludable income earned by U.S. citizens or residents living abroad or in certain U.S. territories.

The credit is allowable against both the regular tax and the alternative minimum tax ("AMT"). To the extent the child tax credit exceeds the taxpayer's tax liability, the taxpayer is eligible for a refundable credit (the additional child tax credit) equal to 15 percent of earned income in excess of a threshold dollar amount (the "earned income" formula). This threshold dollar amount is $10,000 indexed for inflation from 2001. The American Recovery and Reinvestment Act, as subsequently extended by the Tax Relief, Unemployment Insurance Reauthorization, and Job Creation Act of 2010 [342] and the American Taxpayer Relief Act of 2012,[343] set the threshold at $3,000 for taxable years 2009 to 2017.

Families with three or more qualifying children may determine the additional child tax credit using the "alternative formula" if this results in a larger credit than determined under the earned income formula. Under the alternative formula, the additional child tax credit equals the amount by which the taxpayer's social security taxes exceed the taxpayer's earned income tax credit ("EITC").

Earned income is defined as the sum of wages, salaries, tips, and other taxable employee compensation plus net self-employment earnings. Unlike the EITC, which also includes the preceding items in its definition of earned income, the additional child tax credit is based only on earned income to the extent it is included in computing taxable income. For example, some ministers' parsonage allowances are considered self-employment income, and thus are considered earned income for purposes of computing the EITC, but the allowances are excluded from gross income for individual income tax purposes, and thus are not considered earned income for purposes of the additional child tax credit since the income is not included in taxable income.

Explanation of Provision

The provision makes permanent the earned income threshold of $3,000.

May 14, 2015 (H.R. Rep. 114–113), H.R. 765 ("Restaurant and Retail Jobs and Growth Act of 2015") on October 23, 2015 (H.R. Rep No. 114–306), H.R. 961 ("Permanent Active Financing Exception Act of 2015") on October 23, 2015 (H.R. Rep. No. 114–307), H.R. 1430 ("Permanent CFC Look-Through Act of 2015") on October 23, 2015 (H.R. Rep. No. 114–309), H.R. 2940 ("Educator Tax Relief Act of 2015") on October 23, 2015 (H.R. Rep. No. 114–310), and H.R 2510 (relating to bonus depreciation) on October 28, 2015 (H.R. Rep. No. 114–317, Part 1). Each of the bills reported by the House Committee on Ways and Means prior to October passed the House, either separately or in a bill combining certain of the provisions.

[342] Pub. L. No. 111–312.
[343] Pub. L. No. 112–240.

Effective Date

The provision applies to taxable years beginning after the date of enactment (December 18, 2015).

2. American opportunity tax credit made permanent (sec. 102 of the Act and sec. 25A of the Code)

Present Law

Hope credit and American opportunity tax credit

Hope credit

For taxable years beginning before 2009 and after 2017, individual taxpayers are allowed to claim a nonrefundable credit, the Hope credit, against Federal income taxes of up to $1,950 (estimated 2015 level) per eligible student per year for qualified tuition and related expenses paid for the first two years of the student's post-secondary education in a degree or certificate program.[344] The Hope credit rate is 100 percent on the first $1,300 of qualified tuition and related expenses, and 50 percent on the next $1,300 of qualified tuition and related expenses (estimated for 2015). These dollar amounts are indexed for inflation, with the amount rounded down to the next lowest multiple of $100. Thus, for example, a taxpayer who incurs $1,300 of qualified tuition and related expenses for an eligible student is eligible (subject to the AGI phaseout described below) for a $1,300 Hope credit. If a taxpayer incurs $2,600 of qualified tuition and related expenses for an eligible student, then he or she is eligible for a $1,950 Hope credit.

The Hope credit that a taxpayer may otherwise claim is phased out ratably for taxpayers with modified AGI between $55,000 and $65,000 ($110,000 and $130,000 for married taxpayers filing a joint return), as estimated by the JCT staff for 2015. The beginning points of the AGI phaseout ranges are indexed for inflation, with the amount rounded down to the next lowest multiple of $1,000. The size of the phaseout ranges for single and married taxpayers are always $10,000 and $20,000 respectively.

The qualified tuition and related expenses must be incurred on behalf of the taxpayer, the taxpayer's spouse, or a dependent of the taxpayer. The Hope credit is available with respect to an individual student for two taxable years, provided that the student has not completed the first two years of post-secondary education before the beginning of the second taxable year.

The Hope credit is available in the taxable year the expenses are paid, subject to the requirement that the education is furnished to the student during that year or during an academic period beginning during the first three months of the next taxable year. Qualified tuition and related expenses paid with the proceeds of a loan generally are eligible for the Hope credit. The repayment of a loan itself is not a qualified tuition or related expense.

---

[344] Sec. 25A. For taxable years 2009–2017, the American Opportunity tax credit applies (discussed *infra*). Both the Hope credit and the American Opportunity tax credit (in the case of taxable years from 2009–2017) may be claimed against a taxpayer's alternative minimum tax liability.

A taxpayer may claim the Hope credit with respect to an eligible student who is not the taxpayer or the taxpayer's spouse (e.g., in cases in which the student is the taxpayer's child) only if the taxpayer claims the student as a dependent for the taxable year for which the credit is claimed. If a student is claimed as a dependent, the student is not entitled to claim a Hope credit for that taxable year on the student's own tax return. If a parent (or other taxpayer) claims a student as a dependent, any qualified tuition and related expenses paid by the student are treated as paid by the parent (or other taxpayer) for purposes of determining the amount of qualified tuition and related expenses paid by such parent (or other taxpayer) under the provision. In addition, for each taxable year, a taxpayer may claim only one of the Hope credit, the Lifetime Learning credit, or an above-the-line deduction for qualified tuition and related expenses with respect to an eligible student.

The Hope credit is available for qualified tuition and related expenses, which include tuition and fees (excluding nonacademic fees) required to be paid to an eligible educational institution as a condition of enrollment or attendance of an eligible student at the institution. Charges and fees associated with meals, lodging, insurance, transportation, and similar personal, living, or family expenses are not eligible for the credit. The expenses of education involving sports, games, or hobbies are not qualified tuition and related expenses unless this education is part of the student's degree program.

Qualified tuition and related expenses generally include only out-of-pocket expenses. Qualified tuition and related expenses do not include expenses covered by employer-provided educational assistance and scholarships that are not required to be included in the gross income of either the student or the taxpayer claiming the credit. Thus, total qualified tuition and related expenses are reduced by any scholarship or fellowship grants excludable from gross income under section 117 and any other tax-free educational benefits received by the student (or the taxpayer claiming the credit) during the taxable year. The Hope credit is not allowed with respect to any education expense for which a deduction is claimed under section 162 or any other section of the Code.

An eligible student for purposes of the Hope credit is an individual who is enrolled in a degree, certificate, or other program (including a program of study abroad approved for credit by the institution at which such student is enrolled) leading to a recognized educational credential at an eligible educational institution. The student must pursue a course of study on at least a half-time basis. A student is considered to pursue a course of study on at least a half-time basis if the student carries at least one-half the normal full-time work load for the course of study the student is pursuing for at least one academic period that begins during the taxable year. To be eligible for the Hope credit, a student must not have been convicted of a Federal or State felony for the possession or distribution of a controlled substance.

Eligible educational institutions generally are accredited postsecondary educational institutions offering credit toward a bachelor's degree, an associate's degree, or another recognized post-secondary credential. Certain proprietary institutions and post-secondary vocational institutions also are eligible educational institutions. To qualify as an eligible educational institution, an institution must be eligible to participate in Department of Education student aid programs.

American Opportunity tax credit ("AOTC")

The AOTC refers to modifications to the Hope credit that apply for taxable years beginning in 2009 through 2017. The maximum allowable modified credit is $2,500 per eligible student per year for qualified tuition and related expenses paid for each of the first four years of the student's post-secondary education in a degree or certificate program. The modified credit rate is 100 percent on the first $2,000 of qualified tuition and related expenses, and 25 percent on the next $2,000 of qualified tuition and related expenses. For purposes of the modified credit, the definition of qualified tuition and related expenses is expanded to include course materials.

The modified credit is available with respect to an individual student for four years, provided that the student has not completed the first four years of post-secondary education before the beginning of the fourth taxable year. Thus, the modified credit, in addition to other modifications, extends the application of the Hope credit to two more years of post-secondary education.

The modified credit that a taxpayer may otherwise claim is phased out ratably for taxpayers with modified AGI between $80,000 and $90,000 ($160,000 and $180,000 for married taxpayers filing a joint return). The modified credit may be claimed against a taxpayer's AMT liability.

Forty percent of a taxpayer's otherwise allowable modified credit is refundable. However, no portion of the modified credit is refundable if the taxpayer claiming the credit is a child to whom section 1(g) applies for such taxable year (generally, any child who has at least one living parent, does not file a joint return, and is either under age 18 or under age 24 and a student providing less than one-half of his or her own support).

Explanation of Provision

The provision makes the modifications to the Hope credit, known as the AOTC, permanent.

Effective Date

The provision is effective for taxable years beginning after the date of enactment (December 18, 2015).

3. Modification of the earned income tax credit made permanent (sec. 103 of the Act and sec. 32 of the Code)

Present Law

Overview

Low- and moderate-income workers may be eligible for the refundable earned income tax credit ("EITC"). Eligibility for the EITC is based on earned income, adjusted gross income ("AGI"), investment income, filing status, number of children, and immigration and work status in the United States. The amount of the EITC is based on the presence and number of qualifying children in the worker's family, as well as on adjusted gross income and earned income.

The EITC generally equals a specified percentage of earned income up to a maximum dollar amount. The maximum amount applies over a certain income range and then diminishes to zero over a specified phaseout range. For taxpayers with earned income (or AGI, if greater) in excess of the beginning of the phaseout range, the maximum EITC amount is reduced by the phaseout rate multiplied by the amount of earned income (or AGI, if greater) in excess of the beginning of the phaseout range. For taxpayers with earned income (or AGI, if greater) in excess of the end of the phaseout range, no credit is allowed.

An individual is not eligible for the EITC if the aggregate amount of disqualified income of the taxpayer for the taxable year exceeds $3,400 (for 2015). This threshold is indexed for inflation. Disqualified income is the sum of: (1) interest (both taxable and tax exempt); (2) dividends; (3) net rent and royalty income (if greater than zero); (4) capital gains net income; and (5) net passive income that is not self-employment income (if greater than zero).

The EITC is a refundable credit, meaning that if the amount of the credit exceeds the taxpayer's Federal income tax liability, the excess is payable to the taxpayer as a direct transfer payment.

Filing status

An unmarried individual may claim the EITC if he or she files as a single filer or as a head of household. Married individuals generally may not claim the EITC unless they file jointly. An exception to the joint return filing requirement applies to certain spouses who are separated. Under this exception, a married taxpayer who is separated from his or her spouse for the last six months of the taxable year is not considered to be married (and, accordingly, may file a return as head of household and claim the EITC), provided that the taxpayer maintains a household that constitutes the principal place of abode for a dependent child (including a son, stepson, daughter, stepdaughter, adopted child, or a foster child) for over half the taxable year, and pays over half the cost of maintaining the household in which he or she resides with the child during the year.

Presence of qualifying children and amount of the earned income credit

Four separate credit schedules apply: one schedule for taxpayers with no qualifying children, one schedule for taxpayers with one qualifying child, one schedule for taxpayers with two qualifying children, and one schedule for taxpayers with three or more qualifying children.[345]

Taxpayers with no qualifying children may claim a credit if they are over age 24 and below age 65. The credit is 7.65 percent of earnings up to $6,580, resulting in a maximum credit of $503 for 2015. The maximum is available for those with incomes between $6,580 and $8,240 ($13,750 if married filing jointly). The credit be-

---

[345] All income thresholds are indexed for inflation annually.

gins to phase out at a rate of 7.65 percent of earnings above $8,240 ($13,750 if married filing jointly) resulting in a $0 credit at $14,820 of earnings ($20,330 if married filing jointly).

Taxpayers with one qualifying child may claim a credit in 2015 of 34 percent of their earnings up to $9,880, resulting in a maximum credit of $3,359. The maximum credit is available for those with earnings between $9,880 and $18,110 ($23,630 if married filing jointly). The credit begins to phase out at a rate of 15.98 percent of earnings above $18,110 ($23,630 if married filing jointly). The credit is completely phased out at $39,131 of earnings ($44,651 if married filing jointly).

Taxpayers with two qualifying children may claim a credit in 2015 of 40 percent of earnings up to $13,870, resulting in a maximum credit of $5,548. The maximum credit is available for those with earnings between $13,870 and $18,110 ($23,630 if married filing jointly). The credit begins to phase out at a rate of 21.06 percent of earnings $18,110 ($23,630 if married filing jointly). The credit is completely phased out at $44,454 of earnings ($49,974 if married filing jointly).

A temporary provision most recently extended in the American Taxpayer Relief Act of 2012 ("ATRA")[346] allows taxpayers with three or more qualifying children to claim a credit of 45 percent for taxable years through 2017. For example, in 2015 taxpayers with three or more qualifying children may claim a credit of 45 percent of earnings up to $13,870, resulting in a maximum credit of $6,242. The maximum credit is available for those with earnings between $13,870 and $18,110 ($23,630 if married filing jointly). The credit begins to phase out at a rate of 21.06 percent of earnings above $18,110 ($23,630 if married filing jointly). The credit is completely phased out at $47,747 of earnings ($53,267 if married filing jointly).

Under an additional provision most recently extended in ATRA, the phase-out thresholds for married couples were raised to an amount $5,000 (indexed for inflation from 2009) above that for other filers. The increase is $5,520 for 2015. This increase is reflected in the description of the credit, above.

If more than one taxpayer lives with a qualifying child, only one of these taxpayers may claim the child for purposes of the EITC. If multiple eligible taxpayers actually claim the same qualifying child, then a tiebreaker rule determines which taxpayer is entitled to the EITC with respect to the qualifying child. Any eligible taxpayer with at least one qualifying child who does not claim the EITC with respect to qualifying children due to failure to meet certain identification requirements with respect to such children (i.e., providing the name, age and taxpayer identification number of each of such children) may not claim the EITC for taxpayers without qualifying children.

Explanation of Provision

The provision makes permanent the EITC rate of 45 percent for taxpayers with three or more qualifying children.

---

[346] Pub. L. No. 112–240.

The provision makes permanent the higher phase-out thresholds for married couples filing joint returns.

Effective Date

The provision applies to taxable years beginning after December 31, 2015.

4. Extension and modification of deduction for certain expenses of elementary and secondary school teachers (sec. 104 of the Act and sec. 62(a)(2)(D) of the Code)

Present Law

In general, ordinary and necessary business expenses are deductible. However, unreimbursed employee business expenses generally are deductible only as an itemized deduction and only to the extent that the individual's total miscellaneous deductions (including employee business expenses) exceed two percent of adjusted gross income. An individual's otherwise allowable itemized deductions may be further limited by the overall limitation on itemized deductions, which reduces itemized deductions for taxpayers with adjusted gross income in excess of a threshold amount. In addition, miscellaneous itemized deductions are not allowable under the alternative minimum tax.

Certain expenses of eligible educators are allowed as an above-the-line deduction. Specifically, for taxable years beginning prior to January 1, 2015, an above-the-line deduction is allowed for up to $250 annually of expenses paid or incurred by an eligible educator for books, supplies (other than nonathletic supplies for courses of instruction in health or physical education), computer equipment (including related software and services) and other equipment, and supplementary materials used by the eligible educator in the classroom.[347] To be eligible for this deduction, the expenses must be otherwise deductible under section 162 as a trade or business expense. A deduction is allowed only to the extent the amount of expenses exceeds the amount excludable from income under section 135 (relating to education savings bonds), 529(c)(1) (relating to qualified tuition programs), and section 530(d)(2) (relating to Coverdell education savings accounts).

An eligible educator is a kindergarten through grade twelve teacher, instructor, counselor, principal, or aide in a school for at least 900 hours during a school year. A school means any school that provides elementary education or secondary education (kindergarten through grade 12), as determined under State law.

The above-the-line deduction for eligible educators is not allowed for taxable years beginning after December 31, 2014.

Explanation of Provision

The provision makes permanent the deduction for eligible educator expenses.

The provision indexes the $250 maximum deduction amount for inflation, and provides that expenses for professional development

---

[347] Sec. 62(a)(2)(D).

shall also be considered eligible expenses for purposes of the deduction.

Effective Date

The provision making above-the-line deduction permanent applies to taxable years beginning after December 31, 2014.

The provisions pertaining to indexing the $250 maximum deduction amount and qualifying professional development expenses apply to taxable years beginning after December 31, 2015.

5. Extension of parity for exclusion from income for employer-provided mass transit and parking benefits (sec. 105 of the Act and 132(f) of the Code)

Present Law

Qualified transportation fringes

Qualified transportation fringe benefits provided by an employer are excluded from an employee's gross income for income tax purposes and from an employee's wages for employment tax purposes.[348] Qualified transportation fringe benefits include qualified parking, transit passes, vanpool benefits, and qualified bicycle commuting reimbursements.

No amount is includible in the income of an employee merely because the employer offers the employee a choice between cash and qualified transportation fringe benefits (other than a qualified bicycle commuting reimbursement).

Qualified transportation fringe benefits also include a cash reimbursement (under a bona fide reimbursement arrangement) by an employer to an employee for parking, transit passes, or vanpooling. In the case of transit passes, however, in general, a cash reimbursement is considered a qualified transportation fringe benefit only if a voucher or similar item that can be exchanged only for a transit pass is not readily available for direct distribution by the employer to the employee.

Mass transit parity

Before February 17, 2009, the amount that could be excluded as qualified transportation fringe benefits was subject to a monthly limit of $175 for qualified parking benefits and $100 for combined transit pass and vanpool benefits, with each monthly limit adjusted annually for inflation, rounded down to the next lowest multiple of $5.00.[349] Effective for months beginning on or after February 17, 2009, and before January 1, 2015, parity in qualified transportation fringe benefits was provided by temporarily increasing the monthly exclusion for combined employer-provided transit pass and vanpool benefits to the same level as the monthly exclusion for employer-provided parking.[350]

---

[348] Secs. 132(a)(5) and (f), 3121(a)(20), 3231(e)(5), 3306(b)(16) and 3401(a)(19).

[349] The base year used for each adjustment reflects the year for which the particular monthly limit became effective. Specifically, a base year of 1998 is used for qualified parking benefits and a base year of 2001 for combined transit pass and vanpool benefits.

[350] Parity was provided originally by the American Recovery and Reinvestment Act of 2009 ("ARRA"), Pub. L. No. 111–5, effective for months beginning on or after February 17, 2009, the date of enactment of ARRA.

As of January 1, 2015, a lower monthly limit again applies to the exclusion for combined transit pass and vanpool benefits. Specifically, for 2015, the amount that can be excluded as qualified transportation fringe benefits is limited to $130 per month in combined transit pass and vanpool benefits and $250 per month in qualified parking benefits. For 2016, the monthly exclusion limit for combined transit pass and vanpool benefits remains at $130; the monthly exclusion limit for qualified parking benefits increases to $255.

Explanation of Provision

The provision reinstates parity in the exclusion for employer-provided parking benefits and for combined employer-provided transit pass and vanpool benefits (by increasing the monthly exclusion amount for combined transit pass and vanpool benefits to $175 before adjustment for inflation[351]) and makes parity permanent. Thus, for 2015, the monthly limit on the exclusion for combined transit pass and vanpool benefits is $250, the same as the monthly limit on the exclusion for qualified parking benefits. Similarly, for 2016 and later years, the same monthly limit will apply to the exclusion for combined transit pass and vanpool benefits and the exclusion for qualified parking benefits.

In order for the extension to be effective retroactive to January 1, 2015, expenses incurred for months beginning after December 31, 2014, and before the date of enactment of the provision (December 18, 2015), by an employee for employer-provided vanpool and transit benefits may be reimbursed (under a bona fide reimbursement arrangement) by employers on a tax-free basis to the extent they exceed $130 per month and are no more than $250 per month. It is intended that the rule that an employer reimbursement is excludible only if vouchers are not available to provide the benefit continues to apply, except in the case of reimbursements for vanpool or transit benefits between $130 and $250 for months beginning after December 31, 2014, and before enactment of the provision. Further, it is intended that reimbursements of the additional amount for expenses incurred for months beginning after December 31, 2014, and before enactment of the provision, may be made in addition to the provision of benefits or reimbursements of up to the applicable monthly limit for expenses incurred for months beginning after enactment of the provision.

Effective Date

The provision applies to months after December 31, 2014.

6. Deduction for State and local sales taxes (sec. 106 of the Act and sec. 164 of the Code)

Present Law

For purposes of determining regular tax liability, an itemized deduction is permitted for certain State and local taxes paid, includ-

---

[351] The provision failed to include a conforming change to repeal the base year applicable in adjusting the monthly amount for combined transit pass and vanpool benefits. A technical correction is needed to make this change.

ing individual income taxes, real property taxes, and personal property taxes. The itemized deduction is not permitted for purposes of determining a taxpayer's alternative minimum taxable income. For taxable years beginning before January 1, 2015, at the election of the taxpayer, an itemized deduction may be taken for State and local general sales taxes in lieu of the itemized deduction provided under present law for State and local income taxes. As is the case for State and local income taxes, the itemized deduction for State and local general sales taxes is not permitted for purposes of determining a taxpayer's alternative minimum taxable income. Taxpayers have two options with respect to the determination of the sales tax deduction amount. Taxpayers may deduct the total amount of general State and local sales taxes paid by accumulating receipts showing general sales taxes paid. Alternatively, taxpayers may use tables created by the Secretary that show the allowable deduction. The tables are based on average consumption by taxpayers on a State-by-State basis taking into account number of dependents, modified adjusted gross income and rates of State and local general sales taxation. Taxpayers who live in more than one jurisdiction during the tax year are required to pro-rate the table amounts based on the time they live in each jurisdiction. Taxpayers who use the tables created by the Secretary may, in addition to the table amounts, deduct eligible general sales taxes paid with respect to the purchase of motor vehicles, boats, and other items specified by the Secretary. Sales taxes for items that may be added to the tables are not reflected in the tables themselves.

A general sales tax is a tax imposed at one rate with respect to the sale at retail of a broad range of classes of items.[352] No deduction is allowed for any general sales tax imposed with respect to an item at a rate other than the general rate of tax. However, in the case of food, clothing, medical supplies, and motor vehicles, the above rules are relaxed in two ways. First, if the tax does not apply with respect to some or all of such items, a tax that applies to other such items can still be considered a general sales tax. Second, the rate of tax applicable with respect to some or all of these items may be lower than the general rate. However, in the case of motor vehicles, if the rate of tax exceeds the general rate, such excess is disregarded and the general rate is treated as the rate of tax.

A compensating use tax with respect to an item is treated as a general sales tax, provided such tax is complementary to a general sales tax and a deduction for sales taxes is allowable with respect to items sold at retail in the taxing jurisdiction that are similar to such item.

Explanation of Provision

The provision makes permanent the election to deduct State and local sales taxes in lieu of State and local income taxes.

Effective Date

The provision applies to taxable years beginning after December 31, 2014.

---

[352] Sec. 164(b)(5)(B).

Part 2—Incentives for Charitable Giving

7. Special rule for qualified conservation contributions made permanent (sec. 111 of the Act and sec. 170(b) of the Code)

Present Law

Charitable contributions generally

In general, a deduction is permitted for charitable contributions, subject to certain limitations that depend on the type of taxpayer, the property contributed, and the donee organization. The amount of deduction generally equals the fair market value of the contributed property on the date of the contribution. Charitable deductions are provided for income, estate, and gift tax purposes.[353]

In general, in any taxable year, charitable contributions by a corporation are not deductible to the extent the aggregate contributions exceed ten percent of the corporation's taxable income computed without regard to net operating or capital loss carrybacks. Total deductible contributions of an individual taxpayer to public charities, private operating foundations, and certain types of private nonoperating foundations generally may not exceed 50 percent of the taxpayer's contribution base, which is the taxpayer's adjusted gross income for a taxable year (disregarding any net operating loss carryback). To the extent a taxpayer has not exceeded the 50-percent limitation, (1) contributions of capital gain property to public charities generally may be deducted up to 30 percent of the taxpayer's contribution base, (2) contributions of cash to most private nonoperating foundations and certain other charitable organizations generally may be deducted up to 30 percent of the taxpayer's contribution base, and (3) contributions of capital gain property to private foundations and certain other charitable organizations generally may be deducted up to 20 percent of the taxpayer's contribution base.

Contributions in excess of the applicable percentage limits generally may be carried over and deducted over the next five taxable years, subject to the relevant percentage limitations on the deduction in each of those years.

Capital gain property

Capital gain property means any capital asset or property used in the taxpayer's trade or business the sale of which at its fair market value, at the time of contribution, would have resulted in gain that would have been long-term capital gain. Contributions of capital gain property to a qualified charity are deductible at fair market value within certain limitations. Contributions of capital gain property to charitable organizations described in section 170(b)(1)(A) (e.g., public charities, private foundations other than private non-operating foundations, and certain governmental units) generally are deductible up to 30 percent of the taxpayer's contribution base. An individual may elect, however, to bring all these contributions of capital gain property for a taxable year within the 50-percent limitation category by reducing the amount of the con-

---

[353] Secs. 170, 2055, and 2522, respectively.

tribution deduction by the amount of the appreciation in the capital gain property. Contributions of capital gain property to charitable organizations described in section 170(b)(1)(B) (e.g., private non-operating foundations) are deductible up to 20 percent of the taxpayer's contribution base.

For purposes of determining whether a taxpayer's aggregate charitable contributions in a taxable year exceed the applicable percentage limitation, contributions of capital gain property are taken into account after other charitable contributions.

Qualified conservation contributions

Qualified conservation contributions are one exception to the "partial interest" rule, which generally bars deductions for charitable contributions of partial interests in property.[354] A qualified conservation contribution is a contribution of a qualified real property interest to a qualified organization exclusively for conservation purposes. A qualified real property interest is defined as: (1) the entire interest of the donor other than a qualified mineral interest; (2) a remainder interest; or (3) a restriction (granted in perpetuity) on the use that may be made of the real property. Qualified organizations include certain governmental units, public charities that meet certain public support tests, and certain supporting organizations. Conservation purposes include: (1) the preservation of land areas for outdoor recreation by, or for the education of, the general public; (2) the protection of a relatively natural habitat of fish, wildlife, or plants, or similar ecosystem; (3) the preservation of open space (including farmland and forest land) where such preservation will yield a significant public benefit and is either for the scenic enjoyment of the general public or pursuant to a clearly delineated Federal, State, or local governmental conservation policy; and (4) the preservation of an historically important land area or a certified historic structure.

Qualified conservation contributions of capital gain property are subject to the same limitations and carryover rules as other charitable contributions of capital gain property.

Temporary rules regarding contributions of capital gain real property for conservation purposes

In general

Under a temporary provision [355] the 30-percent contribution base limitation on deductions for contributions of capital gain property by individuals does not apply to qualified conservation contributions (as defined under present law). Instead, individuals may deduct the fair market value of any qualified conservation contribution to the extent of the excess of 50 percent of the contribution base over the amount of all other allowable charitable contributions. These contributions are not taken into account in determining the amount of other allowable charitable contributions.

Individuals are allowed to carry over any qualified conservation contributions that exceed the 50-percent limitation for up to 15 years.

---

[354] Secs. 170(f)(3)(B)(iii) and 170(h).
[355] Sec. 170(b)(1)(E).

For example, assume an individual with a contribution base of $100 makes a qualified conservation contribution of property with a fair market value of $80 and makes other charitable contributions subject to the 50-percent limitation of $60. The individual is allowed a deduction of $50 in the current taxable year for the non-conservation contributions (50 percent of the $100 contribution base) and is allowed to carry over the excess $10 for up to 5 years. No current deduction is allowed for the qualified conservation contribution, but the entire $80 qualified conservation contribution may be carried forward for up to 15 years.

Farmers and ranchers

In the case of an individual who is a qualified farmer or rancher for the taxable year in which the contribution is made, a qualified conservation contribution is deductible up to 100 percent of the excess of the taxpayer's contribution base over the amount of all other allowable charitable contributions.

In the above example, if the individual is a qualified farmer or rancher, in addition to the $50 deduction for non-conservation contributions, an additional $50 for the qualified conservation contribution is allowed and $30 may be carried forward for up to 15 years as a contribution subject to the 100-percent limitation.

In the case of a corporation (other than a publicly traded corporation) that is a qualified farmer or rancher for the taxable year in which the contribution is made, any qualified conservation contribution is deductible up to 100 percent of the excess of the corporation's taxable income (as computed under section 170(b)(2)) over the amount of all other allowable charitable contributions. Any excess may be carried forward for up to 15 years as a contribution subject to the 100-percent limitation.[356]

As an additional condition of eligibility for the 100-percent limitation, with respect to any contribution of property in agriculture or livestock production, or that is available for such production, by a qualified farmer or rancher, the qualified real property interest must include a restriction that the property remain generally available for such production. (There is no requirement as to any specific use in agriculture or farming, or necessarily that the property be used for such purposes, merely that the property remain available for such purposes.)

A qualified farmer or rancher means a taxpayer whose gross income from the trade or business of farming (within the meaning of section 2032A(e)(5)) is greater than 50 percent of the taxpayer's gross income for the taxable year.

Termination

The temporary rules regarding contributions of capital gain real property for conservation purposes do not apply to contributions made in taxable years beginning after December 31, 2014.[357]

---

[356] Sec. 170(b)(2)(B).
[357] Secs. 170(b)(1)(E)(vi) and 170(b)(2)(B)(iii).

Explanation of Provision

The provision reinstates and makes permanent the increased percentage limits and extended carryforward period for qualified conservation contributions made in taxable years beginning after December 31, 2014.

The provision also includes special rules for qualified conservation contributions by certain Native Corporations. For this purpose, the term Native Corporation has the meaning given such term by section 3(m) of the Alaska Native Claims Settlement Act.[358] In the case of any qualified conservation contribution which is made by a Native Corporation and is a contribution of property that was land conveyed under the Alaska Native Claims Settlement Act, a deduction for the contribution is allowed to the extent that the aggregate amount of such contributions does not exceed the excess of 100 percent of the taxpayer's taxable income over the amount of all other allowable charitable contributions. Any excess may be carried forward for up to 15 years as a contribution subject to the 100-percent limitation. The provision shall not be construed to modify the existing property rights validly conveyed to Native Corporations under the Alaska Native Claims Settlement Act.

Effective Date

The provision generally applies to contributions made in taxable years beginning after December 31, 2014.

The provision for qualified conservation contributions by certain Native Corporations applies to contributions made in taxable years beginning after December 31, 2015.

8. Tax-free distributions from individual retirement plans for charitable purposes (sec. 112 of the Act and sec. 408(d)(8) of the Code)

Present Law

In general

If an amount withdrawn from a traditional individual retirement arrangement ("IRA") or a Roth IRA is donated to a charitable organization, the rules relating to the tax treatment of withdrawals from IRAs apply to the amount withdrawn and the charitable contribution is subject to the normally applicable limitations on deductibility of such contributions. An exception applies in the case of a qualified charitable distribution.

Charitable contributions

In computing taxable income, an individual taxpayer who itemizes deductions generally is allowed to deduct the amount of cash and up to the fair market value of property contributed to the following entities: (1) a charity described in section 170(c)(2); (2) certain veterans' organizations, fraternal societies, and cemetery companies;[359] and (3) a Federal, State, or local governmental enti-

---

[358] 43 U.S.C. sec. 1602(m) (providing that the term Native Corporation includes "any Regional Corporation, any Village Corporation, any Urban Corporation, and any Group Corporation," as those terms are defined under the Alaska Native Claims Settlement Act).
[359] Secs. 170(c)(3)–(5).

ty, but only if the contribution is made for exclusively public purposes.[360] The deduction also is allowed for purposes of calculating alternative minimum taxable income.

The amount of the deduction allowable for a taxable year with respect to a charitable contribution of property may be reduced depending on the type of property contributed, the type of charitable organization to which the property is contributed, and the income of the taxpayer.[361]

A taxpayer who takes the standard deduction (*i.e.*, who does not itemize deductions) may not take a separate deduction for charitable contributions.[362]

A payment to a charity (regardless of whether it is termed a "contribution") in exchange for which the donor receives an economic benefit is not deductible, except to the extent that the donor can demonstrate, among other things, that the payment exceeds the fair market value of the benefit received from the charity. To facilitate distinguishing charitable contributions from purchases of goods or services from charities, present law provides that no charitable contribution deduction is allowed for a separate contribution of $250 or more unless the donor obtains a contemporaneous written acknowledgement of the contribution from the charity indicating whether the charity provided any good or service (and an estimate of the value of any such good or service provided) to the taxpayer in consideration for the contribution.[363] In addition, present law requires that any charity that receives a contribution exceeding $75 made partly as a gift and partly as consideration for goods or services furnished by the charity (a "quid pro quo" contribution) is required to inform the contributor in writing of an estimate of the value of the goods or services furnished by the charity and that only the portion exceeding the value of the goods or services may be deductible as a charitable contribution.[364]

Under present law, total deductible contributions of an individual taxpayer to public charities, private operating foundations, and certain types of private nonoperating foundations generally may not exceed 50 percent of the taxpayer's contribution base, which is the taxpayer's adjusted gross income for a taxable year (disregarding any net operating loss carryback). To the extent a taxpayer has not exceeded the 50-percent limitation, (1) contributions of capital gain property to public charities generally may be deducted up to 30 percent of the taxpayer's contribution base, (2) contributions of cash to most private nonoperating foundations and certain other charitable organizations generally may be deducted up to 30 percent of the taxpayer's contribution base, and (3) contributions of capital gain property to private foundations and certain other charitable organizations generally may be deducted up to 20 percent of the taxpayer's contribution base.

---

[360] Sec. 170(c)(1).
[361] Secs. 170(b) and (e).
[362] Sec. 170(a).
[363] Sec. 170(f)(8). For any contribution of a cash, check, or other monetary gift, no deduction is allowed unless the donor maintains as a record of such contribution a bank record or written communication from the donee charity showing the name of the donee organization, the date of the contribution, and the amount of the contribution. Sec. 170(f)(17).
[364] Sec. 6115.

Contributions by individuals in excess of the 50-percent, 30-percent, and 20-percent limits generally may be carried over and deducted over the next five taxable years, subject to the relevant percentage limitations on the deduction in each of those years.

In general, a charitable deduction is not allowed for income, estate, or gift tax purposes if the donor transfers an interest in property to a charity (*e.g.*, a remainder) while also either retaining an interest in that property (*e.g.*, an income interest) or transferring an interest in that property to a noncharity for less than full and adequate consideration.[365] Exceptions to this general rule are provided for, among other interests, remainder interests in charitable remainder annuity trusts, charitable remainder unitrusts, and pooled income funds, and present interests in the form of a guaranteed annuity or a fixed percentage of the annual value of the property.[366] For such interests, a charitable deduction is allowed to the extent of the present value of the interest designated for a charitable organization.

IRA rules

Within limits, individuals may make deductible and nondeductible contributions to a traditional IRA. Amounts in a traditional IRA are includible in income when withdrawn (except to the extent the withdrawal represents a return of nondeductible contributions). Certain individuals also may make nondeductible contributions to a Roth IRA (deductible contributions cannot be made to Roth IRAs). Qualified withdrawals from a Roth IRA are excludable from gross income. Withdrawals from a Roth IRA that are not qualified withdrawals are includible in gross income to the extent attributable to earnings. Includible amounts withdrawn from a traditional IRA or a Roth IRA before attainment of age 59½ are subject to an additional 10-percent early withdrawal tax, unless an exception applies. Under present law, minimum distributions are required to be made from tax-favored retirement arrangements, including IRAs. Minimum required distributions from a traditional IRA must generally begin by April 1 of the calendar year following the year in which the IRA owner attains age 70½.[367]

If an individual has made nondeductible contributions to a traditional IRA, a portion of each distribution from an IRA is nontaxable until the total amount of nondeductible contributions has been received. In general, the amount of a distribution that is nontaxable is determined by multiplying the amount of the distribution by the ratio of the remaining nondeductible contributions to the account balance. In making the calculation, all traditional IRAs of an individual are treated as a single IRA, all distributions during any taxable year are treated as a single distribution, and the value of the contract, income on the contract, and investment in the contract are computed as of the close of the calendar year.

In the case of a distribution from a Roth IRA that is not a qualified distribution, in determining the portion of the distribution attributable to earnings, contributions and distributions are deemed

---

[365] Secs. 170(f), 2055(e)(2), and 2522(c)(2).
[366] Sec. 170(f)(2).
[367] Minimum distribution rules also apply in the case of distributions after the death of a traditional or Roth IRA owner.

to be distributed in the following order: (1) regular Roth IRA contributions; (2) taxable conversion contributions;[368] (3) nontaxable conversion contributions; and (4) earnings. In determining the amount of taxable distributions from a Roth IRA, all Roth IRA distributions in the same taxable year are treated as a single distribution.

Distributions from an IRA (other than a Roth IRA) are generally subject to withholding unless the individual elects not to have withholding apply.[369] Elections not to have withholding apply are to be made in the time and manner prescribed by the Secretary.

Qualified charitable distributions

Otherwise taxable IRA distributions from a traditional or Roth IRA are excluded from gross income to the extent they are qualified charitable distributions.[370] The exclusion may not exceed $100,000 per taxpayer per taxable year. Special rules apply in determining the amount of an IRA distribution that is otherwise taxable. The otherwise applicable rules regarding taxation of IRA distributions and the deduction of charitable contributions continue to apply to distributions from an IRA that are not qualified charitable distributions. A qualified charitable distribution is taken into account for purposes of the minimum distribution rules applicable to traditional IRAs to the same extent the distribution would have been taken into account under such rules had the distribution not been directly distributed under the qualified charitable distribution provision. An IRA does not fail to qualify as an IRA as a result of qualified charitable distributions being made from the IRA.

A qualified charitable distribution is any distribution from an IRA directly by the IRA trustee to an organization described in section 170(b)(1)(A) (generally, public charities) other than a supporting organization (as described in section 509(a)(3)) or a donor advised fund (as defined in section 4966(d)(2)). Distributions are eligible for the exclusion only if made on or after the date the IRA owner attains age 70½ and only to the extent the distribution would be includible in gross income (without regard to this provision).

The exclusion applies only if a charitable contribution deduction for the entire distribution otherwise would be allowable (under present law), determined without regard to the generally applicable percentage limitations. Thus, for example, if the deductible amount is reduced because of a benefit received in exchange, or if a deduction is not allowable because the donor did not obtain sufficient substantiation, the exclusion is not available with respect to any part of the IRA distribution.

If the IRA owner has any IRA that includes nondeductible contributions, a special rule applies in determining the portion of a distribution that is includible in gross income (but for the qualified charitable distribution provision) and thus is eligible for qualified charitable distribution treatment. Under the special rule, the dis-

---

[368] Conversion contributions refer to conversions of amounts in a traditional IRA to a Roth IRA.

[369] Sec. 3405.

[370] Sec. 408(d)(8). The exclusion does not apply to distributions from employer-sponsored retirement plans, including SIMPLE IRAs and simplified employee pensions ("SEPs").

tribution is treated as consisting of income first, up to the aggregate amount that would be includible in gross income (but for the qualified charitable distribution provision) if the aggregate balance of all IRAs having the same owner were distributed during the same year. In determining the amount of subsequent IRA distributions includible in income, proper adjustments are to be made to reflect the amount treated as a qualified charitable distribution under the special rule.

Distributions that are excluded from gross income by reason of the qualified charitable distribution provision are not taken into account in determining the deduction for charitable contributions under section 170.

Under present law, the exclusion does not apply to distributions made in taxable years beginning after December 31, 2014.

Explanation of Provision

The provision reinstates and makes permanent the exclusion from gross income for qualified charitable distributions from an IRA.

Effective Date

The provision applies to distributions made in taxable years beginning after December 31, 2014.

9. Extension and expansion of charitable deduction for contributions of food inventory (sec. 113 of the Act and sec. 170 of the Code)

Present Law

Charitable contributions in general

In general, an income tax deduction is permitted for charitable contributions, subject to certain limitations that depend on the type of taxpayer, the property contributed, and the donee organization.[371] In the case of an individual, the deduction is limited to various percentages of the contribution base, depending on the donee and the property contributed. In the case of a corporation,[372] the deduction generally is limited to ten percent of the taxable income (with modifications).[373] Contributions in excess of these limitations may be carried forward for up to five taxable years.

Charitable contributions of cash are deductible in the amount contributed. Subject to several exceptions, contributions of property are deductible at the fair market value of the property. One exception provides that the amount of the charitable contribution is reduced by the amount of any gain which would not have been long-term capital gain if the property contributed had been sold by the taxpayer at its fair market value at the time of the contribution.[374]

---

[371] Sec. 170.
[372] Sec. 170(b)(1). The contribution base is the adjusted gross income determined without regard net operating loss carrybacks.
[373] Sec. 170(b)(2).
[374] Sec. 170(e)(1)(A).

General rules regarding contributions of inventory

As a result of the exception described above, a taxpayer's deduction for charitable contributions of inventory generally is limited to the taxpayer's basis (typically, cost) in the inventory, or, if less, the fair market value of the inventory.

However, for certain contributions of inventory, a C corporation may claim an enhanced deduction equal to the lesser of (1) basis plus one-half of the item's appreciation (*i.e.*, basis plus one-half of fair market value in excess of basis) or (2) two times basis.[375] To be eligible for the enhanced deduction, the contributed property generally must be inventory of the taxpayer and must be contributed to a charitable organization described in section 501(c)(3) (except for private nonoperating foundations), and the donee must (1) use the property consistent with the donee's exempt purpose solely for the care of the ill, the needy, or infants; (2) not transfer the property in exchange for money, other property, or services; and (3) provide the taxpayer a written statement that the donee's use of the property will be consistent with such requirements. In the case of contributed property subject to the Federal Food, Drug, and Cosmetic Act, as amended, the property must satisfy the applicable requirements of such Act on the date of transfer and for 180 days prior to the transfer.[376]

To use the enhanced deduction, the taxpayer must establish that the fair market value of the donated item exceeds basis. The valuation of food inventory has been the subject of disputes between taxpayers and the IRS.[377]

Temporary rule expanding and modifying the enhanced deduction for contributions of food inventory

Under a temporary provision, any taxpayer engaged in a trade or business, whether or not a C corporation, is eligible to claim the enhanced deduction for donations of food inventory.[378] For taxpayers other than C corporations, the total deduction for donations of food inventory in a taxable year generally may not exceed ten percent of the taxpayer's net income for such taxable year from all sole proprietorships, S corporations, or partnerships (or other non C corporations) from which contributions of apparently wholesome food are made. For example, if a taxpayer is a sole proprietor, a shareholder in an S corporation, and a partner in a partnership, and each business makes charitable contributions of food inventory, the taxpayer's deduction for donations of food inventory is limited to ten percent of the taxpayer's net income from the sole proprietorship and the taxpayer's interests in the S corporation and partnership. However, if only the sole proprietorship and the S corporation made charitable contributions of food inventory, the taxpayer's deduction would be limited to ten percent of the net income from the trade or business of the sole proprietorship and the taxpayer's in-

---

[375] Sec. 170(e)(3).
[376] Sec. 170(e)(3)(A)(iv).
[377] Lucky Stores Inc. v. Commissioner, 105 T.C. 420 (1995) (holding that the value of surplus bread inventory donated to charity was the full retail price of the bread rather than half the retail price, as the IRS asserted).
[378] Sec. 170(e)(3)(C).

terest in the S corporation, but not the taxpayer's interest in the partnership.[379]

Under the temporary provision, the enhanced deduction for food is available only for food that qualifies as "apparently wholesome food." Apparently wholesome food is defined as food intended for human consumption that meets all quality and labeling standards imposed by Federal, State, and local laws and regulations even though the food may not be readily marketable due to appearance, age, freshness, grade, size, surplus, or other conditions.

The provision does not apply to contributions made after December 31, 2014.

Explanation of Provision

The provision reinstates and makes permanent the enhanced deduction for contributions of food inventory for contributions made after December 31, 2014.

For taxable years beginning after December 31, 2015, the provision also modifies the enhanced deduction for food inventory contributions by: (1) increasing the charitable percentage limitation for food inventory contributions and clarifying the carryover and coordination rules for these contributions; (2) including a presumption concerning the tax basis of food inventory donated by certain businesses; and (3) including presumptions that may be used when valuing donated food inventory.

First, the ten-percent limitation described above applicable to taxpayers other than C corporations is increased to 15 percent. For C corporations, these contributions are made subject to a limitation of 15 percent of taxable income (as modified). The general ten-percent limitation for a C corporation does not apply to these contributions, but the ten-percent limitation applicable to other contributions is reduced by the amount of these contributions. Qualifying food inventory contributions in excess of these 15-percent limitations may be carried forward and treated as qualifying food inventory contributions in each of the five succeeding taxable years in order of time.

Second, if the taxpayer does not account for inventory under section 471 and is not required to capitalize indirect costs under section 263A, the taxpayer may elect, solely for computing the enhanced deduction for food inventory, to treat the basis of any apparently wholesome food as being equal to 25 percent of the fair market value of such food.

Third, in the case of any contribution of apparently wholesome food which cannot or will not be sold solely by reason of internal standards of the taxpayer, lack of market, or similar circumstances, or by reason of being produced by the taxpayer exclusively for the purposes of transferring the food to an organization described in

---

[379] The ten-percent limitation does not affect the application of the generally applicable percentage limitations. For example, if ten percent of a sole proprietor's net income from the proprietor's trade or business is greater than 50 percent of the proprietor's contribution base which otherwise limits the deduction, the available deduction for the taxable year (with respect to contributions to public charities) is 50 percent of the proprietor's contribution base. Consistent with present law, these contributions may be carried forward because they exceed the 50-percent limitation. Contributions of food inventory by a taxpayer that is not a C corporation that exceed the ten-percent limitation but do not exceed the 50-percent limitation may not be carried forward.

section 501(c)(3), the fair market value of such contribution shall be determined (1) without regard to such internal standards, such lack of market or similar circumstances, or such exclusive purpose, and (2) by taking into account the price at which the same or substantially the same food items (as to both type and quality) are sold by the taxpayer at the time of the contributions (or, if not so sold at such time, in the recent past).

Effective Date

The provision generally applies to contributions made after December 31, 2014.

The modifications to increase the corporate percentage limit and to provide for presumptions relating to basis and valuation apply to taxable years beginning after December 31, 2015.

10. Extension of modification of tax treatment of certain payments to controlling exempt organizations (sec. 114 of the Act and sec. 512 of the Code)

Present Law

In general, organizations exempt from Federal income tax are subject to the unrelated business income tax on income derived from a trade or business regularly carried on by the organization that is not substantially related to the performance of the organization's tax-exempt functions.[380] In general, interest, rents, royalties, and annuities are excluded from the unrelated business income of tax-exempt organizations.[381]

Section 512(b)(13) provides rules regarding income derived by an exempt organization from a controlled subsidiary. In general, section 512(b)(13) treats otherwise excluded rent, royalty, annuity, and interest income as unrelated business taxable income if such income is received from a taxable or tax-exempt subsidiary that is 50-percent controlled by the parent tax-exempt organization to the extent the payment reduces the net unrelated income (or increases any net unrelated loss) of the controlled entity (determined as if the entity were tax exempt).

In the case of a stock subsidiary, "control" means ownership by vote or value of more than 50 percent of the stock. In the case of a partnership or other entity, "control" means ownership of more than 50 percent of the profits, capital, or beneficial interests. In addition, present law applies the constructive ownership rules of section 318 for purposes of section 512(b)(13). Thus, a parent exempt organization is deemed to control any subsidiary in which it holds more than 50 percent of the voting power or value, directly (as in the case of a first-tier subsidiary) or indirectly (as in the case of a second-tier subsidiary).

For payments made pursuant to a binding written contract in effect on August 17, 2006 (or renewal of such a contract on substantially similar terms), the general rule of section 512(b)(13) applies only to the portion of payments received or accrued in a taxable year that exceeds the amount of the payment that would have been

---

[380] Sec. 511.
[381] Sec. 512(b).

paid or accrued if the amount of such payment had been determined under the principles of section 482 (*i.e.*, at arm's length).[382] A 20-percent penalty is imposed on the larger of such excess determined without regard to any amendment or supplement to a return of tax, or such excess determined with regard to all such amendments and supplements. This special rule does not apply to payments received or accrued after December 31, 2014.

Explanation of Provision

The provision reinstates the special rule and makes it permanent. Accordingly, under the provision, payments of rent, royalties, annuities, or interest by a controlled organization to a controlling organization pursuant to a binding written contract in effect on August 17, 2006 (or renewal of such a contract on substantially similar terms), may be includible in the unrelated business taxable income of the controlling organization only to the extent the payment exceeds the amount of the payment determined under the principles of section 482 (*i.e.*, at arm's length). Any such excess is subject to a 20-percent penalty on the larger of such excess determined without regard to any amendment or supplement to a return of tax, or such excess determined with regard to all such amendments and supplements.

Effective Date

The provision applies to payments received or accrued after December 31, 2014.

11. Extension of basis adjustment to stock of S corporations making charitable contributions of property (sec. 115 of the Act and sec. 1367 of the Code)

Present Law

Under present law, if an S corporation contributes money or other property to a charity, each shareholder takes into account the shareholder's pro rata share of the contribution in determining its own income tax liability.[383] A shareholder of an S corporation reduces the basis in the stock of the S corporation by the amount of the charitable contribution that flows through to the shareholder.[384]

In the case of charitable contributions made in taxable years beginning before January 1, 2015, the amount of a shareholder's basis reduction in the stock of an S corporation by reason of a charitable contribution made by the corporation is equal to the shareholder's pro rata share of the adjusted basis of the contributed property. For contributions made in taxable years beginning after December 31, 2014, the amount of the reduction is the shareholder's pro rata share of the fair market value of the contributed property.

---

[382] Sec. 512(b)(13)(E).
[383] Sec. 1366(a)(1)(A).
[384] Sec. 1367(a)(2)(B).

Explanation of Provision

The provision makes the pre-2015 rule relating to the basis reduction on account of charitable contributions of property permanent.

Effective Date

The provision applies to charitable contributions made in taxable years beginning after December 31, 2014.

Part 3—Incentives for Growth, Jobs, Investment, and Innovation

12. Extension and modification of research credit (sec. 121 of the Act and secs. 38 and 41 and new sec. 3111(f) of the Code)

Present Law

Research credit

General rule

For general research expenditures, a taxpayer may claim a research credit equal to 20 percent of the amount by which the taxpayer's qualified research expenses for a taxable year exceed its base amount for that year.[385] Thus, the research credit is generally available with respect to incremental increases in qualified research. An alternative simplified credit (with a 14-percent rate and a different base amount) may be claimed in lieu of this credit.[386]

A 20-percent research tax credit also is available with respect to the excess of (1) 100 percent of corporate cash expenses (including grants or contributions) paid for basic research conducted by universities (and certain nonprofit scientific research organizations) over (2) the sum of (a) the greater of two minimum basic research floors plus (b) an amount reflecting any decrease in nonresearch giving to universities by the corporation as compared to such giving during a fixed-base period, as adjusted for inflation.[387] This separate credit computation commonly is referred to as the basic research credit.

Finally, a research credit is available for a taxpayer's expenditures on research undertaken by an energy research consortium.[388] This separate credit computation commonly is referred to as the energy research credit. Unlike the other research credits, the energy research credit applies to all qualified expenditures, not just those in excess of a base amount.

The research credit, including the basic research credit and the energy research credit, expires for amounts paid or incurred after December 31, 2014.[389]

---

[385] Sec. 41(a)(1).
[386] Sec. 41(c)(5).
[387] Sec. 41(a)(2) and (e). The base period for the basic research credit generally extends from 1981 through 1983.
[388] Sec. 41(a)(3).
[389] Sec. 41(h).

Computation of general research credit

The general research tax credit applies only to the extent that the taxpayer's qualified research expenses for the current taxable year exceed its base amount. The base amount for the current year generally is computed by multiplying the taxpayer's fixed-base percentage by the average amount of the taxpayer's gross receipts for the four preceding years. If a taxpayer both incurred qualified research expenses and had gross receipts during each of at least three years from 1984 through 1988, then its fixed-base percentage is the ratio that its total qualified research expenses for the 1984–1988 period bears to its total gross receipts for that period (subject to a maximum fixed-base percentage of 16 percent). Special rules apply to all other taxpayers (so called start-up firms).[390] In computing the research credit, a taxpayer's base amount cannot be less than 50 percent of its current-year qualified research expenses.

Alternative simplified credit

The alternative simplified credit is equal to 14 percent of qualified research expenses that exceed 50 percent of the average qualified research expenses for the three preceding taxable years.[391] The rate is reduced to 6 percent if a taxpayer has no qualified research expenses in any one of the three preceding taxable years.[392] An election to use the alternative simplified credit applies to all succeeding taxable years unless revoked with the consent of the Secretary.[393]

Eligible expenses

Qualified research expenses eligible for the research tax credit consist of: (1) in-house expenses of the taxpayer for wages and supplies attributable to qualified research; (2) certain time-sharing costs for computer use in qualified research; and (3) 65 percent of amounts paid or incurred by the taxpayer to certain other persons for qualified research conducted on the taxpayer's behalf (so-called contract research expenses).[394] Notwithstanding the limitation for contract research expenses, qualified research expenses include 100 percent of amounts paid or incurred by the taxpayer to an eligible

---

[390] The Small Business Job Protection Act of 1996 expanded the definition of start-up firms under section 41(c)(3)(B)(i) to include any firm if the first taxable year in which such firm had both gross receipts and qualified research expenses began after 1983. A special rule (enacted in 1993) is designed to gradually recompute a start-up firm's fixed-base percentage based on its actual research experience. Under this special rule, a start-up firm is assigned a fixed-base percentage of three percent for each of its first five taxable years after 1993 in which it incurs qualified research expenses. A start-up firm's fixed-base percentage for its sixth through tenth taxable years after 1993 in which it incurs qualified research expenses is a phased-in ratio based on the firm's actual research experience. For all subsequent taxable years, the taxpayer's fixed-base percentage is its actual ratio of qualified research expenses to gross receipts for any five years selected by the taxpayer from its fifth through tenth taxable years after 1993. Sec. 41(c)(3)(B).

[391] Sec. 41(c)(5)(A).
[392] Sec. 41(c)(5)(B).
[393] Sec. 41(c)(5)(C).

[394] Under a special rule, 75 percent of amounts paid to a research consortium for qualified research are treated as qualified research expenses eligible for the research credit (rather than 65 percent under the general rule under section 41(b)(3) governing contract research expenses) if (1) such research consortium is a tax-exempt organization that is described in section 501(c)(3) (other than a private foundation) or section 501(c)(6) and is organized and operated primarily to conduct scientific research, and (2) such qualified research is conducted by the consortium on behalf of the taxpayer and one or more persons not related to the taxpayer. Sec. 41(b)(3)(C).

small business, university, or Federal laboratory for qualified energy research.

To be eligible for the credit, the research not only has to satisfy the requirements of section 174, but also must be undertaken for the purpose of discovering information that is technological in nature, the application of which is intended to be useful in the development of a new or improved business component of the taxpayer, and substantially all of the activities of which constitute elements of a process of experimentation for functional aspects, performance, reliability, or quality of a business component. Research does not qualify for the credit if substantially all of the activities relate to style, taste, cosmetic, or seasonal design factors.[395] In addition, research does not qualify for the credit if: (1) conducted after the beginning of commercial production of the business component; (2) related to the adaptation of an existing business component to a particular customer's requirements; (3) related to the duplication of an existing business component from a physical examination of the component itself or certain other information; (4) related to certain efficiency surveys, management function or technique, market research, market testing, or market development, routine data collection or routine quality control; (5) related to software developed primarily for internal use by the taxpayer; (6) conducted outside the United States, Puerto Rico, or any U.S. possession; (7) in the social sciences, arts, or humanities; or (8) funded by any grant, contract, or otherwise by another person (or government entity).[396]

Relation to deduction

Deductions allowed to a taxpayer under section 174 (or any other section) are reduced by an amount equal to 100 percent of the taxpayer's research tax credit determined for the taxable year.[397] Taxpayers may alternatively elect to claim a reduced research tax credit amount under section 41 in lieu of reducing deductions otherwise allowed.[398]

Specified credits allowed against alternative minimum tax

For any taxable year, the general business credit (which is the sum of the various business credits) generally may not exceed the excess of the taxpayer's net income tax[399] over the greater of (1) the taxpayer's tentative minimum tax or (2) 25 percent of so much

---

[395] Sec. 41(d)(3).

[396] Sec. 41(d)(4).

[397] Sec. 280C(c). For example, assume that a taxpayer makes credit-eligible research expenditures of $1 million during the year and that the base period amount is $600,000. Under the standard credit calculation (*i.e.*, where a taxpayer may claim a research credit equal to 20 percent of the amount by which its qualified expenses for the year exceed its base period amount), the taxpayer is allowed a credit equal to 20 percent of the $400,000 increase in research expenditures, or $80,000 (($1 million – $600,000) * 20% = $80,000). To avoid a double benefit, the amount of the taxpayer's deduction under section 174 is reduced by $80,000 (the amount of the research credit), leaving a deduction of $920,000 ($1 million – $80,000).

[398] Sec. 280C(c)(3). Taxpayers making this election reduce the allowable research credit by the maximum corporate tax rate (currently 35 percent). Continuing with the example from the prior footnote, an electing taxpayer would have its credit reduced to $52,000 ($80,000 – ($80,000 * 0.35%)), but would retain its $1 million deduction for research expenses. This option might be desirable for a taxpayer who cannot claim the full amount of the research credit otherwise allowable due to the limitation imposed by the alternative minimum tax.

[399] The term "net income tax" means the sum of the regular tax liability and the alternative minimum tax, reduced by the credits allowable under sections 21 through 30D. Sec. 38(c)(1).

of the taxpayer's net regular tax liability[400] as exceeds $25,000.[401] Any general business credit in excess of this limitation may be carried back one year and forward up to 20 years.[402] The tentative minimum tax is an amount equal to specified rates of tax imposed on the excess of the alternative minimum taxable income over an exemption amount.[403] Generally, the tentative minimum tax of a C corporation with average annual gross receipts of less than $7.5 million for prior three-year periods is zero.[404]

In applying the tax liability limitation to a list of "specified credits" that are part of the general business credit, the tentative minimum tax is treated as being zero.[405] Thus, the specified credits generally may offset both regular tax and alternative minimum tax ("AMT") liabilities.

For taxable years beginning in 2010, an eligible small business was allowed to offset both the regular and AMT liability with the general business credits determined for the taxable year ("eligible small business credits").[406] For this purpose, an eligible small business was, with respect to any taxable year, a corporation, the stock of which was not publicly traded, a partnership, or a sole proprietor, if the average annual gross receipts did not exceed $50 million.[407] Credits determined with respect to a partnership or S corporation were not treated as eligible small business credits by a partner or shareholder unless the partner or shareholder met the gross receipts test for the taxable year in which the credits were treated as current year business credits.[408]

FICA taxes

The Federal Insurance Contributions Act ("FICA") imposes tax on employers and employees based on the amount of wages (as defined for FICA purposes) paid to an employee during the year, often referred to as "payroll" taxes.[409] The tax imposed on the employer and on the employee is each composed of two parts: (1) the Social Security or old age, survivors, and disability insurance ("OASDI") tax equal to 6.2 percent of covered wages up to the taxable wage base ($118,500 for 2015); and (2) the Medicare or hospital insurance ("HI") tax equal to 1.45 percent of all covered wages.[410] The employee portion of the FICA tax generally must be withheld and remitted to the Federal government by the employer.

---

[400] The term "net regular tax liability" means the regular tax liability reduced by the sum of certain nonrefundable personal and other credits. Sec. 38(c)(1).

[401] Sec. 38(c)(1).

[402] Sec. 39(a)(1).

[403] Sec. 55(b). For example, assume a taxpayer has a regular tax liability of $80,000, a tentative minimum tax of $100,000, and a research credit determined under section 41 of $90,000 for the taxable year (and no other credits). Under present law, the taxpayer's research credit is limited to the excess of $100,000 over the greater of (1) $100,000 or (2) $13,750 (25% of the excess of $80,000 over $25,000). Accordingly, no research credit may be claimed ($100,000 − $100,000 = $0) for the taxable year and the taxpayer's net tax liability is $100,000. The $90,000 research credit may be carried back or forward under the rules applicable to the general business credit.

[404] Sec. 55(e).

[405] See section 38(c)(4)(B) for the list of specified credits, which does not presently include the research credit determined under section 41.

[406] Sec. 38(c)(5)(B).

[407] Sec. 38(c)(5)(C).

[408] Sec. 38(c)(5)(D).

[409] Secs. 3101–3128.

[410] The employee portion of the HI tax under FICA (not the employer portion) is increased by an additional tax of 0.9 percent on wages received in excess of a threshold amount. The

An employer generally files quarterly employment tax returns showing its liability for FICA taxes with respect to its employees' wages for the quarter, as well as the employee FICA taxes and income taxes withheld from the employees' wages.

Explanation of Provision

Research credit

The provision makes permanent the present law credit.[411]

Specified credits allowed against alternative minimum tax

The provision provides that, in the case of an eligible small business (as defined in section 38(c)(5)(C), after application of rules similar to the rules of section 38(c)(5)(D)), the research credit determined under section 41 for taxable years beginning after December 31, 2015, is a specified credit. Thus, these research credits of an eligible small business may offset both regular tax and AMT liabilities.[412]

Payroll tax credit

In general

Under the provision, for taxable years beginning after December 31, 2015, a qualified small business may elect for any taxable year to claim a certain amount of its research credit as a payroll tax credit against its employer OASDI liability, rather than against its income tax liability.[413] If a taxpayer makes an election under this provision, the amount so elected is treated as a research credit for purposes of section 280C.[414]

A qualified small business is defined, with respect to any taxable year, as a corporation (including an S corporation) or partnership (1) with gross receipts of less than $5 million for the taxable year,[415] and (2) that did not have gross receipts for any taxable year before the five taxable year period ending with the taxable year. An individual carrying on one or more trades or businesses also may be considered a qualified small business if the individual meets the conditions set forth in (1) and (2), taking into account its

---

threshold amount is $250,000 in the case of a joint return, $125,000 in the case of a married individual filing a separate return, and $200,000 in any other case.

[411] In making the present law research credit permanent, Congress did not intend to reinstate the previously terminated alternative incremental research credit. See letter dated January 27, 2016, reprinted in Tax Notes Today (Doc 2016–2887, 2016 Tax Notes Today 27–38), from Chairmen Brady and Hatch and Ranking Members Levin and Wyden to Secretary of the Treasury Lew and Commissioner of Internal Revenue Service Koskinen so stating and announcing their intention to introduce technical correction legislation to strike the alternative incremental research credit from the Code, effective as if included in the PATH Act.

[412] Using the above example, under this provision, the limitation would be the excess of $100,000 over the greater of (1) $0 or (2) $13,750. Since $13,750 is greater than $0, the $100,000 would be reduced by $13,750 such that the research credit would be limited to $86,250. Hence, the taxpayer would be able to claim a research credit of $86,250 against its $100,000 net income tax (the sum of $80,000 regular tax liability and $20,000 alternative minimum tax), which would result in $13,750 of total net tax owed ($100,000—$86,250). The remaining $3,750 of its research credit ($90,000—$86,250) may be carried back or forward, as applicable.

[413] The credit does not apply against its employer HI liability or against the employee portion of FICA taxes the employer is required to withhold and remit to the government.

[414] Thus, taxpayers are either denied a section 174 deduction in the amount of the credit or may elect a reduced research credit amount. The election is not taken into account for purposes of determining any amount allowable as a payroll tax deduction.

[415] For this purpose, gross receipts are determined under the rules of section 448(c)(3), without regard to subparagraph (A) thereof.

aggregate gross receipts received with respect to all trades or businesses. A qualified small business does not include an organization exempt from income tax under section 501.

The payroll tax credit portion is the least of (1) an amount specified by the taxpayer that does not exceed $250,000, (2) the research credit determined for the taxable year, or (3) in the case of a qualified small business other than a partnership or S corporation, the amount of the business credit carryforward under section 39 from the taxable year (determined before the application of this provision to the taxable year).

For purposes of this provision, all members of the same controlled group or group under common control are treated as a single taxpayer.[416] The $250,000 amount is allocated among the members in proportion to each member's expenses on which the research credit is based. Each member may separately elect the payroll tax credit, but not in excess of its allocated dollar amount.

A taxpayer may make an annual election under this section, specifying the amount of its research credit not to exceed $250,000 that may be used as a payroll tax credit, on or before the due date (including extensions) of its originally filed return.[417] A taxpayer may not make an election for a taxable year if it has made such an election for five or more preceding taxable years. An election to apply the research credit against OASDI liability may not be revoked without the consent of the Secretary of the Treasury ("Secretary"). In the case of a partnership or S corporation, an election to apply the credit against its OASDI liability is made at the entity level.

Application of credit against OASDI tax liability

The payroll tax portion of the research credit is allowed as a credit against the qualified small business's OASDI tax liability for the first calendar quarter beginning after the date on which the qualified small business files its income tax or information return for the taxable year. The credit may not exceed the OASDI tax liability for a calendar quarter on the wages paid with respect to all employees of the qualified small business.

If the payroll tax portion of the credit exceeds the qualified small business's OASDI tax liability for a calendar quarter, the excess is allowed as a credit against the OASDI liability for the following calendar quarter.

Other rules

The Secretary is directed to prescribe such regulations as are necessary to carry out the purposes of the provision, including (1) to prevent the avoidance of the purposes of the limitations and aggregation rules through the use of successor companies or other means, (2) to minimize compliance and record-keeping burdens, and (3) for recapture of the credit amount applied against OASDI taxes in the case of an adjustment to the payroll tax portion of the

---

[416] For this purpose, all persons or entities treated as a single taxpayer under section 41(f)(1) are treated as a single person.

[417] In the case of a qualified small business that is a partnership, this is the return required to be filed under section 6031. In the case of a qualified small business that is an S corporation, this is the return required to be filed under section 6037. In the case of any other qualified small business, this is the return of tax for the taxable year.

research credit, including requiring amended returns in such a case.

Effective Date

The provision to make the research credit permanent applies to amounts paid or incurred after December 31, 2014.

The provision to allow the research credit against AMT applies to research credits of eligible small businesses determined for taxable years beginning after December 31, 2015.

The provision to allow the research credit against FICA taxes applies to taxable years beginning after December 31, 2015.

13. Extension and modification of employer wage credit for employees who are active duty members of the uniformed services (sec. 122 of the Act and sec. 45P of the Code)

Present Law

Differential pay

In general, compensation paid by an employer to an employee is deductible by the employer unless the expense must be capitalized.[418] In the case of an employee who is called to active duty with respect to the armed forces of the United States, some employers voluntarily pay the employee the difference between the compensation that the employer would have paid to the employee during the period of military service less the amount of pay received by the employee from the military. This payment by the employer is often referred to as "differential pay."

Wage credit for differential pay

If an employer qualifies as an eligible small business employer, the employer is allowed a credit against its income tax liability for a taxable year in an amount equal to 20 percent of the sum of the eligible differential wage payments for each of the employer's qualified employees during the year.

An eligible small business employer means, with respect to a taxable year, an employer that: (1) employed on average less than 50 employees on business days during the taxable year; and (2) under a written plan of the taxpayer, provides eligible differential wage payments to every qualified employee. For this purpose, members of controlled groups, groups under common control, and affiliated service groups are treated as a single employer.[419] The credit is not available with respect to an employer that has failed to comply with the employment and reemployment rights of members of the uniformed services.[420]

Differential wage payment means any payment that: (1) is made by an employer to an individual with respect to any period during which the individual is performing service in the uniformed services of the United States while on active duty for a period of more than 30 days, and (2) represents all or a portion of the wages that

---
[418] Sec. 162(a)(1).
[419] Sec. 414(b), (c), (m) and (o).
[420] Chapter 43 of Title 38 of the United States Code deals with these rights.

the individual would have received from the employer if the individual were performing services for the employer.[421] Eligible differential wage payments are so much of the differential wage payments paid to a qualified employee as does not exceed $20,000. A qualified employee is an individual who has been an employee of the employer for the 91-day period immediately preceding the period for which any differential wage payment is made.

No deduction may be taken for that portion of compensation that is equal to the credit.[422] In addition, the amount of any other income tax credit otherwise allowable with respect to compensation paid to an employee must be reduced by the differential wage payment credit allowed with respect to the employee. The credit is not allowable against a taxpayer's alternative minimum tax liability. Certain rules applicable to the work opportunity tax credit in the case of tax-exempt organizations, estates and trusts, regulated investment companies, real estate investment trusts and certain cooperatives apply also to the differential wage payment credit.[423]

The credit is available with respect to amounts paid after June 17, 2008,[424] and before January 1, 2015.

Explanation of Provision

The provision reinstates the differential wage payment credit and makes it permanent. The provision also modifies the credit by making it available to an employer of any size, rather than only to eligible small business employers.

Effective Date

The provision reinstating the credit and making it permanent applies to payments made after December 31, 2014.

The provision making the credit available to employers of any size applies to taxable years beginning after December 31, 2015.

14. Extension of 15-year straight-line cost recovery for qualified leasehold improvements, qualified restaurant buildings and improvements, and qualified retail improvements (sec. 123 of the Act and sec. 168 of the Code)

Present Law

In general

A taxpayer generally must capitalize the cost of property used in a trade or business and recover such cost over time through annual deductions for depreciation or amortization. Tangible property generally is depreciated under the modified accelerated cost recovery system ("MACRS"), which determines depreciation by applying specific recovery periods, placed-in-service conventions, and depreciation methods to the cost of various types of depreciable property.[425] The cost of nonresidential real property is recovered using the

---

[421] Sec. 3401(h)(2).
[422] Sec. 280C(a).
[423] Sec. 52(c), (d), (e).
[424] The credit was originally provided by the Heroes Earnings Assistance and Relief Tax Act of 2008 ("HEART Act"), Pub. L. No. 110–245, effective for amounts paid after June 17, 2008, the date of enactment of the HEART Act.
[425] Sec. 168.

straight-line method of depreciation and a recovery period of 39 years. Nonresidential real property is subject to the mid-month placed-in-service convention. Under the mid-month convention, the depreciation allowance for the first year in which property is placed in service is based on the number of months the property was in service, and property placed in service at any time during a month is treated as having been placed in service in the middle of the month.

Depreciation of leasehold improvements

Generally, depreciation allowances for improvements made on leased property are determined under MACRS, even if the MACRS recovery period assigned to the property is longer than the term of the lease. This rule applies regardless of whether the lessor or the lessee places the leasehold improvements in service. If a leasehold improvement constitutes an addition or improvement to nonresidential real property already placed in service, the improvement generally is depreciated using the straight-line method over a 39-year recovery period, beginning in the month the addition or improvement was placed in service. However, exceptions exist for certain qualified leasehold improvements, qualified restaurant property, and qualified retail improvement property.

Qualified leasehold improvement property

Section 168(e)(3)(E)(iv) provides a statutory 15-year recovery period for qualified leasehold improvement property placed in service before January 1, 2015. Qualified leasehold improvement property is any improvement to an interior portion of a building that is nonresidential real property, provided certain requirements are met.[426] The improvement must be made under or pursuant to a lease either by the lessee (or sublessee), or by the lessor, of that portion of the building to be occupied exclusively by the lessee (or sublessee). The improvement must be placed in service more than three years after the date the building was first placed in service. Qualified leasehold improvement property does not include any improvement for which the expenditure is attributable to the enlargement of the building, any elevator or escalator, any structural component benefiting a common area, or the internal structural framework of the building.[427] If a lessor makes an improvement that qualifies as qualified leasehold improvement property, such improvement does not qualify as qualified leasehold improvement property to any subsequent owner of such improvement.[428] An exception to the rule applies in the case of death and certain transfers of property that qualify for non-recognition treatment.[429]

Qualified leasehold improvement property is generally recovered using the straight-line method and a half-year convention.[430]

---

[426] Sec. 168(e)(6).
[427] Sec. 168(e)(6) and (k)(3).
[428] Sec. 168(e)(6)(A).
[429] Sec. 168(e)(6)(B).
[430] Sec. 168(b)(3)(G) and (d). An additional first-year depreciation deduction ("bonus depreciation") is allowed equal to 50 percent of the adjusted basis of qualified property acquired and placed in service before January 1, 2015 (January 1, 2016 for certain longer-lived and transportation property). See sec. 168(k). Qualified property eligible for bonus depreciation includes qualified leasehold improvement property. Sec. 168(k)(2)(A)(i)(IV).

Qualified leasehold improvement property placed in service after December 31, 2014 is subject to the general rules described above.

Qualified restaurant property

Section 168(e)(3)(E)(v) provides a statutory 15-year recovery period for qualified restaurant property placed in service before January 1, 2015. Qualified restaurant property is any section 1250 property that is a building or an improvement to a building, if more than 50 percent of the building's square footage is devoted to the preparation of, and seating for on-premises consumption of, prepared meals.[431] Qualified restaurant property is recovered using the straight-line method and a half-year convention.[432] Additionally, qualified restaurant property is not eligible for bonus depreciation unless it also satisfies the definition of qualified leasehold improvement property.[433] Qualified restaurant property placed in service after December 31, 2014 is subject to the general rules described above.

Qualified retail improvement property

Section 168(e)(3)(E)(ix) provides a statutory 15-year recovery period for qualified retail improvement property placed in service before January 1, 2015. Qualified retail improvement property is any improvement to an interior portion of a building which is nonresidential real property if such portion is open to the general public[434] and is used in the retail trade or business of selling tangible personal property to the general public, and such improvement is placed in service more than three years after the date the building was first placed in service.[435] Qualified retail improvement property does not include any improvement for which the expenditure is attributable to the enlargement of the building, any elevator or escalator, any structural component benefiting a common area, or the internal structural framework of the building.[436] In the case of an improvement made by the owner of such improvement, the improvement is a qualified retail improvement only so long as the improvement is held by such owner.[437]

Retail establishments that qualify for the 15-year recovery period include those primarily engaged in the sale of goods. Examples of these retail establishments include, but are not limited to, grocery stores, clothing stores, hardware stores, and convenience stores. Establishments primarily engaged in providing services, such as professional services, financial services, personal services, health services, and entertainment, do not qualify. Generally, it is intended that businesses defined as a store retailer under the current North American Industry Classification System (industry sub-sectors 441

---

[431] Sec. 168(e)(7).

[432] Sec. 168(b)(3)(H) and (d).

[433] Sec. 168(e)(7)(B).

[434] Improvements to portions of a building not open to the general public (e.g., stock room in back of retail space) do not qualify under the provision.

[435] Sec. 168(e)(8).

[436] Sec. 168(e)(8)(C).

[437] Sec. 168(e)(8)(B). Rules similar to section 168(e)(6)(B) apply in the case of death and certain transfers of property that qualify for non-recognition treatment.

through 453) qualify while those in other industry classes do not qualify.[438]

Qualified retail improvement property is recovered using the straight-line method and a half-year convention.[439] Additionally, qualified retail improvement property is not eligible for bonus depreciation unless it also satisfies the definition of qualified leasehold improvement property.[440] Qualified retail improvement property placed in service after December 31, 2014 is subject to the general rules described above.

Explanation of Provision

The provision makes permanent the present-law provisions for qualified leasehold improvement property, qualified restaurant property, and qualified retail improvement property.

Effective Date

The provision applies to property placed in service after December 31, 2014.

15. Extension and modification of increased expensing limitations and treatment of certain real property as section 179 property (sec. 124 of the Act and sec. 179 of the Code)

Present Law

A taxpayer may elect under section 179 to deduct (or "expense") the cost of qualifying property, rather than to recover such costs through depreciation deductions, subject to limitation. For taxable years beginning in 2014, the maximum amount a taxpayer may expense is $500,000 of the cost of qualifying property placed in service for the taxable year.[441] The $500,000 amount is reduced (but not below zero) by the amount by which the cost of qualifying property placed in service during the taxable year exceeds $2,000,000.[442] The $500,000 and $2,000,000 amounts are not indexed for inflation. In general, qualifying property is defined as depreciable tangible personal property that is purchased for use in the active conduct of a trade or business.[443] Qualifying property excludes investments in air conditioning and heating units.[444] For taxable years beginning before 2015, qualifying property also in-

---

[438] Joint Committee on Taxation, *General Explanation of Tax Legislation Enacted in the 110th Congress* (JCS–1–09), March 2009, p. 402.

[439] Sec. 168(b)(3)(I) and (d).

[440] Sec. 168(e)(8)(D).

[441] For the years 2003 through 2006, the relevant dollar amount is $100,000 (indexed for inflation); in 2007, the dollar limitation is $125,000; for the 2008 and 2009 years, the relevant dollar amount is $250,000; and for the years 2010 through 2013, the relevant dollar limitation is $500,000. Sec. 179(b)(1).

[442] For the years 2003 through 2006, the relevant dollar amount is $400,000 (indexed for inflation); in 2007, the dollar limitation is $500,000; for the 2008 and 2009 years, the relevant dollar amount is $800,000; and for the years 2010 through 2013, the relevant dollar limitation is $2,000,000. Sec. 179(b)(2).

[443] Passenger automobiles subject to the section 280F limitation are eligible for section 179 expensing only to the extent of the dollar limitations in section 280F. For sport utility vehicles above the 6,000 pound weight rating, which are not subject to the limitation under section 280F, the maximum cost that may be expensed for any taxable year under section 179 is $25,000. Sec. 179(b)(5).

[444] Sec. 179(d)(1) flush language.

cludes off-the-shelf computer software and qualified real property (*i.e.*, qualified leasehold improvement property, qualified restaurant property, and qualified retail improvement property).[445] Of the $500,000 expense amount available under section 179, the maximum amount available with respect to qualified real property is $250,000 for each taxable year.[446]

For taxable years beginning in 2015 and thereafter, a taxpayer may elect to deduct up to $25,000 of the cost of qualifying property placed in service for the taxable year, subject to limitation. The $25,000 amount is reduced (but not below zero) by the amount by which the cost of qualifying property placed in service during the taxable year exceeds $200,000. The $25,000 and $200,000 amounts are not indexed for inflation. In general, qualifying property is defined as depreciable tangible personal property (not including off-the-shelf computer software, qualified real property, or air conditioning and heating units) that is purchased for use in the active conduct of a trade or business.

The amount eligible to be expensed for a taxable year may not exceed the taxable income for such taxable year that is derived from the active conduct of a trade or business (determined without regard to this provision).[447] Any amount that is not allowed as a deduction because of the taxable income limitation may be carried forward to succeeding taxable years (subject to limitations). However, amounts attributable to qualified real property that are disallowed under the trade or business income limitation may only be carried over to taxable years in which the definition of eligible section 179 property includes qualified real property.[448] Thus, if a taxpayer's section 179 deduction for 2013 with respect to qualified real property is limited by the taxpayer's active trade or business income, such disallowed amount may be carried over to 2014. Any such carryover amounts that are not used in 2014 are treated as property placed in service in 2014 for purposes of computing depreciation. That is, the unused carryover amount from 2013 is considered placed in service on the first day of the 2014 taxable year.[449]

No general business credit under section 38 is allowed with respect to any amount for which a deduction is allowed under section 179.[450] If a corporation makes an election under section 179 to deduct expenditures, the full amount of the deduction does not reduce earnings and profits. Rather, the expenditures that are deducted

---

[445] Sec. 179(d)(1)(A)(ii) and (f).
[446] Sec. 179(f)(3).
[447] Sec. 179(b)(3).
[448] Section 179(f)(4) details the special rules that apply to disallowed amounts with respect to qualified real property.
[449] For example, assume that during 2013, a company's only asset purchases are section 179-eligible equipment costing $100,000 and qualifying leasehold improvements costing $200,000. Assume the company has no other asset purchases during 2013, and has a taxable income limitation of $150,000. The maximum section 179 deduction the company can claim for 2013 is $150,000, which is allocated pro rata between the properties, such that the carryover to 2014 is allocated $100,000 to the qualified leasehold improvements and $50,000 to the equipment.
Assume further that in 2014, the company had no asset purchases and had no taxable income. The $100,000 carryover from 2013 attributable to qualified leasehold improvements is treated as placed in service as of the first day of the company's 2014 taxable year under section 179(f)(4)(C). The $50,000 carryover allocated to equipment is carried over to 2014 under section 179(b)(3)(B).
[450] Sec. 179(d)(9).

reduce corporate earnings and profits ratably over a five-year period.[451]

An expensing election is made under rules prescribed by the Secretary.[452] In general, any election or specification made with respect to any property may not be revoked except with the consent of the Commissioner. However, an election or specification under section 179 may be revoked by the taxpayer without consent of the Commissioner for taxable years beginning after 2002 and before 2015.[453]

Explanation of Provision

The provision provides that the maximum amount a taxpayer may expense, for taxable years beginning after 2014, is $500,000 of the cost of qualifying property placed in service for the taxable year. The $500,000 amount is reduced (but not below zero) by the amount by which the cost of qualifying property placed in service during the taxable year exceeds $2,000,000. The $500,000 and $2,000,000 amounts are indexed for inflation for taxable years beginning after 2015.

In addition, the provision makes permanent the treatment of off-the-shelf computer software as qualifying property. The provision also makes permanent the treatment of qualified real property as eligible section 179 property. For taxable years beginning in 2015, the provision extends the limitation on carryovers and the maximum amount available with respect to qualified real property of $250,000 for such taxable year. The provision removes the limitation related to the amount of section 179 property that may be attributable to qualified real property for taxable years beginning after 2015. Further, for taxable years beginning after 2015, the provision strikes the flush language in section 179(d)(1) that excludes air conditioning and heating units from the definition of qualifying property.

The provision also makes permanent the permission granted to a taxpayer to revoke without the consent of the Commissioner any election, and any specification contained therein, made under section 179.

Effective Date

The provision generally applies to taxable years beginning after December 31, 2014.

The modifications apply to taxable years beginning after December 31, 2015.

16. Extension of treatment of certain dividends of regulated investment companies (sec. 125 of the Act and sec. 871(k) of the Code)

Present Law

A regulated investment company ("RIC") is an entity that meets certain requirements (including a requirement that its income gen-

---

[451] Sec. 312(k)(3)(B).
[452] Sec. 179(c)(1).
[453] Sec. 179(c)(2).

erally be derived from passive investments such as dividends and interest and a requirement that it distribute at least 90 percent of its income) and that elects to be taxed under a special tax regime. Unlike an ordinary corporation, an entity that is taxed as a RIC can deduct amounts paid to its shareholders as dividends. In this manner, tax on RIC income is generally not paid by the RIC but rather by its shareholders. Income of a RIC distributed to shareholders as dividends is generally treated as an ordinary income dividend by those shareholders, unless other special rules apply. Dividends received by foreign persons from a RIC are generally subject to gross-basis tax under sections 871(a) and 881(a), and the RIC payor of such dividends is obligated to withhold such tax under sections 1441 and 1442.

Under a temporary provision of prior law, a RIC that earned certain interest income that generally would not be subject to U.S. tax if earned by a foreign person directly could, to the extent of such net interest income, designate dividends it paid as derived from such interest income for purposes of the treatment of a foreign RIC shareholder. The consequence of that designation was that such dividends were not subject to gross-basis U.S. tax. Also, subject to certain requirements, the RIC was exempt from withholding the gross-basis tax on such dividends. Similar rules applied with respect to the designation of certain short-term capital gain dividends. However, these provisions relating to dividends with respect to interest income and short-term capital gain of the RIC have expired, and therefore do not apply to dividends with respect to any taxable year of a RIC beginning after December 31, 2014.[454]

Explanation of Provision

The provision reinstates and makes permanent the rules exempting from gross-basis tax and from withholding of such tax the interest-related dividends paid by and short-term capital gain dividends paid by a RIC to a foreign person.

Effective Date

The provision applies to dividends paid with respect to any taxable year of a RIC beginning after December 31, 2014.

17. Extension of exclusion of 100 percent of gain on certain small business stock (sec. 126 of the Act and sec. 1202 of the Code)

Present Law

In general

A taxpayer other than a corporation may exclude 50 percent (60 percent for certain empowerment zone businesses) of the gain from the sale of certain small business stock acquired at original issue and held for at least five years.[455] The amount of gain eligible for the exclusion by an individual with respect to the stock of any corporation is the greater of (1) ten times the taxpayer's basis in the

---

[454] Secs. 871(k), 881(e), 1441(a), 1441(c)(12), and 1442(a).
[455] Sec. 1202.

stock or (2) $10 million (reduced by the amount of gain eligible for exclusion in prior years). To qualify as a small business, when the stock is issued, the aggregate gross assets (*i.e.,* cash plus aggregate adjusted basis of other property) held by the corporation may not exceed $50 million. The corporation also must meet certain active trade or business requirements.

The portion of the gain includible in taxable income is taxed at a maximum rate of 28 percent under the regular tax rates applicable to the net capital gain of individuals.[456] Seven percent of the excluded gain is an alternative minimum tax preference.[457]

Special rules for stock acquired after February 17, 2009, and before January 1, 2015

For qualified small business stock acquired after February 17, 2009, and before September 28, 2010, the percent of gain which may be excluded is increased to 75 percent.

For qualified small business stock acquired after September 27, 2010, and before January 1, 2015, the percent of gain which may be excluded is increased to 100 percent and the minimum tax preference does not apply.

Explanation of Provision

The provision makes the post-September 27, 2010, 100-percent exclusion and the exception from minimum tax preference treatment permanent.

Effective Date

The provision applies to stock acquired after December 31, 2014.

18. Extension of reduction in S corporation recognition period for built-in gains tax (sec. 127 of the Act and sec. 1374 of the Code)

Present Law

In general

A "small business corporation" (as defined in section 1361(b)) may elect to be treated as an S corporation. Unlike C corporations, S corporations generally pay no corporate-level tax. Instead, items of income and loss of an S corporation pass through to its shareholders. Each shareholder takes into account separately its share of these items on its own income tax return.[458]

Under section 1374, a corporate level built-in gains tax, at the highest marginal rate applicable to corporations (currently 35 percent), is imposed on an S corporation's net recognized built-in gain[459] that arose prior to the conversion of the C corporation to an S corporation and is recognized by the S corporation during the recognition period, *i.e.,* the 10-year period beginning with the first

---

[456] Sec. 1(h).
[457] Sec. 57(a)(7).
[458] Sec. 1366.
[459] Certain built-in income items are treated as recognized built-in gain for this purpose. Sec. 1374(d)(5).

day of the first taxable year for which the S election is in effect.[460] If the taxable income of the S corporation is less than the amount of net recognized built-in gain in the year such built-in gain is recognized (*e.g.*, because of post-conversion losses), no tax under section 1374 is imposed on the excess of such built-in gain over taxable income for that year. However, the untaxed excess of net recognized built-in gain over taxable income for that year is treated as recognized built-in gain in the succeeding taxable year.[461] Treasury regulations provide that if a corporation sells an asset before or during the recognition period and reports the income from the sale using the installment method under section 453 during or after the recognition period, that income is subject to tax under section 1374.[462]

The built-in gains tax also applies to net recognized built-in gain attributable to any asset received by an S corporation from a C corporation in a transaction in which the S corporation's basis in the asset is determined (in whole or in part) by reference to the basis of such asset (or other property) in the hands of the C corporation.[463] In the case of such a transaction, the recognition period for any asset transferred by the C corporation starts on the date the asset was acquired by the S corporation in lieu of the beginning of the first taxable year for which the corporation was an S corporation.[464]

The amount of the built-in gains tax under section 1374 is treated as a loss by each of the S corporation shareholders in computing its own income tax. The character of the loss is determined by allocating the loss proportionately among the gains giving rise to the tax.[465]

Special rules for 2009, 2010, and 2011

For any taxable year beginning in 2009 and 2010, no tax was imposed on the net recognized built-in gain of an S corporation under section 1374 if the seventh taxable year in the corporation's recognition period preceded such taxable year.[466] Thus, with respect to gain that arose prior to the conversion of a C corporation to an S corporation, no tax was imposed under section 1374 if the seventh taxable year that the S corporation election was in effect preceded the taxable year beginning in 2009 or 2010.

For any taxable year beginning in 2011, no tax was imposed on the net recognized built-in gain of an S corporation under section 1374 if the fifth year in the corporation's recognition period preceded such taxable year.[467] Thus, with respect to gain that arose prior to the conversion of a C corporation to an S corporation, no tax was imposed under section 1374 if the fifth taxable year that the S corporation election was in effect preceded the taxable year beginning in 2011.

---

[460] Sec. 1374(d)(7)(A).
[461] Sec. 1374(d)(2)(B).
[462] Treas. Reg. sec. 1.1374–4(h).
[463] Sec. 1374(d)(8)(A).
[464] Sec. 1374(d)(8)(B).
[465] Sec. 1366(f)(2). Shareholders continue to take into account all items of gain and loss of the S corporation under section 1366.
[466] Sec. 1374(d)(7)(B)(i).
[467] Sec. 1374(d)(7)(B)(ii).

Special rules for 2012, 2013, and 2014

For taxable years beginning in 2012, 2013, and 2014, the term "recognition period" in section 1374, for purposes of determining the net recognized built-in gain, was applied by substituting a five-year period for the otherwise applicable 10-year period.[468] Thus, for such taxable years, the recognition period was the five-year period beginning with the first day of the first taxable year for which the corporation was an S corporation (or beginning with the date of acquisition of assets if the rules applicable to assets acquired from a C corporation applied). If an S corporation with assets subject to section 1374 disposed of such assets in a taxable year beginning in 2012, 2013, or 2014 and the disposition occurred more than five years after the first day of the relevant recognition period, gain or loss on the disposition was not be taken into account in determining the net recognized built-in gain.

The rule requiring the excess of net recognized built-in gain over taxable income for a taxable year to be carried over and treated as recognized built-in gain in the succeeding taxable year applied only to gain recognized within the recognition period.

If an S corporation subject to section 1374 sold a built-in gain asset and reported the income from the sale using the installment method under section 453, the treatment of all payments received was governed by the provisions of section 1374(d)(7) applicable to the taxable year in which the sale was made.[469]

Application to regulated investment trusts and real estate investment trusts

Under Treasury regulations issued under section 337(d), a regulated investment company ("RIC") or a real estate investment trust ("REIT") that was formerly a C corporation (or that acquired assets from a C corporation) generally is subject to the rules of section 1374 as if the RIC or REIT were an S corporation, unless the relevant C corporation elects "deemed sale" treatment.[470] The Treasury regulations include an express reference to the 10-year recognition period in section 1374.[471]

Explanation of Provision

The provision makes the rules applicable to taxable years beginning in 2012, 2013, and 2014 permanent. Under current Treasury regulations, these rules, including the five-year recognition period, also would apply to REITs and RICs that do not elect "deemed sale" treatment.

Effective Date

The provision applies to taxable years beginning after December 31, 2014.

---

[468] Sec. 1374(d)(7)(C).
[469] Sec. 1374(d)(7)(E).
[470] Treas. Reg. sec. 1.337(d)–7(b)(1)(i) and (c)(1).
[471] Treas. Reg. sec. 1.337(d)–7(b)(1)(ii).

19. Extension of subpart F exception for active financing income (sec. 128 of the Act and secs. 953 and 954 of the Code)

Present Law

Under the subpart F rules,[472] 10-percent-or-greater U.S. shareholders of a controlled foreign corporation ("CFC") are subject to U.S. tax currently on certain income earned by the CFC, whether or not such income is distributed to the shareholders. The income subject to current inclusion under the subpart F rules includes, among other things, insurance income and foreign base company income. Foreign base company income includes, among other things, foreign personal holding company income and foreign base company services income (*i.e.,* income derived from services performed for or on behalf of a related person outside the country in which the CFC is organized).

Foreign personal holding company income generally consists of the following: (1) dividends, interest, royalties, rents, and annuities; (2) net gains from the sale or exchange of (a) property that gives rise to the preceding types of income, (b) property that does not give rise to income, and (c) interests in trusts, partnerships, and real estate mortgage investment conduits ("REMICs"); (3) net gains from commodities transactions; (4) net gains from certain foreign currency transactions; (5) income that is equivalent to interest; (6) income from notional principal contracts; (7) payments in lieu of dividends; and (8) amounts received under personal service contracts.

Insurance income subject to current inclusion under the subpart F rules includes any income of a CFC attributable to the issuing or reinsuring of any insurance or annuity contract in connection with risks located in a country other than the CFC's country of organization. Subpart F insurance income also includes income attributable to an insurance contract in connection with risks located within the CFC's country of organization, as the result of an arrangement under which another corporation receives a substantially equal amount of consideration for insurance of other country risks. Investment income of a CFC that is allocable to any insurance or annuity contract related to risks located outside the CFC's country of organization is taxable as subpart F insurance income.[473]

Temporary exceptions from foreign personal holding company income, foreign base company services income, and insurance income apply for subpart F purposes for certain income that is derived in the active conduct of a banking, financing, or similar business, as a securities dealer, or in the conduct of an insurance business (so-called "active financing income").

With respect to income derived in the active conduct of a banking, financing, or similar business, a CFC is required to be predominantly engaged in such business and to conduct substantial activity with respect to such business to qualify for the active financing exceptions. In addition, certain nexus requirements apply,

---

[472] Secs. 951–964.
[473] Prop. Treas. Reg. sec. 1.953–1(a).

which provide that income derived by a CFC or a qualified business unit ("QBU") of a CFC from transactions with customers is eligible for the exceptions if, among other things, substantially all of the activities in connection with such transactions are conducted directly by the CFC or QBU in its home country, and such income is treated as earned by the CFC or QBU in its home country for purposes of such country's tax laws. Moreover, the exceptions apply to income derived from certain cross border transactions, provided that certain requirements are met. Additional exceptions from foreign personal holding company income apply for certain income derived by a securities dealer within the meaning of section 475 and for gain from the sale of active financing assets.

In the case of a securities dealer, the temporary exception from foreign personal holding company income applies to certain income. The income covered by the exception is any interest or dividend (or certain equivalent amounts) from any transaction, including a hedging transaction or a transaction consisting of a deposit of collateral or margin, entered into in the ordinary course of the dealer's trade or business as a dealer in securities within the meaning of section 475. In the case of a QBU of the dealer, the income is required to be attributable to activities of the QBU in the country of incorporation, or to a QBU in the country in which the QBU both maintains its principal office and conducts substantial business activity. A coordination rule provides that this exception generally takes precedence over the exception for income of a banking, financing or similar business, in the case of a securities dealer.

In the case of insurance, a temporary exception from foreign personal holding company income applies for certain income of a qualifying insurance company with respect to risks located within the CFC's country of creation or organization. In the case of insurance, temporary exceptions from insurance income and from foreign personal holding company income also apply for certain income of a qualifying branch of a qualifying insurance company with respect to risks located within the home country of the branch, provided certain requirements are met under each of the exceptions. Further, additional temporary exceptions from insurance income and from foreign personal holding company income apply for certain income of certain CFCs or branches with respect to risks located in a country other than the United States, provided that the requirements for these exceptions are met. In the case of a life insurance or annuity contract, reserves for such contracts are determined under rules specific to the temporary exceptions.

Present law also permits a taxpayer in certain circumstances, subject to approval by the IRS through the ruling process, or as provided in published guidance, to establish that the reserve of a life insurance company for life insurance and annuity contracts is the amount taken into account in determining the foreign statement reserve for the contract (reduced by catastrophe, equalization, or deficiency reserve or any similar reserve). IRS approval or published guidance is to be based on whether the method, the interest rate, the mortality and morbidity assumptions, and any other factors taken into account in determining foreign statement reserves (taken together or separately) provide an appropriate means of measuring income for Federal income tax purposes.

The temporary exceptions apply for taxable years of foreign corporations beginning after December 31, 1998 and before January 1, 2015, and for taxable years of U.S. shareholders with or within which such taxable years of such foreign corporations end.

Explanation of Provision

The provision makes permanent the temporary exceptions from subpart F foreign personal holding company income, foreign base company services income, and insurance income for certain income that is derived in the active conduct of a banking, financing, or similar business, as a securities dealer, or in the conduct of an insurance business.

Effective Date

The provision applies to taxable years of foreign corporations beginning after December 31, 2014, and to taxable years of U.S. shareholders with or within which such taxable years of such foreign corporations end.

Part 4—Incentives for Real Estate Investment

20. Extension of temporary minimum low-income housing tax credit rate for non-Federally subsidized buildings (sec. 131 of the Act and sec. 42 of the Code)

Present Law

In general

The low-income housing credit may be claimed over a 10-year credit period after each low-income building is placed-in-service. The amount of the credit for any taxable year in the credit period is the applicable percentage of the qualified basis of each qualified low-income building.

Present value credit

The calculation of the applicable percentage is designed to produce a credit equal to: (1) 70 percent of the present value of the building's qualified basis in the case of newly constructed or substantially rehabilitated housing that is not Federally subsidized (the "70-percent credit"); or (2) 30 percent of the present value of the building's qualified basis in the case of newly constructed or substantially rehabilitated housing that is Federally subsidized and existing housing that is substantially rehabilitated (the "30-percent credit"). Where existing housing is substantially rehabilitated, the existing housing is eligible for the 30-percent credit and the qualified rehabilitation expenses (if not Federally subsidized) are eligible for the 70-percent credit.

Calculation of the applicable percentage

In general

The credit percentage for a low-income building is set for the earlier of: (1) the month the building is placed in service; or (2) at the election of the taxpayer, (a) the month the taxpayer and the housing credit agency enter into a binding agreement with respect to such building for a credit allocation, or (b) in the case of a tax-exempt bond-financed project for which no credit allocation is required, the month in which the tax-exempt bonds are issued.

These credit percentages (used for the 70-percent credit and 30-percent credit) are adjusted monthly by the IRS on a discounted after-tax basis (assuming a 28-percent tax rate) based on the average of the Applicable Federal Rates for mid-term and long-term obligations for the month the building is placed in service. The discounting formula assumes that each credit is received on the last day of each year and that the present value is computed on the last day of the first year. In a project consisting of two or more buildings placed in service in different months, a separate credit percentage may apply to each building.

Special rule

Under this rule the applicable percentage is set at a minimum of 9 percent for newly constructed non-Federally subsidized buildings placed in service after July 30, 2008, and before January 1, 2015.

Explanation of Provision

The provision makes permanent the minimum applicable percentage of 9 percent for newly constructed non-Federally subsidized buildings.

Effective Date

The provision is effective on January 1, 2015.

21. Extension of military housing allowance exclusion for determining whether a tenant in certain counties is low-income (sec. 132 of the Act and secs. 42 and 142 of the Code)

Present Law

In general

To be eligible for the low-income housing credit, a qualified low-income building must be part of a qualified low-income housing project. In general, a qualified low-income housing project is defined as a project that satisfies one of two tests at the election of the taxpayer. The first test is met if 20 percent or more of the residential units in the project are both rent-restricted, and occupied by individuals whose income is 50 percent or less of area median gross income (the "20–50 test"). The second test is met if 40 percent or more of the residential units in such project are both rent-restricted, and occupied by individuals whose income is 60 percent or less of area median gross income (the "40–60 test"). These income figures are adjusted for family size.

Rule for income determinations before July 30, 2008 and on or after January 1, 2015

The recipients of the military basic housing allowance must include these amounts for purposes of low-income credit eligibility income test, as described above.

Special rule for income determination before January 1, 2015

Under the provision the basic housing allowance (*i.e.*, payments under 37 U.S.C. sec. 403) is not included in income for the low-income credit income eligibility rules with respect to qualified buildings. A qualified building is defined as any building located in:

1. any county which contains a qualified military installation to which the number of members of the Armed Forces assigned to units based out of such qualified military installation has increased by 20 percent or more as of June 1, 2008, over the personnel level on December 31, 2005; and

2. any counties adjacent to a county described in (1), above.

For these purposes, a qualified military installation is any military installation or facility with at least 1000 members of the Armed Forces assigned to it.[474]

The provision applies to income determinations: (1) made after July 30, 2008, and before January 1, 2015, in the case of qualified buildings which received credit allocations on or before July 30, 2008, or qualified buildings placed in service on or before July 30, 2008, to the extent a credit allocation was not required with respect to such building by reason of 42(h)(4) (*i.e.*, such qualified building was at least 50 percent tax-exempt bond financed with bonds subject to the private activity bond volume cap) but only with respect to bonds issued before July 30, 2008; and (2) made after July 30, 2008, in the case of qualified buildings which received credit allocations after July 30, 2008 and before January 1, 2015, or qualified buildings placed in service after July 30, 2008, and before January 1, 2015, to the extent a credit allocation was not required with respect to such qualified building by reason of 42(h)(4) (*i.e.*, such qualified building was at least 50 percent tax-exempt bond financed with bonds subject to the private activity bond volume cap) but only with respect to bonds issued after July 30, 2008, and before January 1, 2015.

Explanation of Provision

The provision makes permanent the special rule that the military basic housing allowance is not included in income for purposes of the low-income housing credit income eligibility rules for qualified buildings.

Effective Date

The provision is effective as if included in the enactment of section 3005 of the Housing Assistance Tax Act of 2008.

---

[474] For a list of qualified military installations, see Notice 2008–79, 2008–40 I.R.B. 726, October 6, 2008, available at https://www.irs.gov/irb/2008-40_IRB/ar10.htm.

22. Extension of RIC qualified investment entity treatment under FIRPTA (sec. 133 of the Act and secs. 897 and 1445 of the Code)

Present Law

Special U.S. tax rules apply to capital gains of foreign persons that are attributable to dispositions of interests in U.S. real property. In general, although a foreign person (a foreign corporation or a nonresident alien individual) is not generally taxed on U.S. source capital gains unless certain personal presence or active business requirements are met, a foreign person who sells a U.S. real property interest ("USRPI") is subject to tax at the same rates as a U.S. person, under the Foreign Investment in Real Property Tax Act ("FIRPTA") provisions codified in section 897 of the Code. Withholding tax is also imposed under section 1445.

A USRPI includes stock or a beneficial interest in any domestic corporation unless such corporation has not been a U.S. real property holding corporation (as defined) during the testing period. In general, if any class of stock of a corporation is regularly traded on an established securities market, stock of such class shall be treated as a USRPI only in the case of a person who, at some time during the testing period, held more than 5 percent of such class of stock.[475] A USRPI also does not include an interest in a domestically controlled "qualified investment entity." A distribution from a "qualified investment entity" that is attributable to the sale of a USRPI is subject to tax under FIRPTA, however, unless the distribution is with respect to an interest that is regularly traded on an established securities market located in the United States and the recipient foreign corporation or nonresident alien individual did not hold more than five percent[476] of that class of stock or beneficial interest within the one-year period ending on the date of distribution.[477] Special rules apply to situations involving tiers of qualified investment entities.

The term "qualified investment entity" includes a real estate investment trust ("REIT") and also includes a regulated investment company ("RIC") that meets certain requirements, although the inclusion of a RIC in that definition does not apply for certain purposes after December 31, 2014.[478]

Explanation of Provision

The provision makes permanent the inclusion of a RIC within the definition of a "qualified investment entity" under section 897 for those situations in which that inclusion would otherwise have expired after December 31, 2014.

---

[475] Sec. 897(c)(3). See section 322 of the Act, described below in item 11 of Title III.B., which, in the case of REIT stock only, increases from five percent to 10 percent the maximum stock ownership a shareholder may have held, during the testing period, of a class of stock that is publicly traded, to avoid having that stock be treated as a USRPI on disposition.

[476] Sec. 897(h)(1). See section 322 of the Act, described below in item 11 of Title III.B., which increases from five percent to 10 percent the percentage ownership threshold for publicly-traded REIT stock.

[477] Sections 857(b)(3)(F), 852(b)(3)(E), and 871(k)(2)(E) require dividend treatment, rather than capital gain treatment, for certain distributions to which FIRPTA does not apply by reason of this exception. See also section 881(e)(2).

[478] Sec. 897(h).

Effective Date

The provision is generally effective on January 1, 2015.

The provision does not apply with respect to the withholding requirement under section 1445 for any payment made before the date of enactment (December 18, 2015), but a RIC that withheld and remitted tax under section 1445 on distributions made after December 31, 2014, and before the date of enactment is not liable to the distributee with respect to such withheld and remitted amounts.

B. Extensions Through 2019

1. Extension of new markets tax credit (sec. 141 of the Act and sec. 45D of the Code)

Present Law

Section 45D provides a new markets tax credit for qualified equity investments made to acquire stock in a corporation, or a capital interest in a partnership, that is a qualified community development entity ("CDE").[479] The amount of the credit allowable to the investor (either the original purchaser or a subsequent holder) is (1) a five-percent credit for the year in which the equity interest is purchased from the CDE and for each of the following two years, and (2) a six-percent credit for each of the following four years.[480] The credit is determined by applying the applicable percentage (five or six percent) to the amount paid to the CDE for the investment at its original issue, and is available to the taxpayer who holds the qualified equity investment on the date of the initial investment or on the respective anniversary date that occurs during the taxable year.[481] The credit is recaptured if at any time during the seven-year period that begins on the date of the original issue of the investment the entity (1) ceases to be a qualified CDE, (2) the proceeds of the investment cease to be used as required, or (3) the equity investment is redeemed.[482]

A qualified CDE is any domestic corporation or partnership: (1) whose primary mission is serving or providing investment capital for low-income communities or low-income persons; (2) that maintains accountability to residents of low-income communities by their representation on any governing board of or any advisory board to the CDE; and (3) that is certified by the Secretary as being a qualified CDE.[483] A qualified equity investment means stock (other than nonqualified preferred stock) in a corporation or a capital interest in a partnership that is acquired at its original issue directly (or through an underwriter) from a CDE for cash, and includes an investment of a subsequent purchaser if such investment was a qualified equity investment in the hands of the prior holder.[484] Substantially all of the investment proceeds must be used by the CDE to make qualified low-income community in-

---

[479] Section 45D was enacted by section 121(a) of the Community Renewal Tax Relief Act of 2000, Pub. L. No. 106–554.
[480] Sec. 45D(a)(2).
[481] Sec. 45D(a)(3).
[482] Sec. 45D(g).
[483] Sec. 45D(c).
[484] Sec. 45D(b).

vestments and the investment must be designated as a qualified equity investment by the CDE. For this purpose, qualified low-income community investments include: (1) capital or equity investments in, or loans to, qualified active low-income community businesses; (2) certain financial counseling and other services to businesses and residents in low-income communities; (3) the purchase from another CDE of any loan made by such entity that is a qualified low-income community investment; or (4) an equity investment in, or loan to, another CDE.[485]

A "low-income community" is a population census tract with either (1) a poverty rate of at least 20 percent or (2) median family income which does not exceed 80 percent of the greater of metropolitan area median family income or statewide median family income (for a non-metropolitan census tract, does not exceed 80 percent of statewide median family income). In the case of a population census tract located within a high migration rural county, low-income is defined by reference to 85 percent (as opposed to 80 percent) of statewide median family income.[486] For this purpose, a high migration rural county is any county that, during the 20-year period ending with the year in which the most recent census was conducted, has a net out-migration of inhabitants from the county of at least 10 percent of the population of the county at the beginning of such period.

The Secretary is authorized to designate "targeted populations" as low-income communities for purposes of the new markets tax credit.[487] For this purpose, a "targeted population" is defined by reference to section 103(20) of the Riegle Community Development and Regulatory Improvement Act of 1994[488] (the "Act") to mean individuals, or an identifiable group of individuals, including an Indian tribe, who are low-income persons or otherwise lack adequate access to loans or equity investments. Section 103(17) of the Act provides that "low-income" means (1) for a targeted population within a metropolitan area, less than 80 percent of the area median family income; and (2) for a targeted population within a non-metropolitan area, less than the greater of—80 percent of the area median family income, or 80 percent of the statewide non-metropolitan area median family income.[489] A targeted population is not required to be within any census tract. In addition, a population census tract with a population of less than 2,000 is treated as a low-income community for purposes of the credit if such tract is within an empowerment zone, the designation of which is in effect under section 1391 of the Code, and is contiguous to one or more low-income communities.

A qualified active low-income community business is defined as a business that satisfies, with respect to a taxable year, the following requirements: (1) at least 50 percent of the total gross income of the business is derived from the active conduct of trade or business activities in any low-income community; (2) a substantial portion of the tangible property of the business is used in a low-

---
[485] Sec. 45D(d).
[486] Sec. 45D(e).
[487] Sec. 45D(e)(2).
[488] Pub. L. No. 103–325.
[489] Pub. L. No. 103–325.

income community; (3) a substantial portion of the services performed for the business by its employees is performed in a low-income community; and (4) less than five percent of the average of the aggregate unadjusted bases of the property of the business is attributable to certain financial property or to certain collectibles.[490]

The maximum annual amount of qualified equity investments was $3.5 million for calendar years 2010, 2011, 2012, 2013, and 2014. The new markets tax credit expired on December 31, 2014. No amount of unused allocation limitation may be carried to any calendar year after 2019.

Explanation of Provision

The provision extends the new markets tax credit for five years, through 2019, permitting up to $3.5 million in qualified equity investments for each of the 2015, 2016, 2017, 2018 and 2019 calendar years. The provision also extends for five years, through 2024, the carryover period for unused new markets tax credits.

Effective Date

The provision applies to calendar years beginning after December 31, 2014.

2. Extension and modification of work opportunity tax credit (sec. 142 of the Act and secs. 51 and 52 of the Code)

Present Law

In general

The work opportunity tax credit is available on an elective basis for employers hiring individuals from one or more of nine targeted groups. The amount of the credit available to an employer is determined by the amount of qualified wages paid by the employer. Generally, qualified wages consist of wages attributable to service rendered by a member of a targeted group during the one-year period beginning with the day the individual begins work for the employer (two years in the case of an individual in the long-term family assistance recipient category).

Targeted groups eligible for the credit

Generally, an employer is eligible for the credit only for qualified wages paid to members of a targeted group.

(1) Families receiving TANF

An eligible recipient is an individual certified by a designated local employment agency (*e.g.*, a State employment agency) as being a member of a family eligible to receive benefits under the Temporary Assistance for Needy Families Program ("TANF") for a period of at least nine months part of which is during the 18-month period ending on the hiring date. For these purposes, members of the family are defined to include only those individuals taken into account for purposes of determining eligibility for the TANF.

---

[490] Sec. 45D(d)(2).

(2) Qualified veteran

Prior to enactment of the "VOW to Hire Heroes Act of 2011" (the "VOW Act"),[491] there were two subcategories of qualified veterans to whom wages paid by an employer were eligible for the credit. Employers who hired veterans who were eligible to receive assistance under a supplemental nutritional assistance program were entitled to a maximum credit of 40 percent of $6,000 of qualified first-year wages paid to such individual.[492] Employers who hired veterans who were entitled to compensation for a service-connected disability were entitled to a maximum wage credit of 40 percent of $12,000 of qualified first-year wages paid to such individual.[493]

The VOW Act modified the work opportunity credit with respect to qualified veterans, by adding additional subcategories. There are now five subcategories of qualified veterans: (1) in the case of veterans who were eligible to receive assistance under a supplemental nutritional assistance program (for at least a three month period during the year prior to the hiring date) the employer is entitled to a maximum credit of 40 percent of $6,000 of qualified first-year wages; (2) in the case of a qualified veteran who is entitled to compensation for a service connected disability, who is hired within one year of discharge, the employer is entitled to a maximum credit of 40 percent of $12,000 of qualified first-year wages; (3) in the case of a qualified veteran who is entitled to compensation for a service connected disability, and who has been unemployed for an aggregate of at least six months during the one year period ending on the hiring date, the employer is entitled to a maximum credit of 40 percent of $24,000 of qualified first-year wages; (4) in the case of a qualified veteran unemployed for at least four weeks but less than six months (whether or not consecutive) during the one-year period ending on the date of hiring, the maximum credit equals 40 percent of $6,000 of qualified first-year wages; and (5) in the case of a qualified veteran unemployed for at least six months (whether or not consecutive) during the one-year period ending on the date of hiring, the maximum credit equals 40 percent of $14,000 of qualified first-year wages.

A veteran is an individual who has served on active duty (other than for training) in the Armed Forces for more than 180 days or who has been discharged or released from active duty in the Armed Forces for a service-connected disability. However, any individual who has served for a period of more than 90 days during which the individual was on active duty (other than for training) is not a qualified veteran if any of this active duty occurred during the 60-

---

[491] Pub. L. No. 112–56 (Nov. 21, 2011).

[492] For these purposes, a qualified veteran must be certified by the designated local agency as a member of a family receiving assistance under a supplemental nutrition assistance program under the Food and Nutrition Act of 2008 for a period of at least three months part of which is during the 12-month period ending on the hiring date. For these purposes, members of a family are defined to include only those individuals taken into account for purposes of determining eligibility for a supplemental nutrition assistance program under the Food and Nutrition Act of 2008.

[493] The qualified veteran must be certified as entitled to compensation for a service-connected disability and (1) have a hiring date which is not more than one year after having been discharged or released from active duty in the Armed Forces of the United States; or (2) have been unemployed for six months or more (whether or not consecutive) during the one-year period ending on the date of hiring. For these purposes, being entitled to compensation for a service-connected disability is defined with reference to section 101 of Title 38, U.S. Code, which means having a disability rating of 10 percent or higher for service connected injuries.

day period ending on the date the individual was hired by the employer. This latter rule is intended to prevent employers who hire current members of the armed services (or those departed from service within the last 60 days) from receiving the credit.

(3) Qualified ex-felon

A qualified ex-felon is an individual certified as: (1) having been convicted of a felony under any State or Federal law; and (2) having a hiring date within one year of release from prison or the date of conviction.

(4) Designated community resident

A designated community resident is an individual certified as being at least age 18 but not yet age 40 on the hiring date and as having a principal place of abode within an empowerment zone, enterprise community, renewal community or a rural renewal community. For these purposes, a rural renewal county is a county outside a metropolitan statistical area (as defined by the Office of Management and Budget) which had a net population loss during the five-year periods 1990–1994 and 1995–1999. Qualified wages do not include wages paid or incurred for services performed after the individual moves outside an empowerment zone, enterprise community, renewal community or a rural renewal community.

(5) Vocational rehabilitation referral

A vocational rehabilitation referral is an individual who is certified by a designated local agency as an individual who has a physical or mental disability that constitutes a substantial handicap to employment and who has been referred to the employer while receiving, or after completing: (a) vocational rehabilitation services under an individualized, written plan for employment under a State plan approved under the Rehabilitation Act of 1973; (b) under a rehabilitation plan for veterans carried out under Chapter 31 of Title 38, U.S. Code; or (c) an individual work plan developed and implemented by an employment network pursuant to subsection (g) of section 1148 of the Social Security Act. Certification will be provided by the designated local employment agency upon assurances from the vocational rehabilitation agency that the employee has met the above conditions.

(6) Qualified summer youth employee

A qualified summer youth employee is an individual: (1) who performs services during any 90-day period between May 1 and September 15; (2) who is certified by the designated local agency as being 16 or 17 years of age on the hiring date; (3) who has not been an employee of that employer before; and (4) who is certified by the designated local agency as having a principal place of abode within an empowerment zone, enterprise community, or renewal community. As with designated community residents, no credit is available on wages paid or incurred for service performed after the qualified summer youth moves outside of an empowerment zone, enterprise community, or renewal community. If, after the end of the 90-day period, the employer continues to employ a youth who was certified during the 90-day period as a member of another targeted group, the limit on qualified first-year wages will take into account wages paid to the youth while a qualified summer youth employee.

(7) Qualified supplemental nutrition assistance program benefits recipient

A qualified supplemental nutrition assistance program benefits recipient is an individual at least age 18 but not yet age 40 certified by a designated local employment agency as being a member of a family receiving assistance under a food and nutrition program under the Food and Nutrition Act of 2008 for a period of at least six months ending on the hiring date. In the case of families that cease to be eligible for food and nutrition assistance under section 6(o) of the Food and Nutrition Act of 2008, the six-month requirement is replaced with a requirement that the family has been receiving food and nutrition assistance for at least three of the five months ending on the date of hire. For these purposes, members of the family are defined to include only those individuals taken into account for purposes of determining eligibility for a food and nutrition assistance program under the Food and Nutrition Act of 2008.

(8) Qualified SSI recipient

A qualified SSI recipient is an individual designated by a local agency as receiving supplemental security income ("SSI") benefits under Title XVI of the Social Security Act for any month ending within the 60-day period ending on the hiring date.

(9) Long-term family assistance recipient

A qualified long-term family assistance recipient is an individual certified by a designated local agency as being: (1) a member of a family that has received family assistance for at least 18 consecutive months ending on the hiring date; (2) a member of a family that has received such family assistance for a total of at least 18 months (whether or not consecutive) after August 5, 1997 (the date of enactment of the welfare-to-work tax credit) if the individual is hired within two years after the date that the 18-month total is reached; or (3) a member of a family who is no longer eligible for family assistance because of either Federal or State time limits, if the individual is hired within two years after the Federal or State time limits made the family ineligible for family assistance.

Qualified wages

Generally, qualified wages are defined as cash wages paid by the employer to a member of a targeted group. The employer's deduction for wages is reduced by the amount of the credit.

For purposes of the credit, generally, wages are defined by reference to the FUTA definition of wages contained in sec. 3306(b) (without regard to the dollar limitation therein contained). Special rules apply in the case of certain agricultural labor and certain railroad labor.

Calculation of the credit

The credit available to an employer for qualified wages paid to members of all targeted groups except for long-term family assistance recipients equals 40 percent (25 percent for employment of 400 hours or less) of qualified first-year wages. Generally, qualified first-year wages are qualified wages (not in excess of $6,000) attributable to service rendered by a member of a targeted group during the one-year period beginning with the day the individual began work for the employer. Therefore, the maximum credit per employee is $2,400 (40 percent of the first $6,000 of qualified first-year wages). With respect to qualified summer youth employees, the maximum credit is $1,200 (40 percent of the first $3,000 of qualified first-year wages). Except for long-term family assistance recipients, no credit is allowed for second-year wages.

In the case of long-term family assistance recipients, the credit equals 40 percent (25 percent for employment of 400 hours or less) of $10,000 for qualified first-year wages and 50 percent of the first $10,000 of qualified second-year wages. Generally, qualified second-year wages are qualified wages (not in excess of $10,000) attributable to service rendered by a member of the long-term family assistance category during the one-year period beginning on the day after the one-year period beginning with the day the individual began work for the employer. Therefore, the maximum credit per employee is $9,000 (40 percent of the first $10,000 of qualified first-year wages plus 50 percent of the first $10,000 of qualified second-year wages).

For calculation of the credit with respect to qualified veterans, see the description of "qualified veteran" above.

Certification rules

Generally, an individual is not treated as a member of a targeted group unless: (1) on or before the day on which an individual begins work for an employer, the employer has received a certification from a designated local agency that such individual is a member of a targeted group; or (2) on or before the day an individual is offered employment with the employer, a pre-screening notice is completed by the employer with respect to such individual, and not later than the 28th day after the individual begins work for the employer, the employer submits such notice, signed by the employer and the individual under penalties of perjury, to the designated local agency as part of a written request for certification. For these purposes, a pre-screening notice is a document (in such form as the Secretary may prescribe) which contains information provided by the individual on the basis of which the employer believes that the individual is a member of a targeted group.

An otherwise qualified unemployed veteran is treated as certified by the designated local agency as having aggregate periods of unemployment (whichever is applicable under the qualified veterans rules described above) if such veteran is certified by such agency as being in receipt of unemployment compensation under a State or Federal law for such applicable periods. The Secretary of the Treasury is authorized to provide alternative methods of certification for unemployed veterans.

Minimum employment period

No credit is allowed for qualified wages paid to employees who work less than 120 hours in the first year of employment.

Qualified tax-exempt organizations employing qualified veterans

The credit is not available to qualified tax-exempt organizations other than those employing qualified veterans. The special rules, described below, were enacted in the VOW Act.

If a qualified tax-exempt organization employs a qualified veteran (as described above) a tax credit against the FICA taxes of the organization is allowed on the wages of the qualified veteran which are paid for the veteran's services in furtherance of the activities related to the function or purpose constituting the basis of the organization's exemption under section 501.

The credit available to such tax-exempt employer for qualified wages paid to a qualified veteran equals 26 percent (16.25 percent for employment of 400 hours or less) of qualified first-year wages. The amount of qualified first-year wages eligible for the credit is the same as those for non-tax-exempt employers (*i.e.,* $6,000, $12,000, $14,000 or $24,000, depending on the category of qualified veteran).

A qualified tax-exempt organization means an employer that is described in section 501(c) and exempt from tax under section 501(a).

The Social Security Trust Funds are held harmless from the effects of this provision by a transfer from the Treasury General Fund.

Treatment of possessions

The VOW Act provided a reimbursement mechanism for the U.S. possessions (American Samoa, Guam, the Commonwealth of the Northern Mariana Islands, the Commonwealth of Puerto Rico, and the United States Virgin Islands). The Secretary of the Treasury is to pay to each mirror code possession (Guam, the Commonwealth of the Northern Mariana Islands, and the United States Virgin Islands) an amount equal to the loss to that possession as a result of the VOW Act changes to the qualified veterans rules. Similarly, the Secretary of the Treasury is to pay to each non-mirror Code possession (American Samoa and the Commonwealth of Puerto Rico) the amount that the Secretary estimates as being equal to the loss to that possession that would have occurred as a result of the VOW Act changes if a mirror code tax system had been in effect in that possession. The Secretary will make this payment to a non-mirror Code possession only if that possession establishes to the satisfaction of the Secretary that the possession has implemented (or, at the discretion of the Secretary, will implement) an income tax benefit that is substantially equivalent to the qualified veterans credit allowed under the VOW Act modifications.

An employer that is allowed a credit against U.S. tax under the VOW Act with respect to a qualified veteran must reduce the amount of the credit claimed by the amount of any credit (or, in the case of a non-mirror Code possession, another tax benefit) that the employer claims against its possession income tax.

Other rules

The work opportunity tax credit is not allowed for wages paid to a relative or dependent of the taxpayer. No credit is allowed for wages paid to an individual who is a more than fifty-percent owner of the entity. Similarly, wages paid to replacement workers during a strike or lockout are not eligible for the work opportunity tax credit. Wages paid to any employee during any period for which the employer received on-the-job training program payments with respect to that employee are not eligible for the work opportunity tax credit. The work opportunity tax credit generally is not allowed for wages paid to individuals who had previously been employed by the employer. In addition, many other technical rules apply.

Expiration

The work opportunity tax credit is not available for individuals who begin work for an employer after December 31, 2014.

Explanation of Provision

The provision extends for five years the present-law employment credit provision (through taxable years beginning on or before December 31, 2019). Additionally, the provision expands the work opportunity tax credit to employers who hire individuals who are qualified long-term unemployment recipients. For purposes of the provision, such persons are individuals who have been certified by the designated local agency as being in a period of unemployment of 27 weeks or more, which includes a period in which the individual was receiving unemployment compensation under State or Federal law. With respect to wages paid to such individuals, employers would be eligible for a 40 percent credit on the first $6,000 of wages paid to such individual, for a maximum credit of $2,400 per eligible employee.

Effective Date

The provision generally applies to individuals who begin work for the employer after December 31, 2014.

The provision relating to wages paid to qualified long-term unemployment recipients applies to individuals who begin work for the employer after December 31, 2015.

3. Extension and modification of bonus depreciation (sec. 143 of the Act and sec. 168(k) of the Code)

Present Law

In general

An additional first-year depreciation deduction is allowed equal to 50 percent of the adjusted basis of qualified property acquired and placed in service before January 1, 2015 (January 1, 2016 for certain longer-lived and transportation property).[494]

---

[494] Sec. 168(k). The additional first-year depreciation deduction is subject to the general rules regarding whether an item must be capitalized under section 263A.

The additional first-year depreciation deduction is allowed for both the regular tax and the alternative minimum tax ("AMT"),[495] but is not allowed in computing earnings and profits.[496] The basis of the property and the depreciation allowances in the year of purchase and later years are appropriately adjusted to reflect the additional first-year depreciation deduction.[497] The amount of the additional first-year depreciation deduction is not affected by a short taxable year.[498] The taxpayer may elect out of additional first-year depreciation for any class of property for any taxable year.[499]

The interaction of the additional first-year depreciation allowance with the otherwise applicable depreciation allowance may be illustrated as follows. Assume that in 2014, a taxpayer purchased new depreciable property and placed it in service.[500] The property's cost is $10,000, and it is five-year property subject to the 200 percent declining balance method and half-year convention. The amount of additional first-year depreciation allowed is $5,000. The remaining $5,000 of the cost of the property is depreciable under the rules applicable to five-year property. Thus, $1,000 also is allowed as a depreciation deduction in 2014.[501] The total depreciation deduction with respect to the property for 2014 is $6,000. The remaining $4,000 adjusted basis of the property generally is recovered through otherwise applicable depreciation rules.

Property qualifying for the additional first-year depreciation deduction must meet all of the following requirements.[502] First, the property must be: (1) property to which the modified accelerated cost recovery system ("MACRS") applies with an applicable recovery period of 20 years or less; (2) water utility property (as defined in section 168(e)(5)); (3) computer software other than computer software covered by section 197; or (4) qualified leasehold improvement property.[503] Second, the original use [504] of the property must commence with the taxpayer.[505] Third, the taxpayer must acquire

---

[495] Sec. 168(k)(2)(G). See also Treas. Reg. sec. 1.168(k)–1(d).
[496] Treas. Reg. sec. 1.168(k)–1(f)(7).
[497] Sec. 168(k)(1)(B).
[498] *Ibid.*
[499] Sec. 168(k)(2)(D)(iii). For the definition of a class of property, see Treas. Reg. sec. 1.168(k)–1(e)(2).
[500] Assume that the cost of the property is not eligible for expensing under section 179 or Treas. Reg. sec. 1.263(a)–1(f).
[501] $1,000 results from the application of the half-year convention and the 200 percent declining balance method to the remaining $5,000.
[502] Requirements relating to actions taken before 2008 are not described herein since they have little (if any) remaining effect.
[503] The additional first-year depreciation deduction is not available for any property that is required to be depreciated under the alternative depreciation system of MACRS. Sec. 168(k)(2)(D)(i).
[504] The term "original use" means the first use to which the property is put, whether or not such use corresponds to the use of such property by the taxpayer. If in the normal course of its business a taxpayer sells fractional interests in property to unrelated third parties, then the original use of such property begins with the first user of each fractional interest (i.e., each fractional owner is considered the original user of its proportionate share of the property). Treas. Reg. sec. 1.168(k)–1(b)(3).
[505] A special rule applies in the case of certain leased property. In the case of any property that is originally placed in service by a person and that is sold to the taxpayer and leased back to such person by the taxpayer within three months after the date that the property was placed in service, the property would be treated as originally placed in service by the taxpayer not earlier than the date that the property is used under the leaseback. If property is originally placed in service by a lessor, such property is sold within three months after the date that the property was placed in service, and the user of such property does not change, then the property is treated as originally placed in service by the taxpayer not earlier than the date of such sale. Sec. 168(k)(2)(E)(ii).

the property within the applicable time period (as described below). Finally, the property must be placed in service before January 1, 2015. An extension of the placed-in-service date of one year (i.e., before January 1, 2016) is provided for certain property with a recovery period of 10 years or longer and certain transportation property.[506]

To qualify, property must be acquired (1) before January 1, 2015, or (2) pursuant to a binding written contract which was entered before January 1, 2015. With respect to property that is manufactured, constructed, or produced by the taxpayer for use by the taxpayer, the taxpayer must begin the manufacture, construction, or production of the property before January 1, 2015.[507] Property that is manufactured, constructed, or produced for the taxpayer by another person under a contract that is entered into prior to the manufacture, construction, or production of the property is considered to be manufactured, constructed, or produced by the taxpayer.[508] For property eligible for the extended placed-in-service date, a special rule limits the amount of costs eligible for the additional first-year depreciation. With respect to such property, only the portion of the basis that is properly attributable to the costs incurred before January 1, 2015 ("progress expenditures") is eligible for the additional first-year depreciation deduction.[509]

The limitation under section 280F on the amount of depreciation deductions allowed with respect to certain passenger automobiles is increased in the first year by $8,000 for automobiles that qualify (and for which the taxpayer does not elect out of the additional first-year deduction).[510] While the underlying section 280F limitation is indexed for inflation,[511] the additional $8,000 amount is not indexed for inflation.

Qualified leasehold improvement property

Qualified leasehold improvement property is any improvement to an interior portion of a building that is nonresidential real property, provided certain requirements are met.[512] The improvement must be made under or pursuant to a lease either by the lessee (or sublessee), or by the lessor, of that portion of the building to be occupied exclusively by the lessee (or sublessee). The improvement must be placed in service more than three years after the date the building was first placed in service. Qualified leasehold improvement property does not include any improvement for which the expenditure is attributable to the enlargement of the building, any el-

---

[506] Property qualifying for the extended placed-in-service date must have an estimated production period exceeding one year and a cost exceeding $1 million. Transportation property generally is defined as tangible personal property used in the trade or business of transporting persons or property. Certain aircraft which is not transportation property, other than for agricultural or firefighting uses, also qualifies for the extended placed-in-service-date, if at the time of the contract for purchase, the purchaser made a nonrefundable deposit of the lesser of 10 percent of the cost or $100,000, and which has an estimated production period exceeding four months and a cost exceeding $200,000.

[507] Sec. 168(k)(2)(E)(i).

[508] Treas. Reg. sec. 1.168(k)–1(b)(4)(iii).

[509] Sec. 168(k)(2)(B)(ii). For purposes of determining the amount of eligible progress expenditures, rules similar to section 46(d)(3) as in effect prior to the Tax Reform Act of 1986 apply.

[510] Sec. 168(k)(2)(F).

[511] Sec. 280F(d)(7).

[512] Sec. 168(k)(3). The additional first-year depreciation deduction is not available for qualified New York Liberty Zone leasehold improvement property as defined in section 1400L(c)(2). Sec. 168(k)(2)(D)(ii).

evator or escalator, any structural component benefiting a common area, or the internal structural framework of the building. For these purposes, a binding commitment to enter into a lease is treated as a lease, and the parties to the commitment are treated as lessor and lessee. A lease between related persons is not considered a lease for this purpose.

Special rule for long-term contracts

In general, in the case of a long-term contract, the taxable income from the contract is determined under the percentage-of-completion method.[513] Solely for purposes of determining the percentage of completion under section 460(b)(1)(A), the cost of qualified property with a MACRS recovery period of seven years or less is taken into account as a cost allocated to the contract as if bonus depreciation had not been enacted for property placed in service before January 1, 2015 (January 1, 2016 in the case of certain longer-lived and transportation property).[514]

Election to accelerate AMT credits in lieu of bonus depreciation

A corporation otherwise eligible for additional first-year depreciation may elect to claim additional AMT credits in lieu of claiming additional depreciation with respect to "eligible qualified property."[515] In the case of a corporation making this election, the straight line method is used for the regular tax and the AMT with respect to eligible qualified property.[516]

Generally, an election under this provision for a taxable year applies to subsequent taxable years. However, each time the provision has been extended, a corporation which has previously made an election has been allowed to elect not to claim additional minimum tax credits, or, if no election had previously been made, to make an election to claim additional credits with respect to property subject to the extension.[517]

A corporation making an election increases the tax liability limitation under section 53(c) on the use of minimum tax credits by the bonus depreciation amount.[518] The aggregate increase in credits allowable by reason of the increased limitation is treated as refundable.[519]

The bonus depreciation amount generally is equal to 20 percent of bonus depreciation for eligible qualified property that could be claimed as a deduction absent an election under this provision.[520] As originally enacted, the bonus depreciation amount for all taxable years was limited to the lesser of (1) $30 million, or (2) six per-

---

[513] Sec. 460.
[514] Sec. 460(c)(6). Other dates involving prior years are not described herein.
[515] Sec. 168(k)(4). Eligible qualified property means qualified property eligible for bonus depreciation with minor effective date differences having little (if any) remaining significance.
[516] Sec. 168(k)(4)(A).
[517] Sec. 168(k)(4)(H), (I), (J), and (K).
[518] Sec. 168(k)(4)(B)(ii).
[519] Sec. 168(k)(4)(F).
[520] For this purpose, bonus depreciation is the difference between (i) the aggregate amount of depreciation determined if section 168(k)(1) applied to all eligible qualified property placed in service during the taxable year and (ii) the amount of depreciation that would be so determined if section 168(k)(1) did not so apply. This determination is made using the most accelerated depreciation method and the shortest life otherwise allowable for each property. Sec. 168(k)(4)(C).

cent of the minimum tax credits allocable to the adjusted net minimum tax imposed for taxable years beginning before January 1, 2006.[521] However, extensions of this provision have provided that this limitation applies separately to property subject to each extension.

All corporations treated as a single employer under section 52(a) are treated as one taxpayer for purposes of the limitation, as well as for electing the application of this provision.[522]

In the case of a corporation making an election which is a partner in a partnership, for purposes of determining the electing partner's distributive share of partnership items, bonus depreciation does not apply to any eligible qualified property and the straight line method is used with respect to that property.[523]

Preproductive period costs of orchards, groves, and vineyards

An orchard, vineyard or grove generally produces annual crops of fruits (*e.g.,* apples, avocadoes, or grapes) or nuts (*e.g.,* pecans, pistachios, or walnuts). During the development period of plants, a farmer generally incurs costs to cultivate, spray, fertilize and irrigate the plants to their crop-producing stage (*i.e.,* preproductive period costs).[524] Preproductive period costs may be deducted or capitalized, depending on the preproductive period of the plant,[525] as well as whether the farmer elects to have section 263A not apply.[526] After the plants start producing fruit or nuts, a farmer can depreciate the capitalized costs of the plants (*i.e.,* the acquisition costs of the seeds, seedlings, or plants and their original planting which were capitalized when incurred, as well as the preproductive period costs if section 263A applied).[527] A 10-year recovery period is assigned to any tree or vine bearing fruits or nuts.[528] A seven-year recovery period generally applies to other plants bearing fruits or nuts.[529]

Explanation of Provision

Bonus depreciation

The provision extends and modifies the additional first-year depreciation deduction for five years, generally through 2019 (through 2020 for certain longer-lived and transportation property

---

[521] Sec. 168(k)(4)(C)(iii).
[522] Sec. 168(k)(4)(C)(iv).
[523] Sec. 168(k)(4)(G)(ii).
[524] See section 263A(e)(3), which defines the "preproductive period" of a plant which will have more than one crop or yield as the period before the first marketable crop or yield from such plant.
[525] See section 263A(d)(1)(A)(ii). Section 263A generally requires certain direct and indirect costs allocable to real or tangible personal property produced by the taxpayer to be included in either inventory or capitalized into the basis of such property, as applicable.
[526] See section 263A(d)(3).
[527] In the case of any tree or vine bearing fruits or nuts, the placed in service date does not occur until the tree or vine first reaches an income-producing stage. Treas. Reg. sec. 1.46–3(d)(2). See also, Rev. Rul. 80–25, 1980–1 C.B. 65, 1980; and Rev. Rul. 69–249, 1969–1 C.B. 31, 1969.
[528] Sec. 168(e)(3)(D)(ii).
[529] Sec. 168(e)(3)(C)(v).

("LLTP" [530])).[531] The 50-percent allowance is phased down for property placed in service in taxable years beginning after 2017 (after 2018 for LLTP). Under the provision, the bonus depreciation percentage rates are as follows:

Placed in Service Year	Bonus Depreciation Percentage	
	Qualified Property—in General	LLTP
2015	50 percent	50 percent
2016	50 percent	50 percent
2017	50 percent	50 percent
2018	40 percent	50 percent [532]
2019	30 percent	40 percent
2020	n/a	30 percent [533]

The $8,000 increase amount in the limitation on the depreciation deductions allowed with respect to certain passenger automobiles is phased down from $8,000 by $1,600 per calendar year beginning in 2018. Thus, the section 280F increase amount for property placed in service in 2018 is $6,400, and for 2019 is $4,800. The increase does not apply to a taxpayer who elects to accelerate AMT credits in lieu of bonus depreciation for a taxable year.

After 2015, the provision allows additional first-year depreciation for qualified improvement property without regard to whether the improvements are property subject to a lease, and also removes the requirement that the improvement must be placed in service more than three years after the date the building was first placed in service.

The provision also extends the special rule for the allocation of bonus depreciation to a long-term contract for five years to property placed in service before January 1, 2020 (January 1, 2021, in the case of certain longer-lived and transportation property).

Expansion of election to accelerate AMT credits in lieu of bonus depreciation

The provision extends, with modifications, the election to increase the AMT credit limitation in lieu of bonus depreciation.

For taxable years ending after December 31, 2014, and before January 1, 2016, a bonus depreciation amount, maximum amount, and maximum increase amount is computed separately with respect to property to which the extension of additional first-year de-

---

[530] LLTP means (i) certain longer-lived and transportation property described in section 168(k)(2)(B), and (ii) certain aircraft described in section 168(k)(2)(C).

[531] Due to the passage of time since the provision's original enactment, the provision eliminates the various acquisition date requirements as no longer relevant. The provision also repeals as deadwood the provision relating to property acquired during certain pre-2012 periods (or certain pre-2013 periods for LLTP).

[532] It is intended that for LLTP placed in service in 2018, 50 percent applies to the entire adjusted basis. Similarly, for LLTP placed in service in 2019, 40 percent applies to the entire adjusted basis. A technical correction may be necessary with respect to LLTP placed in service in 2018 and 2019 so that the statute reflects this intent.

[533] Note that in the case of LLTP described in section 168(k)(2)(B) and placed in service in 2020, 30 percent applies to the adjusted basis attributable to manufacture, construction, or production before January 1, 2020, and the remaining adjusted basis does not qualify for bonus depreciation. Thirty percent applies to the entire adjusted basis of certain aircraft described in section 168(k)(2)(C) and placed in service in 2020.

preciation applies ("round 5 extension property").[534] A corporation that has an election in effect with respect to round 4 extension property claiming minimum tax credits in lieu of bonus depreciation is treated as having an election in effect for round 5 extension property, unless the corporation elects otherwise. The provision also allows a corporation that does not have an election in effect with respect to round 4 extension property to elect to claim minimum tax credits in lieu of bonus depreciation for round 5 extension property. A separate bonus depreciation amount, maximum amount, and maximum increase amount is computed and applied to round 5 extension property.[535]

For taxable years ending after December 31, 2015, the bonus depreciation amount for a taxable year (as defined under present law with respect to all qualified property) is limited to the lesser of (1) 50 percent of the minimum tax credit for the first taxable year ending after December 31, 2015 (determined before the application of any tax liability limitation), or (2) the minimum tax credit for the taxable year allocable to the adjusted net minimum tax imposed for taxable years ending before January 1, 2016 (determined before the application of any tax liability limitation and determined on a first-in, first-out basis).

The provision also provides that in the case of a partnership having a single corporate partner owning (directly or indirectly) more than 50 percent of the capital and profits interests in the partnership, each partner takes into account its distributive share of partnership depreciation in determining its bonus depreciation amount.

Special rules for certain plants

The provision provides an election for certain plants bearing fruits and nuts. Under the election, the applicable percentage of the adjusted basis of a specified plant which is planted or grafted after December 31, 2015 and before January 1, 2020, is deductible for regular tax and AMT purposes in the year planted or grafted by the taxpayer, and the adjusted basis is reduced by the amount of the deduction.[536] The percentage is 50 percent for 2016, and then is phased down by 10 percent per calendar year beginning in 2018. Thus, the percentage for 2018 is 40 percent, and for 2019 is 30 percent. A specified plant is any tree or vine that bears fruits or nuts, and any other plant that will have more than one yield of fruits or nuts and generally has a preproductive period of more than two years from planting or grafting to the time it begins bearing fruits or nuts.[537] The election is revocable only with the consent of the Secretary, and if the election is made with respect to any specified plant, such plant is not treated as qualified property eligi-

---

[534] An election with respect to round 5 extension property is binding for all property that is eligible qualified property solely by reason of the extension of the 50-percent additional first-year depreciation deduction.

[535] In computing the maximum amount, the maximum increase amount for round 5 extension property is reduced by bonus depreciation amounts for preceding taxable years only with respect to round 5 extension property.

[536] Any amount deducted under this election is not subject to capitalization under section 263A.

[537] A specified plant does not include any property that is planted or grafted outside of the United States.

ble for bonus depreciation in the subsequent taxable year in which it is placed in service.

Effective Date

The provision generally applies to property placed in service after December 31, 2014, in taxable years ending after such date.

The modifications relating to bonus depreciation apply to property placed in service after December 31, 2015, in taxable years ending after such date.

The modifications relating to the election to accelerate AMT credits in lieu of claiming bonus depreciation generally applies to taxable years ending after December 31, 2015. For a taxable year beginning before January 1, 2016, and ending after December 31, 2015, a transitional rule applies for purposes of determining the amount eligible for the election to claim additional AMT credits. The transitional rule applies the present-law limitations to property placed in service in 2015 and the revised limitations to property placed in service in 2016.

The provision relating to certain plants bearing fruits and nuts applies to specified plants planted or grafted after December 31, 2015.

4. Extension of look-through treatment of payments between related controlled foreign corporations under foreign personal holding company rules (sec. 144 of the Act and sec. 954(c)(6) of the Code)

Present Law

In general The rules of subpart F [538] require U.S. shareholders with a 10-percent or greater interest in a controlled foreign corporation ("CFC") to include certain income of the CFC (referred to as "subpart F income") on a current basis for U.S. tax purposes, regardless of whether the income is distributed to the shareholders.

Subpart F income includes foreign base company income. One category of foreign base company income is foreign personal holding company income. For subpart F purposes, foreign personal holding company income generally includes dividends, interest, rents, and royalties, among other types of income. There are several exceptions to these rules. For example, foreign personal holding company income does not include dividends and interest received by a CFC from a related corporation organized and operating in the same foreign country in which the CFC is organized, or rents and royalties received by a CFC from a related corporation for the use of property within the country in which the CFC is organized. Interest, rent, and royalty payments do not qualify for this exclusion to the extent that such payments reduce the subpart F income of the payor. In addition, subpart F income of a CFC does not include any item of income from sources within the United States that is effectively connected with the conduct by such CFC of a trade or business within the United States ("ECI") unless such item is exempt from taxation (or is subject to a reduced rate of tax) pursuant to a tax treaty.

---

[538] Secs. 951–964.

The "look-through rule"

Under the "look-through rule" (sec. 954(c)(6)), dividends, interest (including factoring income that is treated as equivalent to interest under section 954(c)(1)(E)), rents, and royalties received or accrued by one CFC from a related CFC are not treated as foreign personal holding company income to the extent attributable or properly allocable to income of the payor that is neither subpart F income nor treated as ECI. For this purpose, a related CFC is a CFC that controls or is controlled by the other CFC, or a CFC that is controlled by the same person or persons that control the other CFC. Ownership of more than 50 percent of the CFC's stock (by vote or value) constitutes control for these purposes.

The Secretary is authorized to prescribe regulations that are necessary or appropriate to carry out the look-through rule, including such regulations as are necessary or appropriate to prevent the abuse of the purposes of such rule.

The look-through rule applies to taxable years of foreign corporations beginning after December 31, 2005 and before January 1, 2015, and to taxable years of U.S. shareholders with or within which such taxable years of foreign corporations end.

Explanation of Provision

The provision extends for five years the application of the look-through rule, to taxable years of foreign corporations beginning before January 1, 2020, and to taxable years of U.S. shareholders with or within which such taxable years of foreign corporations end.

Effective Date

The provision applies to taxable years of foreign corporations beginning after December 31, 2014, and to taxable years of U.S. shareholders with or within which such taxable years of foreign corporations end.

C. Extensions Through 2016

Part 1—Tax Relief for Families and Individuals

1. Extension and modification of exclusion from gross income of discharges of acquisition indebtedness on principal residences (sec. 151 of the Act and sec. 108 of the Code)

Present Law

In general Gross income includes income that is realized by a debtor from the discharge of indebtedness, subject to certain exceptions for debtors in Title 11 bankruptcy cases, insolvent debtors, certain student loans, certain farm indebtedness, and certain real property business indebtedness (secs. 61(a)(12) and 108).[539] In cases involving discharges of indebtedness that are excluded from gross income under the exceptions to the general rule, taxpayers

---

[539] A debt cancellation which constitutes a gift or bequest is not treated as income to the donee debtor (sec. 102).

generally reduce certain tax attributes, including basis in property, by the amount of the discharge of indebtedness.

The amount of discharge of indebtedness excluded from income by an insolvent debtor not in a Title 11 bankruptcy case cannot exceed the amount by which the debtor is insolvent. In the case of a discharge in bankruptcy or where the debtor is insolvent, any reduction in basis may not exceed the excess of the aggregate bases of properties held by the taxpayer immediately after the discharge over the aggregate of the liabilities of the taxpayer immediately after the discharge.

For all taxpayers, the amount of discharge of indebtedness generally is equal to the difference between the adjusted issue price of the debt being cancelled and the amount used to satisfy the debt. These rules generally apply to the exchange of an old obligation for a new obligation, including a modification of indebtedness that is treated as an exchange (a debt-for-debt exchange).

Qualified principal residence indebtedness

An exclusion from gross income is provided for any discharge of indebtedness income by reason of a discharge (in whole or in part) of qualified principal residence indebtedness. Qualified principal residence indebtedness means acquisition indebtedness (within the meaning of section 163(h)(3)(B), except that the dollar limitation is $2 million) with respect to the taxpayer's principal residence. Acquisition indebtedness with respect to a principal residence generally means indebtedness which is incurred in the acquisition, construction, or substantial improvement of the principal residence of the individual and is secured by the residence. It also includes refinancing of such indebtedness to the extent the amount of the indebtedness resulting from such refinancing does not exceed the amount of the refinanced indebtedness. For these purposes, the term "principal residence" has the same meaning as under section 121 of the Code.

If, immediately before the discharge, only a portion of a discharged indebtedness is qualified principal residence indebtedness, the exclusion applies only to so much of the amount discharged as exceeds the portion of the debt which is not qualified principal residence indebtedness. Thus, assume that a principal residence is secured by an indebtedness of $1 million, of which $800,000 is qualified principal residence indebtedness. If the residence is sold for $700,000 and $300,000 debt is discharged, then only $100,000 of the amount discharged may be excluded from gross income under the qualified principal residence indebtedness exclusion.

The basis of the individual's principal residence is reduced by the amount excluded from income under the provision.

The qualified principal residence indebtedness exclusion does not apply to a taxpayer in a Title 11 case; instead the general exclusion rules apply. In the case of an insolvent taxpayer not in a Title 11 case, the qualified principal residence indebtedness exclusion applies unless the taxpayer elects to have the general exclusion rules apply instead.

The exclusion does not apply to the discharge of a loan if the discharge is on account of services performed for the lender or any other factor not directly related to a decline in the value of the residence or to the financial condition of the taxpayer.

The exclusion for qualified principal residence indebtedness is effective for discharges of indebtedness before January 1, 2015.

Explanation of Provision

The provision extends for two additional years (through December 31, 2016) the exclusion from gross income for discharges of qualified principal residence indebtedness. The provision also provides for an exclusion from gross income in the case of those taxpayers' whose qualified principal residence indebtedness was discharged on or after January 1, 2017, if the discharge was subject to a written arrangement entered into prior to January 1, 2017.

Effective Date

The provision generally applies to discharges of indebtedness after December 31, 2014.

The provision relating to discharges pursuant to a written arrangement applies to discharges of indebtedness after December 31, 2015.

2. Extension of mortgage insurance premiums treated as qualified residence interest (sec. 152 of the Act and sec. 163 of the Code)

Present Law

In General

Present law provides that qualified residence interest is deductible notwithstanding the general rule that personal interest is nondeductible.[540]

Acquisition indebtedness and home equity indebtedness Qualified residence interest is interest on acquisition indebtedness and home equity indebtedness with respect to a principal and a second residence of the taxpayer. The maximum amount of home equity indebtedness is $100,000. The maximum amount of acquisition indebtedness is $1 million. Acquisition indebtedness means debt that is incurred in acquiring, constructing, or substantially improving a qualified residence of the taxpayer, and that is secured by the residence. Home equity indebtedness is debt (other than acquisition indebtedness) that is secured by the taxpayer's principal or second residence, to the extent the aggregate amount of such debt does not exceed the difference between the total acquisition indebtedness with respect to the residence, and the fair market value of the residence.

Qualified mortgage insurance

Certain premiums paid or accrued for qualified mortgage insurance by a taxpayer during the taxable year in connection with acquisition indebtedness on a qualified residence of the taxpayer are treated as interest that is qualified residence interest and thus deductible. The amount allowable as a deduction is phased out rat-

---

[540] Sec. 163(h).

ably by 10 percent for each $1,000 (or fraction thereof) by which the taxpayer's adjusted gross income exceeds $100,000 ($500 and $50,000, respectively, in the case of a married individual filing a separate return). Thus, the deduction is not allowed if the taxpayer's adjusted gross income exceeds $109,000 ($54,000 in the case of married individual filing a separate return).

For this purpose, qualified mortgage insurance means mortgage insurance provided by the Department of Veterans Affairs, the Federal Housing Administration, or the Rural Housing Service, and private mortgage insurance (defined in section two of the Homeowners Protection Act of 1998 as in effect on the date of enactment of the provision).

Amounts paid for qualified mortgage insurance that are properly allocable to periods after the close of the taxable year are treated as paid in the period to which they are allocated. No deduction is allowed for the unamortized balance if the mortgage is paid before its term (except in the case of qualified mortgage insurance provided by the Department of Veterans Affairs or Rural Housing Service).

The provision does not apply with respect to any mortgage insurance contract issued before January 1, 2007. The provision terminates for any amount paid or accrued after December 31, 2014, or properly allocable to any period after that date.

Reporting rules apply under the provision.

Explanation of Provision

The provision extends the deduction for private mortgage insurance premiums for two years (with respect to contracts entered into after December 31, 2006). Thus, the provision applies to amounts paid or accrued in 2015 and 2016 (and not properly allocable to any period after 2016).

Effective Date

The provision applies to amounts paid or accrued after December 31, 2014.

3. Extension of above-the-line deduction for qualified tuition and related expenses (sec. 153 of the Act and sec. 222 of the Code)

Present Law

An individual is allowed a deduction for qualified tuition and related expenses for higher education paid by the individual during the taxable year.[541] The deduction is allowed in computing adjusted gross income. The term qualified tuition and related expenses is defined in the same manner as for the Hope and Lifetime Learning credits, and includes tuition and fees required for the enrollment or attendance of the taxpayer, the taxpayer's spouse, or any dependent of the taxpayer with respect to whom the taxpayer may claim a personal exemption, at an eligible institution of higher education for courses of instruction of such individual at such insti-

---

[541] Sec. 222.

tution.[542] The expenses must be in connection with enrollment at an institution of higher education during the taxable year, or with an academic period beginning during the taxable year or during the first three months of the next taxable year. The deduction is not available for tuition and related expenses paid for elementary or secondary education.

The maximum deduction is $4,000 for an individual whose adjusted gross income for the taxable year does not exceed $65,000 ($130,000 in the case of a joint return), or $2,000 for other individuals whose adjusted gross income does not exceed $80,000 ($160,000 in the case of a joint return). No deduction is allowed for an individual whose adjusted gross income exceeds the relevant adjusted gross income limitations, for a married individual who does not file a joint return, or for an individual with respect to whom a personal exemption deduction may be claimed by another taxpayer for the taxable year. The deduction is not available for taxable years beginning after December 31, 2014.

The amount of qualified tuition and related expenses must be reduced by certain scholarships, educational assistance allowances, and other amounts paid for the benefit of such individual,[543] and by the amount of such expenses taken into account for purposes of determining any exclusion from gross income of: (1) income from certain U.S. savings bonds used to pay higher education tuition and fees; and (2) income from a Coverdell education savings account.[544] Additionally, such expenses must be reduced by the earnings portion (but not the return of principal) of distributions from a qualified tuition program if an exclusion under section 529 is claimed with respect to expenses eligible for the qualified tuition deduction. No deduction is allowed for any expense for which a deduction is otherwise allowed or with respect to an individual for whom a Hope or Lifetime Learning credit is elected for such taxable year.

Explanation of Provision

The provision extends the qualified tuition deduction for two years, through 2016.

Effective Date

The provision applies to taxable years beginning after December 31, 2014.

---

[542] The deduction generally is not available for expenses with respect to a course or education involving sports, games, or hobbies, and is not available for student activity fees, athletic fees, insurance expenses, or other expenses unrelated to an individual's academic course of instruction.

[543] Secs. 222(d)(1) and 25A(g)(2).

[544] Sec. 222(c). These reductions are the same as those that apply to the Hope and Lifetime Learning credits.

Part 2—Incentives for Growth, Jobs, Investment, and Innovation

4. Extension of Indian employment tax credit (sec. 161 of the Act and sec. 45A of the Code)

Present Law

In general, a credit against income tax liability is allowed to employers for the first $20,000 of qualified wages and qualified employee health insurance costs paid or incurred by the employer with respect to certain employees.[545] The credit is equal to 20 percent of the excess of eligible employee qualified wages and health insurance costs during the current year over the amount of such wages and costs incurred by the employer during 1993. The credit is an incremental credit, such that an employer's current-year qualified wages and qualified employee health insurance costs (up to $20,000 per employee) are eligible for the credit only to the extent that the sum of such costs exceeds the sum of comparable costs paid during 1993. No deduction is allowed for the portion of the wages equal to the amount of the credit.

Qualified wages means wages paid or incurred by an employer for services performed by a qualified employee. A qualified employee means any employee who is an enrolled member of an Indian tribe or the spouse of an enrolled member of an Indian tribe, who performs substantially all of the services within an Indian reservation, and whose principal place of abode while performing such services is on or near the reservation in which the services are performed. An "Indian reservation" is a reservation as defined in section 3(d) of the Indian Financing Act of 1974 [546] or section 4(10) of the Indian Child Welfare Act of 1978.[547] For purposes of the preceding sentence, section 3(d) is applied by treating "former Indian reservations in Oklahoma" as including only lands that are (1) within the jurisdictional area of an Oklahoma Indian tribe as determined by the Secretary of the Interior, and (2) recognized by such Secretary as an area eligible for trust land status under 25 C.F.R. Part 151 (as in effect on August 5, 1997).

An employee is not treated as a qualified employee for any taxable year of the employer if the total amount of wages paid or incurred by the employer with respect to such employee during the taxable year exceeds an amount determined at an annual rate of $30,000 (which after adjustment for inflation is $45,000 for 2014).[548] In addition, an employee will not be treated as a qualified employee under certain specific circumstances, such as where the employee is related to the employer (in the case of an individual employer) or to one of the employer's shareholders, partners, or grantors. Similarly, an employee will not be treated as a qualified employee where the employee has more than a five percent ownership interest in the employer. Finally, an employee will not be considered a qualified employee to the extent the employee's services

---
[545] Sec. 45A.
[546] Pub. L. No. 93-262.
[547] Pub. L. No. 95-608.
[548] See Instructions for Form 8845, Indian Employment Credit (2014).

relate to gaming activities or are performed in a building housing such activities.

The wage credit is available for wages paid or incurred in taxable years beginning on or before December 31, 2014.

Explanation of Provision

The provision extends for two years the present-law Indian employment credit (through taxable years beginning on or before December 31, 2016).

Effective Date

The provision applies to taxable years beginning after December 31, 2014.

5. Extension and modification of railroad track maintenance credit (sec. 162 of the Act and sec. 45G of the Code)

Present Law

Present law provides a 50-percent business tax credit for qualified railroad track maintenance expenditures paid or incurred by an eligible taxpayer during taxable years beginning before January 1, 2015.[549] The credit is limited to the product of $3,500 times the number of miles of railroad track (1) owned or leased by an eligible taxpayer as of the close of its taxable year, and (2) assigned to the eligible taxpayer by a Class II or Class III railroad that owns or leases such track at the close of the taxable year.[550] Each mile of railroad track may be taken into account only once, either by the owner of such mile or by the owner's assignee, in computing the per-mile limitation. The credit also may reduce a taxpayer's tax liability below its tentative minimum tax.[551] Basis of the railroad track must be reduced (but not below zero) by an amount equal to 100 percent of the taxpayer's qualified railroad track maintenance tax credit determined for the taxable year.[552]

Qualified railroad track maintenance expenditures are defined as gross expenditures (whether or not otherwise chargeable to capital account) for maintaining railroad track (including roadbed, bridges, and related track structures) owned or leased as of January 1, 2005, by a Class II or Class III railroad (determined without regard to any consideration for such expenditure given by the Class II or Class III railroad which made the assignment of such track).[553]

An eligible taxpayer means any Class II or Class III railroad, and any person who transports property using the rail facilities of a Class II or Class III railroad or who furnishes railroad-related property or services to a Class II or Class III railroad, but only with respect to miles of railroad track assigned to such person by such railroad under the provision.[554]

---

[549] Sec. 45G(a) and (f).
[550] Sec. 45G(b)(1).
[551] Sec. 38(c)(4).
[552] Sec. 45G(e)(3).
[553] Sec. 45G(d).
[554] Sec. 45G(c).

The terms Class II or Class III railroad have the meanings given by the Surface Transportation Board.[555]

Explanation of Provision

The provision extends the present law credit for two years, for qualified railroad track maintenance expenditures paid or incurred in taxable years beginning after December 31, 2014, and before January 1, 2017.

The provision also provides that qualified railroad track maintenance expenditures paid or incurred in taxable years beginning after December 31, 2015, are defined as gross expenditures (whether or not otherwise chargeable to capital account) for maintaining railroad track (including roadbed, bridges, and related track structures) owned or leased as of January 1, 2015, by a Class II or Class III railroad (determined without regard to any consideration for such expenditure given by the Class II or Class III railroad which made the assignment of such track).

Effective Date

The provision generally applies to expenditures paid or incurred in taxable years beginning after December 31, 2014.

The modification to the definition of qualified railroad track maintenance expenditures applies to expenditures paid or incurred in taxable years beginning after December 31, 2015.

6. Extension of mine rescue team training credit (sec. 163 of the Act and sec. 45N of the Code)

Present Law

An eligible employer may claim a general business credit against income tax with respect to each qualified mine rescue team employee equal to the lesser of: (1) 20 percent of the amount paid or incurred by the taxpayer during the taxable year with respect to the training program costs of the qualified mine rescue team employee (including the wages of the employee while attending the program); or (2) $10,000.[556] A qualified mine rescue team employee is any full-time employee of the taxpayer who is a miner eligible for more than six months of a taxable year to serve as a mine rescue team member by virtue of either having completed the initial 20 hour course of instruction prescribed by the Mine Safety and Health Administration's Office of Educational Policy and Development, or receiving at least 40 hours of refresher training in such instruction.[557]

An eligible employer is any taxpayer which employs individuals as miners in underground mines in the United States.[558] The term "wages" has the meaning given to such term by section 3306(b)[559]

---

[555] Sec. 45G(e)(1).
[556] Sec. 45N(a).
[557] Sec. 45N(b).
[558] Sec. 45N(c).
[559] Section 3306(b) defines wages for purposes of Federal Unemployment Tax.

(determined without regard to any dollar limitation contained in that section).[560]

No deduction is allowed for the portion of the expenses otherwise deductible that is equal to the amount of the credit.[561] The credit does not apply to taxable years beginning after December 31, 2014.[562] Additionally, the credit is not allowable for purposes of computing the alternative minimum tax.[563]

Explanation of Provision

The provision extends the credit for two years through taxable years beginning on or before December 31, 2016.

Effective Date

The provision applies to taxable years beginning after December 31, 2014.

7. Extension of qualified zone academy bonds (sec. 164 of the Act and sec. 54E of the Code)

Present Law

Tax-exempt bonds

Interest on State and local governmental bonds generally is excluded from gross income for Federal income tax purposes if the proceeds of the bonds are used to finance direct activities of these governmental units or if the bonds are repaid with revenues of the governmental units. These can include tax-exempt bonds which finance public schools.[564] An issuer must file with the Internal Revenue Service certain information about the bonds issued in order for that bond issue to be tax-exempt.[565] Generally, this information return is required to be filed no later the 15th day of the second month after the close of the calendar quarter in which the bonds were issued.

The tax exemption for State and local bonds does not apply to any arbitrage bond.[566] An arbitrage bond is defined as any bond that is part of an issue if any proceeds of the issue are reasonably expected to be used (or intentionally are used) to acquire higher yielding investments or to replace funds that are used to acquire higher yielding investments.[567] In general, arbitrage profits may be earned only during specified periods (*e.g.*, defined "temporary periods") before funds are needed for the purpose of the borrowing or on specified types of investments (*e.g.*, "reasonably required reserve or replacement funds"). Subject to limited exceptions, investment profits that are earned during these periods or on such investments must be rebated to the Federal Government.

---

[560] Sec. 45N(d).
[561] Sec. 280C(e).
[562] Sec. 45N(e).
[563] Sec. 38(c).
[564] Sec. 103.
[565] Sec. 149(e).
[566] Sec. 103(a) and (b)(2).
[567] Sec. 148.

Qualified zone academy bonds

As an alternative to traditional tax-exempt bonds, State and local governments were given the authority to issue "qualified zone academy bonds."[568] A total of $400 million of qualified zone academy bonds is authorized to be issued annually in calendar years 1998 through 2008, $1,400 million in 2009 and 2010, and $400 million in 2011, 2012, 2013 and 2014. Each calendar year's bond limitation is allocated to the States according to their respective populations of individuals below the poverty line. Each State, in turn, allocates the bond authority to qualified zone academies within such State.

A taxpayer holding a qualified zone academy bond on the credit allowance date is entitled to a credit. The credit is includible in gross income (as if it were a taxable interest payment on the bond), and may be claimed against regular income tax and alternative minimum tax liability.

Qualified zone academy bonds are a type of qualified tax credit bond and subject to the general rules applicable to qualified tax credit bonds.[569] The Treasury Department sets the credit rate at a rate estimated to allow issuance of qualified zone academy bonds without discount and without interest cost to the issuer.[570] The Secretary determines credit rates for tax credit bonds based on general assumptions about credit quality of the class of potential eligible issuers and such other factors as the Secretary deems appropriate. The Secretary may determine credit rates based on general credit market yield indexes and credit ratings. The maximum term of the bond is determined by the Treasury Department, so that the present value of the obligation to repay the principal on the bond is 50 percent of the face value of the bond.

"Qualified zone academy bonds" are defined as any bond issued by a State or local government, provided that (1) at least 100 percent of the available project proceeds are used for the purpose of renovating, providing equipment to, developing course materials for use at, or training teachers and other school personnel in a "qualified zone academy" and (2) private entities have promised to contribute to the qualified zone academy certain equipment, technical assistance or training, employee services, or other property or services with a value equal to at least 10 percent of the bond proceeds.

A school is a "qualified zone academy" if (1) the school is a public school that provides education and training below the college level, (2) the school operates a special academic program in cooperation with businesses to enhance the academic curriculum and increase graduation and employment rates, and (3) either (a) the school is located in an empowerment zone or enterprise community designated under the Code, or (b) it is reasonably expected that at least 35 percent of the students at the school will be eligible for free or reduced-cost lunches under the school lunch program established under the National School Lunch Act.

---

[568] See secs. 54E and 1397E.
[569] Sec. 54A.
[570] Given the differences in credit quality and other characteristics of individual issuers, the Secretary cannot set credit rates in a manner that will allow each issuer to issue tax credit bonds at par.

Under section 6431, an issuer of specified tax credit bonds, may elect to receive a payment in lieu of a credit being allowed to the holder of the bond ("direct-pay bonds"). Section 6431 is not available for qualified zone academy bond allocations from the national limitation for years after 2010 or any carry forward of those allocations.

Explanation of Provision

The provision extends the qualified zone academy bond program for two years. The provision authorizes issuance of up to $400 million of qualified zone academy bonds for 2015 and $400 million for 2016. The option to issue direct-pay bonds is not available.

Effective Date

The provision applies to obligations issued after December 31, 2014.

8. Extension of classification of certain race horses as three-year property (sec. 165 of the Act and sec. 168 of the Code)

Present Law

A taxpayer generally must capitalize the cost of property used in a trade or business and recover such cost over time through annual deductions for depreciation or amortization.[571] Tangible property generally is depreciated under the modified accelerated cost recovery system ("MACRS"), which determines depreciation by applying specific recovery periods,[572] placed-in-service conventions, and depreciation methods to the cost of various types of depreciable property.[573] In particular, the statute assigns a three-year recovery period for any race horse (1) that is placed in service after December 31, 2008 and before January 1, 2015[574] and (2) that is placed in service after December 31, 2014 and that is more than two years old at such time it is placed in service by the purchaser.[575] A seven-year recovery period is assigned to any race horse that is placed in service after December 31, 2014 and that is two years old or younger at the time it is placed in service.[576]

---

[571] See secs. 263(a) and 167.

[572] The applicable recovery period for an asset is determined in part by statute and in part by historical Treasury guidance. Exercising authority granted by Congress, the Secretary issued Revenue Procedure 87–56 (1987–2 C.B. 674), laying out the framework of recovery periods for enumerated classes of assets. The Secretary clarified and modified the list of asset classes in Revenue Procedure 88–22 (1988–1 C.B. 785). In November 1988, Congress revoked the Secretary's authority to modify the class lives of depreciable property. Revenue Procedure 87–56, as modified, remains in effect except to the extent that the Congress has, since 1988, statutorily modified the recovery period for certain depreciable assets, effectively superseding any administrative guidance with regard to such property.

[573] Sec. 168.

[574] Sec. 168(e)(3)(A)(i)(I), as in effect after amendment by the Food, Conservation and Energy Act of 2008, Pub. L. No. 110–246, sec. 15344(b).

[575] Sec. 168(e)(3)(A)(i)(II). A horse is more than two years old after the day that is 24 months after its actual birthdate. Rev. Proc. 87–56, 1987–2 C.B. 674, as clarified and modified by Rev. Proc. 88–22, 1988–1 C.B. 785.

[576] Rev. Proc. 87–56, 1987–2 C.B. 674, asset class 01.225.

Explanation of Provision

The provision extends the present-law three-year recovery period for race horses for two years to apply to any race horse (regardless of age when placed in service) which is placed in service before January 1, 2017. Subsequently, the three-year recovery period for race horses will only apply to those which are more than two years old when placed in service by the purchaser after December 31, 2016.

Effective Date

The provision applies to property placed in service after December 31, 2014.

9. Extension of seven-year recovery period for motorsports entertainment complexes (sec. 166 of the Act and sec. 168 of the Code)

Present Law

A taxpayer generally must capitalize the cost of property used in a trade or business and recover such cost over time through annual deductions for depreciation or amortization.[577] Tangible property generally is depreciated under the modified accelerated cost recovery system ("MACRS"), which determines depreciation by applying specific recovery periods,[578] placed-in-service conventions, and depreciation methods to the cost of various types of depreciable property.[579] The cost of nonresidential real property is recovered using the straight-line method of depreciation and a recovery period of 39 years.[580] Nonresidential real property is subject to the mid-month convention, which treats all property placed in service during any month (or disposed of during any month) as placed in service (or disposed of) on the mid-point of such month.[581] All other property generally is subject to the half-year convention, which treats all property placed in service during any taxable year (or disposed of during any taxable year) as placed in service (or disposed of) on the mid-point of such taxable year.[582] Land improvements (such as roads and fences) are recovered using the 150-percent declining balance method and a recovery period of 15 years.[583] An exception

---

[577] See secs. 263(a) and 167.

[578] The applicable recovery period for an asset is determined in part by statute and in part by historical Treasury guidance. Exercising authority granted by Congress, the Secretary issued Revenue Procedure 87–56 (1987–2 C.B. 674), laying out the framework of recovery periods for enumerated classes of assets. The Secretary clarified and modified the list of asset classes in Revenue Procedure 88–22 (1988–1 C.B. 785). In November 1988, Congress revoked the Secretary's authority to modify the class lives of depreciable property. Revenue Procedure 87–56, as modified, remains in effect except to the extent that the Congress has, since 1988, statutorily modified the recovery period for certain depreciable assets, effectively superseding any administrative guidance with regard to such property.

[579] Sec. 168.

[580] Sec. 168(b)(3)(A) and (c).

[581] Sec. 168(d)(2)(A) and (d)(4)(B).

[582] Sec. 168(d)(1) and (d)(4)(A). However, if substantial property is placed in service during the last three months of a taxable year, a special rule requires use of the mid-quarter convention, which treats all property placed in service (or disposed of) during any quarter as placed in service (or disposed of) on the mid-point of such quarter. Sec. 168(d)(3) and (d)(4)(C).

[583] Sec. 168(b)(2)(A) and asset class 00.3 of Rev. Proc. 87–56, 1987–2 C.B. 674. Under the 150-percent declining balance method, the depreciation rate is determined by dividing 150 percent by the appropriate recovery period, switching to the straight-line method for the first taxable

Continued

exists for the theme and amusement park industry, whose assets are assigned a recovery period of seven years.[584] Additionally, a motorsports entertainment complex placed in service on or before December 31, 2014 is assigned a recovery period of seven years.[585] For these purposes, a motorsports entertainment complex means a racing track facility which is permanently situated on land and which during the 36-month period following its placed-in-service date hosts a racing event.[586] The term motorsports entertainment complex also includes ancillary facilities, land improvements (*e.g.*, parking lots, sidewalks, fences), support facilities (*e.g.*, food and beverage retailing, souvenir vending), and appurtenances associated with such facilities (*e.g.*, ticket booths, grandstands).

Explanation of Provision

The provision extends the present-law seven-year recovery period for motorsports entertainment complexes for two years to apply to property placed in service on or before December 31, 2016.

Effective Date

The provision applies to property placed in service after December 31, 2014.

10. Extension and modification of accelerated depreciation for business property on an Indian reservation (sec. 167 of the Act and sec. 168(j) of the Code)

Present Law

With respect to certain property used in connection with the conduct of a trade or business within an Indian reservation, depreciation deductions under section 168(j) are determined using the following recovery periods:

3-year property	2 years
5-year property	3 years
7-year property	4 years
10-year property	6 years
15-year property	9 years
20-year property	12 years
Nonresidential real property	22 years [587]

"Qualified Indian reservation property" eligible for accelerated depreciation includes property described in the table above which is: (1) used by the taxpayer predominantly in the active conduct of a trade or business within an Indian reservation; (2) not used or located outside the reservation on a regular basis; (3) not acquired (directly or indirectly) by the taxpayer from a person who is related to the taxpayer;[588] and (4) is not property placed in service for pur-

---

year where using the straight-line method with respect to the adjusted basis as of the beginning of that year will yield a larger depreciation allowance. Sec. 168(b)(2) and (b)(1)(B).

[584] Asset class 80.0 of Rev. Proc. 87–56, 1987–2 C.B. 674.
[585] Sec. 168(e)(3)(C)(ii).
[586] Sec. 168(i)(15).
[587] Section 168(j)(2) does not provide shorter recovery periods for water utility property, residential rental property, or railroad grading and tunnel bores.
[588] For these purposes, the term "related persons" is defined in section 465(b)(3)(C).

poses of conducting gaming activities.[589] Certain "qualified infrastructure property" may be eligible for the accelerated depreciation even if located outside an Indian reservation, provided that the purpose of such property is to connect with qualified infrastructure property located within the reservation (*e.g.*, roads, power lines, water systems, railroad spurs, and communications facilities).[590]

An "Indian reservation" means a reservation as defined in section 3(d) of the Indian Financing Act of 1974 (25 U.S.C. 1452(d))[591] or section 4(10) of the Indian Child Welfare Act of 1978 (25 U.S.C. 1903(10)).[592] For purposes of the preceding sentence, section 3(d) is applied by treating "former Indian reservations in Oklahoma" as including only lands that are (1) within the jurisdictional area of an Oklahoma Indian tribe as determined by the Secretary of the Interior, and (2) recognized by such Secretary as an area eligible for trust land status under 25 C.F.R. part 151 (as in effect on August 5, 1997).[593]

The depreciation deduction allowed for regular tax purposes is also allowed for purposes of the alternative minimum tax.[594] The accelerated depreciation for qualified Indian reservation property is available with respect to property placed in service on or before December 31, 2014.[595]

Explanation of Provision

The provision extends for two years the present-law accelerated depreciation for qualified Indian reservation property to apply to property placed in service on or before December 31, 2016.

The provision also provides that a taxpayer may annually make an irrevocable election out of section 168(j) on a class-by-class basis for qualified Indian reservation property placed in service in taxable years beginning after December 31, 2015.

Effective Date

The provision generally applies to property placed in service after December 31, 2014.

The modification providing an election out of section 168(j) applies to taxable years beginning after December 31, 2015.

11. Extension of election to expense mine safety equipment (sec. 168 of the Act and sec. 179E of the Code)

Present Law

A taxpayer may elect to treat 50 percent of the cost of any qualified advanced mine safety equipment property as an expense in the taxable year in which the equipment is placed in service.[596] "Qualified advanced mine safety equipment property" means any advanced mine safety equipment property for use in any underground

---

[589] Sec. 168(j)(4)(A).
[590] Sec. 168(j)(4)(C).
[591] Pub. L. No. 93–262.
[592] Pub. L. No. 95–608.
[593] Sec. 168(j)(6).
[594] Sec. 168(j)(3).
[595] Sec. 168(j)(8).
[596] Sec. 179E(a).

mine located in the United States the original use of which commences with the taxpayer and which is placed in service after December 20, 2006, and before January 1, 2015.[597]

Advanced mine safety equipment property means any of the following: (1) emergency communication technology or devices used to allow a miner to maintain constant communication with an individual who is not in the mine; (2) electronic identification and location devices that allow individuals not in the mine to track at all times the movements and location of miners working in or at the mine; (3) emergency oxygen-generating, self-rescue devices that provide oxygen for at least 90 minutes; (4) pre-positioned supplies of oxygen providing each miner on a shift the ability to survive for at least 48 hours; and (5) comprehensive atmospheric monitoring systems that monitor the levels of carbon monoxide, methane, and oxygen that are present in all areas of the mine and that can detect smoke in the case of a fire in a mine.[598]

Explanation of Provision

The provision extends for two years (through December 31, 2016) the present-law placed-in-service date allowing a taxpayer to expense 50 percent of the cost of any qualified advanced mine safety equipment property.

Effective Date

The provision applies to property placed in service after December 31, 2014.

12. Extension of special expensing rules for certain film and television productions; special expensing for live theatrical productions (sec. 169 of the Act and sec. 181 of the Code)

Present Law

Under section 181, a taxpayer may elect[599] to deduct the cost of any qualifying film and television production, commencing prior to January 1, 2015, in the year the expenditure is incurred in lieu of capitalizing the cost and recovering it through depreciation allowances.[600] A taxpayer may elect to deduct up to $15 million of the aggregate cost of the film or television production under this section.[601] The threshold is increased to $20 million if a significant amount of the production expenditures are incurred in areas eligible for designation as a low-income community or eligible for designation by the Delta Regional Authority as a distressed county or isolated area of distress.[602]

A qualified film or television production means any production of a motion picture (whether released theatrically or directly to video cassette or any other format) or television program if at least 75

---

[597] Sec. 179E(c) and (g).
[598] Sec. 179E(d).
[599] See Treas. Reg. section 1.181–2 for rules on making an election under this section.
[600] For this purpose, a production is treated as commencing on the first date of principal photography.
[601] Sec. 181(a)(2)(A).
[602] Sec. 181(a)(2)(B).

percent of the total compensation expended on the production is for services performed in the United States by actors, directors, producers, and other relevant production personnel.[603] The term "compensation" does not include participations and residuals (as defined in section 167(g)(7)(B)).[604] Each episode of a television series is treated as a separate production, and only the first 44 episodes of a particular series qualify under the provision.[605] Qualified productions do not include sexually explicit productions as referenced by section 2257 of title 18 of the U.S. Code.[606]

For purposes of recapture under section 1245, any deduction allowed under section 181 is treated as if it were a deduction allowable for amortization.[607]

Explanation of Provision

The provision extends the special treatment for film and television productions under section 181 for two years to qualified film and television productions commencing prior to January 1, 2017.

The provision also expands section 181 to include any qualified live theatrical production commencing after December 31, 2015. A qualified live theatrical production is defined as a live staged production of a play (with or without music) which is derived from a written book or script and is produced or presented by a commercial entity in any venue which has an audience capacity of not more than 3,000, or a series of venues the majority of which have an audience capacity of not more than 3,000. In addition, qualified live theatrical productions include any live staged production which is produced or presented by a taxable entity no more than 10 weeks annually in any venue which has an audience capacity of not more than 6,500. In general, in the case of multiple live-staged productions, each such live-staged production is treated as a separate production. Similar to the exclusion for sexually explicit productions from the present-law definition of qualified productions, qualified live theatrical productions do not include stage performances that would be excluded by section 2257(h)(1) of title 18 of the U.S. Code, if such provision were extended to live stage performances.

Effective Date

The provision generally applies to productions commencing after December 31, 2014.

The modifications for live theatrical productions apply to productions commencing after December 31, 2015. For purposes of this provision, the date on which a qualified live theatrical production commences is the date of the first public performance of such production for a paying audience.

---

[603] Sec. 181(d)(3)(A).
[604] Sec. 181(d)(3)(B).
[605] Sec. 181(d)(2)(B).
[606] Sec. 181(d)(2)(C).
[607] Sec. 1245(a)(2)(C).

13. Extension of deduction allowable with respect to income attributable to domestic production activities in Puerto Rico (sec. 170 of the Act and sec. 199 of the Code)

Present Law

General

Present law generally provides a deduction from taxable income (or, in the case of an individual, adjusted gross income) that is equal to nine percent of the lesser of the taxpayer's qualified production activities income or taxable income for the taxable year. For taxpayers subject to the 35-percent corporate income tax rate, the nine-percent deduction effectively reduces the corporate income tax rate to slightly less than 32 percent on qualified production activities income.

In general, qualified production activities income is equal to domestic production gross receipts reduced by the sum of: (1) the costs of goods sold that are allocable to those receipts; and (2) other expenses, losses, or deductions which are properly allocable to those receipts.

Domestic production gross receipts generally are gross receipts of a taxpayer that are derived from: (1) any sale, exchange, or other disposition, or any lease, rental, or license, of qualifying production property [608] that was manufactured, produced, grown or extracted by the taxpayer in whole or in significant part within the United States; (2) any sale, exchange, or other disposition, or any lease, rental, or license, of qualified film [609] produced by the taxpayer; (3) any lease, rental, license, sale, exchange, or other disposition of electricity, natural gas, or potable water produced by the taxpayer in the United States; (4) construction of real property performed in the United States by a taxpayer in the ordinary course of a construction trade or business; or (5) engineering or architectural services performed in the United States for the construction of real property located in the United States.

The amount of the deduction for a taxable year is limited to 50 percent of the wages paid by the taxpayer, and properly allocable to domestic production gross receipts, during the calendar year that ends in such taxable year.[610] Wages paid to bona fide residents of Puerto Rico generally are not included in the definition of wages for purposes of computing the wage limitation amount.[611]

Rules for Puerto Rico

When used in the Code in a geographical sense, the term "United States" generally includes only the States and the District of Co-

---

[608] Qualifying production property generally includes any tangible personal property, computer software, and sound recordings.

[609] Qualified film includes any motion picture film or videotape (including live or delayed television programming, but not including certain sexually explicit productions) if 50 percent or more of the total compensation relating to the production of the film (including compensation in the form of residuals and participations) constitutes compensation for services performed in the United States by actors, production personnel, directors, and producers.

[610] For purposes of the provision, "wages" include the sum of the amounts of wages as defined in section 3401(a) and elective deferrals that the taxpayer properly reports to the Social Security Administration with respect to the employment of employees of the taxpayer during the calendar year ending during the taxpayer's taxable year.

[611] Section 3401(a)(8)(C) excludes wages paid to United States citizens who are bona fide residents of Puerto Rico from the term wages for purposes of income tax withholding.

lumbia.[612] A special rule for determining domestic production gross receipts, however, provides that in the case of any taxpayer with gross receipts from sources within the Commonwealth of Puerto Rico, the term "United States" includes the Commonwealth of Puerto Rico, but only if all of the taxpayer's Puerto Rico-sourced gross receipts are taxable under the Federal income tax for individuals or corporations.[613] In computing the 50-percent wage limitation, the taxpayer is permitted to take into account wages paid to bona fide residents of Puerto Rico for services performed in Puerto Rico.[614]

The special rules for Puerto Rico apply only with respect to the first nine taxable years of a taxpayer beginning after December 31, 2005 and before January 1, 2015.

Explanation of Provision

The provision extends the special domestic production activities rules for Puerto Rico to apply for the first eleven taxable years of a taxpayer beginning after December 31, 2005 and before January 1, 2017.

Effective Date

The provision applies to taxable years beginning after December 31, 2014.

14. Extension and modification of empowerment zone tax incentives (sec. 171 of the Act and secs. 1391 and 1394 of the Code)

Present Law

The Omnibus Budget Reconciliation Act of 1993 ("OBRA 93")[615] authorized the designation of nine empowerment zones ("Round I empowerment zones") to provide tax incentives for businesses to locate within certain targeted areas[616] designated by the Secretaries of the Department of Housing and Urban Development ("HUD") and the U.S. Department of Agriculture ("USDA"). The first empowerment zones were established in large rural areas and large cities. OBRA 93 also authorized the designation of 95 enterprise communities, which were located in smaller rural areas and cities. For tax purposes, the areas designated as enterprise communities continued as such for the ten-year period starting in the beginning of 1995 and ending at the end of 2004.

The Taxpayer Relief Act of 1997[617] authorized the designation of two additional Round I urban empowerment zones, and 20 additional empowerment zones ("Round II empowerment zones"). The Community Renewal Tax Relief Act of 2000 ("2000 Community Re-

---

[612] Sec. 7701(a)(9).
[613] Sec. 199(d)(8)(A).
[614] Sec. 199(d)(8)(B).
[615] Pub. L. No. 103–66.
[616] The targeted areas are those that have pervasive poverty, high unemployment, and general economic distress, and that satisfy certain eligibility criteria, including specified poverty rates and population and geographic size limitations.
[617] Pub. L. No. 105–34.

newal Act")[618] authorized a total of 10 new empowerment zones ("Round III empowerment zones"), bringing the total number of authorized empowerment zones to 40.[619] In addition, the 2000 Community Renewal Act conformed the tax incentives that are available to businesses in the Round I, Round II, and Round III empowerment zones, and extended the empowerment zone incentives through December 31, 2009. Subsequent legislation extended the empowerment zone incentives through December 31, 2014.[620]

The tax incentives available within the designated empowerment zones include a Federal income tax credit for employers who hire qualifying employees (the "wage credit"), increased expensing of qualifying depreciable property, tax-exempt bond financing, deferral of capital gains tax on the sale of qualified assets sold and replaced, and partial exclusion of capital gains tax on certain sales of qualified small business stock.

The following is a description of the empowerment zone tax incentives.

Wage credit

A 20-percent wage credit is available to employers for the first $15,000 of qualified wages paid to each employee (*i.e.*, a maximum credit of $3,000 with respect to each qualified employee) who (1) is a resident of the empowerment zone, and (2) performs substantially all employment services within the empowerment zone in a trade or business of the employer.[621]

The wage credit rate applies to qualifying wages paid before January 1, 2015. Wages paid to a qualified employee who earns more than $15,000 are eligible for the wage credit (although only the first $15,000 of wages is eligible for the credit). The wage credit is available with respect to a qualified full-time or part-time employee (employed for at least 90 days), regardless of the number of other employees who work for the employer. In general, any taxable business carrying out activities in the empowerment zone may claim the wage credit, regardless of whether the employer meets the definition of an "enterprise zone business."[622]

---

[618] Pub. L. No. 106–554.

[619] The urban part of the program is administered by HUD and the rural part of the program is administered by the USDA. The eight Round I urban empowerment zones are Atlanta, GA; Baltimore, MD; Chicago, IL; Cleveland, OH; Detroit, MI; Los Angeles, CA; New York, NY; and Philadelphia, PA/Camden, NJ. Atlanta relinquished its empowerment zone designation in Round III. The three Round I rural empowerment zones are Kentucky Highlands, KY; Mid-Delta, MI; and Rio Grande Valley, TX. The 15 Round II urban empowerment zones are Boston, MA; Cincinnati, OH; Columbia, SC; Columbus, OH; Cumberland County, NJ; El Paso, TX; Gary/Hammond/East Chicago, IN; Ironton, OH/Huntington, WV; Knoxville, TN; Miami/Dade County, FL; Minneapolis, MN; New Haven, CT; Norfolk/Portsmouth, VA; Santa Ana, CA; and St. Louis, Missouri/East St. Louis, IL. The five Round II rural empowerment zones are Desert Communities, CA; Griggs-Steele, ND; Oglala Sioux Tribe, SD; Southernmost Illinois Delta, IL; and Southwest Georgia United, GA. The eight Round III urban empowerment zones are Fresno, CA; Jacksonville, FL; Oklahoma City, OK; Pulaski County, AR; San Antonio, TX; Syracuse, NY; Tucson, AZ; and Yonkers, NY. The two Round III rural empowerment zones are Aroostook County, ME; and Futuro, TX.

[620] Pub. L. No. 111–312, sec. 753 (2010), Pub. L. No. 112–240, sec. 327(a) (2013), Pub. L. No. 113–295, sec. 139 (2014).

[621] Sec. 1396. The $15,000 limit is annual, not cumulative, such that the limit is the first $15,000 of wages paid in a calendar year which ends with or within the taxable year.

[622] Secs. 1397C(b) and 1397C(c). However, the wage credit is not available for wages paid in connection with certain business activities described in section 144(c)(6)(B), including a golf course, country club, massage parlor, hot tub facility, suntan facility, racetrack, liquor store, or certain farming activities. In addition, wages are not eligible for the wage credit if paid to: (1) a person who owns more than five percent of the stock (or capital or profits interests) of the

An employer's deduction otherwise allowed for wages paid is reduced by the amount of wage credit claimed for that taxable year.[623] Wages are not to be taken into account for purposes of the wage credit if taken into account in determining the employer's work opportunity tax credit under section 51.[624] In addition, the $15,000 cap is reduced by any wages taken into account in computing the work opportunity tax credit.[625] The wage credit may be used to offset up to 25 percent of the employer's alternative minimum tax liability.[626]

Increased section 179 expensing limitation

An enterprise zone business is allowed up to an additional $35,000 of section 179 expensing for qualified zone property placed in service before January 1, 2015.[627] For taxable years beginning in 2014, the total amount that may be expensed is $535,000 (assuming at least $35,000 of qualified zone property is placed in service during the taxable year).[628] The section 179 expensing allowed to a taxpayer is phased out by the amount by which the cost of qualifying property placed in service during the taxable year exceeds a specified dollar amount.[629] However, only 50 percent of the cost of qualified zone property placed in service during the year by the taxpayer is taken into account in determining the phase out of the limitation amount.[630]

The term "qualified zone property" is defined as depreciable tangible property (including buildings) provided that (i) the property is acquired by the taxpayer (from an unrelated party) after the designation took effect, (ii) the original use of the property in an empowerment zone commences with the taxpayer, and (iii) substantially all of the use of the property is in an empowerment zone in the active conduct of a trade or business by the taxpayer.[631] Special rules are provided in the case of property that is substantially renovated by the taxpayer.

An enterprise zone business means any qualified business entity and any qualified proprietorship. A qualified business entity means any corporation or partnership if for such year: (1) every trade or business of such entity is the active conduct of a qualified business within an empowerment zone; (2) at least 50 percent of the total gross income of such entity is derived from the active conduct of such business; (3) a substantial portion of the use of the tangible property of such entity (whether owned or leased) is within an empowerment zone; (4) a substantial portion of the intangible property of such entity is used in the active conduct of any such busi-

---

employer, (2) certain relatives of the employer, or (3) if the employer is a corporation or partnership, certain relatives of a person who owns more than 50 percent of the business.

[623] Sec. 280C(a).
[624] Sec. 1396(c)(3)(A).
[625] Secs. 1396(c)(3)(B).
[626] Sec. 38(c)(2).
[627] Secs. 1397A.
[628] See sec. 179(b)(1).
[629] For taxable years beginning in 2014, the dollar amount is $2,000,000. Sec. 179(b)(2). Section 124 of the Act permanently extends the section 179 dollar amounts of $500,000 and $2,000,000 for taxable years beginning after 2014.
[630] Secs. 1397A(a)(2).
[631] Sec. 1397D. Note, however, that to be eligible for the increased section 179 expensing, the qualified zone property has to also meet the definition of section 179 property (*e.g.*, building property would only qualify if it constitutes qualified real property under section 179(f)).

ness; (5) a substantial portion of the services performed for such entity by its employees are performed in an empowerment zone; (6) at least 35 percent of its employees are residents of an empowerment zone; (7) less than five percent of the average of the aggregate unadjusted bases of the property of such entity is attributable to collectibles other than collectibles that are held primarily for sale to customers in the ordinary course of such business; and (8) less than five percent of the average of the aggregate unadjusted bases of the property of such entity is attributable to nonqualified financial property.[632]

A qualified proprietorship is any qualified business carried on by an individual as a proprietorship if for such year: (1) at least 50 percent of the total gross income of such individual from such business is derived from the active conduct of such business in an empowerment zone; (2) a substantial portion of the use of the tangible property of such individual in such business (whether owned or leased) is within an empowerment zone; (3) a substantial portion of the intangible property of such business is used in the active conduct of such business; (4) a substantial portion of the services performed for such individual in such business by employees of such business are performed in an empowerment zone; (5) at least 35 percent of such employees are residents of an empowerment zone; (6) less than five percent of the average of the aggregate unadjusted bases of the property of such individual which is used in such business is attributable to collectibles other than collectibles that are held primarily for sale to customers in the ordinary course of such business; and (7) less than five percent of the average of the aggregate unadjusted bases of the property of such individual which is used in such business is attributable to nonqualified financial property.[633]

A qualified business is defined as any trade or business other than a trade or business that consists predominantly of the development or holding of intangibles for sale or license or any business prohibited in connection with the employment credit.[634] In addition, the leasing of real property that is located within the empowerment zone is treated as a qualified business only if (1) the leased property is not residential property, and (2) at least 50 percent of the gross rental income from the real property is from enterprise zone businesses. The rental of tangible personal property is not a qualified business unless at least 50 percent of the rental of such property is by enterprise zone businesses or by residents of an empowerment zone.

Expanded tax-exempt financing for certain zone facilities

States or local governments can issue enterprise zone facility bonds to raise funds to provide an enterprise zone business with qualified zone property.[635] These bonds can be used in areas designated enterprise communities as well as areas designated em-

---

[632] Sec. 1397C(b).
[633] Sec. 1397C(c).
[634] Sec. 1397C(d). Excluded businesses include any private or commercial golf course, country club, massage parlor, hot tub facility, sun tan facility, racetrack or other facility used for gambling, or any store the principal business of which is the sale of alcoholic beverages for off-premises consumption. Sec. 144(c)(6).
[635] Sec. 1394.

powerment zones. To qualify, 95 percent (or more) of the net proceeds from the bond issue must be used to finance: (1) qualified zone property whose principal user is an enterprise zone business, and (2) certain land functionally related and subordinate to such property.

The term enterprise zone business is the same as that used for purposes of the increased section 179 deduction limitation (discussed above) with certain modifications for start-up businesses. First, a business will be treated as an enterprise zone business during a start-up period if (1) at the beginning of the period, it is reasonable to expect the business to be an enterprise zone business by the end of the start-up period, and (2) the business makes bona fide efforts to be an enterprise zone business. The start-up period is the period that ends with the start of the first tax year beginning more than two years after the later of (1) the issue date of the bond issue financing the qualified zone property, and (2) the date this property is first placed in service (or, if earlier, the date that is three years after the issue date).[636]

Second, a business that qualifies as an enterprise zone business at the end of the start-up period must continue to qualify during a testing period that ends three tax years after the start-up period ends. After the three-year testing period, a business will continue to be treated as an enterprise zone business as long as 35 percent of its employees are residents of an empowerment zone or enterprise community.

The face amount of the bonds may not exceed $60 million for an empowerment zone in a rural area, $130 million for an empowerment zone in an urban area with zone population of less than 100,000, and $230 million for an empowerment zone in an urban area with zone population of at least 100,000.

Elective rollover of capital gain from the sale or exchange of any qualified empowerment zone asset

Taxpayers can elect to defer recognition of gain on the sale of a qualified empowerment zone asset held for more than one year and replaced within 60 days by another qualified empowerment zone asset in the same zone.[637] A qualified empowerment zone asset generally means stock or a partnership interest acquired at original issue for cash in an enterprise zone business, or tangible property originally used in an enterprise zone business by the taxpayer. The deferral is accomplished by reducing the basis of the replacement asset by the amount of the gain recognized on the sale of the asset.

Partial exclusion of capital gains on certain small business stock

Generally, individuals may exclude a percentage of gain from the sale of certain small business stock acquired at original issue and held at least five years.[638] For stock acquired prior to February 18, 2009, or after December 31, 2014, the percentage is generally 50 percent, except that for empowerment zone stock the percentage is

---

[636] Sec. 1394(b)(3).
[637] Sec. 1397B.
[638] Sec. 1202.

60 percent for gain attributable to periods before January 1, 2019. For stock acquired after February 17, 2009, and before January 1, 2015, a higher percentage (either 75-percent or 100-percent) applies to all small business stock with no additional percentage for empowerment zone stock.[639]

Other tax incentives

Other incentives not specific to empowerment zones but beneficial to these areas include the work opportunity tax credit for employers based on the first year of employment of certain targeted groups, including empowerment zone residents (up to $2,400 per employee), and qualified zone academy bonds for certain public schools located in an empowerment zone or expected (as of the date of bond issuance) to have at least 35 percent of its students receiving free or reduced lunches.

Explanation of Provision

Extension

The provision extends for two years, through December 31, 2016, the period for which the designation of an empowerment zone is in effect, thus extending for two years the empowerment zone tax incentives, including the wage credit, increased section 179 expensing for qualifying property, tax-exempt bond financing, and deferral of capital gains tax on the sale of qualified assets replaced with other qualified assets. In the case of a designation of an empowerment zone the nomination for which included a termination date which is December 31, 2016, termination shall not apply with respect to such designation if the entity which made such nomination amends the nomination to provide for a new termination date in such manner as the Secretary may provide.

Modification of enterprise zone facility bond employment requirement

The provision also amends the requirements for tax-exempt enterprise zone facility bonds to treat an employee as a resident of an empowerment zone for purposes of the 35 percent in-zone employment requirement if they are a resident of an empowerment zone, an enterprise community, or a qualified low-income community within an applicable nominating jurisdiction. The applicable nominating jurisdiction means, with respect to any empowerment zone or enterprise community, any local government that nominated such community for designation under section 1391. The definition of a qualified low-income community is similar to the definition of a low income community provided in section 45D(e) (concerning eligibility for the new markets tax credit). A "qualified low-income community" is a population census tract with either (1) a poverty rate of at least 20 percent, or (2) median family income which does not exceed 80 percent of the greater of metropolitan area median family income or statewide median family income (for a non-metropolitan census tract, does not exceed 80 percent of statewide median family income). In the case of a population cen-

---

[639] Section 126 of the Act permanently extends the 100-percent exclusion to small business stock for stock acquired after 2014.

sus tract located within a high migration rural county, low-income is defined by reference to 85 percent (as opposed to 80 percent) of statewide median family income. For this purpose, a high migration rural county is any county that, during the 20-year period ending with the year in which the most recent census was conducted, has a net out-migration of inhabitants from the county of at least 10 percent of the population of the county at the beginning of such period.

The Secretary is authorized to designate "targeted populations" as qualified low-income communities. For this purpose, a "targeted population" is defined by reference to section 103(20) of the Riegle Community Development and Regulatory Improvement Act of 1994 (the "Act") to mean individuals, or an identifiable group of individuals, including an Indian tribe, who are low-income persons or otherwise lack adequate access to loans or equity investments. Section 103(17) of the Act provides that "low-income" means (1) for a targeted population within a metropolitan area, less than 80 percent of the area median family income; and (2) for a targeted population within a non-metropolitan area, less than the greater of (a) 80 percent of the area median family income, or (b) 80 percent of the statewide non-metropolitan area median family income.

Effective Date

The provision generally applies to taxable years beginning after December 31, 2014. The provision regarding the special rule for the employee residence test in the context of tax-exempt enterprise zone facility bonds applies to bonds issued after December 31, 2015.

15. Extension of temporary increase in limit on cover over of rum excise taxes to Puerto Rico and the Virgin Islands (sec. 172 of the Act and sec. 7652(f) of the Code)

Present Law

A $13.50 per proof gallon [640] excise tax is imposed on distilled spirits produced in or imported into the United States.[641] The excise tax does not apply to distilled spirits that are exported from the United States, including exports to U.S. possessions (*e.g.*, Puerto Rico and the Virgin Islands).[642]

The Code provides for cover over (payment) to Puerto Rico and the Virgin Islands of the excise tax imposed on rum imported (or brought) into the United States, without regard to the country of origin.[643] The amount of the cover over is limited under Code section 7652(f) to $10.50 per proof gallon ($13.25 per proof gallon before January 1, 2015).

Tax amounts attributable to shipments to the United States of rum produced in Puerto Rico are covered over to Puerto Rico. Tax amounts attributable to shipments to the United States of rum pro-

---

[640] A proof gallon is a liquid gallon consisting of 50 percent alcohol. See sec. 5002(a)(10) and (11).
[641] Sec. 5001(a)(1).
[642] Secs. 5214(a)(1)(A), 5002(a)(15), 7653(b) and (c).
[643] Secs. 7652(a)(3), (b)(3), and (e)(1). One percent of the amount of excise tax collected from imports into the United States of articles produced in the Virgin Islands is retained by the United States under section 7652(b)(3).

duced in the Virgin Islands are covered over to the Virgin Islands. Tax amounts attributable to shipments to the United States of rum produced in neither Puerto Rico nor the Virgin Islands are divided and covered over to the two possessions under a formula.[644] Amounts covered over to Puerto Rico and the Virgin Islands are deposited into the treasuries of the two possessions for use as those possessions determine.[645] All of the amounts covered over are subject to the limitation.

Explanation of Provision

The provision suspends for two years the $10.50 per proof gallon limitation on the amount of excise taxes on rum covered over to Puerto Rico and the Virgin Islands. Under the provision, the cover over limitation of $13.25 per proof gallon is extended for rum brought into the United States after December 31, 2014 and before January 1, 2017. After December 31, 2016, the cover over amount reverts to $10.50 per proof gallon.

Effective Date

The provision applies to articles brought into the United States after December 31, 2014.

16. Extension of American Samoa economic development credit (sec. 173 of the Act and sec. 119 of Pub. L. No. 109–432)

Present Law

A domestic corporation that was an existing credit claimant with respect to American Samoa and that elected the application of section 936 for its last taxable year beginning before January 1, 2006 is allowed a credit based on the corporation's economic activity-based limitation with respect to American Samoa. The credit is not part of the Code but is computed based on the rules of sections 30A and 936. The credit is allowed for the first nine taxable years of a corporation that begin after December 31, 2005, and before January 1, 2015.

A corporation was an existing credit claimant with respect to a American Samoa if (1) the corporation was engaged in the active conduct of a trade or business within American Samoa on October 13, 1995, and (2) the corporation elected the benefits of the possession tax credit[646] in an election in effect for its taxable year that

---

[644] Sec. 7652(e)(2).

[645] Secs. 7652(a)(3), (b)(3), and (e)(1).

[646] For taxable years beginning before January 1, 2006, certain domestic corporations with business operations in the U.S. possessions were eligible for the possession tax credit. Secs. 27(b) and 936. This credit offset the U.S. tax imposed on certain income related to operations in the U.S. possessions. Subject to certain limitations, the amount of the possession tax credit allowed to any domestic corporation equaled the portion of that corporation's U.S. tax that was attributable to the corporation's non-U.S. source taxable income from (1) the active conduct of a trade or business within a U.S. possession, (2) the sale or exchange of substantially all of the assets that were used in such a trade or business, or (3) certain possessions investment. No deduction or foreign tax credit was allowed for any possessions or foreign tax paid or accrued with respect to taxable income that was taken into account in computing the credit under section 936. Under the economic activity-based limit, the amount of the credit could not exceed an amount equal to the sum of (1) 60 percent of the taxpayer's qualified possession wages and allocable employee fringe benefit expenses, (2) 15 percent of depreciation allowances with respect to short-life qualified tangible property, plus 40 percent of depreciation allowances with respect

included October 13, 1995. A corporation that added a substantial new line of business (other than in a qualifying acquisition of all the assets of a trade or business of an existing credit claimant) ceased to be an existing credit claimant as of the close of the taxable year ending before the date on which that new line of business was added.

A corporation will qualify as an existing credit claimant if it acquired all the assets of a trade or business of a corporation that (1) actively conducted that trade or business in a possession on October 13, 1995, and (2) had elected the benefits of the possession tax credit in an election in effect for the taxable year that included October 13, 1995.[647]

The amount of the credit allowed to a qualifying domestic corporation under the provision is equal to the sum of the amounts used in computing the corporation's economic activity-based limitation with respect to American Samoa, except that no credit is allowed for the amount of any American Samoa income taxes. Thus, for any qualifying corporation the amount of the credit equals the sum of (1) 60 percent of the corporation's qualified American Samoa wages and allocable employee fringe benefit expenses and (2) 15 percent of the corporation's depreciation allowances with respect to short-life qualified American Samoa tangible property, plus 40 percent of the corporation's depreciation allowances with respect to medium-life qualified American Samoa tangible property, plus 65 percent of the corporation's depreciation allowances with respect to long-life qualified American Samoa tangible property.

The section 936(c) rule denying a credit or deduction for any possessions or foreign tax paid with respect to taxable income taken into account in computing the credit under section 936 does not apply with respect to the credit allowed by the provision.

For taxable years beginning after December 31, 2011 the credit rules are modified in two ways. First, domestic corporations with operations in American Samoa are allowed the credit even if those corporations are not existing credit claimants. Second, the credit is available to a domestic corporation (either an existing credit claimant or a new credit claimant) only if, in addition to satisfying all the present law requirements for claiming the credit, the corporation also has qualified production activities income (as defined in section 199(c) by substituting "American Samoa" for "the United States" in each place that latter term appears).

In the case of a corporation that is an existing credit claimant with respect to American Samoa and that elected the application of section 936 for its last taxable year beginning before January 1,

---

to medium-life qualified tangible property, plus 65 percent of depreciation allowances with respect to long-life qualified tangible property, and (3) in certain cases, a portion of the taxpayer's possession income taxes. A taxpayer could elect, instead of the economic activity-based limit, a limit equal to the applicable percentage of the credit that otherwise would have been allowable with respect to possession business income, beginning in 1998, the applicable percentage was 40 percent.

To qualify for the possession tax credit for a taxable year, a domestic corporation was required to satisfy two conditions. First, the corporation was required to derive at least 80 percent of its gross income for the three-year period immediately preceding the close of the taxable year from sources within a possession. Second, the corporation was required to derive at least 75 percent of its gross income for that same period from the active conduct of a possession business. Sec. 936(a)(2). The section 936 credit generally expired for taxable years beginning after December 31, 2005.

[647] Sec. 306.

2006, the credit applies to the first nine taxable years of the corporation which begin after December 31, 2005, and before January 1, 2015. For any other corporation, the credit applies to the first three taxable years of that corporation which begin after December 31, 2011 and before January 1, 2015.

Explanation of Provision

The provision extends the credit for two years to apply (a) in the case of a corporation that is an existing credit claimant with respect to American Samoa and that elected the application of section 936 for its last taxable year beginning before January 1, 2006, to the first eleven taxable years of the corporation which begin after December 31, 2005, and before January 1, 2017, and (b) in the case of any other corporation, to the first five taxable years of the corporation which begin after December 31, 2011 and before January 1, 2017.

Effective Date

The provision applies to taxable years beginning after December 31, 2014.

17. Suspension of medical device excise tax (sec. 174 of the Act and sec. 4191 of the Code)

Present Law

Effective for sales after December 31, 2012, a tax equal to 2.3 percent of the sale price is imposed on the sale of any taxable medical device by the manufacturer, producer, or importer of such device.[648] A taxable medical device is any device, as defined in section 201(h) of the Federal Food, Drug, and Cosmetic Act,[649] intended for humans. Regulations further define a medical device as one that is listed by the Food and Drug Administration ("FDA") under section 510(j) of the Federal Food, Drug, and Cosmetic Act and 21 C.F.R. Part 807, pursuant to FDA requirements.[650]

The excise tax does not apply to eyeglasses, contact lenses, hearing aids, or any other medical device determined by the Secretary to be of a type that is generally purchased by the general public at retail for individual use ("retail exemption"). Regulations provide guidance on the types of devices that are exempt under the retail exemption. A device is exempt under these provisions if: (1) it is regularly available for purchase and use by individual consumers who are not medical professionals; and (2) the design of the device demonstrates that it is not primarily intended for use in a medical

---

[648] Sec. 4191.

[649] 21 U.S.C. sec. 321. Section 201(h) defines device as "an instrument, apparatus, implement, machine, contrivance, implant, in vitro reagent, or other similar or related article, including any component, part, or accessory, which is (1) recognized in the official National Formulary, or the United States Pharmacopeia, or any supplement to them, (2) intended for use in the diagnosis of disease or other conditions, or in the cure, mitigation, treatment, or prevention of disease, in man or other animals, or (3) intended to affect the structure or any function of the body of man or other animals, and which does not achieve its primary intended purposes through chemical action within or on the body of man or other animals and which is not dependent upon being metabolized for the achievement of its primary intended purposes."

[650] Treas. Reg. sec. 48.4191–2(a). The regulations also include as devices items that should have been listed as a device with the FDA as of the date the FDA notifies the manufacturer or importer that corrective action with respect to listing is required.

institution or office or by a medical professional.[651] Additionally, the regulations provide certain safe harbors for devices eligible for the retail exemption.[652]

The medical device excise tax is generally subject to the rules applicable to other manufacturers excise taxes. These rules include certain general manufacturers excise tax exemptions including the exemption for sales for use by the purchaser for further manufacture (or for resale to a second purchaser in further manufacture) or for export (or for resale to a second purchaser for export).[653] If a medical device is sold free of tax for resale to a second purchaser for further manufacture or for export, the exemption does not apply unless, within the six-month period beginning on the date of sale by the manufacturer, the manufacturer receives proof that the medical device has been exported or resold for use in further manufacturing.[654] In general, the exemption does not apply unless the manufacturer, the first purchaser, and the second purchaser are registered with the Secretary of the Treasury. Foreign purchasers of articles sold or resold for export are exempt from the registration requirement.

The lease of a medical device is generally considered to be a sale of such device.[655] Special rules apply for the imposition of tax to each lease payment. The use of a medical device subject to tax by manufacturers, producers, or importers of such device, is treated as a sale for the purpose of imposition of excise taxes.[656]

There are also rules for determining the price of a medical device on which the excise tax is imposed.[657] These rules provide for (1) the inclusion of containers, packaging, and certain transportation charges in the price, (2) determining a constructive sales price if a medical device is sold for less than the fair market price, and (3) determining the tax due in the case of partial payments or installment sales.

Explanation of Provision

The provision suspends the medical device excise tax for a period of two years, for sales on or after January 1, 2016 and before January 1, 2018.

Effective Date

The provision applies to sales after December 31, 2015.

---

[651] Treas. Reg. sec. 48.4191–2(b)(2).

[652] Treas. Reg. sec. 48.4191–2(b)(2)(iii). The safe harbors include devices that are described as over-the-counter devices in relevant FDA classification headings as well as certain FDA device classifications listed in the regulations.

[653] Sec. 4221(a). Other general manufacturers excise tax exemptions (*i.e.,* the exemption for sales to purchasers for use as supplies for vessels or aircraft, to a State or local government, to a nonprofit educational organization, or to a qualified blood collector organization) do not apply to the medical device excise tax.

[654] Sec. 4221(b).

[655] Sec. 4217(a).

[656] Sec. 4218.

[657] Sec. 4216.

Part 3—Incentives for Energy Production and Conservation

18. Extension and modification of credit for nonbusiness energy property (sec. 181 of the Act and sec. 25C of the Code)

Present Law

Present law provides a 10-percent credit for the purchase of qualified energy efficiency improvements to existing homes.[658] A qualified energy efficiency improvement is any energy efficiency building envelope component (1) that meets or exceeds the prescriptive criteria for such a component established by the 2009 International Energy Conservation Code as such Code (including supplements) is in effect on the date of the enactment of the American Recovery and Reinvestment Tax Act of 2009[659] (or, in the case of windows, skylights and doors, and metal roofs with appropriate pigmented coatings or asphalt roofs with appropriate cooling granules, meets the Energy Star program requirements); (2) that is installed in or on a dwelling located in the United States and owned and used by the taxpayer as the taxpayer's principal residence; (3) the original use of which commences with the taxpayer; and (4) that reasonably can be expected to remain in use for at least five years. The credit is nonrefundable.

Building envelope components are: (1) insulation materials or systems which are specifically and primarily designed to reduce the heat loss or gain for a dwelling and which meet the prescriptive criteria for such material or system established by the 2009 International Energy Conservation Code, as such Code (including supplements) is in effect on the date of the enactment of the American Recovery and Reinvestment Tax Act of 2009;[660] (2) exterior windows (including skylights) and doors; and (3) metal or asphalt roofs with appropriate pigmented coatings or cooling granules that are specifically and primarily designed to reduce the heat gain for a dwelling.

Additionally, present law provides credits for the purchase of specific energy efficient property originally placed in service by the taxpayer during the taxable year. The allowable credit for the purchase of certain property is (1) $50 for each advanced main air circulating fan, (2) $150 for each qualified natural gas, propane, or oil furnace or hot water boiler, and (3) $300 for each item of energy efficient building property.

An advanced main air circulating fan is a fan used in a natural gas, propane, or oil furnace and which has an annual electricity use of no more than two percent of the total annual energy use of the furnace (as determined in the standard Department of Energy test procedures).

A qualified natural gas, propane, or oil furnace or hot water boiler is a natural gas, propane, or oil furnace or hot water boiler with an annual fuel utilization efficiency rate of at least 95.

Energy-efficient building property is: (1) an electric heat pump water heater which yields an energy factor of at least 2.0 in the

---

[658] Sec. 25C.
[659] Pub. L. No. 111–5, February 17, 2009.
[660] *Ibid.*

standard Department of Energy test procedure, (2) an electric heat pump which achieves the highest efficiency tier established by the Consortium for Energy Efficiency, as in effect on January 1, 2009,[661] (3) a central air conditioner which achieves the highest efficiency tier established by the Consortium for Energy Efficiency as in effect on January 1, 2009,[662] (4) a natural gas, propane, or oil water heater which has an energy factor of at least 0.82 or thermal efficiency of at least 90 percent, and (5) biomass fuel property.

Biomass fuel property is a stove that burns biomass fuel to heat a dwelling unit located in the United States and used as a principal residence by the taxpayer, or to heat water for such dwelling unit, and that has a thermal efficiency rating of at least 75 percent. Biomass fuel is any plant-derived fuel available on a renewable or recurring basis, including agricultural crops and trees, wood and wood waste and residues (including wood pellets), plants (including aquatic plants), grasses, residues, and fibers.

The credit is available for property placed in service prior to January 1, 2015. The maximum credit for a taxpayer for all taxable years is $500, and no more than $200 of such credit may be attributable to expenditures on windows.

The taxpayer's basis in the property is reduced by the amount of the credit. Special proration rules apply in the case of jointly owned property, condominiums, and tenant-stockholders in cooperative housing corporations. If less than 80 percent of the property is used for nonbusiness purposes, only that portion of expenditures that is used for nonbusiness purposes is taken into account.

For purposes of determining the amount of expenditures made by any individual with respect to any dwelling unit, expenditures which are made from subsidized energy financing are not taken into account. The term "subsidized energy financing" means financing provided under a Federal, State, or local program a principal purpose of which is to provide subsidized financing for projects designed to conserve or produce energy.

Explanation of Provision

The provision extends the credit for two years, through December 31, 2016. Additionally, the provision modifies the efficiency standard to require that windows, skylights, and doors meet Energy Star 6.0 standards.

Effective Date

The provision applies to property placed in service after December 31, 2014.

The modification to the credit applies to property placed in service after December 31, 2015.

---

[661] These standards are a seasonal energy efficiency ratio ("SEER") greater than or equal to 15, an energy efficiency ratio ("EER") greater than or equal to 12.5, and heating seasonal performance factor ("HSPF") greater than or equal to 8.5 for split heat pumps, and SEER greater than or equal to 14, EER greater than or equal to 12, and HSPF greater than or equal to 8.0 for packaged heat pumps.

[662] These standards are a SEER greater than or equal to 16 and EER greater than or equal to 13 for split systems, and SEER greater than or equal to 14 and EER greater than or equal to 12 for packaged systems.

19. Extension of credit for alternative fuel vehicle refueling property (sec. 182 of the Act and section 30C of the Code)

Present Law

Taxpayers may claim a 30-percent credit for the cost of installing qualified clean-fuel vehicle refueling property to be used in a trade or business of the taxpayer or installed at the principal residence of the taxpayer.[663] The credit may not exceed $30,000 per taxable year per location, in the case of qualified refueling property used in a trade or business and $1,000 per taxable year per location, in the case of qualified refueling property installed on property which is used as a principal residence.

Qualified refueling property is property (not including a building or its structural components) for the storage or dispensing of a clean-burning fuel or electricity into the fuel tank or battery of a motor vehicle propelled by such fuel or electricity, but only if the storage or dispensing of the fuel or electricity is at the point of delivery into the fuel tank or battery of the motor vehicle. The original use of such property must begin with the taxpayer.

Clean-burning fuels are any fuel at least 85 percent of the volume of which consists of ethanol, natural gas, compressed natural gas, liquefied natural gas, liquefied petroleum gas, or hydrogen. In addition, any mixture of biodiesel and diesel fuel, determined without regard to any use of kerosene and containing at least 20 percent biodiesel, qualifies as a clean fuel.

Credits for qualified refueling property used in a trade or business are part of the general business credit and may be carried back for one year and forward for 20 years. Credits for residential qualified refueling property cannot exceed for any taxable year the difference between the taxpayer's regular tax (reduced by certain other credits) and the taxpayer's tentative minimum tax. Generally, in the case of qualified refueling property sold to a tax-exempt entity, the taxpayer selling the property may claim the credit.

A taxpayer's basis in qualified refueling property is reduced by the amount of the credit. In addition, no credit is available for property used outside the United States or for which an election to expense has been made under section 179.

The credit is available for property placed in service before January 1, 2015.

Explanation of Provision

The provision extends for two years the 30-percent credit for alternative fuel refueling property, through December 31, 2016.

Effective Date

The provision applies to property placed in service after December 31, 2014.

---

[663] Sec. 30C.

20. Extension of credit for electric motorcycles (sec. 183 of the Act and sec. 30D of the Code)

Present Law

For vehicles acquired before 2014, a 10-percent credit was available for qualifying plug-in electric motorcycles and three-wheeled vehicles.[664] Qualifying two- or three-wheeled vehicles needed to have a battery capacity of at least 2.5 kilowatt-hours, be manufactured primarily for use on public streets, roads, and highways, and be capable of achieving speeds of at least 45 miles per hours. The maximum credit for any qualifying vehicle was $2,500.

Explanation of Provision

The provision reauthorizes the credit for electric motorcycles acquired in 2015 and 2016 (but not 2014). The credit for electric three-wheeled vehicles is not extended.

Effective Date

The provision applies to vehicles acquired after December 31, 2014.

21. Extension of second generation biofuel producer credit (sec. 184 of the Act and sec. 40(b)(6) of the Code)

Present Law

The second generation biofuel producer credit is a nonrefundable income tax credit for each gallon of qualified second generation biofuel fuel production of the producer for the taxable year. The amount of the credit per gallon is $1.01. The provision does not apply to qualified second generation biofuel production after December 31, 2014.

"Qualified second generation biofuel production" is any second generation biofuel which is produced by the taxpayer and which, during the taxable year, is: (1) sold by the taxpayer to another person (a) for use by such other person in the production of a qualified second generation biofuel mixture in such person's trade or business (other than casual off-farm production), (b) for use by such other person as a fuel in a trade or business, or (c) who sells such second generation biofuel at retail to another person and places such cellulosic biofuel in the fuel tank of such other person; or (2) used by the producer for any purpose described in (1)(a), (b), or (c).[665] Special rules apply for fuel derived from algae.

"Second generation biofuel" means any liquid fuel that (1) is produced in the United States and used as fuel in the United States, (2) is derived by or from qualified feedstocks and (3) meets the registration requirements for fuels and fuel additives established by the Environmental Protection Agency ("EPA") under section 211 of the Clean Air Act. "Qualified feedstock" means any lignocellulosic

---

[664] Sec. 30D(g).

[665] In addition, for fuels derived from algae, cyanobacterial or lemna, a special rule provides that qualified second generation biofuel includes fuel that is sold by the taxpayer to another person for refining by such other person into a fuel that meets the registration requirements for fuels and fuel additives under section 211 of the Clean Air Act.

or hemicellulosic matter that is available on a renewable or recurring basis, and any cultivated algae, cyanobacteria or lemna. Second generation biofuel does not include fuels that (1) are more than four percent (determined by weight) water and sediment in any combination, (2) have an ash content of more than one percent (determined by weight), or (3) have an acid number greater than 25 ("unprocessed or excluded fuels"). It also does not include any alcohol with a proof of less than 150.

The second generation biofuel producer credit cannot be claimed unless the taxpayer is registered by the Internal Revenue Service ("IRS") as a producer of second generation biofuel. Second generation biofuel eligible for the section 40 credit is precluded from qualifying as biodiesel, renewable diesel, or alternative fuel for purposes of the applicable income tax credit, excise tax credit, or payment provisions relating to those fuels.

Because it is a credit under section 40(a), the second generation biofuel producer credit is part of the general business credits in section 38. However, the credit can only be carried forward three taxable years after the termination of the credit. The credit is also allowable against the alternative minimum tax. Under section 87, the credit is included in gross income.

Explanation of Provision

The provision extends the credit two years, through December 31, 2016.

Effective Date

The provision applies to qualified second generation biofuel production after December 31, 2014.

22. Extension of biodiesel and renewable diesel incentives (sec. 185 of the Act and sec. 40A of the Code)

Present Law

Biodiesel

Present law provides an income tax credit for biodiesel fuels (the "biodiesel fuels credit"). The biodiesel fuels credit is the sum of three credits: (1) the biodiesel mixture credit, (2) the biodiesel credit, and (3) the small agri-biodiesel producer credit. The biodiesel fuels credit is treated as a general business credit. The amount of the biodiesel fuels credit is includible in gross income. The biodiesel fuels credit is coordinated to take into account benefits from the biodiesel excise tax credit and payment provisions discussed below. The credit does not apply to fuel sold or used after December 31, 2014.

Biodiesel is monoalkyl esters of long chain fatty acids derived from plant or animal matter that meet (1) the registration requirements established by the EPA under section 211 of the Clean Air Act (42 U.S.C. sec. 7545) and (2) the requirements of the American Society of Testing and Materials ("ASTM") D6751. Agri-biodiesel is biodiesel derived solely from virgin oils including oils from corn, soybeans, sunflower seeds, cottonseeds, canola, crambe, rapeseeds, safflowers, flaxseeds, rice bran, mustard seeds, camelina, or animal fats.

Biodiesel may be taken into account for purposes of the credit only if the taxpayer obtains a certification (in such form and manner as prescribed by the Secretary) from the producer or importer of the biodiesel that identifies the product produced and the percentage of biodiesel and agri-biodiesel in the product.

Biodiesel mixture credit

The biodiesel mixture credit is $1.00 for each gallon of biodiesel (including agri-biodiesel) used by the taxpayer in the production of a qualified biodiesel mixture. A qualified biodiesel mixture is a mixture of biodiesel and diesel fuel that is (1) sold by the taxpayer producing such mixture to any person for use as a fuel, or (2) used as a fuel by the taxpayer producing such mixture. The sale or use must be in the trade or business of the taxpayer and is to be taken into account for the taxable year in which such sale or use occurs. No credit is allowed with respect to any casual off-farm production of a qualified biodiesel mixture.

Per IRS guidance a mixture need only contain 1/10th of one percent of diesel fuel to be a qualified mixture. Thus, a qualified biodiesel mixture can contain 99.9 percent biodiesel and 0.1 percent diesel fuel.

Biodiesel credit (B–100)

The biodiesel credit is $1.00 for each gallon of biodiesel that is not in a mixture with diesel fuel (100 percent biodiesel or B–100) and which during the taxable year is (1) used by the taxpayer as a fuel in a trade or business or (2) sold by the taxpayer at retail to a person and placed in the fuel tank of such person's vehicle.

Small agri-biodiesel producer credit

The Code provides a small agri-biodiesel producer income tax credit, in addition to the biodiesel and biodiesel mixture credits. The credit is 10 cents per gallon for up to 15 million gallons of agri-biodiesel produced by small producers, defined generally as persons whose agri-biodiesel production capacity does not exceed 60 million gallons per year. The agri-biodiesel must (1) be sold by such producer to another person (a) for use by such other person in the production of a qualified biodiesel mixture in such person's trade or business (other than casual off-farm production), (b) for use by such other person as a fuel in a trade or business, or, (c) who sells such agri-biodiesel at retail to another person and places such agri-biodiesel in the fuel tank of such other person; or (2) used by the producer for any purpose described in (a), (b), or (c).

Biodiesel mixture excise tax credit

The Code also provides an excise tax credit for biodiesel mixtures. The credit is $1.00 for each gallon of biodiesel used by the taxpayer in producing a biodiesel mixture for sale or use in a trade or business of the taxpayer. A biodiesel mixture is a mixture of biodiesel and diesel fuel that (1) is sold by the taxpayer producing such mixture to any person for use as a fuel or (2) is used as a fuel by the taxpayer producing such mixture. No credit is allowed unless the taxpayer obtains a certification (in such form and manner as prescribed by the Secretary) from the producer of the biodiesel that identifies the product produced and the percentage of biodiesel and agri-biodiesel in the product.

The credit is not available for any sale or use for any period after December 31, 2014. This excise tax credit is coordinated with the income tax credit for biodiesel such that credit for the same biodiesel cannot be claimed for both income and excise tax purposes.

Payments with respect to biodiesel fuel mixtures

If any person produces a biodiesel fuel mixture in such person's trade or business, the Secretary is to pay such person an amount equal to the biodiesel mixture credit. The biodiesel fuel mixture credit must first be taken against tax liability for taxable fuels. To the extent the biodiesel fuel mixture credit exceeds such tax liability, the excess may be received as a payment. Thus, if the person has no section 4081 liability, the credit is refundable. The Secretary is not required to make payments with respect to biodiesel fuel mixtures sold or used after December 31, 2014.

Renewable diesel

Renewable diesel is liquid fuel that (1) is derived from biomass (as defined in section 45K(c)(3)), (2) meets the registration requirements for fuels and fuel additives established by the EPA under section 211 of the Clean Air Act, and (3) meets the requirements of the ASTM D975 or D396, or equivalent standard established by the Secretary. ASTM D975 provides standards for diesel fuel suitable for use in diesel engines. ASTM D396 provides standards for fuel oil intended for use in fuel-oil burning equipment, such as furnaces. Renewable diesel also includes fuel derived from biomass that meets the requirements of a Department of Defense specification for military jet fuel or an ASTM specification for aviation turbine fuel.

For purposes of the Code, renewable diesel is generally treated the same as biodiesel. In the case of renewable diesel that is aviation fuel, kerosene is treated as though it were diesel fuel for purposes of a qualified renewable diesel mixture. Like biodiesel, the incentive may be taken as an income tax credit, an excise tax credit, or as a payment from the Secretary. The incentive for renewable diesel is $1.00 per gallon. There is no small producer credit for renewable diesel. The incentives for renewable diesel expired after December 31, 2014.

Explanation of Provision

The provision extends the present law income tax credit, excise tax credit and payment provisions for biodiesel and renewable diesel through December 31, 2016. As it relates to fuel sold or used in 2015, the provision creates a special rule to address claims regarding excise tax credits and claims for payment for the period beginning on January 1, 2015 and ending on December 31, 2015. In particular the provision directs the Secretary to issue guidance within 30 days of the date of enactment. Such guidance is to provide for a one-time submission of claims covering periods occurring during 2015. The guidance is to provide for a 180-day period for the submission of such claims (in such manner as prescribed by the Secretary) to begin no later than 30 days after such guidance is issued. Such claims shall be paid by the Secretary of the Treasury not later than 60 days after receipt. If the claim is not paid within 60 days of the date of the filing, the claim shall be paid with interest from such date determined by using the overpayment rate and method under section 6621 of the Code.

Effective Date

The extension of present law applies to fuel sold or used after December 31, 2014.

23. Extension of credit for the production of Indian coal facilities (sec. 186 of the Act and sec. 45 of the Code)

Present Law

A credit is available for the production of Indian coal sold to an unrelated third party from a qualified facility for a nine-year period beginning January 1, 2006, and ending December 31, 2014. The amount of the credit is $2.00 per ton (adjusted for inflation; $2.317 for 2014). A qualified Indian coal facility is a facility placed in service before January 1, 2009, that produces coal from reserves that on June 14, 2005, were owned by a Federally recognized tribe of Indians or were held in trust by the United States for a tribe or its members.

The credit is a component of the general business credit,[666] allowing excess credits to be carried back one year and forward up to 20 years. The credit is not permitted against the alternative minimum tax.

Explanation of Provision

The provision extends the credit for the production of Indian coal for two years (through December 31, 2016). The provision also removes the placed-in-service limitation for Indian coal facilities (thus permitting facilities placed in service after December 31, 2008, to qualify). The provision also modifies the third party sale requirement to permit related party sales to qualify so long as the Indian coal is subsequently sold to an unrelated third person. Finally, the provision exempts the Indian coal credit from the alternative minimum tax.

Effective Date

The extension of the credit applies to Indian coal produced after December 31, 2014.

The removal of the placed-in-service limitation and the modification to the third party sale requirement apply to coal produced and sold after December 31, 2015.

The provision exempting the credit from the alternative minimum tax applies to credits determined for taxable years beginning after December 31, 2015.

---

[666] Sec. 38(b)(8).

24. Extension of credits with respect to facilities producing energy from certain renewable resources (sec. 187 of the Act and secs. 45 and 48 of the Code)

Present Law

Renewable electricity production credit

An income tax credit is allowed for the production of electricity from qualified energy resources at qualified facilities (the "renewable electricity production credit").[667] Qualified energy resources comprise wind, closed-loop biomass, open-loop biomass, geothermal energy, municipal solid waste, qualified hydropower production, and marine and hydrokinetic renewable energy. Qualified facilities are, generally, facilities that generate electricity using qualified energy resources. To be eligible for the credit, electricity produced from qualified energy resources at qualified facilities must be sold by the taxpayer to an unrelated person.

SUMMARY OF CREDIT FOR ELECTRICITY PRODUCED FROM CERTAIN RENEWABLE RESOURCES

Eligible electricity production activity (sec. 45)	Credit amount for 2015[1] (cents per kilowatt-hour)	Expiration[2]
Wind	2.3	December 31, 2014
Closed-loop biomass	2.3	December 31, 2014
Open-loop biomass (including agricultural livestock waste nutrient facilities)	1.2	December 31, 2014
Geothermal	2.3	December 31, 2014
Municipal solid waste (including landfill gasfacilities and trash combustion facilities).	1.2	December 31, 2014
Qualified hydropower	1.2	December 31, 2014
Marine and hydrokinetic	1.2	December 31, 2014

[1] In general, the credit is available for electricity produced during the first 10 years after a facility has been placed in service.
[2] Expires for property the construction of which begins after this date.

Election to claim energy credit in lieu of renewable electricity production credit

A taxpayer may make an irrevocable election to have certain property which is part of a qualified renewable electricity production facility be treated as energy property eligible for a 30 percent investment credit under section 48. For this purpose, qualified facilities are facilities otherwise eligible for the renewable electricity production credit with respect to which no credit under section 45 has been allowed. A taxpayer electing to treat a facility as energy property may not claim the renewable electricity production credit. The eligible basis for the investment credit for taxpayers making this election is the basis of the depreciable (or amortizable) property that is part of a facility capable of generating electricity eligible for the renewable electricity production credit.

Explanation of Provision

Except for wind facilities, the provision extends for two years the renewable electricity production credit and the election to claim the energy credit in lieu of the electricity production credit (through December 31, 2016).

---

[667] Sec. 45. In addition to the renewable electricity production credit, section 45 also provides income tax credits for the production of Indian coal and refined coal at qualified facilities.

Effective Date

The provision is effective on January 1, 2015.

25. Extension of credit for energy-efficient new homes (sec. 188 of the Act and sec. 45L of the Code)

Present Law

Present law provides a credit to an eligible contractor for each qualified new energy-efficient home that is constructed by the eligible contractor and acquired by a person from such eligible contractor for use as a residence during the taxable year. To qualify as a new energy-efficient home, the home must be: (1) a dwelling located in the United States, (2) substantially completed after August 8, 2005, and (3) certified in accordance with guidance prescribed by the Secretary to have a projected level of annual heating and cooling energy consumption that meets the standards for either a 30-percent or 50-percent reduction in energy usage, compared to a comparable dwelling constructed in accordance with the standards of chapter 4 of the 2006 International Energy Conservation Code as in effect (including supplements) on January 1, 2006, and any applicable Federal minimum efficiency standards for equipment. With respect to homes that meet the 30-percent standard, one-third of such 30-percent savings must come from the building envelope, and with respect to homes that meet the 50-percent standard, one-fifth of such 50-percent savings must come from the building envelope.

Manufactured homes that conform to Federal manufactured home construction and safety standards are eligible for the credit provided all the criteria for the credit are met. The eligible contractor is the person who constructed the home, or in the case of a manufactured home, the producer of such home.

The credit equals $1,000 in the case of a new home that meets the 30-percent standard and $2,000 in the case of a new home that meets the 50-percent standard. Only manufactured homes are eligible for the $1,000 credit.

In lieu of meeting the standards of chapter 4 of the 2006 International Energy Conservation Code, manufactured homes certified by a method prescribed by the Administrator of the Environmental Protection Agency under the Energy Star Labeled Homes program are eligible for the $1,000 credit provided criteria (1) and (2), above, are met.

The credit applies to homes that are purchased prior to January 1, 2015. The credit is part of the general business credit.

Explanation of Provision

The provision extends the credit to homes that are acquired prior to January 1, 2017.

Effective Date

The provision applies to homes acquired after December 31, 2014.

26. Extension of special allowance for second generation biofuel plant property (sec. 189 of the Act and sec. 168(l) of the Code)

Present Law

Present law [668] allows an additional first-year depreciation deduction equal to 50 percent of the adjusted basis of qualified second generation biofuel plant property. In order to qualify, the property generally must be placed in service before January 1, 2015.[669]

Qualified second generation biofuel plant property means depreciable property used in the U.S. solely to produce any liquid fuel that (1) is derived from qualified feedstocks, and (2) meets the registration requirements for fuels and fuel additives established by the Environmental Protection Agency ("EPA") under section 211 of the Clean Air Act.[670] Qualified feedstocks means any lignocellulosic or hemicellulosic matter that is available on a renewable or recurring basis [671] and any cultivated algae, cyanobacteria, or lemna.[672] Second generation biofuel does not include any alcohol with a proof of less than 150 or certain unprocessed fuel.[673] Unprocessed fuels are fuels that (1) are more than four percent (determined by weight) water and sediment in any combination, (2) have an ash content of more than one percent (determined by weight), or (3) have an acid number greater than 25.[674]

The additional first-year depreciation deduction is allowed for both regular tax and alternative minimum tax purposes for the taxable year in which the property is placed in service.[675] The additional first-year depreciation deduction is subject to the general rules regarding whether an item is subject to capitalization under section 263A. The basis of the property and the depreciation allowances in the year of purchase and later years are appropriately adjusted to reflect the additional first-year depreciation deduction.[676] In addition, there is no adjustment to the allowable amount of depreciation for purposes of computing a taxpayer's alternative minimum taxable income with respect to property to which the provision applies.[677] A taxpayer is allowed to elect out of the additional first-year depreciation for any class of property for any taxable year.[678]

In order for property to qualify for the additional first-year depreciation deduction, it must meet the following requirements: (1) the original use of the property must commence with the taxpayer; and (2) the property must be (i) acquired by purchase (as defined under section 179(d)) by the taxpayer, and (ii) placed in service before January 1, 2015.[679] Property that is manufactured, con-

---

[668] Sec. 168(l).
[669] Sec. 168(l)(2)(D).
[670] Secs. 168(l)(2)(A) and 40(b)(6)(E).
[671] For example, lignocellulosic or hemicellulosic matter that is available on a renewable or recurring basis includes bagasse (from sugar cane), corn stalks, and switchgrass.
[672] Sec. 40(b)(6)(F).
[673] Sec. 40(b)(6)(E)(ii) and (iii).
[674] Sec. 40(b)(6)(E)(iii).
[675] Sec. 168(l)(5).
[676] Sec. 168(l)(1)(B).
[677] Sec. 168(l)(5) and (k)(2)(G).
[678] Sec. 168(l)(3)(D).
[679] Sec. 168(l)(2). Requirements relating to actions taken before 2007 are not described herein since they have little (if any) remaining effect.

structed, or produced by the taxpayer for use by the taxpayer qualifies if the taxpayer begins the manufacture, construction, or production of the property before January 1, 2015 (and all other requirements are met).[680] Property that is manufactured, constructed, or produced for the taxpayer by another person under a contract that is entered into prior to the manufacture, construction, or production of the property is considered to be manufactured, constructed, or produced by the taxpayer.

Property any portion of which is financed with the proceeds of a tax-exempt obligation under section 103 is not eligible for the additional first-year depreciation deduction.[681] Recapture rules apply if the property ceases to be qualified second generation biofuel plant property.[682]

Property with respect to which the taxpayer has elected 50 percent expensing under section 179C is not eligible for the additional first-year depreciation deduction.[683]

Explanation of Provision

The provision extends the present law special depreciation allowance for two years, to qualified second generation biofuel plant property placed in service prior to January 1, 2017.

Effective Date

The provision applies to property placed in service after December 31, 2014.

27. Extension of energy efficient commercial buildings deduction (sec. 190 of the Act and sec. 179D of the Code)

Present Law

In general

Code section 179D provides an election under which a taxpayer may take an immediate deduction equal to energy-efficient commercial building property expenditures made by the taxpayer. Energy-efficient commercial building property is defined as property (1) which is installed on or in any building located in the United States that is within the scope of Standard 90.1–2001 of the American Society of Heating, Refrigerating, and Air Conditioning Engineers and the Illuminating Engineering Society of North America ("ASHRAE/IESNA"), (2) which is installed as part of (i) the interior lighting systems, (ii) the heating, cooling, ventilation, and hot water systems, or (iii) the building envelope, and (3) which is certified as being installed as part of a plan designed to reduce the total annual energy and power costs with respect to the interior lighting systems, heating, cooling, ventilation, and hot water systems of the building by 50 percent or more in comparison to a reference building which meets the minimum requirements of Standard 90.1–2001 (as in effect on April 2, 2003). The deduction is limited to an amount equal to $1.80 per square foot of the property

---
[680] Sec. 168(l)(4) and (k)(2)(E).
[681] Sec. 168(l)(3)(C).
[682] Sec. 168(l)(6).
[683] Sec. 168(l)(7).

for which such expenditures are made. The deduction is allowed in the year in which the property is placed in service.

Certain certification requirements must be met in order to qualify for the deduction. The Secretary, in consultation with the Secretary of Energy, will promulgate regulations that describe methods of calculating and verifying energy and power costs using qualified computer software based on the provisions of the 2005 California Nonresidential Alternative Calculation Method Approval Manual or, in the case of residential property, the 2005 California Residential Alternative Calculation Method Approval Manual.

The Secretary is granted authority to prescribe procedures for the inspection and testing for compliance of buildings that are comparable, given the difference between commercial and residential buildings, to the requirements in the Mortgage Industry National Accreditation Procedures for Home Energy Rating Systems.[684] Individuals qualified to determine compliance shall only be those recognized by one or more organizations certified by the Secretary for such purposes.

For energy-efficient commercial building property expenditures made by a public entity, such as public schools, the deduction may be allocated to the person primarily responsible for designing the property in lieu of the public entity.

If a deduction is allowed under this section, the basis of the property is reduced by the amount of the deduction.

The deduction applies to property placed in service prior to January 1, 2015.

Partial allowance of deduction

System-specific deductions

In the case of a building that does not meet the overall building requirement of 50-percent energy savings, a partial deduction is allowed with respect to each separate building system that comprises energy efficient property and which is certified by a qualified professional as meeting or exceeding the applicable system-specific savings targets established by the Secretary. The applicable system-specific savings targets to be established by the Secretary are those that would result in a total annual energy savings with respect to the whole building of 50 percent, if each of the separate systems met the system specific target. The separate building systems are (1) the interior lighting system, (2) the heating, cooling, ventilation and hot water systems, and (3) the building envelope. The maximum allowable deduction is $0.60 per square foot for each separate system.

Interim rules for lighting systems

In general, in the case of system-specific partial deductions, no deduction is allowed until the Secretary establishes system-specific targets.[685] However, in the case of lighting system retrofits, until

---

[684] See IRS Notice 2006–52, 2006–1 C.B. 1175, June 2, 2006; IRS 2008–40, 2008–14 I.R.B. 725 March 11, 2008.

[685] IRS Notice 2008–40, *Supra*, set a target of a 10-percent reduction in total energy and power costs with respect to the building envelope, and 20 percent each with respect to the interior lighting system and the heating, cooling, ventilation and hot water systems. IRS Notice 2012–26 (2012–17 I.R.B. 847 April 23, 2012) established new targets of 10-percent reduction in

such time as the Secretary issues final regulations, the system-specific energy savings target for the lighting system is deemed to be met by a reduction in lighting power density of 40 percent (50 percent in the case of a warehouse) of the minimum requirements in Table 9.3.1.1 or Table 9.3.1.2 of ASHRAE/IESNA Standard 90.1–2001. Also, in the case of a lighting system that reduces lighting power density by 25 percent, a partial deduction of 30 cents per square foot is allowed. A pro-rated partial deduction is allowed in the case of a lighting system that reduces lighting power density between 25 percent and 40 percent. Certain lighting level and lighting control requirements must also be met in order to qualify for the partial lighting deductions under the interim rule.

Explanation of Provision

The provision extends the deduction for two years, through December 31, 2016.

Effective Date

The provision applies to property placed in service after December 31, 2014.

28. Extension of special rule for sales or dispositions to implement FERC or State electric restructuring policy for qualified electric utilities (sec. 191 of the Act and sec. 451(i) of the Code)

Present Law

A taxpayer selling property generally realizes gain to the extent the sales price (and any other consideration received) exceeds the taxpayer's basis in the property.[686] The realized gain is subject to current income tax[687] unless the recognition of the gain is deferred or excluded from income under a special tax provision.[688]

One such special tax provision permits taxpayers to elect to recognize gain from qualifying electric transmission transactions ratably over an eight-year period beginning in the year of sale if the amount realized from such sale is used to purchase exempt utility property within the applicable period[689] (the "reinvestment property").[690] If the amount realized exceeds the amount used to purchase reinvestment property, any realized gain is recognized to the extent of such excess in the year of the qualifying electric transmission transaction.

A qualifying electric transmission transaction is the sale or other disposition of property used by a qualified electric utility to an

---

total energy and power costs with respect to the building envelope, 25 percent with respect to the interior lighting system and 15 percent with respect to the heating, cooling, ventilation and hot water systems, effective beginning March 12, 2012. The targets from Notice 2008–40 may be used until December 31, 2013, but the targets of Notice 2012–26 apply thereafter.

[686] See sec. 1001.
[687] See secs. 61 and 451.
[688] See, e.g., secs. 453, 1031 and 1033.
[689] The applicable period for a taxpayer to reinvest the proceeds is four years after the close of the taxable year in which the qualifying electric transmission transaction occurs.
[690] Sec. 451(i).

independent transmission company prior to January 1, 2015.[691] A qualified electric utility is defined as an electric utility, which as of the date of the qualifying electric transmission transaction, is vertically integrated in that it is both (1) a transmitting utility (as defined in the Federal Power Act[692]) with respect to the transmission facilities to which the election applies, and (2) an electric utility (as defined in the Federal Power Act[693]).[694]

In general, an independent transmission company is defined as: (1) an independent transmission provider[695] approved by the Federal Energy Regulatory Commission ("FERC"); (2) a person (i) who the FERC determines under section 203 of the Federal Power Act[696] (or by declaratory order) is not a "market participant" and (ii) whose transmission facilities are placed under the operational control of a FERC-approved independent transmission provider no later than four years after the close of the taxable year in which the transaction occurs; or (3) in the case of facilities subject to the jurisdiction of the Public Utility Commission of Texas, (i) a person which is approved by that Commission as consistent with Texas State law regarding an independent transmission organization, or (ii) a political subdivision, or affiliate thereof, whose transmission facilities are under the operational control of an organization described in (i).[697]

Exempt utility property is defined as: (1) property used in the trade or business of (i) generating, transmitting, distributing, or selling electricity or (ii) producing, transmitting, distributing, or selling natural gas; or (2) stock in a controlled corporation whose principal trade or business consists of the activities described in (1).[698] Exempt utility property does not include any property that is located outside of the United States.[699]

If a taxpayer is a member of an affiliated group of corporations filing a consolidated return, the reinvestment property may be purchased by any member of the affiliated group (in lieu of the taxpayer).[700]

Explanation of Provision

The provision extends for two years the treatment under the present-law deferral provision to sales or dispositions by a qualified electric utility that occur prior to January 1, 2017.

Effective Date

The provision applies to dispositions after December 31, 2014.

---

[691] Sec. 451(i)(3).

[692] Sec. 3(23), 16 U.S.C. sec. 796, defines "transmitting utility" as any electric utility, qualifying cogeneration facility, qualifying small power production facility, or Federal power marketing agency that owns or operates electric power transmission facilities that are used for the sale of electric energy at wholesale.

[693] Sec. 3(22), 16 U.S.C. sec. 796, defines "electric utility" as any person or State agency (including any municipality) that sells electric energy; such term includes the Tennessee Valley Authority, but does not include any Federal power marketing agency.

[694] Sec. 451(i)(6).

[695] For example, a regional transmission organization, an independent system operator, or an independent transmission company.

[696] 16 U.S.C. sec. 824b.

[697] Sec. 451(i)(4).

[698] Sec. 451(i)(5).

[699] Sec. 451(i)(5)(C).

[700] Sec. 451(i)(7).

29. Extension of excise tax credits and payment provisions relating to alternative fuel (sec. 192 of the Act and secs. 6426 and 6427 of the Code)

Present Law

Alternative fuel and alternative fuel mixture credits and payments

The Code provides two per-gallon excise tax credits with respect to alternative fuel: the alternative fuel credit, and the alternative fuel mixture credit. For this purpose, the term alternative fuel means liquefied petroleum gas, P Series fuels (as defined by the Secretary of Energy under 42 U.S.C. sec. 13211(2)), compressed or liquefied natural gas, liquefied hydrogen, liquid fuel derived from coal through the Fischer-Tropsch process (coal-to-liquids), compressed or liquefied gas derived from biomass, or liquid fuel derived from biomass. Such term does not include ethanol, methanol, or biodiesel.

For coal-to-liquids produced after December 30, 2009, the fuel must be certified as having been derived from coal produced at a gasification facility that separates and sequesters 75 percent of such facility's total carbon dioxide emissions.

The alternative fuel credit is allowed against section 4041 liability, and the alternative fuel mixture credit is allowed against section 4081 liability. Neither credit is allowed unless the taxpayer is registered with the Secretary. The alternative fuel credit is 50 cents per gallon of alternative fuel or gasoline gallon equivalents [701] of nonliquid alternative fuel sold by the taxpayer for use as a motor fuel in a motor vehicle or motorboat, sold for use in aviation or so used by the taxpayer.

The alternative fuel mixture credit is 50 cents per gallon of alternative fuel used in producing an alternative fuel mixture for sale or use in a trade or business of the taxpayer. An alternative fuel mixture is a mixture of alternative fuel and taxable fuel (gasoline, diesel fuel or kerosene) that contains at least 1/10 of one percent taxable fuel. The mixture must be sold by the taxpayer producing such mixture to any person for use as a fuel, or used by the taxpayer producing the mixture as a fuel. The credits expired after December 31, 2014.

A person may file a claim for payment equal to the amount of the alternative fuel credit (but not the alternative fuel mixture credit). The alternative fuel credit must first be applied to the applicable excise tax liability under section 4041 or 4081, and any excess credit may be taken as a payment. These payment provisions generally also expire after December 31, 2014.

For purposes of the alternative fuel credit, alternative fuel mixture credit and related payment provisions, alternative fuel does not include fuel (including lignin, wood residues, or spent pulping liquors) derived from the production of paper or pulp.

---

[701] "Gasoline gallon equivalent" means, with respect to any nonliquid alternative fuel (for example, compressed natural gas), the amount of such fuel having a Btu (British thermal unit) content of 124,800 (higher heating value).

Explanation of Provision

The provision extends the alternative fuel credit and related payment provisions, and the alternative fuel mixture credit through December 31, 2016.[702]

In light of the retroactive nature of the provision, as it relates to alternative fuel sold or used in 2015, the provision creates a special rule to address claims regarding excise credits and claims for payment for the period beginning January 1, 2015 and ending on December 31, 2015. In particular, the provision directs the Secretary to issue guidance within 30 days of the date of enactment. Such guidance is to provide for a one-time submission of claims covering periods occurring during 2015. The guidance is to provide for a 180-day period for the submission of such claims (in such manner as prescribed by the Secretary) to begin no later than 30 days after such guidance is issued.[703] Such claims shall be paid by the Secretary of the Treasury not later than 60 days after receipt. If the claim is not paid within 60 days of the date of the filing, the claim shall be paid with interest from such date determined by using the overpayment rate and method under section 6621 of such Code.

Effective Date

The provision generally applies to fuel sold or used after December 31, 2014.

30. Extension of credit for fuel cell vehicles (sec. 193 of the Act and sec. 30B of the Code)

Present Law

A credit is available through 2014 for vehicles propelled by chemically combining oxygen with hydrogen and creating electricity (fuel cell vehicles). The base credit is $4,000 for vehicles weighing 8,500 pounds or less. Heavier vehicles can get up to a $40,000 credit, depending on their weight. An additional $1,000 to $4,000 credit is available to cars and light trucks to the extent their fuel economy exceeds the 2002 base fuel economy set forth in the Code.

Explanation of Provision

The provision extends the credit for fuel cell vehicles for two years, through December 31, 2016.

Effective Date

The provision applies to property purchased after December 31, 2014.

---

[702] See section 342 of the Act with respect to additional provisions related to liquefied petroleum gas and liquefied natural gas.

[703] This guidance is provided by Notice 2015–3, 2015–6 I.R.B 583.

TITLE II—PROGRAM INTEGRITY

1. Modification of filing dates of returns and statements relating to employee wage information and nonemployee compensation to improve compliance (sec. 201 of the Act and secs. 6071 and 6402 of the Code)

Present Law

Information returns concerning certain payments

Present law requires persons to file an information return concerning certain transactions with other persons.[704] These returns are intended to assist taxpayers in preparing their income tax returns and to help the IRS determine whether such income tax returns are correct and complete.

One of the primary provisions requires every person engaged in a trade or business who makes payments aggregating $600 or more in any taxable year to a single payee in the course of the payor's trade or business to file a return reporting these payments.[705] Payments subject to this reporting requirement include fixed or determinable income or compensation, but do not include payments for goods or certain enumerated types of payments that are subject to other specific reporting requirements. Other reporting requirements are provided for various types of investment income, including interest, dividends, and gross proceeds from brokered transactions (such as a sale of stock) paid to U.S. persons.[706]

The person filing an information return with respect to payments described above is required to provide the recipient of the payment with a written payee statement showing the aggregate payments made and contact information for the payor.[707] The statement must be supplied to payees by the payors by January 31 of the following calendar year.[708] Payors generally must file the information return with the IRS by February 28 of the year following the calendar year for which the return must be filed.[709] However, the due date for most information returns that are filed electronically is March 31.[710]

Information returns regarding wages paid employees

Payors must report wage amounts paid to employees on information returns and provide the employee with an annual statement showing the aggregate wages paid, taxes withheld, and contact information for the payor by January 31 of the following calendar

---

[704] Secs. 6041–6050W.

[705] Sec. 6041(a). The information return generally is submitted electronically as a Form 1099 (*e.g.,* Form 1099–MISC, Miscellaneous Income) or Form 1096, Annual Summary and Transmittal of U.S. Information Returns, although certain payments to beneficiaries or employees may require use of Forms W–3 or W–2, respectively. Treas. Reg. sec. 1.6041–1(a)(2).

[706] Secs. 6042 dividends), 6045 (broker reporting) and 6049 (interest) and the Treasury regulations thereunder.

[707] Sec. 6041(d).

[708] Sec. 6041(d).

[709] Treas. Reg. sec. 31.6071(a)–1(a)(3)(i).

[710] Sections 6011(e) and 6071(b) apply to "returns made under subparts B and C of part III of this subchapter"; Treas. Reg. sec. 301.6011–2(b) mandates use of magnetic media by persons filing information returns identified in the regulation or subsequent or contemporaneous revenue procedures and permits use of magnetic media for all others.

year, using Form W–2, Wage and Tax Statement.[711] For wages paid to employees, and taxes withheld from employee wages, the payors must file an information return with the Social Security Administration ("SSA") on or before the last day of February of the year following the calendar year for which the return must be filed, using Form W–3, Transmittal of Wage and Tax Statements.[712] The due date for these information returns that are filed electronically is March 31.

Under the combined annual wage reporting ("CAWR") system, the SSA and the IRS have an agreement, in the form of a Memorandum of Understanding, to share wage data and to resolve, or reconcile, the differences in the wages reported to them. Employers submit Forms W–2, (listing Social Security wages earned by individual employees), and W–3, (providing an aggregate summary of wages paid and taxes withheld) directly to SSA.[713] After it records the wage information from Forms W–2 and W–3 in its individual Social Security wage account records, SSA forwards the information to IRS.[714]

Rules relating to refunds and certain refundable credits

A refund is due to a taxpayer with respect to a taxable year if the taxpayer has made an overpayment of Federal income taxes,[715] to the extent that such overpayment is not required to be applied to offset other liabilities.[716]

An individual may reduce his or her tax liability by any available tax credits. In some instances, a permissible credit is "refundable," i.e., it may result in a refund in excess of any credits for withheld taxes or estimated tax payments available to the individual. Two such credits are the child tax credit and the earned income tax credit ("EITC").

An individual may claim a tax credit for each qualifying child under the age of 17. The amount of the credit per child is $1,000. The aggregate amount of child credits that may be claimed is phased out for individuals with income over certain threshold amounts. Specifically, the otherwise allowable child tax credit is reduced by $50 for each $1,000 (or fraction thereof) of modified adjusted gross income over $75,000 for single individuals or heads of households, $110,000 for married individuals filing joint returns, and $55,000 for married individuals filing separate returns. To the extent the child credit exceeds the taxpayer's tax liability, the taxpayer is eligible for a refundable credit[717] (the additional child tax credit) equal to 15 percent of earned income in excess of $3,000.[718]

---

[711] Sec. 6051(a).

[712] Treas. Reg. sec. 31.6051–2; IRS, "Filing Information Returns Electronically," Pub. 3609 (Rev. 12–2011); Treas. Reg. sec. 31.6071(a)–1(a)(3)(i).

[713] Pub. L. No. 94–202, sec. 232, 89 Stat. 1135 (1976) (effective with respect to statements reporting income received after 1977).

[714] Employers submit quarterly reports to IRS on Form 941, Employer's Quarterly Federal Tax Return, regarding aggregate quarterly totals of wages paid and taxes due. IRS then compares the W–3 wage totals to the Form 941 wage totals.

[715] Sec. 6402(a).

[716] Such liabilities include past-due support payments (sec. 6402(c)), debts owed to other Federal agencies (sec. 6402(d)), certain State income tax debts (sec. 6402(e)), or unemployment compensation debts (sec. 6402(f)).

[717] The refundable credit may not exceed the maximum credit per child of $1,000.

[718] Families with three or more children may determine the additional child tax credit using an alternative formula, if this results in a larger credit than determined under the earned in-

The EITC is available to low-income workers who satisfy certain requirements. The amount of the EITC varies depending upon the taxpayer's earned income and whether the taxpayer has one, two, more than two, or no qualifying children. In 2015, the maximum EITC is $6,242 for taxpayers with more than two qualifying children, $5,548 for taxpayers with two qualifying children, $3,359 for taxpayers with one qualifying child, and $503 for taxpayers with no qualifying children. The credit amount begins to phaseout at an income level of $23,630 for joint-filers with children, $18,110 for other taxpayers with children, $13,750 for joint-filers with no children and $8,240 for other taxpayers with no qualifying children. The phaseout percentages are 15.98 for taxpayers with one qualifying child, 21.06 for two or more qualifying children and 7.65 for no qualifying children.

For purposes of computing a taxpayer's overpayment of tax, the amount of refundable credits in excess of income tax liability is considered to be an overpayment of tax.[719] Thus, the Internal Revenue Service pays the value of these credits, to the extent they are in excess of a taxpayer's income tax liability, and not applied to offset other liabilities, to the taxpayer as a refund of tax.

At the time that the taxpayer files a return claiming a refundable credit, the Internal Revenue Service is generally not in possession of information needed to confirm the taxpayer's eligibility for such credit, even though payors must report wage amounts paid to employees on information returns and provide the employee with an annual statement showing the aggregate payments made and contact information for the payor by January 31 of the following calendar year.[720]

Explanation of Provision

The provision requires that certain information returns be filed by January 31, generally the same date as the due date for employee and payee statements, and that such returns are no longer eligible for the extended filing date for electronically filed returns under section 6071(b). Specifically, the provision accelerates the filing of information on wages reportable on Form W–2 and nonemployee compensation. The due date for employee and payee statements remains the same. Nonemployee compensation generally includes fees for professional services, commissions, awards, travel expense reimbursements, or other forms of payments for services performed for the payor's trade or business by someone other than in the capacity of an employee.

Additionally, the provision requires that no credit or refund for an overpayment for a taxable year shall be made to a taxpayer before the 15th day of the second month following the close of that taxable year, if the taxpayer claimed the EITC or additional child tax credit on the tax return. Individual taxpayers are generally calendar year taxpayers, thus, for most taxpayers who claim the EITC or additional child tax credit this rule would apply such that a refund of tax would not be made to such taxpayer prior to February

---

come formula. Under the alternative formula, the additional child tax credit equals the amount by which the taxpayer's social security taxes exceed the taxpayer's EITC.

[719] Sec. 6401(b).
[720] Sec. 6051(a).

15th of the year following the calendar year to which the taxes relate.

Effective Date

The provision is effective for returns and statements relating to calendar years beginning after the date of enactment (December 18, 2015). The provision pertaining to the payment of certain refunds shall apply to credits or refunds made after December 31, 2016.

2. Safe harbor for *de minimis* errors on information returns, payee statements, and withholding (sec. 202 of the Act and secs. 6721 and 6722 of the Code)

Present Law

Failure to comply with the information reporting requirements results in penalties, which may include a penalty for failure to file the information return,[721] to furnish payee statements,[722] or to comply with other various reporting requirements.[723] No penalty is imposed if the failure is due to reasonable cause.[724]

Any person who is required to file an information return, or furnish a payee statement, but who fails to do so on or before the prescribed due date, is subject to a penalty that varies based on when, if at all, the information return is filed. Both the failure to file and failure to furnish penalties are adjusted annually to account for inflation. In the Trade Preferences Extension Act of 2015,[725] the penalties were increased for information returns or payee statements due after December 31, 2015. The penalty amounts, whether they are limited to a maximum amount in a calendar year, and the changes enacted in the Trade Preferences Extension Act, are described below.

Penalties with respect to returns or statement due before January 1, 2016.

If a person files an information return after the prescribed filing date but on or before the date that is 30 days after the prescribed filing date, the amount of the penalty is $30 per return ("first-tier penalty"), with a maximum penalty of $250,000 per calendar year. If a person files an information return after the date that is 30 days after the prescribed filing date but on or before August 1, the amount of the penalty is $60 per return ("second-tier penalty"), with a maximum penalty of $500,000 per calendar year. If an information return is not filed on or before August 1 of any year, the amount of the penalty is $100 per return ("third-tier penalty"), with a maximum penalty of $1,500,000 per calendar year. If a failure to file is due to intentional disregard of a filing requirement, the minimum penalty for each failure is $250, with no calendar year limit.

---

[721] Sec. 6721.
[722] Sec. 6722.
[723] Sec. 6723. The penalty for failure to comply timely with a specified information reporting requirement is $50 per failure, not to exceed $100,000 per calendar year.
[724] Sec. 6724.
[725] Trade Preferences Extension Act of 2015, Pub. L. No. 114–27, sec. 806 (June 29, 2015).

Lower maximum levels for this failure to file correct information return penalty apply to small businesses. Small businesses are defined as firms having average annual gross receipts for the most recent three taxable years that do not exceed $5 million. The maximum penalties for small businesses are: $75,000 (instead of $250,000) if the failures are corrected on or before 30 days after the prescribed filing date; $200,000 (instead of $500,000) if the failures are corrected on or before August 1; and $500,000 (instead of $1,500,000) if the failures are not corrected on or before August 1.

Any person who is required to furnish a payee statement who fails to do so on or before the prescribed filing date is subject to a penalty that varies based on when, if at all, the payee statement is furnished, similar to the penalty for filing an information return discussed above. A first-tier penalty is $30, subject to a maximum of $250,000, a second-tier penalty is $60 per statement, up to $500,000, and a third-tier penalty is $100, up to a maximum of $1,500,000. Lower maximum levels for this failure to furnish correct payee statement penalty apply to small businesses. Small businesses are defined as firms having average annual gross receipts for the most recent three taxable years that do not exceed $5 million. The maximum penalties for small businesses are: $75,000 (instead of $250,000) if the failures are corrected on or before 30 days after the prescribed filing date; $200,000 (instead of $500,000) if the failures are corrected on or before August 1; and $500,000 (instead of $1,500,000) if the failures are not corrected on or before August 1.

In cases in which the failure to file an information return or to furnish the correct payee statement is due to intentional disregard, the minimum penalty for each failure is $250, with no calendar year limit. No distinction is made between small businesses and other persons required to report.

Penalties with respect to returns or statements due after December 31, 2015

The Trade Preferences Extension Act of 2015 increased the penalties to the following amounts for information returns or payee statements due after December 31, 2015. The first-tier penalty is $50 per return, with a maximum penalty of $500,000 per calendar year. The second-tier penalty increases to $100 per return, with a maximum penalty of $1,500,000 per calendar year. The third-tier penalty increases to $250 per return, with a maximum penalty of $3,000,000 per calendar year.

The lower maximum levels applicable to small businesses also were increased, as follows. The maximum penalties for small businesses are: $175,000 if the failures are corrected on or before 30 days after the prescribed filing date; $500,000 if the failures are corrected on or before August 1; and $1,000,000 if the failures are not corrected on or before August 1.

For failures or misstatements due to intentional disregard, the penalty per return or statement increased to $500, with no calendar year limit. No distinction between small businesses and other persons required to report is made in such cases.

Explanation of Provision

The provision creates a safe harbor from the application of the penalty for failure to file a correct information return and the penalty for failure to furnish a correct payee statement in circumstances in which the information return or payee statement is otherwise correctly filed but includes a *de minimis* error of the amount required to be reported on such return or statement. In general, a *de minimis* error of an amount on the information return or statement need not be corrected if the error for any single amount does not exceed $100. A lower threshold of $25 is established for errors with respect to the reporting of an amount of withholding or backup withholding. The provision requires broker reporting to be consistent with amounts reported on uncorrected returns which are eligible for the safe harbor. If any person receiving payee statements requests a corrected statement, the penalty for failure to file a correct information return and the penalty for failure to furnish a correct payee statement would continue to apply in the case of a *de minimis* error.

Effective Date

The provision applies to information returns required to be filed and payee statements required to be furnished after December 31, 2016.

3. Requirements for the issuance of ITINs (sec. 203 of the Act and sec. 6109 of the Code)

Present Law

Any individual filing a U.S. tax return is required to state his or her taxpayer identification number on such return. Generally, a taxpayer identification number is the individual's Social Security number ("SSN").[726] However, in the case of individuals who are not eligible to be issued an SSN, but who still have a tax filing obligation, the IRS issues IRS individual taxpayer identification numbers ("ITIN") for use in connection with the individual's tax filing requirements.[727] An individual who is eligible to receive an SSN may not obtain an ITIN for purposes of his or her tax filing obligations.[728] An ITIN does not provide eligibility to work in the United States or claim Social Security benefits.

Examples of individuals who potentially need an ITIN in order to file a U.S. return include nonresident aliens filing a claim for a reduced withholding rate under treaty benefits, a nonresident alien required to file a U.S. tax return, a U.S. resident alien filing a U.S. tax return, a dependent or spouse of a U.S. citizen or resident alien, or a dependent or spouse of a nonresident alien visa holder.

Taxpayers applying for an ITIN must complete a Form W-7, "Application For IRS Individual Taxpayer Identification Number." For identification purposes, the Form W-7 requires that taxpayers include original documentation such as passports and birth certificates, or certified copies of these documents by the issuing agency.

---

[726] Sec. 6109(a).
[727] Treas. Reg. Sec. 301.6109–1(d)(3)(i).
[728] Treas. Reg. Sec. 301.6109–1(d)(3)(ii).

Notarized or apostilized copies of such documentation are insufficient.[729] Supporting documentation to establish a taxpayer's identity includes: passport, USCIS photo identification, visa issued by U.S. Department of State, U.S. driver's license, U.S. military identification card, foreign driver's license, foreign military identification card, national identification card (must be current and contain name, photograph, address, DOB, and expiration date), U.S. state identification card, foreign voter registration card, civil birth certificate, medical records (valid only for dependents under age 6), and school records (valid only for dependents under age 14).

The Form W–7, and accompanying original documentation, may be submitted by mail.[730] Additionally, a taxpayer may file for an ITIN by bringing completed documentation and forms to an IRS Taxpayer Assistance Center in the United States (which can authenticate passports or national identification cards, and forward the application on for processing) or an IRS office abroad. Taxpayers may also visit an acceptance agent, an individual who may submit a W–7 application on behalf of the taxpayer along with documentary evidence, or, in the case of a certifying acceptance agent, who is authorized by the IRS to verify identifying documents in addition to submitting the Form W–7. Applications submitted with the use of a certifying acceptance agent must be accompanied by a certificate of accuracy, attached to the Form W–7.

Under a policy announced in November 2012 for ITINs issued on or after January 1, 2013, ITINs would automatically expire after five years of the issuance date.[731] That is, a taxpayer would be required to reapply for a new ITIN after five years if he or she still needed the ITIN for tax filing purposes. On June 30, 2014, the IRS announced that it was revising this policy. Under the revised policy, ITINs would be deactivated only if the ITIN was not used during any tax year for a period of five consecutive years.[732]

Explanation of Provision

The provision modifies certain rules related to ITIN application procedures, and adds rules regarding the term of existing and new ITINs.

ITIN application procedures

Under the provision, the Secretary is authorized to issue ITINs to individuals either in person or via mail. In-person applications may be submitted to either: (1) an employee of the Internal Revenue Service or (2) a community-based certified acceptance agent approved by the Secretary.[733] In the case of individuals residing outside of the United States, in-person applications may be sub-

---

[729] See Instructions for Form W–7 (Rev. December, 2014), available at https://www.irs.gov/pub/irs-pdf/iw7.pdf.

[730] Ibid.

[731] IR–2012–98 (Nov. 29, 2012), available at https://www.irs.gov/uac/Newsroom/IRS-Strengthens-Integrity-of-ITIN-System;-Revised-Application-Procedures-in-Effect-for-Upcoming-Filing-Season.

[732] IR–2014–76 (June 30, 2014), available at https://www.irs.gov/uac/Newsroom/Unused-ITINS-to-Expire-After-Five-Years%3B-New-Uniform-Policy-Eases-Burden-on-Taxpayers,-Protects-ITIN-Integrity.

[733] The community-based certified acceptance agent program is intended to expand the existing IRS acceptance agent program. See Rev. Proc. 2006–10, 2006–1 C.B. 293 (December 16, 2005).

mitted to an employee of the Internal Revenue Service or a designee of the Secretary at a United States diplomatic mission or consular post. The provision authorizes the Secretary to establish procedures to accept ITIN applications via mail.

The provision directs the Secretary to maintain a program for certifying and training community-based acceptance agents. Persons eligible to be acceptance agents may include financial institutions, colleges and universities, Federal agencies, State and local governments, including State agencies responsible for vital records, persons that provide assistance to taxpayers in the preparation of their tax returns, and other persons or categories of persons as authorized by regulations or in other guidance by the Secretary.

The provision allows the Secretary to determine what documents are acceptable for purposes of proving an individual's identity, foreign status and residency. However, only original documentation or certified copies meeting the requirements set forth by the Secretary will be acceptable. Additionally, the provision requires the Secretary to develop procedures that distinguish ITINs used by individuals solely for the purpose of obtaining treaty benefits, so as to ensure that such numbers are used only to claim treaty benefits.

Term of ITINs

General rule

Under the provision, any ITIN issued after December 31, 2012 shall expire if not used on a Federal income tax return for a period of three consecutive taxable years (expiring on December 31 of such third consecutive year). The IRS is provided with math error authority related to returns filed with an ITIN that has expired, been revoked by the Secretary, or that is otherwise invalid.

Special rule in the case of ITINs issued prior to 2013

Under the provision, ITINs issued prior to 2013, while remaining subject to the general rule described above,[734] will, regardless of whether such ITIN has been used on Federal income tax returns, no longer be valid as of the applicable date, as follows:

Year ITIN Issued	Applicable Date
Pre-2008	January 1, 2017
2008	January 1, 2018
2009 or 2010	January 1, 2019
2011 or 2012	January 1, 2020

The provision also requires that the Treasury Office of Inspector General conduct an audit two years after the date of enactment (and every two years after) of the ITIN application process. Additionally, the provision requires the Secretary to conduct a study on the effectiveness of the application process for ITINs prior to the implementation of the amendments made by this provision, the effects of such amendments, the comparative effectiveness of an in-

---

[734] In the case of ITINs that, including taxable year 2015, have been unused on Federal income tax returns for three (or more) consecutive taxable years, such ITINs shall expire on December 31, 2015.

person review process versus other methods of reducing fraud in the ITIN program and improper payments to ITIN holders as a result, and possible administrative and legislative recommendations to improve such process.

Effective Date

The provision relating to ITIN application procedures is effective for applications for ITINs made after the date of enactment (December 18, 2015). The provision relating to the term of ITINs is effective on the date of enactment.

4. Prevention of retroactive claims of earned income credit, child tax credit, and American Opportunity Tax Credit (secs. 204, 205, and 206 of the Act and secs. 24, 25A and 32 of the Code)

Present Law

Refundable credits

An individual may reduce his or her tax liability by any available tax credits. In some instances, a permissible credit is "refundable," *i.e.*, it may result in a refund in excess of any credits for withheld taxes or estimated tax payments available to the individual. Three major credits are the child tax credit, the earned income tax credit ("EITC") and the American opportunity tax credit.

An individual may claim a tax credit for each qualifying child under the age of 17. The amount of the credit per child is $1,000. The aggregate amount of child credits that may be claimed is phased out for individuals with income over certain threshold amounts. Specifically, the otherwise allowable child tax credit is reduced by $50 for each $1,000 (or fraction thereof) of modified adjusted gross income over $75,000 for single individuals or heads of households, $110,000 for married individuals filing joint returns, and $55,000 for married individuals filing separate returns. To the extent the child credit exceeds the taxpayer's tax liability, the taxpayer is eligible for a refundable credit [735] (the additional child tax credit) equal to 15 percent of earned income in excess of $3,000.[736]

The EITC is available to low-income workers who satisfy certain requirements. The amount of the EITC varies depending upon the taxpayer's earned income and whether the taxpayer has one, two, more than two, or no qualifying children. In 2015, the maximum EITC is $6,242 for taxpayers with more than two qualifying children, $5,548 for taxpayers with two qualifying children, $3,359 for taxpayers with one qualifying child, and $503 for taxpayers with no qualifying children. The credit amount begins to phaseout at an income level of $23,630 for joint-filers with children, $18,110 for other taxpayers with children, $13,750 for joint-filers with no children and $8,240 for other taxpayers with no qualifying children. The phaseout percentages are 15.98 for taxpayers with one quali-

---

[735] The refundable credit may not exceed the maximum credit per child of $1,000.

[736] Families with three or more children may determine the additional child tax credit using an alternative formula, if this results in a larger credit than determined under the earned income formula. Under the alternative formula, the additional child tax credit equals the amount by which the taxpayer's social security taxes exceed the taxpayer's earned income tax credit.

fying child, 21.06 for two or more qualifying children and 7.65 for no qualifying children.

Certain individual taxpayers are allowed to claim a nonrefundable credit, the Hope credit, against Federal income taxes for qualified tuition and related expenses paid for the first two years of the student's post-secondary education in a degree or certificate program. The American Opportunity tax credit, refers to modifications to the Hope credit that apply for taxable years beginning in 2009 and extended through 2017.[737] The maximum allowable modified credit is $2,500 per eligible student per year for qualified tuition and related expenses paid for each of the first four years of the student's post-secondary education in a degree or certificate program. The modified credit rate is 100 percent on the first $2,000 of qualified tuition and related expenses, and 25 percent on the next $2,000 of qualified tuition and related expenses. Forty percent of a taxpayer's otherwise allowable American opportunity tax credit is refundable.

Identification requirements with respect to refundable credits

In order to claim the earned income credit, a taxpayer must include his or her taxpayer identification number (and if the taxpayer is married filing a joint return, the taxpayer identification number of the taxpayer's spouse) on the tax return.[738] For these purposes, a taxpayer identification number must be a Social Security number ("SSN") issued by the Social Security Administration.[739] Similarly, any child claimed by a taxpayer for purposes of determining the earned income credit must also be affiliated with a taxpayer identification number on the tax return.[740] Again, for these purposes, such number must be an SSN issued by the Social Security Administration.[741]

The child credit may not be claimed with respect to any qualifying child unless the taxpayer includes the name and taxpayer identification number of such qualifying child on the tax return for the taxable year.[742] For these purposes, taxpayer identification number is not limited to an SSN, as is the case for the earned income credit. Thus, a taxpayer may claim a child using an IRS individual taxpayer identification number ("ITIN"), issued by the IRS for those who are not eligible to be issued an SSN but who still have tax filing obligations. Additionally, a child may be identified on the return using an adoption taxpayer identification number ("ATIN"). There are no specific rules regarding the identifying number affiliated with the taxpayer claiming the child credit. Thus, the general rules applicable to all taxpayers, requiring that an identifying number accompany the return, are applicable.[743]

For the American opportunity credit (in addition to the other credits with respect to amounts paid for educational expenses), no

---

[737] These modifications are made permanent by section 102 of the Act. See Part Thirteen, Division Q, Title II, item 10, *supra*.
[738] Sec. 32(c)(1)(E)(i) and (ii).
[739] Sec. 32(m).
[740] Sec. 32(c)(3)(D).
[741] Sec. 32(m).
[742] Sec. 24(e).
[743] Sec. 6109.

credit may be claimed by a taxpayer with respect to the qualifying tuition and related expenses of an individual, unless that individual's taxpayer identification number is included on the tax return.[744] As with the child credit, for these purposes a taxpayer identification number is not limited to a Social Security number. Thus, a taxpayer may claim the credit with the use of an ITIN (either the taxpayer's own ITIN, if they are filing as a non-dependent and claiming tuition expenses incurred on their own behalf, or the ITIN of a dependent to whom the credit relates).

Explanation of Provision

The provision denies to any taxpayer the EITC, child credit, and American opportunity tax credit, with respect to any taxable year for which such taxpayer has a taxpayer identification number that has been issued after the due date (or extended due date) for filing the return for such taxable year. Similarly, a qualifying child (in the case of the EITC and child credit) or a student (in the case of the American opportunity credit) is not taken into account with respect to any taxable year for which such child or student is associated with a taxpayer identification number that has been issued after the due date (or extended due date) for filing the return for such taxable year.

Effective Date

The provision generally applies to any return of tax, and any amendment or supplement to any return of tax, which is filed after the date of the enactment. However, the provision shall not apply to any return of tax (other than an amendment or supplement to any return of tax) for any taxable year which includes the date of the enactment, if such return is filed on or before the due date for such return of tax.

5. Procedures to reduce improper claims (sec. 207 of the Act and secs. 24, 25A, 32, and 6695 of the Code)

Present Law

Eligibility requirements for certain credits

Two credits available to individuals use both income level and the presence and number of qualifying children as factors in determining eligibility for the credit: the child tax credit[745] and the earned income tax credit ("EITC").[746] Additionally, the Hope credit, the Lifetime Learning credit, and the American opportunity tax credit ("AOTC") are available to taxpayers who meet adjusted gross income requirements as well as specific requirements regarding the payment of tuition and related expenses for secondary-education.

---

[744] Sec. 25A(g)(1).
[745] Sec. 24.
[746] Sec. 32. Additionally, the child and dependent care credit is determined in part with respect to income and the presence of qualifying children, but this credit is not implicated by the provision.

EITC eligibility

Eligibility for the EITC is based on earned income, adjusted gross income, investment income, filing status, number of children, and immigration and work status in the United States. The EITC generally equals a specified percentage of earned income up to a maximum dollar amount. The maximum amount applies over a certain income range and then diminishes to zero over a specified phaseout range. For taxpayers with earned income (or adjusted gross income ("AGI"), if greater) in excess of the beginning of the phaseout range, the maximum EITC amount is reduced by the phaseout rate multiplied by the amount of earned income (or AGI, if greater) in excess of the beginning of the phaseout range. For taxpayers with earned income (or AGI, if greater) in excess of the end of the phaseout range, no credit is allowed.

An individual is not eligible for the EITC if the aggregate amount of disqualified income of the taxpayer for the taxable year exceeds $3,400 (for 2015). This threshold is indexed for inflation. Disqualified income is the sum of: (1) interest (both taxable and tax exempt); (2) dividends; (3) net rent and royalty income (if greater than zero); (4) capital gains net income; and (5) net passive income that is not self-employment income (if greater than zero).

No credit is allowed unless the taxpayer includes the Social Security number of the taxpayer and such taxpayer's spouse, on the tax return. Additionally, a qualifying child is not taken into account for purposes of the EITC unless the child's Social Security number is listed on the tax return.

Child credit eligibility

An individual may claim a child tax credit of $1,000 for each qualifying child under the age of 17,[747] provided that the child is a citizen, national, or resident of the United States.[748] The aggregate amount of child credits that may be claimed is phased out for individuals with income over certain threshold amounts. Specifically, the otherwise allowable child tax credit is reduced by $50 for each $1,000 (or fraction thereof) of modified adjusted gross income over $75,000 for single individuals or heads of households, $110,000 for married individuals filing joint returns, and $55,000 for married individuals filing separate returns. For purposes of this limitation, modified adjusted gross income includes certain otherwise excludable income earned by U.S. citizens or residents living abroad or in certain U.S. territories.[749] If the resulting child credit exceeds the tax liability of the taxpayer, the taxpayer is eligible for a refundable credit (known as the additional child tax credit)[750] equal to 15 percent of earned income in excess of a threshold dollar amount (the "earned income" formula). Prior to 2009, the threshold dollar amount was $10,000 and was indexed for inflation. For taxable years beginning after 2009 and before January 1, 2018, the threshold amount is $3,000, and is not indexed for inflation. The $3,000 threshold is currently scheduled to expire for taxable years

---

[747] Sec. 24(a).
[748] Sec. 24(c).
[749] Sec. 24(b).
[750] Sec. 24(d).

beginning after December 31, 2017, after which the threshold reverts to the indexed $10,000 amount.[751]

Families with three or more children may determine the additional child tax credit using the "alternative formula," if this results in a larger credit than determined under the earned income formula. Under the alternative formula, the additional child tax credit equals the amount by which the taxpayer's social security taxes exceed the taxpayer's EIC.

Hope credit, Lifetime Learning credit, and AOTC eligibility

The Hope credit, the Lifetime learning credit, and the AOTC are available to certain taxpayers who incur tuition and related expenses on secondary education.[752] The AOTC is a modification of the Hope credit, and applies only for taxable years from 2009–2017.[753] In the case of the Hope and Lifetime Learning credits, the credit that a taxpayer may otherwise claim is phased out ratably for taxpayers with modified adjusted gross income between $55,000 and $65,000 ($110,000 and $130,000 for married taxpayers filing a joint return). The AOTC is phased out ratably for taxpayers with modified adjusted gross income between $80,000 and $90,000 ($160,000 and $180,000 for married taxpayers filing a joint return), and may be claimed against a taxpayer's AMT liability. 40 percent of a taxpayer's otherwise allowable AOTC is refundable.

The credits vary in availability: The Hope credit is available with respect to an individual student for two years, the AOTC is available for four years, while the Lifetime Learning credit has no limit on availability. For all credits, qualified tuition and related expenses must be incurred on behalf of the taxpayer, the taxpayer's spouse, or a dependent of the taxpayer. The credits are available in the taxable year the tuition and related expenses are paid, subject to the requirement that the education is furnished to the student during that year or during an academic period beginning during the first three months of the next taxable year. Qualified tuition and related expenses paid with the proceeds of a loan generally are eligible for the credits, but repayment of a loan itself is not a qualified tuition or related expense.

A taxpayer may claim the Hope credit, Lifetime Learning credit, or AOTC with respect to an eligible student who is not the taxpayer or the taxpayer's spouse (*e.g.*, in cases in which the student is the taxpayer's child) only if the taxpayer claims the student as a dependent for the taxable year for which the credit is claimed. If a student is claimed as a dependent, the student is not entitled to claim any of the credits for education expenses for that taxable year on the student's own tax return. If a parent (or other tax-

---

[751] An earlier provision of this Act makes the $3,000 threshold permanent. See the description of sec. 101 of the Act.

[752] Sec. 25A. The Hope credit rate is 100 percent on the first $1,300 of qualified tuition and related expenses, and 50 percent on the next $1,300 of qualified tuition and related expenses (estimated for 2015). For the AOTC, the maximum credit is $2,500 per eligible student per year for qualified tuition and related expenses paid for each of the first four years of the student's post-secondary education in a degree or certificate program. The credit rate is 100 percent on the first $2,000 of qualified tuition and related expenses, and 25 percent on the next $2,000 of qualified tuition and related expenses. For the Lifetime Learning credit, 20 percent of up to $10,000 of qualified tuition and related expenses per taxpayer return is eligible for the credit (*i.e.*, the maximum credit per taxpayer return is $2,000).

[753] An earlier provision of this Act makes the modifications to the Hope credit known as the AOTC permanent. See the description of sec. 102 of the Act.

payer) claims a student as a dependent, any qualified tuition and related expenses paid by the student are treated as paid by the parent (or other taxpayer) for purposes of determining the amount of qualified tuition and related expenses paid by such parent (or other taxpayer) under the provision.

An eligible student for purposes of the Hope credit and AOTC is an individual who is enrolled in a degree, certificate, or other program (including a program of study abroad approved for credit by the institution at which such student is enrolled) leading to a recognized educational credential at an eligible educational institution. The student must pursue a course of study on at least a half-time basis. A student is considered to pursue a course of study on at least a half-time basis if the student carries at least one-half the normal full-time work load for the course of study the student is pursuing for at least one academic period that begins during the taxable year.

Unlike the Hope credit and AOTC, the Lifetime Learning credit is available to students who are enrolled on a part-time basis. To be eligible for the Hope credit and the AOTC, a student must not have been convicted of a Federal or State felony for the possession or distribution of a controlled substance. The Lifetime Learning credit does not contain this requirement.

Diligence required by preparers returns for EITC claimants

Under Section 6695(g) of the Code, a penalty of $500 may be imposed on a person who, as a tax return preparer,[754] prepares a tax return for a taxpayer claiming the EITC, unless the tax return preparer exercises due diligence with respect to that claim. The due diligence requirements extend to both the determination of eligibility for the credit and the amount of the credit, as prescribed by regulations, which also detail how to document one's compliance with those requirements.[755] The position taken with respect to the EITC must be based on current and reasonable information that the paid preparer develops, either directly from the taxpayer or by other reasonable means. The preparer may not ignore implications of information provided by taxpayers, and is expected to make reasonable inquiries about incorrect, inconsistent or incomplete information.

The conclusions about eligibility and computation, as well as the steps taken to develop those conclusions, must be documented, using Form 8867, "Paid Preparer's Earned Income Credit Checklist," which is filed with the return.[756] The basis for the computation of the credit must also be documented, either on a Computation Worksheet, or in an alternative record containing the requisite information. The preparer is required to maintain that documentation for three years.

---

[754] Sec. 7701(a)(36) provides a general definition of tax return preparer to include persons who are compensated to prepare all or a substantial portion of a return or claim for refund, with certain exceptions.

[755] Treas. Reg. sec. 1.6695–2(b).

[756] If the return preparer electronically files the return or claim for the taxpayer, the Form 8867 is filed electronically with the return. If the prepared return or claim is given to the taxpayer to file, the Form 8867 is provided to the taxpayer at the same time, to submit with the return or claim for refund.

The penalty may be waived with respect to a particular return or claim for refund on the basis of all facts and circumstances. The preparer must establish that he routinely follows reasonable office procedures to ensure compliance. The failure to comply with the requirements must be isolated and inadvertent.[757] The enhanced duties of due diligence required with respect to the EITC do not extend to other refundable credits.

There are no separately stated due diligence requirements for paid tax return preparers who prepare Federal income tax returns on which a child tax credit or the AOTC is claimed.

Explanation of Provision

The provision requires paid tax return preparers who prepare Federal income tax returns on which a child (or additional child) tax credit is claimed and on which the AOTC is claimed to meet due diligence requirements similar to those applicable to returns claiming an earned income tax credit.

The provision also requires the Secretary to conduct a study evaluating the effectiveness of tax return preparer due diligence requirements for the EITC, child tax credit and AOTC. The study with respect to the EITC shall be completed one year from the date of enactment (December 18, 2015), and the study regarding the child credit and the AOTC shall be due two years from the date of enactment.

Effective Date

The provision is effective for taxable years beginning after December 31, 2015.

6. Restrictions on taxpayers who improperly claimed credits in prior year (sec. 208 of the Act and secs. 24, 25A and 6213 of the Code)

Present Law

Refundable credits

An individual may reduce his or her tax liability by any available tax credits. In some instances, a permissible credit is "refundable," *i.e.*, it may result in a refund in excess of any credits for withheld taxes or estimated tax payments available to the individual. Three major credits are the child tax credit, the earned income credit and the American opportunity tax credit.

An individual may claim a tax credit for each qualifying child under the age of 17. The amount of the credit per child is $1,000. The aggregate amount of child credits that may be claimed is phased out for individuals with income over certain threshold amounts. Specifically, the otherwise allowable child tax credit is reduced by $50 for each $1,000 (or fraction thereof) of modified adjusted gross income over $75,000 for single individuals or heads of households, $110,000 for married individuals filing joint returns, and $55,000 for married individuals filing separate returns. To the extent the child credit exceeds the taxpayer's tax liability, the tax-

---

[757] Treas. Reg. sec. 1.6695–2(d).

payer is eligible for a refundable credit [758] (the additional child tax credit) equal to 15 percent of earned income in excess of $3,000.[759]

A refundable earned income tax credit ("EITC") is available to low-income workers who satisfy certain requirements. The amount of the EITC varies depending upon the taxpayer's earned income and whether the taxpayer has one, two, more than two, or no qualifying children. In 2015, the maximum EITC is $6,242 for taxpayers with more than two qualifying children, $5,548 for taxpayers with two qualifying children, $3,359 for taxpayers with one qualifying child, and $503 for taxpayers with no qualifying children. The credit amount begins to phaseout at an income level of $23,630 for joint-filers with children, $18,110 for other taxpayers with children, $13,750 for joint-filers with no children and $8,240 for other taxpayers with no qualifying children. The phaseout percentages are 15.98 for taxpayers with one qualifying child, 21.06 for two or more qualifying children and 7.65 for no qualifying children.

Certain individual taxpayers are allowed to claim a nonrefundable credit, the Hope credit, against Federal income taxes for qualified tuition and related expenses paid for the first two years of the student's post-secondary education in a degree or certificate program. The American Opportunity tax credit, refers to modifications to the Hope credit that apply for taxable years beginning in 2009 and extended through 2017.[760] The maximum allowable modified credit is $2,500 per eligible student per year for qualified tuition and related expenses paid for each of the first four years of the student's post-secondary education in a degree or certificate program. The modified credit rate is 100 percent on the first $2,000 of qualified tuition and related expenses, and 25 percent on the next $2,000 of qualified tuition and related expenses. 40 percent of a taxpayer's otherwise allowable American opportunity tax credit is refundable.

Disallowance period with respect to the earned income credit

A taxpayer who was previously disallowed the EITC may not claim the EITC for a period of ten taxable years after the most recent taxable year for which there was a final determination that the taxpayer's claim of credit was due to fraud. Such disallowance period is two years in the case of a taxpayer for which there was a final determination that the taxpayer's EITC claim was due to reckless or intentional disregard of rules and regulations (but not to fraud).

Additionally, in the case of a taxpayer who was previously denied the EITC for any taxable year as a result of IRS deficiency procedures, the taxpayer may not claim an EITC in subsequent years unless the taxpayer provides a Form 8862 with the tax return, so as to demonstrate eligibility for the EITC in that taxable year.

---

[758] The refundable credit may not exceed the maximum credit per child of $1,000.

[759] The $3,000 threshold was a temporary number that is made permanent by section 101 of the Act. Families with three or more children may determine the additional child tax credit using an alternative formula, if this results in a larger credit than determined under the earned income formula. Under the alternative formula, the additional child tax credit equals the amount by which the taxpayer's social security taxes exceed the taxpayer's earned income tax credit.

[760] The modifications to the Hope credit, known as the American opportunity credit, are made permanent by section 102 of the Act.

Math error authority

The Federal income tax system relies upon self-reporting and assessment. A taxpayer is expected to prepare a report of his liability[761] and submit it to the Internal Revenue Service ("IRS") with any payment due. The Code provides general authority for the IRS to assess all taxes shown on returns,[762] other than certain Federal unemployment tax and estimated income taxes.[763] The assessment is required to be made by recording the liability in the "office of the Secretary" in a manner determined under regulations.[764] If the IRS determines that the assessment was materially incorrect, additional tax must be assessed within the limitations period.[765]

The authority to assess the additional tax may be subject to certain restrictions on assessment known as the deficiency procedures.[766] A deficiency of tax occurs if the amount of certain taxes[767] assessed for a period, after reduction for any rebates of tax, is less than the liability determined under the Code. Generally, in the case of income taxes, if the IRS questions whether the correct tax liability has been self-assessed by a taxpayer, the IRS generally first informs the taxpayer by letter. Most discrepancies in income tax liability identified by the IRS are resolved through such "correspondence audits." In other cases, an examining agent reviews the return and determines whether an adjustment in income tax reported on the return is required. The determination by the examining agent that an adjustment to the return is required results in a notice to the taxpayer that provides an opportunity for the taxpayer to invoke rights to an administrative appeal or to agree to the adjustments within 30 days. If the taxpayer responds timely and disputes the adjustments, the case is referred to an independent administrative appeals officer for review. In most cases, the taxpayer and the IRS agree on the merit or lack of merit of the adjustments proposed, and the cases are closed without issuance of a notice of deficiency. If the parties do not reach agreement administratively, the IRS must issue a formal notice of deficiency to a taxpayer,[768] which begins a period within which a taxpayer may petition the U.S. Tax Court. During that period, as well as during the pendency of any proceeding in Tax Court, assessment of the deficiency is not permitted.[769]

There are several exceptions to the restrictions on assessment of taxes that are generally subject to the deficiency procedures.[770]

---

[761] Secs. 6011 and 6012.

[762] See sec. 6201(a), which authorizes assessment of tax computed by the taxpayer as well as amounts computed by the IRS at the election of the taxpayer, under section 6014.

[763] Sec. 6201(b).

[764] Sec. 6203.

[765] Secs. 6204.

[766] Secs. 6211 through 6215.

[767] The taxes to which deficiency procedures apply are income, estate and gift and excise taxes arising under chapters 41, 42, or 44. Secs. 6211 and 6213.

[768] Sec. 6212.

[769] Sec. 6213(a). If a taxpayer wishes to contest the merits in a different court, the taxpayer may agree to assessment of the tax, reserving his or her rights to contest the merits, pay the disputed amount, and pursue a claim for refund reviewable in a suit in Federal district court or Court of Federal Claims.

[770] Section 6213 provides that a taxpayer may waive the restrictions on assessment, permits immediate assessment to reflect payments of tax remitted to the IRS and to correct amounts credited or applied as a result of claims for carrybacks under section 1341(b), and requires as-

Continued

One of the principal exceptions is the authority to assess without issuance of a notice of deficiency if the error is a result of a mathematical or clerical error, generally referred to as math error authority. If the mistake on the return is of a type that is within the meaning of mathematical or clerical error, the IRS assesses the tax and sends notice of the math error to the taxpayer. Purely mathematical or clerical issues are often identified early in the processing of a return, prior to issuance of any refund; they are not typically identified as a result of an examination of a return.[771] Although most math errors identified by the IRS resulted in the assessment of additional tax, over 2.6 million of the 6.6 million math errors identified in FY2011 [772] involved adjustments in taxpayers' favor for credits to which taxpayers were entitled but had failed to claim, mostly commonly the "Making Work Pay Credit" for taxable year 2010.

Since 1976, the issuance of a notice of math error begins a 60 day period within which a taxpayer may submit a request for abatement of the math error adjustment, which then requires the IRS to abate the assessment and refer the unresolved issue for examination.[773] The IRS Data Books do not report the number of abatements of math error assessments.

The scope of IRS math error authority now encompasses numerous issues, many of which concern rules regarding refundable credits.[774] The summary assessment is used to deny a claimed credit or deduction, either during initial processing of a return on which the credit is claimed or in an examination of the return after the refund has been issued. For example, in 2009, the authority was expanded to cover several grounds on which a homebuyer credit could be disallowed.[775] These grounds include (1) an omission of any increase in tax required by the recapture provisions of the credit; (2) information from the person issuing the taxpayer identification number of the taxpayer that indicates that the taxpayer does not meet the age requirement of the credit; (3) information provided to the Secretary by the taxpayer on an income tax return for at least one of the two preceding taxable years that is inconsistent with eligibility for such credit; or (4) failure to attach to the return a properly executed copy of the settlement statement used to complete the purchase.

Explanation of Provision

The provision expands the disallowance rules that apply to the EITC to the child tax credit and the American opportunity tax credit. Thus, if an individual claims the child tax credit or the

---

sessment of amounts ordered as criminal restitution. Assessment is also permitted in certain circumstances in which collection of the tax would be in jeopardy. Sections 6851, 6852 or 6861.

[771] See, Treasury Inspector General for Tax Administration, *Some Taxpayer Responses to Math Error Adjustments Were Not Worked Timely and Accurately* (TIGTA No. 2011–40–059), July 11, 2011.

[772] 2011 IRS Data Book, Table 15.

[773] Although the exception to restrictions on assessment to correct mathematical errors had long been in the Code, the requirement to abate upon timely request was added in 1976 when the authority was expanded to include correction of clerical errors. Sec. 6213(b)(2)(A); Tax Reform Act of 1976, Pub. L. 94–55, Sec. 1206(a). In order to reassess the amount abated, the IRS must comply with the deficiency procedures.

[774] Math error authority currently applies to certain errors related to the earned income tax credit and the child tax credit. Sec. 6213(g)(2)(F), (G), (I), (K), (L), and (M).

[775] Sec. 6213(g)(2)(O) and (P).

American opportunity credit in a taxable year, that individual is denied the credit, and such claim for credit was determined to be due to fraud, or reckless or intentional disregard of the rules, that individual may not claim the credit for the next ten or two years, respectively.

Additionally, the provision requires that taxpayers who were previously denied the child tax credit or the American opportunity tax credit in any taxable year as a result of IRS deficiency procedures to provide additional information demonstrating eligibility for such credit, as required by the Secretary.

The provision would add the following items to the list of circumstances in which the IRS has authority to make an assessment as a math error: (1) a taxpayer claimed the EITC,[776] child tax credit, or the AOTC during the period in which a taxpayer is not permitted to claim such credit as a consequence of having made a prior fraudulent or reckless claim; and (2) there was an omission of information required by the Secretary relating to a taxpayer making improper prior claims of the child tax credit or the AOTC.

Effective Date

The provision is effective for taxable years beginning after December 31, 2015.

7. Treatment of credits for purposes of certain penalties (sec. 209 of the Act and secs. 6664 and 6676 of the Code)

Present Law

Underpayment penalties

Under present law, an accuracy-related penalty or a fraud penalty may be imposed on certain underpayments of tax.[777] The Code imposes a 20-percent penalty on the portion of an underpayment attributable to: negligence or disregard of rules or regulations, a substantial understatement, a substantial valuation overstatement, a substantial overstatement of pension liabilities, a substantial estate or gift tax valuation understatements, any disallowance of tax benefits by reason of lacking economic substance, or any undisclosed foreign financial asset understatement.[778] A penalty of 75 percent of an underpayment is imposed in the case of fraud. An exception to these penalties for reasonable cause generally applies.[779] An underpayment, for this purpose, means the excess of the amount of tax imposed over the amount of tax shown on the return.[780]

---

[776] Sec. 32(k)(1).

[777] Secs. 6662 and 6663. Present law also imposes a separate accuracy-related 20-percent penalty on portions of an underpayment attributable to a listed or reportable transaction. Sec. 6662A(a). The penalty increases to 30 percent if the transaction is not adequately disclosed. Secs. 6662A(c) and 6664(d)(2)(A).

[778] The 20-percent penalty is increased to 40 percent when there is a gross valuation misstatement involving a substantial valuation overstatement, a substantial overstatement of pension liabilities, a substantial estate or gift tax valuation understatement, or when a transaction lacking economic substance is not properly disclosed. Secs. 6662(h) and 6662(i).

[779] Sec. 6664(c). There is no reasonable cause exception for tax benefits disallowed by reason of a transaction lacking economic substance and certain valuation overstatements related to charitable deduction property.

[780] Sec. 6664(a). Previous assessments and rebates may also be taken into account.

These penalties are assessed in the same manner as taxes.[781] In the case of income taxes, a taxpayer may contest any deficiency in tax determined by the IRS in the Tax Court before an assessment of the tax may be made.[782] Generally a deficiency in tax is the excess of the amount of tax imposed over the amount of tax shown on the return.[783]

The Code allows certain credits against the income tax.[784] Most of the credits may not exceed the taxpayer's income tax. However certain credits ("refundable credits") may exceed the tax and the amount of these credits in excess of the tax imposed (reduced by the other credits) is an overpayment which creates a refund or credit.[785] Refundable credits include a portion of the child credit, the American opportunity tax credit, and the earned income credit.[786]

In determining a deficiency in tax, the refundable credits in excess of tax are treated as negative amounts of tax.[787] Thus, the amounts of tax imposed and the tax shown on the return may be negative amounts. The Code does not provide a similar rule for the determination of an underpayment for purposes of the penalties.[788]

The Tax Court ruled that for purposes of determining the amount of an underpayment for purposes of the penalty provisions, the tax shown on the return may not be less than zero.[789] Thus, no accuracy-related penalty or fraud penalty may be imposed to the extent the refundable credits reduce the tax imposed below zero.

Erroneous claims

Present law imposes a penalty of 20 percent on the amount by which a claim for refund or credit exceeds the amount allowable unless it is shown that the claim has a reasonable basis.[790] The penalty does not apply to claims relating to the earned income credit. The penalty does not apply to the portion of any claim to which the accuracy-related and fraud penalties apply. The deficiency procedures do not apply to this penalty.

Explanation of Provision

The provision amends the definition of underpayment applicable to the determination of accuracy-related and fraud penalties by incorporating in the definition the rule that in determining the tax imposed and the amount of tax shown on the return, the excess of the refundable credits over the tax is taken into account as negative amount of tax. Thus, if a taxpayer files an income tax return erroneously claiming refundable credits in excess of tax, there is an

---

[781] Sec. 6665(a).
[782] Sec. 6211–6215.
[783] Sec. 6211. Previous assessments and rebates may also be taken into account.
[784] Secs. 21–54AA.
[785] Sec. 6401(b).
[786] Refundable credits include credits for withholding of taxes. Treas. Reg. secs. 1–6664–2(b) and (c) provide special rules for the withholding credits.
[787] Sec. 6211(b)(4).
[788] The Improved Penalty Administration and Compliance Tax Act (the "Act"), Pub. L. No. 101–239, sec. 7721(c), revised the penalties to provide a single accuracy-related penalty for various types of misconduct. The definition of underpayment for purposes of similar penalties prior to that Act was defined by reference to the definition of a deficiency. See sec. 6653(c)(1) prior to its repeal by the Act.
[789] *Rand v. Commissioner*, 141 T.C. No. 12 (November 18, 2013).
[790] Sec. 6676.

underpayment on which an accuracy-related or fraud penalty may be imposed.

The provision also repeals the exception from the erroneous claims penalty for the earned income credit and changes the standard for penalty relief from reasonable basis to reasonable cause.

Effective Date

The provision amending the definition of underpayment is effective for returns filed after the date of enactment (December 18, 2015) and for returns filed on or before the date of enactment if the statute of limitations period for assessment has not expired.

The provision repealing the exception from the erroneous claim penalty is effective for claims filed after the date of enactment.

The provision relating to reasonable cause is effective for claims filed after the date of enactment.[791]

8. Increase the penalty applicable to paid tax preparers who engage in willful or reckless conduct (sec. 210 of the Act and sec. 6694 of the Code)

Present Law

Tax return preparers are subject to a penalty for preparation of a return or refund claim with respect to which an understatement of tax liability results. If the understatement is due to an "unreasonable position," the penalty is the greater of $1,000 or 50 percent of the income derived (or to be derived) by the return preparer with respect to that return.[792] Any position that a return preparer does not reasonably believe is more likely than not to be sustained on its merits is an "unreasonable position" unless the position is disclosed on the return or there is "substantial authority" for the position.[793] There is a substantial authority for a position if the weight of the authorities supporting the treatment is substantial in relation to the weight of authorities supporting contrary treatment. If the position taken meets the definition of a tax shelter (as defined in section 6662(d)(2)(B)(ii)(I)) or a listed or reportable transaction (as referenced in 6662A), the preparer must have a reasonable belief that the position would more likely than not be sustained on its merits. If the understatement is due to willful or reckless conduct, the penalty increases to the greater of $5,000 or 50 percent of the income derived (or to be derived) by the return preparer with respect to that return.[794]

Explanation of Provision

The provision increases the penalty rate on paid tax return preparers for understatements due to willful or reckless conduct to the greater of $5,000 or 75 percent of the income derived (or to be derived) by the preparer with respect to the return or claim for refund.

---

[791] A technical correction is needed to provide the effective date.
[792] Sec. 6694(a)(1).
[793] Sec. 6694(a)(2).
[794] Sec. 6694(b).

Effective Date

The provision is effective for returns prepared for taxable years ending after the date of enactment (December 18, 2015).

9. Employer identification number required for American opportunity tax credit (sec. 211 of the Act and secs. 25A and 6050S of the Code)

Certain individual taxpayers are allowed to claim a nonrefundable credit, the Hope credit, against Federal income taxes for qualified tuition and related expenses paid for the first two years of the student's post-secondary education in a degree or certificate program. The American Opportunity tax credit, refers to modifications to the Hope credit that apply for taxable years beginning in 2009 and extended through 2017.[795] The maximum allowable modified credit is $2,500 per eligible student per year for qualified tuition and related expenses paid for each of the first four years of the student's post-secondary education in a degree or certificate program. The modified credit rate is 100 percent on the first $2,000 of qualified tuition and related expenses, and 25 percent on the next $2,000 of qualified tuition and related expenses. 40 percent of a taxpayer's otherwise allowable American opportunity tax credit is refundable.

For the American opportunity credit (in addition to the other credits with respect to amounts paid for educational expenses), no credit may be claimed by a taxpayer with respect to the qualifying tuition and related expenses of an individual, unless that individual's taxpayer identification number is included on the tax return.[796] The Code imposes no reporting requirement with respect to the identity of the educational institution attended by the individual.

Section 6050S of the Code imposes reporting requirements, related to higher education tax benefits, on eligible educational institutions and certain other persons.[797] Eligible educational institutions are subject to the reporting requirements if the institution enrolls any individual for any academic period. The information return must include the name, address, and taxpayer identification number of any individual (a) who is or has been enrolled at an eligible education institution and with respect to whom certain transactions are made or (b) with respect to whom certain payments were made or received. Additionally, eligible educational institutions are required to provide the following information: (a) the aggregate amount of payments received or the aggregate amount billed for qualified tuition and related expenses during the calendar year; (b) the aggregate amount of grants received by the individual for payment of costs of attendance that are administered and processed by the institution during the calendar year; and (c) the amount of any adjustments to the aggregate amounts reported

---

[795] The American opportunity credit was made permanent in another section of this Act. See the description of sec. 102 of this Act.

[796] Sec. 25A(g)(1).

[797] In addition to eligible educational institutions, the relevant reporting requirements discussed herein are imposed on persons who are engaged in a trade or business of making payments to any individual under an insurance arrangements as reimbursements or refunds (or similar amounts) of qualified tuition and related expenses.

under (a) or (b) with respect to the individual for a prior calendar year.

Explanation of Provision

The provision requires that taxpayers claiming the American opportunity tax credit provide the employer identification number of the educational institution attended by the individual to whom the credit relates.

The provision modifies the reporting requirements under section 6050S of the Code to require an educational institution to provide its employer identification number on the Form 1098–T.[798]

Effective Date

The provision requiring the employer identification number is effective for taxable years beginning after December 31, 2015.

The provision modifying the information reporting requirements is effective for expenses paid after December 31, 2015, for education furnished in academic periods beginning after such date.

10. Higher education information reporting only to include qualified tuition and related expenses actually paid (sec. 212 of the Act and sec. 6050S of the Code)

Present Law

Section 6050S of the Code imposes reporting requirements, related to higher education tax benefits, on eligible educational institutions and certain other persons.[799] Eligible educational institutions are subject to the reporting requirements if the institution enrolls any individual for any academic period. The information return must include the name, address, and taxpayer identification number of any individual (a) who is or has been enrolled at an eligible education institution and with respect to whom certain transactions are made or (b) with respect to whom certain payments were made or received. Additionally, eligible educational institutions are required to provide the following information: (a) the aggregate amount of payments received or the aggregate amount billed for qualified tuition and related expenses during the calendar year; (b) the aggregate amount of grants received by the individual for payment of costs of attendance that are administered and processed by the institution during the calendar year; and (c) the amount of any adjustments to the aggregate amounts reported under (a) or (b) with respect to the individual for a prior calendar year.

Explanation of Provision

The provision requires eligible educational institutions that have a reporting obligation to report the aggregate amount of payments

---

[798] This is already required under Treasury regulations. See Treas. Reg. secs. 1.6050S–1(b)(2)(ii)(A) and 1.6050S–1(b)(3)(ii)(A).

[799] In addition to eligible educational institutions, the relevant reporting requirements discussed herein are imposed on persons who are engaged in a trade or business of making payments to any individual under an insurance arrangements as reimbursements or refunds (or similar amounts) of qualified tuition and related expenses.

of qualified tuition and related expenses received during the calendar year.

Effective Date

The provision is effective for expenses paid after December 31, 2015, for education furnished in academic periods beginning after such date.

TITLE III—MISCELLANEOUS PROVISIONS

A. Family Tax Relief

1. Exclusion for amounts received under the work colleges program (sec. 301 of the Act and sec. 117 of the Code) [800]

Present Law

Under present law, an individual who is a candidate for a degree at a qualifying educational organization may exclude amounts received as a qualified scholarship from gross income and wages. In addition, present law provides an exclusion from gross income and wages for qualified tuition reductions for certain education provided to employees of certain educational organizations. The exclusions for qualified scholarships and qualified tuition reductions do not apply to any amount received by a student that represents payment for teaching, research, or other services by the student required as a condition for receiving the scholarship or tuition reduction. Payments for such services are includible in gross income and wages. An exception to this rule applies in the case of the National Health Services Corps Scholarship Program and the F. Edward Herbert Armed Forces Health Professions Scholarship and Financial Assistance Program.

Explanation of Provision

The provision exempts from gross income any payments from a comprehensive student work-learning-service program (as defined in section 448(e) of the Higher Education Act of 1965) operated by a work college (as defined in such section). Specifically, a work college must require resident students to participate in a work-learning-service program that is an integral and stated part of the institution's educational philosophy and program.

Effective Date

The provision is effective for amounts received in taxable years beginning after the date of enactment (December 18, 2015).

---

[800] The Senate Committee on Finance reported S. 912 on April 14, 2015 (S. Rep. No. 114–22).

2. Modification of rules relating to section 529 programs (sec. 302 of the Act and sec. 529 of the Code)[801]

Present Law

Section 529 qualified tuition programs

In general

A qualified tuition program is a program established and maintained by a State or agency or instrumentality thereof, or by one or more eligible educational institutions, which satisfies certain requirements and under which a person may purchase tuition credits or certificates on behalf of a designated beneficiary that entitle the beneficiary to the waiver or payment of qualified higher education expenses of the beneficiary (a "prepaid tuition program"). Section 529 provides specified income tax and transfer tax rules for the treatment of accounts and contracts established under qualified tuition programs.[802] In the case of a program established and maintained by a State or agency or instrumentality thereof, a qualified tuition program also includes a program under which a person may make contributions to an account that is established for the purpose of satisfying the qualified higher education expenses of the designated beneficiary of the account, provided it satisfies certain specified requirements (a "savings account program"). Under both types of qualified tuition programs, a contributor establishes an account for the benefit of a particular designated beneficiary to provide for that beneficiary's higher education expenses.

In general, prepaid tuition contracts and tuition savings accounts established under a qualified tuition program involve prepayments or contributions made by one or more individuals for the benefit of a designated beneficiary. Decisions with respect to the contract or account are typically made by an individual who is not the designated beneficiary. Qualified tuition accounts or contracts generally require the designation of a person (generally referred to as an "account owner")[803] whom the program administrator (oftentimes a third party administrator retained by the State or by the educational institution that established the program) may look to for decisions, recordkeeping, and reporting with respect to the account established for a designated beneficiary. The person or persons who make the contributions to the account need not be the same person who is regarded as the account owner for purposes of administering the account. Under many qualified tuition programs, the account owner generally has control over the account or contract, including the ability to change designated beneficiaries and to withdraw funds at any time and for any purpose. Thus, in practice, qualified tuition accounts or contracts generally involve a contributor, a designated beneficiary, an account owner (who often-

---

[801] The House Committee on Ways and Means reported H.R. 529 on February 20, 2015 (H.R. Rep. No. 114–25). The House passed the bill on February 25, 2015. The Senate Committee on Finance reported S. 335 on May 21, 2015 (S. Rep. No. 114–56).

[802] For purposes of this description, the term "account" is used interchangeably to refer to a prepaid tuition benefit contract or a tuition savings account established pursuant to a qualified tuition program.

[803] Section 529 refers to contributors and designated beneficiaries, but does not define or otherwise refer to the term "account owner," which is a commonly used term among qualified tuition programs.

times is not the contributor or the designated beneficiary), and an administrator of the account or contract.

Qualified higher education expenses

For purposes of receiving a distribution from a qualified tuition program that qualifies for favorable tax treatment under the Code, qualified higher education expenses means tuition, fees, books, supplies, and equipment required for the enrollment or attendance of a designated beneficiary at an eligible educational institution, and expenses for special needs services in the case of a special needs beneficiary that are incurred in connection with such enrollment or attendance. Qualified higher education expenses generally also include room and board for students who are enrolled at least half-time. For taxable years 2009 and 2010 only, qualified higher education expenses included the purchase of any computer technology or equipment, or Internet access or related services, if such technology or services were to be used by the beneficiary or the beneficiary's family during any of the years a beneficiary was enrolled at an eligible institution.

Contributions to qualified tuition programs

Contributions to a qualified tuition program must be made in cash. Section 529 does not impose a specific dollar limit on the amount of contributions, account balances, or prepaid tuition benefits relating to a qualified tuition account; however, the program is required to have adequate safeguards to prevent contributions in excess of amounts necessary to provide for the beneficiary's qualified higher education expenses. Contributions generally are treated as a completed gift eligible for the gift tax annual exclusion. Contributions are not tax deductible for Federal income tax purposes, although they may be deductible for State income tax purposes. Amounts in the account accumulate on a tax-free basis (i.e., income on accounts in the plan is not subject to current income tax).

A qualified tuition program may not permit any contributor to, or designated beneficiary under, the program to direct (directly or indirectly) the investment of any contributions (or earnings thereon) more than two times in any calendar year, and must provide separate accounting for each designated beneficiary. A qualified tuition program may not allow any interest in an account or contract (or any portion thereof) to be used as security for a loan.

Distributions from qualified tuition programs

Distributions from a qualified tuition program are excludable from the distributee's gross income to the extent that the total distribution does not exceed the qualified higher education expenses incurred for the beneficiary.[804]

If a distribution from a qualified tuition program exceeds the qualified higher education expenses incurred for the beneficiary, the amount includible in gross income is determined, first, by applying the annuity rules of section 72[805] to determine the amount which would be includible in gross income if none of the amount

---

[804] Sec. 529(c)(3)(B)(i) and (ii)(I).

[805] Under section 72, a distribution is includible in income to the extent that the distribution represents earnings on the contribution to the program, determined on a pro rata basis.

distributed was for qualified higher education expenses and, then, reducing that amount by an amount which bears the same ratio to that amount as the qualified higher education expenses bear to the amount of the distribution.[806]

For example, assume a taxpayer had $5,000 in a qualified tuition program account, $4,000 of which was the amount contributed. Also assume the taxpayer withdraws $1,000 from the account and $500 is used for qualified higher education expenses. First, the taxpayer applies the annuity rules of section 72 which results in $200 being included in income under section 72 assuming none of the distribution is used for qualified higher education expenses. Then the taxpayer reduces the $200 by one-half because 50 percent of the distribution was used for qualified higher education expenses. Thus, $100 is includible in gross income. This amount is subject to an additional 10-percent tax (unless an exception applies).

The Code provides that, except as provided by the Secretary of the Treasury ("Secretary"), for purposes of this calculation, the taxpayer's account value, income, and investment amount, are generally measured as of December 31st of the taxable year in which the distribution was made. The Secretary has issued guidance providing that the earnings portion of a distribution is to be computed on the date of each distribution.[807]

In the case of an individual who is the designated beneficiary for more than one qualified tuition program, all such accounts are aggregated for purposes of calculating the earnings in the account under section 72. The Secretary has provided in guidance that this aggregation is required only in the case of accounts contained within the same 529 program, having the same account owner and the same designated beneficiary.[808]

Explanation of Provision

The provision makes three modifications to section 529.

First, the provision provides that qualified higher education expenses include the purchase of computer or peripheral equipment (as defined in section 168(i)(2)(B)), computer software (as defined in section 197(e)(3)(B)), or Internet access and related services if the equipment, software, or services are to be used primarily by the beneficiary during any of the years the beneficiary is enrolled at an eligible education institution.

Second, the provision repeals the rules providing that section 529 accounts must be aggregated for purposes of calculating the amount of a distribution that is included in a taxpayer's income. Thus, in the case of a designated beneficiary who has received multiple distributions from a qualified tuition program in the taxable year, the portion of a distribution that represents earnings is now to be computed on a distribution-by-distribution basis, rather than an aggregate basis, such that the computation applies to each distribution from an account. The following example illustrates the operation of this provision: Assume that two designated savings ac-

---

[806] Sec. 529(c)(3)(A) and (B)(ii).
[807] Notice 2001–81, 2001–2 C.B. 617, December 10, 2001.
[808] *Ibid.*

counts [809] have been established by the same account owner within the same qualified tuition program for the same designated beneficiary. Account A contains $20,000, all of which consists of contributed amounts (i.e., it has no earnings). Account B contains $30,000, $20,000 of which constitutes an investment in the account, and $10,000 attributable to earnings on that investment. Assume a taxpayer were to receive a $10,000 distribution from Account A, with none of the proceeds being spent on qualified higher education expenses. Under present law, both of the designated beneficiary's accounts would be aggregated for purposes of computing earnings. Thus, $2,000 of the $10,000 distribution from Account A ($10,000 * $10,000/$50,000) would be included in the designated beneficiary's income. Under the provision, the accounts would not be aggregated for purposes of determining earnings on the account. Thus, because Account A has no earnings, no amount of the distribution would be included in the designated beneficiary's income for the taxable year.

Third, the provision creates a new rule that provides, in the case of a designated beneficiary who receives a refund of any higher education expenses, any distribution that was used to pay the refunded expenses shall not be subject to tax if the designated beneficiary recontributes the refunded amount to the qualified tuition program within 60 days of receiving the refund, only to the extent that such recontribution is not in excess of the refund. A transition rule allows for recontributions of amounts refunded after December 31, 2014, and before the date of enactment (December 18, 2015) to be made not later than 60 days after the enactment of this provision.

Effective Date

The provision allowing computer technology to be considered a higher education expense is effective for taxable years beginning after December 31, 2014. The provision removing the aggregation requirement in the case of multiple distributions is effective for distributions made after December 31, 2014. The provision allowing a recontribution of refunded tuition amounts is effective for tuition refunded after December 31, 2014.

3. Modification to qualified ABLE programs (sec. 303 of the Act and sec. 529A of the Code)

Present Law

In general

The Code provides for a tax-favored savings program intended to benefit disabled individuals, known as qualified ABLE programs.[810] A qualified ABLE program is a program established and maintained by a State or agency or instrumentality thereof. A qualified ABLE program must meet the following conditions: (1) under the provisions of the program, contributions may be made to

---

[809] As used in this example, the term 'account' refers to a sum of money set aside in a qualified tuition program, and does not refer to the allocation of such money into differing investment options offered by such program.
[810] Sec. 529A.

an account (an "ABLE account"), established for the purpose of meeting the qualified disability expenses of the designated beneficiary of the account; (2) the program must limit a designated beneficiary to one ABLE account; (3) the program must allow for the establishment of ABLE accounts only for a designated beneficiary who is either a resident of the State maintaining such ABLE program or a resident of a State that has not established an ABLE program (a "contracting State") which has entered into a contract with such State to provide the contracting State's residents with access to the State's ABLE program; and (4) the program must meet certain other requirements discussed below. A qualified ABLE program is generally exempt from income tax, but is otherwise subject to the taxes imposed on the unrelated business income of tax-exempt organizations.

A designated beneficiary of an ABLE account is the owner of the ABLE account. A designated beneficiary must be an eligible individual (defined below) who established the ABLE account and who is designated at the commencement of participation in the qualified ABLE program as the beneficiary of amounts paid (or to be paid) into and from the program.

Contributions to an ABLE account must be made in cash and are not deductible for Federal income tax purposes. Except in the case of a rollover contribution from another ABLE account, an ABLE account must provide that it may not receive aggregate contributions during a taxable year in excess of the amount under section 2503(b) of the Code (the annual gift tax exemption). For 2015, this is $14,000.[811] Additionally, a qualified ABLE program must provide adequate safeguards to ensure that ABLE account contributions do not exceed the limit imposed on accounts under the qualified tuition program of the State maintaining the qualified ABLE program. Amounts in the account accumulate on a tax-deferred basis (*i.e.*, income on accounts under the program is not subject to current income tax).

A qualified ABLE program may permit a designated beneficiary to direct (directly or indirectly) the investment of any contributions (or earnings thereon) no more than two times in any calendar year and must provide separate accounting for each designated beneficiary. A qualified ABLE program may not allow any interest in the program (or any portion thereof) to be used as security for a loan.

Distributions from an ABLE account are generally includible in the distributee's income to the extent consisting of earnings on the account.[812] Distributions from an ABLE account are excludable from income to the extent that the total distribution does not exceed the qualified disability expenses of the designated beneficiary during the taxable year. If a distribution from an ABLE account exceeds the qualified disability expenses of the designated bene-

---

[811] This amount is indexed for inflation. In the case that contributions to an ABLE account exceed the annual limit, an excise tax in the amount of six percent of the excess contribution to such account is imposed on the designated beneficiary. Such tax does not apply in the event that the trustee of such account makes a corrective distribution of such excess amounts by the due date (including extensions) of the individual's tax return for the year within the taxable year.

[812] The rules of section 72 apply in determining the portion of a distribution that consists of earnings.

ficiary, a pro rata portion of the distribution is excludable from income. The portion of any distribution that is includible in income is subject to an additional 10-percent tax unless the distribution is made after the death of the beneficiary. Amounts in an ABLE account may be rolled over without income tax liability to another ABLE account for the same beneficiary [813] or another ABLE account for the designated beneficiary's brother, sister, stepbrother or stepsister who is also an eligible individual.

Except in the case of an ABLE account established in a different ABLE program for purposes of transferring ABLE accounts,[814] no more than one ABLE account may be established by a designated beneficiary. Thus, once an ABLE account has been established by a designated beneficiary, no account subsequently established by such beneficiary shall be treated as an ABLE account.

A contribution to an ABLE account is treated as a completed gift of a present interest to the designated beneficiary of the account. Such contributions qualify for the per-donee annual gift tax exclusion ($14,000 for 2015) and, to the extent of such exclusion, are exempt from the generation skipping transfer ("GST") tax. A distribution from an ABLE account generally is not subject to gift tax or GST tax.

Eligible individuals

As described above, a qualified ABLE program may provide for the establishment of ABLE accounts only if those accounts are established and owned by an eligible individual, such owner referred to as a designated beneficiary. For these purposes, an eligible individual is an individual either (1) for whom a disability certification has been filed with the Secretary for the taxable year, or (2) who is entitled to Social Security Disability Insurance benefits or SSI benefits [815] based on blindness or disability, and such blindness or disability occurred before the individual attained age 26.

A disability certification means a certification to the satisfaction of the Secretary, made by the eligible individual or the parent or guardian of the eligible individual, that the individual has a medically determinable physical or mental impairment, which results in marked and severe functional limitations, and which can be expected to result in death or which has lasted or can be expected to last for a continuous period of not less than 12 months, or is blind (within the meaning of section 1614(a)(2) of the Social Security Act). Such blindness or disability must have occurred before the date the individual attained age 26. Such certification must include a copy of the diagnosis of the individual's impairment and be signed by a licensed physician.[816]

Qualified disability expenses

As described above, the earnings on distributions from an ABLE account are excluded from income only to the extent total distributions do not exceed the qualified disability expenses of the des-

---

[813] For instance, if a designated beneficiary were to relocate to a different State.

[814] In which case the contributor ABLE account must be closed 60 days after the transfer to the new ABLE account is made.

[815] These are benefits, respectively, under Title II or Title XVI of the Social Security Act.

[816] No inference may be drawn from a disability certification for purposes of eligibility for Social Security, SSI or Medicaid benefits.

ignated beneficiary. For this purpose, qualified disability expenses are any expenses related to the eligible individual's blindness or disability which are made for the benefit of the designated beneficiary. Such expenses include the following expenses: education, housing, transportation, employment training and support, assistive technology and personal support services, health, prevention and wellness, financial management and administrative services, legal fees, expenses for oversight and monitoring, funeral and burial expenses, and other expenses, which are approved by the Secretary under regulations and consistent with the purposes of section 529A.

Transfer to State

In the event that the designated beneficiary dies, subject to any outstanding payments due for qualified disability expenses incurred by the designated beneficiary, all amounts remaining in the deceased designated beneficiary's ABLE account not in excess of the amount equal to the total medical assistance paid such individual under any State Medicaid plan established under title XIX of the Social Security Act shall be distributed to such State upon filing of a claim for payment by such State. Such repaid amounts shall be net of any premiums paid from the account or by or on behalf of the beneficiary to the State's Medicaid Buy-In program.

Treatment of ABLE accounts under Federal programs

Any amounts in an ABLE account, and any distribution for qualified disability expenses, shall be disregarded for purposes of determining eligibility to receive, or the amount of, any assistance or benefit authorized by any Federal means-tested program. However, in the case of the SSI program, a distribution for housing expenses is not disregarded, nor are amounts in an ABLE account in excess of $100,000. In the case that an individual's ABLE account balance exceeds $100,000, such individual's SSI benefits shall not be terminated, but instead shall be suspended until such time as the individual's resources fall below $100,000. However, such suspension shall not apply for purposes of Medicaid eligibility.

Treatment of ABLE accounts in bankruptcy

Property of a bankruptcy estate may not include certain amounts contributed to an ABLE account, if the designated beneficiary of such account was a child, stepchild, grandchild or stepgrandchild of the debtor during the taxable year in which funds were placed in the account. Such funds shall be excluded from the bankruptcy estate only to the extent that they were contributed to an ABLE account at least 365 days prior to the filing of the title 11 petition, are not pledged or promised to any entity in connection with any extension of credit, and are not excess contributions as defined in new section 4973(h). In the case of funds contributed to an ABLE account that are contributed not earlier than 720 days (and not later than 365 days) prior to the filing of the petition, only up to $6,225 may be excluded.

Explanation of Provision

The provision eliminates the requirement that ABLE accounts may be established only in the State of residence of the ABLE account owner.[817]

Effective Date

The provision applies to taxable years beginning after December 31, 2014.

4. Exclusion from gross income of certain amounts received by wrongly incarcerated individuals (sec. 304 of the Act and new sec. 139F of the Code)

Present Law

The taxability of damages, *i.e.*, the amounts received as a result of a claim or legal action for compensation for injury, depends upon the nature of the underlying claim. If a direct payment on the underlying claim would be includible as income under section 61, and no specific exemption for that type of income is otherwise provided in the Code, then damages intended to compensate for loss of that includible income are themselves includible income.[818] Section 104 of the Code specifically excludes from gross income most compensation for physical injuries or physical sickness. Damages for nonphysical injuries, such as mental anguish, damage to reputation, discrimination, or lost income, are not within the purview of the section 104 exclusion. Compensation related to wrongful incarceration but not physical injuries or physical sickness is not specifically addressed by the Code.

Explanation of Provision

Under the provision, with respect to any wrongfully incarcerated individual, gross income shall not include any civil damages, restitution, or other monetary award (including compensatory or statutory damages and restitution imposed in a criminal matter) relating to the incarceration of such individual for the covered offense for which such individual was convicted.

A wrongfully incarcerated individual means an individual:

(1) who was convicted of a covered offense;

(2) who served all or part of a sentence of imprisonment relating to that covered offense; and

(3)(i) was pardoned, granted clemency, or granted amnesty for such offense because the individual was innocent, or

(ii) for whom the judgment of conviction for the offense was reversed or vacated, and whom the indictment, infor-

---

[817] The Joint Committee staff's technical explanation of the PATH Act of 2015 incorrectly stated that the provision allowed for rollovers to ABLE accounts from qualified tuition programs (also known as 529 accounts). See Joint Committee on Taxation, *Technical Explanation of the Revenue Provisions of the Protecting Americans from Tax Hikes Act of 2015, House Amendment #2 to the Senate Amendment to H.R. 2029 (Rules Committee Print 114–40)*, (JCX–144–15), December 17, 2015, p. 151. The provision does not change the rules relating to rollovers to ABLE accounts.

[818] For example, a claim for lost wages results in taxable damages, because the wages themselves would have been taxable, but an award for damage to property may not result in includible income if the award does not exceed the recipient's basis in the property.

mation, or other accusatory instrument for that covered offense was dismissed or who was found not guilty at a new trial after the judgment of conviction for that covered offense was reversed or vacated.

For these purposes, a covered offense is any criminal offense under Federal or State law, and includes any criminal offense arising from the same course of conduct as that criminal offense.

The provision contains a special rule allowing individuals to make a claim for credit or refund of any overpayment of tax resulting from the exclusion, even if such claim would be disallowed under the Code or by operation of any law or rule of law (including *res judicata*), if the claim for credit or refund is filed before the close of the one-year period beginning on the date of enactment (December 18, 2015).

Effective Date

The provision is effective for taxable years beginning before, on, or after the date of enactment (December 18, 2015).

5. Clarification of special rule for certain governmental plans (sec. 305 of the Act and sec. 105(j) of the Code)[819]

Present Law

Reimbursements under an employer-provided accident or health plan for medical care expenses for employees, their spouses, their dependents, and adult children under age 27 are excludible from gross income.[820] However, in order for these reimbursements to be excluded from income, the plan may reimburse expenses of only the employee and the employee's spouse, dependents, and children under age 27. In the case of a deceased employee, the plan generally may reimburse medical expenses of only the employee's surviving spouse, dependents and children under age 27. If a plan reimburses expenses of any other beneficiary, all expense reimbursements under the plan are included in income, including reimbursements of expenses of the employee and the employee's spouse, dependents and children under age 27 (or the employee's surviving spouse, dependents and children under age 27).[821]

Under a limited exception, reimbursements under a plan do not fail to be excluded from income solely because the plan provides for reimbursements of medical expenses of a deceased employee's beneficiary, without regard to whether the beneficiary is the employee's surviving spouse, dependent, or child under age 27.[822] In order for the exception to apply, the plan must have provided, on or before January 1, 2008, for reimbursement of the medical expenses of a deceased employee's beneficiary. In addition, the plan must be funded by a medical trust (1) that is established in connection with a public retirement system, and (2) that either has been authorized by a State legislature, or has received a favorable ruling from the

---

[819] The Senate Committee on Finance reported S.910 on April 14, 2015 (S. Rep. No. 114–21).
[820] Sec. 105(b).
[821] Rev. Rul. 2006–36, 2006–2 C.B. 353. The ruling is effective for plan years beginning after December 31, 2008, in the case of plans including certain reimbursement provisions on or before August 14, 2006.
[822] Sec. 105(j).

IRS that the trust's income is not includible in gross income by reason of the exclusion for income of a State or political subdivision.[823] This exception preserves the exclusion for reimbursements of expenses of the employee and the employee's spouse, dependents, and children under age 27 (or the employee's surviving spouse, dependents, and children under age 27). Reimbursements of expenses of other beneficiaries are included in income.

Explanation of Provision

The provision expands the exception to apply to additional plans. As expanded, the exception applies to a plan funded by a medical trust (1) that is either established in connection with a public retirement system or established by or on behalf of a State or political subdivision thereof, and (2) that either has been authorized by a State legislature or has received a favorable ruling from the IRS that the trust's income is not includible in gross income by reason of either the exclusion for income of a State or political subdivision or the exemption from income tax for a voluntary employees' beneficiary association ("VEBA").[824] As under present law, the plan is still required to have provided, on or before January 1, 2008, for reimbursement of the medical expenses of a deceased employee's beneficiary, without regard to whether the beneficiary is the employee's surviving spouse, dependent, or child under age 27.

The provision also clarifies that this exception preserves the exclusion for reimbursements of expenses of the employee and the employee's spouse, dependents, and children under age 27, or the employee's surviving spouse, dependents, and children under age 27 (referred to under the provision as "qualified taxpayers") and that, as under present law, reimbursements of expenses of other beneficiaries are included in income.

Effective Date

The provision is effective with respect to payments after the date of enactment (December 18, 2015).

6. Rollovers permitted from other retirement plans into SIMPLE retirement accounts (sec. 306 of the Act and sec. 408(p)(1)(B) of the Code)

Present Law

Certain small businesses can establish a simplified retirement plan called the savings incentive match plan for employees ("SIMPLE") retirement plan. SIMPLE plans can be adopted by employers: (1) that employ 100 or fewer employees who received at least $5,000 in compensation during the preceding year; and (2) that do not maintain another employer-sponsored retirement plan.[825] A SIMPLE plan can be either an individual retirement arrangement

---

[823] This exclusion is provided under section 115.
[824] Tax-exempt status for a VEBA is provided under Code section 501(c)(9).
[825] Sec. 408(p)(2)(C)(i). There is a two-year grace period for an employer that establishes and maintains a SIMPLE IRA for one or more years and satisfies the 100 employee limit but fails to meet the 100 employer limit in a subsequent year, provided that the reason for the failure is not due to an acquisition, disposition, or similar transaction involving the employer.

(an "IRA") for each employee[826] or part of a qualified cash or deferred arrangement (a "section 401(k) plan").[827] The rules applicable to SIMPLE IRAs and SIMPLE section 401(k) plans are similar, but not identical.

Distributions from employer-sponsored retirement plans and IRAs (including SIMPLE plans) are generally includible in gross income, except to the extent the amount distributed represents a return of after-tax contributions (that is, basis). The portion of a distribution made before age 59½, death, or disability that is includible in gross income is generally subject to an additional 10-percent income tax.[828] Early withdrawals from a SIMPLE plan generally are subject to the additional 10-percent tax. However, in the case of a SIMPLE IRA, early withdrawals during the two-year period beginning on the date the employee first participated in the SIMPLE IRA are subject to an additional 25 percent tax.[829]

If certain requirements are met, distributions from employer-sponsored retirement plans and IRAs generally may generally be rolled over on a nontaxable basis to another employer-sponsored retirement plan or IRA. However, a distribution from a SIMPLE IRA during the two-year period beginning on the date the employee first participated in the SIMPLE IRA may be rolled over only to another SIMPLE IRA. In addition, because the only contributions that may be made to a SIMPLE IRA are contributions under a SIMPLE plan, distributions from other employer-sponsored retirement plans and IRAs cannot be rolled over to a SIMPLE IRA, even after this two-year period.

Explanation of Provision

The provision permits rollovers of distributions from employer-sponsored retirement plans and traditional IRAs (that are not SIMPLE IRAs) into a SIMPLE IRA after the expiration of the two-year period following the date the employee first participated in the SIMPLE IRA (the two-year period during which the additional income tax on distributions from a SIMPLE IRA is 25 percent instead of 10 percent).

Effective Date

The provision applies to contributions to SIMPLE IRAs made after the date of enactment (December 18, 2015).

---

[826] Sec. 408(p). A SIMPLE IRA may not be in the form of a Roth IRA.
[827] Sec. 401(k)(11).
[828] Sec. 72(t). There are other exceptions to the 10-percent additional income tax, besides attainment of age 59½, death, or disability.
[829] Sec. 72(t)(6).

7. Technical amendment relating to rollover of certain airline payment amounts (sec. 307 of the Act and sec. 1106 of the FAA Modernization and Reform Act of 2012)

Present Law

Individual retirement arrangements

The Code provides for two types of individual retirement arrangements ("IRAs"): traditional IRAs and Roth IRAs.[830]

Contributions to a traditional IRA may be deductible from gross income, or nondeductible contributions may be made, which result in "basis." Distributions from a traditional IRA are includible in gross income to the extent not treated as a return of basis (that is, if attributable to deductible contributions or earnings).

Contributions to a Roth IRA are not deductible (and result in basis), and qualified distributions from a Roth IRA are excludable from gross income. Distributions from a Roth IRA that are not qualified distributions are includible in gross income to the extent not treated as a return of basis (that is, if attributable to earnings). In general, a qualified distribution from a Roth IRA is a distribution that (1) is made after the five taxable year period beginning with the first taxable year for which the individual first made a contribution to a Roth IRA, and (2) is made on or after the individual attains age 59½, death, or disability or which is a qualified special purpose distribution.

The total amount that an individual may contribute to one or more IRAs for a year (other than a rollover contribution, discussed below) is generally limited to the lesser of: (1) a dollar amount ($5,500 for 2015, plus $1,000 if the individual is age 50 or older); or (2) the amount of the individual's compensation that is includible in gross income for the year. In the case of married individuals filing a joint return, a contribution up to the dollar limit for each spouse may be made, provided the combined compensation of the spouses is at least equal to the contributed amount.

Subject to certain requirements, an individual may roll a distribution from an IRA over to an IRA of the same type on a nontaxable basis (that is, without income inclusion). In addition, an individual generally may convert a traditional IRA to a Roth IRA. In that case, the amount converted is includible in income as if a distribution from the traditional IRA had been made.

Rollover of airline payments to traditional IRAs

Under the FAA Modernization and Reform Act of 2012 ("2012 FAA Act"), if a qualified airline employee contributes any portion of an airline payment amount to a traditional IRA within 180 days of receipt of the amount (or, if later, within 180 days of February 14, 2012, the date of enactment of the 2012 FAA Act), the amount contributed is treated as a rollover contribution to the IRA.[831] A

---

[830] Traditional IRAs are described in section 408, and Roth IRAs are described in section 408A.

[831] Sec. 1106 of Pub. L. No. 112–95. Under section 125 of the Worker, Retiree, and Employer Recovery Act of 2008 ("WRERA"), Pub. L. No. 110–458, a qualified airline employee is permitted to contribute any portion of an airline payment amount to a Roth IRA within 180 days of receipt of such amount (or, if later, within 180 days of December 23, 2008, the date of enactment of WRERA), and the amount contributed is treated as a rollover contribution to the Roth IRA. The

qualified airline employee making such a rollover contribution may exclude the contributed amount from gross income for the taxable year in which the airline payment amount was paid to the qualified airline employee.

For this purpose, a qualified airline employee is an employee or former employee of a commercial passenger airline carrier who was a participant in a qualified defined benefit plan maintained by the carrier that was terminated or that became subject to the benefit accrual and other restrictions applicable to certain plans under the Pension Protection Act of 2006 ("PPA").[832] If a qualified airline employee dies after receiving an airline payment amount, or if an airline payment amount is paid to a surviving spouse of a qualified airline employee, the surviving spouse may receive the same rollover contribution treatment (and the related exclusion from income) as the employee could have received.

An airline payment amount is any payment of any money or other property payable by a commercial passenger airline to a qualified airline employee: (1) under the approval of an order of a Federal bankruptcy court in a case filed after September 11, 2001, and before January 1, 2007, and (2) in respect of the qualified airline employee's interest in a bankruptcy claim against the airline carrier, any note of the carrier (or amount paid in lieu of a note being issued), or any other fixed obligation of the carrier to pay a lump sum amount. An airline payment amount does not include any amount payable on the basis of the carrier's future earnings or profits. The amount of any airline payment amount is determined without regard to the withholding of the employee's share of taxes under the Federal Insurance Contributions Act ("FICA") or income tax.[833] Thus, for purposes of the rollover provision and the related exclusion from income, the gross amount of the airline payment amount (before withholding) applies.

The ability to contribute airline payment amounts to a traditional IRA as a rollover contribution (and the related exclusion from income) is subject to limitations. First, a qualified airline employee is not permitted to contribute an airline payment amount to a traditional IRA for a taxable year if, at any time during the taxable year or a preceding taxable year, the employee was a "covered employee," that is, the principal executive officer (or an individual acting in such capacity) within the meaning of the Securities Exchange Act of 1934 or among the three most highly compensated officers for the taxable year (other than the principal executive officer), of the commercial passenger airline carrier making the airline payment amount.[834] Second, in the case of a qualified airline em-

---

2012 FAA Act permitted an employee who had previously made a rollover contribution of an airline payment amount to a Roth IRA to recharacterize all or a portion of the rollover contribution as a rollover contribution to a traditional IRA and to exclude the recharacterized amount from income.

[832] Pub. L. No. 109–280. Section 402 of PPA provides funding relief with respect to certain defined benefit plans maintained by commercial passenger airlines, subject to meeting the benefit accrual and other restrictions under PPA section 402(b)(2) and (3).

[833] Secs. 3102 and 3402. An airline payment amount that is excluded from income under the 2012 FAA Act continues to be wages for FICA and Social Security earnings purposes.

[834] Covered employee status is defined by reference to section 162(m) (limiting deductions for compensation of covered employees), which defines a covered employee as (1) the chief executive officer of the corporation (or an individual acting in such capacity) as of the close of the taxable year, and (2) the four most highly compensated officers for the taxable year (other than the chief

Continued

ployee who was not at any time a covered employee, the amount that may be contributed to a traditional IRA for a taxable year cannot exceed the excess (if any) of (1) 90 percent of the aggregate airline payment amounts received during the taxable year and all preceding taxable years, over (2) the aggregate amount contributed to a traditional IRA (and excluded from income) for all preceding taxable years ("90 percent limitation").

Under the 2012 FAA Act, a qualified airline employee who excludes from income an airline payment amount contributed to a traditional IRA may file a claim for a refund until the later of: (1) the usual period of limitation (generally, three years from the time the return was filed or two years from the time the tax was paid, whichever period expires later),[835] or (2) April 15, 2013.

The definition of qualified airline employee under the 2012 FAA Act was amended in 2014 to include an employee or former employee of a commercial passenger airline carrier who was a participant in a qualified defined benefit plan maintained by the carrier that was frozen (that is, under which all benefit accruals ceased) as of November 1, 2012 ("2014 amendments").[836] The 2014 amendments also amended the definition of airline payment amount under the 2012 FAA Act to include any payment of any money or other property payable by a commercial passenger airline (but not any amount payable on the basis of the carrier's future earnings or profits) to a qualified airline employee: (1) under the approval of an order of a Federal bankruptcy court in a case filed on November 29, 2011, and (2) in respect of the qualified airline employee's interest in a bankruptcy claim against the airline carrier, any note of the carrier (or amount paid in lieu of a note being issued), or any other fixed obligation of the carrier to pay a lump sum amount. Thus, as a result of the 2014 amendments, if a qualified airline employee (other than a covered employee as described above) under a qualified defined benefit plan that was frozen as of November 1, 2012, receives an airline payment amount under a Federal bankruptcy order in a case filed on November 29, 2011, and, subject to the 90 percent limitation described above, contributes any portion of the airline payment amount to a traditional IRA within 180 days of receipt of the amount, the amount contributed is treated as a rollover contribution to the traditional IRA and may be excluded from gross income for the taxable year in which the airline payment amount was paid to the qualified airline employee.[837]

---

executive officer), whose compensation is required to be reported to shareholders under the Securities Exchange Act of 1934. Treas. Reg. sec. 1.162–27(c)(2) provides that whether an employee is the chief executive officer or among the four most highly compensated officers is determined pursuant to the executive compensation disclosure rules promulgated under the Securities Exchange Act of 1934. To reflect 2006 changes made to the disclosure rules by the Securities and Exchange Commission, Notice 2007–49, 2007–25 I.R.B. 1429, provides that "covered employee" means any employee who is (1) the principal executive officer (or an individual acting in such capacity) within the meaning of the amended disclosure rules, or (2) among the three most highly compensated officers for the taxable year (other than the principal executive officer).

[835] Sec. 6511(a).

[836] An act to amend certain provisions of the FAA Modernization and Reform Act of 2012, Pub. L. No. 113–243, enacted December 18, 2014. The 2014 amendments allow a qualified airline employee who excludes from income an airline payment amount contributed to a traditional IRA to file a claim for a refund until the later of (1) the usual period of limitation (generally, three years from the time the return was filed or two years from the time the tax was paid, whichever period expires later), or (2) April 15, 2015.

[837] As permitted under present law, after the contribution, an individual may convert the traditional IRA to a Roth IRA.

Unlike the 2012 FAA Act, the 2014 amendments did not contain a provision to allow previously made payments that came within the definition of airline payment amounts as a result of the amendments to be rolled over within 180 days after enactment.[838]

Explanation of Provision

The provision allows any amount that comes within the definition of an airline payment amount as a result of the 2014 amendments to be rolled over within 180 days of receipt or, if later, within the period beginning on December 18, 2014, and ending 180 days after enactment of the provision.

Effective Date

The provision is effective as if included in the 2014 amendments.

8. Treatment of early retirement distributions for nuclear materials couriers, United States Capitol Police, Supreme Court Police, and diplomatic security special agents (sec. 308 of the Act and sec. 72(t) of the Code)

Present Law

An individual who receives a distribution from a qualified retirement plan before age 59½, death, or disability is subject to a 10-percent early withdrawal tax on the amount includible in income unless an exception to the tax applies.[839] Among other exceptions, the early distribution tax does not apply to distributions made to an employee who separates from service after age 55 (the "separation from service" exception), or to distributions that are part of a series of substantially equal periodic payments made for the life, or life expectancy, of the employee or the joint lives, or life expectancies, of the employee and his or her beneficiary (the "equal periodic payments" exception).[840]

Under a special rule for qualified public safety employees, the separation from service exception applies to distributions from a governmental defined benefit pension plan if the employee separates from service after age 50 (rather than age 55). A qualified public safety employee is an employee of a State or political subdivision of a State if the employee provides police protection, firefighting services, or emergency medical services for any area within the jurisdiction of such State or political subdivision.

The special rule for applying the separation from service exception to qualified public safety employees was revised by the Defending Public Safety Employees' Retirement Act, effective for distributions after December 31, 2015.[841] First, the definition of qualified

---

[838] As described above, the WRERA provision enacted in 2008 also contained a provision allowing rollovers within 180 days of receipt of an airline payment amount or, if later, within 180 days of the date of enactment of WRERA.

[839] Sec. 72(t).

[840] Sec. 72(t)(2)(iv) and (v). Section 72(t)(4) provides a recapture rule under which, in general, if the series of payments eligible for the equal periodic payments exception is modified within five years of the first payment or before age 59½, an additional tax applies equal to the early withdrawal tax that would have applied in the absence of the exception.

[841] Sec. 2 of Pub. L. No. 114–26, enacted June 29, 2015, discussed in Part Five. This provision also allows a qualified public safety employee to modify a series of payments to which the equal

Continued

public safety employee was expanded to include Federal law enforcement officers, Federal customs and border protection officers, Federal firefighters, and air traffic controllers.[842] In addition, the special rule was extended to distributions from governmental defined contribution plans (rather than just governmental defined benefit plans).[843]

Explanation of Provision

The provision amends the definition of qualified public safety employee to include nuclear materials couriers,[844] members of the United States Capitol Police, members of the Supreme Court police, and diplomatic security special agents of the United States Department of State.

Effective Date

The provision applies to distributions after December 31, 2015.

9. Prevention of extension of tax collection period for members of the Armed Forces who are hospitalized as a result of combat zone injuries (sec. 309 of the Act and secs. 6502 and 7508(e) of the Code)[845]

Present Law

The Code provides active duty military and civilians in designated combat zones additional time in which to file tax returns, pay tax liabilities and take other actions required in order to comply with their tax obligations.[846] A commensurate amount of time is provided for the IRS to complete actions required with respect to assessment and collection of the obligations of such active duty military and civilian taxpayers. The additional time provided equals the actual time in duty status, which includes hospitalization resulting from service, plus 180 days. In other words, in determining how much time remains in which to perform a task required by the Code, both the taxpayer and the IRS may disregard the period of active duty.

The Code provides that collection activities generally may only occur within ten years after assessment.[847] The effect of the provisions described above is to extend the 10-year collection period for combat zone taxpayers.

Explanation of Provision

Under the provision, the collection period for taxpayers hospitalized for combat zone injuries shall not be suspended by reason of any period of continuous hospitalization or the 180 days after hos-

---

periodic payments exception has applied without being subject to the recapture rule described above.

[842] These positions are defined by reference to the provisions of the Civil Service Retirement System (CSRS) and the Federal Employees Retirement System (FERS).

[843] Under section 7701(j), the Federal Thrift Savings Plan is treated as a qualified defined contribution plan.

[844] These positions are defined by reference to the provisions of CSRS and FERS.

[845] The Senate Committee on Finance reported S. 907 on April 14, 2015 (S. Rep. No. 114–18).

[846] Sec. 7508.

[847] Sec. 6502.

pitalization. Accordingly, the collection period expires 10 years after assessment, plus the actual time spent in a combat zone, regardless of the length of the postponement period available for hospitalized taxpayers to comply with their tax obligations.

Effective Date

The provision applies to taxes assessed before, on, or after the date of the enactment (December 18, 2015).

B. Real Estate Investment Trusts

Overview

In general

A real estate investment trust ("REIT") is an entity that otherwise would be taxed as a U.S. corporation but elects to be taxed under a special REIT tax regime. To qualify as a REIT, an entity must meet a number of requirements. At least 90 percent of REIT income (other than net capital gain) must be distributed annually;[848] the REIT must derive most of its income from passive, generally real estate-related, investments; and REIT assets must be primarily real estate-related. In addition, a REIT must have transferable interests and at least 100 shareholders, and no more than 50 percent of the REIT interests may be owned by five or fewer individual shareholders (as determined using specified attribution rules). Other requirements also apply.[849]

If an electing entity meets the requirements for REIT status, the portion of its income that is distributed to its shareholders as a dividend or qualifying liquidating distribution each year is deductible by the REIT (whereas a regular subchapter C corporation cannot deduct such distributions).[850] As a result, the distributed income of the REIT is not taxed at the entity level; instead, it is taxed only at the investor level. Although a REIT is not required to distribute more than the 90 percent of its income described above to retain REIT status, it is taxed at ordinary corporate rates on amounts not distributed or treated as distributed.[851]

A REIT may designate a capital gain distribution to its shareholders, who treat the designated amount as long-term capital gain when distributed. A REIT also may retain net capital gain and pay corporate income tax on the amount retained, while the shareholders include the undistributed capital gain in income, obtain a credit for the corporate tax paid, and step up the basis of their

---

[848] Even if a REIT meets the 90-percent income distribution requirement for REIT qualification, more stringent distribution requirements must be met in order to avoid an excise tax under section 4981.

[849] Secs. 856 and 857.

[850] Liquidating distributions are covered to the extent of earnings and profits, and are defined to include redemptions of stock that are treated by shareholders as a sale of stock under section 302. Secs. 857(b)(2)(B), 561, and 562(b).

[851] An additional four-percent excise tax is imposed to the extent a REIT does not distribute at least 85 percent of REIT ordinary income and 95 percent of REIT capital gain net income within a calendar year period. In addition, to the extent a REIT distributes less than 100 percent of its ordinary income and capital gain net income in a year, the difference between the amount actually distributed and 100 percent is added to the distribution otherwise required in a subsequent year to avoid the excise tax. Sec. 4981.

REIT stock for the amount included in income.[852] In this manner, capital gain also is taxed only once, whether or not distributed, rather than at both the entity and investor levels.

Income tests

A REIT is restricted to earning certain types of generally passive income. Among other requirements, at least 75 percent of the gross income of a REIT in each taxable year must consist of real estate-related income. Such income includes: rents from real property; gain from the sale or other disposition of real property (including interests in real property) that is not stock in trade of the taxpayer, inventory, or other property held by the taxpayer primarily for sale to customers in the ordinary course of its trade or business; interest on mortgages secured by real property or interests in real property; and certain income from foreclosure property (the "75-percent income test").[853] Qualifying rents from real property include rents from interests in real property and charges for services customarily furnished or rendered in connection with the rental of real property,[854] but do not include impermissible tenant service income.[855] Impermissible tenant service income includes amounts for services furnished by the REIT to tenants or for managing or operating the property, other than amounts attributable to services that are provided by an independent contractor or taxable REIT subsidiary, or services that certain tax exempt organizations could perform under the section 512(b)(3) rental exception from unrelated business taxable income.[856] Qualifying rents from real property include rent attributable to personal property which is leased under, or in connection with, a lease of real property, but only if the rent attributable to such personal property for the taxable year does not exceed 15 percent of the total rent for the taxable year attributable to both the real and personal property leased under, or in connection with, the lease.[857]

In addition, rents received from any entity in which the REIT owns more than 10 percent of the vote or value generally are not qualifying income.[858] However, there is an exception for certain rents received from taxable REIT subsidiaries (described further below), in which a REIT may own more than 10 percent of the vote or value.

In addition, 95 percent of the gross income of a REIT for each taxable year must be from the 75-percent income sources and a sec-

---

[852] Sec. 857(b)(3).
[853] Secs. 856(c)(3) and 1221(a)(1). Income from sales that are not prohibited transactions solely by virtue of section 857(b)(6) also is qualified REIT income.
[854] Sec. 856(d)(1)(A) and (B).
[855] Sec. 856(d)(2)(C).
[856] Sec. 856(d)(7)(A) and (C). If impermissible tenant service income with respect to any real or personal property is more than one percent of all amounts received or accrued during the taxable year directly or indirectly with respect to such property, then the impermissible tenant service income with respect to such property includes all such amounts. Sec. 856(d)(7)(B). The amount treated as received for any service (or management or operation) shall not be less than 150 percent of the direct cost of the trust in furnishing or rendering the service (or providing the management or operation). Sec. 856(d)(7)(D). For purposes of the 75-percent and 95-percent income tests, impermissible tenant service income is included in gross income of the REIT. Sec. 856(d)(7)(E).
[857] Sec. 856(d)(1)(C).
[858] Sec. 856(d)(2)(B).

ond permitted category of other, generally passive sources such as dividends and interest (the "95-percent income test").[859]

A REIT must be a U.S. domestic entity, but it is permitted to hold foreign real estate or other foreign assets, provided the 75-percent and 95-percent income tests and the other requirements for REIT qualification are met.[860]

Asset tests

At least 75 percent of the value of a REIT's assets must be real estate assets, cash and cash items (including receivables), and Government securities[861] (the "75-percent asset test").[862] Real estate assets are real property (including interests in real property and interests in mortgages on real property) and shares (or transferable certificates of beneficial interest) in other REITs.[863] No more than 25 percent of a REIT's assets may be securities other than such real estate assets.[864]

Except with respect to securities of a taxable REIT subsidiary, not more than five percent of the value of a REIT's assets may be securities of any one issuer, and the REIT may not possess securities representing more than 10 percent of the outstanding value or voting power of any one issuer.[865] In addition, not more than 25 percent of the value of a REIT's assets may be securities of one or more taxable REIT subsidiaries.[866]

The asset tests must be met as of the close of each quarter of a REIT's taxable year. However, a REIT that has met the asset tests as of the close of any quarter does not lose its REIT status solely because of a discrepancy during a subsequent quarter between the value of the REIT's investments and such requirements, unless such discrepancy exists immediately after the acquisition of any security or other property and is wholly or partly the result of such acquisition.[867]

Taxable REIT subsidiaries

A REIT generally cannot own more than 10 percent of the vote or value of a single entity. However, there is an exception for ownership of a taxable REIT subsidiary ("TRS") that is taxed as a corporation, provided that securities of one or more TRSs do not represent more than 25 percent of the value of REIT assets.

A TRS generally can engage in any kind of business activity except that it is not permitted directly or indirectly to operate either a lodging facility or a health care facility, or to provide to any other person (under a franchise, license, or otherwise) rights to any

---

[859] Sec. 856(c)(2).

[860] See Rev. Rul. 74–191, 1974–1 C.B. 170.

[861] Government securities are defined for this purpose under section 856(c)(5)(F), by reference to the Investment Company Act of 1940. The term includes securities issued or guaranteed by the United States or persons controlled or supervised by and acting as an instrumentality thereof, but does not include securities issued or guaranteed by a foreign, state, or local government entity or instrumentality.

[862] Sec. 856(c)(4)(A).

[863] Temporary investments in certain stock or debt instruments also can qualify if they are temporary investments of new capital, but only for the one-year period beginning on the date the REIT receives such capital. Sec. 856(c)(5)(B).

[864] Sec. 856(c)(4)(B)(i).

[865] Sec. 856(c)(4)(B)(iii).

[866] Sec. 856(c)(4)(B)(ii).

[867] Sec. 856(c)(4). In the case of such an acquisition, the REIT also has a grace period of 30 days after the close of the quarter to eliminate the discrepancy.

brand name under which any lodging facility or health care facility is operated.[868]

However, a TRS may rent a lodging facility or health care facility from its parent REIT and is permitted to hire an independent contractor[869] to operate such facility. Rent paid to the parent REIT by the TRS with respect to hotel, motel, or other transient lodging facility operated by an independent contractor is qualified rent for purposes of the REIT's 75-percent and 95-percent income tests.[870] This lodging facility rental rule is an exception to the general rule that rent paid to a REIT by any corporation (including a TRS) in which the REIT owns 10 percent or more of the vote or value is not qualified rental income for purposes of the 75-percent or 95-percent REIT income tests.[871] There is also an exception to the general rule in the case of a TRS that rents space in a building owned by its parent REIT if at least 90 percent of the space in the building is rented to unrelated parties and the rent paid by the TRS to the REIT is comparable to the rent paid by the unrelated parties.[872]

REITs are subject to a tax equal to 100 percent of redetermined rents, redetermined deductions, and excess interest. These are defined generally as the amounts of specified REIT transactions with a TRS of the REIT, to the extent such amounts differ from an arm's length amount.[873]

Prohibited transactions tax

REITs are subject to a prohibited transaction tax ("PTT") of 100 percent of the net income derived from prohibited transactions. For this purpose, a prohibited transaction is a sale or other disposition of property by the REIT that is "stock in trade of a taxpayer or other property which would properly be included in the inventory of the taxpayer if on hand at the close of the taxable year, or property held for sale to customers by the taxpayer in the ordinary course of his trade or business"[874] and is not foreclosure property. The PTT for a REIT does not apply to a sale if the REIT satisfies certain safe harbor requirements in section 857(b)(6)(C) or (D), including an asset holding period of at least two years.[875] If the conditions are met, a REIT may either (1) make no more than seven sales within a taxable year (other than sales of foreclosure property or involuntary conversions under section 1033), or (2) sell either no more than 10 percent of the aggregate bases, or no more than 10

---

[868] The latter restriction does not apply to rights provided to an independent contractor to operate or manage a lodging or health care facility if such rights are held by the corporation as a franchisee, licensee, or in similar capacity and such lodging facility or health care facility is either owned by such corporation or is leased by such corporation from the REIT. Sec. 856(l)(3).

[869] An independent contractor will not fail to be treated as such for this purpose because the TRS bears the expenses of operation of the facility under the contract, or because the TRS receives the revenues from the operation of the facility, net of expenses for such operation and fees payable to the operator pursuant to the contract, or both. Sec. 856(d)(9)(B).

[870] Sec. 856(d)(8)(B).
[871] Sec. 856(d)(2)(B).
[872] Sec. 856(d)(8)(A).
[873] Sec. 857(b)(7).

[874] This definition is the same as the definition of certain property the sale or other disposition of which would produce ordinary income rather than capital gain under section 1221(a)(1).

[875] Additional requirements for the safe harbor limit the amount of expenditures the REIT can make during the two-year period prior to the sale that are includible in the adjusted basis of the property, require marketing to be done by an independent contractor, and forbid a sales price that is based on the income or profits of any person.

percent of the aggregate fair market value, of all its assets as of the beginning of the taxable year (computed without regard to sales of foreclosure property or involuntary conversions under section 1033), without being subject to the PTT tax.[876]

REIT shareholder tax treatment

Although a REIT typically does not pay corporate level tax due to the deductible distribution of its income, and thus is sometimes compared to a partnership or S corporation, REIT equity holders are not treated as being engaged in the underlying activities of the REIT as are partners or S corporation shareholders, and the activities at the REIT level that characterize its income do not generally flow through to equity owners to characterize the tax treatment of REIT distributions to them. A distribution to REIT shareholders out of REIT earnings and profits is generally treated as an ordinary income REIT dividend and is treated as ordinary income taxed at the shareholder's normal rates on such income.[877] However, a REIT is permitted to designate a "capital gain dividend" to the extent a distribution is made out of its net capital gain.[878] Such a dividend is treated as long-term capital gain to the shareholders.[879]

REIT shareholders are not taxed on REIT income unless the income is distributed to them (except in the case of REIT net capital gain retained by the REIT and designated for inclusion in the shareholder's income as explained in the preceding footnote). However, since a REIT must distribute 90 percent of its ordinary income annually, and typically will distribute or designate its income as capital gain dividends to avoid a tax at the REIT level, REIT income generally is taxed in full at the shareholder level annually.

REIT shareholders are not entitled to any share of REIT losses to offset against other shareholder income. However, if the REIT itself has income, its losses offset its income in determining how much it is required to distribute to meet the distribution requirements. Also, REIT losses that reduce earnings and profits can cause a distribution that exceeds the REIT's earnings and profits to be treated as a nontaxable return of capital to its shareholders.

Tax exempt shareholders

A tax exempt shareholder is exempt from tax on REIT dividends, and is not treated as engaging in any of the activities of the REIT. As one example, if the REIT borrowed money and its income at the REIT level were debt-financed, a tax exempt shareholder would not

---

[876] Sec. 857(b)(6).

[877] Because a REIT dividend is generally paid out of income that was not taxed to the distributing entity, the dividend is not eligible for the dividends received deductions to a corporate shareholder. Sec. 243(d)(3). A REIT dividend is not eligible for the 20 percent qualified dividend rate to an individual shareholder, except to the extent such dividend is attributable to REIT income from nondeductible C corporation dividends, or to certain income of the REIT that was subject to corporate level tax. Sec. 857(c).

[878] Sec. 857(b)(3)(C). Net capital gain is the excess of the net long-term capital gain for the taxable year over the net short-term capital loss for the taxable year. Sec. 1222.

[879] A REIT may also retain its net capital gain without distribution, while designating a capital gain dividend for inclusion in shareholder income. In this case, the REIT pays corporate-level tax on the capital gain, but the shareholder includes the undistributed capital gain in income, receives a credit for the corporate level tax paid, and steps up the basis of the REIT stock for the amount included in income, with the result that the net tax paid is the shareholder-level capital gain tax. Sec. 857(b)(3)(D).

have debt-financed unrelated business income from the REIT dividend.

Foreign shareholders

Except as provided by the Foreign Investment in Real Property Tax Act of 1980 ("FIRPTA"),[880] a REIT shareholder that is a foreign corporation or a nonresident alien individual normally treats its dividends as fixed and determinable annual and periodic income that is subject to withholding under section 1441 but not treated as active business income that is effectively connected with the conduct of a U.S. trade or business, regardless of the level of real estate activity of the REIT in the United States.[881] A number of treaties permit a lower rate of withholding on REIT dividends than the Code would otherwise require.

Although FIRPTA applies in many cases to foreign investment in U.S. real property through a REIT, REITs offer foreign investors some ability to invest in U.S real property interests without subjecting gain on the sale of REIT stock to FIRPTA (for example, if the REIT is domestically controlled).[882] In general, if any class of stock of a corporation is regularly traded on an established securities market, stock of such class is subject to FIRPTA only in the case of a person who, at some time during the testing period, held more than 5 percent of such class of stock.[883] Also, if the REIT stock is publicly traded and the foreign investor does not own more than five percent of such stock, the investor can receive distributions from the sale by the REIT of U.S. real property interests without such distributions being subject to FIRPTA.[884]

1. Restriction on tax-free spinoffs involving REITs (sec. 311 of the Act and secs. 355 and 856 of the Code)

Present Law

A corporation generally is required to recognize gain on the distribution of property (including stock of a subsidiary) to its shareholders as if the corporation had sold such property for its fair market value.[885] In addition, the shareholders receiving the distributed property are ordinarily treated as receiving a dividend equal to the value of the distribution (to the extent of the distributing corporation's earnings and profits),[886] or capital gain in the case of an acquisition of its stock that significantly reduces the shareholder's interest in the parent corporation.[887]

An exception to these rules applies if the distribution of the stock of a controlled corporation satisfies the requirements of section 355.

---

[880] Pub. L. No. 96–499. FIRPTA treats income of a foreign investor from the sale or disposition of U.S. real property interests as effectively connected with the operation of a trade or business in the United States. Such income is taxed at regular U.S. rates and withholding obligations are imposed on payors of the income. Secs. 897 and 1445.

[881] As noted above, REITs are not permitted to receive income from property that is inventory or that is held for sale to customers in the ordinary course of the REIT's business. However, REITs may engage in certain activities, including acquisition, development, lease, and sale of real property, and may provide "customary services" to tenants.

[882] Sec. 897(h)(2).
[883] Sec. 897(c)(3).
[884] Sec. 897(h)(1).
[885] Sec. 311(b).
[886] Sec. 301(b)(1) and (c)(1).
[887] Sec. 302(a) and (b)(2).

If all the requirements are satisfied, there is no tax to the distributing corporation or to the shareholders on the distribution.

One requirement to qualify for tax-free treatment under section 355 is that both the distributing corporation and the controlled corporation must be engaged immediately after the distribution in the active conduct of a trade or business that has been conducted for at least five years and was not acquired in a taxable transaction during that period (the "active business test").[888]

For this purpose, the active business test is satisfied only if (1) immediately after the distribution, the corporation is engaged in the active conduct of a trade or business, or (2) immediately before the distribution, the corporation had no assets other than stock or securities in the controlled corporations and each of the controlled corporations is engaged immediately after the distribution in the active conduct of a trade or business.[889] For this purpose, the active business test is applied by reference to the relevant affiliated group rather than on a single corporation basis. For the parent distributing corporation, the relevant affiliated group consists of the distributing corporation as the common parent and all corporations affiliated with the distributing corporation through stock ownership described in section 1504(a)(1) (regardless of whether the corporations are otherwise includible corporations under section 1504(b)),[890] immediately after the distribution. The relevant affiliated group for a controlled distributed subsidiary corporation is determined in a similar manner (with the controlled corporation as the common parent).

In determining whether a corporation is directly engaged in an active trade or business that satisfies the requirement, IRS ruling practice formerly required that the value of the gross assets of the trade or business being relied on must ordinarily constitute at least five percent of the total fair market value of the gross assets of the corporation directly conducting the trade or business.[891] The IRS suspended this specific rule in connection with its general administrative practice of moving IRS resources away from advance rulings on factual aspects of section 355 transactions in general.[892]

Section 355 does not apply to an otherwise qualifying distribution if, immediately after the distribution, either the distributing or the controlled corporation is a disqualified investment corporation and any person owns a 50 percent interest in such corporation and did not own such an interest before the distribution. A disqualified investment corporation is a corporation of which two-thirds or more

---

[888] Sec. 355(b).

[889] Sec. 355(b)(1).

[890] Sec. 355(b)(3).

[891] Rev. Proc. 2003–3, sec. 4.01(30), 2003–1 I.R.B. 113.

[892] Rev. Proc. 2003–48, 2003–29 I.R.B. 86. Since then, the IRS discontinued private rulings on whether a transaction generally qualifies for nonrecognition treatment under section 355. Nonetheless, the IRS may still rule on certain significant issues. See Rev. Proc. 2016–1, 2016–1 I.R.B. 1; Rev. Proc. 2016–3, 2016–1 I.R.B. 126. Recently, the IRS announced that it will not rule in certain situations in which property owned by any distributing or controlled corporation becomes the property of a RIC or a REIT; however, the IRS stated that the policy did not extend to situations in which, immediately after the date of the distribution, both the distributing and controlled corporation will be RICs, or both of such corporations will be REITs, and there is no plan or intention on the date of the distribution for either the distributing or the controlled corporation to cease to be a RIC or a REIT. See Rev. Proc. 2015–43, 2015–40 I.R.B. 467.

of its asset value is comprised of certain passive investment assets. Real estate is not included as such an asset.[893]

The IRS has ruled that a REIT may satisfy the active business requirement through its rental activities.[894] More recently, the IRS has issued a private ruling indicating that a REIT that has a TRS can satisfy the active business requirement by virtue of the active business of its TRS.[895] Thus, a C corporation that owns REIT-qualified assets may create a REIT to hold such assets and spin off that REIT without tax consequences to it or its shareholders (if the newly-formed REIT satisfies the active business requirement through its rental activities or the activities of a TRS). Following the spin-off, income from the assets held in the REIT is no longer subject to corporate level tax (unless there is a disposition of such assets that incurs tax under the built in gain rules).

Explanation of Provision

The provision makes a REIT generally ineligible to participate in a tax-free spin-off as either a distributing or controlled corporation under section 355. There are two exceptions, however. First, the general rule does not apply if, immediately after the distribution, both the distributing and the controlled corporations are REITs.[896] Second, a REIT may spin off a TRS if (1) the distributing corporation has been a REIT at all times during the 3-year period ending on the date of the distribution, (2) the controlled corporation has been a TRS of the REIT at all times during such period, and (3) the REIT has had control (as defined in section 368(c)[897] applied by taking into account stock owned directly or indirectly, including through one or more partnerships, by the REIT) of the TRS at all times during such period. For this purpose, control of a partnership means ownership of at least 80 percent of the profits interest and at least 80 percent of the capital interests.

A controlled corporation will be treated as meeting the control requirements if the stock of such corporation was distributed by a TRS in a transaction to which section 355 (or so much of section 356 as relates to section 355) applies and the assets of such corporation consist solely of the stock or assets held by one or more TRSs of the distributing corporation meeting the control requirements noted above.

If a corporation that is not a REIT was a distributing or controlled corporation with respect to any distribution to which section 355 applied, such corporation (and any successor corporation) shall not be eligible to make a REIT election for any taxable year beginning before the end of the 10-year period beginning on the date of such distribution.

---

[893] Sec. 355(g).

[894] Rev. Rul. 2001–29, 2001–1 C.B. 1348.

[895] Priv. Ltr. Rul. 201337007. A private ruling may be relied upon only by the taxpayer to which it is issued. However, private rulings provide some indication of administrative practice.

[896] As long as a REIT election for each corporation is effective immediately after the distribution, the elections may be made after that time.

[897] Under section 368(c), the term "control" means the ownership of stock possessing at least 80 percent of the total combined voting power of all classes of stock entitled to vote and at least 80 percent of the total number of shares of all other classes of stock of the corporation.

Effective Date

The provision generally applies to distributions on or after December 7, 2015,[898] but does not apply to any distribution pursuant to a transaction described in a ruling request initially submitted to the Internal Revenue Service on or before such date, which request has not been withdrawn and with respect to which a ruling has not been issued or denied in its entirety as of such date.

2. Reduction in percentage limitation on assets of REIT which may be taxable REIT subsidiaries (sec. 312 of the Act and sec. 856 of the Code)

Present Law

A REIT generally is not permitted to own securities representing more than 10 percent of the vote or value of any entity, nor is it permitted to own securities of a single issuer comprising more than 5 percent of REIT value.[899] In addition, rents received by a REIT from a corporation of which the REIT directly or indirectly owns more than 10 percent of the vote or value generally are not qualified rents for purposes of the 75-percent and 95-percent income tests.[900]

There is an exception from these rules in the case of a TRS.[901] No more than 25 percent of the value of total REIT assets may consist of securities of one or more TRSs.[902]

Explanation of Provision

The provision reduces to 20 percent the permitted percentage of total REIT assets that may be securities of one or more TRSs.

Effective Date

The provision applies to taxable years beginning after December 31, 2017.

3. Prohibited transaction safe harbors (sec. 313 of the Act and sec. 857 of the Code)

Present Law

REITs are subject to a prohibited transaction tax ("PTT") of 100 percent of the net income derived from prohibited transactions. For this purpose, a prohibited transaction is a sale or other disposition of property by the REIT that is "stock in trade of a taxpayer or other property which would properly be included in the inventory of the taxpayer if on hand at the close of the taxable year, or property held for sale to customers by the taxpayer in the ordinary

---

[898] The provision does not apply to distributions by a corporation pursuant to a plan under which stock constituting control (within the meaning of section 368(c)) of the controlled corporation was distributed before December 7, 2015.
[899] Sec. 856(c)(4)(B)(iii).
[900] Sec. 856(d)(2)(B).
[901] Sec. 856(d)(8).
[902] Sec. 856(c)(4)(B)(ii).

course of his trade or business"[903] and is not foreclosure property. The PTT for a REIT does not apply to a sale if the REIT satisfies certain safe harbor requirements in section 857(b)(6)(C) or (D), including an asset holding period of at least two years.[904] If the conditions are met, a REIT may either (1) make no more than seven sales within a taxable year (other than sales of foreclosure property or involuntary conversions under section 1033), or (2) sell either no more than 10 percent of the aggregate bases, or no more than 10 percent of the aggregate fair market value, of all its assets as of the beginning of the taxable year (computed without regard to sales of foreclosure property or involuntary conversions under section 1033), without being subject to the PTT tax.[905]

The additional requirements for the safe harbor limit the amount of expenditures the REIT or a partner of the REIT can make during the two-year period prior to the sale that are includible in the adjusted basis of the property. Also, if more than seven sales are made during the taxable year, substantially all marketing and development expenditures with respect to the property must have been made through an independent contractor from whom the REIT itself does not derive or receive any income.

Explanation of Provision

The provision expands the amount of property that a REIT may sell in a taxable year within the safe harbor provisions, from 10 percent of the aggregate basis or fair market value, to 20 percent of the aggregate basis or fair market value. However, in any taxable year, the aggregate adjusted bases and the fair market value of property (other than sales of foreclosure property or sales to which section 1033 applies) sold during the three taxable year period ending with such taxable year may not exceed 10 percent of the sum of the aggregate adjusted bases or the sum of the fair market value of all of the assets of the REIT as of the beginning of each of the 3 taxable years that are part of the period.

The provision clarifies that the determination of whether property is described in section 1221(a)(1) is made without regard to whether or not such property qualifies for the safe harbor from the prohibited transactions rules.

Effective Date

The provision generally applies to taxable years beginning after the date of enactment (December 18, 2015). However, the provision clarifying the determination of whether property is described in section 1221(a)(1) has retroactive effect, but does not apply to any sale of property to which section 857(b)(6)(G) applies.

---

[903] This definition is the same as the definition of certain property the sale or other disposition of which would produce ordinary income rather than capital gain under section 1221(a)(1).

[904] Additional requirements for the safe harbor limit the amount of expenditures the REIT can make during the two-year period prior to the sale that are includible in the adjusted basis of the property, require marketing to be done by an independent contractor, and forbid a sales price that is based on the income or profits of any person.

[905] Sec. 857(b)(6).

4. Repeal of preferential dividend rule for publicly offered REITs; authority for alternative remedies to address certain REIT distribution failures (secs. 314 and 315 of the Act and sec. 562 of the Code)

Present Law

A REIT is allowed a deduction for dividends paid to its shareholders.[906] In order to qualify for the deduction, a dividend must not be a "preferential dividend."[907] For this purpose, a dividend is preferential unless it is distributed pro rata to shareholders, with no preference to any share of stock compared with other shares of the same class, and with no preference to one class as compared with another except to the extent the class is entitled to a preference.

Similar rules apply to regulated investment companies ("RICs").[908] However, the preferential dividend rule does not apply to a publicly offered RIC (as defined in section 67(c)(2)(B)).[909]

Explanation of Provision

The provision repeals the preferential dividend rule for publicly offered REITs. For this purpose, a REIT is publicly offered if it is required to file annual and periodic reports with the Securities and Exchange Commission under the Securities Exchange Act of 1934.

For other REITs, the provision provides the Secretary of the Treasury with authority to provide an appropriate remedy to cure the failure of the REIT to comply with the preferential dividend requirements in lieu of not considering the distribution to be a dividend for purposes of computing the dividends-paid deduction where the Secretary determines the failure to comply is inadvertent or is due to reasonable cause and not due to willful neglect, or the failure is a type of failure identified by the Secretary as being so described.

Effective Date

The provision to repeal the preferential dividend rule for publicly offered REITs applies to distributions in taxable years beginning after December 31, 2014.

The provision granting authority to the Secretary of the Treasury to provide alternative remedies addressing certain REIT distribution failures applies to distributions in taxable years beginning after December 31, 2015.

5. Limitations on designation of dividends by REITs (sec. 316 of the Act and sec. 857 of the Code)

Present Law

A REIT that has a net capital gain for a taxable year may designate dividends that it pays or is treated as paying during the

---

[906] Sec. 857(b)(2)(B).
[907] Sec. 562(c).
[908] Sec. 852(b)(2)(D).
[909] Sec. 562(c).

year as capital gain dividends.[910] A capital gain dividend is treated by the shareholder as gain from the sale or exchange of a capital asset held more than one year.[911] The amount that may be designated as capital gain dividends for any taxable year may not exceed the REIT's net capital gain for the year.

A REIT may designate dividends that it pays or is treated as paying during the year as qualified dividend income.[912] Qualified dividend income is taxed to individuals at the same tax rate as net capital gain, under rules enacted by the Taxpayer Relief Act of 1997.[913] The amount that may be designated as qualified dividend income for any taxable year is limited to qualified dividend income received by the REIT plus some amounts subject to corporate taxation at the REIT level.

The IRS has ruled that a RIC may designate the maximum amount permitted under each of the provisions allowing a RIC to designate dividends even if the aggregate of all the designated amounts exceeds the total amount of the RIC's dividends distributions.[914]

The IRS also has ruled that if a RIC has two or more classes of stock and it designates the dividends that it pays on one class as consisting of more than that class's proportionate share of a particular type of income, the designations are not effective for federal tax purposes to the extent that they exceed the class's proportionate share of that type of income.[915] The Internal Revenue Service announced that it would provide guidance that RICs and REITs must use in applying the capital gain provision enacted by the Taxpayer Relief Act of 1997.[916] The announcement referred to the designation limitations of Revenue Ruling 89-91.

Explanation of Provision

The provision limits the aggregate amount of dividends designated by a REIT for a taxable year under all of the designation provisions to the amount of dividends paid with respect to the taxable year (including dividends described in section 858 that are paid after the end of the REIT taxable year but treated as paid by the REIT with respect to the taxable year).

The provision provides the Secretary of the Treasury authority to prescribe regulations or other guidance requiring the proportionality of the designation for particular types of dividends (for example, capital gain dividends) among shares or beneficial interests in a REIT.

Effective Date

The provision applies to distributions in taxable years beginning after December 31, 2015.

---

[910] Sec. 857(b)(3)(C).
[911] Sec. 857(b)(3)(B).
[912] Sec. 857(c)(2).
[913] Sec. 1(h)(11) enacted in Pub. L. No. 105-34.
[914] Rev. Rul. 2005-31, 2005-1 C.B.1084.
[915] Rev. Rul. 89-81, 1989-1 C.B. 226.
[916] Notice 97-64, 1997-2 C.B. 323. Recently, the IRS modified Notice 97-64 and provided certain new rules for RICs; the designation limitations in Revenue Ruling 89-81, however, continue to apply. Notice 2015-41, 2015-24 I.R.B. 1058.

6. Debt instruments of publicly offered REITs and mortgages treated as real estate assets (sec. 317 of the Act and sec. 856 of the Code)

Present Law

At least 75 percent of the value of a REIT's assets must be real estate assets, cash and cash items (including receivables), and Government securities (the "75-percent asset test").[917] Real estate assets are real property (including interests in real property and mortgages on real property) and shares (or transferable certificates of beneficial interest) in other REITs.[918] No more than 25 percent of a REIT's assets may be securities other than such real estate assets.[919]

Except with respect to a TRS, not more than five percent of the value of a REIT's assets may be securities of any one issuer, and the REIT may not possess securities representing more than 10 percent of the outstanding value or voting power of any one issuer.[920] No more than 25 percent of the value of a REIT's assets may be securities of one or more TRSs.[921]

The asset tests must be met as of the close of each quarter of a REIT's taxable year.[922]

At least 75 percent of a REIT's gross income must be from certain real estate related and other items. In addition, at least 95 percent of a REIT's gross income must be from specified sources that include the 75 percent items and also include interest, dividends, and gain from the sale or other disposition of securities (whether or not real estate-related).

Explanation of Provision

Under the provision, debt instruments issued by publicly offered REITs are treated as real estate assets, as are interests in mortgages on interests in real property (for example, an interest in a mortgage on a leasehold interest in real property). Such assets therefore are qualified assets for purposes of meeting the 75-percent asset test, but are subject to special limitations described below.

As under present law, income from debt instruments issued by publicly offered REITs that is interest income or gain from the sale or other disposition of a security is treated as qualified income for purposes of the 95-percent gross income test. Income from debt instruments issued by publicly offered REITs that would not have been treated as real estate assets but for the new provision, however, is not qualified income for purposes of the 75-percent income

---

[917] Sec. 856(c)(4)(A).
[918] Such term also includes any property (not otherwise a real estate asset) attributable to the temporary investment of new capital, but only if such property is stock or a debt instrument, and only for the one-year period beginning on the date the REIT receives such capital. Sec. 856(c)(5)(B).
[919] Sec. 856(c)(4)(B)(i).
[920] Sec. 856(c)(4)(B)(iii).
[921] Sec. 856(c)(4)(B)(ii).
[922] Sec. 856(c)(4). However, a REIT that has met the asset tests as of the close of any quarter does not lose its REIT status solely because of a discrepancy during a subsequent quarter between the value of the REIT's investments and such requirements, unless such discrepancy exists immediately after the acquisition of any security or other property and is wholly or partly the result of such acquisition. Sec. 856(c)(4).

test, and not more than 25 percent of the value of a REIT's total assets is permitted to be represented by such debt instruments.

Effective Date

The provision is effective for taxable years beginning after December 31, 2015.

7. Asset and income test clarification regarding ancillary personal property (sec. 318 of the Act and sec. 856 of the Code)

Present Law

75-percent income test

Among other requirements, at least 75 percent of the gross income of a REIT in each taxable year must consist of real estate-related income. Such income includes: rents from real property; income from the sale or exchange of real property (including interests in real property) that is not stock in trade, inventory, or held by the taxpayer primarily for sale to customers in the ordinary course of its trade or business; interest on mortgages secured by real property or interests in real property; and certain income from foreclosure property (the "75-percent income test"). Amounts attributable to most types of services provided to tenants (other than certain "customary services"), or to more than specified amounts of personal property, are not qualifying rents.

The Code definition of rents from real property includes rent attributable to personal property which is leased under, or in connection with, a lease of real property, but only if the rent attributable to such property for the taxable year does not exceed 15 percent of the total rent for the taxable year attributable to both the real and personal property leased under, or in connection with, such lease.[923]

For purposes of determining whether interest income is from a mortgage secured by real property, Treasury regulations provide that where a mortgage covers both real property and other property, an apportionment of the interest must be made. If the loan value of the real property is equal to or exceeds the amount of the loan, then the entire interest income is apportioned to the real property. However, if the amount of the loan exceeds the loan value of the real property, then the interest income apportioned to the real property is an amount equal to the interest income multiplied by a fraction, the numerator of which is the loan value of the real property and the denominator of which is the amount of the loan.[924] The remainder of the interest income is apportioned to the other property.

The loan value of real property is defined as the fair market value of the property determined as of the date on which the commitment by the REIT to make the loan becomes binding on the REIT. In the case of a loan purchased by a REIT, the loan value

---

[923] Sec. 856(d)(1)(C).
[924] Treas. Reg. sec. 1.856–5(c)(1). The amount of the loan for this purpose is defined as the highest principal amount of the loan outstanding during the taxable year. Treas. Reg. sec. 1.856–5(c)(3).

of the real property is the fair market value of the real property determined as of the date on which the commitment of the REIT to purchase the loan becomes binding.[925]

75-percent asset test

At the close of each quarter of the taxable year, at least 75 percent of the value of a REIT's total assets must be represented by real estate assets, cash and cash items, and Government securities.

Real estate assets generally mean real property (including interests in real property and interests in mortgages on real property) and shares (or transferable certificates of beneficial interest) in other REITs.

Neither the Code nor regulations address the allocation of value in cases where real property and personal property may both be present.

Explanation of Provision

The provision allows certain ancillary personal property leased with real property to be treated as real property for purposes of the 75-percent asset test, applying the same threshold that applies under present law for purposes of determining rents from real property under section 856(d)(1)(C) for purposes of the 75-percent income test.

The provision also modifies the present-law rules for determining when an obligation secured by a mortgage is considered secured by a mortgage on real property if the security includes personal property as well. Under the provision, in the case of an obligation secured by a mortgage on both real property and personal property, if the fair market value of such personal property does not exceed 15 percent of the total fair market value of all such property, such personal property is treated as real property for purposes of the 75-percent income and 75-percent asset test computations.[926] In making this determination, the fair market value of all property (both personal and real) is determined at the same time and in the same manner as the fair market value of real property is determined for purposes of apportioning interest income between real property and personal property under the rules for determining whether interest income is from a mortgage secured by real property.

Effective Date

The provision is effective for taxable years beginning after December 31, 2015.

8. Hedging provisions (sec. 319 of the Act and sec. 857 of the Code)

Present Law

Except as provided by Treasury regulations, income from certain REIT hedging transactions that are clearly identified, including gain from the sale or disposition of such a transaction, is not included as gross income under either the 95-percent income or 75-

---

[925] Special rules apply to construction loans. Treas. Reg. sec. 1.856–5(c)(2).
[926] Sec. 856(c)(3)(B) and (4)(A).

percent income test. Transactions eligible for this exclusion include transactions that hedge indebtedness incurred or to be incurred by the REIT to acquire or carry real estate assets and transactions entered primarily to manage risk of currency fluctuations with respect to items of income or gain described in section 856(c)(2) or (3).[927]

Explanation of Provision

The provision expands the scope of the present-law exception of certain hedging income from gross income for purposes of the income tests, under section 856(c)(5)(G). Under the provision, if (1) a REIT enters into one or more positions described in clause (i) of section 856(c)(5)(G) with respect to indebtedness described therein or one or more positions described in clause (ii) of section 856(c)(5)(G) with respect to property that generates income or gain described in section 856(c)(2) or (3); (2) any portion of such indebtedness is extinguished or any portion of such property is disposed of; and (3) in connection with such extinguishment or disposition, such REIT enters into one or more transactions which would be hedging transactions described in subparagraph (B) or (C) of section 1221(b)(2) with respect to any position referred to in (1) above, if such position were ordinary property,[928] then any income of such REIT from any position referred to in (1) and from any transaction referred to in (3) (including gain from the termination of any such position or transaction) shall not constitute gross income for purposes of the 75-percent or 95-percent gross income tests, to the extent that such transaction hedges such position.

The provision is intended to extend the current treatment of income from certain REIT hedging transactions as income that is disregarded for purposes of the 75-percent and 95-percent income tests to income from positions that primarily manage risk with respect to a prior hedge that a REIT enters in connection with the extinguishment or disposal (in whole or in part) of the liability or asset (respectively) related to such prior hedge, to the extent the new position qualifies as a section 1221 hedge or would so qualify if the hedged position were ordinary property.

The provision also clarifies that the identification requirement that applies to all hedges under the hedge gross income rules is the requirement described in section 1221(a)(7), determined after taking account of any curative provisions provided under the regulations referred to therein.

Effective Date

The provision is effective for taxable years beginning after December 31, 2015.

---

[927] Sec. 856(c)(5)(G).

[928] Such definition of a hedging transaction is applied for purposes of this provision without regard to whether or not the position referred to is ordinary property.

9. Modification of REIT earnings and profits calculation to avoid duplicate taxation (sec. 320 of the Act and secs. 562 and 857 of the Code)

Present Law

For purposes of computing earnings and profits of a corporation, the alternative depreciation system, which generally is less accelerated than the system used in determining taxable income, is used in the case of the depreciation of tangible property. Also, certain amounts treated as currently deductible for purposes of computing taxable income are allowed as a deduction ratably over a period of five years for computing earnings and profits. Finally, the installment method is not allowed in computing earnings and profits from the installment sale of property.[929]

In the case of a REIT, the current earnings and profits of a REIT are not reduced by any amount which is not allowable as a deduction in computing its taxable income for the taxable year.[930] In addition, for purposes of computing the deduction for dividends paid by a REIT for a taxable year, earnings and profits are increased by the total amount of gain on the sale or exchange of real property by the trust during the year.[931]

These rules can by illustrated by the following example:

Example.—Assume that a REIT had $100 of taxable income and earnings and profits in each of five consecutive taxable years (determined without regard to any energy efficient commercial building deduction[932] and without regard to any deduction for dividends paid). Assume that in the first of the five years, the REIT had an energy efficient commercial building deduction in computing its taxable income of $10, reducing its pre-dividend taxable income to $90. Assume further that the deduction is allowable at a rate of $2 per year over the five-year period beginning with the first year in computing its earnings and profits.

Under present law, the REIT's earnings and profits in the first year are $98 ($100 less $2). In each of the next four years, the REIT's current earnings and profits are $100 ($98 as computed for the first year plus an additional $2 under section 857(d)(1) for the $2 not deductible in computing taxable income for the year).

Assume the REIT distributes $100 to its shareholders at the close of each of the five years. Under present law, the shareholders have $98 dividend income in the first year and a $2 return of capital and $100 dividend income in each of the following four years, for a total of $498 dividend income, notwithstanding that the REIT had only $490 pre-dividend taxable income over the period. The dividends paid by the REIT reduce its taxable income to zero in each of the taxable years.

Explanation of Provision

Under the provision, the current earnings and profits of a REIT for a taxable year are not reduced by any amount that (1) is not

---

[929] Sec. 312(k)(3) and (n)(5).
[930] Sec. 857(d)(1). This provision applies to a REIT without regard to whether it meets the requirements of section 857(a) for the taxable year.
[931] Sec. 562(e).
[932] Sec. 179D.

allowable as a deduction in computing its taxable income for the current taxable year and (2) was not so allowable for any prior taxable year. Thus, under the provision, if an amount is allowable as a deduction in computing taxable income in year one and is allowable in computing earnings and profits in year two (determined without regard to present-law section 857(d)(1)), section 857(d)(1) no longer applies and the deduction in computing the year two earnings and profits of the REIT is allowable. Thus, a lesser maximum amount will be a dividend to shareholders in that year. This provision does not change the present-law determination of current earnings and profits for purposes of computing a REIT's deduction for dividends paid.

In addition, the provision provides that the current earnings and profits of a REIT for a taxable year for purposes of computing the deduction for dividends paid are increased by any amount of gain on the sale or exchange of real property taken into account in determining the taxable income of the REIT for the taxable year (to the extent the gain is not otherwise so taken into account). Thus, in the case of an installment sale of real property, current earnings and profits for purposes of the REIT's deduction for dividends paid for a taxable year are increased by the amount of gain taken into account in computing its taxable income for the year and not otherwise taken into account in computing the current earnings and profits.

The following illustrates the application of the provision:

Example.—Assume the same facts as in the above example. Under the provision, as under present law, in the first taxable year, the earnings and profits of the REIT were $98 and the shareholders take into account $98 dividend income and $2 is a return of capital. Under the provision, in each of the next four years, the earnings and profits are $98 (i.e., section 857(d)(1) does not apply) so that the shareholders take into account $98 of dividend income in each year and $2 is a return of capital each year.

For purposes of the REIT's deduction for dividends paid, present law remains unchanged so that the REIT's taxable income will be reduced to zero in each of the taxable years.

Effective Date

The provision is effective for taxable years beginning after December 31, 2015.

10. Treatment of certain services provided by taxable REIT subsidiaries (sec. 321 of the Act and sec. 857 of the Code)

Present Law

Taxable REIT subsidiaries

A TRS generally can engage in any kind of business activity except that it is not permitted directly or indirectly to operate either a lodging facility or a health care facility, or to provide to any other person (under a franchise, license, or otherwise) rights to any brand name under which any lodging facility or health care facility is operated.

REITs are subject to a tax equal to 100 percent of redetermined rents, redetermined deductions, and excess interest. These are defined generally as the amounts of specified REIT transactions with a TRS of the REIT, to the extent such amounts differ from an arm's length amount.

Prohibited transactions tax

REITs are subject to a prohibited transaction tax ("PTT") of 100 percent of the net income derived from prohibited transactions.[933] For this purpose, a prohibited transaction is a sale or other disposition of property by the REIT that is stock in trade of a taxpayer or other property that would properly be included in the inventory of the taxpayer if on hand at the close of the taxable year, or property held for sale to customers by the taxpayer in the ordinary course of his trade or business and is not foreclosure property. The PTT for a REIT does not apply to a sale of property which is a real estate asset if the REIT satisfies certain criteria in section 857(b)(6)(C) or (D).

Section 857(b)(6)(C) provides that a prohibited transaction does not include a sale of property which is a real estate asset (as defined in section 856(c)(5)(B)) and which is described in section 1221(a)(1) if (1) the REIT has held the property for not less than two years; (2) aggregate expenditures made by the REIT, or any partner of the REIT, during the two year period preceding the date of sale which are includible in the basis of the property do not exceed 30 percent of the net selling price of the property; (3) either: (A) the REIT does not make more than seven sales of property[934] during the taxable year, or (B) the aggregate adjusted bases (as determined for purposes of computing earnings and profits) of property[935] sold during the taxable year does not exceed 10 percent of the aggregate bases (as so determined) of all of the assets of the REIT as of the beginning of the taxable year, or (C) the fair market value of property[936] sold during the taxable year does not exceed 10 percent of the aggregate fair market value of all the assets of the REIT as of the beginning of the taxable year; (4) in the case of land or improvements, not acquired through foreclosure (or deed in lieu of foreclosure), or lease termination, the REIT has held the property for not less than two years for production of rental income; and (5) if the requirement of (3)(A) above is not satisfied, substantially all of the marketing and development expenditures with respect to the property were made through an independent contractor (as defined in section 856(d)(3)) from whom the REIT does not derive or receive any income.

Section 857(b)(6)(D) provides that a prohibited transaction does not include a sale of property which is a real estate asset (as defined in section 856(c)(5)(B)) and which is described in section 1221(a)(1) if (1) the REIT has held the property for not less than two years in connection with the trade or business of producing timber; (2) the aggregate expenditures made by the REIT, or any partner of the REIT, during the two year period preceding the date

---

[933] Sec. 857(b)(6).
[934] Sales of foreclosure property or sales to which section 1033 applies are excluded.
[935] Sales of foreclosure property or sales to which section 1033 applies are excluded.
[936] Sales of foreclosure property or sales to which section 1033 applies are excluded.

of sale which (A) are includible in the basis of the property (other than timberland acquisition expenditures), and (B) are directly related to operation of the property for the production of timber or for the preservation of the property for use as a timberland, do not exceed 30 percent of the net selling price of the property; (3) the aggregate expenditures made by the REIT, or a partner of the REIT, during the two year period preceding the date of sale which (A) are includible in the basis of the property (other than timberland acquisition expenditures), and (B) are not directly related to operation of the property for the production of timber or for the preservation of the property for use as a timberland, do not exceed five percent of the net selling price of the property; (4) either: (A) the REIT does not make more than seven sales of property [937] during the taxable year, or (B) the aggregate adjusted bases (as determined for purposes of computing earnings and profits) of property [938] sold during the taxable year does not exceed 10 percent of the aggregate bases (as so determined) of all of the assets of the REIT as of the beginning of the taxable year, or (C) the fair market value of property [939] sold during the taxable year does not exceed 10 percent of the aggregate fair market value of all the assets of the REIT as of the beginning of the taxable year; (5) if the requirement of (4)(A) above is not satisfied, substantially all of the marketing expenditures with respect to the property were made through an independent contractor (as defined in section 856(d)(3)) from whom the REIT does not derive or receive any income, or, in the case of a sale on or before the termination date, a TRS; and (6) the sales price of the property sold by the trust is not based in whole or in part on income or profits derived from the sale or operation of such property.

Foreclosure property

Under current law, certain income and gain derived from foreclosure property satisfies the 95-percent and 75-percent REIT income tests.[940] Property will cease to be foreclosure property, however, if used in a trade or business conducted by the REIT, other than through an independent contractor from which the REIT itself does not derive or receive any income, more than 90 days after the day on which the REIT acquired such property.[941]

Explanation of Provision

For purposes of the exclusion from the prohibited transactions excise tax, the provision modifies the requirement of section 857(b)(6)(C)(v), that substantially all of the development expenditures with respect to the property were made through an independent contractor from whom the REIT itself does not derive or receive any income, to allow a TRS to have developed the property.[942]

---

[937] Sales of foreclosure property or sales to which section 1033 applies are excluded.
[938] Sales of foreclosure property or sales to which section 1033 applies are excluded.
[939] Sales of foreclosure property or sales to which section 1033 applies are excluded.
[940] Sec. 856(c)(2)(F) and (3)(F).
[941] Sec. 856(e)(4)(C).
[942] The requirement limiting the amount of expenditures added to basis that the REIT, or a partner of the REIT, may make within two years prior to the sale, as well as other requirements for the exclusion, are retained.

The provision also allows a TRS to make marketing expenditures with respect to property under section 857(b)(6)(C)(v) or 857(b)(6)(D)(v) without causing property that is otherwise eligible for the prohibited transaction exclusion to lose such qualification.

The provision allows a TRS to operate foreclosure property without causing loss of foreclosure property status, under section 856(e)(4)(C).

The items subject to the 100-percent excise tax on certain non-arm's-length transactions between a TRS and a REIT are expanded to include "redetermined TRS service income." Such income is defined as gross income of a TRS of a REIT attributable to services provided to, or on behalf of, such REIT (less the deductions properly allocable thereto) to the extent the amount of such income (less such deductions) would be increased on distribution, apportionment, or allocation under section 482 (but for the exception from section 482 if the 100-percent excise tax applies). The term does not include gross income attributable to services furnished or rendered to a tenant of the REIT (or deductions properly attributable thereto), since that income is already subject to a separate provision of the 100-percent excise tax rules.

Effective Date

The provision is effective for taxable years beginning after December 31, 2015.

11. Exception from FIRPTA for certain stock of REITs; exception for interests held by foreign retirement and pension funds (secs. 322 and 323 of the Act and secs. 897 and 1445 of the Code) [943]

Present Law

General rules relating to FIRPTA

A foreign person that is not engaged in the conduct of a trade or business in the United States generally is not subject to any U.S. tax on capital gain from U.S. sources, including capital gain from the sale of stock or other capital assets.[944]

However, the Foreign Investment in Real Property Tax Act of 1980 ("FIRPTA")[945] generally treats a foreign person's gain or loss from the disposition of a U.S. real property interest ("USRPI") as income that is effectively connected with the conduct of a U.S. trade or business, and thus taxable at the income tax rates applica-

---

[943] The Senate Committee on Finance reported S.915 on April 14, 2015 (S. Rep. No. 114–25). Section 2 of that bill contained a provision similar to section 322 of the Protecting Americans from Tax Hikes Act of 2015 (Division Q of Pub. L. No. 114–113).

[944] Secs. 871(b) and 882(a). Property is treated as held by a person for use in connection with the conduct of a trade or business in the United States, even if not so held at the time of sale, if it was so held within 10 years prior to the sale. Sec. 864(c)(7). Also, all gain from an installment sale is treated as from the sale of property held in connection with the conduct of such a trade or business if the property was so held during the year in which the installment sale was made, even if the recipient of the payments is no longer engaged in the conduct of such trade or business when the payments are received. Sec. 864(c)(6).

[945] Pub. L. No. 96–499. The rules governing the imposition and collection of tax under FIRPTA are contained in a series of provisions enacted in 1980 and subsequently amended. See secs. 897, 1445, 6039C, and 6652(f).

ble to U.S. persons, including the rates for net capital gain.[946] With certain exceptions, if a foreign corporation distributes a USRPI, gain is recognized on the distribution (including a distribution in redemption or liquidation) of a USRPI, in an amount equal to the excess of the fair market value of the USRPI (as of the time of distribution) over its adjusted basis.[947] A foreign person subject to tax on FIRPTA gain is required to file a U.S. tax return under the normal rules relating to receipt of income effectively connected with a U.S. trade or business.[948]

The payor of amounts that FIRPTA treats as effectively connected with a U.S. trade or business ("FIRPTA income") to a foreign person generally is required to withhold U.S. tax from the payment.[949] Withholding generally is 10 percent of the sales price, in the case of a direct sale by the foreign person of a USRPI (but withholding is not required in certain cases, including on any sale of stock that is regularly traded on an established securities market[950]), and 10 percent of the amount realized by the foreign shareholder in the case of certain distributions by a corporation that is or has been a U.S. real property holding corporation ("USRPHC") during the applicable testing period.[951] The withholding is generally 35 percent of the amount of a distribution to a foreign person of net proceeds attributable to the sale of a USRPI from an entity such as a partnership, REIT, or RIC.[952] The foreign person can request a refund with its U.S. tax return, if appropriate, based on that person's total U.S. effectively connected income and deductions (if any) for the taxable year.

USRPHCs and five-percent public shareholder exception

USRPIs include not only interests in real property located in the United States or the U.S. Virgin Islands, but also stock of a USRPHC, generally defined as any domestic corporation, unless the taxpayer establishes that the fair market value of the corporation's USRPIs was less than 50 percent of the combined fair market value of all its real property interests (U.S. and worldwide) and all its assets used or held for use in a trade or business, at all times during a "testing period," which is the shorter of the duration of the taxpayer's ownership of the stock after June 18, 1980, or the five-year period ending on the date of disposition of the stock.[953]

Under an exception, even if a corporation is a USRPHC, a shareholder's shares of a class of stock that is regularly traded on an established securities market are not treated as USRPIs if the shareholder holds (applying attribution rules) no more than five percent

---

[946] Sec. 897(a).
[947] Sec. 897(d). In addition, such gain may also be subject to the branch profits tax at a 30-percent rate (or lower treaty rate).
[948] In addition, section 6039C authorizes regulations that would require a return reporting foreign direct investments in U.S. real property interests. No such regulations have been issued, however.
[949] Sec. 1445(a).
[950] Sec. 1445(b)(6).
[951] Sec. 1445(e)(3). Withholding at 10 percent of a gross amount may also apply in certain other circumstances under regulations. See sec. 1445(e)(4) and (5).
[952] Sec. 1445(e)(6) and Treasury regulations thereunder. The Treasury Department is authorized to issue regulations that would reduce the 35 percent withholding on distributions to 20 percent during the time that the maximum income tax rate on dividends and capital gains of U.S. persons is 20 percent.
[953] Sec. 897(c)(1) and (2).

of that class of stock at any time during the testing period.[954] Among other things, the relevant attribution rules require attribution between a corporation and a shareholder that owns five percent or more in value of the stock of such corporation.[955] The attribution rules also attribute stock ownership between spouses and between children, grandchildren, parents, and grandparents.

FIRPTA rules for foreign investment through REITs and RICs

Special FIRPTA rules apply to foreign investment through a "qualified investment entity," which includes any REIT and certain RICs that invest largely in USRPIs (including stock of one or more REITs).[956]

Stock of domestically controlled qualified investment entities not a USRPI

If a qualified investment entity is "domestically controlled" (defined to mean that less than 50 percent in value of the qualified investment entity has been owned (directly or indirectly) by foreign persons during the relevant testing period[957]), stock of such entity is not a USRPI and a foreign shareholder can sell the stock of such entity without being subject to tax under FIRPTA, even if the stock would otherwise be stock of a USRPHC. Treasury regulations provide that for purposes of determining whether a REIT is domestically controlled, the actual owner of REIT shares is the "person who is required to include in his return the dividends received on the stock."[958] The IRS has issued a private letter ruling concluding that the term "directly or indirectly" for this purpose does not require looking through corporate entities that, in the facts of the ruling, were represented to be fully taxable domestic corporations for U.S. federal income tax purposes "and not otherwise a REIT, RIC, hybrid entity, conduit, disregarded entity, or other flow-through or look-through entity."[959]

---

[954] Sec. 897(c)(3). The constructive ownership attribution rules are specified in section 897(c)(6)(C).

[955] If a person owns, directly or indirectly, five percent or more in value of the stock in a corporation, such person is considered as owning the stock owned directly or indirectly by or for such corporation, in that proportion which the value of the stock such person so owns bears to the value of all the stock in such corporation. Sec. 318(c)(2)(C) as modified by section 897(c)(6)(C). Also, if five percent or more in value of the stock in a corporation is owned directly or indirectly, by or for any person, such corporation shall be considered as owning the stock owned, directly or indirectly, by or for such person. Sec. 318(c)(3)(C) as modified by section 897(c)(6)(C).

[956] Sec. 897(h)(4)(A)(i). The provision including certain RICs in the definition of qualified investment entity previously expired December 31, 2014. Section 133 of the Protecting Americans from Tax Hikes Act of 2015 (Division Q of Pub. L. No. 114–113) reinstated the provision and made it permanent as of January 1, 2015, as described above in item 22 of Title I.A.

[957] The testing period for this purpose if the shorter of (i) the period beginning on June 19, 1980, and ending on the date of disposition or distribution, as the case may be, (ii) the five-year period ending on the date of the disposition or distribution, as the case may be, or (iii) the period during which the qualified investment entity was in existence. Sec. 897(h)(4)(D).

[958] Treas. Reg. sec. 1.897–1(c)(2)(i) and –8(b).

[959] PLR 200923001. A private letter ruling may be relied upon only by the taxpayer to which it is issued. However, private letter rulings provide some indication of administrative practice.

FIRPTA applies to qualified investment entity (REIT and certain RIC) distributions attributable to gain from sale or exchange of USRPIs, except for distributions to certain five-percent or smaller shareholders

A distribution by a REIT or other qualified investment entity, to the extent attributable to gain from the entity's sale or exchange of USRPIs, is treated as FIRPTA income.[960] The FIRPTA character is retained if the distribution occurs from one qualified investment entity to another, through a tier of REITs or RICs.[961] An IRS notice (Notice 2007–55) states that this rule retaining the FIRPTA income character of distributions attributable to the sale of USRPIs applies to any distributions under sections 301, 302, 331, and 332 (i.e., to dividend distributions, distributions treated as sales or exchanges of stock by the investor, and both nonliquidating and liquidating distributions) and that the IRS will issue regulations to that effect.[962]

There is an exception to this rule in the case of distributions to certain public shareholders. If an investor has owned no more than five percent of a class of stock of a REIT or other qualified investment entity that is regularly traded on an established securities market located in the United States during the one-year period ending on the date of the distribution, then amounts attributable to gain from entity sales or exchanges of USRPIs can be distributed to such a shareholder without being subject to FIRPTA tax.[963] Such distributions that are dividends are treated as dividends from the qualified investment entity,[964] and thus generally would be subject to U.S. dividend withholding tax (as reduced under any applicable treaty), but are not treated as income effectively connected with the conduct of a U.S. trade or business. An IRS Chief Counsel advice memorandum concludes that such distributions which are made in complete liquidation of a REIT are not treated as dividends from the qualified investment entity and thus generally would not be subject to U.S. dividend withholding tax (in addition to not being treated as income effectively connected with the conduct of a U.S. trade or business).[965]

Explanation of Provision

Exception from FIRPTA for certain REIT stock

In the case of REIT stock only, the provision increases from five percent to 10 percent the maximum stock ownership a shareholder may have held, during the testing period, of a class of stock that is publicly traded, to avoid having that stock be treated as a USRPI on disposition.

---

[960] Sec. 897(h)(1).

[961] In 2006, the Tax Increase Prevention and Reconciliation Act of 2005 ("TIPRA"), Pub. L. No. 109–222, sec. 505, specified the retention of this FIRPTA character on a distribution to an upper-tier qualified investment entity, and added statutory withholding requirements.

[962] Notice 2007–55, 2007–2 C.B.13. The Notice also states that in the case of a foreign government investor, because FIRPTA income is treated as effectively connected with the conduct of a U.S. trade or business, proceeds distributed by a qualified investment entity from the sale of USRPIs are not exempt from tax under section 892. The Notice cites and compares existing temporary regulations and indicates that Treasury will apply those regulations as well to certain distributions. See Temp. Treas. Reg. secs. 1.892–3T, 1.897–9T(e), and 1.1445–10T(b).

[963] Sec. 897(h)(1), second sentence.

[964] Secs. 852(b)(3)(E) and 857(b)(3)(F).

[965] AM 2008–003, February 15, 2008.

The provision likewise increases from five percent to 10 percent the percentage ownership threshold that, if not exceeded, results in treating a distribution to holders of publicly traded REIT stock, attributable to gain from sales of exchanges of USRPIs, as a dividend, rather than as FIRPTA gain.

The attribution rules of section 897(c)(6)(C) retain the present-law rule that requires attribution between a shareholder and a corporation if the shareholder owns more than five percent of a class of stock of the corporation. The attribution rules now apply, however, to the determination of whether a person holds more than 10 percent of a class of publicly traded REIT stock.

The provision also provides that REIT stock held by a qualified shareholder, including stock held indirectly through one or more partnerships, is not a U.S real property interest in the hands of such qualified shareholder, except to the extent that an investor in the qualified shareholder (other than an investor that is a qualified shareholder) holds more than 10 percent of that class of stock of the REIT (determined by application of the constructive ownership rules of section 897(c)(6)(C)). Thus, so long as the "more than 10 percent" rule is not exceeded, a qualified shareholder may own and dispose of any amount of stock of a REIT (including stock of a privately-held, non-domestically controlled REIT that is owned by such qualified shareholder) without the application of FIRPTA.

If an investor in the qualified shareholder (other than an investor that is a qualified shareholder) directly, indirectly, or constructively holds more than 10 percent of such class of REIT stock (an "applicable investor"), then a percentage of the REIT stock held by the qualified shareholder equal to the applicable investor's percentage ownership of the qualified shareholder is treated as a USRPI in the hands of the qualified shareholder and is subject to FIRPTA. In that case, an amount equal to such percentage multiplied by the disposition proceeds and REIT distribution proceeds attributable to underlying USRPI gain is treated as FIRPTA gain in the hands of the qualified shareholder.

The provision is intended to override in certain cases one of the conclusions reached in AM 2008–003. Specifically, the provision contains special rules with respect to certain distributions that are treated as a sale or exchange of REIT stock under section 301(c)(3), 302, or 331 with respect to a qualified shareholder. Any such amounts attributable to an applicable investor are ineligible for the FIRPTA exception for qualified shareholders, and thus are subject to FIRPTA. Any such amounts attributable to other investors are treated as a dividend received from a REIT for purposes of U.S. dividend withholding tax and the application of income tax treaties, notwithstanding their general treatment under the Code.

A qualified shareholder is defined as a foreign person that (i) either is eligible for the benefits of a comprehensive income tax treaty which includes an exchange of information program and whose principal class of interests is listed and regularly traded on one or more recognized stock exchanges (as defined in such comprehensive income tax treaty), or is a foreign partnership that is created or organized under foreign law as a limited partnership in a jurisdiction that has an agreement for the exchange of information with respect to taxes with the United States and has a class of limited partnership units representing greater than 50 percent of the value of all the partnership units that is regularly traded on the NYSE or NASDAQ markets, (ii) is a qualified collective investment vehicle (as defined below), and (iii) maintains records on the identity of each person who, at any time during the foreign person's taxable year, is the direct owner of 5 percent or more of the class of interests or units (as applicable) described in (i), above.

A qualified collective investment vehicle is defined as a foreign person that (i) would be eligible for a reduced rate of withholding under the comprehensive income tax treaty described above, even if such entity holds more than 10 percent of the stock of such REIT,[966] (ii) is publicly traded, is treated as a partnership under the Code, is a withholding foreign partnership, and would be treated as a USRPHC if it were a domestic corporation, or (iii) is designated as such by the Secretary of the Treasury and is either (a) fiscally transparent within the meaning of section 894, or (b) required to include dividends in its gross income, but is entitled to a deduction for distributions to its investors.

The provision also contains rules with respect to partnership allocations of USRPI gains to applicable investors. If an applicable investor's proportionate share of USRPI gain for the taxable year exceeds such partner's distributive share of USRPI gain for the taxable year then such partner's distributive share of non-USRPI income or gain is recharacterized as USRPI gain for the taxable year in the amount that the distributive share of USRPI gain exceeds the proportionate share of USRPI gain. For purposes of these partnership allocation rules, USRPI gain is defined to comprise the net of gain recognized on disposition of a USRPI, distributions from a REIT that are treated as USRPI gain, and loss from the disposition of USRPIs. An investor's proportionate share of USRPI gain is determined based on the applicable investor's largest proportionate share of income or gain for the taxable year, and if such proportionate amount may vary during the existence of the partnership, such share is the highest share the applicable investor may receive.

Domestically controlled qualified investment entity

The provision redefines the term "domestically controlled qualified investment entity" to provide a number of new rules and presumptions relating to whether a qualified investment entity is domestically controlled. First, a qualified investment entity shall be permitted to presume that holders of less than five percent of a class of stock regularly traded on an established securities market in the United States are U.S. persons throughout the testing period, except to the extent that the qualified investment entity has actual knowledge that such persons are not U.S. persons. Second, any stock in the qualified investment entity held by another qualified investment entity (I) which has issued any class of stock that is regularly traded on an established stock exchange, or (II) which is a RIC that issues redeemable securities (within the meaning of section 2 of the Investment Company Act of 1940) shall be treated

---

[966] The qualified collective investment vehicle must be eligible for a reduced rate of withholding under a provision in the dividends article of the relevant treaty dealing specifically with dividends paid by REITs. For example, the U.S. income tax treaties with Australia and the Netherlands provide such a reduced rate of withholding under certain circumstances.

as held by a foreign person unless such other qualified investment entity is domestically controlled (as determined under the new rules) in which case such stock shall be treated as held by a U.S. person. Finally, any stock in a qualified investment entity held by any other qualified investment entity not described in (I) or (II) of the preceding sentence shall only be treated as held by a U.S. person to the extent that the stock of such other qualified investment entity is (or is treated under the new provision as) held by a U.S. person.

Exception for interests held by foreign retirement and pension funds

The provision exempts from the rules of section 897 any USRPI held directly (or indirectly through one or more partnerships) by, or to any distribution received from a real estate investment trust by, a qualified foreign pension fund or by a foreign entity wholly-owned by a qualified foreign pension fund. A qualified foreign pension fund means any trust, corporation, or other organization or arrangement [967] (A) which is created or organized under the law of a country other than the United States, (B) which is established to provide retirement or pension benefits to participants or beneficiaries that are current or former employees (or persons designated by such employees) of one or more employers in consideration for services rendered,[968] (C) which does not have a single participant or beneficiary with a right to more than five percent of its assets or income, (D) which is subject to government regulation and provides annual information reporting about its beneficiaries to the relevant tax authorities in the country in which it is established or operates, and (E) with respect to which, under the laws of the country in which it is established or operates, (i) contributions to such organization or arrangement that would otherwise be subject to tax under such laws are deductible or excluded from the gross income of such entity or taxed at a reduced rate, or (ii) taxation of any investment income of such organization or arrangement is deferred or such income is taxed at a reduced rate.

The provision also makes conforming changes to section 1445 to eliminate withholding on sales by qualified foreign pension funds (and their wholly-owned foreign subsidiaries) of USRPIs.

The Secretary of the Treasury may provide such regulations as are necessary to carry out the purposes of the provision.

Effective Date

The provision to extend exceptions from FIRPTA for certain REIT stock applies to dispositions and distributions on or after the date of enactment (December 18, 2015).

The provision to modify the definition of a domestically controlled qualified investment entity is effective on the date of enactment (December 18, 2015).

---

[967] Foreign pension funds may be structured in a variety of ways, and may comprise one or more separate entities. The word "arrangement" encompasses such alternative structures.

[968] Multi-employer and government-sponsored public pension funds that provide pension and pension-related benefits may satisfy this prong of the definition. For example, such pension funds may be established for one or more companies or professions, or for the general working public of a foreign country.

The exception for interests held by foreign retirement and pension funds generally applies to dispositions and distributions after the date of enactment (December 18, 2015).

12. Increase in rate of withholding of tax on dispositions of United States real property interests (sec. 324 of the Act and sec. 1445 of the Code) [969]

Present Law

A purchaser of a USRPI from any person is obligated to withhold 10 percent of gross purchase price unless certain exceptions apply.[970] The obligation does not apply if the transferor furnishes an affidavit that the transferor is not a foreign person. Even absent such an affidavit, the obligation does not apply to the purchase of publicly traded stock.[971] Also, the obligation does not apply to the purchase of stock of a nonpublicly traded domestic corporation, if the corporation furnishes the transferee with an affidavit stating the corporation is not and has not been a USRPHC during the applicable period (unless the transferee has actual knowledge or receives a notification that the affidavit is false).[972]

Treasury regulations[973] generally provide that a domestic corporation must, within a reasonable period after receipt of a request from a foreign person holding an interest in it, inform that person whether the interest constitutes a USRPI.[974] No particular form is required. The statement must be dated and signed by a responsible corporate officer who must verify under penalties of perjury that the statement is correct to his knowledge and belief. If a foreign investor requests such a statement, then the corporation must provide a notice to the IRS that includes the name and taxpayer identification number of the corporation as well as the investor, and indicates whether the interest in question is a USRPI. However, these requirements do not apply to a domestically controlled REIT or to a corporation that has issued any class of stock which is regularly traded on an established securities market at any time during the calendar year. In such cases a corporation may voluntarily choose to comply with the notice requirements that would otherwise have applied.[975]

In addition to these exceptions that might be determined at the entity level, even if a corporation is a USRPHC, its stock is not a USRPI in the hands of the seller if the stock is of a class that is publicly traded and the foreign shareholder disposing of the stock has not owned (applying attribution rules) more than five percent of such class of stock during the relevant period.

---

[969] The Senate Committee on Finance reported S.915 on April 14, 2015 (S. Rep. No. 114–25). Section 3 of that bill contained an identical provision.
[970] Sec. 1445.
[971] Sec. 1445(b)(6).
[972] Sec. 1445(b)(3). Other exceptions also apply. Sec. 1445(b).
[973] Treas. Reg. Sec. 1.897–2(h).
[974] As described previously, stock of a U.S. corporation is not generally a USRPI unless it is stock of a USRPHC. However, all U.S. corporate stock is deemed to be such stock, unless it is shown that the corporation's U.S. real property interests do not amount to the relevant 50 percent or more of the corporation's relevant assets. Also, even if a REIT is a USRPHC, if it is domestically controlled its stock is not a USRPI.
[975] Treas. Reg. sec. 1.897–2(h)(3).

Explanation of Provision

The provision generally increases the rate of withholding of tax on dispositions and certain distributions of URSPIs, from 10 percent to 15 percent. There is an exception to this higher rate of withholding (retaining the 10 percent withholding tax rate under present law) for sales of residences intended for personal use by the acquirer, with respect to which the purchase price does not exceed $1,000,000. Thus, if the present law exception for personal residences (where the purchase price does not exceed $300,000) does not apply, the 10 percent withholding rate is retained so long as the purchase price does not exceed $1,000,000.

Effective Date

The provision applies to dispositions after the date which is 60 days after the date of enactment (December 18, 2015).

13. Interests in RICs and REITs not excluded from definition of United States real property interests (sec. 325 of the Act and sec. 897 of the Code)[976]

Present Law

An interest in a corporation is not a USRPI if (1) as of the date of disposition of such interest, such corporation did not hold any USRPIs and (2) all of the USRPIs held by such corporation during the shorter of (i) the period of time after June 18, 1980, during which the taxpayer held such interest, or (ii) the five-year period ending on the date of disposition of such interest, were either disposed of in transactions in which the full amount of the gain (if any) was recognized, or ceased to be USRPIs by reason of the application of this rule to one or more other corporations (the so-called "cleansing rule").[977]

Explanation of Provision

Under the provision, the cleansing rule applies to stock of a corporation only if neither such corporation nor any predecessor of such corporation was a RIC or a REIT at any time during the shorter of the period after June 18, 1980 during which the taxpayer held such stock, or the five-year period ending on the date of the disposition of such stock.

Effective Date

The provision applies to dispositions on or after the date of enactment (December 18, 2015).

---

[976] The Senate Committee on Finance reported S.915 on April 14, 2015 (S. Rep. No. 114–25). Section 6 of that bill contained an identical provision.
[977] Sec. 897(c)(1)(B).

14. Dividends derived from RICs and REITs ineligible for deduction for United States source portion of dividends from certain foreign corporations (sec. 326 of the Act and sec. 245 of the Code) [978]

Present Law

A corporation is generally allowed to deduct a portion of the dividends it receives from another corporation. The deductible amount is a percentage of the dividends received. The percentage depends on the level of ownership that the corporate shareholder has in the corporation paying the dividend. The dividends-received deduction is 70 percent of the dividend if the recipient owns less than 20 percent of the stock of the payor corporation, 80 percent if the recipient owns at least 20 percent but less than 80 percent of the stock of the payor corporation, and 100 percent if the recipient owns 80 percent or more of the stock of the payor corporation.[979]

Dividends from REITs are not eligible for the corporate dividends received deduction.[980] Dividends from a RIC are eligible only to the extent attributable to dividends received by the RIC from certain other corporations, and are treated as dividends from a corporation that is not 20-percent owned.[981]

Dividends received from a foreign corporation are not generally eligible for the dividends-received deduction. However, section 245 provides that if a U.S. corporation is a 10-percent shareholder of a foreign corporation, the U.S. corporation is generally entitled to a dividends-received deduction for the portion of dividends received that are attributable to the post-1986 undistributed U.S. earnings of the foreign corporation. The post-1986 undistributed U.S. earnings are measured by reference to earnings of the foreign corporation effectively connected with the conduct of a trade or business within the United States, or received by the foreign corporation from an 80-percent-owned U.S. corporation.[982] A 2013 IRS chief counsel advice memorandum advised that dividends received by a 10-percent U.S. corporate shareholder from a foreign corporation controlled by the shareholder are not eligible for the dividends-received deduction if the dividends were attributable to interest income of an 80-percent owned RIC.[983] Treasury regulations section 1.246–1 states that the deductions provided in sections "243 . . . 244 . . . and 245 (relating to dividends received from certain foreign corporations)" are not allowable with respect to any dividend received from certain entities, one of which is a REIT.

---

[978] The Senate Committee on Finance reported S.915 on April 14, 2015 (S. Rep. No. 114–25). Section 7 of that bill contained an identical provision.

[979] Sec. 243.

[980] Secs. 243(d)(3) and 857(c)(1).

[981] Secs. 243(d)(2) and 854(b)(1)(A) and (C).

[982] Sec. 245

[983] IRS CCA 201320014. The situation addressed in the memorandum involved a controlled foreign corporation that had terminated its "CFC" status before year end, through a transfer of stock to a partnership. The advice was internal IRS advice to the Large Business and International Division. Such advice is not to be relied upon or cited as precedent by taxpayers, but may offer some indication of administrative practice.

Explanation of Provision

Under the provision, for purposes of determining whether dividends from a foreign corporation (attributable to dividends from an 80-percent owned domestic corporation) are eligible for a dividends-received deduction under section 245, dividends from RICs and REITs are not treated as dividends from domestic corporations.

Effective Date

The provision applies to dividends received from RICs and REITs on or after the date of enactment (December 18, 2015). No inference is intended with respect to the proper treatment under section 245 of dividends received from RICs or REITs before such date.

C. Additional Provisions

1. Provide special rules concerning charitable contributions to, and public charity status of, agricultural research organizations (sec. 331 of the Act and secs. 170(b) and 501(h) of the Code) [984]

Present Law

Public charities and private foundations

An organization qualifying for tax-exempt status under section 501(c)(3) of the Internal Revenue Code of 1986, as amended (the "Code") is further classified as either a public charity or a private foundation. An organization may qualify as a public charity in several ways.[985] Certain organizations are classified as public charities per se, regardless of their sources of support. These include churches, certain schools, hospitals and other medical organizations (including medical research organizations), certain organizations providing assistance to colleges and universities, and governmental units.[986] Other organizations qualify as public charities because they are broadly publicly supported or support specific public charities. First, a charity may qualify as publicly supported if at least one-third of its total support is from gifts, grants or other contributions from governmental units or the general public.[987] Alternatively, it may qualify as publicly supported if it receives more than one-third of its total support from a combination of gifts, grants, and contributions from governmental units and the public plus revenue arising from activities related to its exempt purposes (*e.g.*, fee for service income). In addition, this category of public charity must not rely excessively on endowment income as a source of support.[988] A supporting organization, i.e., an organization that

---

[984] The Senate Committee on Finance reported S. 906 on April 14, 2015 (S. Rep. No. 114–19).

[985] The Code does not expressly define the term "public charity," but rather provides exceptions to those entities that are treated as private foundations.

[986] Sec. 509(a)(1) (referring to sections 170(b)(1)(A)(i) through (iv) for a description of these organizations).

[987] Treas. Reg. sec. 1.170A–9(f)(2). Failing this mechanical test, the organization may qualify as a public charity if it passes a "facts and circumstances" test. Treas. Reg. sec. 1.170A–9(f)(3).

[988] To meet this requirement, the organization must normally receive more than one-third of its support from a combination of (1) gifts, grants, contributions, or membership fees and (2) certain gross receipts from admissions, sales of merchandise, performance of services, and fur-

Continued

provides support to another section 501(c)(3) entity that is not a private foundation and meets certain other requirements of the Code, also is classified as a public charity.[989]

A section 501(c)(3) organization that does not fit within any of the above categories is a private foundation. In general, private foundations receive funding from a limited number of sources (e.g., an individual, a family, or a corporation).

The deduction for charitable contributions to private foundations is in some instances less generous than the deduction for charitable contributions to public charities. For example, an individual taxpayer who makes a cash charitable contribution may deduct the contribution up to 50 percent of her contribution base (generally, adjusted gross income, with modifications) if the contribution is made to a public charity, but only up to 30 percent of her contribution base if the contribution is made to a non-operating private foundation.[990]

In addition, private foundations are subject to a number of operational rules and restrictions that do not apply to public charities, as well as a tax on their net investment income.[991]

Medical research organizations

A medical research organization is treated as a public charity per se, regardless of its sources of financial support, and charitable contributions to a medical research organization may qualify for the more preferential 50-percent limitation.[992]

To qualify as a medical research organization, an organization's principal purpose or functions must be medical research, and it must be directly engaged in the continuous active conduct of medical research in conjunction with a hospital.[993] For a contribution to a medical research organization to qualify for the more preferential 50-percent limitation of section 170(b)(1)(A), during the calendar year in which the contribution is made, the organization must be committed to spend such contribution for the active conduct of medical research before January 1 of the fifth calendar year beginning after the date such contribution is made.[994]

---

nishing of facilities in connection with activities that are related to the organization's exempt purposes. Sec. 509(a)(2)(A). In addition, the organization must not normally receive more than one-third of its support in each taxable year from the sum of (1) gross investment income and (2) the excess of unrelated business taxable income as determined under section 512 over the amount of unrelated business income tax imposed by section 511. Sec. 509(a)(2)(B).

[989] Sec. 509(a)(3). Organizations organized and operated exclusively for testing for public safety also are classified as public charities. Sec. 509(a)(4). Such organizations, however, are not eligible to receive deductible charitable contributions under section 170.

[990] Secs. 170(b)(1)(A) and (B).

[991] Unlike public charities, private foundations are subject to tax on their net investment income at a rate of two percent (one percent in some cases). Sec. 4940. Private foundations also are subject to more restrictions on their activities than are public charities. For example, private foundations are prohibited from engaging in self-dealing transactions (sec. 4941), are required to make a minimum amount of charitable distributions each year (sec. 4942), are limited in the extent to which they may control a business (sec. 4943), may not make jeopardizing investments (sec. 4944), and may not make certain expenditures (sec. 4945). Violations of these rules result in excise taxes on the foundation and, in some cases, may result in excise taxes on the managers of the foundation.

[992] Secs. 170(b)(1)(A)(iii) and 509(a)(1).

[993] Treas. Reg. sec. 1.170A–9(d)(2)(i).

[994] *Ibid.*

Lobbying activities of section 501(c)(3) organizations

Charitable organizations face limits on the amount of permissible lobbying activity. An organization does not qualify for tax-exempt status as a charitable organization unless "no substantial part" of its activities constitutes "carrying on propaganda, or otherwise attempting, to influence legislation" (commonly referred to as "lobbying").[995] Public charities may engage in limited lobbying activities, provided that such activities are not substantial, without losing their tax–exempt status and generally without being subject to tax. In contrast, private foundations are subject to a restriction that lobbying activities, even if insubstantial, may result in the foundation being subject to penalty excise taxes.[996]

For purposes of determining whether lobbying activities are a substantial part of a public charity's overall functions, a public charity may choose between two standards, the "substantial part" test or the "expenditure" test.[997] The substantial part test derives from the statutory language quoted above and uses a facts and circumstances approach to measure the permissible level of lobbying activities. The expenditure test sets specific dollar limits, calculated as a percentage of a charity's total exempt purpose expenditures, on the amount a charity may spend to influence legislation.[998]

Explanation of Provision

The provision amends section 170(b)(1)(A) to provide special treatment for certain agricultural research organizations, consistent with the present-law treatment for medical research organizations. The effect of the proposed amendment, therefore, is to: (1) allow certain charitable contributions to qualifying agricultural research organizations to qualify for the 50-percent limitation; and (2) treat qualifying agricultural research organizations as public charities (*i.e.*, non-private foundations) per se, regardless of their sources of financial support.

To qualify, an agricultural research organization must be engaged in the continuous active conduct of agricultural research (as defined in section 1404 of the Agricultural Research, Extension, and Teaching Policy Act of 1977) in conjunction with a land-grant college or university (as defined in such section) or a non-land grant college of agriculture (as defined in such section). In addition, for a contribution to an agricultural research organization to qualify for the 50-percent limitation, during the calendar year in which a contribution is made to the organization, the organization must be committed to spend the contribution for such research before January 1 of the fifth calendar year which begins after the date of the contribution. It is intended that the provision be interpreted in like manner to and consistent with the rules applicable to medical research organizations.

An agricultural research organization is permitted to use the expenditure test of section 501(h) for purposes of determining whether a substantial part of its activities consist of carrying on propa-

---

[995] Sec. 501(c)(3).
[996] Sec. 4945(d)(1).
[997] Secs. 501(c)(3), 501(h), and 4911. Churches and certain church-related entities may not choose the expenditure test. Sec. 501(h)(5).
[998] Secs. 501(h) and 4911.

ganda, or otherwise attempting, to influence legislation (*i.e.*, lobbying).

Effective Date

The provision is effective for contributions made on or after the date of enactment (December 18, 2015).

2. Remove bonding requirements for certain taxpayers subject to Federal excise taxes on distilled spirits, wine, and beer (sec. 332 of the Act and secs. 5061(d), 5173(a), 5351, 5401 and 5551 of the Code)

Present Law

An excise tax is imposed on all distilled spirits, wine, and beer produced in, or imported into, the United States.[999] The tax liability legally comes into existence the moment the alcohol is produced or imported but payment of the tax is not required until a subsequent withdrawal or removal from the distillery, winery, brewery, or, in the case of an imported product, from customs custody or bond.[1000] The excise tax is paid on the basis of a return [1001] and is paid at the time of removal unless the taxpayer has a withdrawal bond in place. In that case, the taxes are paid with semimonthly returns, the periods for which run from the 1st to the 15th of the month and from the 16th to the last day of the month, with the returns and payments due not later than 14 days after the close of the respective return period.[1002] For example, payments of taxes with respect to removals occurring from the 1st to the 15th of the month are due with the applicable return on the 29th. Taxpayers who expect to be liable for not more than $50,000 in excise taxes for the calendar year may pay quarterly.[1003] Under regulations, wineries with less than $1,000 in annual excise taxes may file and pay on an annual basis.[1004] Taxpayers who were liable for a gross amount of taxes of $5,000,000 or more for the preceding calendar year must make deposits of tax for the current calendar year by electronic funds transfer.[1005]

Certain removals or transfers are exempt from tax. For example, distilled spirits, wine, and beer may be removed either free of tax or without immediate payment of tax for certain uses,[1006] such as for export or an industrial use. Bulk distilled spirits, as well as wine and beer, may be transferred without payment of the tax between bonded premises under certain conditions specified in the regulations; [1007] such bulk products, if imported, may be transferred without payment of the tax to domestic bonded premises

---

[999] Secs. 5001, 5041, and 5051.

[1000] Secs. 5006, 5043, and 5054. In general, proprietors of distilled spirit plants, proprietors of bonded wine cellars, brewers, and importers are liable for the tax. Secs. 5005, 5043, and 5054. Customs and Border Protection (CBP) collects the excise tax on imported products.

[1001] Sec. 5061.

[1002] Under a special rule, September has three return periods. Sec. 5061.

[1003] Sec. 5061.

[1004] 27 CFR sec. 24.273.

[1005] Sec. 5061.

[1006] Such uses are specified in sections 5053, 5214, 5362, and 5414.

[1007] See, *e.g.*, sec. 5212. Domestic bottled distilled spirits cannot be transferred in bond between distilleries. See 27 CFR sec. 19.402.

under certain conditions.[1008] The tax liability accompanies such a product that is transferred in bond.

Before commencing operations, a distiller must register, a winery must qualify, and a brewery must file a notice with the Alcohol and Tobacco Tax and Trade Bureau (TTB) and receive approval to operate.[1009] Various types of bonds (including operations bonds and tax deferral or withdrawal bonds) are required for any person operating a distilled spirits plant, winery, or brewery.[1010] The bond amounts are generally set by regulations and determined based on the underlying excise tax liability.[1011]

Explanation of Provision

The provision allows any distilled spirits, wine, or beer taxpayer who reasonably expects to be liable for not more than $50,000 per year in alcohol excise taxes (and who was liable for not more than $50,000 in such taxes in the preceding calendar year) to file and pay such taxes quarterly, rather than semi-monthly. The provision also creates an exemption from the bond requirement in the Code for these taxpayers. The provision includes conforming changes to the other sections of the Code describing bond requirements.

Additionally, the provision allows any distilled spirits, wine, or beer taxpayer with a reasonably expected alcohol excise tax liability of not more than $1,000 per year to file and pay such taxes annually rather than on a quarterly basis.

Effective Date

The provision is effective for calendar quarters beginning more than one year after the date of enactment (December 18, 2015).

3. Modification to alternative tax for certain small insurance companies (sec. 333 of the Act and sec. 831(b) of the Code) [1012]

Present Law

Under present law, the taxable income of a property and casualty insurance company is the sum of the amount earned from underwriting income and from investment income (as well as gains and other income items), reduced by allowable deductions. For this purpose, underwriting income and investment income are computed on

---

[1008] Secs. 5005, 5232, 5364, and 5418. Imported bottled distilled spirits, wine, and beer cannot be transferred in bond from customs custody to a distillery, winery, or brewery. See sec. 5061(d)(2)(B).

[1009] Secs. 5171, 5351–53, and 5401; 27 CFR sec. 19.72(b) (distilled spirits plant), 27 CFR sec. 24.106 (wine producer), 27 CFR sec. 25.61(a) (brewer).

[1010] Secs. 5173, 5354, 5401, and 5551; 27 CFR parts 19 (Distilled Spirits), 24 (Wine), and 25 (Beer).

[1011] See, *e.g.*, 27 CFR sec. 19.166(c) requiring a withdrawal bond for distilled spirits in the amount of excise tax that has not been paid (up to a maximum of $1 million); 27 CFR sec. 24.148(a)(2) requiring a wine bond to cover the amount of tax deferred (up to a maximum of $250,000); 27 CFR sec. 25.93(a) requiring a bond equal to 10 percent of the maximum excise tax for which the brewer will be liable to pay during a calendar year for brewers required to file tax returns and remit excise taxes semimonthly and a bond equal to $1,000 for brewers who were liable for not more than $50,000 in excise taxes with respect to beer in the previous year and who reasonably expect to be liable for not more than $50,000 in such taxes during the current year.

[1012] The Senate Committee on Finance reported S. 905 on April 14, 2015 (S. Rep. No. 114–16).

the basis of the underwriting and investment exhibit of the annual statement approved by the National Association of Insurance Commissioners. Insurance companies are subject to tax at regular corporate income tax rates.

In lieu of the tax otherwise applicable, certain property and casualty insurance companies may elect to be taxed only on taxable investment income under section 831(b). The election is available to mutual and stock companies with net written premiums or direct written premiums (whichever is greater) that do not exceed $1,200,000.

For purposes of determining whether a company meets this dollar limit, the company is treated as receiving during the taxable year amounts of net or direct written premiums that are received during that year by all other companies that are members of the same controlled group as the company. A controlled group means any controlled group of corporations as defined in section 1563(a), but applying a "more than 50 percent" threshold in lieu of the "at least 80 percent" threshold in the requirement that one of the corporations own at least 80 percent of the total combined voting power of all classes of stock entitled to vote or at least 80 percent of the total value of share of all classes of stock of each of the corporations; without treating insurance companies as a separate controlled group; and without treating life insurance companies as excluded members.[1013]

Explanation of Provision

The provision modifies the section 831(b) eligibility rules for a property and casualty insurance company to elect to be taxed only on taxable investment income.

Increase and indexing of dollar limits

The provision increases the amount of the limit on net written premiums or direct written premiums (whichever is greater) from $1,200,000 to $2,200,000 and indexes this amount for inflation starting in 2016. The base year for calculating the inflation adjustment is 2013. If the amount, as adjusted, is not a multiple of $50,000, it is rounded to the next lowest multiple of $50,000.

Diversification requirements

The provision adds diversification requirements to the eligibility rules. A company can meet these in one of two ways.

Risk diversification test

An insurance company meets the diversification requirement if no more than 20 percent of the net written premiums (or, if greater, direct written premiums) of the company for the taxable year is attributable to any one policyholder. In determining the attribution of premiums to any policyholder, all policyholders that are related [1014] or are members of the same controlled group [1015] are treated as one policyholder.

[1013] Sec. 1563(a)(1) and (4), and (b)(2)(D), as modified by sec. 831(b)(2)(B).

[1014] For this purpose, persons are related within the meaning of section 267(b) or 707(b).

[1015] Members of the same controlled group are determined as under present law for purposes determining whether a company meets the dollar limit applicable to net written premiums (or,

Relatedness test

If the company does not meet this 20-percent requirement, an alternative diversification requirement applies for the company to be eligible to elect 831(b) treatment.[1016] Under this requirement, no person who holds (directly or indirectly) an interest in the company is a specified holder who holds (directly or indirectly) aggregate interests in the company that constitute a percentage of the entire interests in the company that is more than a de minimis percentage higher than the percentage of interests in the specified assets with respect to the company held (directly or indirectly) by the specified holder. Except as otherwise provided in regulations or other guidance, two percentage points or less is treated as de minimis. An indirect interest for this purpose includes any interest held through a trust, estate, partnership, or corporation.

A specified holder means, with respect to an insurance company, any individual who holds (directly or indirectly) an interest in the insurance company and who is a spouse or lineal descendant (including by adoption) of an individual who holds an interest (directly or indirectly) in the specified assets with respect to the insurance company.

The specified assets with respect to an insurance company mean the trades or businesses, rights, or assets with respect to which the net written premiums (or direct written premiums) of the company are paid.

For example, assume that in 2017, a captive insurance company does not meet the requirement that no more than 20 percent of its net (or direct) written premiums is attributable to any one policyholder. The captive has one policyholder, Business, certain of whose property and liability risks the captive covers (the specified assets), and Business pays the captive $2 million in premiums in 2017. Business is owned 70 percent by Father and 30 percent by Son. The captive is owned 100 percent by Son (whether directly, or through a trust, estate, partnership, or corporation). Son is Father's lineal descendant. Son, a specified holder, has a non-de minimis percentage greater interest in the captive (100 percent) than in the specified assets with respect to the captive (30 percent). Therefore, the captive is not eligible to elect section 831(b) treatment.

If, by contrast, all the facts were the same except that Son owned 30 percent and Father owned 70 percent of the captive, Son would not have a non-de minimis percentage greater interest in the captive (30 percent) than in the specified assets with respect to the captive (30 percent). The captive would meet the diversification requirement for eligibility to elect section 831(b) treatment. The same result would occur if Son owned less than 30 percent of the captive

---

if greater, direct written premiums). The provision relocates the controlled group definition, as modified for purposes of section 831, in section 831(b)(2)(C).

[1016] These added eligibility rules reflect the concern expressed by the Senate Committee on Finance upon reporting out S. 905, "An Act to Amend the Internal Revenue Code of 1986 to Increase the Limitation on Eligibility for the Alternative Tax for Certain Small Insurance Companies," when the Committee stated, "The Committee notes that the provision does not include a related proposal that would narrow eligibility to elect the alternative tax in a manner intended to address abuse potential, but that may cause problems for certain States. The Committee therefore wants the Treasury Department to study the abuse of captive insurance companies for estate planning purposes, so Congress can better understand the scope of this problem and whether legislation is necessary to address it." S. Rep. 114–16, April 14, 2015, page 2.

(and Father more than 70 percent), and the other facts remained unchanged.

Any insurance company for which an 831(b) election is in effect for a taxable year must report information required by the Secretary relating to the diversification requirements imposed under the provision.

The provision also makes a technical amendment striking an unnecessary redundant parenthetical reference to interinsurers and reciprocal underwriters.

Effective Date

The provision is effective for taxable years beginning after December 31, 2016.

4. Treatment of timber gain (sec. 334 of the Act and sec. 1201 of the Code)

Present Law

Treatment of certain timber gain

Under present law, if a taxpayer cuts standing timber, the taxpayer may elect to treat the cutting as a sale or exchange eligible for capital gains treatment (sec. 631(a)). The fair market value of the timber on the first day of the taxable year in which the timber is cut is used to determine the gain attributable to such cutting. Such fair market value is thereafter considered the taxpayer's cost of the cut timber for all purposes, such as to determine the taxpayer's income from later sales of the timber or timber products. Also, if a taxpayer disposes of the timber with a retained economic interest or makes an outright sale of the timber, the gain is eligible for capital gain treatment (sec. 631(b)). This treatment under either section 631(a) or (b) requires that the taxpayer has owned the timber or held the contract right for a period of more than one year.

The maximum regular rate of tax on the net capital gain of an individual is 20 percent.[1017] Certain gains are subject to an additional 3.8-percent tax.[1018]

The net capital gain of a corporation is taxed at the same rates as ordinary income, up to a maximum rate of 35 percent.[1019]

Explanation of Provision

The Act provides a 23.8-percent alternative tax rate for corporations on the portion of a corporation's taxable income that consists of qualified timber gain (or, if less, the net capital gain) for a taxable year.

Qualified timber gain means the net gain described in section 631(a) and (b) for the taxable year, determined by taking into account only trees held more than 15 years.

[1017] Sec. 1(h).
[1018] Sec. 1411.
[1019] Secs. 11 and 1201.

Effective Date

The provision applies to taxable years beginning in 2016.

5. Modification of definition of hard cider (sec. 335 of the Act and sec. 5041 of the Code) [1020]

Present Law

An excise tax is imposed on all distilled spirits, wine, and beer produced in, or imported into, the United States.[1021] The tax liability legally comes into existence the moment the alcohol is produced or imported but payment of the tax is not required until a subsequent withdrawal or removal from the distillery, winery, brewery, or, in the case of an imported product, from customs custody or bond.[1022]

Distilled spirits, wine, and beer produced or imported into the United States are taxed at the following rates per specified volumetric measure:

Item	Current Tax Rate
Distilled Spirits	$13.50 per proof gallon [1023]
Wine [1024]	
Still Wines:	
Not more than 14 percent alcohol	$1.07 per wine gallon [1025]
More than 14 percent but not more than 21 percent alcohol	$1.57 per wine gallon
More than 21 percent but not more than 24 percent alcohol	$3.15 per wine gallon
More than 24 percent alcohol	Taxed as distilled spirits [1026] ($13.50 per proof gallon)
Hard cider	$0.226 per wine gallon
Sparkling Wines—	
Champagne and other naturally sparkling wines	$3.40 per wine gallon
Artificially carbonated wines	$3.30 per wine gallon
Beer [1027]	$18.00 per barrel [1028]

Hard cider is a still wine derived primarily from apples or apple concentrate and water, containing no other fruit product, and containing at least one-half of one percent and less than seven percent alcohol by volume.[1029] Still wines are wines containing not more than 0.392 grams of carbon dioxide per hundred milliliters of wine.

[1020] The Senate Committee on Finance reported S.906 on April 14, 2015 (S. Rep. No. 114–17).
[1021] Secs. 5001 (distilled spirits), 5041 (wines), and 5051 (beer).
[1022] Secs. 5006, 5043, and 5054. In general, proprietors of distilled spirit plants, proprietors of bonded wine cellars, brewers, and importers are liable for the tax.
[1023] A "proof gallon" is a U.S. liquid gallon of proof spirits, or the alcoholic equivalent thereof. Generally a proof gallon is a U.S. liquid gallon consisting of 50 percent alcohol. On lesser quantities, the tax is paid proportionately. Credits are allowed for wine content and flavors content of distilled spirits. Sec. 5010.
[1024] Small domestic wine producers (*i.e.*, those producing not more than 250,000 wine gallons in a calendar year) are allowed a credit of $0.90 per wine gallon ($0.056 per wine gallon in the case of hard cider) on the first 100,000 wine gallons (other than champagne and other sparkling wines) removed. The credit is reduced by one percent for each 1,000 wine gallons produced in excess of 150,000 wine gallons per calendar year.
[1025] A "wine gallon" is a U.S. gallon of liquid measure equivalent to the volume of 231 cubic inches. On lesser quantities, the tax is paid proportionately.
[1026] Sec. 5001(a)(4).
[1027] A small domestic brewer (one who produces not more than 2 million barrels in a calendar year) is subject to a per barrel rate of $7.00 on the first 60,000 barrels produced in that year.
[1028] A "barrel" contains not more than 31 gallons, each gallon equivalent to the volume of 231 cubic inches. On lesser quantities, the tax is paid proportionately.
[1029] Sec. 5041(b)(6).

Other wines made from apples, apple concentrate or other fruit products are taxed at the rates applicable in accordance with the alcohol and carbon dioxide content of the wine.

Explanation of Provision

The provision would amend the definition of hard cider to mean a wine with a carbonation level that does not exceed 0.64 grams of carbon dioxide per hundred milliliters of wine. Additionally, the provision would expand the hard cider definition to include pears, or pear juice concentrate and water, in addition to apples and apple juice concentrate and water. Under the provision, the Secretary may, by regulation, prescribe tolerance to the limitation as may be reasonably necessary in good commercial practice. The provision would change the allowable alcohol content of cider to at least one-half of one percent and less than 8.5 percent alcohol by volume.

Effective Date

The provision applies to hard cider removed during calendar years beginning after December 31, 2016.

6. Church plan clarification (sec. 336 of the Act and sec. 414 of the Code)

Present Law

Tax-favored retirement plans

Tax-favored employer-sponsored retirement plans include qualified retirement plans and section 403(b) plans.[1030] A qualified retirement plan may be maintained by any type of employer. Section 403(b) plans may be maintained only by (1) certain tax-exempt organizations,[1031] and (2) educational institutions of State or local governments (*i.e.,* public schools, including colleges and universities).

Qualified retirement plans and section 403(b) plans are subject to various requirements to receive tax-favored treatment, such as nondiscrimination requirements, vesting requirements, and limits on contributions and benefits, discussed below. In the case of plans subject to the Employee Retirement Income Security Act of 1974 ("ERISA"), requirements similar to some of the requirements under the Code, such as vesting requirements, apply also under ERISA.

Under the Code, these plans generally are prohibited from discriminating in favor of highly compensated employees [1032] with respect to contributions and benefits under the plan ("general nondiscrimination rule") and with respect to the group of employees eligible to participate in a plan ("minimum coverage rule").[1033]

[1030] Secs. 401(a) and 403(b).

[1031] These are organizations exempt from tax under section 501(c)(3).

[1032] Under section 414(q), an employee generally is treated as highly compensated if the employee (1) was a five-percent owner of the employer at any time during the year or the preceding year, or (2) had compensation for the preceding year in excess of $120,000 (for 2015).

[1033] Sections 401(a)(3) and 410(b) deal with the minimum coverage requirement; section 401(a)(4) deals with the general nondiscrimination requirements, with related rules in section 401(a)(5). In addition to the minimum coverage and general nondiscrimination requirements, under section 401(a)(26), the group of employees who accrue benefits under a defined benefit plan for a year must consist of at least 50 employees, or, if less, 40 percent of the workforce, subject to a minimum of two employees accruing benefits. Special tests apply to elective defer-

Special rules for plans maintained by churches or church-related organizations

Special rules apply with respect to qualified retirement plans that are church plans and to section 403(b) plans that are maintained by churches or qualified church-controlled organizations.

A qualified retirement plan that is a church plan is excepted from various requirements applicable to qualified plans generally under the Code unless an election is made for the plan to be subject to these requirements.[1034] A church plan with respect to which this election is not made is generally referred to as a "nonelecting church plan."[1035] A nonelecting church plan is also exempt from ERISA.[1036]

For this purpose, a church plan generally is a plan established and maintained for its employees (or their beneficiaries) by a church or by a convention or association of churches that is tax-exempt.[1037] For this purpose, employees of a tax-exempt organization that is controlled by or associated with a church or a convention or association of churches are treated as employed by a church or convention or association of churches. Associated with a church or a convention or association of churches for this purpose means sharing common religious bonds and convictions. Finally, a church plan also includes a plan maintained by an organization that is controlled by or associated with a church or convention or association of churches and has as its principal purpose or function the administration or funding of a plan or program for providing retirement or welfare benefits, or both, for the employees of the church or convention or association of churches (a "church plan organization").

A section 403(b) plan maintained by a church or qualified church-controlled organization is not subject to the nondiscrimination requirements otherwise applicable to section 403(b) plans.[1038] For this purpose, church means a church, a convention or association of churches, or an elementary or secondary school that is controlled, operated, or principally supported by a church or by a convention or association of churches and includes a qualified church-

---

rals under section 401(k) and employer matching contributions and after-tax employee contributions under section 401(m). Detailed regulations implement these statutory requirements. The nondiscrimination rules, with some modifications, apply to a section 403(b) plan by cross-reference in section 403(b)(12).

[1034] Secs. 401(a), last sentence, 410 (c) and (d), and 411(e). The requirements from which a church plan is exempt include the minimum participation, vesting, anti-alienation, and qualified joint and survivor requirements. With respect to the nondiscrimination requirements applicable to qualified retirement plans, Notice 2001-46, 2001-2 C.B. 122, provides that, until further notice, nonelecting church plans may be operated in accordance with a reasonable, good faith interpretation of the statutory requirements, rather than having to comply with the requirements in the nondiscrimination regulations.

[1035] Under section 411(e)(2), a nonelecting church plan is subject to the vesting, participation, and nondiscriminatory vesting requirements in effect before the enactment of ERISA (the pre-ERISA vesting requirements). Under the pre-ERISA vesting requirements, a participant's accrued benefit is not required to become nonforfeitable (or vested) until the participant attains normal retirement age under the plan, rather than in accordance with a prescribed schedule as is generally required for qualified retirement plans. In addition, the pattern of vesting under the plan may not have the effect of discriminating in favor of a prohibited group of officers, shareholders, supervisors, and highly compensated employees.

[1036] ERISA sec. 4(b)(2).

[1037] Secs. 414(e) and 501. A similar definition applies under ERISA section 3(33). The definition of church plan is not limited to retirement plans. For example, a health plan may be a church plan.

[1038] Sec. 403(b)(1)(D).

controlled organization.[1039] A qualified church-controlled organization is any church-controlled tax-exempt organization [1040] other than an organization that (1) offers goods, services, or facilities for sale, other than on an incidental basis, to the general public, other than goods, services, or facilities that are sold at a nominal charge substantially less than the cost of providing the goods, services, or facilities; and (2) normally receives more than 25 percent of its support from either governmental sources, or receipts from admissions, sales of merchandise, performance of services, or furnishing of facilities, in activities that are not unrelated trades or businesses, or from both. Church controlled organizations that are not qualified church-controlled organizations are generally referred to as "non-qualified church-controlled organizations."

Aggregation rules for groups under common control

General rule

In general, in applying the requirements for tax-favored treatment, employees of employers (including corporations and other entities) that are members of a group under common control are treated as employed by a single employer (referred to as aggregation rules).[1041] For example, in applying the nondiscrimination requirements, the employees of all the members of a group, and the benefits provided under plans maintained by any member of the group, are generally taken into account. In the case of taxable entities, common control is generally based on the percentage of equity ownership with a general threshold of 80 percent ownership. Other tests apply for entities that do not involve ownership.

Rules for tax-exempt organizations (other than churches)

Treasury regulations provide rules for determining whether tax-exempt organizations are under common control.[1042]

Under one rule, common control exists between an exempt organization and another organization if at least 80 percent of the directors or trustees of one organization are either representatives of, or directly or indirectly controlled by, the other organization. A trustee or director is treated as a representative of another exempt organization if he or she also is a trustee, director, agent, or employee of the other exempt organization. A trustee or director is controlled by another organization if the other organization has the general power to remove the trustee or director and designate a new trustee or director. Whether a person has the power to remove or designate a trustee or director is based on facts and circumstances.

Under a permissive aggregation rule, exempt organizations that maintain a plan that covers one or more employees from each orga-

---

[1039] Sec. 403(b)(12)(B), which incorporates by reference the definitions in section 3121(w)(3)(A) and (B).

[1040] For this purpose, exempt status under section 501(c)(3) is required.

[1041] Sec. 414(c) and the regulations thereunder provide for aggregation of groups under common control. Section 414 (b), (m) and (o) also provide aggregation rules for a controlled group of corporations and affiliated service groups. Under section 414(t), the aggregation rules apply also for purposes of various benefits other than retirement benefits. In addition, other provisions incorporate the aggregation rules by reference, such as section 4980H, requiring certain employers to offer health coverage to full-time employees.

[1042] Treas. Reg. sec. 1.414(c)–5.

nization may treat themselves as under common control (and, thus, as a single employer) if each of the organizations regularly coordinates their day-to-day exempt activities.[1043] The regulations also permit the IRS, in published guidance, to permit other types of combinations of entities that include exempt organizations to elect to be treated as under common control for one or more specified purposes if (1) there are substantial business reasons for maintaining each entity in a separate trust, corporation, or other form, and (2) the treatment would be consistent with the anti-abuse standards described below.

The regulations provide an anti-abuse rule under which the IRS may treat an entity as under common control with an exempt organization in certain cases. These include any case in which the IRS determines that the structure of one or more exempt organizations (which may include an exempt organization and a taxable entity) or the positions taken by the organizations have the effect of avoiding or evading any requirements for tax-favored retirement plans (or any other requirement for purposes of which the common control rules apply).[1044]

Rules for churches and qualified church-controlled organizations

The regulations for determining common control of tax-exempt organizations generally do not apply to churches or qualified church-controlled organizations, as defined for purposes of the exception to the section 403(b) nondiscrimination rules.[1045] The regulations do, however, provide a rule for permissive disaggregation between churches and qualified church-controlled organizations and other entities. In the case of a church plan (as defined above) to which contributions are made by two or more entities that are common law employers, any employer may apply the general aggregation rules for tax-exempt entities (as described above) to entities that are not a church or qualified church-controlled organization separately from entities that are churches or qualified church-controlled organizations. For example, in the case of a group of entities consisting of a church, a secondary school (which is a qualified church-controlled organization), and several nursing homes each of which receives more than 25 percent of its support from fees paid by residents (so that none of them is a qualified church-controlled organization), the nursing homes may treat themselves as being under common control with each other, but not as being under common control with the church and the school, even though the nursing homes would be under common control with the school

---

[1043] The regulations give as an example an entity that provides a type of emergency relief within one geographic region and another that provides that type of emergency relief within another geographic region and indicates that the two organizations may treat themselves as under common control if they have a single plan covering employees of both entities and regularly coordinate their day-to-day exempt activities. Similarly, a hospital that is an exempt organization and another exempt organization with which it coordinates the delivery of medical services or medical research may treat themselves as under common control if there is a single plan covering employees of the hospital and employees of the other exempt organization and the coordination is a regular part of their day-to-day exempt activities.

[1044] Treas. Reg. sec. 1.414(c)–5(f).

[1045] Under Treas. Reg. sec. 1.414(c)–5(e), the rules for churches and qualified church-controlled organizations are reserved.

and the church under the general aggregation rules for tax-exempt entities.

The preamble to the Treasury regulations also indicates that churches and qualified church-controlled organizations maintaining section 403(b) plans can continue to rely on previous guidance [1046] that provides a safe harbor standard for determining the members of a controlled group.[1047] Under this safe harbor, a controlled group includes each entity of which at least 80 percent of the directors, trustees or other individual members of the entity's governing body are either representatives of or directly or indirectly control, or are controlled by, the contributing employer. In addition, under the safe harbor, an entity is included in the same controlled group as the contributing employer if the entity provides directly or indirectly at least 80 percent of the contributing employer's operating funds and there is a degree of common management or supervision between the entities. A degree of common management or supervision exists if the entity providing the funds has the power to appoint or nominate officers, senior management or members of the board of directors (or other governing board) of the entity receiving the funds. A degree of common management or supervision also exists if the entity providing the funds is involved in the day-to-day operations of the entity.

Limits on contributions and benefits

Contributions or benefits under a qualified retirement plan are subject to limits. The limit that applies is generally based on whether the plan is a defined contribution plan or a defined benefit plan.[1048]

Total contributions to a defined contribution plan on behalf of an employee (other than catch-up contributions for an employee age 50 or older) for a year cannot exceed the lesser of $53,000 (for 2015) and the employee's compensation.[1049] Contributions made by an employer to more than one plan are aggregated for purposes of this limit, and employee contributions to a defined benefit plan, if any, are also taken into account in applying the limit.

An employee's annual benefit under all defined benefit plans of an employer generally must be limited to the lesser of $210,000 (for 2015) and the employee's average compensation for the three years resulting in the highest average.[1050] The dollar limit applies to benefits commencing between age 62 and age 65 in the form of a straight life annuity for the life of the employee. If benefits under a plan are paid in a form other than a straight life annuity commencing between age 62 and age 65, the benefits payable under the other form (including any benefit subsidies) generally cannot exceed the dollar limit when actuarially converted to a straight life annuity commencing at age 62.[1051]

[1046] Notice 89–23, 1989–1 C.B. 654, Part V.B.2.a.

[1047] 72 Fed. Reg. 41128, 41138 (July 26, 2007).

[1048] Sec. 415(a)(1).

[1049] Sec. 415(c).

[1050] Sec. 415(b). In general, the dollar limit is prorated in the case of a participant with fewer than 10 years of participation in a plan, and the compensation limit is prorated in the case of a participant with fewer than 10 years of service with the employer.

[1051] Specified interest and, in some cases, mortality assumptions apply in doing this conversion.

Section 403(b) plans are generally defined contribution plans and are subject to the limits on contributions to defined contribution plans.[1052] However, under the Tax Equity and Fiscal Responsibility Act of 1982, certain defined benefit arrangements established by church-related organizations and in effect on September 3, 1982, are treated as section 403(b) plans ("section 403(b) defined benefit plans").[1053] Under Treasury regulations, the present value of an employee's annual accrual under a section 403(b) defined benefit plan is subject to the limit on contributions to a defined contribution plan, and the benefits under the plan are subject to the limit on benefits under a defined benefit plan.[1054] Thus, the plan is subject to both limits.

Automatic enrollment

Qualified defined contribution plans and section 403(b) plans may include a feature under which an employee may elect between the receipt of cash compensation and plan contributions, referred to as elective deferrals.[1055] Plans are commonly designed so that an employee will receive cash compensation unless the employee affirmatively elects to make elective deferrals. Alternatively, some plans provide for automatic enrollment, a design under which elective deferrals are made at a specified rate for an employee, instead of cash compensation, unless the employee elects not to make deferrals or to make deferrals at a different rate. The Code provides various rules to accommodate automatic enrollment arrangements.[1056]

In the case of a plan subject to ERISA, ERISA generally preempts State laws relating to employee benefit plans.[1057] ERISA also expressly exempts any State laws that would impede a plan from providing an automatic enrollment arrangement, as described in the ERISA preemption provision.[1058] However, ERISA preemption does not apply with respect to plans that are exempt from ERISA, including nonelecting church plans.

Vesting requirements and transfers between plans

In general, employer-provided benefits under a qualified retirement plan are subject to minimum vesting requirements, which depend on whether the plan is a defined contribution plan or a defined benefit plan.[1059] In addition, under either type of plan, a par-

---

[1052] Secs. 403(b)(1), first sentence, and 415(k)(4). However, section 415(a)(2), last sentence, suggests that a section 403(b) plan could be subject instead to the limit on benefits under a defined benefit plan.

[1053] Sec. 251(e)(5) of Pub. L. No. 97–248.

[1054] Treas. Reg. secs. 1.403(b)–10(f) and 1.415–1(b)(2) and (3).

[1055] Secs. 401(k) and 403(b)(1) and (12). The amount of elective deferrals an employee may make is subject to limits.

[1056] See, for example, secs. 401(k)(13) and (m)(12), 414(w), and 4979(f)(1). For a discussion of automatic enrollment, see Joint Committee on Taxation, *Present Law and Background Relating to Tax-Favored Retirement Savings* (JCX–98–14), September 15, 2014, pages 36–38, available at www.jct.gov.

[1057] ERISA sec. 514(a).

[1058] ERISA sec. 514(e).

[1059] Sec. 411(a) and ERISA sec. 203. Under a defined contribution plan, a participant must vest in benefits attributable to employer contributions under one of two vesting schedules: 100 percent vesting after three years of service or graduated vesting over two to six years of service. With respect to employer-provided benefits under a defined benefit plan, a participant generally must vest under one of two vesting schedules: 100 percent vesting after five years of service,

Continued

ticipant must be fully vested at all times in benefits attributable to his or her own contributions. However, a nonelecting church plan is exempt from these vesting requirements. In contrast, contributions to a section 403(b) plan, including a section 403(b) that is a church plan, must be fully vested at all times.[1060]

A distribution to a participant from a qualified retirement plan or a section 403(b) plan generally may be rolled over to the other type of plan, including by a direct transfer to the recipient plan. In addition, in some cases, benefits and assets from one type of plan may be transferred to another plan of the same type or two plans of the same type may be merged into a single plan. However, transfers of benefits and assets between a qualified retirement plan and a section 403(b) plan are not permitted through a trustee-to-trustee transfer (other than a rollover of a distribution) or through a merger of two plans.[1061]

Group trusts

Assets of a tax-favored retirement plan generally must be set aside in a trust or other fund and used for the exclusive benefit of participants and beneficiaries. IRS guidance allows the assets of different qualified retirement plans, including plans maintained by unrelated employers, to be pooled and held by a "group trust," thus enabling employers of various sizes to benefit from economies of scale for administrative and investment purposes.[1062] In addition to qualified retirement plan assets, a group trust may also hold assets associated with certain other tax-favored retirement arrangements, including section 403(b) plans. However, a group trust may not hold other assets, such as the assets of employers sponsoring the plans.

The assets of a section 403(b) plan generally must be invested in annuity contracts or stock of regulated investment companies (that is, mutual funds).[1063] Under a special rule, certain defined contribution arrangements, referred to as retirement income accounts, established or maintained by a church, or a convention or association of churches, including a church plan organization (as described above), are treated as annuity contracts and thus are treated as section 403(b) plans, the assets of which may be invested in a group trust.[1064] The assets of retirement income accounts may also be commingled in a common fund with assets of a church itself (that is, assets that are not retirement plan assets) that are devoted exclusively to church purposes.[1065] However, unless permitted by the IRS, the assets of a church plan sponsor may not be combined with other types of retirement plan assets, such as in a group trust.[1066]

---

or graduated vesting over three to seven years of service. Under certain defined benefit plans, full vesting must occur after three years of service.

[1060] Sec. 403(b)(1)(C).
[1061] Treas. Reg. sec. 1.403(b)–10(b)(1).
[1062] Rev. Rul. 81–100, 1981–1 C.B. 326, most recently modified by Rev. Rul. 2014–24, 2014–2 C.B. 529.
[1063] Sec. 403(b)(1)(A) and (7).
[1064] Sec. 403(b)(9); Treas. Reg. sec. 1.403(b)–8(f).
[1065] Treas. Reg. sec. 1.403(b)–9(a)(6).
[1066] Ibid.

Explanation of Provision

Application of controlled group rules to church plans

General rule

For purposes of applying the controlled group rules with respect to employers that are organizations eligible to maintain church plans, the general rule under the provision is that one organization is not aggregated with another organization and treated as a single employer unless two conditions are satisfied. First, one of the organizations provides directly or indirectly at least 80 percent of the operating funds for the other organization during the preceding taxable year of the recipient organization, and, second, there is a degree of common management or supervision between the organizations, such that the organization providing the operating funds is directly involved in the day-to-day operations of the other organization.

Nonqualified church-controlled organizations

Notwithstanding the general rule, an organization that is a nonqualified church-controlled organization ("first organization") is aggregated with one or more other nonqualified church-controlled organizations or an organization that is not a tax-exempt organization ("other organization") and thus treated as a single employer if at least 80 percent of the directors or trustees of the other organization or organizations are either representatives of, or directly or indirectly controlled by, the first organization.

Permissive aggregation among church-related organizations

With respect to organizations associated with a church or convention or association of churches and eligible to maintain a church plan, an election may be made to treat the organizations as a single employer even if they would not otherwise be aggregated. The election must be made by the church or convention or association of churches with which such organizations are associated, or by an organization designated by the church or convention or association of churches. The election, once made, applies to all succeeding plan years unless revoked with notice provided to the Secretary of the Treasury ("Secretary") in such manner as the Secretary prescribes.

Permissive disaggregation of church-related organizations

For purposes of applying the general rule above, in the case of a church plan, an employer may elect to treat entities that are churches or qualified church-controlled organizations separately from other entities, regardless of whether the entities maintain separate church plans. The election, once made, applies to all succeeding plan years unless revoked with notice provided to the Secretary in such manner as the Secretary prescribes.

Anti-abuse rule

Under the provision, the anti-abuse rule in the regulations continues to apply for purposes of the rules for determining whether entities are under common control.

Contribution and benefit limits for section 403(b) defined benefit plans

Under the provision, a section 403(b) defined benefit plan is subject to the limit on benefits under a defined benefit plan and is not subject to the limit on contributions to a defined contribution plan.

Automatic enrollment by church plans

The provision preempts any State law relating to wage, salary or payroll payment, collection, deduction, garnishment, assignment, or withholding that would directly or indirectly prohibit or restrict the inclusion of an automatic contribution arrangement in a church plan. For this purpose, an automatic contribution arrangement is an arrangement under which a plan participant (1) may elect to have the plan sponsor or the employer make payments as contributions under the plan on behalf of the participant, or to the participant directly in cash, and (2) is treated as having elected to have the plan sponsor or the employer make contributions equal to a uniform percentage of compensation provided under the plan until the participant specifically elects not to have contributions made or to have contributions made at a different percentage.

Within a reasonable period before the first day of each plan year, the plan sponsor, plan administrator or employer maintaining the arrangement must provide each participant with notice of the participant's rights and obligations under the arrangement. The notice must include an explanation of (1) the participant's right under the arrangement not to have contributions made on the participant's behalf (or to elect to have contributions made at a different percentage) and (2) how contributions made under the arrangement will be invested in the absence of any investment election by the participant. The notice must be sufficiently accurate and comprehensive to apprise the participant of such rights and obligations and must be written in a manner calculated to be understood by the average participant to whom the arrangement applies.

The participant must have a reasonable period of time, after receipt of the explanation described above and before the first contribution is made, to make an election not to have contributions made or to have contributions made at a different percentage. If a participant has not made an affirmative investment election, contributions made under the arrangement must be invested in a default investment selected with the care, skill, prudence, and diligence that a prudent person selecting an investment option would use.

Allow certain plan transfers and mergers

Under the provision, if a qualified retirement plan that is a church plan and a section 403(b) plan are both maintained by the same church or convention or association of churches, and two requirements are satisfied, a transfer of all or a portion of a participant's or beneficiary's accrued benefit from one plan to the other, or a merger of the two plans, is permitted. The two requirements are that (1) the total accrued benefit of each participant or beneficiary immediately after the transfer or merger be equal to or greater than the participant's or beneficiary's total accrued benefit immediately before the transfer or merger, and (2) the total accrued benefit be nonforfeitable (i.e., 100 percent vested) after the transfer or merger and at all times thereafter. The permitted transfer or merger does not result in any income inclusion by the participant or beneficiary and does not affect the tax-favored status of the qualified retirement plan or section 403(b) plan.

Investment of church plan and church assets in group trusts

The provision allows the investment in a group trust of the assets of a church plan, including a qualified retirement plan and a retirement income account, as well as the assets of a church plan organization with respect to a church plan or retirement income account and any other assets permitted to be commingled for investment purposes with the assets of a church plan, retirement income account, or a church plan organization, without adversely affecting the tax status of the group trust, the church plan, the retirement income account, the church plan organization, or any other plan or trust that invests in the group trust.

Effective Date

The changes made to the controlled group rules and the provision relating to limits on defined benefit section 403(b) plans apply to years beginning before, on, or after the date of enactment (December 18, 2015).

The provision relating to automatic enrollment is effective on the date of enactment.

The provision relating to plan transfers and mergers applies to transfers or mergers occurring after the date of enactment.

The provision relating to investments in group trusts applies to investments made after the date of enactment.

D. Revenue Provisions

1. Updated ASHRAE standards for energy efficient commercial buildings deduction (sec. 341 of the Act and sec. 179D of the Code) [1067]

Present Law

In general

Code section 179D provides an election under which a taxpayer may take an immediate deduction equal to energy-efficient commercial building property expenditures made by the taxpayer. Energy-efficient commercial building property is defined as property (1) which is installed on or in any building located in the United States that is within the scope of Standard 90.1–2001 of the American Society of Heating, Refrigerating, and Air Conditioning Engineers and the Illuminating Engineering Society of North America ("ASHRAE/IESNA"), (2) which is installed as part of (i) the interior lighting systems, (ii) the heating, cooling, ventilation, and hot water systems, or (iii) the building envelope, and (3) which is certified as being installed as part of a plan designed to reduce the total annual energy and power costs with respect to the interior

---

[1067] The Senate Committee on Finance reported S. 1946 on August 5, 2015 (S. Rep. No. 114–118). See sec. 160.

lighting systems, heating, cooling, ventilation, and hot water systems of the building by 50 percent or more in comparison to a reference building which meets the minimum requirements of Standard 90.1–2001 (as in effect on April 2, 2003). The deduction is limited to an amount equal to $1.80 per square foot of the property for which such expenditures are made. The deduction is allowed in the year in which the property is placed in service.

Certain certification requirements must be met in order to qualify for the deduction. The Secretary, in consultation with the Secretary of Energy, will promulgate regulations that describe methods of calculating and verifying energy and power costs using qualified computer software based on the provisions of the 2005 California Nonresidential Alternative Calculation Method Approval Manual or, in the case of residential property, the 2005 California Residential Alternative Calculation Method Approval Manual.

The Secretary is granted authority to prescribe procedures for the inspection and testing for compliance of buildings that are comparable, given the difference between commercial and residential buildings, to the requirements in the Mortgage Industry National Accreditation Procedures for Home Energy Rating Systems.[1068] Individuals qualified to determine compliance shall only be those recognized by one or more organizations certified by the Secretary for such purposes.

For energy-efficient commercial building property expenditures made by a public entity, such as public schools, the deduction may be allocated to the person primarily responsible for designing the property in lieu of the public entity.

If a deduction is allowed under this section, the basis of the property is reduced by the amount of the deduction.

The deduction is effective for property placed in service prior to January 1, 2015.

Partial allowance of deduction

System-specific deductions

In the case of a building that does not meet the overall building requirement of 50-percent energy savings, a partial deduction is allowed with respect to each separate building system that comprises energy efficient property and which is certified by a qualified professional as meeting or exceeding the applicable system-specific savings targets established by the Secretary. The applicable system-specific savings targets to be established by the Secretary are those that would result in a total annual energy savings with respect to the whole building of 50 percent, if each of the separate systems met the system specific target. The separate building systems are (1) the interior lighting system, (2) the heating, cooling, ventilation and hot water systems, and (3) the building envelope. The maximum allowable deduction is $0.60 per square foot for each separate system.

[1068] See IRS Notice 2006–52, 2006–1 C.B. 1175, June 2, 2006; IRS 2008–40, 2008–14 I.R.B. 725 March 11, 2008.

Interim rules for lighting systems

In general, in the case of system-specific partial deductions, no deduction is allowed until the Secretary establishes system-specific targets.[1069] However, in the case of lighting system retrofits, until such time as the Secretary issues final regulations, the system-specific energy savings target for the lighting system is deemed to be met by a reduction in lighting power density of 40 percent (50 percent in the case of a warehouse) of the minimum requirements in Table 9.3.1.1 or Table 9.3.1.2 of ASHRAE/IESNA Standard 90.1–2001. Also, in the case of a lighting system that reduces lighting power density by 25 percent, a partial deduction of 30 cents per square foot is allowed. A pro-rated partial deduction is allowed in the case of a lighting system that reduces lighting power density between 25 percent and 40 percent. Certain lighting level and lighting control requirements must also be met in order to qualify for the partial lighting deductions under the interim rule.

Explanation of Provision

The provision increases the efficiency standards for property placed in service after December 31, 2015, such that qualifying buildings are determined relative to the ASHRAE/IESNA 90.1–2007 standards. A separate section of the Act, section 190, extends the deduction for two years, through December 31, 2016.

Effective Date

The provision applies to property placed in service after December 31, 2015.

2. Excise tax equivalency for liquefied petroleum gas and liquefied natural gas (sec. 342 of the Act and sec. 6426 of the Code) [1070]

Present Law

Fuel excise taxes

The alternative fuel and alternative fuel excise tax credits are allowable as credits against the fuel excise taxes imposed by sections 4081 and 4041. Fuel excise taxes are imposed on taxable fuel (gasoline, diesel fuel or kerosene) under section 4081. In general, these fuels are taxed when removed from a refinery, terminal rack, upon entry into the United States, or upon sale to an unregistered person. A back-up tax under section 4041 is imposed on previously untaxed fuel and alternative fuel used or sold for use as fuel in a motor vehicle or motorboat to the supply tank of a highway vehicle. In general, the rates of tax are 18.3 cents per gallon (or in the case

---

[1069] IRS Notice 2008–40, Supra, set a target of a 10-percent reduction in total energy and power costs with respect to the building envelope, and 20 percent each with respect to the interior lighting system and the heating, cooling, ventilation and hot water systems. IRS Notice 2012–26 (2012–17 I.R.B. 847 April 23, 2012) established new targets of 10-percent reduction in total energy and power costs with respect to the building envelope, 25 percent with respect to the interior lighting system and 15 percent with respect to the heating, cooling, ventilation and hot water systems, effective beginning March 12, 2012. The targets from Notice 2008–40 may be used until December 31, 2013, but the targets of Notice 2012–26 apply thereafter.

[1070] The Senate Committee on Finance reported S. 1946 on August 5, 2015 (S. Rep. No. 114–118). See sec. 303.

of compressed natural gas 18.3 cents per gasoline gallon equivalent), and in the case of liquefied natural gas, and liquid fuel derived from coal or biomass, 24.3 cents per gallon.

For fuel sold or used after December 31, 2015, liquefied petroleum gas will be taxed at 18.3 cents per energy equivalent of a gallon of gasoline (defined as 5.75 pounds of liquefied petroleum gas); liquefied natural gas will be taxed at 24.3 cents per energy equivalent of a gallon of diesel (defined as 6.06 pounds of liquefied natural gas); and compressed natural gas will be taxed at 18.3 cents per energy equivalent of a gallon of gasoline (defined as 5.66 pounds of compressed natural gas.

Excise tax credits and payments

The alternative fuel and alternative fuel excise tax credit provides a 50 cents per gallon credit for specific alternative fuels. Non-liquid alternative fuels receive a credit of 50 cents per gasoline gallon equivalent (defined as the amount of such fuel having a Btu content of 128,700 (higher heating value). Liquefied natural gas and liquefied petroleum gas are afforded a credit of 50 cents per gallon. To the extent the alternative fuel credit exceeds tax, it is refundable as a payment under section 6427(e)(2). The alternative fuel mixture credit is not eligible for the payment incentive.

Explanation of Provision

The alternative fuel excise tax credits and outlay payment provisions (extended by section 192 of the Act) related to liquefied natural gas and liquefied petroleum gas are converted to the same energy equivalent basis used for the purpose of the section 4041 tax for fuel sold or used after December 31, 2015. For liquefied natural gas the credit is 50 cents per energy equivalent of diesel fuel (6.06 pounds of liquefied natural gas) and for liquefied petroleum gas the credit is 50 cents per energy equivalent of gasoline (5.75 pounds of liquefied petroleum gas).

Effective Date

The provision is effective for fuel sold or used after December 31, 2015.

3. Exclusion from gross income of certain clean coal power grants (sec. 343 of the Act) [1071]

Present Law

Section 402 of the Energy Policy Act of 2005 provides criteria for Federal financial assistance under the Clean Coal Power Initiative. To the extent this financial assistance comes in the form of a grant, award, or allowance, it must generally be included in income under section 61 of the Internal Revenue Code (the "Code").

Corporate taxpayers may be eligible to exclude such financial assistance from gross income as a contribution of capital under section 118 of the Code. The basis of any property acquired by reason of such a contribution of capital must be reduced by the amount

---

[1071] The Senate Committee on Finance reported S. 1946 on August 5, 2015 (S. Rep. No. 114–118). See sec. 301.

of the contribution. This exclusion is not available to non-corporate taxpayers.

Explanation of Provision

With respect to eligible non-corporate recipients, the provision excludes from gross income and alternative minimum taxable income any grant, award, or allowance made pursuant to section 402 of the Energy Policy Act of 2005. The provision requires that, to the extent the grant, award or allowance is related to depreciable property, the adjusted basis is reduced by the amount excluded from income under the provision. The provision requires eligible non-corporate recipients to pay an upfront payment to the Federal government equal to 1.18 percent of the value of the grant, award, or allowance.

Under the provision, eligible non-corporate recipients are defined as (1) any recipient (other than a corporation) of any grant, award, or allowance made pursuant to Section 402 of the Energy Policy Act of 2005 that (2) makes the upfront 1.18-percent payment, where (3) the grant, award, or allowance would have been excludable from income by reason of Code section 118 if the taxpayer had been a corporation. In the case of a partnership, the eligible non-corporate recipients are the partners.

Effective Date

The provision is effective for payments received in taxable years beginning after December 31, 2011.

4. Clarification of valuation rule for early termination of certain charitable remainder unitrusts (sec. 344 of the Act and sec. 664(e) of the Code)

Present Law

Charitable remainder trusts

A charitable remainder trust may be structured as a charitable remainder annuity trust ("CRAT") or a charitable remainder unit trust ("CRUT"). A CRAT is a trust that is required to pay, at least annually, a fixed dollar amount of at least five percent of the initial value of the trust to a noncharity for the life of an individual or for a period of 20 years or less, with the remainder passing to charity.[1072] A CRUT is a trust that generally is required to pay, at least annually, a fixed percentage of at least five percent of the fair market value of the trust's assets determined at least annually to a noncharity (the income beneficiary) for the life of an individual or for a period 20 years or less, with the remainder passing to charity.[1073]

The Code provides two exceptions under which the trustee of a CRUT may pay the income beneficiary an amount different from the fixed percentage of the value of the trust's assets, as described above. First, in a net income only CRUT ("NICRUT"), the trustee pays the income beneficiary the lesser of the trust income for the

---
[1072] Sec. 664(d)(1).
[1073] Sec. 664(d)(2).

year or the fixed percentage of the value of the trust assets, described above.[1074] Stated differently, the distribution that otherwise would be made to the income beneficiary is limited by the trust income. Second, in a net income CRUT with a make-up feature ("NIMCRUT"), the trustee makes make-up distributions when a CRUT has distributed less than the fixed percentage of the value of the trust assets in a prior year by reason of the net income limit.[1075]

A trust does not qualify as a CRAT if the annuity for a year is greater than 50 percent of the initial fair market value of the trust's assets. A trust does not qualify as a CRUT if the percentage of assets that are required to be distributed at least annually is greater than 50 percent. A trust does not qualify as a CRAT or a CRUT unless the value of the remainder interest in the trust is at least 10 percent of the value of the assets contributed to the trust.

Distributions from a CRAT or CRUT are treated in the following order as: (1) ordinary income to the extent of the trust's undistributed ordinary income for that year and all prior years; (2) capital gains to the extent of the trust's undistributed capital gain for that year and all prior years; (3) other income (*e.g.*, tax-exempt income) to the extent of the trust's undistributed other income for that year and all prior years; and (4) corpus.[1076]

In general, distributions to the extent they are characterized as income are includible in the income of the beneficiary for the year that the annuity or unitrust amount is required to be distributed even though the annuity or unitrust amount is not distributed until after the close of the trust's taxable year.[1077]

CRATs and CRUTs are exempt from Federal income tax for a tax year unless the trust has any unrelated business taxable income for the year. Unrelated business taxable income includes certain debt financed income. A charitable remainder trust that loses exemption from income tax for a taxable year is taxed as a regular complex trust. As such, the trust is allowed a deduction in computing taxable income for amounts required to be distributed in a taxable year, not to exceed the amount of the trust's distributable net income for the year.

Valuation of interests in a charitable remainder trust

When the grantor funds a CRAT or a CRUT, the grantor generally may take an income tax charitable deduction equal to the present value of the charitable remainder interest of the trust[1078] determined on the date of the transfer (or, in the case of a testamentary transfer, on the date of the decedent's death or an alternate valuation date). For purposes of determining the amount of the grantor's charitable contribution, the remainder interest of a CRAT or CRUT (whether a standard CRUT, a NICRUT, or NIMCRUT) is computed on the basis that an amount equal to five percent of the net fair market value of its assets (or a greater amount, if required under the terms of the trust instrument) is to

---
[1074] Sec. 664(d)(3)(A).
[1075] Sec. 664(d)(3)(B).
[1076] Sec. 664(b).
[1077] Treas. Reg. sec. 1.664–1(d)(4).
[1078] Sec. 170(f)(2)(A).

be distributed each year to the income beneficiary.[1079] Thus, in the case of a NICRUT or a NIMCRUT, the net income limitation is disregarded.

The Code does not provide a rule for valuing the interests in a charitable remainder trust in the event of an early termination of the trust.

Explanation of Provision

Under the provision, in the case of the early termination of a NICRUT or NIMCRUT, the remainder interest is valued using rules similar to the rules for valuing the remainder interest of a charitable remainder trust when determining the amount of the grantor's charitable contribution deduction. In other words, the remainder interest is computed on the basis that an amount equal to five percent of the net fair market value of the trust assets (or a greater amount, if required under the terms of the trust instrument) is to be distributed each year, with any net income limit being disregarded.[1080]

Effective Date

The provision is effective for terminations of trusts occurring after the date of enactment (December 18, 2015).

5. Prevention of transfer of certain losses from tax indifferent parties (sec. 345 of the Act and sec. 267 of the Code)

Present Law

Related party sales

Sections 267(a)(1) and 707(b) generally disallow a deduction for a loss on the sale or exchange of property, directly or indirectly, to certain related parties or controlled partnerships. When a loss has been so disallowed, section 267(d) provides that the transferee may reduce any gain that the transferee later recognizes on a disposition of the asset by the amount of loss disallowed to the transferor.[1081] Thus, the application of section 267(d) shifts the benefit of the loss to the transferee to the extent of post-sale appreciation.

[1079] Sec. 664(e).

[1080] The provision was introduced in the House of Representatives on December 8, 2015, as H.R. 4192 (114th Cong., 1st Sess.). For a statement of the bill sponsors' intent, see 161 Cong. Rec. E1726 (Dec. 8, 2015) (statement of Rep. Tiberi) ("My bill provides that, on an early termination of a charitable remainder trust, the donor and the charity will apportion the value of the trust using the same methodology that was used to determine the value of the remainder interest on formation. The donor will recognize capital gain on the total value received, the charity will receive its share of the trust's assets, and the early termination will not constitute self-dealing or otherwise disqualify the charitable remainder trust.").

[1081] The loss disallowance rules of sections 267(a) and 707(b) together, and the corresponding rule under section 267(d), apply to transactions between the following parties:

(1) Members of a family, which include ancestors, lineal descendants, spouse and siblings (whether by the whole or half blood).

(2) An individual and a corporation more than 50 percent in value of the outstanding stock of which is owned, directly or indirectly, by or for the individual.

(3) Two corporations which are members of the same controlled group (as defined in sec. 267(f)).

(4) A grantor and a fiduciary of any trust.

(5) A fiduciary of a trust and a fiduciary of another trust, if the same person is a grantor of both trusts.

Continued

A different rule applies in the case of a sale or exchange between two corporations that are members of the same controlled group. Under section 267(f), the loss to the transferor is not denied entirely, but rather is deferred until such time as the property is transferred outside the controlled group and there would be recognition of loss under consolidated return principles, or such other time as may be prescribed in regulations. While the loss is deferred, it is not transferred to another party.

Sections 267 and 707 generally operate on an item-by-item basis, so that if a transferor sells several items of separately acquired property to a related or controlled party in a single transaction, the disallowance at the time of the sale applies to each loss regardless of any gains recognized on other property in the same transfer.[1082]

Transferee basis in gift cases

In the case of property acquired by gift, the basis generally is the basis in the hands of the transferor. If the basis exceeds the fair market value at the time of the gift, however, the basis for purposes of determining loss is the fair market value at that time.[1083] This rule has the same effect as the rule in section 267(d), in effect allowing the loss at the time of the transfer to offset post-transfer appreciation.

Transferee basis in certain nontaxable corporate organizations and reorganizations

In the case of certain nontaxable organizations and reorganizations, the transferee corporation takes the same basis in property that the property had in the hands of the transferor, increased by the amount of any gain recognized by the transferor.[1084] However, in cases involving the importation of a net built-in loss, the transferee's aggregate adjusted basis may not exceed the fair market value of the property immediately after the transaction.[1085] This rule applies to a transfer of property if (i) gain or loss with respect to such property is not subject to Federal income tax in the hands

---

(6) A fiduciary of a trust and a beneficiary of such trust.

(7) A fiduciary of a trust and a beneficiary of another trust, if the same person is a grantor of both trusts.

(8) A fiduciary of a trust and a corporation more than 50 percent in value of the outstanding stock of which is owned, directly or indirectly, by or for the trust or by or for a person who is a grantor of the trust.

(9) A person and an organization to which section 501 applies and which is controlled directly or indirectly by the person or (if such person is an individual) by members of the family of the individual.

(10) A corporation and a partnership if the same persons own more than 50 percent in value of the outstanding stock of the corporation and more than 50 percent of the capital interest or profits interest in the partnership.

(11) Two S corporations in which the same persons own more than 50 percent in value of the outstanding stock of each corporation.

(12) An S corporation and a C corporation if the same persons own more than 50 percent in value of the outstanding stock of each corporation.

(13) Except in the case of a sale or exchange in satisfaction of a pecuniary bequest, an executor of an estate and a beneficiary of the estate.

(14) A partnership and a person owning, directly or indirectly, more than 50 percent of the capital interest or profits interest in the partnership.

(15) Two partnerships in which the same persons own, directly or indirectly, more than 50 percent of the capital interests or profits interests.

[1082] This rule in effect prevents a transferor from selectively realizing certain losses to offset gains in a transaction with a related party.

[1083] Sec. 1015.

[1084] Sec. 362(a) and (b).

[1085] Sec. 362(e)(1).

of the transferor immediately before the transfer and (ii) gain or loss with respect to such property is subject to such tax in the hands of the transferee immediately after such transfer.

Explanation of Provision

The provision provides that the general rule of section 267(d) does not apply to the extent gain or loss with respect to property that has been sold or exchanged is not subject to Federal income tax in the hands of the transferor immediately before the transfer but any gain or loss with respect to the property is subject to Federal income tax in the hands of the transferee immediately after the transfer. Thus, the basis of the property in the hands of the transferee will be its cost for purposes of determining gain or loss, thereby precluding a loss importation result.

Effective Date

The provision applies to sales and other dispositions of property acquired after December 31, 2015, by the taxpayer in a sale or exchange to which section 267(a)(1) applied.

6. Treatment of certain persons as employers with respect to motion picture projects (sec. 346 of the Act and new sec. 3512 of the Code)

Present Law

FICA and FUTA taxes

The Federal Insurance Contributions Act ("FICA") imposes tax on employers and employees based on the amount of wages (as defined for FICA purposes) paid to an employee during the year.[1086] The tax imposed on the employer and on the employee is each composed of two parts: (1) the Social Security or old age, survivors, and disability insurance ("OASDI") tax equal to 6.2 percent of covered wages up to the OASDI wage base ($118,500 for 2015); and (2) the Medicare or hospital insurance ("HI") tax equal to 1.45 percent of all covered wages.[1087] The employee portion of the FICA tax generally must be withheld and remitted to the Federal government by the employer.

The Federal Unemployment Tax Act ("FUTA") imposes a tax on employers of six percent of wages up to the FUTA wage base of $7,000.[1088] An employer may take a credit against its FUTA tax liability for its contributions to a State unemployment fund and, in certain cases, an additional credit for contributions that would have been required if the employer had been subject to a higher contribution rate under State law. For purposes of the credit, the term "contributions" means payments required by State law to be

---

[1086] Secs. 3101–3128. FICA taxes, FUTA taxes (discussed herein), taxes under the Railroad Retirement Tax Act or "RRTA" (secs. 3201–3241) and income tax withholding (secs. 3401–3404) are commonly referred to collectively as employment taxes. Sections 3501–3511 provide additional employment tax rules.

[1087] For taxable years beginning after 2012, the employee portion of the HI tax under FICA (not the employer portion) is increased by an additional tax of 0.9 percent on wages received in excess of a threshold amount. The threshold amount is $250,000 in the case of a joint return, $125,000 in the case of a married individual filing a separate return, and $200,000 in any other case.

[1088] Secs. 3301–3311.

made by an employer into an unemployment fund, to the extent the payments are made by the employer without being deducted or deductible from employees' remuneration.

Responsibility for employment tax compliance

FICA and FUTA tax responsibility generally rests with the person who is the employer of an employee under a common-law test that has been incorporated into Treasury regulations.[1089] Under the regulations, an employer-employee relationship generally exists if the person for whom services are performed has the right to control and direct the individual who performs the services, not only as to the result to be accomplished by the work, but also as to the details and means by which that result is accomplished. That is, an employee is subject to the will and control of the employer, not only as to what is to be done, but also as to how it is to be done. It is not necessary that the employer actually control the manner in which the services are performed; rather, it is sufficient that the employer have a right to control. Whether the requisite control exists is determined on the basis of all the relevant facts and circumstances. The test of whether an employer-employee relationship exists often arises in determining whether a worker is an employee or an independent contractor. However, the same test applies in determining whether a worker is an employee of one person or another.

In some cases, a person other than the common-law employer (a "third party") may be liable for employment taxes. In particular, if wages are paid to an employee by a third party and the third party, rather than the employer, has control of the payment of the wages, the third party is the "statutory" employer responsible for complying with applicable employment tax requirements.[1090]

As indicated above, remuneration with respect to employment with a particular employer for a year is excepted from OASDI or FUTA taxes to the extent it exceeds the applicable OASDI or FUTA wage base.[1091] In contrast, if an employee works for multiple employers during a year, a separate wage base generally applies in determining the employer share of OASDI tax and FUTA tax with respect to remuneration for employment with each employer, even if the wages earned with all the employers are paid by the same third party.[1092]

[1089] Treas. Reg. secs. 31.3121(d)–1(c)(1) and 31.3306(i)–1(a).

[1090] Sec. 3401(d)(1) (for purposes of income tax withholding, if the employer does not have control of the payment of wages, the person having control of the payment of such wages is treated as the employer); *Otte v. United States*, 419 U.S. 43 (1974) (the person who has the control of the payment of wages is treated as the employer for purposes of withholding the employee's share of FICA taxes from wages); *In re Armadillo Corporation*, 561 F.2d 1382 (10th Cir. 1977), and *In re The Laub Baking Company v. United States*, 642 F.2d 196 (6th Cir. 1981) (the person who has control of the payment of wages is the employer for purposes of the employer's share of FICA taxes and FUTA tax). The mere fact that wages are paid by a person other than the employer does not necessarily mean that the payor has control of the payment of the wages. Rather, control depends on the facts and circumstances. See, for example, *Consolidated Flooring Services v. United States*, 38 Fed. Cl. 450 (1997), and *Winstead v. United States*, 109 F. 2d 989 (4th Cir. 1997).

[1091] An employee is subject to OASDI tax only with respect to remuneration up to the applicable wage base for a year, regardless of whether the employee works for only one employer or for more than one employer during the year. If, as a result of working for more than one employer, OASDI tax is withheld with respect to remuneration above the applicable wage base, the employee is allowed a credit under section 31(b).

[1092] *Cencast Services, L.P. v. United States*, 729 F.3d 1352 (Fed. Cir. 2013).

Explanation of Provision

Under the provision, for purposes of the OASDI and FUTA wage bases, remuneration paid by a "motion picture project employer" during a calendar year to a "motion picture project worker" is treated as remuneration paid with respect to employment of the motion picture project worker by the motion picture project employer. As a result, all remuneration paid by the motion picture project employer to a motion picture project worker during a calendar year is subject to a single OASDI wage base and a single FUTA wage base, without regard to the worker's status as a common law employee of multiple clients of the motion picture project employer during the year.

A person must meet several criteria to be treated as a motion picture project employer. The person (directly or through an affiliate [1093]) must (1) be a party to a written contract covering the services of motion picture project workers with respect to motion picture projects [1094] in the course of the trade or business of a client of the motion picture project employer, (2) be contractually obligated to pay remuneration to the motion picture project workers without regard to payment or reimbursement by any other person, (3) control the payment (within the meaning of the Code) of remuneration to the motion picture project workers and pay the remuneration from its own account or accounts, (4) be a signatory to one or more collective bargaining agreements with a labor organization that represents motion picture project workers, and (5) have treated substantially all motion picture project workers whom the person pays as employees (and not as independent contractors) during the calendar year for purposes of determining FICA, FUTA and other employment taxes. In addition, at least 80 percent of all FICA remuneration paid by the person in the calendar year must be paid to motion picture project workers.

A motion picture project worker means any individual who provides services on motion picture projects for clients of a motion picture project employer that are not affiliated with the motion picture project employer.

Effective Date

The provision applies to remuneration paid after December 31, 2015. Nothing in the amendments made by the provision is to be construed to create any inference as to the law before the date of enactment (December 18, 2015).

[1093] For purposes of the provision, "affiliate" and "affiliated" status are based on the aggregation rules applicable for retirement plan purposes under section 414(b) and (c).

[1094] For purposes of the provision, a motion picture project generally means a project for the production of a motion picture film or video tape as described in section 168(f)(3).

TITLE IV—TAX ADMINISTRATION

A. Internal Revenue Service Reforms[1095]

1. Duty to ensure that Internal Revenue Service employees are familiar with and act in accordance with certain taxpayer rights (sec. 401 of Act and sec. 7803 of the Code)

Present Law

The Code[1096] provides that the Commissioner has such duties and powers as prescribed by the Secretary. Unless otherwise specified by the Secretary, such duties and powers include the power to administer, manage, conduct, direct, and supervise the execution and application of the internal revenue laws or related statutes and tax conventions to which the United States is a party, and to recommend to the President a candidate for Chief Counsel (and recommend the removal of the Chief Counsel). If the Secretary determines not to delegate such specified duties to the Commissioner, such determination will not take effect until 30 days after the Secretary notifies the House Committees on Ways and Means, Government Reform and Oversight, and Appropriations, and the Senate Committees on Finance, Governmental Affairs, and Appropriations. The Commissioner is to consult with the Oversight Board on all matters within the Board's authority (other than the recommendation of candidates for Commissioner and the recommendation to remove the Commissioner).

Unless otherwise specified by the Secretary, the Commissioner is authorized to employ such persons as the Commissioner deems proper for the administration and enforcement of the internal revenue laws and is required to issue all necessary directions, instructions, orders, and rules applicable to such persons. Unless otherwise provided by the Secretary, the Commissioner will determine and designate the posts of duty.

Explanation of Provision

The provision adds to the Commissioner's duties the requirement to ensure that employees of the IRS are familiar with and act in accord with taxpayer rights as afforded by other provisions of the Internal Revenue Code. These rights are enumerated as follows: (A) the right to be informed, (B) the right to quality service, (C) the right to pay no more than the correct amount of tax, (D) the right to challenge the position of the Internal Revenue Service and be heard, (E) the right to appeal a decision of the Internal Revenue Service in an independent forum, (F) the right to finality, (G) the right to privacy, (H) the right to confidentiality, (I) the right to retain representation, and (J) the right to a fair and just tax system.

[1095] The House Committee on Ways and Means reported H.R. 1058 on April 13, 2015 (H.R. Rep. 114–70). The House passed the bill on April 15, 2015.
[1096] Sec. 7803(a).

Effective Date

The provision is effective on the date of enactment (December 18, 2015).

2. Prohibition of use of personal e-mail for official government business (sec. 402 of the Act)

Present Law

Federal executive agencies are required to maintain and preserve Federal records,[1097] whether in paper or electronic form, and protect against unauthorized removal of such records. Policies for the retention and disposal of records must conform to the requirements of the record-management procedures, as implemented by the Archivist of the United States.[1098] Email accounts are specifically included within the scope of records subject to the record-retention policies.[1099] Each agency is required to provide instruction and guidance to persons conducting business on behalf of the agency, including employees, officers and contractors, and use of personal email accounts for agency business is to be discouraged.[1100]

The government-wide record-management requirements are in addition to the obligations to protect the sensitive information for which the IRS is responsible. Tax information is sensitive and confidential.[1101] The Code imposes civil and criminal penalties to protect it from unauthorized use, inspection or disclosure.[1102] As a condition of receiving tax data, outside agencies must establish to the satisfaction of the IRS that they have adequate programs and security protocols in place to protect the data received.[1103] Personal email computer storage systems are not inspected by the IRS for security.

Given the sensitive and confidential nature of the information handled by the IRS and the need to be accountable for all agency records, the IRS has in place policies restricting the use of email accounts.[1104] Transmission of Federal tax information is only permitted outside the IRS in limited circumstances. In 2012, the IRS published a revised section of its manual in which it updated its administrative rules on e-records generally, and banned use of non-IRS/Treasury email for any governmental or official purpose.[1105]

[1097] 44 U.S.C. sec. 3101. See 44 U.S.C. sec. 3301 for a definition of Federal records that generally includes all documentary materials that agencies receive or create in the conduct of official business and that may have evidentiary value with respect to official business, regardless of the physical form of the materials.

[1098] See generally Title 44, at chapter 29 (records management by the Archivist of the United States and the General Services Administration), chapter 31 (records management of Federal agencies) and chapter 33 (disposal of records).

[1099] 36 CFR sec. 1236.22(a).

[1100] A quarterly bulletin published by the National Archives and Records Administration provides guidance to executive agencies. See generally NARA Bulletin 2013–03, available at http://www.archives.gov/records-mgmt/bulletins/2013/2013–03.html.

[1101] Sec. 6103(a).

[1102] See secs. 7213 (criminal unauthorized disclosure), 7213A (criminal unauthorized inspection) and 7431 (civil remedy for unauthorized inspection or disclosure).

[1103] Sec. 6103(p)(4).

[1104] I.R.M. paragraphs 1.10.3 *et seq.*, and 11.3.1.

[1105] I.R.M. paragraph 10.8.1.4.6.3.1, "Privately Owned E-Mail Accounts." (May 3, 2012).

Explanation of Provision

The provision bars use of personal email accounts by IRS employees for official government business.

Effective Date

The provision is effective on the date of enactment (December 18, 2015).

3. Release of information regarding the status of certain investigations (sec. 403 of the Act and sec. 6103 of the Code)

Present Law

Section 6103: Rules and penalties associated with the disclosure of confidential returns and return information

In general

Generally, tax returns and return information ("tax information") are confidential and may not be disclosed unless authorized in the Code.[1106] Return information includes data received, collected or prepared by the Secretary with respect to the determination of the existence or possible existence of liability of any person under the Code for any tax, penalty, interest, fine, forfeiture, or other imposition or offense. Information received, collected, or prepared by the Secretary with respect to a Title 26 offense is the return information of the person being investigated. Thus, generally, the Secretary may not disclose the status of an investigation to a person alleging a violation of their privacy (*i.e.*, an unauthorized disclosure of their return information) or other offense under the Code committed by a third party.

Exceptions to the general rule

Section 6103 provides exceptions to the general rule of confidentiality, detailing permissible disclosures. Among those exceptions are disclosures to specified persons with a "material interest" in the return or return information.[1107] For example, upon written request, an individual can obtain that individual's return, joint returns are available to either spouse with respect to whom the return was filed, and the administrator of an estate can obtain the return of an estate. Similarly, return information may be disclosed to those authorized to receive the return. However, the Secretary may withhold return information the disclosure of which the Secretary determines would seriously impair Federal tax administration.[1108]

Under section 6103(c), the Secretary may disclose a taxpayer's return or return information to such person or persons as the taxpayer may designate in a request for or consent to such disclosure. There are no restrictions placed on the recipient of tax information received pursuant to the consent of the taxpayer, and the penalties for unauthorized disclosure or inspection (discussed below) do not

---

[1106] Sec. 6103(a).
[1107] Sec. 6103(e).
[1108] Sec. 6103(e)(7).

apply to persons receiving tax information pursuant to a taxpayer's consent.

Criminal and civil penalties (sections 7213, 7213A, and 7431)

Criminal penalties apply for the unauthorized inspection or disclosure of tax information. Willful unauthorized disclosure is a felony under section 7213 and the willful unauthorized inspection of tax information is a misdemeanor under section 7213A. Under section 7431, taxpayers may also pursue a civil cause of action for disclosures and inspections not authorized by section 6103.[1109]

Section 7214: Other offenses by officers and employees of the United States

Section 7214 concerns offenses by officers and employees of the United States. It provides, upon conviction, for the dismissal from office, a $10,000 fine and/or five years imprisonment of any officer or employee:

    1. who is guilty of any extortion or willful oppression under color of law; or

    2. who knowingly demands other or greater sums than are authorized by law, or receives any fee, compensation, or reward, except as by law prescribed, for the performance of any duty; or

    3. who with intent to defeat the application of any provision of this title fails to perform any of the duties of his office or employment; or

    4. who conspires or colludes with any other person to defraud the United States; or

    5. who knowingly makes opportunity for any person to defraud the United States; or

    6. who does or omits to do any act with intent to enable any other person to defraud the United States; or

    7. who makes or signs any fraudulent entry in any book, or makes or signs any fraudulent certificate, return, or statement; or

    8. who, having knowledge or information of the violation of any revenue law by any person, or of fraud committed by any person against the United States under any revenue law, fails to report, in writing, such knowledge or information to the Secretary; or

    19. who demands, or accepts, or attempts to collect, directly or indirectly as payment or gift, or otherwise, any sum of money or other thing of value for the compromise, adjustment, or settlement of any charge or complaint for any violation or alleged violation of law, except as expressly authorized by law so to do.

In the discretion of the court, up to one-half of the amount of fine for a section 7214 violation may be awarded for the use of the informer. In addition, the court is to render judgment against said officer or employee for the amount of damages sustained in favor of the party injured.

[1109] Sec. 7431.

Section 7214 also provides that any internal revenue officer or employee interested, directly or indirectly, in the manufacture of tobacco, snuff, cigarettes, or in the production, rectification or redistillation of distilled spirits is to be dismissed from office and each such officer or employee so interested in any such manufacture or production, rectification, or redistillation of fermented liquors is to be fined not more than $5,000.

Explanation of Provision

The provision amends section 6103(e) to provide that in the case of an investigation involving the return or return information of an individual alleging a violation of sections 7213, 7213A or 7214, the Secretary may disclose to the complainant (or such person's designee) whether an investigation, based on the person's provision of information indicating a violation of sections 7213, 7213A or 7214 of the Code, has been initiated, is open or is closed. The Secretary may disclose whether the investigation substantiated a violation of sections 7213, 7213A or 7214 of the Code, and whether action has been taken with respect to the individual who committed the substantiated violation, including whether any referral has been made for prosecution of such individual. As under present law section 6103(e), the Secretary may disclose return information if the disclosure would not seriously impair Federal tax administration.

Effective Date

The provision is effective for disclosures made on or after the date of enactment (December 18, 2015).

4. Require the Secretary of the Treasury to describe administrative appeals procedures relating to adverse determinations of tax-exempt status of certain organizations (sec. 404 of the Act and sec. 7123 of the Code)

Present Law

Section 501(c) organizations

Section 501(c) describes certain organizations that are exempt from Federal income tax under section 501(a). Section 501(c) organizations include, among others, charitable organizations (501(c)(3)), social welfare organizations (501(c)(4)),[1110] labor organizations (501(c)(5)), and trade associations and business leagues (501(c)(6)). In addition to being exempt from Federal income tax, section 501(c)(3) organizations generally are eligible to receive tax

---

[1110] Section 501(c)(4) provides tax exemption for civic leagues or organizations not organized for profit but operated exclusively for the promotion of social welfare, and no part of the net earnings of which inures to the benefit of any private shareholder or individual. An organization is operated exclusively for the promotion of social welfare if it is engaged primarily in promoting in some way the common good and general welfare of the people of a community. Treas. Reg. sec. 1.501(c)(4)–1(a)(2). The promotion of social welfare does not include direct or indirect participation or intervention in political campaigns on behalf of or in opposition to any candidate for public office; however, social welfare organizations are permitted to engage in political activity so long as the organization remains engaged primarily in activities that promote social welfare. The lobbying activities of a social welfare organization generally are not limited. An organization is not operated primarily for the promotion of social welfare if its primary activity is operating a social club for the benefit, pleasure, or recreation of its members, or is carrying on a business with the general public in a manner similar to organizations that are operated for profit.

deductible contributions. Section 501(c)(3) organizations are subject to operational rules and restrictions that do not apply to many other types of tax-exempt organizations.

Application for tax exemption

Section 501(c)(3) organizations

Section 501(c)(3) organizations (with certain exceptions) are required to seek formal recognition of tax-exempt status by filing an application with the Internal Revenue Service ("IRS") (Form 1023 or Form 1023 EZ for small organizations).[1111] In response to the application, the IRS issues a determination letter or ruling either recognizing the applicant as tax-exempt or not. Certain organizations are not required to apply for recognition of tax-exempt status in order to qualify as tax-exempt under section 501(c)(3) but may do so. These organizations include churches, certain church-related organizations, organizations (other than private foundations) the gross receipts of which in each taxable year are normally not more than $5,000, and organizations (other than private foundations) subordinate to another tax-exempt organization that are covered by a group exemption letter.

A favorable determination by the IRS on an application for recognition of tax-exempt status will generally be retroactive to the date that the section 501(c)(3) organization was created if it files a completed Form 1023 or Form 1023 EZ within 15 months of the end of the month in which it was formed.[1112] If the organization does not file either form or files a late application, it will not be treated as tax-exempt under section 501(c)(3) for any period prior to the filing of an application for recognition of tax exemption.[1113] Contributions to section 501(c)(3) organizations that are subject to the requirement that the organization apply for recognition of tax-exempt status generally are not deductible from income, gift, or estate tax until the organization receives a determination letter from the IRS.[1114]

Information required on Form 1023 includes, but is not limited to: (1) a detailed statement of actual and proposed activities; (2) compensation and financial information regarding officers, directors, trustees, employees, and independent contractors; (3) a statement of revenues and expenses for the current year and the three preceding years (or for the years of the organization's existence, if less than four years); (4) a balance sheet for the current year; (5) a description of anticipated receipts and contemplated expenditures; (6) a copy of the articles of incorporation, trust document, or other organizational or enabling document; (7) organization bylaws (if any); and (8) information about previously filed Federal income

---

[1111] See sec. 508(a).

[1112] Pursuant to Treas. Reg. sec. 301.9100–2(a)(2)(iv), organizations are allowed an automatic 12-month extension as long as the application for recognition of tax exemption is filed within the extended, i.e., 27-month, period. The IRS also may grant an extension beyond the 27-month period if the organization is able to establish that it acted reasonably and in good faith and that granting relief will not prejudice the interests of the government. Treas. Reg. secs. 301.9100–1 and 301.9100–3.

[1113] Treas. Reg. sec. 1.508–1(a)(1).

[1114] Sec. 508(d)(2)(B). Contributions made prior to receipt of a favorable determination letter may be deductible prior to the organization's receipt of such favorable determination letter if the organization has timely filed its application to be recognized as tax-exempt. Treas. Reg. secs. 1.508–1(a) and 1.508–2(b)(1)(i)(b).

tax and exempt organization returns, if applicable. The Form 1023 EZ requires less information and relies primarily on attestations of the applicant.

A favorable determination letter issued by the IRS will state that the application for recognition of tax exemption and supporting documents establish that the organization submitting the application meets the requirements of section 501(c)(3) and will classify the organization as either a public charity or a private foundation.

Organizations that are classified as public charities (or as private operating foundations) and not as private nonoperating foundations may cease to satisfy the conditions that entitled the organization to such status. The IRS makes an initial determination of public charity or private foundation status that is subsequently monitored by the IRS through annual return filings. The IRS periodically announces in the Internal Revenue Bulletin a list of organizations that have failed to establish, or have been unable to maintain, their status as public charities or as private operating foundations, and that become private nonoperating foundations.

If the IRS denies an organization's application for recognition of exemption under section 501(c)(3), the organization may seek a declaratory judgment regarding its tax status.[1115] Prior to utilizing the declaratory judgment procedure, the organization must have exhausted all administrative remedies available to it within the IRS.

Other section 501(c) organizations

Most section 501(c) organizations—including organizations described within sections 501(c)(4) (social welfare organizations, etc.), 501(c)(5) (labor organizations, etc.), or 501(c)(6) (business leagues, etc.)—are not required to provide notice to the Secretary that they are requesting recognition of exempt status. Rather, organizations are exempt under these provisions if they satisfy the requirements applicable to such organizations. However, in order to obtain certain benefits such as public recognition of tax-exempt status, exemption from certain State taxes, and nonprofit mailing privileges, such organizations voluntarily may request a formal recognition of exempt status by filing a Form 1024.

If such an organization voluntarily requests a determination letter by filing Form 1024 within 27 months of the end of the month in which it was formed, its determination of exempt status, once provided, generally will be effective as of the organization's date of formation.[1116] If, however, the organization files Form 1024 after the 27-month deadline has passed, its exempt status will be formally recognized only as of the date the organization filed Form 1024.

The declaratory judgment process available to organizations seeking exemption under section 501(c)(3) is not available to organizations seeking exemption under other subsections of the Code, including sections 501(c)(4), 501(c)(5), and 501(c)(6).

[1115] Sec. 7428.
[1116] Rev. Proc. 2015–9, sec. 11, 2015–2 I.R.B. 249.

Revocation (and suspension) of exempt status

An organization that has received a favorable tax-exemption determination from the IRS generally may continue to rely on the determination as long as there is not a "material change, inconsistent with exemption, in the character, the purpose, or the method of operation of the organization, or a change in the applicable law."[1117] A ruling or determination letter concluding that an organization is exempt from tax may, however, be revoked or modified: (1) by notice from the IRS to the organization to which the ruling or determination letter was originally issued; (2) by enactment of legislation or ratification of a tax treaty; (3) by a decision of the United States Supreme Court; (4) by issuance of temporary or final Regulations by the Treasury Department; (5) by issuance of a revenue ruling, a revenue procedure, or other statement in the Internal Revenue Bulletin; or (6) automatically, in the event the organization fails to file a required annual return or notice for three consecutive years.[1118] A revocation or modification of a determination letter or ruling may be retroactive if, for example, there has been a change in the applicable law, the organization omitted or misstated a material fact, or the organization has operated in a manner materially different from that originally represented.[1119]

The IRS generally issues a letter revoking recognition of an organization's tax-exempt status only after: (1) conducting an examination of the organization; (2) issuing a letter to the organization proposing revocation; and (3) allowing the organization to exhaust the administrative appeal rights that follow the issuance of the proposed revocation letter. In the case of a section 501(c)(3) organization, the revocation letter immediately is subject to judicial review under the declaratory judgment procedures of section 7428. To sustain a revocation of tax-exempt status under section 7428, the IRS must demonstrate that the organization no longer is entitled to exemption.

Upon revocation of tax-exemption or change in the classification of an organization (e.g., from public charity to private foundation status), the IRS publishes an announcement of such revocation or change in the Internal Revenue Bulletin. Contributions made to organizations by donors who are unaware of the revocation or change in status ordinarily will be deductible if made on or before the date of publication of the announcement.

The IRS may suspend the tax-exempt status of an organization for any period during which an organization is designated or identified by U.S. authorities as a terrorist organization or supporter of terrorism.[1120] Such an organization also is ineligible to apply for tax exemption. The period of suspension runs from the date the organization is first designated or identified to the date when all designations or identifications with respect to the organization have been rescinded pursuant to the law or Executive Order under which the designation or identification was made. During the pe-

---

[1117] *Ibid.*
[1118] *Ibid.*, sec. 12.
[1119] *Ibid.*
[1120] Sec. 501(p) (enacted by Pub. L. No. 108–121, sec. 108(a), effective for designations made before, on, or after November 11, 2003).

riod of suspension, no deduction is allowed for any contribution to a terrorist organization.

Appeals of adverse determinations or revocations of exempt status

Adverse determination

If the IRS reaches the conclusion that an organization does not qualify for exempt status, the exempt organizations Rulings and Agreements unit ("EO Rulings and Agreements") will issue a proposed adverse determination letter or ruling. The proposed adverse determination will advise the taxpayer of its opportunity to appeal the determination by requesting Appeals Office consideration.[1121]

If an organization protests an adverse determination, EO Rulings and Agreements (if it maintains its adverse position) will forward the protest and the application case file to the Appeals Office, which will consider the organization's appeal. If the Appeals Office agrees with EO Rulings and Agreements, it will issue a final adverse determination letter or, if a conference was requested, schedule a conference with the organization. At the end of the conference process, the Appeals Office will issue a final adverse determination letter or a favorable determination letter.[1122]

Prior to early 2015, certain cases were referred to EO Technical, and that unit would issue the proposed adverse determination. Under interim guidance issued on May 19, 2014, by the Acting Director, Rulings and Agreements (Exempt Organizations), an organization that receives a proposed adverse determination with regard to an application that has been transferred to EO Technical (or its successor) may request a conference with EO Technical in addition to requesting Appeals Office Consideration.[1123] Prior to that time, however, a determination letter issued on the basis of technical advice from EO Technical could not be appealed to the Appeals Office on issues that were the subject of the technical advice.[1124] The procedure described in the interim guidance has since been added to the IRS Revenue Procedure relating to exempt status determinations.[1125]

Revocation or modification of a determination

As stated above, a determination letter or ruling recognizing exemption may be revoked or modified. In the case of a revocation or modification of a determination letter or ruling, the appeal and conference procedures are essentially the same as described above in connection with initial determinations of exempt status.[1126]

Explanation of Provision

The provision effectively codifies the May 19, 2014, interim guidance by requiring the Secretary to describe procedures under which a section 501(c) organization may request an administrative appeal

---

[1121] Rev. Proc. 2015–9, 2015–2 I.R.B. 249, secs. 5 and 7.
[1122] *Ibid*, sec. 7.
[1123] IRS Memorandum, *Appeals Office Consideration of All Proposed Adverse Rulings Relating to Tax-Exempt Status from EO Technical by Request,* May 19, 2014.
[1124] Rev. Proc. 2014–9, 2014–2 I.R.B. 281, sec. 7.
[1125] Rev. Proc. 2015–9, 2015–2 I.R.B. 249, secs. 5 and 7.
[1126] *Ibid.*, sec. 12.

(including a conference relating to such an appeal, if requested) to the Internal Office of Appeals of an adverse determination. For this purpose, an adverse determination includes a determination adverse to the organization relating to:

1. the initial qualification or continuing classification of the organization as exempt from tax under section 501(a);

2. the initial qualification or continuing classification of the organization as an organization described in section 170(c)(2) (generally describing certain corporations, trusts, community chests, funds, and foundations that are eligible recipients of tax deductible contributions);

3. the initial or continuing classification of the organization as a private foundation under section 509(a); or

4. the initial or continuing classification of the organization as a private operating foundation under section 4942(j)(3).

Effective Date

The provision is effective for determinations made on or after May 19, 2014.

5. Require section 501(c)(4) organizations to provide notice of formation (sec. 405 of the Act, secs. 6033 and 6652 of the Code, and new sec. 506 of the Code) [1127]

Present Law

Section 501(c)(4) organizations

Section 501(c)(4) provides tax exemption for civic leagues or organizations not organized for profit but operated exclusively for the promotion of social welfare, or certain local associations of employees, provided that no part of the net earnings of the entity inures to the benefit of any private shareholder or individual. An organization is operated exclusively for the promotion of social welfare if it is engaged primarily in promoting in some way the common good and general welfare of the people of a community.[1128] The promotion of social welfare does not include direct or indirect participation or intervention in political campaigns on behalf of or in opposition to any candidate for public office; however, social welfare organizations are permitted to engage in political activity so long as the organization remains engaged primarily in activities that promote social welfare. The lobbying activities of a social welfare organization generally are not limited. An organization is not operated primarily for the promotion of social welfare if its primary activity is operating a social club for the benefit, pleasure, or recreation of its members, or is carrying on a business with the general public in a manner similar to organizations that are operated for profit.

[1127] The House Committee on Ways and Means reported H.R.1295 on April 13, 2015 (H.R. Rep. 114–71). The House passed the bill on April 15, 2015.

[1128] Treas. Reg. sec. 1.501(c)(4)–1(a)(2).

Application for tax exemption

Section 501(c)(3) organizations

Section 501(c)(3) organizations (with certain exceptions) are required to seek formal recognition of tax-exempt status by filing an application with the IRS (Form 1023).[1129] In response to the application, the IRS issues a determination letter or ruling either recognizing the applicant as tax-exempt or not. Certain organizations are not required to apply for recognition of tax-exempt status in order to qualify as tax-exempt under section 501(c)(3) but may do so. These organizations include churches, certain church-related organizations, organizations (other than private foundations) the gross receipts of which in each taxable year are normally not more than $5,000, and organizations (other than private foundations) subordinate to another tax-exempt organization that are covered by a group exemption letter.

A favorable determination by the IRS on an application for recognition of tax-exempt status will generally be retroactive to the date that the section 501(c)(3) organization was created if it files a completed Form 1023 or Form 1023 EZ within 15 months of the end of the month in which it was formed.[1130] If the organization does not file either form or files a late application, it will not be treated as tax-exempt under section 501(c)(3) for any period prior to the filing of an application for recognition of tax exemption.[1131] Contributions to section 501(c)(3) organizations that are subject to the requirement that the organization apply for recognition of tax-exempt status generally are not deductible from income, gift, or estate tax until the organization receives a determination letter from the IRS.[1132]

Information required on Form 1023 includes, but is not limited to: (1) a detailed statement of actual and proposed activities; (2) compensation and financial information regarding officers, directors, trustees, employees, and independent contractors; (3) a statement of revenues and expenses for the current year and the three preceding years (or for the years of the organization's existence, if less than four years); (4) a balance sheet for the current year; (5) a description of anticipated receipts and contemplated expenditures; (6) a copy of the articles of incorporation, trust document, or other organizational or enabling document; (7) organization bylaws (if any); and (8) information about previously filed Federal income tax and exempt organization returns, if applicable. The Form 1023 EZ requires less information and relies primarily on attestations of the applicant.

[1129] See sec. 508(a).

[1130] Pursuant to Treas. Reg. sec. 301.9100–2(a)(2)(iv), organizations are allowed an automatic 12-month extension as long as the application for recognition of tax exemption is filed within the extended, i.e., 27-month, period. The IRS also may grant an extension beyond the 27-month period if the organization is able to establish that it acted reasonably and in good faith and that granting relief will not prejudice the interests of the government. Treas. Reg. secs. 301.9100–1 and 301.9100–3.

[1131] Treas. Reg. sec. 1.508–1(a)(1).

[1132] Sec. 508(d)(2)(B). Contributions made prior to receipt of a favorable determination letter may be deductible prior to the organization's receipt of such favorable determination letter if the organization has timely filed its application to be recognized as tax-exempt. Treas. Reg. secs. 1.508–1(a) and 1.508–2(b)(1)(i)(b).

A favorable determination letter issued by the IRS will state that the application for recognition of tax exemption and supporting documents establish that the organization submitting the application meets the requirements of section 501(c)(3) and will classify the organization as either a public charity or a private foundation.

Organizations that are classified as public charities (or as private operating foundations) and not as private nonoperating foundations may cease to satisfy the conditions that entitled the organization to such status. The IRS makes an initial determination of public charity or private foundation status that is subsequently monitored by the IRS through annual return filings. The IRS periodically announces in the Internal Revenue Bulletin a list of organizations that have failed to establish, or have been unable to maintain, their status as public charities or as private operating foundations, and that become private nonoperating foundations.

If the IRS denies an organization's application for recognition of exemption under section 501(c)(3), the organization may seek a declaratory judgment regarding its tax status.[1133] Prior to utilizing the declaratory judgment procedure, the organization must have exhausted all administrative remedies available to it within the IRS.

Other section 501(c) organizations

Most section 501(c) organizations—including organizations described within sections 501(c)(4) (social welfare organizations, etc.), 501(c)(5) (labor organizations, etc.), or 501(c)(6) (business leagues, etc.)—are not required to provide notice to the Secretary that they are requesting recognition of exempt status. Rather, organizations are exempt under these provisions if they satisfy the requirements applicable to such organizations. However, in order to obtain certain benefits such as public recognition of tax-exempt status, exemption from certain State taxes, and nonprofit mailing privileges, such organizations voluntarily may request a formal recognition of exempt status by filing a Form 1024.

If such an organization voluntarily requests a determination letter by filing Form 1024 within 27 months of the end of the month in which it was formed, its determination of exempt status, once provided, generally will be effective as of the organization's date of formation.[1134] If, however, the organization files Form 1024 after the 27-month deadline has passed, its exempt status will be formally recognized only as of the date the organization filed Form 1024.

The declaratory judgment process available to organizations seeking exemption under section 501(c)(3) is not available to organizations seeking exemption under other subsections of the Code, including sections 501(c)(4), 501(c)(5), and 501(c)(6).

[1133] Sec. 7428.

[1134] Rev. Proc. 2013–9, 2013–2 I.R.B. 255. Prior to the issuance of Revenue Procedure 2013–9 in early 2013, an organization that filed an application for exemption on Form 2014 generally could obtain a determination that it was exempt as of its date of formation, regardless of when it filed Form 1024.

Revocation (and suspension) of exempt status

An organization that has received a favorable tax-exemption determination from the IRS generally may continue to rely on the determination as long as "there are no substantial changes in the organization's character, purposes, or methods of operation."[1135] A ruling or determination letter concluding that an organization is exempt from tax may, however, be revoked or modified: (1) by notice from the IRS to the organization to which the ruling or determination letter was originally issued; (2) by enactment of legislation or ratification of a tax treaty; (3) by a decision of the United States Supreme Court; (4) by issuance of temporary or final Regulations by the Treasury Department; (5) by issuance of a revenue ruling, a revenue procedure, or other statement in the Internal Revenue Bulletin; or (6) automatically, in the event the organization fails to file a required annual return or notice for three consecutive years.[1136] A revocation or modification of a determination letter or ruling may be retroactive if, for example, there has been a change in the applicable law, the organization omitted or misstated a material fact, or the organization has operated in a manner materially different from that originally represented.[1137]

The IRS generally issues a letter revoking recognition of an organization's tax-exempt status only after: (1) conducting an examination of the organization; (2) issuing a letter to the organization proposing revocation; and (3) allowing the organization to exhaust the administrative appeal rights that follow the issuance of the proposed revocation letter. In the case of a section 501(c)(3) organization, the revocation letter immediately is subject to judicial review under the declaratory judgment procedures of section 7428. To sustain a revocation of tax-exempt status under section 7428, the IRS must demonstrate that the organization no longer is entitled to exemption.

Upon revocation of tax-exemption or change in the classification of an organization (e.g., from public charity to private foundation status), the IRS publishes an announcement of such revocation or change in the Internal Revenue Bulletin. Contributions made to organizations by donors who are unaware of the revocation or change in status ordinarily will be deductible if made on or before the date of publication of the announcement.

The IRS may suspend the tax-exempt status of an organization for any period during which an organization is designated or identified by U.S. authorities as a terrorist organization or supporter of terrorism.[1138] Such an organization also is ineligible to apply for tax exemption. The period of suspension runs from the date the organization is first designated or identified to the date when all designations or identifications with respect to the organization have been rescinded pursuant to the law or Executive Order under which the designation or identification was made. During the pe-

---

[1135] Treas. Reg. sec. 1.501(a)–1(a)(2).
[1136] Rev. Proc. 2013–9, 2013–2 I.R.B. 255.
[1137] Ibid.
[1138] Sec. 501(p) (enacted by Pub. L. No. 108–121, sec. 108(a), effective for designations made before, on, or after November 11, 2003).

riod of suspension, no deduction is allowed for any contribution to a terrorist organization.

Explanation of Provision

Under the provision, an organization described in section 501(c)(4) must provide to the Secretary notice of its formation and intent to operate as such an organization, in such manner as the Secretary may prescribe. The notice, together with a reasonable user fee in an amount to be established by the Secretary, must be provided no later than 60 days following the organization's establishment and must include the following information: (1) the name, address, and taxpayer identification number of the organization; (2) the date on which, and the State under the laws of which, the organization was organized; and (3) a statement of the purpose of the organization. The Secretary may extend the 60-day deadline for reasonable cause. Any such fees collected may not be expended by the Secretary unless provided by an appropriations Act. Within 60 days of receipt of a notice of an organization's formation and intent to operate as an organization described in section 501(c)(4), the Secretary shall issue to the organization an acknowledgment of the notice.

The provision amends section 6652(c) (which provides for penalties in the event of certain failures to file an exempt organization return or disclosure) to impose penalties for failure to file the notice required under the proposal. An organization that fails to file a notice within 60 days of its formation (or, if an extension is granted for reasonable cause, by the deadline established by the Secretary) is subject to a penalty equal to $20 for each day during which the failure occurs, up to a maximum of $5,000. In the event such a penalty is imposed, the Secretary may make a written demand on the organization specifying a date by which the notice must be provided. If any person fails to comply with such a demand on or before the date specified in the demand, a penalty of $20 is imposed for each day the failure continues, up to a maximum of $5,000.

With its first annual information return (Form 990, Form 990–EZ, or Form 990–N) filed after providing the notice described above, a section 501(c)(4) organization must provide such information as the Secretary may require, and in the form prescribed by the Secretary, to support its qualification as an organization described in section 501(c)(4). The Secretary is not required to issue a determination letter following the organization's filing of the expanded first annual information return.

A section 501(c)(4) organization that desires additional certainty regarding its qualification as an organization described in section 501(c)(4) may file a request for a determination, together with the required user fee, with the Secretary. Such a request is in addition to, not in lieu of, filing the required notice described above. It is intended that such a request for a determination be submitted on a new form (separate from Form 1024, which may continue to be used by certain other organizations) that clearly states that filing such a request is optional. The request for a determination is treated as an application subject to public inspection and disclosure under sections 6104(a) and (d).

Effective Date

The provision generally is effective for organizations organized after the date of enactment (December 18, 2015).

Organizations organized on or before the date of enactment that have not filed an application for exemption (Form 1024) or annual information return or notice (under section 6033) on or before the date of enactment must provide the notice required under the provision within 180 days of the date of enactment.

6. Declaratory judgments for section 501(c)(4) and other exempt organizations (sec. 406 of the Act and sec. 7428 of the Code) [1139]

Present Law

In order for an organization to be granted tax exemption as a charitable entity described in section 501(c)(3), it must file an application for recognition of exemption with the IRS and receive a favorable determination of its status.[1140] For most section 501(c)(3) organizations, eligibility to receive tax-deductible contributions similarly is dependent upon its receipt of a favorable determination from the IRS. In general, a section 501(c)(3) organization can rely on a determination letter or ruling from the IRS regarding its tax-exempt status, unless there is a material change in its character, purposes, or methods of operation. In cases where an organization violates one or more of the requirements for tax exemption under section 501(c)(3), the IRS generally may revoke an organization's tax exemption, notwithstanding an earlier favorable determination.

Present law authorizes an organization to seek a declaratory judgment regarding its tax-exempt status as a remedy if the IRS denies its application for recognition of exemption under section 501(c)(3), fails to act on such an application, or informs a section 501(c)(3) organization that it is considering revoking or adversely modifying its tax-exempt status.[1141] The right to seek a declaratory judgment arises in the case of a dispute involving a determination by the IRS with respect to: (1) the initial qualification or continuing qualification of an organization as a charitable organization for tax exemption purposes or for charitable contribution deduction purposes; (2) the initial classification or continuing classification of an organization as a private foundation; (3) the initial classification or continuing classification of an organization as a private operating foundation; or (4) the failure of the IRS to make a determination with respect to (1), (2), or (3).[1142] A "determination" in this context generally means a final decision by the IRS affecting the tax qualification of a charitable organization. Section 7428 vests jurisdiction over controversies involving such a determination in the U.S. District Court for the District of Columbia, the U.S. Court of Federal Claims, and the U.S. Tax Court.[1143]

[1139] The House Committee on Ways and Means reported H.R. 1295 on April 13, 2015 (H.R. Rep. 114–71). The House passed the bill on April 15, 2015.
[1140] Sec. 508(a).
[1141] Sec. 7428.
[1142] Sec. 7428(a)(1).
[1143] Sec. 7428(a)(2).

Prior to utilizing the declaratory judgment procedure, an organization must have exhausted all administrative remedies available to it within the IRS.[1144] For the first 270 days after a request for a determination is made and before the IRS informs the organization of its decision, an organization is deemed not to have exhausted its administrative remedies. If no determination is made during the 270-day period, the organization may initiate an action for declaratory judgment after the period has elapsed. If, however, the IRS makes an adverse determination during the 270-day period, an organization may immediately seek declaratory relief. The 270-day period does not begin with respect to applications for recognition of tax-exempt status until the date a substantially completed application is submitted.

Under present law, a non-charity (*i.e.*, an organization not described in section 501(c)(3)) may not seek a declaratory judgment with respect to an IRS determination regarding its tax-exempt status. In general, such an organization must petition the U.S. Tax Court for relief following the issuance of a notice of deficiency or pay any tax owed and file a refund action in Federal district court or the U.S. Court of Federal Claims.

Explanation of Provision

The provision extends the section 7428 declaratory judgment procedure to the initial determination or continuing classification of an organization as tax-exempt under section 501(a) as an organization described in: (1) any subsection of section 501(c) (including social welfare and certain other organizations described in section 501(c)(4)); or (2) section 501(d) (religious and apostolic organizations).

Effective Date

The provision is effective for pleadings filed after the date of enactment (December 18, 2015).

7. Termination of employment of Internal Revenue Service employees for taking official actions for political purposes (sec. 407 of the Act and sec. 1203(b) of the Internal Revenue Service Restructuring and Reform Act of 1998)

Present Law

The IRS Restructuring and Reform Act of 1998 (the "Restructuring Act")[1145] requires the IRS to terminate an employee for certain proven violations committed by the employee in connection with the performance of official duties. The violations include: (1) willful failure to obtain the required approval signatures on documents authorizing the seizure of a taxpayer's home, personal belongings, or business assets; (2) providing a false statement under oath material to a matter involving a taxpayer; (3) with respect to a taxpayer, taxpayer representative, or other IRS employee, the violation of any right under the U.S. Constitution, or any civil right established under titles VI or VII of the Civil Rights Act of 1964,

---

[1144] Sec. 7428(b)(2).
[1145] Pub. L. No. 105–206, sec. 1203(b), July 22, 1998.

title IX of the Educational Amendments of 1972, the Age Discrimination in Employment Act of 1967, the Age Discrimination Act of 1975, sections 501 or 504 of the Rehabilitation Act of 1973 and title I of the Americans with Disabilities Act of 1990; (4) falsifying or destroying documents to conceal mistakes made by any employee with respect to a matter involving a taxpayer or a taxpayer representative; (5) assault or battery on a taxpayer or other IRS employee, but only if there is a criminal conviction or a final judgment by a court in a civil case, with respect to the assault or battery; (6) violations of the Internal Revenue Code, Treasury Regulations, or policies of the IRS (including the Internal Revenue Manual) for the purpose of retaliating or harassing a taxpayer or other IRS employee; (7) willful misuse of section 6103 for the purpose of concealing data from a Congressional inquiry; (8) willful failure to file any tax return required under the Code on or before the due date (including extensions) unless failure is due to reasonable cause; (9) willful understatement of Federal tax liability, unless such understatement is due to reasonable cause; and (10) threatening to take an official action, such as an audit, or delay or fail to take official action with respect to a taxpayer for the purpose of extracting personal gain or benefit.

The Act provides non-delegable authority to the Commissioner to determine that mitigating factors exist, that, in the Commissioner's sole discretion, mitigate against terminating the employee. The Act also provides that the Commissioner, in his sole discretion, may establish a procedure to determine whether an individual should be referred for such a determination by the Commissioner. The Treasury Inspector General ("IG") is required to track employee terminations and terminations that would have occurred had the Commissioner not determined that there were mitigation factors and include such information in the IG's annual report to Congress.

Explanation of Provision

The provision amends the Restructuring Act to expand the scope of the violation concerning an IRS employee threatening to audit a taxpayer for the purpose of extracting personal gain or benefit to include actions taken for political purposes. As a result, the provision requires the IRS to terminate an employee who, for political purposes or personal gain, undertakes official action with respect to a taxpayer or, depending on the circumstances, fails to do so, delays action or threatens to perform, delay or omit such official action. Official actions for purposes of this provision include audits or examinations.

Effective Date

The provision is effective on the date of enactment (December 18, 2015).

8. Gift tax not to apply to gifts made to certain exempt organizations (sec. 408 of the Act and sec. 2501(a) of the Code)[1146]

Present Law

Overview

The Code imposes a tax for each calendar year on the transfer of property by gift during such year by any individual, whether a resident or nonresident of the United States.[1147] The amount of taxable gifts for a calendar year is determined by subtracting from the total amount of gifts made during the year: (1) the gift tax annual exclusion (described below); and (2) allowable deductions.

Gift tax for the current taxable year is determined by: (1) computing a tentative tax on the combined amount of all taxable gifts for the current and all prior calendar years using the common gift tax and estate tax rate table; (2) computing a tentative tax only on all prior-year gifts; (3) subtracting the tentative tax on prior-year gifts from the tentative tax computed for all years to arrive at the portion of the total tentative tax attributable to current-year gifts; and, finally, (4) subtracting the amount of unified credit not consumed by prior-year gifts.

Unified credit (exemption) and tax rates

Unified credit

A unified credit is available with respect to taxable transfers by gift and at death.[1148] The unified credit offsets tax, computed using the applicable estate and gift tax rates, on a specified amount of transfers, referred to as the applicable exclusion amount, or exemption amount. The exemption amount was set at $5 million for 2011 and is indexed for inflation for later years.[1149] For 2015, the inflation-indexed exemption amount is $5.43 million.[1150] Exemption used during life to offset taxable gifts reduces the amount of exemption that remains at death to offset the value of a decedent's estate. An election is available under which exemption that is not used by a decedent may be used by the decedent's surviving spouse (exemption portability).

Common tax rate table

A common tax-rate table with a top marginal tax rate of 40 percent is used to compute gift tax and estate tax. The 40-percent rate applies to transfers in excess of $1 million (to the extent not exempt). Because the exemption amount currently shields the first $5.43 million in gifts and bequests from tax, transfers in excess of the exemption amount generally are subject to tax at the highest marginal 40-percent rate.

[1146] The House Committee on Ways and Means reported H.R. 1104 on April 13, 2015 (H.R. Rep. 114–64). The House passed the bill on April 15, 2015.
[1147] Sec. 2501(a).
[1148] Sec. 2010.
[1149] For 2011 and later years, the gift and estate taxes were reunified, meaning that the gift tax exemption amount was increased to equal the estate tax exemption amount.
[1150] For 2015, the $5.43 exemption amount results in a unified credit of $2,117,800, after applying the applicable rates set forth in section 2001(c).

Transfers by gift

The gift tax applies to a transfer by gift regardless of whether: (1) the transfer is made outright or in trust; (2) the gift is direct or indirect; or (3) the property is real or personal, tangible or intangible.[1151] For gift tax purposes, the value of a gift of property is the fair market value of the property at the time of the gift.[1152] Where property is transferred for less than full consideration, the amount by which the value of the property exceeds the value of the consideration is considered a gift and is included in computing the total amount of a taxpayer's gifts for a calendar year.[1153]

For a gift to occur, a donor generally must relinquish dominion and control over donated property. For example, if a taxpayer transfers assets to a trust established for the benefit of his or her children, but retains the right to revoke the trust, the taxpayer may not have made a completed gift, because the taxpayer has retained dominion and control over the transferred assets. A completed gift made in trust, on the other hand, often is treated as a gift to the trust beneficiaries.

By reason of statute, certain transfers are not treated as transfers by gift for gift tax purposes. These include, for example, certain transfers for educational and medical purposes [1154] and transfers to section 527 political organizations.[1155]

Under present law, there is no explicit exception from the gift tax for a transfer to a tax-exempt organization described in section 501(c)(4) (generally, social welfare organizations), 501(c)(5) (generally, labor and certain other organizations), or section 501(c)(6) (generally, trade associations and business leagues).

Taxable gifts

As stated above, the amount of a taxpayer's taxable gifts for the year is determined by subtracting from the total amount of the taxpayer's gifts for the year the gift tax annual exclusion and any available deductions.

Gift tax annual exclusion

Under present law, donors of lifetime gifts are provided an annual exclusion of $14,000 per donee in 2015 (indexed for inflation from the 1997 annual exclusion amount of $10,000) for gifts of present interests in property during the taxable year.[1156] If the non-donor spouse consents to split the gift with the donor spouse, then the annual exclusion is $28,000 per donee in 2015. In general, unlimited transfers between U.S. spouses are permitted without imposition of a gift tax. Special rules apply to the contributions to a qualified tuition program ("529 Plan") including an election to treat a contribution that exceeds the annual exclusion as a contribution made ratably over a five-year period beginning with the year of the contribution.[1157]

[1151] Sec. 2511(a).
[1152] Sec. 2512(a).
[1153] Sec. 2512(b).
[1154] Sec. 2503(e).
[1155] Sec. 2501(a)(4).
[1156] Sec. 2503(b).
[1157] Sec. 529(c)(2).

Transfers between spouses

A 100-percent marital deduction generally is permitted for the value of property transferred between U.S. spouses.[1158]

Transfers to charity

Contributions to section 501(c)(3) charitable organizations and certain other organizations may be deducted from the value of a gift for Federal gift tax purposes.[1159] The effect of the deduction generally is to remove the full fair market value of assets transferred to charity from the gift tax base; unlike the income tax charitable deduction, there are no percentage limits on the deductible amount. A charitable contribution of a partial interest in property, such as a remainder or future interest, generally is not deductible for gift tax purposes.[1160]

Explanation of Provision

Under the provision, the gift tax shall not apply to the transfer of money or other property to an organization described in section 501(c)(4), 501(c)(5), or 501(c)(6) and exempt from tax under section 501(a) for the use of such organization.

Effective Date

The provision is effective for gifts made after the date of enactment (December 18, 2015). The provision shall not be construed to create an inference with respect to whether any transfer of property to such an organization, whether made before, on, or after the date of enactment, is a transfer by gift for gift tax purposes.

9. Extend the Internal Revenue Service authority to require a truncated Social Security Number ("SSN") on Form W–2 (sec. 409 of the Act and sec. 6051 of the Code)

Present Law

Section 6051(a) generally requires that an employer provide a written statement to each employee on or before January 31 of the succeeding year showing the remuneration paid to that employee during the calendar year and other information including the employee's Social Security number. The Form W–2, Wage and Tax Statement, is used to provide this information to employees and contains the taxpayer's SSN, wages paid, taxes withheld, and other information.

Other statements provided to taxpayers, such as Forms 1099, generally issued to any individual or unincorporated business paid in excess of $600 per calendar year for services rendered, are subject to rules under section 6109 dealing with identifying numbers. Section 6109 requires that the filer provide the taxpayer's "identifying number" which is an individual's SSN except as otherwise specified in regulations.[1161] Accordingly, for Forms 1099, the De-

---
[1158] Sec. 2523.
[1159] Sec. 2522.
[1160] Sec. 2522(c)(2).
[1161] See Treas. Reg. sec. 301.6109–1.

partment of the Treasury has the authority to require or permit filers to use a number other than a taxpayer's SSN, including a truncated SSN (the last four numbers of the SSN).

Explanation of Provision

The provision revises section 6051 to require employers to include an "identifying number" for each employee, rather than an employee's SSN, on Form W–2. This change will permit the Department of the Treasury to promulgate regulations requiring or permitting a truncated SSN on Form W–2, under authority currently provided in section 6109(d).

Effective Date

The provision is effective on the date of enactment (December 18, 2015).

10. Clarification of enrolled agent credentials (sec. 410 of the Act)

Present Law

Treasury Department Circular No. 230 provides rules relating to practice before the IRS by attorneys, certified public accountants, enrolled agents, enrolled actuaries, and others.

Explanation of Provision

The provision amends Title 31 of the U.S. Code to permit enrolled agents meeting the Secretary's qualifications to use the designation "enrolled agent," "EA," or "E.A."

Effective Date

The provision is effective on the date of enactment (December 18, 2015).

11. Partnership audit rules (sec. 411 of the Act and secs. 6225, 6226, 6234, 6235, and 6031 of the Code)

Present Law

Under recent amendments to Chapter 63,[1162] relating to partnership audit rules, the returns filed for partnership taxable years beginning after 2017 are subject to a centralized system for audit, adjustment and collection of tax that applies to all partnerships, except those eligible partnerships that have filed a valid election out. The Secretary may initiate an examination of a partnership by

---

[1162] Sections 6221 through 6241, as amended by section 1101, "The Bipartisan Budget Act of 2015," Pub. L. 114–74. For years prior to the effective date of the new provisions, there remain three sets of rules for tax audits of partners and partnerships. Partnerships with more than 100 partners may elect the electing large partnership audit rules of sections 6240 through 6256. Partnerships with more than 10 partners (and that are not electing large partnerships) are subject to the TEFRA partnership audit rules enacted in 1982, found in sections 6221 through 6234. Under these two sets of rules, partnership items generally are determined at the partnership level under unified audit procedures. All other partnerships (those with 10 or fewer partners that have not elected the TEFRA audit rules) are subject to the audit rules applicable generally, with the tax treatment of an adjustment to a partnership's items of income, gain, loss, deduction, or credit determined for each partner in separate proceedings, both administrative and judicial.

issuing a notice of administrative proceeding to the partnership or its designated representative.[1163] Any adjustment to items of income, gain, loss, deduction, or credit of a partnership for a partnership taxable year, and any partner's distributive share thereof, generally is determined at the partnership level.[1164] The Secretary is required to notify the partnership and the partnership representative of any proposed partnership adjustment before the Secretary may issue a notice of final partnership adjustment.[1165] A notice of proposed adjustment issued to the partnership identifies both the substance of the adjustment and informs the partnership of the amount of any imputed underpayment that results. If the adjustments result in any underpayment of tax attributable to these items, the tax is generally imputed to the partnership and may be assessed and collected at the partnership level in the year that the partnership adjustment becomes final (the adjustment year).[1166] As an alternative to partnership payment of the imputed underpayment, a partnership may elect to furnish a statement of each partner's share of any adjustments (similar to a Schedule K–1) to each reviewed-year partner, who is then required to pay tax attributable to the partnership adjustment.[1167]

An imputed underpayment of tax with respect to a partnership adjustment for any reviewed year is determined by netting all adjustments of items of income, gain, loss, or deduction and multiplying the net amount by the highest rate of Federal income tax applicable either to individuals or to corporations that is in effect for the reviewed year.[1168] Any adjustments to items of credit are taken into account as an increase or decrease of the product of this multiplication. Any net increase or decrease in loss is treated as a decrease or increase, respectively, in income. Netting is done taking into account applicable limitations, restrictions, and special rules under present law.

Modification of an imputed underpayment generally

If the partnership disagrees with the computation of the imputed underpayment during an administrative proceeding, it may seek modification of the computation, subject to the approval of the Secretary.[1169] Modification procedures permit redetermination of the imputed underpayment (1) to take into account amounts paid with amended returns filed by reviewed year partners, (2) to disregard the portion allocable to a tax-exempt partner, and (3) to take into account a rate of tax lower than the highest tax rate for individuals or corporations for the reviewed year. In addition, regulations or guidance may provide for additional procedures to modify imputed underpayment amounts on the basis of other necessary or appro-

---

[1163] Sec. 6231(a)(1).
[1164] Sec. 6221(a).
[1165] Sec. 6231(a)(1) and (2).
[1166] For purposes of the centralized system, the reviewed year means the partnership taxable year to which the item being adjusted relates (sec. 6225(d)(1)). The adjustment year means (1) in the case of an adjustment pursuant to the decision of a court (under the centralized system's judicial review provisions), the partnership taxable year in which the decision becomes final; (2) in the case of an administrative adjustment request, the partnership taxable year in which it is made; or (3) in any other case, the partnership taxable year in which the notice of final partnership adjustment is mailed (sec. 6225(d)(2)).
[1167] Sec. 6226.
[1168] Sec. 6225(b)(1).
[1169] Sec. 6225(c).

priate factors. In the case of a publicly traded partnership, such other appropriate factors could include taking into account the present-law section 469(k) rule requiring that deductions that exceed income (passive activity losses) be carried forward and applied against income from the publicly traded partnership, not against other income of the partners.

Modifying an imputed underpayment based on applicable highest tax rates

The partnership may seek to modify an imputed underpayment amount by demonstrating that a lower tax rate is applicable to partners.[1170] For example, the partnership may demonstrate that a portion of an imputed underpayment is allocable to a partner that is a C corporation, and for that C corporation partner, the highest marginal rate of Federal income tax (35 percent in 2015, for example) for ordinary income for the reviewed year is lower than the highest marginal rate of Federal income tax for individuals (39.6 percent in 2015, for example). The statutory language refers to ordinary income but does not refer to capital gain of a corporation, which is generally subject to tax at the same rate as ordinary income of a corporation.

Limitations period for partnership adjustments

In general, the Secretary may adjust an item on a partnership return at any time within three years of the date a return is filed (or the return due date, if the return is not filed) or an administrative adjustment request is made. The time within which the adjustment is made by the Secretary may be later if a notice of proposed adjustment[1171] is issued, because the issuance of a notice of proposed partnership adjustment begins the running of a period of 270 days in which the partnership may seek a modification of the imputed underpayment. Although the partnership generally is limited to 270 days from the issuance of that notice to seek a modification of the imputed underpayment, extensions may be permitted by the IRS. During the 270-day period, the Secretary may not issue a notice of final partnership adjustment.

After a notice of proposed adjustment resulting in an imputed underpayment is issued, the final partnership notice may be issued no later than either the date which is 270 days after the partnership has completed its response seeking a revision of an imputed underpayment, or, if the partnership provides an incomplete or no response, no later than 270 days after the date of a notice of proposed adjustment.

Forum for judicial review

A partnership may seek judicial review of a notice of final partnership adjustment within 90 days after the notice is mailed, in the U.S. Tax Court, the Court of Federal Claims or a U.S. district court for the district in which the partnership has its principal place of business. The statutory language refers to the Claims Court rather than the Court of Federal Claims.

[1170] Sec. 6225(c)(4).
[1171] Sec. 6231.

Restriction on authority to amend partner information statements

Partner information returns (currently Schedules K–1) required to be furnished by the partnership may not be amended after the due date of the partnership return to which the partner information returns relate.[1172] A conforming amendment inadvertently strikes newly added language relating to the restriction on amended partner information statements.

Explanation of Provision

The provision corrects and clarifies several provisions relating to partnership audits to express the intended rule.

Modifying an imputed underpayment based on applicable highest tax rates

The provision strikes the reference to ordinary income of corporations in the rule that provides procedures for modification of an imputed underpayment to make clear that a lower rate of tax may be taken into account in the case of either capital gain or ordinary income of a partner that is a C corporation.

Modifying an imputed underpayment based on certain passive losses of publicly traded partnerships

Under the provision, certain section 469(k) passive activity losses can reduce the imputed underpayment of a publicly traded partnership under the centralized system. The imputed underpayment can be determined without regard to the portion of the underpayment that the partnership demonstrates is attributable to (i.e., would be offset by) specified passive activity losses attributable to a specified partner. The amount of the specified passive activity loss is concomitantly decreased, and the partnership takes the net decrease into account as an adjustment in the adjustment year with respect to the specified partners to which the net decrease relates.

A specified passive activity loss for any specified partner of a publicly traded partnership means the lesser of the section 469(k) passive activity loss of that partner which is separately determined with respect to the partnership (1) for the partner's taxable year in which or with which the reviewed year of the partnership ends, or (2) for the partner's taxable year in which or with which the adjustment year of the partnership ends. A specified partner is a person who continuously meets each of three requirements for the period starting with the partner's taxable year in which or with which the partnership reviewed year ends through the partner's taxable year in which or with which the partnership adjustment year ends. These three requirements are that the person is a partner of the publicly traded partnership; the person is an individual, estate, trust, closely held C corporation, or personal service corporation; and the person has a specified passive activity loss with respect to the publicly traded partnership.

[1172] After that date, a timely administrative adjustment request may address Schedule K–1 errors. Sec. 6227.

Limitations period for partnership adjustments

The provision clarifies the unintended conflict between section 6231 (barring the Secretary from issuing the notice of final partnership adjustment earlier than the expiration of the 270 days after the notice of a proposed adjustment) and section 6235 (requiring that a notice of final partnership adjustment be filed no later than 270 days after the notice of proposed adjustment in the case of a partnership that does not seek modification of the imputed underpayment). As amended, section 6235 provides that a notice of final partnership adjustment to a partnership that does not seek modification of an underpayment in response to a notice of proposed adjustment may be issued up to 330 days (plus any additional number of days that were agreed upon as an extension of time for taxpayer response) after the notice of proposed adjustment.

Forum for judicial review

The provision correctly identifies the Court of Federal Claims in section 6234.

The provision adds a cross reference within the alternative payment rules [1173] to the time period for seeking judicial review,[1174] clarifying that judicial review is available to a partnership that has made the election [1175] under the alternative payment rules.

Restriction on authority to amend partner information statements

The provision corrects the conforming amendment so that it correctly strikes the last sentence of section 6031(b) under prior law, which sentence related to repealed provisions on electing large partnerships.

Effective Date

The provision is effective as if included in section 1101 of the Bipartisan Budget Act of 2015.[1176]

B. United States Tax Court [1177]

Part 1—Taxpayer Access to United States Tax Court

1. Filing period for interest abatement cases (sec. 421 of the Act and sec. 6404 of the Code)

Present Law

The United States Tax Court (herein the "Tax Court") has jurisdiction over actions brought by a taxpayer for review of a denial of a request for interest abatement if (1) the taxpayer meets certain net worth requirements, and (2) the petition is filed within 180 days of mailing of a final determination by the Secretary not to

---

[1173] Sec. 6226.
[1174] Sec. 6234(a).
[1175] Sec. 6226(a)(1).
[1176] Pub. L. No. 114–74, enacted November 2, 2015.
[1177] The Senate Committee on Finance reported S. 903 on April 14, 2015 (S. Rep. No. 114–14).

abate interest.[1178] In the absence of the mailing of a final determination by the Secretary, the Code does not authorize the filing of a Tax Court petition, and the taxpayer is unable to seek judicial review of the claim.

Explanation of Provision

The provision amends the Code to authorize a petition with the Tax Court to seek review of a claim for interest abatement upon the expiration of a 180-day period after the filing with the IRS of a claim for abatement of interest, in instances in which the Secretary has failed to issue a final determination within that period.

Effective Date

The provision is effective for claims filed after the date of enactment (December 18, 2015).

2. Small tax case election for interest abatement cases (sec. 422 of the Act and secs. 6404 and 7463 of the Code)

Present Law

The Code provides certain proceedings for small tax cases, generally those that involve disputes of $50,000 or less.[1179] Under the Code, the Tax Court has exclusive jurisdiction to review a failure by the Secretary to abate interest.[1180] However, the Code presently does not authorize cases to be conducted using small tax case procedures, unless the issue arises as part of a request for review of collection actions.[1181]

Explanation of Provision

The provision amends the Code to extend the small tax case procedures to petitions brought under section 6404(h), for review of a decision by the Secretary not to abate interest in cases in which the total amount of interest for which abatement is sought does not exceed $50,000.

Effective Date

The provision applies to cases pending as of the day after the date of enactment (December 18, 2015), and cases commencing after the date of enactment.

[1178] Sec. 6404(h).

[1179] Sec. 7463. These cases are handled under less formal procedures than regular cases. The Tax Court's decision in a small tax case is final and cannot be appealed to any court by the IRS or by the petitioner. See sec. 7463, Title XVII of the United States Tax Court rules, and http://www.ustaxcourt.gov/forms/Petition_Kit.pdf.

[1180] Sec. 6404(h). *Hinck v. United States,* 127 S.Ct. 2011 (2007).

[1181] Secs. 7463, 6330.

3. Venue for appeal of spousal relief and collection cases (sec. 423 of the Act and sec. 7482 of the Code)

Present Law

The jurisdiction of the Tax Court includes authority to render decisions on a taxpayer's entitlement to relief from joint and several liability and collection of taxes by lien and levy.[1182]

Venue for appellate review of Tax Court decisions by the U.S. Court of Appeals is determined for certain specified cases by the taxpayer's legal residence, principal place of business, or principal office or agency is located. A default rule prescribes that venue for review of all other cases lies in the U.S. Court of Appeals for the District of Columbia.[1183] Cases involving relief from joint or several liability or collection by lien and levy are not among those expressly identified as appealable to the circuit of residence or principal business/office. However, routine practice since enactment, on the part of both the litigants and the courts, has been to treat such cases as appealable to the U.S. Court of Appeals for the circuit corresponding to the petitioner's residence or principal business or office.

Explanation of Provision

The provision amends section 7482(b) to clarify that Tax Court decisions rendered in cases involving petitions under sections 6015, 6320, or 6330 follow the generally applicable rule for appellate review. That rule provides that the cases are appealable to the U.S. Court of Appeals for the circuit in which is located the petitioner's legal residence in the case of an individual or the petitioner's principal place of business or principal office of agency in the case of an entity other than an individual.

Effective Date

The provision applies to petitions filed after the date of enactment. No inference is intended with respect to the application of section 7482 to petitions filed on or before the date of enactment.

4. Suspension of running of period for filing petition of spousal relief and collection cases (sec. 424 of the Act and secs. 6015 and 6330 of the Code)

Present Law

Section 6015(e) addresses procedures by which taxpayers may petition the Tax Court to determine the appropriate relief available to the individual in matters involving spousal relief from joint and several liability and collection of taxes by lien and levy. It also provides for suspension of the running of a period of limitations[1184] on the collection of assessments that may apply, limits on tax court jurisdictions in certain circumstances, and rules for providing adequate notice of proceedings to the other spouse.

[1182] Secs. 6015, 6320, and 6330.
[1183] Sec. 7482.
[1184] Sec. 6502.

Section 6330 disallows levies to be made on property or rights to property unless the Secretary has notified the taxpayer in writing of their right to a hearing before such levy is made. Under subsection (d), once a determination is made, the taxpayer may appeal the determination to the Tax Court within 30 days. Under subsection (e), the levy actions which are the subject of the requested hearing and the running of any relevant period of limitations[1185] are suspended for the period during which such hearing and appeals are pending.

Neither section 6015 or 6330 includes a rule similar to the coordination rule found in the general provisions regarding filing a petition with the Tax Court for taxpayers in bankruptcy.[1186] Under that rule, the period of the automatic stay in bankruptcy is disregarded, and the taxpayer may file its petition with the Tax Court within 60 days after the stay is lifted.

Explanation of Provision

The provision adds to existing rules a suspension of the running of a period of limitations on filing a petition as described in section 6015(e) for a taxpayer who is prohibited from filing such a petition under U.S.C. Title 11. The suspension is for the period during which the taxpayer is prohibited from filing such a petition and for 60 days thereafter.

The provision also adds to existing rules a suspension of the running of a period of limitations on filing a petition as described in section 6330(e) for a taxpayer who is prohibited from filing such a petition under U.S.C. Title 11. The suspension is for the period during which the taxpayer is prohibited from filing such a petition and for 30 days thereafter.

Effective Date

The provision applies to petitions filed under section 6015(e) of the Code after the date of enactment and to petitions filed under section 6330 of the Code after the date of enactment.

5. Application of Federal rules of evidence (sec. 425 of the Act and sec. 7453 of the Code)

Present Law

In general, the Code provides that the proceedings of the Tax Court shall be conducted in accordance with rules of practice and procedure (other than rules of evidence) as prescribed by the Tax Court, and in accordance with the rules of evidence applicable in trials without a jury in the United States District Court of the District of Columbia.[1187] The Tax Court has interpreted the Code to require the Tax Court to apply the evidentiary precedent of the D.C. Circuit in all cases[1188], an exception to the Tax Court's regular practice under *Golsen v. Commissioner*[1189] of applying the

---
[1185] Secs. 6502, 6531, and 6532.
[1186] Sec. 6213(f).
[1187] Sec. 7453.
[1188] All cases except those cases in which section 7453 does not apply, *e.g.*, small tax cases.
[1189] 54 T.C. 742 (1970), aff'd, 445 F.2d 985 (10th Cir. 1971).

precedent of the circuit court of appeals to which its decision is appealable ("the *Golsen* rule").

The Federal Rules of Evidence [1190] are the applicable rules of evidence for all Federal district courts in all judicial districts, including the District of Columbia. In addition, the United States Code includes specific rules and procedures for evidence.[1191] Rule 143 of the Rules of Practice and Procedure promulgated by the Tax Court, states "those rules include the rules of evidence in the Federal Rules of Civil Procedure and any rules of evidence generally applicable in the Federal courts (including the United States District Court for the District of Columbia)."

Explanation of Provision

The provision amends the Code to provide that proceedings of the Tax Court be conducted in accordance with rules of practice and procedure as prescribed by the Tax Court, and in accordance with Federal Rules of Evidence. Thus, under the *Golsen* rule, the Tax Court will apply the evidentiary precedent of the circuit court of appeals to which its decision is appealable.

Effective Date

The provision applies to proceedings commenced after the date of enactment, and to the extent that it is just and practicable, to all proceedings pending on such date.

Part 2—United States Tax Court Administration

6. Judicial conduct and disability procedures (sec. 431 of the Act and new sec. 7466 of the Code)

Present Law

Under Title 28 of the United States Code, any person is authorized to file a complaint alleging that an Article III Judge has engaged in conduct prejudicial to the effective and expeditious administration of the business of the courts; the law also permits any person to allege conduct reflecting a covered Judge's inability to perform his or her duties because of mental or physical disability.[1192] A judicial council exercises specific powers in investigating and taking action with respect to such complaints, including paying certain fees and allowances incurred in conducting hearings and awarding reimbursement of reasonable expenses in appropriate circumstances from appropriated funds.[1193] Title 28 directs other Article I courts, including the Court of Federal Claims [1194] and the Court of Appeals for Veterans Claims,[1195] to prescribe similar rules for the filing of complaints with respect to the conduct

---

[1190] The Federal Rules of Evidence, as amended through 2012, under the authority of 28 U.S.C. sec. 2074, is available at http://www.uscourts.gov/uscourts/rules/rules-evidence.pdf. "The Act to Establish Rules of Evidence for Certain Courts and Proceedings," Pub. L. No. 93–595 (January 2, 1975).

[1191] 28 U.S.C. secs. 1731 through 1828.

[1192] Judicial Conduct and Disability Act of 1980, 28 U.S.C. secs. 351–364. On March 11, 2008, the Judicial Conference of the United States promulgated rules governing such proceedings.

[1193] 28 U.S.C. chapter 16.

[1194] 28 U.S.C. sec. 363.

[1195] 38 U.S.C. sec. 7253(g).

or disability of any Judge and for the investigation and resolution of such complaints.

Unlike the prescriptions of Title 28 for Article III courts and other Article I courts, there is no statutory provision related to complaints regarding the conduct or disability of a Tax Court Judge, Senior Judge, or Special Trial Judge, although they voluntarily agree to follow the rules contained in the Code of Conduct for U.S. Judges.[1196]

Explanation of Provision

The provision authorizes the Tax Court to prescribe procedures for the filing of complaints with respect to the conduct of any judge or special trial judge of the Tax Court and for the investigation and resolution of such complaints. In investigating and taking action with respect to such a complaint, the provision authorizes the Tax Court to exercise the powers granted to a judicial council under Title 28.

Effective Date

The provision applies to proceedings commenced after the date which is 180 days after the date of enactment, and to the extent that it is just and practicable, to all proceedings pending on such date.

7. Administration, judicial conference, and fees (sec. 432 of the Act; Code sec. 7473 and new secs. 7470 and 7470A of the Code)

Present Law

Congress established the Tax Court as a court of law under Article I with its governing provisions in the Code. However, provisions governing most Federal courts are codified in Title 28 of the United States Code. Congress has, from time to time, amended the governing laws of other Federal courts and the laws that apply to the Administrative Office of the United States Courts relating to administering certain authorities of the judiciary.[1197]

Federal courts, including Article I courts such as the Court of Appeals for Veterans Claims, have express statutory authority to conduct an annual judicial conference.[1198] The Tax Court has conducted periodic judicial conferences in order to consider the business of the Tax Court and to discuss means of improving the administration of justice within the Tax Court's jurisdiction. The Tax Court's judicial conferences have been attended by persons admitted to practice before the Tax Court, including representatives of the Internal Revenue Service, the Department of Justice, private practitioners, low-income taxpayer clinics, and by other persons active in the legal profession.

[1196] Available at http://www.uscourts.gov/uscourts/RulesAndPolicies/conduct/vol02a-ch02.pdf.
[1197] These authorities are available to Article III courts either directly or through the laws enacted for the Administrative Office of the United States Court under U.S.C. title 28 (see *e.g.*, 28 U.S.C. secs. 601, et seq.) and to other Article I courts such as the U.S. Court of Appeals for Veterans Claims under 38 U.S.C. sec. 7287.
[1198] 38 U.S.C. sec. 7286.

Federal courts are authorized to deposit certain court fees into a special fund of the Treasury to be available to offset funds appropriated for the operation and maintenance of the courts.[1199] The Tax Court's filing fees are statutorily set at "not in excess of $60" and are covered into the Treasury as miscellaneous receipts.[1200]

Explanation of Provision

The provision amends the Code to provide the Tax Court with the same general management, administrative, and expenditure authorities that are available to other Article I courts.

The provision amends the Code to provide the Tax Court with express authority to conduct an annual judicial conference and charge a reasonable registration fee.

The provision amends the Code to authorize the Tax Court to deposit certain fees into a special fund of the Treasury to be available to offset funds appropriated for the operation and maintenance of the Tax Court.

Effective Date

The provision is effective on the date of enactment.

Part 3—Clarification Relating to the United States Tax Court

8. Clarification relating to the United States Tax Court (sec. 441 of the Act and sec. 7441 of the Code)

Present Law

The Tax Court was created in 1969 as a court of record established under Article I of the U.S. Constitution with jurisdiction over tax matters as conferred upon it under the Code.[1201] It superseded an independent agency of the Executive Branch known as the Tax Court of the United States, which itself superseded the Board of Tax Appeals.[1202]

As judges of an Article I court, Tax Court judges do not have lifetime tenure nor do they enjoy the salary protection afforded judges in Article III courts. They are subject to removal only for cause, by the President.[1203] The authority to remove a judge for cause was the basis for a recent unsuccessful challenge to an order of the Tax Court, in which the taxpayer invoked the separation of powers doctrine to argue that the removal authority is an unconstitutional interference of the executive branch with the exercise of judicial powers. In rejecting that challenge, the Court of Appeals for the District of Columbia held in *Kuretski v. Commissioner*[1204] that the

---

[1199] 28 U.S.C. secs. 1941(A) and 1931.

[1200] Sec. 7473.

[1201] Sec. 7441.

[1202] The Board of Tax Appeals was created in 1924 to review deficiency determinations. In 1942, it was renamed the Tax Court of the United States.

[1203] Section 7443(f) permits the President to remove a Tax Court judge for inefficiency, neglect of duty, or malfeasance in office, after notice and opportunity for a public hearing.

[1204] *Kuretski v. Commissioner*, 755 F.3d 929 (D.C. Cir. 2014), *petition for cert. filed* (U.S. Nov. 26, 2014) (No. 14–622), available at http://www.procedurallytaxing.com/wp-content/uploads/2014/12/Kuretski-Supreme-Court-Petition.pdf. For an explanation of the status of Article I courts in comparison to the Article III judiciary, see, *Federal Courts: A Legal Overview* (Report No. R43746), October 1, 2014, available at http://www.fas.org/sgp/crs/misc/R43746.pdf.

Tax Court is an independent Executive Branch agency, while acknowledging that the Tax Court is a "Court of Law" for purposes of the Appointments Clause.[1205]

Explanation of Provision

To avoid confusion about the independence of the Tax Court as an Article I court, the provision clarifies that the Tax Court is not an agency of the Executive Branch.

Effective Date

The provision is effective on the date of enactment.

[1205] *Kuretski v. Commissioner*, p. 932, distinguishing *Freytag v. Commissioner*, 501 U.S. 868 (1991).

APPENDIX: ESTIMATED BUDGET EFFECTS OF TAX LEGISLATION ENACTED IN 2015

APPENDIX:
ESTIMATED BUDGET EFFECTS OF TAX LEGISLATION ENACTED IN 2015

Fiscal Years 2015-2025

[Millions of Dollars]

Provision	Effective	2015	2016	2017	2018	2019	2020	2021	2022	2023	2024	2025	2015-25
PART ONE: SLAIN OFFICER FAMILY SUPPORT ACT OF 2015 - Accelerate the Income Tax Benefits for Charitable Cash Contributions for Relief of the Families of New York Police Department Detectives Wenjian Liu and Rafael Ramos and Clarify that Payments made by Charitable Organizations to Families of Victims are Treated as Exempt Payments (Public Law 114-7, signed into law by the President on April 1, 2015)	[1]	[2]	[2]	---	---	---	---	---	---	---	---	---	[2]
PART TWO: MEDICARE ACCESS AND CHIP REAUTHORIZATION ACT OF 2015 - 100 Percent Continuous Levy Authority on Payment to Medicare Providers and Suppliers (Public Law 114-10, signed into law by the President on April 16, 2015)	pma 180da DOE	---	54	55	56	57	58	60	61	62	63	64	591
PART THREE: DON'T TAX OUR FALLEN PUBLIC SAFETY HEROES ACT - Exclude from Gross Income Any Compensation Received by Public Safety Officers or Their Dependents for Injuries or Death Suffered in the Line of Duty (Public Law 114-14, signed into law by the President on May 22, 2015)	DOE	------ No Revenue Effect ------
PART FOUR: HIGHWAY AND TRANSPORTATION FUNDING ACT OF 2015 - Extension of Highway Trust Fund Expenditure Authority (sunset 7/31/15) (Public Law 114-21, signed into law by the President on May 29, 2015)	DOE	------ No Revenue Effect ------
PART FIVE: DEFENDING PUBLIC SAFETY EMPLOYEES' RETIREMENT ACT - Allow Federal Law Enforcement Officers, Firefighters, and Air Traffic Controllers to Make Penalty-Free Withdrawals from Governmental Plans after Age 50 (Public Law 114-26, signed into law by the President on June 29, 2015)	da 12/31/15	---	5	1	-1	-1	-2	-2	-1	-1	-1	-1	-5
PART SIX: TRADE PREFERENCES EXTENSION ACT OF 2015 (Public Law 114-27, signed into law by the President on June 29, 2015)													
IV - Extension of Trade Adjustment Assistance													
A. Extension and Modification of the Health Coverage Tax Credit (sunset 12/31/19) [3]	cmi tyba 12/31/13	---	-47	-45	-35	-35	-12	---	---	---	---	---	-173

350

Provision	Effective	2015	2016	2017	2018	2019	2020	2021	2022	2023	2024	2025	2015-25
VIII - Offsets													
A. Increase the Amount of Any Required Installment of Corporate Estimated Tax Otherwise Due in July, August, or September of 2020 by 8 Percent for Corporations with Assets of at Least $1 Billion	DOE	---	---	---	---	---	5,761	-5,761	---	---	---	---	---
B. Payee Statement Required to Claim Certain Education Tax Benefits [3]	tyba DOE	---	21	106	94	48	49	50	51	52	52	53	576
C. Special Rule for Educational Institutions Unable to Collect TINs of Individuals with Respect to Higher Education Tuition and Related Expenses	[4]	---	[2]	[2]	[2]	[2]	[2]	[2]	[2]	[2]	[2]	[2]	[2]
D. Increase Penalty for Failure to File Correct Information Returns and Provide Payee Statements	rasrtbfa 12/31/15	---	5	13	13	14	14	15	15	15	16	16	136
E. Child Tax Credit Not Refundable for Taxpayers Electing to Exclude Foreign Earned Income from Tax [3]	tyba 12/31/14	---	38	36	35	28	27	26	26	25	26	26	293
TOTAL OF PART SIX		---	**17**	**110**	**107**	**55**	**5,839**	**-5,670**	**92**	**92**	**94**	**95**	**832**
PART SEVEN: SURFACE TRANSPORTATION AND VETERANS HEALTH CARE CHOICE IMPROVEMENT ACT OF 2015 (Public Law 114-41, signed into law by the President on July 31, 2015)													
II - Revenue Provisions													
A. Extension of Highway Trust Fund Expenditure Authority (sunset 10/29/15)	DOE	---	---	---	---	---	--- No Revenue Effect ---						
B. Funding of the Highway Trust Fund - transfer $6.068 billion from the General Fund to the Highway Account of the Highway Trust Fund and $2.0 billion from the General Fund to the Mass Transit Account of the Highway Trust Fund	DOE	---	---	---	---	---	--- No Revenue Effect ---						
C. Modification of Mortgage Information Reporting Requirements	[5]	---	22	147	152	164	172	191	207	227	251	273	1,806
D. Require Consistency Between Estate Tax Value and Income Tax Basis of Assets Acquired From a Decedent	[6]	17	117	132	141	148	154	159	164	167	170	173	1,542
E. Clarify the 6-Year Statute of Limitations in the Case of Overstatement of Basis	[7]	3	40	70	87	98	110	126	146	168	177	182	1,209
F. Change the Filing Due Dates of Certain Tax and Information Returns	rf tyba 12/31/15	---	---	251	13	1	1	5	8	11	13	13	314
G. Extend Section 420 Transfers of Excess Pension Assets to Retiree Health and Life Insurance Accounts (sunset 12/31/25)	tmta 12/31/21	---	---	---	---	---	---	---	24	48	49	50	172
H. Equalization of Excise Taxes on Liquefied Natural Gas, Liquefied Petroleum Gas, and Compressed Natural Gas	fsota 12/31/15	---	-6	-8	-8	-9	-9	-10	-9	-10	-11	-12	-90
IV - Veterans Provisions													
A. Treatment of Employees with Health Coverage Under TRICARE or the Veterans Health Administration for Purposes of the Employer Mandate Under the Patient Protection and Affordable Care Act [8]	mba 12/31/13	---	-63	-66	-70	-74	-78	-83	-88	-93	-99	-104	-816

Provision	Effective	2015	2016	2017	2018	2019	2020	2021	2022	2023	2024	2025	2015-25
B. Eligibility for Health Savings Account not Affected by Receipt of Medical Care for Service-Connected Disability [9]	mba 12/31/15	---	-11	-17	-22	-27	-34	-40	-48	-55	-61	-69	-384
TOTAL OF PART SEVEN		20	99	509	293	301	316	348	404	463	489	506	3,753
PART EIGHT: AIRPORT AND AIRWAY EXTENSION ACT OF 2015 - Extension of Airport and Airway Trust Fund Expenditure Authority and Funding of Airport and Airway Trust Fund (sunset 3/31/16) (Public Law 114-55, signed into law by the President on September 30, 2015)	DOE	------- No Revenue Effect -------
PART NINE: SURFACE TRANSPORTATION EXTENSION ACT OF 2015 - Extension of Highway Trust Fund Expenditure Authority (sunset 11/20/15) (Public Law 114-73, signed into law by the President on October 29, 2015)	DOE	------- No Revenue Effect -------
PART TEN: BIPARTISAN BUDGET ACT OF 2015 (Public Law 114-74, signed into law by the President on November 2, 2015)													
V - Pensions													
A. Mortality Tables and Extension of Current Funding Stabilization Percentages to 2018, 2019, and 2020													
1. Mortality tables [10] [11]	pyba 12/31/15	---	3	6	9	22	36	92	216	280	250	205	1,118
2. Extension of current funding stabilization [10] [12] [13]	pyba 12/31/15	---	---	---	174	797	1,704	2,303	2,024	875	-120	-1,223	6,534
XI - Revenue Provisions Related to Tax Compliance													
A. Partnership Audits and Adjustments	rffp tyba 12/31/17	---	[14]	[14]	[14]	843	1,165	1,260	1,383	1,505	1,565	1,604	9,325
B. Partnership interests Created by Gift	tyba 12/31/15	---	266	325	282	240	199	161	124	99	97	101	1,894
TOTAL OF PART TEN		---	269	331	465	1,902	3,104	3,816	3,747	2,759	1,792	687	18,871
PART ELEVEN: SURFACE TRANSPORTATION EXTENSION ACT OF 2015, PART II - Extension of Highway Trust Fund Expenditure Authority (sunset 12/4/15) (Public Law 114-87, signed into law by the President on November 20, 2015)	DOE	------- No Revenue Effect -------
PART TWELVE: FIXING AMERICA'S SURFACE TRANSPORTATION ("FAST") ACT (Public Law 114-94, signed into law by the President on December 4, 2015)													
Division C - Finance													
XXXI - Highway Trust Fund and Related Taxes													
A. Extension of Highway Trust Fund Expenditure Authority (sunset 9/30/20)	DOE	------- No Revenue Effect -------
B. Extension of Highway-Related Taxes (present-law taxes sunset 9/30/22; the heavy vehicle use tax sunsets 9/30/23)	10/1/16	------- No Revenue Effect -------
C. Additional Transfers to Highway Trust Fund - transfer $51.9 billion from the General Fund to the Highway Account of the Highway Trust Fund and $18.1 billion from the General Fund to the Mass Transit Account of the Highway Trust Fund	DOE	------- No Revenue Effect -------

Provision	Effective	2015	2016	2017	2018	2019	2020	2021	2022	2023	2024	2025	2015-25
D. Transfer to Highway Trust Fund of Certain Motor Vehicle Safety Penalties	aca DOE	---------- No Revenue Effect ----------											
E. Appropriation from Leaking Underground Storage Tank Trust Fund - transfer $0.3 billion from the Leaking Underground Storage Tank Trust Fund to the highway account of the Highway Trust Fund	[15]	---------- No Revenue Effect ----------											
XXXII - Offsets													
A. Revocation or Denial of Passports in Cases of Certain Unpaid Taxes	DOE	---	18	57	65	48	39	35	32	33	34	35	395
B. Reform of Rules Related to Qualified Tax Collection Contracts [3] and Special Compliance Personnel Program	[16] & acarbsa DOE		[17]	187	235	246	257	269	282	296	310	325	2,408
C. Repeal of Modification of Automatic Extension of Return Due Date for Certain Employee Benefit Plans	dtyba 12/31/15	---------- Negligible Revenue Effect ----------											
TOTAL OF PART TWELVE		---	18	244	300	294	296	304	314	329	344	360	2,803
PART THIRTEEN: CONSOLIDATED APPROPRIATIONS ACT, 2016 (Public Law 114-113, signed into law by the President on December 18, 2015)													
Division P - Tax-Related Provisions													
A. High Cost Employer-Sponsored Health Coverage Excise Tax Provisions													
1. Two-year moratorium of the ACA excise tax on certain high-cost plans (2018 and 2019) [3] [18] [19]	DOE	---	---	---	-2,234	-7,171	-6,472	-1,836	-2,202	-2,444	-2,583	-2,684	-15,877
2. Deductibility of excise tax on high cost employer-sponsored health coverage [20]	DOE	---	---	---	---	---	-151	-538	-656	-764	-849	-936	-3,894
3. Study on suitable benchmarks for age and gender adjustment of excise tax on high cost employer-sponsored health coverage	DOE	---------- No Revenue Effect ----------											
B. Annual Fee on Health Insurance Providers - One-Year Moratorium on Annual Fee on Health Insurance Providers (2017)	DOE	---	---	-10,952	-1,217	---	---	---	---	---	---	---	-12,169
C. Miscellaneous Provisions													
1. Beginning-of-construction date for wind renewable power facilities eligible to claim the electricity production credit or investment credit in lieu of the production credit (sunset 12/31/19)	1/1/15	---	---	-109	-429	-891	-1,366	-1,836	-2,202	-2,444	-2,583	-2,684	-14,545
2. Extension and phaseout of higher credit rate of solar energy credit (sunset 12/31/21)	DOE	---	---	-340	-636	-753	-802	-786	-601	-449	-402	-224	-4,995
3. Extension and phaseout of credits with respect to residential qualified solar electric property and qualified solar water heating property (sunset 12/31/21)	1/1/17	---	-2	-183	-869	-872	-881	-825	-700	---	---	---	-4,333
4. Allow independent refiners to exclude 75% of oil transportation costs from the calculation of their qualified production activities income (sunset 12/31/21)	tyba 12/31/15	---	-119	-299	-305	-310	-315	-323	-197	---	---	---	-1,868
Total of Division P - Tax Related Provisions		---	-121	-11,883	-5,690	-9,997	-9,987	-4,308	-4,356	-3,657	-3,834	-3,844	-57,681

354

Division Q - Protecting Americans from Tax Hikes Act of 2015
I. Extenders
A. Permanent Extensions

Provision	Effective	2015	2016	2017	2018	2019	2020	2021	2022	2023	2024	2025	2015-25
1. Reduce the earnings threshold for the refundable portion of the child tax credit to $3,000 made permanent [3]	tyba DOE	---	---	---	---	-12,373	-12,455	-12,452	-12,534	-12,597	-12,694	-12,733	-87,839
2. American opportunity tax credit made permanent [3]	tyba DOE	---	---	---	-2,361	-11,789	-11,649	-11,326	-11,115	-10,738	-10,564	-10,316	-79,858
3. Modification of the earned income tax credit made permanent:													
a. Credit percentage of 45% for three or more qualifying children made permanent [3]	tyba DOE	---	---	---	-25	-2,541	-2,601	-2,672	-2,733	-2,804	-2,897	-2,973	-19,245
b. Increase beginning and ending income levels for joint returns by $5,000 indexed after 2009 made permanent [3]	tyba DOE	---	---	---	-16	-1,602	-1,596	-1,592	-1,593	-1,596	-1,605	-1,604	-11,204
4. Permanently extend and modify the deduction for certain expenses of elementary and secondary school teachers	tyba 12/31/14 & tyba 12/31/15	---	-257	-236	-241	-260	-302	-306	-311	-319	-332	-335	-2,898
5. Parity for exclusion from income for employer-provided mass transit and parking benefits made permanent [21]	ma 12/31/14	---	-115	-146	-151	-157	-162	-184	-198	-208	-219	-231	-1,771
6. Deduction for State and local general sales taxes made permanent	tyba 12/31/14	---	-3,480	-3,462	-3,656	-3,872	-4,074	-4,298	-4,539	-4,772	-5,021	-5,267	-42,440
7. Permanently extend and modify the special rule for qualified conservation contributions	Cmi tyba 12/31/14 & Ctmi tyba 12/31/15	---	-81	-83	-89	-94	-101	-116	-133	-147	-162	-176	-1,184
8. Tax-free distributions from IRAs to certain public charities for individuals age 70-1/2 or older, not to exceed $100,000 per taxpayer per year made permanent	dmi tyba 12/31/14	---	-556	-700	-776	-822	-866	-911	-964	-1,013	-1,055	-1,104	-8,768
9. Permanently extend and expand the enhanced charitable deduction for contributions of food inventory	cma 12/31/14 & tyba 12/31/15	---	-162	-195	-202	-209	-216	-223	-231	-239	-248	-256	-2,182
10. Modification of tax treatment of certain payments under existing arrangements to controlling exempt organizations made permanent	proaa 12/31/14	---	-30	-16	-15	-14	-13	-13	-12	-11	-11	-10	-146
11. Basis adjustment to stock of S corporations making charitable contributions of property made permanent	Cmi tyba 12/31/14	---	-73	-53	-55	-57	-59	-61	-64	-68	-71	-75	-636
12. Research credit permanently extended and modified	apoia 12/31/14 & tyba 12/31/14	---	-8,345	-6,902	-8,256	-9,538	-10,758	-11,912	-12,994	-14,077	-14,894	-15,569	-113,245
13. Permanently extend and modify employer wage credit for activated military reservists	pma 12/31/14 & tyba 12/31/15	---	-2	-10	-20	-23	-23	-23	-24	-24	-24	-24	-196
14. 15-year straight-line cost recovery for qualified leasehold improvements, qualified restaurant buildings and improvements, and qualified retail improvements made permanent [22]	ppisa 12/31/14	---	-350	-582	-920	-1,297	-1,706	-2,151	-2,622	-3,098	-3,580	-3,998	-20,305
15. Permanently extend and modify increased expensing limitations and treatment of certain real property as section 179 property	tyba 12/31/14 & tyba 12/31/15 [23]	---	-22,299	-10,995	-8,749	-6,963	-5,583	-4,843	-4,103	-4,077	-4,650	-4,789	-77,051
16. Treatment of certain dividends of RICs made permanent	tyba 12/31/15	---	-176	-111	-116	-122	-128	-134	-140	-147	-154	-161	-1,389
17. Exclusion of 100 percent of gain on certain small business stock made permanent	saa 12/31/14	---	17	15	16	16	-215	-1,546	-1,645	-1,727	-1,804	-1,879	-8,750
18. Reduction in S corporation recognition period for built-in gains tax made permanent	tyba 12/31/14	---	-282	-285	-223	-146	-101	-80	-81	-91	-97	-99	-1,485
19. Exception under subpart F for active financing income made permanent	[24]	---	-9,975	-7,050	-7,097	-7,150	-7,247	-7,347	-7,698	-8,036	-8,151	-8,254	-78,005

355

Provision	Effective	2015	2016	2017	2018	2019	2020	2021	2022	2023	2024	2025	2015-25
20. Minimum LIHTC rate for non-federally subsidized new buildings (9%) made permanent.	1/1/15	---	[2]	[2]	-1	-2	-2	-2	-3	-3	-3	-3	-19
21. Military housing allowance exclusion for determining LIHTC eligibility made permanent.	ido a 1/1/15	---	[2]	-3	-5	-5	-7	-9	-11	-13	-15	-15	-83
22. Treatment of RICs as "qualified investment entities" under section 897 (FIRPTA) made permanent.	1/1/15 [25]	---	-86	-57	-63	-68	-71	-77	-85	-93	-103	-113	-816
B. Extensions Through 2019													
1. New markets tax credit (sunset 12/31/19).	cyba 12/31/14	---	-5	-28	-97	-198	-297	-365	-408	-434	-423	-346	-2,602
2. Extend and modify the work opportunity tax credit (sunset 12/31/19).	iwbwftea 12/31/14 & twbwftea 12/31/15	---	-1,376	-1,341	-1,513	-1,640	-1,294	-719	-510	-353	-151	-72	-8,969
3. Bonus depreciation extended, modified, and phased down:													
a. Additional first-year depreciation for 50% of basis of qualified property (sunset 12/31/19) [26].	ppisa 12/31/14 tyeasd & ppisa 12/31/15 tyeasd	---	-90,635	-39,370	-20,913	-92	34,169	43,156	28,064	18,065	10,661	5,612	-11,344
b. Election to accelerate AMT credit in lieu of bonus depreciation (sunset 12/31/19).	tyea 12/31/14 & tyea 12/31/15	---	-2,492	-3,931	-4,231	-4,558	-1,655	-30	-26	-16	-9	-6	-16,953
c. Special rules for certain plants bearing fruits and nuts. (sunset 12/31/19).	sppega 12/31/15	---	---	---	---	---- Estimate Included In Part Thirteen, Division Q, Item 1.B.3.a ----							
4. Look-through treatment of payments between related CFCs under foreign personal holding company income rules (sunset 12/31/19).	[24]	---	-2,296	-1,527	-1,666	-1,792	-548	---	---	---	---	---	-7,829
C. Extensions Through 2016													
1. Extend and modify discharge of indebtedness on principal residence excluded from gross income of individuals (sunset 12/31/16).	doia 12/31/14 & doia 12/31/15	---	-3,344	-1,799									-5,143
2. Mortgage insurance premiums treated as qualified residence interest (sunset 12/31/16).	apooa 12/31/14	---	-1,314	-1,004									-2,318
3. Above-the-line deduction for qualified tuition and related expenses (sunset 12/31/16).	tyba 12/31/14	---	-360	-248									-608
4. Indian employment tax credit (sunset 12/31/16).	tyba 12/31/14	---	-74	-40	-11	-1							-126
5. Extend and modify the railroad track maintenance credit (sunset 12/31/16).	epoit tyba 12/31/14 & epoit tyba 12/31/15	---	-288	-141	[2]	[2]							-428
6. Mine rescue team training credit (sunset 12/31/16).	tyba 12/31/14	---	-2	-1	[2]	[2]	[2]	[2]					-4
7. Qualified zone academy bonds (sunset 12/31/16).	oia 12/31/14	---	[2]	-10	-16	-24	-27	-26	-25	-24	-22	-22	-196
8. Classification of certain race horses as three-year property (sunset 12/31/16).	ppisa 12/31/14	---	-22	-42	-20	9	20	22	19	11	3		---
9. Seven-year recovery period for motorsports entertainment complexes (sunset 12/31/16) [27].	ppisa 12/31/14	---	-20	-24	-20	-13	-9	-8	-6	-2	3	5	-95
10. Extend and modify accelerated depreciation for business property on an Indian reservation (sunset 12/31/16).	ppisa 12/31/14 & tyba 12/31/15	---	-215	-137	-32	32	66	73	49	17	-4	-8	-159
11. Election to expense mine safety equipment (sunset 12/31/16).	ppisa 12/31/14	---	-24	1	6	5	4	3	3	1	[17]		---
12. Special expensing rules for certain film and television productions and live theatrical productions (sunset 12/31/16).	pca 12/31/14 & pca 12/31/15	---	-351	-84	102	89	56	43	36	30	26	26	-26
13. Deduction allowable with respect to income attributable to domestic production activities in Puerto Rico (sunset 12/31/16).	tyba 12/31/14	---	-154	-80									-234
14. Extend and modify empowerment zone tax incentives (sunset 12/31/16).	tyba 12/31/14 & bia 12/31/15	---	-350	-165	6	4	3	2	1	1			-498

Provision	Effective	2015	2016	2017	2018	2019	2020	2021	2022	2023	2024	2025	2015-25
15. Increase in limit on cover over of rum excise tax revenues (from $10.50 to $13.25 per proof gallon) to Puerto Rico and the Virgin Islands (sunset 12/31/16) [3] [28]	abiUSa 12/31/14	---	-308	-28	---	---	---	---	---	---	---	---	-336
16. American Samoa economic development credit (sunset 12/31/16)	tyba 12/31/14	---	-27	-5	---	---	---	---	---	---	---	---	-32
17. Two-year moratorium of the ACA medical device excise tax (sales in calendar year 2016 and 2017)	sa 12/31/15	---	-1,398	-1,958	-556	---	---	---	---	---	---	---	-3,911
18. Extend and modify the credit for section 25C nonbusiness energy property (sunset 12/31/16)	ppisa 12/31/14 & ppisa 12/31/15	---	-826	-505	---	---	---	---	---	---	---	---	-1,331
19. Credit for alternative fuel vehicle refueling property (sunset 12/31/16)	ppisa 12/31/14	---	-81	-24	-7	-4	-2	1	1	1	1	1	-112
20. Credit for two-wheeled plug-in electric vehicles (sunset 12/31/16)	vaa 12/31/14	---	-3	-1	[2]	[2]	---	---	---	---	---	---	-4
21. Second generation biofuel producer credit (sunset 12/31/16)	fpa 12/31/16	---	-30	-15	---	---	---	---	---	---	---	---	-45
22. Incentives for biodiesel and renewable diesel - extend present-law income tax credits, excise tax credit, and outlay payments (sunset 12/31/16)	fsoua 12/31/14	---	-2,210	-353	---	---	---	---	---	---	---	---	-2,563
23. Extend and modify the credit for Indian coal production facilities (sunset 12/31/16)	cpa 12/31/14 & cpasa 12/31/15 ityeasd	---	-39	-17	-9	-6	-3	-1	---	---	---	---	-75
24. Beginning-of-construction date for non-wind renewable power facilities eligible to claim the electricity production credit or investment credit in lieu of the production credit (sunset 12/31/16)	1/1/15	---	---	---	-22	-84	-146	-186	-210	-228	-237	-243	-1,356
25. Credit for construction of energy-efficient new homes (sunset 12/31/16)	haa 12/31/14	---	-361	-139	-68	-60	-52	-45	-28	-7	---	---	-760
26. Special allowance for second generation biofuel plant property (sunset 12/31/16)	ppisa 12/31/14	---	-6	-1	2	1	1	1	1	[17]	[17]	[17]	[2]
27. Energy efficient commercial buildings deduction (sunset 12/31/16)	ppisa 12/31/14	---	-301	-61	8	7	6	5	4	4	3	2	-324
28. Special rule for sales or dispositions to implement Federal Energy Regulatory Commission ("FERC") or State electric restructuring policy for qualified electric utilities (sunset 12/31/16)	Da 12/31/14	---	-597	-48	110	110	110	110	110	75	20	---	---
29. Excise tax credits and outlay payments for alternative fuel, and excise tax credits for alternative fuel mixtures (sunset 12/31/16)	fsoua 12/31/14	---	-794	-124	---	---	---	---	---	---	---	---	-918
30. Alternative motor vehicle credit for qualified fuel cell motor vehicles (sunset 12/31/16)	tyba 12/31/14	---	-5	-1	---	---	---	---	---	---	---	---	-6
II. Program Integrity													
1. Modifications of filing dates of returns and statements relating to employee wage information and other nonemployee compensation to improve compliance; change earliest date of certain refunds to improve compliance [3]	rasrt cyba DOE & corma 12/31/16	---	---	9	45	75	98	101	106	110	115	120	779
2. Safe harbor for de minimis errors on information returns and payee statements	[29]	---	---	[2]	[2]	[2]	[2]	[2]	[2]	[2]	[2]	[2]	[2]
3. Requirements for the issuance of ITINs [3]	afITIN Ma DOE	---	---	470	474	477	440	381	364	310	268	238	3,424

356

357

Provision	Effective	2015	2016	2017	2018	2019	2020	2021	2022	2023	2024	2025	2015-25
4. Prevention of retroactive claims of earned income credit, child tax credit, and American opportunity tax credit:													
a. Prevention of retroactive claims of earned income credit after issuance of Social Security number [3]	[30]	---	---	38	40	42	44	47	49	51	54	57	422
b. Prevention of certain retroactive claims of child tax credit [3]	[30]	---	---	106	101	93	81	71	65	57	49	41	665
c. Prevention of certain retroactive claims of American opportunity tax credit [3]	[30]	---	[17]	3	4	4	4	4	4	4	4	4	32
5. Procedures to reduce improper claims [3]	tyba 12/31/15	---	---	5	5	5	5	5	5	5	5	5	47
6. Restrictions on taxpayers who improperly claimed credits in prior year [3]	tyba 12/31/15	---	---	---	12	12	12	11	11	11	10	10	88
7. Treatment of credits for purposes of certain penalties	[31]	---	25	54	70	72	53	55	56	58	60	62	564
8. Increase the penalty applicable to paid tax preparers who engage in willful or reckless conduct	npf tvca DOE	---	[17]	[17]	1	1	1	1	1	1	1	1	9
9. Employer identification number required for American opportunity tax credit [3]	tyba 12/31/15 & [32]	---	18	91	92	92	92	92	91	90	90	89	837
10. Higher education information reporting only to include qualified tuition and related expenses actually paid	[32]	---	[17]	[17]	[17]	[17]	[17]	[17]	[17]	[17]	[17]	[17]	2
III. Miscellaneous Provisions													
A. Family Tax Relief													
1. Exclusion for amounts received under the Work Colleges Program	arri tyba DOE	---	[2]	[2]	[2]	[2]	[2]	[2]	[2]	[2]	[2]	[2]	-2
2. Improvements to section 529 accounts:													
a. Computer technology and equipment permanently allowed as a qualified higher education expense for section 529 accounts	tyba 12/31/14	---	-3	-2	-3	-3	-4	-5	-6	-7	-8	-10	-51
b. Elimination of distribution aggregation requirements	da 12/31/14 generally	---	---	---	-----	Estimate Included in Part Thirteen, Division Q, Item III.A.2.a -----							
c. Recontribution of refunded amounts	rohcea 12/31/14	---	---	---	-----	Estimate Included in Part Thirteen, Division Q, Item III.A.2.a -----							
3. Elimination of residency requirement for qualified ABLE programs [33]	tyba 12/31/14	---	-1	-4	-8	-12	-13	-13	-13	-13	-13	-12	-103
4. Exclusion for wrongfully incarcerated individuals	tybbo'a DOE	---	-2	-2	-1	-1	-1	-1	-1	-1	-1	-1	-10
5. Clarification of special rule for certain governmental plans [34]	pa DOE	---	[2]	[2]	[2]	[2]	[2]	[2]	[2]	[2]	[2]	[2]	-5
6. Rollovers permitted from other retirement plans into simple retirement accounts	cma DOE	---	-1	-1	-1	-1	-1	-1	-1	-1	-1	-1	
7. Technical amendment relating to rollover of certain airline payment amounts	[35]	-----	No Revenue Effect -----										
8. Treatment of early retirement distributions for nuclear materials couriers, United States Capitol Police, Supreme Court Police, and State Department special agents	da 12/31/15	---	[2]	[2]	[2]	[2]	[2]	[2]	[2]	[2]	[2]	[2]	[2]
9. Prevention of extension of tax collection period for members of the Armed Forces who are hospitalized as a result of combat zone injuries	tabo a DOE	---	[2]	[2]	[2]	[2]	[2]	[2]	[2]	[2]	[2]	[2]	[2]
B. Real Estate Investment Trusts ("REITs")													
1. Restriction on tax-free spinoffs involving REITs, including transition rules	do a 12/7/15 generally	---	42	73	90	132	173	215	254	286	310	328	1,902
2. Reduction in percentage limitation on assets of REIT which may be taxable REIT subsidiaries	tyba 12/31/17	---	[17]	[17]	7	15	18	20	23	26	28	31	167

Provision	Effective	2015	2016	2017	2018	2019	2020	2021	2022	2023	2024	2025	2015-25
3. Prohibited transaction safe harbors	generally tyba DOE	---	27	22	5	-2	-3	-4	-6	-9	-11	-13	7
4. Repeal of preferential dividend rule for publicly offered REITs; authority for alternative remedies to address certain failures:													
a. Repeal of preferential dividend rule for publicly offered REITs	di tyba 12/31/14	---	----------	----------	----------	----------	Negligible Revenue Effect	----------	----------	----------	----------	----------	----------
b. Authority for alternative remedies to address certain failures	di tyba 12/31/15	---	-1	-1	-1	-1	-1	-1	-1	[2]	[2]	[2]	-4
5. Limitations on designation of dividends by REITs	di tyba 12/31/15	---	1	1	1	1	1	1	1	[17]	[17]	[17]	4
6. Debt instruments of publicly offered REITs and mortgages treated as real estate assets	tyba 12/31/15	---	[2]	[2]	[2]	[2]	[2]	-1	-1	-1	-2	-2	-7
7. Asset and income test clarification regarding ancillary personal property	tyba 12/31/15	---	[2]	[2]	[2]	-1	-1	-1	-1	-1	-1	-2	-8
8. Hedging provisions	tyba 12/31/15	---	[2]	[2]	[2]	[2]	[2]	[2]	[2]	[2]	-1	-1	-2
9. Modification of REIT earnings and profits calculation to avoid duplicate taxation	tyba 12/31/15	---	-1	-1	-1	-1	-1	-1	-1	[2]	[2]	[2]	-4
10. Treatment of certain services provided by taxable REIT subsidiaries	tyba 12/31/15	---	-1	-1	-4	-4	-5	-7	-8	-9	-12	-14	-65
11. Exception from FIRPTA for certain stock of REITs; exception for interests held by foreign retirement and pension funds:													
a. Exception from FIRPTA for certain stock of REITs [37]		---	-108	-142	-168	-191	-216	-240	-266	-293	-321	-351	-2,297
b. Exception for interests held by foreign retirement or pension funds [36]	dada DOE	---	-120	-144	-163	-175	-188	-201	-216	-233	-249	-266	-1,953
12. Increase in rate of withholding of tax on dispositions of United States real property interests	[38]	---	21	20	17	18	19	20	21	23	24	26	209
13. Interests in RICs and REITs not excluded from definition of United States real property interests	Do/a DOE	---	9	22	21	14	16	22	29	36	41	45	256
14. Dividends derived from RICs and REITs ineligible for deduction for United States source portion of dividends from certain foreign corporations	[39]	---	20	47	60	71	82	90	93	96	100	104	762
C. Additional Provisions													
1. Deductibility of charitable contributions to agricultural research organizations	cmoaa DOE	---	-2	-3	-3	-3	-3	-3	-4	-4	-4	-4	-32
2. Removal of bond requirements and extending filing periods for certain taxpayers with limited excise tax liability	aoxfbmt 1ya DOE	---	----------	----------	----------	----------	Negligible Revenue Effect	----------	----------	----------	----------	----------	----------
3. Modifications to alternative tax for certain small insurance companies	tyba 12/31/16	---	---	-3	-5	-6	-7	-9	-10	-11	-14	-15	-80
4. Treatment of timber gains (sunset 12/31/16)	tyba 12/31/15	---	-25	-11	---	---	---	---	---	---	---	---	-35
5. Modification of definition of hard cider	cra cyba 12/31/16	---	-1	-1	-1	-1	-1	-1	-1	-2	-2	-2	-12
6. Church plan clarification [40]	generally after DOE	---	---	-7	-10	-11	-11	-12	-12	-13	-14	-14	-104
D. Revenue Provisions													
1. Updated ASHRAE standards for energy efficient commercial buildings deduction	ppisa 12/31/15	---	6	3	[2]	[2]	[2]	[2]	[2]	[2]	[2]	[2]	8
2. Excise tax credit equivalency for liquefied petroleum gas and liquefied natural gas	fsoua 12/31/15	---	46	17	---	---	---	---	---	---	---	---	63
3. Exclusion from gross income of certain clean coal power grants to non-corporate taxpayers	[41]	---	-148	-28	8	41	47	34	24	17	8	2	6
4. Clarify the valuation rule for early termination of certain charitable remainder unitrusts	totoa DOE	---	4	40	21	15	9	5	6	5	4	4	113

Provision	Effective	2015	2016	2017	2018	2019	2020	2021	2022	2023	2024	2025	2015-25
5. Prevention of transfer of certain losses from tax indifferent parties	[42]	---	29	97	119	124	129	136	141	148	155	162	1,240
6. Treatment of certain persons as employers with respect to motion picture projects [43]	rpa 12/31/15	---	10	7	3	3	3	4	4	4	4	4	45
IV. Tax Administration													
A. Internal Revenue Service Reforms													
1. Duty to ensure that IRS employees are familiar with and act in accord with certain taxpayer rights	DOE	-----	-----	-----	-----	-----	-----	*No Revenue Effect*	-----	-----	-----	-----	-----
2. IRS employees prohibited from using personal email accounts for official business	DOE	-----	-----	-----	-----	-----	-----	*No Revenue Effect*	-----	-----	-----	-----	-----
3. Release of information regarding the status of certain investigations	dmo a DOE	-----	-----	-----	-----	-----	-----	*No Revenue Effect*	-----	-----	-----	-----	-----
4. Administrative appeal relating to adverse determinations of tax-exempt status of certain organizations	Dmo a 5/19/14	-----	-----	-----	-----	-----	-----	*Negligible Revenue Effect*	-----	-----	-----	-----	-----
5. Organizations required to notify Secretary of intent to operate under 501(c)(4)	generally ooa DOE	---	[17]	1	1	1	1	1	1	1	1	1	7
6. Declaratory judgment remedy extended to all 501(c) and (d) organizations	pfia DOE	---	-1	-1	-1	-1	-1	-1	-2	-2	-2	-2	-15
7. Termination of employment of Internal Revenue Service employees for taking official actions for political purposes	DOE	-----	-----	-----	-----	-----	-----	*No Revenue Effect*	-----	-----	-----	-----	-----
8. Gift tax not to apply to contributions to certain exempt organizations	gma DOE	-----	-----	-----	-----	-----	-----	*No Revenue Effect*	-----	-----	-----	-----	-----
9. Extend Internal Revenue Service authority to require truncated Social Security numbers on Form W-2	DOE	-----	-----	-----	-----	-----	-----	*Negligible Revenue Effect*	-----	-----	-----	-----	-----
10. Clarification of enrolled agent credentials	DOE	-----	-----	-----	-----	-----	-----	*Negligible Revenue Effect*	-----	-----	-----	-----	-----
11. Partnership audit rules	[44]	-----	-----	-----	-----	-----	-----	*No Revenue Effect*	-----	-----	-----	-----	-----
B. United States Tax Court													
1. Filing period for interest abatement cases	efa DOE	---	[2]	[2]	[2]	[2]	[2]	[2]	[2]	[2]	[2]	[2]	[2]
2. Small tax case election for interest abatement cases	[45]	---	[2]	[2]	[2]	[2]	[2]	[2]	[2]	[2]	[2]	[2]	[2]
3. Venue for appeal of spousal relief and collection cases	Pfa DOE	-----	-----	-----	-----	-----	-----	*No Revenue Effect*	-----	-----	-----	-----	-----
4. Suspension of running of period for filing petition of spousal relief and collection cases	Pfa DOE	---	[2]	[2]	[2]	[2]	[2]	[2]	[2]	[2]	[2]	[2]	[2]
5. Application of Federal Rules of Evidence	[46]	-----	-----	-----	-----	-----	-----	*No Revenue Effect*	-----	-----	-----	-----	-----
6. Judicial conduct and disability procedures	[47]	-----	-----	-----	-----	-----	-----	*No Revenue Effect*	-----	-----	-----	-----	-----
7. Administration, judicial conference, and fees	DOE	-----	-----	-----	-----	-----	-----	*No Revenue Effect*	-----	-----	-----	-----	-----
8. Clarification relating to United States Tax Court	DOE	-----	-----	-----	-----	-----	-----	*No Revenue Effect*	-----	-----	-----	-----	-----
Total of Division Q - Protecting Americans from Tax Hikes Act of 2015		---	-156,715	-83,347	-61,139	-66,408	-28,722	-19,427	-35,959	-48,018	-57,808	-64,411	-621,951
TOTAL OF PART THIRTEEN		---	-156,836	-95,230	-66,829	-76,405	-38,709	-23,735	-40,314	-51,675	-61,642	-68,255	-679,632

Joint Committee on Taxation

NOTE: Details may not add to totals due to rounding.

[Legend and Footnotes for the Appendix appear on the following pages]

360

Legend and Footnotes for the Appendix:

Legend for "Effective" column:

abiUSa = articles brought into the United States after
aca = amounts collected after
acarbsa = amounts collected and retained by the Secretary after
acqbmt = any calendar quarters beginning more than
af = applications for
apoaa = amounts paid or accrued after
apoia = amounts paid or incurred after
ari = amounts received in
bia = bonds issued after
cfa = claims filed after
cma = contributions made after
cmi = coverage months in
Cmi = contributions made in
cmoaa = contributions made on and after
corma = credits or refunds made after
cra = cider removed after
cpa = coal produced after
cpasa = coal produced and sold after
cyba = calendar years beginning after
da = distributions after
Da = dispositions after
dada = dispositions and distributions after
di = distributions in
dmi = distributions made in
dmo/a = disclosures made on or after

Dmo/a = determinations made on or after
doia = discharge of indebtedness after
do/a = distributions on or after
Do/a = dispositions on or after
DOE = date of enactment
epoii = expenses paid or incurred in
fpa = fuel produced after
fsoua = fuel sold or used after
gma = gifts made after
haa = homes acquired after
ido/a = income determinations on or after
ITIN = individual taxpayer identification number
ityeasd = in taxable years ending after such date
iwbwftea = individuals who begin work for the employer after
ma = months after
Ma = made after
mba = months beginning after
oia = obligations issued after
ooa = organizations organized after
pa = payments after
pca = productions commencing after
pfa = pleadings filed after
Pfa = petitions filed after
pma = payments made after
ppisa = property placed in service after

proaa = payments received or accrued after
pyba = plan years beginning after
rasrt = returns and statements relating to
rasrtbfa = returns and statements required to be filed after
rf = returns for
rffp = returns filed for partnership
rohoea = refunds of higher education expenses after
rpa = remuneration paid after
rpf = returns prepared for
sa = sales after
saa = stock acquired after
sppoga = specified plants planted or grafted after
tabo/a = taxes assessed before, on, or after
tma = transfers made after
totoa = terminations of trusts occurring after
tyba = taxable years beginning after
tybo/a = taxable years beginning before, on, or after
tyea = taxable years ending after
vaa = vehicles acquired after
1ya = 1 year after
180da = 180 days after

[1] The provision allowing acceleration of a donor's charitable deduction applies to contributions made between January 1, 2015, and April 15, 2015. The provision clarifying that distributions from an organization will be treated as related to the organization's tax-exempt status applies to payments made on or after December 20, 2014, and on or before October 15, 2015.
[2] Loss of less than $500,000.
[3] Estimate includes the following outlay effects:

	2015	2016	2017	2018	2019	2020	2021	2022	2023	2024	2025	2015-25
Extension and modification of the Health Coverage Tax Credit.	---	5	20	28	28	7	---	---	---	---	---	87
Payee statement required to claim certain education tax benefits.	---	---	-39	-40	---	---	---	---	---	---	---	-79
Child tax credit not refundable for taxpayers electing to exclude foreign earned income from tax.	---	-38	-36	-35	-28	-27	-26	-26	-25	-26	-26	-293
Reform of rules related to qualified tax collection contracts.	---	[48]	187	235	246	257	269	282	296	310	325	2,408
Two-year moratorium of the ACA excise tax on certain high-cost plans (2018 and 2019).	---	---	---	-656	-923	-278	---	---	---	---	---	-1,857
Reduce the earnings threshold for the refundable portion of the child tax credit to $3,000 made permanent.	---	---	---	---	12,373	12,455	12,452	12,534	12,597	12,694	12,733	87,839
American opportunity tax credit made permanent.	---	---	---	---	6,258	6,252	6,230	6,255	6,230	6,235	6,253	43,713
Modification of the earned income tax credit made permanent:												
a. Credit percentage of 45% for three or more qualifying children made permanent.	---	---	---	---	2,433	2,491	2,557	2,610	2,673	2,757	2,827	18,348
b. Increase beginning and ending income levels for joint returns by $5,000 indexed after 2009 made permanent.	---	---	---	---	1,342	1,334	1,325	1,318	1,313	1,317	1,316	9,265

[Footnotes for the Appendix are continued on the following pages]

Footnotes for the Appendix continued:

[3] Estimate includes the following outlay effects (continued):

	2015	2016	2017	2018	2019	2020	2021	2022	2023	2024	2025	2015-25
Increase in limit on cover over of rum excise tax revenues to Puerto Rico and the Virgin Islands [28]	---	308	28	---	---	---	---	---	---	---	---	336
Modifications of filing dates of returns and statements relating to employee wage information and other nonemployee compensation to improve compliance, change earliest date of certain refunds to improve compliance	---	---	-2	-10	-17	-23	-24	-25	-26	-27	-28	-182
Requirement for the issuance of ITINs	---	---	-428	-433	-435	-401	-345	-328	-277	-237	-209	-3,094
Prevention of retroactive claims of earned income credit after issuance of Social Security number	---	---	-37	-39	-41	-43	-45	-48	-50	-53	-55	-412
Prevention of certain retroactive claims of child tax credit	---	---	-99	-90	-83	-72	-64	-58	-51	-43	-37	-597
Prevention of certain retroactive claims of American opportunity tax credit	---	---	-3	-3	-3	-3	-3	-3	-3	-3	-3	-27
Procedures to reduce improper claims	---	---	-4	-4	-4	-4	-4	-4	-4	-3	-4	-40
Restrictions on taxpayers who improperly claimed credits in prior year	---	---	---	-12	-11	-11	-11	-11	-10	-10	-10	-86
Employer identification number required for American opportunity tax credit	---	---	-36	-37	-38	-38	-38	-38	-38	-38	-38	-338

[4] Effective for returns required to be made, and statements required to be furnished, after December 31, 2015.
[5] Effective for returns required to be made, and statements required to be furnished, after December 31, 2016.
[6] Effective for property with respect to which an estate tax return is filed after the date of enactment.
[7] Effective for all returns for which the assessment period is open as of the date of enactment and for returns filed after such date.
[8] Estimate provided by the staff of the Joint Committee on Taxation and the Congressional Budget Office.
[9] Estimate includes the following budget effects:

	2015	2016	2017	2018	2019	2020	2021	2022	2023	2024	2025	2015-25
On-budget effects	---	-9	-15	-19	-23	-29	-35	-41	-47	-52	-59	-328
Off-budget effects	---	-2	-2	-3	-4	-5	-6	-7	-8	-9	-10	-56

[10] Estimate does not include effects on PBGC premiums, which are estimated by the Congressional Budget Office.
[11] Estimate includes the following effects:

	2015	2016	2017	2018	2019	2020	2021	2022	2023	2024	2025	2015-25
Total Revenue Effect	---	3	6	9	22	36	92	216	289	250	205	1,118
On-budget effects	---	2	6	9	21	35	87	204	267	239	196	1,064
Off-budget effects	---	---	---	---	1	1	5	12	13	12	9	54

[12] This estimate is the net effect of the funding stabilization provision with pension package interaction.
[13] Estimate includes the following effects:

	2015	2016	2017	2018	2019	2020	2021	2022	2023	2024	2025	2015-25
Total Revenue Effect	---	---	---	174	797	1,704	2,303	2,024	875	-120	-1,223	6,534
On-budget effects	---	---	---	163	753	1,619	2,198	1,940	853	-104	-1,159	6,263
Off-budget effects	---	---	---	11	44	85	105	84	22	-16	-64	271

[14] Gain or loss of less than $500,000.
[15] Out of amounts in the Leaking Underground Storage Tank Trust Fund, the following amounts are transferred to the Highway Account of the Highway Trust Fund: $100 million on the date of enactment, $100 million on October 1, 2016, and $100 million on October 1, 2017.
[16] There are four different effective dates for this provision. (1) the provision generally applies to tax receivables identified by the Secretary after the date of enactment, (2) the Secretary is required to enter into qualified tax collection contracts within three months after the date of enactment, (3) the provision applies to disclosures made after the date of enactment, and (4) the provision relating to reports is effective on the date of enactment.
[17] Gain of less than $500,000.
[18] Estimate includes the following

	2015	2016	2017	2018	2019	2020	2021	2022	2023	2024	2025	2015-25
off-budget effects	---	---	---	-646	-893	-300	---	---	---	---	---	-1,838

[19] Estimate provided by the staff of the Joint Committee on Taxation and the Congressional Budget Office.
[20] Estimate includes interaction with Part Thirteen, Division P, Item A.1.

[Footnotes for the Appendix are continued on the following page]

362

Footnotes for the Appendix continued:

[21] Estimate includes the following effects:

	2015	2016	2017	2018	2019	2020	2021	2022	2023	2024	2025	2015-25
Total Revenue Effects	---	-115	-146	-151	-157	-162	-184	-198	-208	-219	-231	-1,771
On-budget effects	---	-76	-96	-99	-103	-107	-121	-130	-137	-144	-152	-1,164
Off-budget effects	---	-40	-50	-52	-54	-56	-63	-68	-71	-75	-79	-608

[22] Estimate includes interaction with section 179 and bonus depreciation.
[23] Effective for dividends paid with respect to any taxable year of regulated investment companies beginning after December 31, 2014.
[24] Effective for taxable years of foreign corporations beginning after December 31, 2014, and for taxable years of U.S. shareholders with or within which taxable years of such foreign corporations end.
[25] The provision does not apply with respect to the withholding requirement under section 1445 for any payment made before the date of the enactment.
[26] Estimate includes interaction with section 179. The percentage is phased down from 50 percent by 10 percent per calendar year beginning in 2018 (2019 for certain longer-lived and transportation property).
[27] Estimate includes interaction with bonus depreciation.
[28] Estimate provided by the Congressional Budget Office.
[29] Effective for returns required to be filed, and payee statements required to be provided, after December 31, 2016.
[30] Effective for all returns filed after date of enactment except with respect to timely returns for the taxable year that includes the date of enactment.
[31] The provision amending the definition of underpayment is effective for returns filed after the date of enactment and for returns filed on or before the date of enactment if the statute of limitations period for assessment has not expired. The provision repealing the exception from the erroneous claim penalty is effective for claims filed after the date of enactment.
[32] Effective for expenses paid after December 31, 2015, for education furnished in academic periods beginning after such date.
[33] This provision could also affect direct spending. Any estimates of changes to direct spending would be provided by the Congressional Budget Office.
[34] Estimate includes the following effects:

	2015	2016	2017	2018	2019	2020	2021	2022	2023	2024	2025	2015-25
off-budget effects	---	[2]	[2]	[2]	[2]	[2]	[2]	[2]	[2]	[2]	[2]	-3

[35] Effective as if included in Public Law 113-243.
[36] Estimate includes interactions with Part Thirteen, Division Q, Item III.B.1.
[37] Effective as of date of enactment for determinations of control, dispositions of USRPI, or deductible REIT distributions, except that the technical correction to section 8897(b)(4)(A) takes effect as of January 1, 2015.
[38] Effective for dispositions after the date which is 60 days after the date of enactment.
[39] Effective for dividends received from RICs and REITs on or after the date of enactment.
[40] Estimate includes the following effects:

	2015	2016	2017	2018	2019	2020	2021	2022	2023	2024	2025	2015-25
Total Revenue Effects	---	---	-7	-10	-11	-11	-12	-12	-13	-14	-14	-104
On-budget effects	---	---	-6	-9	-10	-10	-11	-11	-12	-12	-13	-94
Off-budget effects	---	---	-1	-1	-1	-1	-1	-1	-1	-1	-1	-10

[41] Effective for amounts received under section 402 of the Energy Policy Act of 2005 in taxable years beginning after December 31, 2011.
[42] Effective for sales and other dispositions of property acquired after December 31, 2015, by the taxpayer in a sale or exchange to which section 267(a)(1) of the Internal Revenue Code of 1986 applied.
[43] Estimate includes the following

	2015	2016	2017	2018	2019	2020	2021	2022	2023	2024	2025	2015-25
off-budget effects	---	-1	-2	-4	-5	-5	-6	-6	-6	-6	-6	-47

[44] Effective as if included in section 1101 of the Bipartisan Budget Act of 2015, Public Law 114-74.
[45] Effective for cases pending as of the day after the date of the enactment, and cases commencing after the date of enactment.
[46] Effective for proceedings commenced after the date of enactment and, to the extent that it is just and practicable, to all proceedings pending on such date.
[47] Effective for proceedings commenced after the date which is 180 days after the date of enactment and, to the extent that it is just and practicable, to all proceedings pending on such date.
[48] Increase in outlays of less than $500,000.

www.ingramcontent.com/pod-product-compliance
Lightning Source LLC
Chambersburg PA
CBHW060244240426
43673CB00047B/1873